W9-CHY-849

TAKING ISSUE charts

Taking Issue charts present arguments on both sides of controversial topics in the education field.

OVERVIEW charts

Overview charts identify key information on issues such as employment, organizations, historical events and laws, and guidelines and approaches.

"Home to a Dirty Street" Useni Perkins

"There are no children here" Alex Kotlowitz

FOUNDATIONS
of EDUCATION

7th Edition

FOUNDATIONS
of EDUCATION

Allan C. Ornstein
Loyola University of Chicago

Daniel U. Levine
University of Nebraska at Omaha

Houghton Mifflin Company   Boston   New York

Senior Sponsoring Editor: Loretta Wolozin
Associate Editor: Lisa A. Mafrici
Senior Project Editor: Carol Newman
Senior Production/Design Coordinator: Carol Merrigan
Senior Manufacturing Coordinator: Marie Barnes
Associate Marketing Manager: Jean Zielinski DeMayo

Cover design: Cat & Mouse

Cover image: Sonia Delauney, scarf designs for Diaghilev ballet "Cleopatre,"
Sonia Delauney Archives, Amsterdam.

Part opener credits: Part One, page 3: Tom McCarthy/The Picture Cube; Part Two,
page 65: The Granger Collection POL/84-2; Part Three, page 175: Bob Daemmrich;
Part Four, page 275: Elizabeth Crews; Part Five, page 387: Elizabeth Crews; Part Six,
page 489: Elizabeth Crews.

Printed in the U.S.A.
Library of Congress Catalog Card Number: 99-71956
ISBN: 0-395-95576-9

1 2 3 4 5 6 7 8 9–QH–03 02 01 00 99

CONTENTS

v

PART TWO   Historical Foundations   65

3   World Roots of American Education   66

4   Pioneers in Education   105

5   Historical Development of American Education   135

14 Curriculum and Instruction 452

PART SIX Effective Education: International and American Perspectives 489

15 International Education 490

16 School Effectiveness and Reform in the United States 519

PREFACE

The Seventh Edition of *Foundations of Education* provides a comprehensive overview and analysis of topics and material typically taught in foundations courses in the United States. We have written it for students who are preparing for a teaching career as well as those who simply wish to learn more about the key educational issues and policies affecting American education.

Audience and Purpose

This text is designed for use in both introductory courses in the foundations of education and in a variety of upper-level foundations courses. For beginning students in education, it provides a clear understanding of the teaching profession and the issues and controversies confronting American education today. The book also is appropriate for upper-level courses because of its solid research base and documentation drawn extensively from primary sources and its systematic attention to providing up-to-date references.

Our purposes in writing this book remain the same as in the previous six editions: to provide a comprehensive body of knowledge and information on the various foundations of education and significant contemporary issues, while incorporating relevant interdisciplinary perspectives. We have sought to summarize and synthesize fundamental concepts and research findings in a practical way and to provide balanced treatment of controversial issues without making the text either too simplistic or too complicated.

Goals and Features of the Revision

Three goals directed the work on this new edition: 1) to make sure it is contemporary and substantive in identifying and analyzing appropriate subject matter; 2) to increase the effectiveness of the text for student learning; and 3) to provide material that instructors are likely to want emphasized in preparing their students for teaching careers.

In order to meet our first goal, of including an appropriate mix of contemporary and substantive classic subject matter, we have worked to refine the emphases, or themes, that recur throughout the book:

- **Diversity** We continue to place emphasis, throughout this revision, on student diversity and multiculturalism. For example, we discuss the importance of diverse populations in the teaching profession, the current status of desegregation and other important equal opportunity trends, and educational responses to the increasing diversity of students in the United States.
- **Technology** We have systematically placed greater emphasis on the emerging role of technology in education. Our increased emphasis on technology includes new sections on the history of technology in education, the place of technology in school reform, and the effects of digital technologies on children.

■ **Developing One's Own Philosophy of Education**   New sections stressing development of a personal philosophy of education include the professional planning for the first-year feature described below, as well as questions or sections in many chapters stressing the relevance and importance of a personal philosophy of education to the realities of day-to-day teaching.

Other current and important topics that receive particular emphasis in the Seventh Edition include professional development, school-based management, character education, the history of education in China and India, legal protections regarding assaults on teachers and students, school choice and charter schools, curriculum and testing standards, promising instructional innovations and interventions, approaches for helping disadvantaged students and for equalizing educational opportunity, collaboration between schools and other institutions, research on class size, and international achievement patterns.

We have worked diligently to obtain the latest available data on contemporary topics such as teacher employment trends, student and school demographics, adolescent substance abuse, school finance trends, changes in the family, school governance changes, and student performance. Over forty percent of the citations in this edition are from 1996 or later.

Our updating has drawn to a considerable extent on resources available on the Internet. For this reason, many of the citations do not have page references. Students can explore areas of personal interest by scrutinizing the printed versions of many sources we cite — including news sources such as the *New York Times* and *Education Week* and journal sources such as the *American School Board Journal, Educational Resources Information Clearing House,* and *Scientific American* — at college, community, and university libraries. (For *Education Week,* most articles can be accessed easily by searching the Archives.) But in general, instructors should recognize that a substantial proportion of our citations are available to their students on the Internet. To facilitate access, we frequently provide URLs that students can access from any computer linked to the World Wide Web. (The web sites were active at the time we prepared this text, but we, of course, are not responsible for their continued presence.)

In order to meet our second goal, the enhancement of student understanding, we have retained and thoroughly updated key pedagogical features that helped students in previous editions, including focusing questions, marginal notes, Getting to the Source and Taking Issue features, topical overview charts, chapter summaries, key terms lists and an extensive glossary, discussion questions, and lists of selected Internet and reading resources. In addition, we have paid considerable attention to making our textual descriptions of both new and continuing topics as clear and informative as possible, revising many of the discussions retained from previous editions to further enhance readability and understanding.

Finally, we have added **two new features** that highlight our third goal of helping students prepare for teaching careers:

■ **"Professional Planning for Your First Year"** sections in each chapter describe plausible situations that teachers may well confront during their first year, and then ask the reader how he or she might respond and what concepts rooted in one's philosophy of education might be drawn on in doing so.

■ **"Suggested Projects for Professional Development"** sections at the end of each chapter provide readers with opportunities to extend their knowledge about chapter ideas by engaging in such activities as conducting surveys; engaging in debates, role-plays, and group activities; researching and presenting in-depth information; and visiting schools. Several chapters include suggestions that may serve as the basis for elements of a portfolio for certification or interviewing.

Content and Organization

The text consists of sixteen chapters divided into six parts. Part One ("Understanding the Teaching Profession") considers the climate in which teachers work today and its impact on teaching. Changes in the job market and in the status of the profession and issues such as teacher empowerment, school-based management, and alternative certification are treated in detail.

The three chapters in Part Two ("Historical Foundations") provide historical context for understanding current educational practices and trends by examining the events and ideas that have influenced the development of education in the United States. Chapter 3 has been revised in accordance with its new title, "World Roots of American Education."

Part Three ("Political, Economic, and Legal Foundations") presents an overview of the organization, governance, and administration of elementary and secondary education; the financing of public education; and the legal aspects of education.

Part Four ("Social Foundations") examines the relationships between society and the schools that society has established to serve its needs. The three chapters in this part discuss culture and socialization, the complex relationship between social class, race, and educational achievement, and the various programs aimed at providing equal educational opportunity for all students.

Part Five ("Philosophical and Curricular Foundations") examines the ideas and concepts that have shaped education and the ways in which changes in societies have led to changes in educational goals, curriculum, and instructional methods. Throughout these three chapters we explicitly point out how particular philosophical ideas are linked to goals, curriculum, and other facets of contemporary education. This section concludes with a look at emerging curriculum trends.

Part Six ("Effective Education: International and American Perspectives") provides a comparative look at schools and their development throughout the world and an in-depth analysis of current efforts to improve school effectiveness in the United States.

Special Pedagogic Features

The Seventh Edition of *Foundations of Education* includes many special features designed to help students easily understand and master the material in the text. Six pedagogical features are particularly noteworthy:

- **"Professional Planning for Your First Year"** features in each chapter describe situations that teachers may well confront during their first year, and then asks the reader how he or she might respond based on his or her philosophy of education. These response situations connect chapter ideas to the real world of teaching as experienced by beginning professionals.

- **"Suggested Projects for Professional Development"** at the end of each chapter provide readers with opportunities to extend their knowledge about chapter ideas by conducting surveys; engaging in debates, role-plays, and group activities; researching and presenting in-depth information; and visiting schools to observe and interview faculty and administrators. Several chapters include suggestions that may serve as the basis for elements of a portfolio for certification or interviewing.

- **Internet and video resources** at the end of each chapter connect both the reader and instructor to emerging new technologies.

- **"Getting to the Source"** offers students the opportunity to become familiar with a wide variety of primary source materials. Appearing in every chapter, this feature consists of one-page excerpts from a variety of high-interest, significant, and relevant primary source materials, along with author commentary and questions. New material involving this feature includes "A Confucianist View of Good Teaching," "Rousseau on Natural Education," and "Every Child Reading."

- **Charts entitled "Taking Issue"** present controversial issues in the field of education, offering arguments on both sides of a question so that students can understand why the topic is important and how it affects contemporary schools. One of these charts appears in each chapter, covering issues such as alternative certification, merit pay, magnet schools, character education, and establishing a national curriculum. New material involving this feature includes "Universal Truth or Cultural Relativism?" and "Should Education Be Child-Centered?" Instructors may wish to use these charts as the basis for class discussion or essay assignments.

- **Topical overview charts,** set off in screened boxes throughout the text, summarize and compare key developments and topics.

To help you easily locate these six features above, special indexes for each of them appear on the inside cover at the back of this book.

In addition, other key pedagogic features of the preceding edition have been retained, including the following:

- *Focusing questions* at the beginning of each chapter highlight the major topics to be discussed.

- *Marginal notations* reinforce central points throughout the text.

- *Annotated lists of selected readings and resources for further learning* that may be of special interest to readers appear at the end of each chapter.

- *A list of key terms,* with cross-references to text pages, appears near the end of each chapter as a convenient recapitulation and guide for the student.

- *End-of-chapter features* also include *summary lists* that facilitate understanding and analysis of content and *discussion questions* to stimulate class participation in examining text material.

- *An extensive glossary* at the end of the book defines important terms and concepts.

Ancillaries

Accompanying the text is an *Instructor's Resource Manual with Test Items*. It contains hundreds of test items, developed according to sound principles and standards of test construction. The multiple-choice items have been extensively revised and include many items that test for higher-order thinking skills. In addition, the instructional resource material of the manual has been thoroughly updated and revised to reflect new text content; it offers for each chapter of the text a chapter outline, a chapter overview, student objectives, lecture and discussion topics, student projects, selected references and resources, a transition guide, and model syllabi.

The test items contained in the Instructor's Resource Manual are also available in an electronic format in a *Computerized Test Generator.*

A set of *transparencies,* both two- and one-color, is available to each instructor upon adoption of the text. The transparencies include figures from the text and new material as well.

Acknowledgments

The Seventh Edition would not have been possible without the contributions and feedback from many individuals. In particular, James Lawlor, Professor of Education at Towson University, planned and carried out many quite substantial revisions in Chapters 2, 6, 7, 13, and 14. His outstanding contributions to this volume are in themselves a testimonial to the breadth of his knowledge and the acuity of his insight as an educator dedicated to improving professional preparation. Gerald Gutek, Professor Emeritus of Education and History at Loyola University of Chicago, has also made an outstanding contribution to the book as the author of Chapters 3, 4, 5, and 12, which he thoroughly revised and updated for this edition.

A number of reviewers made useful suggestions and provided thoughtful reactions that guided us in this revision. We wish to thank the following individuals for their conscientiousness and for their contributions to the content of this edition:

H. Rose Adesiyan, *Purdue University, Calumet*

John A. Bucci, *Rhode Island College*

Virden Evans, *Florida A & M University*

John R. Petry, *The University of Memphis*

Richard R. Renner, *University of Florida*

Roderick M. Thronson, *Carroll College*

We also want to acknowledge and express appreciation for the work of Sheralee Connors who, as Development Editor, made crucial contributions in every aspect involved in revising this text. At Houghton Mifflin, Associate Editor Lisa Mafrici and Senior Sponsoring Editor Loretta Wolozin continued to provide overall leadership and supervision to make sure that this edition would be worthwhile and timely. Other persons who made creative contributions included Carol Newman, Senior Project Editor, Carol Merrigan, Senior Production/Design Coordinator, and Marie Barnes, Senior Manufacturing Coordinator. We'd also like to thank Susan Zorn, who copyedited the manuscript.

FOUNDATIONS
of EDUCATION

PART ONE

Understanding the Teaching Profession

CHAPTER ONE

Motivation, Status, and Preparation of the Teacher

Some of your relatives or friends may have questioned you about your interest in becoming a teacher. "Are you sure you want to deal with kids?" they may have asked. "Why don't you pick a high-tech field like computer science, where you get a lot of prestige, a big salary, and you won't have to worry about children unless you have some of your own?"

In response, you may try to explain the importance of helping children and young people become capable and responsible adults. You may point out that teachers in today's schools are gaining more power and more responsibilities, not to mention higher salaries. Still, you may be pondering your own motives for teaching, as well as the potential opportunities, rewards, and difficulties of a teaching career. This chapter will examine such topics, including the motivation to become a teacher, the status of teachers, pay scales, career preparation, and efforts to improve the teaching work force and to give teachers more decision-making power. As you read, think about how you might explain your interest in teaching the next time someone asks you. To help focus your thoughts, keep the following questions in mind:

- What are the usual reasons for becoming a teacher, and how do your own reasons compare with them?
- What is satisfying and dissatisfying about teaching?
- How does the prestige of teaching compare with that of other occupations?
- What do teachers earn? How does this compare with other occupations?
- What are the employment trends for teachers?
- How are teachers prepared? How are they certified?
- What are the trends in teacher education?
- What developments are taking place in the quality of the teacher work force and the conditions of teaching?

Choosing a Career in Teaching

There are many motives, both idealistic and practical, for choosing a career in teaching. Often, a person's reasons for wanting to teach stem from his or her own *personal philosophy of education,* a topic we will revisit throughout the book. People who are thinking of entering the teaching profession — and even those who are already teaching — should ask themselves why they are making this choice. Their motives may include (1) a love of children, (2) a desire to impart knowledge, (3) an interest in and excitement about teaching, and (4) a desire to perform a valuable service to society. Other reasons may include job security, pension benefits, and the relative ease of preparing for teaching compared with the training required by some other professions.

Reasons for entering the profession

Reasons for teaching

One study of future teachers from a representative sample of seventy-six schools and colleges of teacher education examined reasons for selecting the teaching profession. Ninety percent of the respondents cited "helping children grow and learn" as one of their reasons. Next highest was the statement "seems to be a challenging field" (63 percent), followed closely by "like work conditions" (54 percent), "inspired by favorite teachers" (53 percent), and "sense of vocation and honor of teaching" (52 percent). These reasons were basically similar to those cited in several other studies conducted during the past fifteen years. Some of these studies also concluded that admiration for one's own elementary and secondary teachers is often important in shaping decisions to become a teacher.[1]

Satisfaction with Teaching

Once people become teachers, are they generally satisfied with their work? In a poll conducted for the Metropolitan Life Insurance Company, teachers have been asked, "All in all, how satisfied would you say you are with teaching as a career?" Nearly 90 percent of the respondents say that they are either "very satisfied" or "somewhat satisfied." Nearly half report that they are more enthusiastic about teaching than when they began their careers, and the percentage reporting that they can make a decent living in teaching has nearly tripled since the early 1980s.[2]

National surveys

One important reason for teachers' job satisfaction is that they often feel successful in advancing their students' learning and growth. Recent increases in teacher salaries, widespread recognition of teachers' expertise, and the quality of their interpersonal relationships with students and parents also promote satisfaction. Since teachers appear to be mostly positive about these and other aspects of their jobs, it is not surprising that they generally indicate they have high satisfaction in their work.

Reasons for satisfaction

In recent years much attention has been paid to the problems of American schools, and this book will not shy away from that subject. It is important to recognize, however, that most teachers do not find such problems overwhelming.

Teachers' reactions to problems

[1]Pamela B. Joseph and Nancy Green, "Perspectives on Reasons for Becoming Teachers," *Journal of Teacher Education* (November–December 1986), pp. 28–33; Donald B. Cruickshank, *Research That Informs Teachers and Teacher Educators* (Bloomington, Ind.: Phi Delta Kappa, 1990); and "What It Takes to Teach" (undated paper posted at the internet site of Recruiting New Teachers, available at **www.rnt.org**).
[2]National Center for Education Statistics, *America's Teachers Ten Years After "A Nation at Risk"* (Washington, D.C.: U.S. Department of Education, 1995); *The Metropolitan Life Survey of the American Teacher 1984–1995* (New York: Metropolitan Life, 1995); and Andrew S. Latham, "Teacher Satisfaction," *Educational Leadership* (February 1998), pp. 82–83.

There are many motives for becoming a teacher, but perhaps the most powerful is the desire to work with young people. *(© John Maher/Stock Boston)*

Figure 1.1 shows the responses of teachers when they were asked whether possible problems in their schools were "serious." On matters ranging from physical safety to student apathy, large majorities reported that the problems were not serious.

Aspects of dissatisfaction   Many teachers do, however, report dissatisfaction with certain aspects of their work that they think interfere with their ability to teach and to establish positive relationships with students. Nationwide surveys show that many teachers believe they have insufficient time for counseling students, planning lessons, and other instructional functions. Other complaints include ambiguity in the expectations of

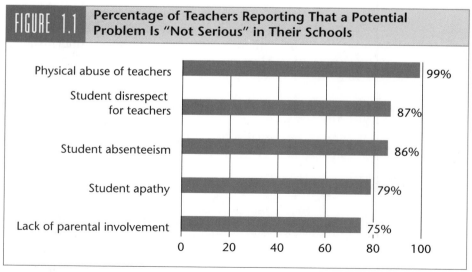

FIGURE 1.1   **Percentage of Teachers Reporting That a Potential Problem Is "Not Serious" in Their Schools**

Physical abuse of teachers — 99%
Student disrespect for teachers — 87%
Student absenteeism — 86%
Student apathy — 79%
Lack of parental involvement — 75%

Source: Adapted from data in Thomas D. Snyder and Charlene M. Hoffman, *Digest of Educational Statistics* (Washington, D.C.: U.S. Government Printing Office, 1994), Table 27, p. 34.

supervisors; obligations to participate in staff development perceived as irrelevant or ineffective; lack of supplies and equipment; extensive paperwork and record keeping; and insufficient opportunity to participate in organizational decisions. Improvements in teacher salaries and teaching conditions (described later in this chapter) may reduce these aspects of dissatisfaction in the future.[3]

Coping with Stress

Teaching can be stressful

Like other occupations, teaching has its difficult and stressful moments. Research indicates that elementary and secondary teaching has become more stressful than it was in earlier periods and that greater stress is causing burnout among some teachers. Definitions of *burnout* generally characterize it as emotional and, in many cases, physical exhaustion. These reactions often stem from the feeling that one's students have serious problems that impede learning or the belief that time pressures and administrative regulations are interfering with instruction.[4]

Coping techniques

Efforts are being made to help stressed professionals develop coping techniques. Counselors point out that exercise, rest, hobbies, good nutrition, meditation or other relaxation techniques, efficient scheduling of personal affairs, and vacations can help individuals cope with high-stress jobs. Recommendations for avoiding burnout also advise teachers to participate in professional renewal activities or support groups, to separate their jobs from their home life, and to try to maintain an open-minded attitude toward change. Many professional organizations and school districts offer courses or workshops emphasizing coping techniques and other stress-reduction approaches. Specialists on this topic also point out that some educators see stressful conditions as a challenge, an attitude that evidently helps them cope with the stress they experience.[5]

Overall, we have seen that most teachers are motivated by a desire to work with young people and to enter a challenging and honorable field. Most teachers are satisfied with most aspects of their jobs. There is some dissatisfaction, however, with various "nonteaching" considerations, and stress can be a problem for teachers who have not yet learned to cope with it. As we shall see later in this chapter, nationwide efforts are under way to address some of the teaching conditions that teachers find difficult.

Status and Supply of Teachers

What kind of social status do teachers have? Two of the major determinants of social status are occupational prestige and salary level. Prestige and salary in turn are affected by **supply and demand.** When the supply of people in an occupation exceeds demand, their prestige and salaries tend to decline, leading to a decrease in

[3]"Who's in Charge? Teachers' Views on Control over School Policy and Classroom Practices," *Education Research Reports* (August 1994), pp. 1–4; Judith Anderson, "Who's in Charge?" *U.S. Department of Education Research Reports* (October 1995), pp. 1–8; and Judith Rényi, "Building Learning into the Teaching Job," *Educational Leadership* (February 1998), pp. 70–74.
[4]Barry A. Farber, *Crisis in Education* (San Francisco: Jossey-Bass, 1991); Anne Cockburn, *Teaching Under Pressure* (Bristol, Pa.: Falmer, 1996); and R. Sergio Guglielmi and Kristin Tatrow, "Occupational Stress, Burnout, and Health in Teachers," *Review of Educational Research* (Spring 1998), pp. 61–99.
[5]Edward F. Pajak, Deborah Williams, and Carl D. Glickman, "Teacher Stress: Implications for Supervision," *Educational Leadership* (December 1987–January 1988), p. 95; John J. Byrne, "Teacher As Hunger Artist," *Contemporary Education* (Winter 1998), pp. 86–91; and Connie Anderson, "Time Well Spent," *Teaching K–8* (January 1999), pp. 80–81.

GETTING TO THE SOURCE

Teacher in America
BY
JACQUES BARZUN

AN ATLANTIC MONTHLY PRESS BOOK
LITTLE, BROWN AND COMPANY · BOSTON
1947

Teachers and Teaching

JACQUES BARZUN

Jacques Barzun, who emigrated from France to the United States, was admitted to Columbia University at age sixteen in 1923 and later served as a professor of history at that institution for more than 30 years. Many of his publications provide thoughtful analysis of teaching and learning at all levels of education. In the following excerpt, from a book published in 1944, he discusses the status and power of teachers and the "American state of mind about Education."

There is an age-old prejudice against teaching. Teachers must share with doctors the world's most celebrated sneers, and with them also the world's unbounded hero-worship. Always and everywhere, "He is a schoolteacher" has meant "He is an underpaid pitiable drudge." Even a politician stands higher, because power in the street seems less of a mockery than power in the classroom. But when we speak of Socrates, Jesus, Buddha, and "other great teachers of humanity," the atmosphere somehow changes and the politician's power begins to look shrunken and mean. August examples show that no limit can be set to the power of a teacher. . . .

The odd thing is that almost everybody is a teacher at some time or other during his life. Besides Socrates and Jesus, the great teachers of mankind are mankind itself — your parents and mine. First and last, parents do a good deal more teaching than doctoring, yet so natural and necessary is this duty that they never seem aware of performing it. It is only when they are beyond it, when they have thoroughly ground irremediable habits of speech, thought, and behavior into their offspring that they discover the teacher as an institution and hire him to carry on the work.

. . . [N]ot long ago, I joined a club which described its membership as made up of Authors, Artists, and Amateurs — an excellent reason for joining. Conceive

social status. Conversely, high demand and low supply tend to increase salaries, prestige, and social status.

Occupational Prestige

Occupations with high prestige

Occupational prestige refers to the esteem in which an occupation is held in a particular society. Occupations rate high in prestige if they are generally perceived as making an especially valuable contribution to society. Those occupations that require a high level of education or skill and little manual or physical labor also tend to be prestigious. On these aspects of social status, the job of elementary or secondary teacher historically has ranked relatively high.

Prestige of teachers

Perhaps the best-known studies of occupational prestige are those conducted by the National Opinion Research Center (NORC). In these studies of more than 500 occupations, the highest average score for a major occupation was 82 for physicians and surgeons, and the lowest was 9 for shoe shiners. Elementary school teachers were rated at 60 and secondary school teachers at 63 — both above the 90th percentile. In addition, the percentage of teachers who say they "feel respected in today's society" has increased substantially in recent decades. In one cross-national

my disappointment when I found that the classifications had broken down and I was now entered as an Educator. Doubtless we shall have to keep the old pugilistic title of Professor, [but] we can and must get rid of "Educator." Imagine the daily predicament: someone asks, "What do you do?" — "I profess and I educate." It is unspeakable and absurd.

Don't think this frivolous, but regard it as a symbol. Consider the American state of mind about Education at the present time. An unknown correspondent writes to me: "Everybody seems to be dissatisfied with education except those in charge of it." This is a little less than fair, for a great deal of criticism has come from the profession. But let it stand. Dissatisfaction is the keynote. Why dissatisfaction? Because Americans believe in Education, because they pay large sums for Education, and because Education does not seem to yield results. At this point one is bound to ask: "What results do you expect?"

The replies are staggering. Apparently Education is to do everything that the rest of the world leaves undone. . . . An influential critic, head of a large university, wants education to generate a classless society; another asks that education root out racial intolerance (in the third or the ninth grade, I wonder?); still another requires that college courses be designed to improve labor relations. One man, otherwise sane,

thinks the solution of the housing problem has bogged down — in the schools; and another proposes to make the future householders happy married couples — through the schools. . . .

Well, this is precisely where the use of the right word comes in. . . . The advantage of [the word] "teaching" is that in using it you must recognize — if you are in your sober senses — that practical limits exist. You know by instinct that it is impossible to "teach" democracy, or citizenship or a happy married life. I do not say that these virtues and benefits are not somehow connected with good teaching. They are, but they occur as by-products. They come, not from a course, but from a teacher; not from a curriculum, but from a human soul.

Questions

1. When you become a teacher, do you want to be known as an "educator"? What are the positives and negatives attached to this designation?
2. What noninstructional problems and tasks have been thrust at least in part on the schools in recent years?

Source: Jacques Barzun, *The Teacher in America* (Boston: Little, Brown, 1944). Copyright 1944, 1945 by Jacques Barzun. Copyright © renewed 1972 by Jacques Barzun. By permission of Little, Brown and Company.

Reasons for higher teacher status

study, 70 percent of U.S. respondents believed that high-school teachers are either "very respected" or "fairly respected."[6]

One reason why teachers have maintained or even increased their occupational prestige is that their average level of education has risen greatly over the past century. As requirements for entering teaching increase (as detailed later in this chapter) and as more teachers earn graduate degrees, the occupational prestige and status of teachers should improve still more. Rising salaries, discussed in the next section, will also boost status. Other trends that may raise the status of teaching include a growing national concern for the quality and effectiveness of education. Evidence pointing to recent gains in the status of teachers was clear in a 1998 national

---

[6]C. C. North and Paul K. Hatt, "Jobs and Occupation: A Popular Evaluation," *Opinion News*, September 1, 1947, pp. 3–13; Robert W. Hodge, Paul M. Siegel, and Peter H. Rossi, "Occupational Prestige in the United States, 1925–63," *American Journal of Sociology* (November 1964), pp. 286–302; Donald J. Treiman, *Occupational Prestige in Comparative Perspective* (New York: Academic Press, 1977); and Brian Rowan, "Comparing Teachers' Work with Work in Other Occupations: Notes on the Professional Status of Teaching," *Educational Researcher* (August–September 1994), pp. 4–17.

Teachers often supplement their salaries by taking on additional responsibilities, such as athletics, drama, or other extracurricular activities. *(© Spencer Grant/Stock Boston)*

poll in which 75 percent of respondents — up from 57 percent in 1996 — said that teaching, more than medicine and six other professions, "provides the most benefit to society."[7]

Pay Scales and Trends

Increase in salaries

Traditionally, teachers had relatively high occupational prestige but relatively low salaries. In 1960, for example, the average teacher salary in current dollars was slightly less than $26,000. By 1997 this figure had risen to $38,436. Today it is not uncommon for some experienced teachers in wealthy school districts to earn $65,000 to $75,000. Moreover, teachers have opportunities to supplement their income by supervising after-school programs, athletics, drama, and other extracurricular activities, and some can advance to administrative positions with annual salaries well over $90,000. In addition, one should keep in mind that public-school teachers usually have excellent benefits (such as pensions and health insurance) compared to other workers.[8]

Differences among states

Teaching pay varies considerably among and within states. Figure 1.2 shows the range of variation among states. Average overall salaries in the three highest-paying states (Connecticut, New Jersey, and Alaska) were nearly twice as high as those in the three lowest-paying states (North Dakota, Mississippi, and South

[7]*Education at a Glance* (Paris: Organization for Economic Cooperation and Development, 1995) and David Haselkorn and Louis Harris, *The Essential Profession* (Belmont, Mass.: Recruiting New Teachers, 1998), available at **www.rnt.org.**

[8]Allan C. Ornstein, "Teacher Salaries Look Good for the 1990s," *Education Digest* (December 1990), pp. 21–23; Jay Chambers and Sharon Bobbitt, *The Patterns of Teacher Compensation* (Washington D.C.: U.S. Department of Education 1996); and F. Howard Nelson and Krista Schneider, *Survey and Analysis of Salary Trends 1997* (Washington, D.C.: American Federation of Teachers, AFL-CIO, 1998), available at **www.aft.org.**

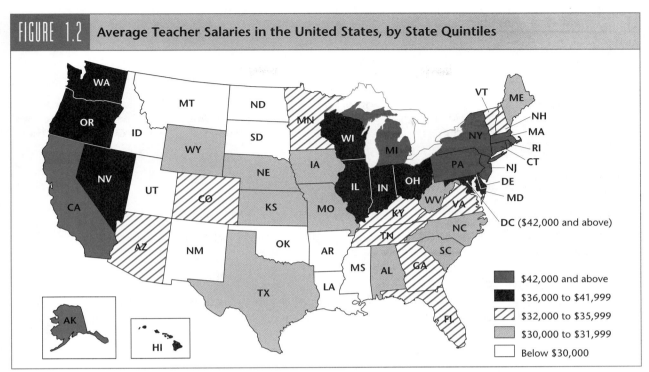

FIGURE 1.2 **Average Teacher Salaries in the United States, by State Quintiles**

Legend:
- $42,000 and above
- $36,000 to $41,999
- $32,000 to $35,999
- $30,000 to $31,999
- Below $30,000

DC ($42,000 and above)

Source: Adapted from F. Howard Nelson and Krista Schneider, *Survey and Analysis of Salary Trends 1997* (Washington, D.C.: American Federation of Teachers, AFL-CIO, 1998), available at **www.aft.org**.

Dakota). Of course, comparative living costs must be taken into account. It is much more expensive to live in Alaska, for example, than to live in the Southeast or the North Central states. Salary differences within states are also wide, especially in states where average state pay scales are high. For example, in Niles, Illinois, the average teacher salary in 1998 was more than $20,000 higher than the average for Illinois teachers statewide. Salary schedules in wealthy suburban districts generally are substantially higher than those in most other school districts.

Salaries vary with experience and education

The greatest variation in salaries is accounted for by years of experience and education. Teachers with more years of experience and more education earn more than those with less of either. Table 1.1 shows the range based on years of experience and additional education in a typical salary schedule — that of the Kansas City, Missouri, public schools. The salary schedule negotiated for 1998 provided $24,539 for a first-year teacher with a B.A. degree and $46,457 for a teacher at the highest level of experience and education. The particular numbers will change from district to district and state to state, but the wide difference between the upper and lower pay levels is fairly common.

Starting salaries

Although a teacher at the top of the salary schedule can earn an attractive salary (especially considering that the academic year is less than ten months long), starting salaries still tend to be lower than in some other professions. Recognizing this problem, many political and educational leaders have been working to increase salaries for both first-year and experienced teachers in order to attract and retain high-quality staff. Figure 1.3 shows the results of efforts to improve teacher salaries. During the inflationary period of the 1970s, teachers' salaries declined relative to

TABLE 1.1	Selected Steps in the Salary Schedule for the Kansas City, Missouri, Public Schools, 1998			
	Bachelor's Degree	**Master's Degree or Bachelor's Degree + 36 Graduate Hours**	**Master's Degree + 32 Graduate Hours**	**Doctorate or Master's Degree + 60 Graduate Hours**
First year (Step 1)	$24,539	$27,068	$28,756	$29,599
Fifth year (Step 5)	27,912	31,164	33,318	34,416
Tenth year (Step 10)	32,129	36,285	39,020	40,436
Maximum (Step 15)	—	41,402	44,722	46,457

Note: Teachers with a bachelor's degree must earn at least thirty-six graduate hours by their thirteenth year of teaching.

Source: Reference sheet distributed by Kansas City, Missouri, Public Schools, 1998.

inflation and to the average salary of all workers, but large gains in both these measures of teacher compensation have been registered since 1980.[9]

Supply and Demand

From 1950 until the mid-1960s, the schools were bursting at the seams with record enrollments that originated in the post–World War II baby boom. These high-birthrate groups had to rely on teachers born during the low-birthrate years of the Great Depression — a trickle of teachers for a flood of students. In the 1960s and 1970s, a falling birthrate reversed the teacher supply situation, resulting in a surplus of teachers. As college students, teacher educators, and state government officials realized that there was a substantial oversupply of teachers, enrollment in teacher-education pro-

Changing patterns

grams decreased, and the percentage of college freshmen interested in becoming teachers declined from 23 percent in 1968 to 5 percent in 1982. Since then, the trend has reversed once more. In part because the decline in the production of new teachers helped to reduce the surplus, the percentage of college students interested in teaching has again increased, rising by nearly 100 percent during the late 1980s and 1990s.[10]

What, then, is the trend for the next ten or fifteen years? Many analysts predict a shortage of teachers, for several reasons:[11]

Reasons to expect a teacher shortage

1. When the original baby boom grew up and began to produce its own children, a "mini" baby boom developed. In addition, many immigrant families have entered the United States in recent years. As a result, school enrollment has been increasing (see Table 1.2).

---

[9]Gary Sykes, "Present Views of Teachers Past," *Educational Researcher* (January–February 1991), pp. 31–32; Peter Brimelow and Leslie Spencer, "Apple for the Teacher," *Forbes*, April 24, 1995, pp. 46–48; and "U.S. Teacher Pay Rises Slightly," National Education Association press release, February 27, 1997.

[10]Beverly T. Watkins, "Teacher–Education Update," *Chronicle of Higher Education*, April 25, 1990, p. A18; and Somini Sepgupta, "A Traditional Career Gains New Class," *New York Times*, August 3, 1997.

[11]"Good to Know," *Future Teacher* (February 1995), p. 4; Ethan Bronner, "Teachers Union Pursuing Quality Control," *New York Times*, July 20, 1998; "The Supply Side of the Labor Market," *Work Force Economics* (June 1998), pp. 3–8; and Richard W. Riley, "High Quality Teachers for Every Classroom," *Teaching K–8* (January 1999), p. 6.

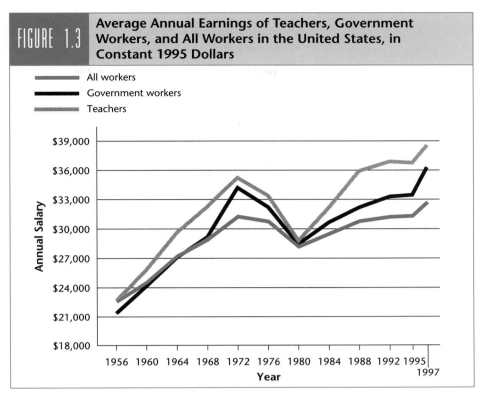

FIGURE 1.3 **Average Annual Earnings of Teachers, Government Workers, and All Workers in the United States, in Constant 1995 Dollars**

Source: Adapted from F. Howard Nelson and Krista Schneider, *Survey and Analysis of Salary Trends 1997* (Washington, D.C.: American Federation of Teachers, AFL-CIO, 1998), available at **www.aft.org**.

2. A significant proportion of the current teaching force will reach retirement age within the next ten years.

3. Educational reformers in some locations are attempting to reduce class size, expand preschool education, place greater emphasis on science and mathematics, and introduce other changes that require more teachers.

4. Higher standards for becoming a teacher are serving to limit the supply of new teachers.

5. Many states are moving to reduce the number of teachers who are not certified for the courses they teach; this reduction in "out-of-field" assignments will require hiring of more teachers.

Reasons to expect no shortage

Other educators, however, argue that there will not be a major shortage of teachers in the next several years. On the supply side, fewer teachers seem to be leaving the profession than in earlier years. Improved salaries may also bring ex-teachers back to the schools and attract people who trained as teachers but did not originally enter the profession. Moreover, many states are making it easier to become a teacher through the process of alternative certification (discussed later in this chapter).[12]

Given the arguments on each side of the issue, it is difficult to determine whether teacher shortages will be widespread in the next decade. However, shortages

[12]*The Supply Side of the Teacher Labor Market in the Southeast* (Research Triangle Park, N.C.: Southeastern Educational Improvement Laboratory, 1990); and Thomas D. Snyder et al., *The Condition of Education 1998* (Washington, DC: U.S. Government Printing Office, 1998).

Shortages in "special needs" fields

should continue to exist in such "special-needs" fields as education of students with disabilities, remedial education, bilingual education, science and mathematics, and foreign languages. In addition, teachers will remain in short supply in many rural areas and in some city and suburban communities that register significant population growth, particularly in the South and Southwest.[13]

Opportunities in Nonpublic Schools.   Numerous job opportunities may be available for prospective teachers in nonpublic schools during the next decade. As Table 1.2 shows, private schools enroll more than 11 percent of the nation's elementary and secondary students. Like the public schools, many private schools are trying to upgrade their instructional programs, often by hiring more teachers who specialize in such areas as science, math, computers, education of children with disabilities, and bilingual education.

Upgraded programs

Changing enrollment patterns

Years ago a large majority of students attending nonpublic schools were in Catholic schools, but this situation has now changed. In the past three decades Catholic enrollment has declined and many other nonpublic schools have been established. Enrollment has increased most in the independent (nonreligious) sector and in schools sponsored by evangelical and fundamentalist church groups. Moreover, many Catholic schools have been increasing the percentage of lay teachers on their faculties, and this trend is likely to continue.[14]

Regardless of whether a large teacher shortage does or does not develop in the next few years, prospective teachers can and should take certain steps to enhance their opportunities for rewarding employment.[15] Some of these are outlined in Overview 1.1.

TABLE 1.2	Public- and Private-School K–12 Enrollments, 1965–2008 (in millions)			
	Total K–12	Public K–12	Private K–12	Private as Percentage of Total
1965	49.4	43.1	6.3	12.9%
1970	51.3	45.9	5.4	10.6
1980	46.2	40.9	5.3	12.1
1985	45.0	39.4	5.6	14.0
1990	46.4	41.2	5.2	11.2
1998	52.7	46.8	5.9	11.3
2008 (projected)	54.3	48.2	6.1	11.2

Source: The Condition of Education, 1991 (Washington, D.C.: U.S. Government Printing Office, 1991), Projections of Education Statistics to 2008 (Washington, D.C.: U.S. Government Printing Office, 1997); and "Enrollment Hits Another Record High, Study Finds," Education Week, September 1998.

[13]Mark Littleton and Jack Holcomb, "New Routes to the Classroom," *American School Board Journal* (May 1994), pp. 37–39; Tamra Fitzpatrick, "Seattle Searches Nationwide for Teachers," *Seattle Times,* June 22, 1998; and Betsy Streisand and Thomas Toch, "Many Millions of Kids, and Too Few Teachers," *U.S. News and World Report,* September 9, 1998.
[14]"Catholic Educators Come out Fighting," *Teacher Magazine* (January 1992), p. 9; and David Baker and Cornelius Riordan, "The 'Eliting' of the Common American Catholic School and the National Education Crisis," *Phi Delta Kappan* (September 1998), pp. 16–23.
[15]See, for example, Maria Mihalik, "Thirty Minutes to Sell Yourself," *Teacher Magazine* (April 1990), pp. 78–80; Diane H. Nettles and Pamela B. Petrick, *Portfolio Development for Preservice Teachers* (Bloomington, Ind.: Phi Delta Kappa, 1995); and Beth Hurst, Cindy Wilson, and Genny Cramer, "Professional Teaching Portfolios," *Phi Delta Kappan* (April 1998), pp. 578–582.

OVERVIEW 1.1   Ways to Improve Your Employment Prospects

Advance Preparation

Check the certification requirements of your state and follow them correctly.

Acquire adjunct skills so that you can be multidimensional, ready to assist in activities like coaching or supervising the student newspaper.

Maintain an up-to-date file listing of all your professional activities, accomplishments, and awards.

Keep well-organized notes on what you learn from classroom observations.

Begin a journal specifically related to teaching concerns. Use it to reflect on what you see and hear and to develop your own ideas.

Scouting and Planning

Collect information on school districts that have vacant positions. Possible sources of information include your career planning or placement office and the state education department's office of teacher employment. Look into computerized job banks operated by professional organizations or available through the Internet.

For school districts in which you are particularly interested, contact them directly.

Plan your application strategy in advance.

Assembling Materials

Prepare a neat, accurate, clear résumé.

Prepare a professional portfolio including lesson plans, peer critiques, descriptions of relevant experience, supervisors' evaluations, and, if possible, a videotape of your teaching.

Ask your career planning or placement office for advice on other materials to include with the credentials you will submit.

Applying for a Job

Begin applying for teaching jobs as soon as possible.

Apply for several vacancies at once.

Preparing for an Interview

Take time to clarify your philosophy of education and learning. Know what you believe, and be able to explain it.

Be prepared for other interview questions as well. In particular, anticipate questions that deal with classroom management, lesson design, and your employment history.

Learn as much as you can about the school district *before* the interview: for instance, its organization, its levels of teaching positions, its types of schools, and its use of technology.

Preparation of Teachers

Evolution of teacher training

During the colonial period and well into the early nineteenth century, anyone who wanted to become a teacher usually obtained approval from a local minister or a board of trustees associated with a religious institution. A high-school or college diploma was not considered necessary. If you could read, write, and spell and were of good moral character, you could teach school. By the 1820s, future teachers had begun attending normal schools (discussed in Chapter 5), although formal certification procedures still were not required. Eventually, the normal schools became teacher colleges, and most of the teacher colleges have now become diversified colleges and universities. Today, except for alternative certification or temporary certification, all states require a bachelor's degree or five years of college work for entrance into teaching.

Preservice Teacher Education

Major components of pre-service preparation

The preparation of teachers usually consists of three major components: (1) liberal (or general) education, (2) specialized subject-field education, and (3) professional education. In general, the purpose of a *liberal education* is to liberate the mind, to provide knowledge of self and culture worthy of a citizen in a free society. A liberal program combines the arts and sciences and seeks to give the student a broad cultural background. The *specialized subject field* comprises a cluster of courses in a specific subject area and provides the prospective teacher with in-depth preparation for his or her chosen teaching field. In most colleges and universities this subject field is called the student's "major" or "minor." Whereas secondary teachers are typically certified in one subject field, and for this reason usually complete a greater amount of coursework in one or two areas, most elementary teachers are responsible for many subject fields. However, elementary teachers may also specialize in areas such as music, art, physical education, and foreign language. *Professional education* consists of courses designed to provide knowledge and skills regarding the art and science of teaching.

Almost all educators agree that the preparation of good teachers rests on these three components. There are strong arguments, however, about the relative emphasis that each component should receive. How much time, for example, should the education student devote to courses in liberal education, versus courses in a specialized subject field and professional education? Viewpoints also differ concerning the extent to which clinical experience, which emphasizes practice in actual school settings, should be incorporated in professional education courses.

Credit requirements

The typical school of education requires about 25 semester hours of professional studies for elementary teacher candidates and 20 hours for secondary teacher candidates. Of course, some colleges of education encourage or require more than this number of credits or specify courses beyond state certification requirements. Most colleges and universities distribute education courses throughout the four-year program, but some cluster them during the last year. Others have a fifth-year component consisting of subject-field and professional courses. Still others have a five-year program involving fieldwork in schools beginning the second or third year and culminating in a graduate-credit internship in schools during the fifth year.

Certification

Requirements for certification

In order to teach in a U.S. public school, prospective teachers must be certificated by the state in the subject areas or grade levels they wish to teach. Until recently, most states granted **certification** based on documentation that the candidate possessed appropriate professional preparation and good moral character. However, increasing public dissatisfaction with the quality of education has led to the widespread use of competency tests for future teachers.[16]

Renewable certificates

In past decades teaching certificates usually were issued for life. Now some states issue certificates valid for only three to five years. Teachers currently holding life certificates are not affected, but those with renewable certificates usually have to furnish proof of positive evaluations or university coursework to have their certificates renewed.

---

[16]John Tryneski, ed., *Requirements for Certification,* 63rd ed. (Chicago: University of Chicago Press, 1998).

Wide differences among states

Variation in Certification Requirements. One of the things that makes the preparation of teachers such a bedeviling problem is that certification requirements vary so widely from state to state. The situation can be summarized as follows: The power to determine requirements for teacher certification is divided among legislatures, state departments of education, schools and colleges of education, superintendents of public instruction, and boards of education. The range of semester hours in general education (that is, arts and sciences) required for a secondary certificate varies nationwide from about 30 hours at the low end to about 75 at the high end. The minimum hours required in professional education courses and the number of semester or quarter hours needed to teach an academic subject also vary in accordance with state requirements. But throughout the country, it is usually the responsibility of the teacher-preparation institution, not the state, to decide what courses in the subject field will be used to meet the semester requirements. Add to this the fact that courses with the same title may differ widely in content from one institution to another, and the result is that state and institutional requirements, even when taken together, do not guarantee that teachers have studied a uniform set of skills and concepts.

Interstate movement of teachers

Reciprocity of Teacher Certificates. Differences in the certification requirements of the individual states traditionally have inhibited the movement of teachers throughout the country. A teacher certified to teach in New York, for example, might not meet the requirements for teaching in Illinois. Organizations concerned with the quality of education generally criticize this lack of reciprocity among states. Many educators argue that freer interstate movement of teachers would be helpful in (1) balancing teacher supply and demand, (2) improving opportunities for teachers, (3) reducing inbreeding and provincialism in local school systems, and (4) increasing morale among teachers.

Regional certificates

With varying degrees of success, reciprocity compacts were established between some states as early as 1900. In recent years, action has been taken to establish two regional teaching certificates, one that provides reciprocity among Iowa, Kansas, Missouri, and Nebraska, and another that provides reciprocity among the New England states. In addition, various organizations are working to develop nationwide approaches that will facilitate teachers' geographic mobility.[17]

Where formal reciprocity agreements exist, people graduating from approved programs leading to certification in one state are supposed to be automatically eligible for similar certification in other participating states. However, certified teachers who expect to move from one state to another should always obtain information on requirements and interpretations that may affect their status and employability.

Nontraditional preparation

Alternative Certification. Partly to attract more talented candidates to teaching, and partly in reaction to current or anticipated shortages in teaching fields such as science and math, most states have introduced **alternative certification** programs. These allow prospective teachers to obtain certification without following the traditional preparation path at schools and colleges of education. New Jersey, for example,

---

[17]The organizations include the National Association of State Directors of Teacher Education Certification (NASDTEC), the Council of Chief State School Officers, and the Educational Testing Service. For commentary, see "One Small Step for Teachers, One Giant Leap for Bureaucrats," *Teacher Magazine* (April 1990), p. 54; Arthur E. Wise, "Professionalization and Standards," *Education Week,* June 1, 1994, pp. 37, 48; and "Information about NASDTEC Activities and Accomplishments," (Undated posting at the Internet site maintained by the NASDTEC), available at **www.nasdtec.org.**

TAKING ISSUE

Alternative Certification

Alternative certification programs that bypass traditional teacher education requirements have been introduced in many states. In general, these programs provide orientation experiences for college graduates and then place them in full-time teaching positions where they receive training leading to certification at the same time they are learning about teaching and education.

Arguments PRO

1 Learning to teach on the job is potentially more effective because it provides better opportunities to determine what does and doesn't work in the real world and to talk with, observe, and emulate successful teachers.

2 Professional studies are likely to be more meaningful and practical when they are integrated with full-time teaching than when they are presented in largely theoretical college courses.

3 Alternative programs, which do not require years of study for certification, can help attract teacher candidates to shortage areas such as mathematics, science, and bilingual education.

4 Alternative programs help attract minority teachers, retired persons with special skills in technical subjects, and other candidates who can make important contributions in improving the education system.

5 The existence of competing alternative programs will stimulate colleges and universities to improve their teacher-training programs.

Arguments CON

1 Learning to teach on the job generally will prove unsuccessful because many or most participants will be overwhelmed by the immediate demands placed on a new teacher and will be unable to develop and hone their skills adequately.

2 In practice, school districts either lack sufficient resources to provide professional studies for participants or have other priorities. Initial data on several alternative certification programs support this point.

3 These programs offer short-term relief only. Many participants will withdraw during or soon after the first year of teaching, once they realize they are not suited for or interested in the work.

4 Alternative certification reinforces inequity in education because it often places inexperienced persons at inner-city schools, which have high turnover and the most need for well-trained and experienced faculty.

5 Competing alternative programs may distract colleges and universities from offering training that develops the understanding and skills of reflective teachers over several years of study.

has a program to attract "talented persons who did not study education in college." Nationwide, more than 75,000 teachers have been certified through alternative certification programs. Many new teachers within this group are persons pursuing teaching careers after leaving the armed forces.[18]

---

[18]Ann Bradley, "Expiring 'Troops to Teachers' Project Outfits Classrooms with Teachers in Demand," *Education Week* (October 14, 1998); and C. Emily Feistritzer, "Alternative Teacher Certification: An Overview" (Paper prepared for the National Center for Education Information, February 1998), available at **www.ncei.com**.

Alternative certification programs try to provide for intense supervision and compressed formal coursework during the first few years of assignment to a teaching position. Many educators, however, are troubled by alternative certification. Short-term preparation cannot prove as adequate as traditional training programs, and pressures to respond rapidly to shortages of personnel in key teaching areas may lead schools to tolerate superficial preparation and supervision. In addition, alternative certification may undercut efforts to improve the quality of the teacher force through reform of teacher-education programs and preservice testing of future teachers' competencies.[19]

Several systematic examinations of alternative certification programs have provided some encouraging indications that well-educated individuals with a "sincere interest in teaching" are being attracted and that "intense supervision" is being provided. However, some recent assessments have raised questions. For example, data on several alternative certification programs indicate that many participants received little or none of the training or supervision that school districts were supposed to provide. Some of the participants acquired large debts and were unable to find teaching jobs afterward.[20]

Probably the best-known alternative certification program is a national effort called Teach for America. Designed to attract recent graduates from colleges at which students have high achievement scores, Teach for America has spent millions of dollars to recruit potential teachers, train them intensively for eight weeks, and place them in school districts with severe urban problems. Some of the initial reports were promising. For example, in some years more than one-quarter of the participants were minority individuals, and many of the secondary-school participants had much-needed skills in math or science. But the data also indicated that many of these potential new teachers were frustrated by conditions in difficult schools and/or withdrew before completing their initial assignments. Critics also raised questions about the adequacy of the eight-week training, the possible "arrogance" inherent in a program that recruits high-ability but thinly trained teachers from elite colleges for placement in low-income schools, and the failure of some participating schools and districts to provide recruits with promised support.[21]

Trends in Preservice Education

Over the past two decades, many teacher-education programs have placed significant emphasis on competency-based preparation, on school-based field centers, and on earlier field experience. In recent years major developments also have included movements toward fifth-year and five-year programs; increased emphasis on producing

---

[19]Roy A. Edelfelt, "Final Thoughts on Alternative Certification," *Educational Forum* (Winter 1994), pp. 220–223; and Denise McKeon, "The Promise of Alternative Certification: Has It Materialized?" (1998 Posting on the Internet site of the American Educational Research Association), available at **aera.net/outreach**.

[20]Joe M. Smith, "The Alternate Route: Flaws in the New Jersey Plan," *Educational Leadership* (November 1991), pp. 32–36; C. Emily Feistritzer, "The Evolution of Alternative Teacher Certification," *Educational Forum* (Winter 1994), pp. 132–138; and John M. Miller and Michael C. McKenna, "A Comparison of Alternatively and Traditionally Prepared Teachers," *Journal of Teacher Education* (May–June 1998), pp. 167–176.

[21]Julie L. Nicklin, "Alternative Teacher–Education Project Draws Mixed Review," *Chronicle of Higher Education*, June 19, 1991, pp. A21–A22; Rachel Shteir, "Teach for America: Learning the Hard Way," *The New York Times Education Life*, January 7, 1996, pp. 25, 30; Wendy Kopp, "A Case for Professional Corps," *National Civic Review* (Fall 1997), pp. 211–217; and Elizabeth Greenspan, "A Look at . . . the Desire to Teach," *Washington Post*, November 8, 1998.

"reflective" teachers; growing use of computers and other technology; requirements that future teachers learn about methods for teaching students with disabilities and other "special" populations; and programs to prepare teaching candidates for the diverse cultural and ethnic settings of contemporary American schools.

Testing of teachers'
performance

Competency-Based Teacher Education and Performance Assessment. A program using **competency-based teacher education** (CBTE) requires prospective teachers to demonstrate minimum levels of performance on specified teaching tasks. For example, rather than identifying an appropriate teaching strategy by writing a brief essay or selecting from multiple-choice alternatives, a candidate may be required to teach a simulated class and then discuss the reasons for his or her teaching behaviors. The skills and understandings tested are based on research findings about the characteristics of effective teachers.

In the 1970s as many as half the teacher-training institutions in the United States used some degree of CBTE in their preservice programs, but this figure declined as colleges and universities experienced financial problems (CBTE is expensive if done well) and as questions were raised about CBTE's utility and feasibility. However, during the 1990s Kentucky, Oklahoma, and some other states moved to introduce or expand performance-based competency assessment.[22]

Criticisms directed at CBTE and other performance-based approaches have included the following:[23]

Criticisms of CBTE

1. Performance-assessment approaches fragment teacher education by introducing too many separate skills. For example, some implementations have included hundreds of skill modules.

2. The reliability and validity of competency tests are not well established.

3. It is difficult to translate assessment information about prospective teachers into certification units and licensing requirements.

4. Valid performance-assessment approaches are too expensive for many teacher-preparation programs.

School-Based Field Centers. One innovation designed to make teacher preparation more realistic and practical involves field centers at cooperating elementary or secondary schools. Much of the training previously provided at the college or university campus is now conducted at these **school-based field centers,** which frequently have office space for college faculty, special equipment for use in teacher training, and outstanding teachers who serve as supervisors and models.

School-based centers
on the rise

Whereas in 1968 less than 20 percent of higher education teacher-training institutions had established or designated school-based centers, approximately half had done so by 1994. The trend toward establishing these centers was particularly evident among public colleges and universities: about two-thirds of the public higher education institutions have established a school-based center of some kind. The number of centers seems to have been increasing in the 1980s and 1990s, as

---

[22]Kenneth M. Zeichner and Daniel P. Liston, *Traditions of Reform in U.S. Teacher Education* (East Lansing, Mich.: National Center for Research on Teacher Education, 1990); Claudia Long and Kendyll Stansbury, "Performance Assessments for Beginning Teachers," *Phi Delta Kappan* (December 1994), pp. 318–326; and "Teacher Preparation," *NEGP Monthly,* May 27, 1998, available at **www.negp.gov.**
[23]Sam J. Yarger and Bruce R. Joyce, "Going Beyond the Data: Reconstructing Teacher Education," *Journal of Teacher Education* (November–December 1977), pp. 21–25; and Mary E. Diez, *Changing the Practice of Teacher Education* (Washington, DC: American Association of Colleges of Teacher Education, 1998).

reform-minded educators have explored possibilities for establishing "professional development schools" (described later in this chapter).[24]

Early assignments in schools

Early Field Experience.　Many teacher-education programs have become more practical by requiring or encouraging future teachers to spend a significant amount of time in elementary or secondary schools early in their preparation. Professional courses dealing with subjects such as introduction to education, educational psychology, or pedagogical methods are closely coordinated with classroom observation, assignments as a teacher aide, or other field experiences in local schools. Institutions that require early and continual field experience have constructed a sequence by which students move from observation, to service as a teacher's aide, to relatively full-scale teaching responsibility much as in the traditional "practice teaching" semester.[25]

Scheduling of professional-study components

Fifth-Year and Five-Year Programs.　During the 1980s several states and numerous schools and colleges of education either introduced fifth-year programs or expanded teacher education across five years of preparation. We define *fifth-year programs* as those that include few or no professional-study components during the four years in which the future teacher earns a bachelor's degree; professional preparation is concentrated in the fifth year. In contrast, *five-year programs* spread professional preparation across the undergraduate years and focus increasingly on clinical experience and training. Some institutions modify these programs by shifting some professional studies to a fifth year while retaining substantial undergraduate teacher-education requirements.

State mandates

　　Fifth-year programs sometimes arise as a response to state government mandates to greatly reduce or eliminate undergraduate teacher-education courses. This would ensure that future teachers spend more time acquiring a comprehensive general education and more adequate knowledge of subjects they eventually will teach. In Virginia, for example, the state has placed a maximum of eighteen hours on teacher-education courses taken as part of a four-year preparation program; additional education courses are taken during the fifth year of study. More commonly, though, teacher-education institutions create five-year programs in which the professional studies begin with orientation in the freshman or sophomore year and conclude with concentrated field experience (sometimes as an intern) in the fifth year. Some institutions have further complicated training by establishing a program that requires more than five years.[26]

"Thoughtful" practitioners

Reflective Teaching.　In accordance with the recent stress on improving students' thinking and comprehension skills, many institutions emphasize **reflective teaching** as a central theme in teacher education. Reflective teachers frequently reflect on the

---

[24]Edward J. Meade, Jr., "Reshaping the Clinical Phase of Teacher Preparation," *Phi Delta Kappan* (May 1991), pp. 666–669; Kate Hawkes, "Learning from Peers," *Journal of Teacher Education* (May–June 1995), pp. 175–183; and Robin H. McBee, "Readying Teachers for Real Classrooms," *Educational Leadership* (February 1998), pp. 56–58.

[25]Catherine Cornbleth and Jeanne Ellsworth, "Teachers and Teacher Education: Clinical Faculty Roles and Relationships," *American Educational Research Journal* (Spring 1994), pp. 49–70; Judy Swanson, "Systemic Reform in the Professionalism of Educators," *Phi Delta Kappan* (September 1995), pp. 36–39; and Pamela G. Fry and Linda J. McKinney, "A Qualitative Study of Preservice Teachers' Early Field Experiences in an Urban, Culturally Different School," *Urban Education* (May 1997), pp. 184–201.

[26]"Herbst's Recommendations," *The Holmes Group Forum* (Winter 1992), p. 7; Julie Nicklin, "A Plethora of Reforms," *Chronicle of Higher Education* (March 9, 1994), pp. A16, A18; and Linda Darling-Hammond, "Teachers and Teaching," *Educational Researcher* (January–February, 1998), pp. 5–15.

PROFESSIONAL PLANNING

for your first year

Maintaining Your Commitments and Goals as a Teacher

The Situation

Faculty members with whom you study in your teacher-education program may point out that it can be difficult to practice what you have been taught when you obtain a teaching position. In some of your courses you will learn that it is important to teach students how to understand complex material and how to solve problems in your subject-matter field. You also will learn how to help them do this. In concluding parts of this chapter you will see that helping students in this way is an overriding goal of nationwide efforts that are under way to improve and reform elementary and secondary schools.

But when you actually begin to teach, you may well encounter obstacles. You might find that you do not have sufficient, appropriate materials to emphasize meaningful learning. Your class or classes could be too large, or include too many very-low-achieving students, to allow you to easily apply what you have learned. Most insidiously, some of your new colleagues may disparage your efforts to emphasize growth in students' comprehension and thinking skills. These colleagues may have concluded that many students are not willing to work hard. They will often tell you that you should "stick to the basics" that some students have not mastered. It is not too early for you to begin to consider, as you study this textbook, how you might respond productively if you find yourself in this situation.

Thought Questions

1. How many years of teaching might be required for you to acquire the experience necessary to teach effectively in a difficult situation?
2. What might you do to "hold on" to your philosophical commitments to help students acquire meaningful skills and subject matter if or when you have difficulty applying what you have learned in your own classroom?
3. Which teaching approaches and strategies in your professional preparation courses seem to be most practical in terms of application in "real" classrooms?
4. To what extent should you be willing to modify your goals and commitments based on what happens to you when you become a certified teacher? To what extent should you resist doing this?

results of their teaching and adjust their methods accordingly. Closely related terms such as *inquiry-oriented teacher education, expert decision making,* and *higher-order self-reflection* also have been used to describe this concept. Hundreds of schools of education have reorganized their programs to try to prepare reflective teachers, but the programs are very diverse, and there is little agreement on what reflective teaching should mean.[27]

---

[27]Dorothy K. Stewart, "Reflective Teaching in Preservice Teacher Education," *Journal of Teacher Education* (September 1994), pp. 298–302; Linda Darling-Hammond, "The Right to Learn and the Advancement of Teaching," *Educational Researcher* (August–September, 1996), pp. 5–17; and Terry L. Wentzlaff, "Dispositions and Portfolio Development," *Education* (Summer 1998), pp. 564–572.

*Technology training
for teachers*

Computer and Technology Use.   National surveys of teacher-education programs indicate that more than 90 percent have established computer or technology laboratories. These laboratories encompass a wide variety of activities and objectives, such as orienting future teachers in computer use, introducing hardware and software developed for elementary and secondary schools, and strengthening interest and capability in technology for lesson design or delivery. Many students are also being exposed to technology in their teaching methods courses. However, some programs apparently do not have sufficient funds to support high-quality efforts to prepare their future teachers to use contemporary technologies.[28]

Help for schools of education

The incorporation of knowledge and skills regarding the use of technology as part of teacher preparation is a worldwide trend. For example, the compulsory, nationwide curriculum for initial teacher training in the United Kingdom now includes a listing of IT (Information Technology) skills that students must acquire before the end of their courses. In the United States, the Panel on Educational Technology formed by President William Clinton recommended that government should help schools of education improve their capability for "preparing the next generation of American teachers to make effective use of technology," and the Higher Education Reauthorization Act of 1998 subsequently provided funds for a variety of activities that in part involve technology in teacher training. Emphasis on the use of technology in both preservice and in-service teacher-development programs undoubtedly will continue to increase in the future.[29]

Preparation for mainstreaming and inclusion

Requirements for Teaching of Disabled Students.   Many states and teacher-training institutions now require that all future teachers receive some preparation in working with students who have significant disabilities. The law demands that disabled students be *mainstreamed* in regular classes as much as is possible and feasible, and there has been a growing trend toward full *inclusion* of disabled students no matter how extensive their special needs. (See Chapter 11 for information about mainstreaming, inclusion, and related topics.) As a consequence, most teachers can expect to have some responsibility for working with special-needs students. Typical teacher-training requirements include the following:[30]

Typical requirements

- Cooperative, interdisciplinary efforts in which both higher-education faculty and knowledgeable field educators help future teachers learn approaches for working with students with disabilities
- Arrangements that reduce or eliminate the separation between programs and courses that prepare "regular" teachers and those that prepare "special-education" teachers

---

[28]Dianne I. Novak and Carl F. Berger, "Integrating Technology into Teacher-Education," *T.H.E. Journal* (April 1991), pp. 83–86; "The Use of Technology by Schools, Colleges, and Departments of Education." Statement published by the American Association of Colleges of Teacher Education, Fall, 1996; and Donald R. Coker and Mary Wilson, "Reconceptualizing the Process of Teacher Preparation," *Education* (Summer 1997), pp. 500–506.

[29]Niki Davis, "Information Technology in Teacher Education," *Journal of Information Technology and Teacher Education* (Number 3, 1997), available at **www.triangle.co.uk;** and "Statement by U.S. Secretary of Education Richard W. Riley on Senate Passage of S. 1882," available at **www.ed.gov.**

[30]Carol Strawderman and Pamela Lindsey, "Keeping Up with the Times," *Journal of Teacher Education* (March–April 1995), pp. 95–100; and Charles C. Mackey, "A National Perspective on Professional Certification" (Paper prepared for First Southeast Comprehensive System for Personnel Development Network, 1998).

■ Requirements in many states that all future teachers complete one or more courses in education for special-needs students, and/or that existing courses incorporate substantial amounts of material on the subject

Preparing for multicultural classrooms

Preparation for Teaching in Diverse Settings.   In line with increases in the enrollment of racial and ethnic minority groups in U.S. schools, programs to prepare future teachers have been adding components designed to ensure that teacher candidates will function successfully in diverse settings. Similar efforts are under way in teacher licensing. For example, the Praxis III teacher performance assessment approach, developed by the Educational Testing Service (ETS), specifies that a candidate for a teaching license should be able to demonstrate a "comprehensive understanding" of why it is important to become familiar with students' background knowledge and experiences, and to describe several procedures that can be used to obtain such information. Although multiculturalism has become a controversial topic, many educators believe strongly that teacher-preparation programs should emphasize ways to celebrate, not merely tolerate, the cultural and ethnic diversity in U.S. classrooms.[31]

Efforts to Improve the Teaching Force

In recent years, there has been much discussion about possibilities for improving the quality of the teaching work force. Much of the effort to improve the quality of teachers and teaching has centered on testing of teachers, on the shortage of minority teachers, and on a variety of recommendations publicized in influential national reports on the problems of the U.S. educational system.

Ability of Teachers

Standardized test scores

Discussions of the "quality" of the teaching work force frequently focus on "ability" scores derived from standardized tests such as the Scholastic Aptitude Test (SAT) and the American College Test (ACT). Among potential teachers, such test scores declined in the 1970s, as they did for students majoring in business and numerous other subjects. For example, between 1973 and 1981, the average SAT verbal score of college students intending to teach fell from 418 to 397. Since 1982, however, the test scores of college students who say they intend to become teachers have appreciably increased, and appear to be generally similar to those of students majoring in business, psychology, and the health professions. Other encouraging data have been provided by the American Association of Colleges for Teacher Education (AACTE), which reported that a national sample of school administrators rated teacher-education graduates significantly higher than earlier graduates on eight characteristics such as "ability to organize the classroom" and "motivating all students to reach their maximum potential." In addition, more than two-thirds of education faculty report that their students are well prepared in instructional methods and approaches.[32]

---

[31]Mary L. Gomez, "Prospective Teachers' Perspectives on Teaching Diverse Children," *Journal of Negro Education* (Fall 1993), pp. 459–474; "Public School Teachers," *Daily Report Card,* July 9, 1997; and G. Pritchy Smith, *Common Sense About Uncommon Knowledge* (Washington, D.C.: American Association of Colleges of Teacher Education, 1998).

[32]Daniel Koretz, *Educational Achievement: Explanations and Implications of Recent Trends* (Washington, D.C.: Congressional Budget Office, 1987); "SAT Scores," *Teacher Education Reports,* September 7, 1995, p. 3; and Catherine E. Cardina and John K. Roden, "Academic Proficiency of Students Who Reported Intentions of Majoring in Education," *Journal of Teacher Education* (January–February, 1998), pp. 38–46.

Funding questions

In considering students' readiness to teach, it should be noted that clinical preparation for many future teachers consists of less than a semester of "practice" or "student" teaching, and that the average annual per-student expenditure for training teachers typically is much less than the average annual per-student expenditure in elementary and secondary schools. Some observers trace this problem at least in part to the tendency of schools and colleges of education to serve as "cash cows" that generate revenue used to fund other campus units. Resulting inadequacies in teacher-preparation programs became a matter of widespread national concern when a number of well-publicized reports on problems in education were released in the 1980s. We will review these reports' implications for teachers and teaching later in this chapter and in subsequent chapters.[33]

Testing of Teachers

Testing basic skills

Some of the efforts to improve the teaching force focus on **basic skills testing** of preservice teachers, new teachers, and sometimes experienced teachers. Drawing on the argument that teachers who have very low reading, mathematics, communications, and/or professional knowledge probably are ineffective in their teaching, many states have introduced requirements that prospective teachers pass some form of minimum skills test in reading and language, math, subject-area specialty, and/or professional knowledge. More than forty states now use the Praxis test developed by the Educational Testing Service for this purpose.[34]

Praxis examination

Criticism of testing

Testing of prospective and current teachers has become a controversial topic that is not likely to be resolved soon. Many political leaders see testing as one of the few feasible steps they can take to improve public confidence in the teaching force. Opponents argue that the process unjustifiably excludes people who do poorly on paper-and-pencil tests. Many opponents also believe that existing tests are biased against minorities and other candidates not from the cultural mainstream. Critics also cite data indicating that scores on standardized tests such as the NTE do not correlate well with subsequent on-the-job measures of teaching effectiveness.[35]

Support of testing

Proponents of testing generally counter that all or nearly all teachers must be able to demonstrate that they can function at least at the seventh- or eighth-grade level in reading, writing, and math — the minimum level currently specified on some of the tests — if they are to perform effectively in their jobs. Many proponents also argue that research has provided enough information to justify minimum standards and to allow for the creation of more valid exams.[36]

---

[33]"New Respect for Teacher Education?" *Teacher Magazine* (January 1992), pp. 8–9; Hendrik D. Gideonese, "Appointments with Ourselves," *Phi Delta Kappan* (October 1993), pp. 174–180; and Linda Darling-Hammond and Barnett Berry, "Investing in Teaching," *Education Week*, May 27, 1998, pp. 34, 48.
[34]Linda Darling-Hammond, *The Evolution of Teacher Policy* (Santa Monica, Calif.: Rand, 1988); and Richard Whitmire, "Scrutiny Falls on Teacher Testing," *Seattle Times*, July 6, 1998.
[35]Ayres G. D'Costa, "The Impact of Courts on Teacher Competence Testing," *Theory into Practice* (Spring 1993), pp. 104–112; Linda Darling-Hammond, Arthur E. Wise, and Stephen P. Klein, *A License to Teach* (Boulder, Colo.: Westview, 1995); and David G. Imig, "The Seventy Percent Solution," *AACTE Briefs*, May 4, 1998, available at **www.aacte.org**.
[36]W. James Popham and W. N. Kirby, "Recertification Tests for Teachers: A Defensible Safeguard for Society," *Phi Delta Kappan* (September 1987), pp. 45–49; Richard J. Murname, "The Case for Performance-Based Licensing," *Phi Delta Kappan* (October 1991), pp. 137–142; and Allen Glenn, "Passing the Test," *AACTE Briefs*, August 10, 1998, available at **www.aacte.org**.

Controversy in Massachusetts

Controversy regarding testing of prospective teachers became nationally prominent in 1998 after Massachusetts administered its first statewide test for this purpose. Thirty percent of the candidates failed the reading and writing test, and 63 percent of candidates for mathematics certification failed the subject-matter test in their field. After the chairman of the state board of education stated that "the real story . . . is that so many prospective public school teachers failed a test that a bright 10th grader could pass without difficulty," that the real "casualties" of the test included "grammar, syntax, diction, spelling, and logic," and that "no responsible person would subject anyone's children, much less his own, to teachers who had failed these topics," legislators and educators in Massachusetts and elsewhere initiated an ongoing debate concerning the levels of test performance that should be imposed for entering and exiting teacher-preparation programs and for obtaining teaching certificates.[37]

Help for Beginning Teachers

State initiatives to assist new teachers

In addition to expanding testing of teachers, many states and school districts have established programs to improve the teaching force by assisting beginning teachers. Since the early 1980s, more than thirty states have mandated statewide initiatives or have provided funds for this purpose. Some general themes in these efforts include the following:[38]

- The programs often use a support team rather than a single mentor teacher.
- Mentor teachers serve as peer coaches and receive released time and/or stipends for helping new teachers.
- Formal training materials are available on a statewide or districtwide basis.
- Performance-assessment approaches are used to determine whether new teachers have mastered some of the most important teaching skills.

Recommendations of National Reports

Since the mid-1980s a large number of reports — prepared by various national commissions as well as individuals supported by philanthropic and government grants — have focused on problems of education in the United States. Frequently referred to collectively as the **national reports**, they are discussed in detail in Chapter 13.

Problems identified in A Nation at Risk

A Nation at Risk (1983), the best known and most influential of the national reports, was prepared by the National Commission on Excellence in Education sponsored by the U.S. Department of Education. Arguing that the United States is "at risk" in the sense that its "once unchallenged preeminence in commerce, industry, service, and technological innovation is being overtaken by competitors

---

[37]John Silber, "Those Who Can't Teach," *New York Times*, July 7, 1998.
[38]Leslie Huling-Austin, "Beginning Teacher Assistance Programs: An Overview," in *Assisting the Beginning Teacher* (Reston, Va.: Association of Teacher Educators, 1994), pp. 5–13; Carol B. Furtwengler, "Beginning Teachers Programs: Analysis of State Actions During the Reform Era," *Education Policy Analysis Archives* (February 1995), available at **olam.ed.asu.edu**; Del Schalock, Mark Schalock, and David Myton, "Effectiveness — Along with Quality — Should Be the Focus," *Phi Delta Kappan* (February 1998), pp. 468–470; and Jimmie Cook, "Mid-Year Memorandum," *Teaching K–8* (January 1999) pp. 40–41.

throughout the world," the commission concluded that one major aspect of decline has been a "rising tide of mediocrity" in the schools. The report's recommendations are summarized in Overview 13.2. Here, we should take special note of the report's suggestions for making teaching a more rewarding and respected profession:[39]

Proposals for the teaching profession

- Set higher standards for entry into the profession
- Increase teacher salaries so they are "professionally competitive, market-sensitive, and performance-based," thus making them part of a system that gives greater rewards to superior teachers (in other words, institute merit pay, a practice discussed in Chapter 2)
- Add an additional month of employment with pay for teachers
- Institute a *career ladder* that distinguishes among different levels of teachers, so that qualified people progress from beginning teacher to experienced teacher and finally to the level of *master* teacher
- Use incentives such as grants and loans to attract outstanding candidates into teaching, particularly into shortage areas such as science and mathematics
- Involve master teachers in preparing and supervising probationary teachers

Carnegie recommendations

In 1986, three years after the publication of *A Nation at Risk,* the Carnegie Task Force on Teaching as a Profession released *A Nation Prepared: Teachers for the 21st Century.* This report stressed the urgent need to improve education for the nation's growing proportion of low-income and minority students and the importance of teaching "complex, non-routine intellectual" skills. Like *A Nation at Risk,* the Carnegie report recommended increasing teachers' salaries and establishing a career hierarchy so that teachers at the top of the hierarchy, called "lead teachers" (a category similar to "master teachers"), would exercise leadership responsibilities in the schools. The report also called for incentives to increase the pool of minority teachers. It further proposed the establishment of a national board, as in medicine and law, to set high standards for teachers and certify those who met them.[40]

NBPTS certification

In 1987, in accordance with this last recommendation, the Carnegie Corporation helped establish the **National Board for Professional Teaching Standards** (NBPTS), a nonprofit organization whose purpose is to issue certificates to teachers who meet the board's standards for professional ability and knowledge. As of 1998, the board had awarded contracts to identify standards and develop assessments for 33 certification fields, and the first candidates had earned certification in several of the fields, including "English Language Arts," and "Generalist" studies for early adolescents. The standards, which focus on both content knowledge and effective teaching methods, are designed to be considerably more rigorous than those for state certification tests. Assessment methods include interviews, portfolios, computer

---

[39]National Commission on Excellence in Education, *A Nation at Risk: The Imperative for Education Reform* (Washington, D.C.: U.S. Department of Education, 1983), p. 5; and National Education Commission on Time and Learning, *Prisoners of Time* (Washington, D.C.: U.S. Department of Education, 1994). The latter report, which builds on parts of *A Nation at Risk,* is available at **nces.ed.gov**. See also William J. Bennett et al., "A Nation Still at Risk," *Policy Review* (July–August 1998), available at **www.heritage.com.**, and Paul D. Houston, "Do we Suffer from Educational Glaucoma?" *School Administrator* (January 1999).
[40]Carnegie Task Force on Teaching as a Profession, *A Nation Prepared: Teachers in the 21st Century* (New York: Carnegie Corporation, 1986). See also Rick Ginsberg and David N. Plank, eds., *Commissions, Reports, Reforms, and National Policy* (Westport, Conn.: Greenwood, 1995); and "Alliance Advocates Higher Standards for Teachers in New Partnerships," *Work America* (January 1998), pp. 1–3.

and video simulations, and other innovative elements. To be eligible for national board certification, teachers must have a bachelor's degree and at least three years of successful teaching. Several states and a number of school districts have decided to pay the application fee and/or to provide salary increases for teachers who pass the NBPTS certification exams.[41]

INTASC standards

Standards for the performance of teachers — in this case beginning teachers — are also being developed by the Interstate New Teacher Assessment and Support Consortium (INTASC) with funding from the U.S. Department of Education. Current information concerning INTASC can be obtained on the Internet by accessing **www.cesso.org/intasc.html**. More than 30 states are participating in INTASC.[42]

Holmes Group recommendations

Holmes and Other Groups.   Since 1986, reform of the teaching profession has been a primary concern of the Holmes Group, a consortium of deans of education at major research universities. Subsequently renamed the Holmes Partnership, Holmes commissioned a series of reports, including *Tomorrow's Teachers, Tomorrow's Schools,* and *Tomorrow's Schools of Education.* In addition to the reforms stressed in other reports, the Holmes Group has emphasized the need for teacher-education students to have early experience in schools. Consequently, the group has focused on the creation of **professional development schools** (PDSs). Like a traditional "laboratory" school, the PDS is designed to link a local school district with a college or school of education, but in a more comprehensive and systematic fashion. College faculty members function as classroom teachers and serve as mentors for new teachers. According to the Holmes Group, PDSs will encourage thoughtful, long-term inquiry into teaching and learning. Experienced teachers, beginning teachers, teacher educators, and administrators will work together to create a community of learners, and to improve educational opportunities for low-achieving students.[43]

Support for PDSs

Other groups, including the American Federation of Teachers, the American Association of Colleges of Teacher Education (AACTE), and the National Education Association, have been working to establish plans for schools similar to PDSs. The efforts are in the early stages, but AACTE surveys indicate that many schools and colleges of education are cooperating with professional development schools or similar institutions. On the other hand, progress has been hampered by lack of funds among both school districts and higher-education institutions.[44]

---

[41]*Towards High and Rigorous Standards* (Detroit: National Board for Professional Teaching Standards, 1990); "Assessing Accomplished Teaching, *ERIC Review* (Winter 1995), pp. 14–15 (available at **www.ed.gov**); Barbara C. Shapiro, "The NBTS Sets Standards for Accomplished Teaching," *Educational Leadership* (March 1995), pp. 55–57; and Iris C. Rotberg, Mary H. Futrell, and Joyce M. Lieberman, "National Board Certification," *Phi Delta Kappan* (February 1998), pp. 462–466.

[42]"Teacher Preparation," *National Education Goals Panel Monthly*, May 27, 1998, available at **www.negp.gov**; and Ernest W. Brewer and Connie Hollingsworth, eds., *Promising Practices* (Scottsdale, Ariz.: Holcomb Hathaway, 1999).

[43]Holmes Group, *Tomorrow's Teachers* (East Lansing, Mich.: Holmes Group, 1986); Holmes Group, *Tomorrow's Schools* (East Lansing, Mich.: Holmes Group, 1990); Holmes Group, *Tomorrow's Schools of Education* (East Lansing, Mich.: Holmes Group, 1995). See also Linda Valli, David Cooper, and Lisa Frankes, "Professional Development Schools and Equity," in Michael W. Apple, ed., *Review of Research in Education 22* (Washington, D.C.: American Educational Research Association, 1997), pp. 251–304.

[44]Ann Lieberman and Lynne Miller, "Teacher Development in Professional Practice Schools," *Teachers College Record* (Fall 1990), pp. 105–122; Ismat Abdal-Haqq, "Professional Development Schools," *ERIC Review* (Winter 1995), pp. 16–17; and Peter Murrell, Jr., *Like Stone Soup* (Washington, D.C.: American Association of Colleges of Teacher Education, 1998).

Renaissance Group proposals

Additional support for reform of the teaching profession has come from the Renaissance Group (a consortium of higher-education institutions composed primarily of former teacher-training colleges) and the U.S. Department of Education (DOE). The Renaissance Group contends that teacher training should be integrated throughout a student's university experience rather than reserved for the student's final year and should incorporate extensive, sequenced field and clinical experience. The DOE supports several national initiatives aimed at improving teaching and teacher preparation through research and development.[45]

Reactions to the National Reports and Subsequent Developments.   Reactions to the plethora of national reports and subsequent developments described above have been mixed. There is no doubt that the reports have helped focus attention on the problems of education, and the specific proposals have generated a great deal of support. However, many educators believe that the reports have been too simplistic in their diagnoses and solutions, and some of the proposals have met with substantial resistance and criticism.[46]

Critiques of national reports

For example, many teachers and administrators as well as researchers have criticized the emphasis on "lead teacher" and "career ladder" approaches that give some teachers greater authority and remuneration than their colleagues. The NBPTS was attacked by the president of the American Association of School Administrators, who described the national board as "an attempted takeover of American schools by teacher unions." Others have pointed out the enormous expense involved in implementing NBPTS practices and the difficulties the board faces in constructing valid tests of teachers' skills and knowledge. Similarly, critics of professional development schools have focused on the high costs of PDSs and the lack of available funds, as well as the divergent interests that hamper collaboration between school districts and higher education institutions. There is concern, as well, that teachers participating in reform activities will be overburdened by numerous and conflicting demands for change.[47]

State reforms

Despite the lack of consensus, nearly all state governments have taken actions consistent with one or another of the national reports. Many states have raised teacher salaries, stiffened entrance and exit requirements for teacher education, and/or expanded testing of new teachers.[48] These efforts were supported and

---

[45]J. T. Sandefur, *Analysis of Teacher Education Reform Initiatives* (Bowling Green, Ky.: Western Kentucky University, 1991); Joseph C. Vaughan, "OERI Launches Professional Development Initiatives," *ERIC Review* (Winter 1995), pp. 18–19 (a free subscription to the review can be obtained by calling 1-800-ASK ERIC); and "The Federal Role in Developing the 'Best Teachers,'" *Policy Forum* (October 1997).

[46]For examples, see Thomas B. Timar and David L. Kirp, *Managing Educational Excellence* (New York: Falmer, 1988); Joseph Murphy, ed., *The Educational Reform Movement of the 1980s* (Berkeley, Calif.: McCutchan, 1990); and Michael Fullan, et al. *The Rise and Stall of Teacher Education Reform* (Washington, D.C.: American Association of Colleges of Teacher Education, 1998).

[47]William R. Johnson, "Empowering Practitioners: Holmes, Carnegie, and the Lessons of History," *History of Education Quarterly* (Summer 1987), pp. 221–240; Ann Bradley, "Wait a Minute . . ." *Teacher Magazine* (March 1990), pp. 16, 18; and Mary L. Collins, "The Reform of Teacher Education," *Contemporary Education*, Fall 1997, pp. 48–51.

[48]Carole Furtwengler, "State Actions for Personnel Evaluation," *Education Policy Analysis Archives* (February, 1995), available at **olam.ed.asu.edu**; and Diane Kassell, Michael Kirst, and Margaret Hoppe, "Persistence and Change, *CPRE Policy Briefs* (March 1997), available at **www.negp.gov**.

expanded by passage of the national **Higher Education Reauthorization Act of 1998**, which included funding for the following activities:[49]

Higher Education Reauthorization Act

■ To improve "teacher preparation through grants to partnerships . . . between teacher education institutions and school districts to produce teachers who have strong teaching skills, are highly competent in the academic content areas in which they plan to teach, and know how to use technology as a tool for teaching and learning"

■ To recruit "additional teachers for high-need areas through . . . grants to partnerships between high-quality teacher education programs and local schools to offer scholarships, support, and services" to candidates who agree to work at least three years in high-need schools

■ To support "state-level efforts to improve teacher quality through State Teacher Quality Enhancement grants to strengthen state certification standards, create alternative pathways into teaching, hold higher education institutions accountable for the quality of teachers they prepare, and recruit high-quality teachers"

■ To strengthen "accountability in teacher education by requiring that states and teacher education institutions report on teacher preparation, including their students' performance on teacher licensing exams"

Diversity of the Teaching Force: A Growing Concern

Although the U.S. school population is becoming increasingly diverse, the teaching force has not kept pace. For example, African Americans and Hispanics make up nearly one-third of the student population in public schools, but the proportion of elementary and secondary teachers who are African American or Hispanic is generally estimated at 10 percent or less. The situation is particularly acute in the largest urban districts, where minority students comprise nearly 90 percent of enrollment but less than 20 percent of teachers are from minority groups. This underrepresentation of minority groups in the teaching force is expected to grow even more severe in the future. Currently, only about 10 percent of teacher-education majors are African American or Hispanic; yet members of these minority groups are predicted to constitute a still higher percentage of elementary and secondary students in the near future.[50]

Need for teacher diversity

Reasons for increasing teacher diversity

Increasing the diversity of the teaching force to better reflect the student population is widely viewed as an important goal. For one thing, teachers from a cultural or ethnic minority group generally are in a better position than nonminority teachers to serve as positive role models for minority students. In many cases, minority teachers also may have a better understanding of minority students' expectations and learning styles (see Chapters 10 and 11), particularly if minority teachers working with low-income students grew up in working-class homes themselves. For example, Lisa Delpit, Jacqueline Irvine, and other analysts have pointed out that

---

[49]"A Better Deal for Students and Families," 1998 presidential press release available at **www.ed.gov.**
[50]Julie L. Nicklin, "Shape Up or Shut Down," *The Chronicle of Higher Education,* February 3, 1995, p. A17; Michelle N-K. Collison, "Getting Minority Students Turned On to Teaching," *The New York Times Education Life,* January 7, 1996, pp. 25, 30; and Judy Taylor with Lenaya Raock, "Are Urban Teachers Ready to Teach?," *Cityschools,* (Spring 1998), pp. 13–17.

The shortage of minority teachers has been characterized as a "crisis-like situation," and efforts are being made to increase the number of minority teacher-education candidates.
(© David Young Wolff/ Photo Edit)

African American teachers may be less prone than middle-class nonminority teachers to mistakenly assume that low-income black students will respond well to a teacher who is informal and overly friendly. In addition, teachers from Asian American, Hispanic American, and other minority groups frequently are needed to work with students who have limited English skills.[51]

Problems of written tests

Widespread testing of teachers has led to further concerns. Many teacher candidates from ethnic or cultural minorities have not performed well on typical paper-and-pencil tests. In Alabama, for example, only about one-third of African American students completing teacher-education programs passed the state teacher candidacy exams during the 1980s, compared to approximately three-fourths of

---

[51]Lisa D. Delpit, "The Silenced Dialogue: Power and Pedagogy in Educating Other People's Children," *Harvard Educational Review* (August 1988), pp. 280–298; William Ayers, "Justice and Equity," *Rethinking Schools* (Summer 1995), pp. 28–30, available at **www.rethinkingschools.org;** Deneese L. Jones and Rosetta F. Sandidge, "Recruiting and Retaining Teachers in Urban Schools," *Education and Urban Society* (February 1997), pp. 192–203; and Maruin Wideen, Jolie Mayer-Smith, and Barbara Moon, "A Critical Analysis of the Research on Learning to Teach," *Review of Educational Research* (Summer 1998), pp. 130–178.

nonminority candidates. Low passing rates for African American or Hispanic candidates also have been reported in other states, including Arizona, California, Georgia, Mississippi, New Mexico, Oklahoma, and Texas. Some observers believe that testing of prospective teachers has eliminated more than 50,000 African American and Hispanic candidates during the past fifteen years, and that recent trends toward raising minimum scores may disqualify 70 percent of minority candidates in the future.[52]

Proposals for promoting diversity

After reviewing data on the low proportion of minority teachers and the low passing rates of prospective minority teachers, AACTE officials have stated that these figures reflect a "devastating" crisis. Along with other organizations, the AACTE has proposed and helped initiate legislation for a variety of new programs to increase the number of minority teachers. The proposals include increasing financial aid for prospective minority teachers, enhancing recruitment of minority candidates, initiating precollegiate programs to attract minority students, and providing coursework to improve admissions test scores of minority students interested in teaching.[53]

Educational Reform and Teacher Empowerment

Standardizing teaching methods

In conjunction with reform efforts, many states and local school districts have prescribed particular methods to be used in planning and delivering instruction. Teachers are evaluated, in large part, by their ability to follow these standard methods. In Arkansas, Missouri, and Texas, to take three examples, guidelines for teacher assessment have specified the general instructional sequence — for instance, introduce the topic, present material, check for understanding, provide guided and independent practice, and discuss homework — that teachers should follow in executing a "model" lesson.

Adverse effects of standardized methods

To some extent, this type of reform appears to have magnified rather than alleviated the problems in education. As noted earlier, teachers frequently express dissatisfaction with their limited opportunities to participate in decision making. Reforms that dictate particular instructional methods tend to reduce teachers' autonomy even further. As Linda McNeil's study in Texas concluded, legislative requirements for extensive testing of students, combined with administrative prescriptions of appropriate teaching methods, have contributed to "deprofessionalization" and "deskilling" of the teaching force. **Deprofessionalization** occurs when policies encourage or require teachers to simplify curriculum and instruction in order to ensure that students demonstrate mastery on easy-to-grade tests. McNeil, Robert Rothman, and other observers have reported that many teachers respond with "defensive teaching" in which they fragment the curriculum to fit tests, "mystify" topics by emphasizing factual regurgitation over understanding, and simplify material to gain the compliance of students.[54]

[52]"Tests Keep Thousands of Minorities out of Teaching," *Fair Test Examiner* (Winter 1989), pp. 8–9; David F. Allen, "From Analysis to Policy," *Teacher Education and Practice* (Fall–Winter 1993–1994), pp. 5–12; and Jeff Archer, "States Raising Bar for Teachers Despite Pending Shortage," *Education Week*, March 25, 1998.

[53]*Minority Teacher Supply and Demand* (Washington, D.C.: American Association of Colleges of Teacher Education, 1990), p. 3. See also Xue Lan Rong and Judith Pressie, "The Continuing Decline in Asian American Teachers," *American Educational Research Journal* (Summer 1997), pp. 267–293; and Susan Melnick and Kenneth Zeichner, "Teacher Education Responsibilities to Address Diversity Issues," *Theory into Practice* (Spring 1998).

[54]Linda M. McNeil, *Contradictions of Control* (New York: Routledge and Kegan Paul, 1986). See also Susan Moore Johnson, *Teachers at Work* (New York: Basic, 1990); Robert Rothman, *Measuring Up* (San Francisco: Jossey-Bass, 1995); William L. Sanders and Sandra P. Horn, "Educational Assessment Reassessed," *Educational Policy Analysis Archives*, March 3, 1995, available at **olam.ed.asu.edu;** and Chris Richards, "Popular Culture, Politics, and the Curriculum," *Educational Researcher* (June–July 1998), pp. 32–34.

Rewarding passivity

The consequences of specifying instructional methods seem to have been similarly negative with respect to teacher evaluation. As described by one observer in the Southwest, evaluative approaches frequently reward teachers who "lecture and question a relatively passive class but not teachers who help students struggle through difficult tasks — such as science experiments, English composition, or computer programming — on their own." Researchers elsewhere have described cases in which prescription of specific teaching methods has led teachers to emphasize passive learning and memorization of low-level material.[55]

School-based management

Although resistance to this trend has been sporadic, progress is being made in some locations. Some reform efforts deal specifically with **teacher empowerment,** which usually involves *decentralization* and *school-based management* to increase the role of teachers in decision making. For example, contractual agreements reached between teacher associations and school boards in many districts have given teachers a larger role in determining school policies and practices. Such provisions typically give faculties greater opportunities to select instructional methods and materials and to determine how funds will be spent in their schools. (School-based management is discussed in detail in Chapter 2.)

Self-governance in Dade County

Some recent experiments to improve education through teacher empowerment are even more ambitious and comprehensive. For example, in Dade County, Florida, many schools are participating in a self-governance experiment in which teachers and administrators work together to redesign the educational programs in their schools. To a significant extent, faculties can determine the number of staff to be employed and how they will function. As part of this project, the board of education has suspended requirements in such areas as maximum class size, length of the school day, and number of minutes per subject. The Dade County Federation of Teachers has agreed to waive contractual provisions so that teachers can work longer hours without more pay and can assist in evaluating other teachers.[56]

Comprehensive reforms in Rochester

From some points of view, the approach in Rochester, New York, has been even more comprehensive. Since 1987 contracts between the board of education and the Rochester Teachers Association have included the following key provisions:[57]

1. Based on the Carnegie model for "lead" teachers, a career in teaching program was established. In this program, teachers move through four stages: (a) *intern* (new) teachers working under the supervision of experienced colleagues; (b) *resident* teachers with a completed internship but only provisional certification; (c) *professional* teachers with a permanent certificate; and (d) *lead* teachers with at least ten years of experience who work 10 percent longer hours and devote as much as half their time to serving as mentors, to planning instructional improvements, or to other leadership roles. Lead teachers, who are selected by panels consisting of four teachers and three administrators, earn approximately $75,000 per year.

---

[55]Harriett Tyson-Bernstein, "The Texas Teacher Appraisal System," *American Educator* (Spring 1987), pp. 26–31; Arthur E. Wise, "Legislative Learning Revisited," *Phi Delta Kappan* (January 1988), pp. 328–333; Daniel U. Levine and Rayna F. Levine, *Society and Education*, 9th ed. (Needham Heights, Mass.: Allyn and Bacon, 1996); and John Smyth, Geoff Shacklock, and Rob Hattam, "Teacher Development in Difficult Times," *Teacher Development* (Nov. 1, 1997), available at **www.triangle.co.uk.**

[56]Brian Peterson, "How School-Based Management Is Faring in Miami," *Education Week,* June 12, 1991, p. 26; and Susan H. Fuhrman and Richard F. Elmore, *Ruling Out Rules* (New Brunswick, N.J.: CPRE, 1995). See also Allan Odden, "Implementing Site-Based Management," *WCER Highlights* (Spring 1997).

[57]Joanna Richardson, "Rochester, N.Y., Contract Links Accountability, Resources," *Education Week,* December 15, 1993, p. 3; and Christine E. Murray, Gerald Grant, and Raji Swaminathan, "Rochester's Reforms," *Phi Delta Kappan* (October 1997), pp. 148–155.

2. Instead of following traditional seniority practices in determining teachers' assignments, a faculty committee in each school interviews teachers who wish to transfer and makes decisions based on the needs of that school. At the same time, professional teachers and lead teachers are assigned on the basis of need rather than seniority and thus more frequently teach the lowest-achieving students and classes. As Rochester Teachers Association President Adam Urbanski put it, "Success with these students shouldn't be expected of first-year teachers, who have enough to do just to learn the job. Rookie teachers taking on the toughest assignments would be tantamount in the medical profession to interns performing open-heart surgery while master surgeons treat skin abrasions."[58]

3. Building on Rochester's already sizable magnet-school program, all schools have become "schools of choice" that offer specialized learning opportunities and compete with each other to attract students. Teachers play a large role in selecting and implementing the unique combination of curricular themes and instructional arrangements in each school.[59]

It is still premature to reach conclusions about the success or failure of such experiments. These reform efforts will encounter many obstacles, and educators involved in them will have to learn how to translate teacher empowerment into improved school functioning.[60]

Outlook for Teaching

Bright prospects for teachers

Until the school reform movement of the 1980s, college students majoring in education were confronted with a buyer's market for teachers, and many wondered whether it was wise to enter a field that seemed to be declining in salary, status, and general attractiveness. Now national attention has focused on education, and there is good news regarding teachers' prospects. The pattern of teacher oversupply has been reversed, and governments at all levels are acting to improve salaries and teaching conditions as well as teacher recruitment and preparation. Individuals dedicated to helping young people learn and grow in the schools should have considerable professional opportunities to realize their ambitions. In the years to come, the teaching profession should experience a renewed excitement and an even greater sense that the work is of vital importance to American society.

Summing Up

1. Although there are many reasons for entering the teaching profession, research indicates that most teachers do so to help young children and to provide a service to society.

2. Most teachers are satisfied with most aspects of their jobs, though there is some dissatisfaction with starting salaries and certain other aspects of the profession.

---

[58]Adam Urbanski, "Restructuring the Teaching Profession," *Education Week,* October 28, 1987, p. 32.
[59]Magnet schools offer special curriculum or instruction for students who enroll voluntarily and may not live nearby.
[60]Daniel U. Levine and Eugene E. Eubanks, "Site–Based Management: Engine for Reform or Pipedream?" in John J. Lane and Edgar Epps, eds., *Restructuring the Schools* (Berkeley, Calif.: McCutchan, 1992); Bill Geraci, "Local Decision Making," *Educational Leadership* (December 1995–January 1996), pp. 50–52; and *Teachers Leading the Way* (Washington D.C.: U.S. Department of Education, 1988), available at **www.ed.gov.**

3. Teacher salaries have improved rapidly in recent years.

4. There was a sharp drop in demand relative to supply of teachers in the 1970s. This situation has been reversed, and there may be a serious shortage of teachers in the future.

5. The preservice preparation of teachers involves three major components: a liberal education, specialized subject-field education, and professional studies. Each of these interrelated areas is important in preparing successful teachers.

6. Requirements for teacher certification vary from state to state and among institutions of higher learning.

7. In general, teacher education is becoming more practical and reality oriented. Trends in this direction include competency-based teacher education, the establishment of school-based centers for preparing future teachers, and the provision of early field experience in elementary and secondary classrooms. Other important trends include the introduction of five-year and fifth-year programs and the interest in developing reflective teachers. Teachers also are being increasingly prepared to use up-to-date technology, to work with students who have special needs, and to teach in widely diverse settings.

8. Despite these trends in teacher education, there is still a widespread national concern with the quality of the teaching work force. Efforts to address this concern include the increasing use of basic skills testing for new and future teachers. More help is also being supplied for beginning teachers. The major national reports on education have proposed tying salaries to performance, setting higher national standards for licensing, and establishing the highly paid position of "lead" or "master" teacher.

9. Besides the competence of teachers, many educators are focusing on ways to increase the diversity of the teaching work force to better reflect the student population.

10. Many school districts are attempting to work out approaches for empowering teachers in order to make schools more effective.

11. Increasing public concern for education, changes occurring in the schools, and improvements in the outlook for teachers are bringing new excitement and importance to the role of the teacher.

Key Terms

The numbers in parentheses indicate the pages where explanations of the key terms can be found.

supply and demand *(7)*

occupational prestige *(8)*

certification *(16)*

alternative certification *(17)*

competency-based teacher education *(20)*

school-based field centers *(20)*

reflective teaching *(21)*

basic skills testing *(25)*

national reports *(26)*

A Nation at Risk (26)

National Board for Professional Teaching Standards *(27)*

professional development schools *(28)*

Higher Education Reauthorization Act of 1998 *(30)*

deprofessionalization *(32)*

teacher empowerment *(33)*

Discussion Questions

1. What are your reasons for becoming a teacher? How do these reasons compare with those of your classmates, and with research cited in this chapter?

2. Do you believe that the trends in teacher education identified in this chapter are desirable? Do you think they will result in improved education in the schools? What conditions are necessary to make them effective?

3. What steps can be taken to improve teacher salaries? Which are most likely to be successful? What will determine whether they are successful?

4. What jobs other than teaching in elementary or secondary schools may be open to persons with a teaching certificate? What additional preparation might be necessary or helpful in obtaining such jobs?

Suggested Projects for Professional Development

1. Collect and analyze information on teacher salary schedules in several nearby school districts. Compare your data with information other members of your class acquire from additional districts. What patterns do you see? What might be the advantages and disadvantages involved in teaching in these districts?

2. Investigate the level of funding for teacher education at your campus. Is there any reason to believe that your school or college of education serves as a "cash cow" that provides substantial funding for other campus units?

3. Explore Internet resources to obtain current information about the National Board for Professional Teaching Standards and other organizations working to improve the preparation or performance of teachers. (See the board's Internet site at **www.nbtps.org**, and the Readings and Resources section below for a starting point.)

4. Interview an elementary school teacher and a high-school teacher about their level of satisfaction with their work and their reasons for being satisfied or dissatisfied. Compare your findings with those of other students in your class.

5. Individually or as a team member, prepare a report on activities of projects and organizations that work to ensure that teachers possess a high level of preparation for their jobs. Projects and organizations that might be examined include Praxis III (**www.ets.org**), Intasc (**www.ccsso.org/intasc.html**) and the NBPTS (**www.nbpts.org**).

Suggested Readings and Resources

Internet Resources

The federal government maintains various sites on the World Wide Web. Many of the topics in this chapter (as well as most others in this book) can be explored at **www.ed.gov**. The Educational Resources Information Center (ERIC) can be accessed at **www.ericir.syr.edu.** Various professional organizations such as the Association for Supervision and Curriculum Development (**www.ascd.org**) and Phi Delta Kappa (**www.pdkintl.org**) also sponsor relevant sites.

Publications

The ASCUS Annual: A Job Search Handbook for Educators. Evanston, Ill.: Association for School, College and University Staffing. *This annual publication is designed to help either prospective or current teachers find a position. It can be obtained from career planning offices or from ASCUS, 1600 Dodge Avenue, S-330, Evanston, Illinois 60201-3451, telephone 708-864-1999.*

Freedman, Samuel G. *Small Victories.* New York: Harper, 1990; and Cristina Rathbone, *On the Outside Looking In.* Boston: Atlantic Monthly Press, 1998. *These books describe the highs and lows in the work of dedicated teachers at big-city high schools.*

Herndon, Joseph. *The Way It Spozed to Be.* New York: Bantam, 1968. *A classic when it was published, this book, which describes the satisfactions and difficulties of teaching in the inner city, is still relevant in the new millenium.*

Journal of Teacher Education. Regularly provides information and analysis regarding important issues in preservice and in-service education.

McNeil, Linda M. *Contradictions of Control.* New York: Routledge and Kegan Paul, 1986. *Analyzes teachers' reactions to legislative and administrative mandates that sometimes distort instruction toward low-level concentration on facts.*

Nettles, D. H., and Pamela B. Petrick. *Portfolio Development for Preservice Teachers.* Bloomington, Ind.: Phi Delta Kappa, 1995. *Describes major steps involved in preparing a professional portfolio.*

The New Teacher Page. Well-written, interesting, and useful, this Internet site provides material relevant for future as well as new teachers, available at **www.geocities.com/Athens/Delphi.**

Rothman, Robert. *Measuring Up.* San Francisco: Jossey-Bass, 1995. *Portrays testing practices and requirements that detract from meaningful instruction, then develops an "agenda for reform" in testing and teaching.*

Teacher Development. This international on-line journal is available at **www.triangle.co.uk.**

Theory into Practice. The Spring, 1998 issue of this journal is devoted to the theme "Preparing Teachers for Cultural Diversity."

CHAPTER TWO

The Teaching Profession

Until the twentieth century, teachers had relatively little preparation for their jobs and relatively little voice in determining the conditions of their employment. Teacher training consisted of one or two years and sometimes less at a normal school or teachers college, and teachers had to follow strict rules and regulations concerning their behavior outside the school. Unorganized and isolated from one another in small schools and school districts, teachers could be summarily dismissed by a board of education. Many were told they could not teach any material that someone in the community might find objectionable.

Times have changed. Today, teachers aspire to be professionals with expert knowledge concerning the content and methods of instruction in their particular fields. In addition, they are well organized as a group and have gained greater rights to be judged mainly on the basis of their performance rather than on the basis of their behavior outside the school. Often, too, they participate in making decisions about the conditions in which they work. In many cases, they are forging stronger links with school administrators, university researchers, government officials, and the communities they serve. The first part of this chapter describes the ways in which teachers are striving for full professional status; the second discusses how teacher organizations have grown in power and prominence. As you read Chapter 2, think about the following questions:

- What trends show that teaching is becoming a full-fledged profession?
- In what ways is teaching *not* fully a profession?
- How does merit pay help or hinder the teaching profession?
- What are the essential differences between the NEA and the AFT? Can these differences be reconciled?
- What are some other important professional organizations for teachers?
- What professional organizations might education students and beginning teachers join?

This chapter was revised by Dr. James Lawlor, Towson University

Is Teaching a Profession?

Whether teaching can be considered a profession in the fullest sense has been a great concern to educators for many decades. A number of educators have tried to identify the ideal characteristics of professions and, by rating teachers on these items, determine whether teaching is a profession. Here are some characteristics of a full **profession**, based on the works of noted authorities over a twenty-five-year period.[1]

Characteristics of a profession

1. A sense of public service; a lifetime commitment to career
2. A defined body of knowledge and skills beyond that grasped by laypersons
3. A lengthy period of specialized training
4. Control over licensing standards and/or entry requirements
5. Autonomy in making decisions about selected spheres of work
6. An acceptance of responsibility for judgments made and acts performed related to services rendered; a set of standards of performance
7. A self-governing organization composed of members of the profession
8. Professional associations and/or elite groups to provide recognition for individual achievements
9. A code of ethics to help clarify ambiguous matters or doubtful points related to services rendered
10. High prestige and economic standing

Teaching as a "semi-profession"

The general consensus is that teaching is not a profession in the fullest sense because it does not possess some of the above characteristics. In some ways, teaching may be viewed as a "semiprofession" or an "emerging profession" that is in the process of achieving these characteristics.[2] Several sociologists contend that nursing and social work are also semiprofessions.

In particular, teaching seems to lag behind professions like law and medicine in four important areas: (1) a defined body of knowledge and skills beyond that grasped by laypersons, (2) control over licensing standards and/or entry requirements, (3) autonomy in making decisions about selected spheres of work, and (4) high prestige and economic standing. In the following sections we explore these four aspects of teaching.

A Defined Body of Knowledge

No agreed-upon knowledge

All professions have a monopoly on a certain kind of knowledge that separates their members from the general public and allows them to exercise control over the vocation. By mastering this defined body of knowledge, members of the profession establish their expertise, and by denying membership to those who have not mastered it, they protect the public from quacks and untrained amateurs. In the past there has been no agreed-upon specialized body of knowledge that is "education"

---

[1]Ronald G. Corwin, *Sociology of Education* (New York: Appleton-Century-Crofts, 1965); Robert B. Howsam et al., *Educating a Profession* (Washington, D.C.: American Association of Colleges for Teacher Education, 1976); and Susan J. Rosenholtz, *Teachers' Workplace: The Social Organization of Schools* (New York: Longman, 1989).
[2]Amitai Etzioni, *The Semiprofessions and Their Organizations: Teachers, Nurses, and Social Workers* (New York: Free Press, 1969), p. v.

or "teaching."[3] Nor has teaching been guided by the extensive rules of procedure and established methodologies found in professions like the physical sciences and health care. As a result, too many people, especially the lay public, talk about education as if they were experts — a situation that causes a great deal of conflicting and sometimes negative conversation.[4]

Lack of agreement on teacher education

Another result of the ill-defined body of knowledge is that the content of teacher-education courses varies from state to state and even among teacher-training institutions within a given state. At the very least, there should be some national agreement on the mix of teacher-training courses devoted to liberal education, subject-matter specialization, and professional knowledge. But agreement on this topic has eluded educators for the last forty years. James Koerner described the problem further in his highly critical book *The Miseducation of American Teachers.* Koerner argued that by requiring too many education courses — as many as 60 hours at some state teacher colleges — and by making these courses too "soft," colleges of education were producing teachers versed in pedagogy at the expense of academic content.[5] While critics have helped reduce the number of required education courses, the controversy continues,[6] making it especially difficult to establish clear national standards for teacher preparation.

NCATE standards

The situation is gradually changing, however. **The National Council for Accreditation of Teacher Education** (NCATE) has set standards that specify the courses to be taken and the qualifications of the faculty who teach those courses. At this point, a large number of teacher-education institutions still do not meet NCATE's standards; as recently as 1998, 58 percent of the 1,200 colleges involved in training teachers were not accredited by NCATE. However, most NCATE members have worked diligently to meet NCATE standards, and 89 percent had obtained NCATE approval by 1998.[7] Moreover, the American Association of Colleges for Teacher Education (AACTE) decided in 1995 to promote the pursuit of NCATE accreditation. To further this end, AACTE is expanding technical assistance, such as consultants to nonaccredited institutions, during the accreditation process.[8]

Control over Requirements for Entry and Licensing

Variations in certification

Whereas most professions have uniform requirements for entry and licensing, historically this has not been the case in teaching. As indicated in Chapter 1, recent re-

---

[3]David Dill, *What Teachers Need to Know* (San Francisco: Jossey-Bass, 1990); and John I. Goodlad, *Teachers for Our Nation's Schools* (San Francisco: Jossey-Bass, 1990).

[4]Hendrik D. Gideonse, *Relating Knowledge to Teacher Education* (Washington, D.C.: American Association of Colleges for Teacher Education, 1989); Brian Rowan, "Comparing Teachers' Work with Work in Other Occupations: Notes on the Professional Status of Teaching," *Educational Researcher* (August–September 1994), pp. 4–17, 21; and Jonathan Saphier, *Bonfires and Magic Bullets. Making Teaching a True Profession* (Carlisle, Mass.: Research for Better Teaching, 1995).

[5]James D. Koerner, *The Miseducation of American Teachers* (Boston: Houghton Mifflin, 1963).

[6]See, for example, Pamela C. Boyd, "Professional School Reform and Public School Renewal: Portrait of a Partnership," *Journal of Teacher Education* (March–April 1994), pp. 132–139; and Robert A. Roth, "The University Can't Train Teachers: Transformation of a Profession," *Journal of Teacher Education* (September–October 1994), pp. 261–268.

[7]National Council for the Accreditation of Teacher Education, *NCATE Facts* (Washington, D.C.: National Council for Accreditation of Teacher Education, 1998), pp. 1, 6; and Arthur E. Wise, "We Need More Than a Redesign," *Educational Leadership* (November 1991), p. 7.

[8]"AACTE Strategic Plan Includes Focus on Accreditation," *NCATE Reporter* (Washington, D.C.: National Council for Accreditation of Teacher Education, 1998), p. 5; and *Restructuring the Education of Teachers,* Report of the Commission on the Education of Teachers into the 21st Century (Washington, D.C.: Association of Teacher Educators, 1992).

forms have required prospective teachers in most states to pass minimum competency tests, and bodies such as the National Board for Professional Teaching Standards are establishing methods for measuring a person's ability to teach. However, certification requirements still vary greatly from state to state, and the trend toward testing of teachers has generated widespread controversy. Moreover, it is estimated that many teachers working in the secondary schools are teaching out of license — in other words, outside their recognized areas of expertise. This problem is especially acute in science and mathematics.

Debate about alternative certification

The outlook is further clouded by the trend toward alternative certification. As discussed in Chapter 1, this is a process by which teachers are recruited from the ranks of college-educated retirees, part-time industrial personnel, and experienced people seeking second careers. Intended to eliminate teacher shortages in certain subject areas (such as mathematics, science, and computer instruction) or to upgrade the quality of new teachers, alternative certification is often praised as practical and innovative by laypeople and school board members. Most teacher organizations, on the other hand, see alternative certification as a threat to the profession. One critic wrote, "The assumption that those who know something can automatically teach . . . [will] not solve the problem of teacher quality."[9] The AACTE has taken a middle position, supporting alternative licensing procedures only at the master's degree level and in conjunction with supervised field training.[10]

Involvement of teacher organizations

Whatever they may think about differing requirements for certification, teachers traditionally have had little to say on these matters. However, teacher organizations are beginning to cooperate with state legislatures and departments of education to modify certification standards and establish professional practice boards (discussed later in this chapter). The more input teachers have — the more control they exercise over their own licensing procedures — the more teaching will be recognized as a full profession.

Autonomy in Deciding About Spheres of Work

Professional control vs. lay control

In a profession, every member of the group, but no outsider, is assumed to be qualified to make professional judgments on the nature of the work involved. Indeed, control by laypersons is considered the natural enemy of professions; it limits the power of the professional and opens the door to outside interference. Professionals usually establish rules and customs that give them exclusive jurisdiction over their area of competence and their relationships with clients.

Traditional lack of teacher input

Teachers, in contrast, have traditionally had little input in curriculum decisions, and they are vulnerable when they seek to introduce textbooks or discuss topics considered controversial by pressure groups. In fact, school officials often hire outside "experts" with little teaching experience to help them select books, write grant proposals, or resolve local school-community issues.[11] Even in school

---

[9]Lee S. Shulman, "Knowledge and Teaching: Foundations and the New Reform," *Harvard Educational Review* (February 1987), p. 324.
[10]*Alternative Paths to Teaching* (Washington, D.C.: American Association of Colleges for Teacher Education, 1995); Glen Buck, et al., "Alternative Certification Programs," *Teacher Education and Special Education* (Winter 1995), pp. 39–48.
[11]Michael W. Apple, "Is There a Curriculum Voice to Reclaim?" *Phi Delta Kappan* (March 1990); Alfred G. Hess, "The Changing Role of Teacher: Moving from Interested Spectators to Engaged Planners," *Education and Urban Society* (May 1994), pp. 248–263; and John J. DiNatale, "School Improvement and Restructuring: A Threefold Approach," *NASSP Bulletin* (October 1994), pp. 79–83.

reform, the initiative often comes from government officials, business leaders, and civic groups rather than from teachers. Taxpayers and their representatives are said to "reasonably" claim a large share in decision making because they foot the bill and provide the clients. Only recently, with the advent of school-based management (discussed later in this chapter) and other forms of teacher participation, has this situation begun to change.

Accountability to the public

Although collective bargaining has resulted in new arrangements between teachers and administrators, most people still believe that teachers are public servants and are therefore accountable to the people and to the school officials who are hired, elected, or appointed by the people. Thus, in many situations, teachers can be told what to do by parents, principals, superintendents, and school board members, even when these directives go against the teachers' professional judgments.

High Prestige and Economic Standing

Salary trends

As pointed out in Chapter 1, teachers have registered major gains in salary and status during the past decades. Although teachers' salaries since 1930 have increased more than those of the average worker in industry, teacher pay remains lower than that of the average college graduate, such as an engineer, nurse, accountant, or business major.[12] In addition, teachers still earn far less than lawyers, business executives, and some other professionals with similar levels of formal education.

Prestige deriving from complex work

In terms of occupational prestige, teachers have fared somewhat better. Brian Rowan, comparing teachers' work with other occupations, found that complexity of work was directly related to occupational prestige. Since teaching was more complex than 75 percent of all other occupations, it ranked quite high in prestige. The complexity of teachers' work is manifested in their need to apply principles of logical or scientific thinking to define problems, collect data, establish facts, and draw conclusions. They must be highly proficient in language (reading, writing, and speaking), and, most of all, they must work effectively with many kinds of people — children, adolescents, parents, colleagues, and superiors. This work with people sets teaching apart from most other occupations. However, society accords higher prestige (and, of course, higher pay) to professionals such as physicians, academics, lawyers, and engineers, mainly because they must deal with information generally regarded as more abstract (complex) and because these fields require more rigorous academic preparation and licensure.[13]

Status-consistency hypothesis

It may seem unrealistic to compare the prestige and salaries of teachers with those of physicians, lawyers, dentists, or top business executives. For example, despite a level of formal education similar to that of a teacher, business executives might earn $150,000 per year, and some might earn $500,000 or more. Nevertheless, the *status-consistency hypothesis* holds that a group tends to compare its achievements (both prestige and salary) with those of other groups, striving to match the rewards of people with similar jobs and similar years of education.[14] If this is true, we can expect teachers to make comparisons with other groups and to feel somewhat dissatisfied. In the past this dissatisfaction has been one of the major

---

[12]Victor R. Lindquist and Frank S. Endicott, *The Northwestern Lindquist-Endicott Report: Employment Trends for College Graduates,* Forty-sixth Annual Survey (Evanston, Ill.: Northwestern University, 1992); "Teacher Salaries," *NEA Today* (February 1995), p. 9; and "Teaching Low on the Pay Scale," *NEA Today* (March 1995), p. 5.

[13]Rowan, "Comparing Teachers' Work," pp. 4–13.

[14]Ronald G. Corwin, *Militant Professionalism: A Study of Militant Conflict in High Schools* (New York: Appleton-Century-Crofts, 1970).

reasons for teacher militancy, and it has motivated some teachers to leave the profession.[15]

Teacher status on the rise

To its credit, educational reform has put teachers in the limelight and has brought pressure on school districts to increase salaries. Though optimistic projections have not always been fulfilled,[16] the earnings gap between teachers and other highly educated groups may now begin to close. With help from their own professional organizations, coupled with pressure to upgrade educational standards, teachers should continue to experience increased status.

Trends Toward Professionalism

Although teaching probably should not be considered a fully professionalized occupation, some trends have helped it move in that direction. Collective bargaining, for example, can enhance teachers' capacity to make decisions about their work in the classroom. Several other major aspects of a long-range trend toward the professionalization of teaching are also apparent, as discussed below.

The Scope of Collective Bargaining

By 1980 teachers had won the right to have their representatives formally bargain with their employers in most of the United States. The extent and nature of **collective bargaining** varied from negotiations conducted in the absence of a law allowing or forbidding it to full-scale contract bargaining backed by the right to strike.

Is collective bargaining professional?

In some ways, collective bargaining may be considered a nonprofessional or even an antiprofessional activity. In law, medicine, or the ministry, for example, few professionals work in organizations in which terms of employment are determined by collective bargaining. From another point of view, however, collective bargaining can significantly enhance the professionalization of teaching by giving teachers greater authority to determine their work conditions and their effectiveness as teachers.

Changing focus of collective bargaining

The trend in collective bargaining has been to include a growing number of concerns other than the fundamental salary issue. Today, the focus is often on peer review, career ladders, merit pay, standards setting, and school-based management,[17] subjects discussed in later sections of this chapter. Teachers' bargaining units often feel the "push/pull" of addressing bread-and-butter issues as opposed to professional concerns.[18] As the new century begins, the movements toward school reform, school restructuring, and teacher empowerment will give teachers more professional autonomy, union strength, and higher salaries, in exchange for greater accountability and reduced adversarial bargaining.

---

[15]Jo Anna Natale, "Why Teachers Leave," *Executive Educator* (November 1993), pp. 8–15; Patricia Gonzales, "Strategies for Teacher Retention," *NSTEP Information Brief* (Alexandria, Va.: National Association of State Directors of Special Education, 1995).

[16]Allan C. Ornstein, "Teacher Salaries in Social Context," *High School Journal* (December–January 1990), pp. 129–132; and "Teacher Salaries," *NEA Today* (February 1995), p. 9; Southern Regional Education Board, "SREB Teacher Salaries: Update for 1995–96 and Estimated Increases for 1997 (Atlanta, Ga.: SREB, 1996).

[17]Dennis Sparks, "Insights on School Improvement," *Journal of Staff Development* (Summer 1993), pp. 18–21; Lynn M. Cornett, "Lessons from 10 Years of Teacher Improvement Reforms," *Educational Leadership* (February 1995), pp. 26–30; and William A. Firestone, "Redesigning Teacher Salary Systems for Educational Reform," *American Educational Research Journal* (Fall 1994), pp. 549–574.

[18]Sharon Cowley, "A Coalition View of Site-Based Management: Implications for School Administrators in Collective Bargaining Agreements," *Planning and Changing* (1993), pp. 147–159.

Sharing of power

Collective bargaining is an integral part of the teaching profession. In the early 1960s and 1970s, school boards and school administrators often saw the militant teachers' unions as obsessed with wages and working conditions.[19] Today, educators on both sides of the negotiating table have gained experience and become more comfortable with collective bargaining. School board members, superintendents, principals, and teachers are learning to share power and to work as partners to improve the schools. Continuing in this vein, collective bargaining can not only resolve conflicts between school boards and teachers but can also raise the overall status of the profession.[20]

Professional Practice Boards

Setting professional standards

It is not likely that educators will be given complete autonomy in setting standards for professional practice, but recently they have gained a greater role. Today all states except two (Maine and South Dakota) have established state **professional practice boards,** or similar bodies, which set standards for teacher certification. These boards upgrade the profession by defining standards for minimum competency, by reprimanding teachers for unprofessional or unproductive behavior, and in extreme cases by suspending teachers' certificates. However, few of these state boards are composed of a majority of teachers, and some states do not even require teacher participation on the board.[21]

NEA's position

The National Education Association (NEA) has endorsed the idea of professional practice boards but believes they should be controlled by teachers — with other groups, such as school administrators and universities, given minority representation. The NEA argues that teachers are just as capable of governing their own profession as are attorneys, doctors, and accountants.[22] Other educators favor a single national board rather than independent state boards. This has always been the position of the American Federation of Teachers (AFT), and the idea has been welcomed by many of the national task force groups. As mentioned in Chapter 1, the Carnegie Corporation has helped to found the **National Board for Professional Teaching Standards** (NBPTS). The NEA now supports this organization, since two-thirds of the directors of the NBPTS are "teaching professionals" — that is, representatives of teacher unions, subject-area associations, and teachers noted for classroom excellence.[23] Currently, the NBPTS has granted national certification to over 500 teachers in seven areas:

A national board

---

[19]Charles T. Kearchner and Douglas Mitchell, *The Changing Idea of a Teacher's Union* (New York: Falmer Press, 1988).

[20]Charles T. Kearchner, "Building the Airplane As It Rolls Down the Runway," *School Administrator* (November 1993), pp. 8–15; Del Stover, "Report from the Picket Line," *American School Board Journal* (December 1991), pp. 46–47; and William Keene, *"Win/Win or Else": Collective Bargaining in an Age of Public Discontent* (Thousand Oaks, CA.: Corwin Press, 1996).

[21]*Teacher Education Policy in the States: A 50 State Survey of Legislative and Administrative Actions* (Washington, D.C.: American Association of Colleges for Teacher Education, 1990); and telephone interview with Penny Early, Research Specialist, American Association of Colleges of Teacher Education, August, 21, 1998.

[22]Keith Geiger, "Holding America Accountable," *Washington Post,* May 6, 1991, p. 34; and National Education Association, "Professional Standards Boards," *NEA Handbook, 1994–95* (Washington, D.C.: NEA, 1994), p. 311.

[23]John W. Porter, "A Call for National Certification of Teachers," *NASSP Bulletin* (October 1990), pp. 64–70; Arthur E. Wise, "Teaching the Teachers," *American School Board Journal* (June 1994), pp. 22–25; Donna H. Leuker, "Certification: Teachers at the Top of Their Profession," *American School Board Journal* (June 1994), p. 24; and Albert Shanker, "Quality Assurance: What Must Be Done to Strengthen the Teaching Profession," *Phi Delta Kappan* (November, 1996), pp. 220–224.

- Early childhood/generalists
- Early adolescence/generalists
- Early adolescence/English-language arts
- Middle childhood/generalist
- Early adolescence, young adulthood/art
- Adolescence and young adulthood/mathematics
- Adolescence and young adulthood/science.

Eventually the program is expected to cover over thirty separate certification areas. Although NBPTS certification is voluntary and cannot be required as a condition of hiring, many educators hope that local school boards and superintendents will develop incentives to encourage teachers to apply for national certification.[24] Twenty-one states have already initiated some form of support in the form of certification fee reimbursement or salary supplements.[25]

Mediated Entry

Mediated entry refers to the practice of inducting persons into a profession through carefully supervised stages that help them learn how to apply professional knowledge successfully in a concrete situation. For example, in the medical profession, aspiring physicians serve one or more years as interns and then as residents before being considered full-fledged professionals.

Dan Lortie has studied the teacher's job from a sociological perspective and has concluded that, in terms of sequenced professional entry, teaching ranks in between occupations characterized by "casual" entry and those that place difficult demands on would-be members.[26] The lack of more carefully mediated entry has profound consequences because it means that new teachers have relatively little opportunity to benefit from the principles and practices developed by earlier educators. Teachers too often report that they learned to teach through trial and error in the classroom. They also report that the beginning years of teaching can be a period of anxiety, loneliness, and fear, even of trauma.[27] Although the beginning period of almost any occupation or profession has its problems and anxieties, a more systematic mediated entry would probably alleviate some of these problems.

Lack of assistance for new teachers

There is an increasing trend for colleges and universities to use professional development schools (described in Chapter 1) as clinical settings where aspiring teachers engage in year-long classroom experiences with students prior to student teaching (residency). This multisemester approach — in actual classrooms under the guidance of experienced teachers and their university professors — provides a more systematic induction into the teaching profession.[28]

Professional development schools as clinical settings

---

[24]National Board for Professional Teaching Standards, *Teacher to Teacher* (Washington, D.C.: National Board for Professional Teaching Standards, Spring, 1997); Bob Reising, "National Certification of Teachers," *Clearing House* (July–August 1995), pp. 332–333.
[25]James Kelly, "Message from the President," *Portfolio* (Fall/Winter, 1996), p. 4.
[26]Dan C. Lortie, *Schoolteacher: A Sociological Study* (Chicago: University of Chicago Press, 1975).
[27]Barry A. Farber, *Crisis in Education: Stress and Burnout in the American Teacher* (San Francisco: Jossey-Bass, 1991); Pamela L. Grossman, *The Making of a Teacher* (New York: Teachers College Press, 1990); Susan Moore Johnson, *Teachers at Work* (New York: Harper and Row, 1990); and Anne Cockburn, *Teaching Under Pressure* (Bristol, Pa.: Falmer, 1996).
[28]Ismat Abdul-Haqq, *Professional Development Schools: Weighing the Evidence* (Thousand Oaks, Calif.: Corwin Press, 1997).

Establishing a transition period

The teaching profession now recognizes the need to develop a period of induction and transition into teaching. Some school districts, such as Toledo, Ohio, provide the probationary or intern teacher with feedback and assistance from experienced teachers. Other districts assign especially trained mentor teachers to work closely with new teachers, particularly those teachers assigned to teach "high-risk" students.[29] In many other school districts, all teachers are evaluated, but there are different expectations and training sessions for probationary teachers and experienced teachers.[30] Some colleges and universities are providing transitional guidance for their graduates who enter teaching, either through direct supervision or through staff development or both. Overall, the trend toward more carefully mediated entry should continue because it is supported by major teacher unions and several education reform groups.

Staff Development

Keeping up to date

Teaching demands rigorous and continuous training. **Staff development** is the further education and training of a school district's teaching staff. To stay up to date in their preparation and to acquire new classroom skills, teachers have traditionally participated in various kinds of in-service training.

Rising importance of staff development

Both the NEA and the AFT support the concept of staff development as an integral part of a teacher's professional growth. Given the fact that U.S. teachers are an aging group (the average teacher is about fifty years old and has twenty years of experience), many states now require teachers to participate in staff development programs in order to retain their teaching certificates. Younger teachers, those with less than ten years' experience, tend to use staff development programs to pursue new degrees (mostly master's degrees), whereas veteran teachers with ten or more years' experience are more likely to participate in specialized workshops or in-service training.[31]

Training in educational technology and research

One important focus for staff development is improving teachers' knowledge and skills in using educational technology. This effort ranges from teaching basic computer literacy, such as word processing and making grade spreadsheets, to teaching more sophisticated use of Internet resources, interactive video, CD-ROM videodisks, and distance learning.[32] The AFT has also developed an Educational Research and Dissemination (ER&D) Program to expose teachers to the growing body of important research findings in education. Through a series of collegial workshops, participants learn about the latest research and explore practical classroom

---

[29]Tom Ganser, "The Contribution of Service as a Cooperating Teacher and Mentor Teacher to the Professional Development of Teachers." (Paper Presented at the Annual Meeting of the American Educational Research Association, Chicago, Ill. March 24–28, 1997, ERIC Document Number: ED408279.)

[30]Arthur E. Wise, Linda Darling-Hammond, and Barnett Berry, *Effective Teacher Selection: From Recruitment to Retention* (Santa Monica, Calif.: Rand Corporation, 1987). See also David Holdzkom, "Teacher Performance Appraisal in North Carolina: Preferences and Practices," *Phi Delta Kappan* (June 1991), pp. 782–784; and Joseph Kretovics, Kathleen Farber, and William Armaline, "Reform from the Bottom Up," *Phi Delta Kappan* (December 1991), pp. 295–299.

[31]*The Condition of Education* (Washington, D.C.: U.S. Government Printing Office, 1997), p. 138.

[32]Judith Duffield, "Trials, Tribulations and Minor Successes: Integrating Technology into a Preservice Teacher Preparation Program," *Tech Trends* (September 1997), pp. 22–26; James Harvey, ed., *Technology and Teacher Professional Development* (Santa Monica, Calif.: Rand Corporation, 1995).

Staff development programs, such as the in-service workshop these teachers are participating in, keep teachers up to date and help them acquire additional classroom skills. *(© Michael Newmann/ Photo Edit)*

applications. Over 1,500 teachers have already been trained by universities to act as workshop leaders, and the program continues to grow.[33]

Taken as a whole, the new varieties of staff development programs give teachers a major voice in decisions that affect their professional careers. These programs also help to establish the concept that teaching requires lengthy and ongoing periods of training, like other full-fledged professions. See Figure 2.1 for recent trends in staff development.

Merit Pay

Critiques of merit pay

Real changes in teacher remuneration are under way. A growing number of school boards have taken the position that **merit pay** (a supplement to a teacher's base salary to reward superior performance) is a cost-effective method of motivating teachers and encouraging excellence in teaching. However, teacher unions and other critics have expressed reservations about merit pay plans. Some argue that because what teachers do is very complicated and difficult to measure, assessments of merit are too often subjective, especially when left in the hands of a single person — the school principal.[34] Teachers and their professional organizations feel more comfortable when teachers are evaluated by their peers. Where merit plans have been implemented, some reports claim, teachers have often felt that the wrong people were selected for preferential pay. Some observers fear that rewards given to a relatively small number of teachers will be at the expense of many others, thereby

---

[33]*AFT Educational Research and Dissemination Program* (Washington, D.C.: AFT, 1990); and telephone conversation with Deanna Woods, Assistant Director of the Educational Research and Dissemination Program, American Federation of Teachers, November 14, 1995.
[34]Ron Brandt, "On Research on Teaching," *Educational Leadership* (April 1992), pp. 14–19; and Stephen Jacobsen, "Money Incentives and the Reform of Teacher Compensation: A Persistent Dilemma," *International Journal of Educational Reform* (January 1995), pp. 29–35.

FIGURE 2.1 Trends in Staff Development

Approach	Example
Developing the individual *and* the organization, that is, the school or school district	Strategic planning or school-based management workshops, for example, foster teacher and administrator cohesiveness by focusing on the actual needs of the school
Efforts driven by a coherent strategic plan for the district and the school	Districtwide efforts to define the school district's "essential curriculum"
Focus on students' needs, working *backward* to what educators need to promote appropriate student outcomes	Constructing lesson plans that focus on student performance outcomes
Training on the job	Support by mentor teachers and administrators to help teachers grow as they gain experience
Active study by teachers of the teaching and learning process	School districts offering a wide variety of in-service courses to broaden teachers' knowledge and skills as they work with students
Stress on a combination of generic skills (such as mastery instruction) and content-specific skills (pertaining to particular subject areas, such as math or social studies)	Providing special workshops in instructional strategies and recent trends in teaching specialized disciplines
Staff developers who provide consultation, planning, and facilitation services as well as training	Use of specialists within and outside the school district to share expertise with teachers, principals, and central office administrators
Staff development as a critical function performed by all administrators and teacher leaders	Development of a cadre of mentor teachers and peer coaches with released time to assist new teachers
Staff development as an essential and indispensible process	Commitment by school districts to provide the financial and human resources to help teachers achieve success in their careers

Career ladders

threatening the unity and collegiality among educators. Moreover, the funding for merit pay plans has often been inadequate. The need, critics say, is to increase all teachers' salaries, not just a few, and not to pit teachers against one another.[35]

Even as the arguments continue, the concept of merit pay has spread to many school districts and to entire states. Today, merit pay plans are sometimes linked with *career ladders,* which establish clear-cut stages through which a teacher may advance. In the Rochester, New York, school system, for example, there are four ranks that culminate in the position of lead teacher, which can pay nearly $75,000 per year. On a statewide level, North Carolina in 1991 implemented a merit plan called "differential pay," whereby local school districts receive up to 3 percent above their normal salary totals to allocate to teachers on the basis of merit or additional responsibilities.[36] Overall, the trend toward raising the ceiling on teachers' salaries, and making distinctions based on merit, should attract brighter students into the profession and keep good teachers from leaving classrooms for more competitive salaries in other fields.

School-Based Management

Decision making at the school level

Many educational reforms, as we have seen, involve a movement toward teacher empowerment — increasing teachers' participation in decisions that affect their own work and careers. One such reform is **school-based management** (also known as *site-based management, site-based decision making,* or *collaborative decision making*), a system in which many decisions about curriculum, instruction, staff development, allocation of funds, and staffing assignments are made at the individual school level rather than by the superintendent or the board of education. Working together, the school's teachers, administrators, and often parents develop their own plan for the school's future.

Teachers as experts

The assumption underlying school-based management is that people who share in responsibilities and decisions will believe in what they are doing and will work more effectively toward common goals. This concept of reform also recognizes that teachers are experts whose talents should be put to use in planning. The reform plans in Dade County, Florida, and Rochester, New York (described in Chapter 1), include a generous dose of school-based management. Other districts with similar plans include Louisville, Chicago, Denver, Los Angeles, Philadelphia, and Baltimore.

Willingness to get involved

The fate of school-based management rests especially on the relationship between principals and their teachers, on the willingness of teachers to take responsibility for directing their own behavior, and on the amount of extra time teachers are willing to devote to working out problems and reaching consensus.[37] Advocates

---

[35]Dale Ballou and Michael Podgursky, "Teachers' Attitude Toward Merit Pay," *Industrial and Labor Relations Review* (October 1993), pp. 50–61; See also "Salaries and Benefits," *NEA Handbook 1997–98* (Washington, D.C.: National Education Association, 1994), pp. 297–298; and Allen Odden and Carolyn Kelley, *Paying Teachers for What They Know and Do* (Thousand Oaks, Calif.: Corwin Press, 1997).

[36]Lou Ann Dickson et al., "Teacher Attitudes Toward a Career Ladder," *ERS-Spectrum* (Spring 1992), pp. 27–33; and telephone conversations with Thomas Gillette, Chief Negotiator, Rochester Teachers Association, July 10, 1991, and David Holdzkom, Chief Consultant for the North Carolina Department of Public Instruction, July 8, 1991.

[37]Gordon Cawelti, "Key Elements of Site-Based Management," *Educational Leadership* (May 1989), pp. 46–54; and Oneida Martin and John Heflin, "Redefining Leadership Roles for Site-Based Management Systems." (Paper Presented at Annual Meeting of the Midsouth Educational Research Association, Biloxi, Mississippi, November 8–10, 1995.)

TAKING ISSUE

Merit Pay

Traditionally, teachers have earned salaries based on their number of years in teaching and their highest degree obtained. Some recent plans, however, offer extra pay to teachers judged to be above average in teaching skills, work habits, leadership, or student achievement.

QUESTION   Should individual teachers be chosen to receive special increases in pay on the basis of merit?

Arguments PRO

1 Teachers whose students consistently score high on achievement tests or have healthy social attitudes must be outstanding teachers or models for citizenship. Such teachers merit extra compensation for their work.

2 Teachers who provide their students with creative and interesting educational experiences, work hard in preparation, and give many hours of their own time to their students also deserve special compensation.

3 Merit pay reduces teaching conformity by encouraging teachers to develop different teaching approaches, become more independent in thought, and exceed what is presented in texts or asked for in teaching guides.

4 Some merit pay plans allow teachers to earn $75,000 or more. Without such opportunities, as in business, to earn above the base salary, capable and ambitious people will not go into teaching.

5 Merit pay promotes excellence in teaching by acting as an incentive for teachers to improve their performance. Each teacher is encouraged to develop better teaching behaviors and a deeper concern for student welfare. Such incentives are found in business and most other professions: why not in teaching?

Arguments CON

1 Factors related to achievement and social attitudes are so diverse that it is impossible to identify the teacher's contribution. Influences from the home, social class, and peer groups cannot readily be separated from the effects of teaching.

2 Hard work can perhaps be measured. But many "creative" activities do not necessarily correlate with good teaching. If creativity is a criterion, merit pay may be awarded more for the teacher's apparent inventiveness than for students' learning.

3 Those who evaluate teachers' merit may unconsciously favor people who do not challenge district policy or seem to threaten the stability of the school with innovative approaches. Thus, merit pay may encourage conformity.

4 The taxpayers will never be able or willing to support extensive merit pay rewards. Business can offset such rewards by raising prices. But merit pay in schools requires higher taxes, which are often not feasible.

5 Incentive pay, by definition, can be given to only a few. Such a plan penalizes equally qualified teachers who are not chosen simply because there are not enough positions. Moreover, competition for merit pay pits one teacher against another, encourages political games, and destroys the collegial cooperation essential to good education.

of school-based management claim that most teachers welcome the increased involvement and that teacher morale and the overall climate of the school dramatically improve.[38]

Critics contend that the result of collaboration is often not useful. Considerable time, they say, is devoted to discussing daily teaching problems such as classroom management, equipment needs, clerical routines, and working conditions; thus little time remains for the larger issue of school effectiveness. In addition, some administrators argue that many teachers are ill-equipped for shared leadership because they have little or no staff development training in it; instead of cooperating, teachers may revert to a hostile collective bargaining stance.[39] In addition, some districts have found it difficult to develop meaningful parental involvement in school-based decision making.[40]

Critiques of school-based management

The expansion of school-based management will require patience and a willingness to work out differences in expectations. Once it is put into practice, however, shared decision making helps empower teachers and further enhances their professional status.

Teacher Organizations

A critical factor in the development of teaching as a profession has been the growth of professional organizations for teachers. Although today's working conditions still need improvement, they sharply contrast with the restrictions teachers once endured. For example, a Wisconsin teacher's contract for 1922, reputedly required the teacher to agree:

A 1922 teacher contract

1. Not to get married. This contract becomes null and void immediately if the teacher marries.

2. Not to keep company with men.

3. To be home between the hours of 8 P.M. to 6 A.M. unless in attendance at a school function.

4. Not to loiter downtown in ice-cream parlors.

5. Not to leave town at any time without the permission of the chairman of the Trustees.

6. Not to smoke cigarettes.

7. Not to drink beer, wine, or whiskey.

8. Not to ride in a carriage or automobile with any man except her brother or father.

---

[38]Priscilla Wholstetter and Kerri L. Briggs, "The Principal's Role in School-Based Management," *Principal* (November 1994), pp. 14, 16–17; Hess, "The Changing Role," pp. 248–263; and Lew Allen and Carl D. Glickman, "School Improvement: The Elusive Faces of Shared Governance," *NASSP Bulletin* (March 1992), pp. 80–87.

[39]Mary L. Radnofsky, "Empowerment and the Power Not to Change: Teachers' Perceptions of Restructuring," *International Journal of Educational Reform* (April 1994), pp. 154–164; Ellen Marie Rice and Gail T. Schneider, "A Decade of Teacher Empowerment: An Empirical Analysis of Teacher Involvement in Decision Making, 1980–1991," *Journal of Educational Administration* (January 1994), pp. 43–58; and Jane David, "The Who, What, and Why of Site-Based Management," *Educational Leadership* (December–January, 1995–1996), pp. 4–9.

[40]Eddy Van Meter, "Implementing School Based Decision Making in Kentucky," *NASSP Bulletin* (September 1994), pp. 61–70; Alan Riley, "Parent Empowerment: An Idea for the Nineties," *Education Canada* (Fall 1994), pp. 14–20; and Joel Westheimer and Joseph Kahne, "Building School Communities: An Experienced Based Model," *Phi Delta Kappan* (December 1993), pp. 324–328.

9. Not to dress in bright colors.

10. Not to dye her hair.

11. Not to wear less than two petticoats.

12. Not to wear dresses shorter than two inches above the ankles.

13. To keep the schoolroom clean:

   a. To sweep the classroom floor at least once daily.

   b. To scrub the classroom floor at least once weekly.

   c. To clean the blackboard at least once daily.

   d. To start the fire at 7 A.M. so that the room will be warm at 8 A.M. when the children arrive.

14. Not to wear face powder, mascara, or to paint the lips.[41]

Consider these requirements in the context of the times: the status of women, the image of teachers, and what Small Town, U.S.A., was like. Most of the schools then were still rural, and provincial and puritanical values prevailed. Although teaching was a serious calling in the 1920s, it was hardly a "profession" or even a "semiprofession."

NEA and AFT

Obviously, the foregoing conditions no longer exist, and to a large extent the growth of teacher organizations and teacher militancy have played a role in changing them. The **National Education Association (NEA)** and the **American Federation of Teachers (AFT)** are the two most important organizations. They usually are considered rivals, competing for members, recognition, and power. Although some educators believe that perpetuation of this division is a healthy form of professional competition, others view it as detrimental to the teaching profession — a splitting

Although the number of teacher strikes has declined in recent years, teacher organizations still consider the strike—or the threat to strike—to be an important tactic for improving teachers' salaries and working conditions. *(Mary Kate Denny)*

of power and a waste of resources. Some argue, too, that teachers will not attain full professional status until one unified voice speaks for them.

Benefits of organizational membership

Regardless of which teacher organization you prefer or are inclined to join, the important step is to make a commitment and be an active member. Organizational membership will not only increase your own professionalism and gain you collegial relationships; your support also helps to improve salary, working conditions, and benefits. In addition, reading the journals, magazines, or newsletters that most professional organizations publish will keep you abreast of the latest developments in the field.

National Education Association (NEA)

The National Education Association is a complex, multifaceted organization involved in many areas of education on local, state, and national levels. Unlike the AFT, the NEA includes both teachers and administrators at the national level. As shown in Table 2.1, membership totaled 2.3 million by 1998 and was projected to reach 2.4 million by the year 2000.[42] Among NEA members in 1998 more than 2 million were classroom teachers.[43] This figure comprises three-fourths of the nation's 2.6 million public school teachers. Primarily suburban and rural in its membership, the NEA represents the fifth largest lobbying force in the country. The state affiliates are usually among the most influential education lobbies at the state level.[44]

NEA membership

NEA services

The NEA offers a wide range of professional services. The Research Division conducts annual studies on the status of the profession; it also publishes research memos and opinion surveys on an annual basis. The NEA's major publication is a monthly newspaper called *NEA Today*. Most of the fifty state affiliates publish a monthly magazine as well.

TABLE 2.1	Recent Membership of the NEA and AFT	
Year	**NEA Membership**	**AFT Membership**
1960	714,000	59,000
1970	1,100,000	205,000
1980	1,650,000	550,000
1990	2,050,000	750,000
1995	2,200,000	875,000
1998	2,300,000	950,000
2000 (projected)	2,400,000	1,000,000

Source: "The AFT Soars," *The 1988–90 Report of the Officers of the American Federation of Teachers* (Washington, D.C.: AFT, 1990), p. 15; *NEA Handbook, 1986–87* (Washington, D.C.: NEA, 1986), Table 4, p. 142; *NEA Handbook, 1994–95* (Washington, D.C.: NEA, 1995), Table 1, p. 164; and *NEA Handbook, 1997–98,* Table 1, p. 166.

---

[42]Robert Chase, "NEA President Speaks," *NEA Today* (January 1998), p. 2.
[43]*NEA Handbook, 1997–98*, Table 1, p. 166.
[44]"NEA Budget 1997–98," *NEA Handbook, 1997–98*, p. 406.

OVERVIEW 2.1	Comparison of the National Education Association (NEA) and the American Federation of Teachers (AFT)	
	NEA	**AFT**
Total membership (1998)	2,300,000	950,000
Members who are classroom teachers	2,000,000	500,000
President	Robert Chase	Sandra Feldman
President's term	2 years (maximum 6 years per person)	2 years (no maximum)
Organizational view	Professional association	Union affiliation with AFL-CIO
Organizational atmosphere (blue collar)	Relatively formal (white collar)	Relatively informal
Geographic strength	Suburban and rural areas	Large and medium-size cities

American Federation of Teachers (AFT)

AFT membership

Formed in 1916, the AFT is affiliated with the AFL-CIO. Originally it was open only to classroom teachers. In 1976, however, in order to increase membership, the AFT started to target professional employees such as nurses and nonprofessional school personnel such as cafeteria, custodial, maintenance, and transportation workers. Membership in 1998 stood at 950,000 (Table 2.1), of whom 500,000 were teachers.

AFT services

In the past, the AFT has not been involved with research and publication to the extent that the NEA has, but the union does publish a professional magazine, *Changing Education,* a *Consortium Yearbook,* and a monthly newspaper, *American Teacher.* In addition, the local affiliates each put out a monthly newsletter. Unlike the NEA, the AFT has always required its members to join the local, state (twenty-two in all), and national organizations simultaneously.

The AFT and teacher militancy

The AFT expanded rapidly in the 1960s and 1970s when its affiliates spearheaded a dramatic increase in teacher strikes and other militant actions. The AFT became the dominant teacher organization in many large urban centers where unions have traditionally flourished, where militant tactics have been common, and where teachers in general have perceived a need for a powerful organization to represent them. In rural and suburban areas, where union tactics have received less support, the NEA remains dominant.

Rivalry Between the NEA and AFT

Professionalism vs. unionism

For years the NEA and the AFT have competed for members and for exclusive local rights to represent teachers. Overview 2.1 sums up some major differences between the two organizations. The NEA has historically viewed itself as a professional association, not a union. For many years it shunned collective bargaining, strikes, and militant tactics. It vehemently criticized the AFT for its labor affiliation, maintaining that this relationship and the AFT's use of the strike were detrimental to the professional image of teachers. For its part, the AFT criticized the NEA's more conciliatory tactics as unrealistic and argued that union affiliation provided teachers with political and economic clout; it also criticized the NEA for permitting administrators to join the organization.

Differences waning

The differences between the two organizations were most pronounced in the late 1960s and 1970s, when the AFT led the surge in teacher strikes. Since then, however, both organizations have toned down their militancy, and strikes have become a less frequent occurrence.[45]

Areas of Agreement Between the NEA and AFT

Agreement on many issues

Despite their continuing differences, the NEA and AFT agree on most big issues concerning teachers and schools, including improved salaries and working conditions, smaller classrooms, reduced teacher patrol and clerical duties, free time for preparation, and released time with pay for attending professional conferences. Both organizations promote full academic freedom for teachers, including the right to participate in textbook selection committees, as well as due process and grievance procedures to protect teachers. They seek a credentialed position (not provisional) for all educators as a means of enhancing the image of the profession. Both organizations wish to increase financial support of all public schools and to extend free public education to all children and young people from prekindergarten to grade fourteen (or junior college).

Codes of ethics

The two organizations share a concern for a professional ethics code. Their respective codes of ethics clarify the roles and responsibilities of teachers and stress the special commitment that teachers must make to students and the profession. The AFT code also emphasizes a commitment to the public and the school districts. Both codes of ethics highlight the dignity of the individual, fulfillment of the student's human potential, the importance of truth, and respect for democratic principles.

Upgrading the profession

Both the NEA and AFT wish to increase teacher involvement and influence in teacher-education programs, and they condemn recent assaults on teachers' tenure and security.[46] The two organizations have played an important role in the current effort to upgrade the teaching profession and academic standards in schools. They are active in promoting special education, compensatory education (especially Head Start), drug education, sex education and AIDS education, environmental education, and global education.[47]

Political activities

In the political arena, the NEA and AFT recognize the need to elect pro-teacher and pro-education political representatives. Through their national and state political action committees (PACs), they now spend millions of dollars annually on political campaigns and lobbying efforts, and they encourage their teachers to volunteer time in election contests and to run for political office.[48] They have been so successful in this approach that by 1995 teachers represented 15 percent of elected school board members nationwide.[49]

Ending the rivalry

A Possible Merger. If the two organizations are compatible enough to back the same political candidates, why shouldn't they end their rivalry? Many educators,

---

[45]Telephone conversations with Charmaine Marsh, Assistant Director of Public Relations, American Federation of Teachers, July 6, 1995, and Daniel Ashyk, *Public Sector Collective Bargaining in Ohio, 1984–1993* (Columbus, Ohio.: Ohio State University, Center for Labor Research, 1995).

[46]"What to Do About Teacher Quality," Commentary in *Education Week*, July 12, 1995, p. 37; Sam Ellis, "Laying Siege to Seniority," *Time,* December 23, 1991, p. 64.

[47]These issues are continuously discussed in *Education Week* in news items or paid advertisements. Also, the annual NEA handbook and AFT report regularly discuss the organizations' agendas and issues.

[48]One controversial example of this direct electoral participation was provided by Edward Doherty, president of the Boston Teacher Union, who ran against two-term incumbent mayor Raymond Flynn in 1992.

[49]Marsh, AFT, July 6, 1995.

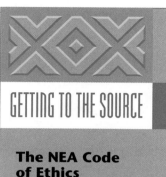

GETTING TO THE SOURCE

The NEA Code of Ethics

Nearly everyone agrees that a profession should have a code of ethics. Accordingly, both the NEA and the AFT have developed such codes, attempting to clarify the relationship between teachers and students as well as the behavior expected of teachers. Although the laws applying to teachers vary from state to state, courts are often influenced by the NEA and AFT codes. The NEA code printed here, established originally in 1929, has been revised six times, most recently in 1975. Although similar to the AFT code, the NEA Code of Ethics is more comprehensive.

Preamble

The educator, believing in the worth and dignity of each human being, recognizes the supreme importance of the pursuit of truth, devotion to excellence, and the nurture of democratic principles. Essential to these goals is the protection of freedom to learn and to teach and the guarantee of equal educational opportunity for all. The educator accepts the responsibility to adhere to the highest ethical standards.

The educator recognizes the magnitude of the responsibility inherent in the teaching process. The desire for the respect and confidence of one's colleagues, of students, of parents, and of the members of the community provides the incentive to attain and maintain the highest possible degree of ethical conduct. The Code of Ethics of the Education Profession indicates the aspiration of all educators and provides standards by which to judge conduct.

The remedies specified by the NEA and/or its affiliates for the violation of any provision of this Code shall be exclusive and no such provision shall be enforceable in any form other than one specifically designated by the NEA or its affiliates.

Principle I—Commitment to the Student. The educator strives to help each student realize his or her potential as a worthy and effective member of society. The educator therefore works to stimulate the spirit of inquiry, the acquisition of knowledge and understanding, and the thoughtful formulation of worthy goals.

In fulfillment of the obligation to the student, the educator—

1. Shall not unreasonably restrain the student from independent action in the pursuit of learning.
2. Shall not unreasonably deny the student access to varying points of view.
3. Shall not deliberately suppress or distort subject matter relevant to the student's progress.

Steps toward a merger

faced with important questions about working conditions, tenure, teacher accountability, and teacher evaluation, have concluded that the best way to promote the interests of the teaching profession is for the two organizations to move toward greater unity — and ultimately toward merger.

The possibility of merging the two national organizations has surfaced several times in recent decades. Merger discussions in 1990 and 1995 were unproductive. A resolution to merge the two organizations was defeated at the NEA's annual convention in 1998. Although a majority of members of both organizations are in favor of merger, they have yet to agree on a merger plan. Strong sentiment exists in both

4. Shall make reasonable effort to protect the student from conditions harmful to learning or to health and safety.
5. Shall not intentionally expose the student to embarrassment or disparagement.
6. Shall not on the basis of race, color, creed, sex, national origin, marital status, political or religious beliefs, family, social or cultural background, or sexual orientation, unfairly:
   a. Exclude any student from participation in any program;
   b. Deny benefits to any student;
   c. Grant any advantage to any student.
7. Shall not use professional relationships with students for private advantage.
8. Shall not disclose information about students obtained in the course of professional service, unless disclosure serves a compelling professional purpose or is required by law.

Principle II—Commitment to the Profession. The education profession is vested by the public with a trust and responsibility requiring the highest ideals of professional service.

In the belief that the quality of the services of the education profession directly influences the nation and its citizens, the educator shall exert every effort to raise professional standards, to promote a climate that encourages the exercise of professional judgment, to achieve conditions which attract persons worthy of the trust to careers in education, and to assist in preventing the practice of the profession by unqualified persons.

In fulfillment of the obligation to the profession, the educator—
1. Shall not in an application for a professional position deliberately make a false statement or fail to disclose a material fact related to competency and qualifications.

2. Shall not misrepresent his/her professional qualifications.
3. Shall not assist entry into the profession of a person known to be unqualified in respect to character, education, or other relevant attribute.
4. Shall not knowingly make a false statement concerning the qualifications of a candidate for a professional position.
5. Shall not assist a noneducator in the unauthorized practice of teaching.
6. Shall not disclose information about colleagues obtained in the course of professional service unless disclosure serves a compelling professional purpose or is required by law.
7. Shall not knowingly make false or malicious statements about a colleague.
8. Shall not accept any gratuity, gift, or favor that might impair or appear to influence professional decisions or actions.

Questions

1. How does a code of ethics strengthen a profession? Are there any ways in which it could weaken a profession?
2. What is the best procedure for dealing with individuals who violate a code of ethics: closed hearings, arbitration, adjustments during contract negotiation, litigation? Why?
3. If you had the opportunity to add one clause and omit another one, what changes would you make in the NEA code?

Source: National Education Association, *Code of Ethics of the Educational Profession,* adopted by the NEA Representative Assembly, 1975. Cover and excerpt reprinted by permission of the Association.

organizations that their unification would provide a 3.3 million teacher voice to fight what union leaders see as an unprecedented assault against public education.[50] Should such a united, "super" organization emerge from these negotiations, it would presumably be better organized, stronger, and more efficient, and it would give teachers enormous political power.[51]

50 "Educators Reject Union Merger Plan," *The Sun,* July 6, 1998, p. A3.
51 "NEA Delegates Agree to Open Merger Talks with AFT," *Education Week,* July 12, 1995, p. 10.

PROFESSIONAL PLANNING

for your first year

Professional Planning for Your First Year: New Teacher Decisions and Dilemmas

The Situation

Imagine this scene: It is late in the day; you are both exhilarated and exhausted and desperate to sit down for a few minutes. However, you have to attend your first faculty meeting. The *Faculty Bulletin* indicates that someone from the central office will present the school board's merit pay proposal. She will be followed by a representative from the local teacher's association who will make a pitch for new teachers to join the local and state organizations as well as the National Education Association (NEA). Afterward your principal will talk about the school district's intention to shift to a school-based management plan.

You sit down at a table with two other new teachers and Sally Thomas, your "mentor" teacher. One new teacher asks Sally if an AFT representative is going to be present. Sally smiles, says "No," and explains that although the American Federation of Teachers often represents teachers in large cities, it is not popular with teachers in many suburban districts. Sally then engages two other faculty members in a spirited discussion about the school board's merit pay plan and the new concept of school-based management.

As your principal starts the meeting, questions begin to form in your head. What benefits will you receive from membership in the NEA and its local and state affiliates? Are there different benefits connected with AFT membership? What other professional organizations might you join? Is school-based management just a fad, or will it change the way your school is run? Considering the proposed new pay system, should you begin work on a master's degree, as Sally thinks you should?

Thought Questions

1. How important do you believe it is that teachers continue to strive for recognition as professionals?
2. What benefits would you gain from professional organization membership?
3. Are there any disadvantages to joining professional organizations?
4. At this point in your career, which of the two major professional organizations looks more attractive to you? Why?
5. What types of professional development do you plan to pursue during and after your first year of teaching?

General Professional Organizations for Teachers

In addition to the NEA and AFT, there are more than 325 other national teacher organizations.[52] In the following sections we describe some of the basic types.

Specialized Professional Organizations

At the working level of the classroom, the professional organization of greatest benefit to a teacher (and education student) is usually one that focuses on his or her

---

[52]See *Directory of Education Associations, 1997–98* (Washington, D.C.: U.S. Department of Education, 1997).

OVERVIEW 2.2 — Major Specialized Professional Organizations for Teachers

Organizations That Focus on Specific Subject Matter

1. American Alliance for Health, Physical Education, Recreation and Dance
2. American Council on the Teaching of Foreign Languages
3. American Industrial Arts Association
4. American School Health Association
5. American Vocational Association
6. Association for Education in Journalism
7. International Reading Association
8. Modern Language Association
9. Music Teachers National Association
10. National Art Education Association
11. National Business Education Association
12. National Council for the Social Studies
13. National Council of Teachers of English
14. National Council of Teachers of Mathematics
15. National Science Teachers Association

Organizations That Focus on a Type or Age Level of Student

1. American Association for Gifted Children
2. American Association of Workers for the Blind
3. American Association for Asian Studies
4. American Montessori Society
5. American Speech-Language-Hearing Association
6. Association for Childhood Education International
7. Association for Children with Learning Disabilities
8. Council for Exceptional Children
9. National Association for Bilingual Children
10. National Association for the Education of Young Children
11. National Association for Multicultural Children
12. National Middle School Association
13. National Rehabilitation Association
14. National Scholarship Service and Fund for Negro Students
15. Rural Education Association

Subject-related associations

major field. Each such subject-centered professional association provides a meeting ground for teachers of similar interests. The activities of these professional organizations customarily consist of regional and national meetings and the publication of professional journals, that provide current teaching tips, enumerate current issues in the discipline, and summarize current research and its relationship to practice. The left-hand column of Overview 2.2 lists fifteen major organizations that focus on specific subject matter.

Student-related organizations

Other organizations, also national in scope, focus on the needs and rights of particular kinds of students, ensuring that these children and youth are served by well-prepared school personnel. Fifteen such organizations are listed in the second column of Overview 2.2. These associations hold regional and national meetings and publish monthly or quarterly journals.

Other professional associations

Still another type of organization is the professional organization whose members cut across various subjects and student types, such as the Association for Supervision and Curriculum Development and Phi Delta Kappa. These organizations tend to highlight general innovative teaching practices, describe new trends and policies affecting the entire field of education, have a wide range of membership, and work for the advancement of the teaching profession in general.

Religious Education Organizations

Catholic education organizations

In grades K–12 there are approximately 378,000 nonpublic school teachers, of whom 135,000 belong to religious education associations. One of the largest religious teacher organizations is the National Association of Catholic School Teachers (NACST), founded in 1978 and now comprising over 5,000 teachers, mainly from large cities.[53] Few Catholic K–12 schoolteachers belong to either the NEA or the AFT.

The largest and oldest Catholic education organization is the National Catholic Education Association, comprising 23,000 institutions and 200,000 Catholic educators. Most members are administrators, serving as principals, supervisors, or superintendents of their respective schools. Few teachers are members.[54]

Parent-Teacher Groups

A forum for parents and teachers to work together in resolving educational problems on the local, state, and national levels is provided by **parent-teacher groups.** Teachers usually take an active part in these associations and work with parents on curriculum and instructional programs, student policy, and school-community relations.

PTA membership

Founded in 1897, the **Parent-Teacher Association (PTA)** — the most prominent of the groups — is a loose confederation of fifty-three branches and 25,538 local units, with over 6.5 million members (mostly mothers) in 1998. Every PTA unit devises its own pattern of organization and service to fit its school and neighborhood. (Some units now use the acronym PTSA, emphasizing their inclusion of students.) Membership in the PTA is open to anyone interested in promoting the welfare of children and youth, working with teachers and schools, and supporting the goals of the PTA.[55] *PTA Today* and *What's Happening in Washington* are the official monthly magazines of the association.[56]

National PTA activities

As the nation's largest child-advocacy organization, the National PTA is constantly assessing children's welfare so that it can respond to changes in society and in children's needs. For a number of years, the National PTA has lobbied to reduce violence on television and to improve the quality of children's television programming. It is also very active in programs related to reading, urban education, sex education and AIDS education, child nutrition and safety education, and drug abuse prevention, as well as in improving school discipline and combating censorship of school and library materials.

Organizations for Prospective Teachers

Help in understanding the profession

Students who are thinking of or are committed to careers as teachers may join a number of professional organizations. These organizations help answer many questions; develop an understanding of the profession; stimulate ideals of professional ethics, standards, and training; provide an opportunity to meet other education

---

[53]Letter from and telephone conversation with Heidi Wunder, Public Relations Assistant, National Catholic Education Association, July 12, 1995; telephone conversation with Virginia Crowther, Office Manager–Membership, National Association of Catholic School Teachers, November 9, 1995.
[54]Wunder, NCEA, July 12, 1995.
[55]*Partners in Education: Teachers in the PTA* (Chicago: The National PTA, 1987); and telephone conversation with Tom Joseph, Director, The National PTA, July 20, 1998.
[56]*The National PTA Handbook* (Chicago: The National PTA, 1998).

OVERVIEW 2.3   Professional Organizations for Students to Join

Name and Location	Membership Profile	Focus	Major Journals
Student National Education Association, Washington, D.C.	Undergraduate students (46,000)	Future teachers; understanding the profession; liability coverage	*Today's Education* (annual); *NEA Handbook* (annual)
Pi Lambda Theta, Bloomington, Ind.	Undergraduate and graduate students; teachers and administrators (11,500)	Honorary association; teaching	*Educational Horizons* (quarterly)
Phi Delta Kappa, Bloomington, Ind.	Undergraduate and graduate students; teachers, administrators, and professors (130,000)	Honorary association; research; service, leadership, and teaching; issues, trends, and policies	*Phi Delta Kappan* (monthly); *Fastbacks* at reduced rates
Kappa Delta Pi, Lafayette, Ind.	Graduate students, teachers, administrators, and professors (29,700); undergraduate students (25,300)	Honorary association; teaching	*Educational Forum* (quarterly); *Kappa Delta Pi Record* (quarterly)
American Educational Research Association, Washington, D.C.	Graduate students and professors (22,500); undergraduate students (4,500)	Research and its application to education	*Educational Researcher* (bimonthly); *American Educational Research Journal* (quarterly), *Review of Educational Research* (quarterly); *Educational Evaluation and Policy Analysis* (quarterly)

students and educators at local and national meetings; and publish materials that help members keep up with current trends in the profession. Overview 2.3 describes five such organizations.

Students interested in joining any of these organizations can ask their professors for appropriate information. If you visit your college library, you can track down the respective journals for each organization. The first or second page of each issue will list the membership and Internet address and membership dues; some journals will also indicate lower membership rates for students.

Summing Up

1. It is generally agreed that teaching is not yet a full profession, although it is moving toward becoming one.
2. Collective bargaining is an integral part of the teaching profession, giving teachers greater authority to determine working conditions and their effectiveness as teachers.
3. Many trends in education are raising the level of teacher professionalism. State professional practice boards and the National Board for Professional Teaching Standards, for example, enable teachers to participate in setting

criteria for entering the profession. Mediated entry and staff development programs help to establish the idea that teaching is a full-fledged profession requiring lengthy and continued training. Merit pay and school-based management provide opportunities for increased salaries and more professional responsibilities.

4. The NEA and AFT now represent the large majority of classroom teachers; these organizations have improved teachers' salaries and working conditions and have gained them a greater voice in decisions that affect teaching and learning in the schools.

5. Although several differences in philosophy and practice separate the NEA and AFT, the possibility of merger may become a reality in the near future.

6. There are many professional organizations that are open to undergraduate students or to graduate students and teachers. All provide valuable information and services to educators at different career levels.

Key Terms

profession *(39)*

National Council for Accreditation of Teacher Education *(40)*

collective bargaining *(43)*

professional practice boards *(44)*

National Board for Professional Teaching Standards *(44)*

mediated entry *(45)*

staff development *(46)*

merit pay *(47)*

school-based management *(49)*

National Education Association (NEA) *(52)*

American Federation of Teachers (AFT) *(52)*

parent-teacher groups *(60)*

Parent-Teacher Association (PTA) *(60)*

Discussion Questions

1. In your opinion, is teaching a profession or not? What changes might be needed for teaching to gain a truly professional status? What does teacher professionalism mean to you?

2. What kind of special relationships does your college of education have with area school districts and/or schools? How do these relationships enhance your preparation as well as that of the teachers and administrators in the schools? How could these be improved?

3. Are staff development programs essential for maintaining high-quality teaching? If so, what should their main focus be? By whom and how should these programs be decided?

4. Do you believe that teachers should have a greater role in managing schools, as the proponents of school-based management argue? As a teacher, what kinds of decisions would you like to be involved in? Are there any areas of school management in which you would rather *not* be involved, and if so, why?

Projects for Professional Development

1. Either by telephone or over the Internet, contact your local NEA and AFT affiliates and ask for information on membership costs, benefits, and services and for position statements on key educational issues. Talk with teachers in the schools you visit, asking them which of the organizations tend to represent teachers in your area and why. Make a chart to display your information and share it with the class.

2. Survey local public-school teachers and your education faculty regarding their views on merit pay. Compare and contrast your results with the views expressed in the Taking Issue feature on page 50. What is your opinion? What are you uncertain about? How can you find more information to clear up these uncertainties?

3. Talk with teachers in the schools and your education professors to find out which professional organizations they belong to — and why. Review the list of specialized professional organizations in Overview 2.2 and select two or three of most interest to you. Using the Internet addresses below, contact these organizations about student membership costs, special benefits, publications, and special programs.

4. Using local newspapers, professional journal articles, and conversations with teachers and administrators, identify an educational issue or trend of importance in a local school district. Why is the issue or trend so important? What are the differing views on the issue (for/against; pro/con)? What implications do you see for teachers and administrators as professional people? Talk with your instructor about selecting several of your classmates to present their issue and its analysis as a panel before the class.

Suggested Readings and Resources

Internet Resources

Information about many of the organizations discussed in this chapter can be found on the World Wide Web. For example, the NEA maintains a home page at **www.nea.org**; the AFT is at **www.aft.org**; and the National PTA is at **www.pta.org**. In addition, the Usenet offers access to many news and discussion groups related to education; some of them, such as k12.chat. teacher, focus on topics of particular concern to elementary and secondary school teachers.

For specific topics such as staff development and educational technology, the biggest problem often lies in deciding which of the many good sites to visit first. For staff development, try the National Staff Development Council at **www.nsdc.org**. For educational technology, search the federal government site at **www.ed.gov**. For either term a general net search will provide a good start.

Publications

Abdul-Haqq, Ismat, *Professional Development Schools: Weighing the Evidence.* Thousand Oaks: Corwin Press, 1997. *An excellent book on professional development school partnerships in teacher education.*

Bascia, Nina. *Unions in Teachers' Professional Lives.* New York: Teachers College Press, 1994. *A case study book on teachers' unions.*

Conant, James B. *The Education of American Teachers.* New York: McGraw-Hill, 1964. *A classic text on improving teacher education and teacher professionalism.*

Johnson, Susan Moore. *Teachers at Work*. New York: Harper and Row, 1990. *The rules and responsibilities teachers adopt in classrooms and schools.*

Lieberman, Myron, and Gene Geisert. *Teacher Union Bargaining: Practice and Policy.* Chicago: Precept Press, 1994. *A book on collective bargaining issues and teachers' unions.*

Murray, Frank. *The Teacher Educator's Handbook: Building a Knowledge Base for the Preparation of Teachers.* San Francisco: Jossey-Bass, 1996. *This is a thorough examination of the need for a knowledge base in teaching, based on research and school reform issues.*

National PTA. *National Standards for Parent/Family Involvement.* Chicago: The National PTA, 1997. *A comprehensive set of standards to help schools, families and parent groups work cooperatively to help children and effect educational change.*

Ornstein, Allan C. *Teaching: Theory into Practice.* Boston: Allyn and Bacon, 1995. *Designed to have students reflect on teaching in both the theoretical and the practical sense.*

Reynolds, Larry J. *Successful Site-Based Management: A Practical Guide.* Thousand Oaks: Corwin Press, 1997. *An excellent guidebook for introducing a system-wide approach to site-based management as a strategy for school improvement.*

Rosenholtz, Susan J. *Teachers' Workplace: The Social Organization of Schools.* New York: Longman, 1989. *A discussion of the profession of teaching and how teachers interact in school settings.*

Walling, Donovan R., ed. *Teachers as Leaders: Perspectives on the Professional Development of Teachers.* Bloomington, Ind.: Phi Delta Kappa Educational Foundation, 1994. *A handbook for recruiting teachers, especially minorities, with general information on the teaching profession and professional development.*

Warner, Jack, and Clyde Bryan. *The Unauthorized Teacher's Survival Guide.* Indianapolis: Park Avenue Publications, 1995. *Must reading for all new teachers — a how-to-survive guide that covers everything a young professional needs to know, from "soup to nuts."*

PART TWO

Historical Foundations

CHAPTER THREE

World Roots of American Education

As part of their professional knowledge base, preservice teachers need to understand how education and schooling originated, developed, and reached their present condition. Even the most urgent contemporary educational issues remain confused unless we examine their historical roots. As the Bradley Commission put it, students "need to confront the diverse cultural heritages of the world's many peoples, and they need to know the origins and evolution of the political, religious, and social ideas that have shaped our institutions and those of others."[1]

Chapter 3 examines how diverse cultural heritages have shaped education today. Though the chapter examines Western historical influences on American education, it also takes a world or global view by discussing developments in ancient China, India, and Egypt.[2] By showing how some of today's issues and practices arose in the past, it seeks to empower us to understand the present and build the future.

Throughout history, teachers have dealt with many questions that remain unresolved today. These important queries address the nature of knowledge, education, schooling, and teaching and learning. They deal with such issues as personal and group rights to participate in schooling and how educational opportunities were often limited by gender, race, and socioeconomic class biases. As you read Chapter 3, consider the following questions:

- How were knowledge, education, schooling, teaching, and learning defined in the major historical periods?

- What concepts of the educated person were dominant during each period of history discussed in this chapter?

- How did racial, gender, and socioeconomic factors limit educational opportunities in the past?

- Historically, has schooling been used for cultural transmission or change?

- What curriculum (the content of education) and what teaching methods were used in the various historical periods?

- How did the ideas of leading educators contribute to modern education?

---

[1]The Bradley Commission on History in Schools, *Building a History Curriculum: Guidelines for Teaching History in Schools* (Washington, D.C.: Educational Excellence Network, 1988), pp. 3–4.
[2]For a discussion of history in its larger world context, see Peter Gram, *Beyond Eurocentrism: A New View of Modern World History* (Syracuse, N.Y.: Syracuse University Press, 1996).

Education in Preliterate Societies

Cultural transmission

Trial-and-error learning

Moral codes

Oral tradition

Storytelling

Literacy

Our narrative begins in preliterate times before the invention of reading and writing. Our preliterate ancestors preserved their culture by transmitting it orally from one generation to the next. We can find the origins of informal learning in families and appreciate why it remains so powerful even today. Although we live in a time when information is electronically stored and retrieved in computers, an examination of preliterate education can help us understand why schools often tend to be conservative institutions, often resisting change as they train the young in essential "survival" skills.

Preliterate people faced the almost overwhelming problems of surviving in an environment that pitted them against drought and floods, wild animals, and attacks from hostile groups. By trial and error, they developed survival skills that over time became cultural patterns. For culture to continue, it had to be transmitted deliberately from the group's adults to its children, a process called **acculturation.** As children learned the group's language, skills, and values, they inherited and perpetuated their culture.

Over time, the patterns of group life—the survival skills—evolved into moral codes that were inculcated in the young. The codes were part of rituals used when children entered adulthood. These rituals incorporated dancing, music, and dramatic acting that gave them a powerful supernatural meaning. Then as now, children learned the group's prescriptions (things they should do) as well as its proscriptions or taboos (behaviors that were forbidden).

Lacking writing to record their past, preliterate societies relied on oral tradition—storytelling—to transmit their cultural heritage. Elders or priests, often gifted storytellers, sang or recited narratives of the group's past. Combining myths and legends, the oral tradition informed the young about the group's heroes, victories, and defeats. The songs and stories helped young people learn the group's spoken language and develop more abstract thinking about time and space. Today, storytelling remains an entertaining but important way for children to learn about their past and themselves.

As toolmakers, humans made and used spears, axes, and other tools, the earliest examples of a human-made technology. Similarly, as language users, they created, used, and manipulated symbols. When these symbols came to be expressed in signs, pictographs, and letters, creating a written language, humans made the great cultural leap to literacy and then to schooling.

A global frame of reference helps to understand the worldwide movement to develop schools in literate societies. For that reason, our historical survey begins with the ancient empires of China, India, and Egypt.

Education in Ancient Chinese Civilization

Because of its long history and vast influence, Chinese civilization offers significant insights into education's evolution. With the world's largest population, modern China is an important global power. Historically, it was a great empire whose civilization reached high pinnacles of political, social, and educational development. The empire was ruled by a series of dynasties spanning more than forty centuries, from 2200 B.C. to A.D. 1912.[3] Although the educational traditions discussed in this section originated in the ancient era, many still survive. (See Overview 3.1 for key periods in China an other countries).

---

[3]Ray Huang, *China: A Macro History* (Armonk, N.Y.: M. E. Sharpe, 1997).

OVERVIEW 3.1   Key Periods in Educational History

Historical Group or Period	Educational Goals	Students
Preliterate societies 7000 B.C.–5000 B.C.	To teach group survival skills; to cultivate group cohesiveness	Children in the group
China 3000 B.C.–A.D. 1900	To prepare elite officials to govern the empire according to Confucian principles	Males of gentry class
India 3000 B.C.–present	To learn behavior and rituals based on the Vedas	Males of upper castes
Egypt 3000 B.C.–300 B.C.	To prepare priest-scribes to administer the empire	Males of upper classes
Greek 1600 B.C.–300 B.C.	*Athens:* To cultivate civic responsibility and identification with city-state *Athens:* to develop well-rounded persons *Sparta:* to train soldiers and military leaders	Male children of citizens; ages 7–20
Roman 750 B.C.–A.D. 450	To develop civic responsibility for republic and then empire; to develop administrative and military skills	Male children of citizens; ages 7–20
Arabic A.D. 700–A.D. 1350	To cultivate religious commitment to Islamic beliefs; to develop expertise in mathematics, medicine, and science	Male children of upper classes; ages 7–20
Medieval A.D. 500–A.D. 1400	To develop religious commitment, knowledge, and ritual; to reestablish social order; to prepare persons for appropriate roles	Male children of upper classes or those entering religious life; girls and young women entering religious communities; ages 7–20
Renaissance A.D. 1350–A.D. 1500	To cultivate a humanist expert in the classics (Greek and Latin); to prepare courtiers for service to dynastic leaders	Male children of aristocracy and upper classes; ages 7–20
Reformation A.D. 1500–A.D. 1600	To cultivate a commitment to a particular religious denomination; to cultivate general literacy	Boys and girls, ages 7–12, in vernacular schools; young men, ages 7–12, of upper-class backgrounds in humanist schools

Instructional Methods	Curriculum	Agents	Influences on Education
Informal means of education; children imitating adult skills and values	Practical skills of hunting, fishing, food gathering; stories, myths, songs, poems, dances	Parents, tribal elders, and priests	Emphasis on informal education in transmission of skills and values
Memorization and recitation of classic texts	Confucian classics	Government officials	Written examinations for civil service and other professions
Memorizing and intepreting sacred texts	Vedas and religious texts	Brahmin priest-scholars	Cultural transmission and assimilation; spiritual detachment
Memorizing and copying dictated texts	Religious or technical texts	Priest and scribes	Restriction of educational controls and services to a priestly elite; use of education to prepare bureaucracies
Drill, memorization, recitation in primary schools; lecture, discussion, and dialogue in higher schools	*Athens:* reading, writing, arithmetic, drama, music, physical education, literature, poetry *Sparta:* drill, military songs, and tactics	*Athens:* private teachers and schools, Sophists, philosophers *Sparta:* military teachers	*Athens:* the concept of the well-rounded, liberally educated person *Sparta:* the concept of the military state
Drill, memorization, and recitation in *ludus;* declamation in rhetorical schools	Reading, writing, arithmetic, Laws of Twelve Tables, law, philosophy	Private schools and teachers; schools of rhetoric	Emphasis on education for practical administrative skills; relating education to civic responsibility
Drill, memorization, and recitation in lower schools; imitation and discussion in higher schools	Reading, writing, mathematics, religious literature, scientific studies	Mosques; court schools	Arabic numerals and computation; reentry of classical materials on science and medicine
Drill, memorization, recitation, chanting in lower schools; textual analysis and disputation in universities and in higher schools	Reading, writing, arithmetic, liberal arts; philosophy, theology; crafts; military tactics and chivalry	Parish, chantry, and cathedral schools; universities; apprenticeship; knighthood	Establishment of the structure, content, and organization of the university as a major institution of higher education; the institutionalization and preservation of knowledge
Memorization, translation, and analysis of Greek and Roman classics	Latin, Greek, classical literature, poetry, art	Classical humanist educators and schools such as lycée, gymnasium, Latin school	An emphasis on literary knowledge, excellence, and style as expressed in classical literature; a two-track system of schools
Memorization, drill, indoctrination, catechetical instruction in vernacular schools; translation and analysis of classical literature in humanist schools	Reading, writing, arithmetic, catechism, religious concepts and ritual; Latin and Greek; theology	Vernacular elementary schools for the masses; classical schools for the upper classes	A commitment to universal education to provide literacy to the masses; the origins of school systems with supervision to ensure doctrinal conformity; the dual-track school system based on socioeconomic class and career goals

Cultural continuity

The Chinese educational heritage reveals persistent efforts to maintain unbroken cultural continuity.[4] These efforts help us understand questions educators still ask: What is the relationship between cultural continuity and change, and how does education promote one or the other?

Center of world

Culturally, the Chinese, like the ancient Greeks, saw their country as the center of the civilized world.[5] Like many people, the Chinese were ethnocentric and believed that their language and culture were superior to all others. Regarding foreigners as barbarians, the Chinese were inward-looking, seeing little of value in other cultures. Eventually, imperial China's reluctance to adapt technology from other cultures isolated and weakened the empire and made it, by the nineteenth century, vulnerable to foreign exploitation. The issue of how to adapt to new ideas, especially in science and technology, and still preserve one's own culture remains important in China today and in other countries as well.

The Confucian Code

Ordered relationships

In imperial China, Confucian ethics regulated political, social, economic, and educational relationships. A philosopher and government official, **Confucius** (551–478 B.C.) feared violence and political unrest. Therefore, he devised an ethical system that stressed family values and political and social stability. Confucius used two important concepts — hierarchy and subordination — to guide human relationships.[6] He envisioned the vast Chinese empire as one great extended family, paternalistically governed by the imperial father, the emperor. All the empire's subjects were to be compliantly subordinate and show deep piety toward their ruler.[7]

Scholarships and Hierarchies

Hierarchical society

At the summit of the Chinese social hierarchy were the emperor and imperial court. Somewhat lower but still very prestigious and powerful were the scholar officials who governed China for the emperor. Next came the wealthy landowners, the gentry, and then the smaller landowning farmers, artisans, and merchants. At the bottom were landless workers.

Intellectual leadership

Like Plato's Republic (discussed later in the chapter) the Chinese system rested on the rationale that only intellectuals were suited to rule. Since intellectual activity was valued more than applied and manual work, schools aimed to reproduce the intellectual elite by preparing the ongoing generations of scholar-officials.

Confucian ethics

Dominating education in imperial China, Confucian ethics tried to develop personal virtue, morality, and loyalty. These values, in turn, would create a harmonious society. Schools emphasized learning the Confucian classics, especially the *Analects,* a collection of Confucius's lectures recorded and interpreted by his students. Also important in Chinese education was Mencius (371–289 B.C.), who refined and developed Confucius's ideas.[8] Informal education, carried on in kinship

---

[4]David Grossman, "Teaching About a Changing China," *Social Education* (February 1986), p. 100.
[5]Roxann Prazniak, *Dialogues Across Civilizations: Sketches in World History from the Chinese and European Experiences* (Boulder, Colo.: Westview of HarperCollins, 1996).
[6]For primary sources on Confucius, see Confucius, *The Analects,* trans., D.C. Lau (New York: Penguin Books, 1979); See also Chi Yun, *Shadows in a Chinese Landscape: The Notes of a Confucian Scholar,* ed. and trans. David L. Keenan (Armonk, N.Y.: M. E. Sharpe, 1998).
[7]John K. Fairbanks, Edwin O. Reichsauer, and Albert M. Craig, *East Asia: The Modern Transformation,* vol. 2 (London: Allen and Unwin, 1965), pp. 80–85.
[8]Conrad Schirokauer, *A Brief History of Chinese Civilization* (New York: Harcourt Brace Jovanovich, 1991), pp. 40–41.

The Situation

In a flight of historical imagination, assume that Confucius is visiting the present-day United States and its schools. He still holds the same beliefs that he did in imperial China. You are a teacher in one of the schools that he visits. How would you answer the following questions that he asks about American society, education, and schools?

Thought Questions

1. I have read newspaper articles and seen television news about violence in American society and schools. Why don't you try to curb violence by instilling strong values of order and harmony like we did in imperial China?
2. I noticed several students who were talking to each other rather than listening to you. This behavior seems to show disrespect for teachers. Why doesn't American society instill greater respect for teachers?
3. I observed that in your class you asked students to give their opinion. What makes the opinion of young people worth listening to? Isn't it better to hear the wisdom of the elders in your society?

groups, emphasized the wisdom of elders, the desirability of maintaining traditional values, and the dangers of departing from custom. These traditional family relationships and values were the foundation of China's civic and social order. Confucianist ethical doctrines were also carried to Japan and Korea, which were influenced by Chinese culture.

China's Contribution to World and Western Education

Importance of examinations

An important educational legacy from ancient China was its system of national examinations. Chinese educators developed comprehensive written examinations to assess students' academic competence. Students prepared for the examinations by studying ancient Chinese literature and Confucian texts with master teachers at imperial or temple schools. The examinations emphasized recalling memorized information rather than solving actual problems. The examination process, like the society, operated hierarchically and selectively. Students had to pass a series of rigorous examinations in ascending order; if they failed, they were dismissed from the process.[9] In imperial days, only a small number of finalists were eligible for the empire's highest civil service positions. The educational and examination systems were reserved exclusively for upper-class males. Ineligible for government positions, women were excluded from schools as well. China's examination system perpetuated tradition rather than bringing about change. It created and sustained an immense social gulf between the educated elite and the mass of illiterates.

Currently, national examinations, especially for university entrance, dominate education in modern China and Japan. Other countries such as the United Kingdom have recently developed national tests. In the United States, national volun-

[9]John K. Fairbanks, Edwin O. Reichsauer, and Albert M. Craig, *East Asia: The Modern Transformation,* vol. 2 (London: Allen and Unwin, 1965), pp. 87–88.

GETTING TO THE SOURCE

A Confucian View of Good Teaching

CONFUCIUS

Plutarch
Plato Locke
Quintilian Moses
Saint Basil Erasmus
Saint Jerome Al-Ghazali
Aristotle Gerson Comenius
Ibn Khaldoun Saint Augustine
Maimonides Luther Montaigne
Bacon Descartes Galileo Franklin
Luzzatto Emerson Dewey Jefferson
Pestalozzi Froebel Herbart Rousseau

Three Thousand Years of Educational Wisdom
Selections from Great Documents
Edited by Robert Ulich Second edition, enlarged

Confucius (551–479 B.C.) developed the ethical system that governed society, politics, and education in ancient China. Concerned with maintaining social and cultural harmony, Confucius's ideas on education emphasized the proper attitudes and relationships between teachers and students. Confucian philosophy has had and continues to exercise an important influence on culture and education in China, Japan, Korea, and in other Asian countries. The following selection is from Confucius's "Record on the Subject of Education."

13. When a superior man knows the causes which make instruction successful, and those which make it of no effect, he can become a teacher of others. Thus in his teaching, he leads and does not drag; he strengthens and does not discourage; he opens the way but does not conduct to the end without the learner's own efforts. Leading and not dragging produces harmony. Strengthening and not discouraging makes attainment easy. Opening the way and not conducting to the end makes the learner thoughtful. He who produces such harmony, easy attainment, and thoughtfulness may be pronounced a skilful teacher.

14. Among learners there are four defects with which the teacher must make himself acquainted. Some err in the multitude of their studies; some, in their fewness; some, in the feeling of ease with which they proceed; and some, in the readiness with which they stop. These four defects arise from the difference of their minds. When a teacher knows the character of his mind, he can save the learner from the defect to which he is liable. Teaching should be directed to develop that in which the pupil excels, and correct the defects to which he is prone.

tary tests have been proposed. Although national tests contribute to uniformity across a country, they tend to force teachers to teach for the examination rather than for students' interests and needs.

Education in Ancient Indian Civilization

Cultural equilibrium

Brief history

Like China, India is an ancient civilization. As in Egypt's Nile Valley, river valley civilizations flourished on the banks of India's Indus River at Mohenjo-daro and Harrapa from 3000 B.C. to 1500 B.C. These civilizations developed an elaborate urban culture with well-plotted brick houses, copper tools, and drainage and sanitation systems.

India's educational history reveals a general pattern of intrusion by invaders, followed by a cultural clash with the indigenous people, and then the restoration of sociocultural equilibrium. In this cultural equilibrium, the invaders were brought into India's culture while at the same time the indigenous people borrowed some of the invaders' ideas.[10]

The first invaders were the Aryans, ancestors of India's Hindi-speaking majority. The Aryans conquered India around 1500 B.C. and imposed their rule over the indigenous Dravidian peoples. They introduced their religion, Hinduism, and their

---

[10]For India's history and culture, see Ranbir Vohra, *The Making of India: A Historical Survey* (Armonk, N.Y.: M. E. Sharpe, 1997); and Herman Kulke and Dietmar Rothermund, *A History of India* (New York: Routledge, 1998).

15. The good singer makes men able to continue his notes, and so the good teacher makes them able to carry out his ideas. His words are brief, but far-reaching; unpretentious, but deep; with few illustrations, but instructive. In this way he may be said to perpetuate his ideas.

16. When a man of talents and virtue knows the difficulty on the one hand and the facility on the other in the attainment of learning, and knows also the good and bad qualities of his pupils, he can vary his methods of teaching. When he can vary his methods of teaching, he can be a master indeed. When he can be a teacher indeed, he can be the Head of an official department. When he can be such a Head, he can be the Ruler of a state. Hence it is from the teacher indeed that one learns to be a ruler, and the choice of a teacher demands the greatest care; as it is said in the Record, "The three kings and the four dynasties were what they were by their teachers."

Questions

1. According to Confucius, what principles contribute to successful teaching and learning?

2. What deficiencies may interfere with students' learning?
3. When should teachers vary their teaching methods?
4. What did Confucius believe was an appropriate teacher-learner relationship?
5. What are your ideas of good teaching — which are part of your philosophy of education — and how do they agree with or differ from Confucius's ideas?

Source: Robert Ulich, ed., *Three Thousand Years of Educational Wisdom.* (Cambridge, Mass.: Harvard University Press, 1954), pp. 21–22.

highly stratified hierarchical social order, the **caste** system. They were followed by Muslims, who established the Mughul dynasty in the thirteenth century. Then, in the eighteenth century, Europeans — the French, Portuguese, and British — penetrated the subcontinent. Defeating their colonialist rivals, the British gained control over India.

Hinduism

Hinduism, a powerful cultural force in India, incorporates a wide range of religious beliefs and elaborate rituals. Believing in the transmigration of souls, Hinduism emphasizes that a person's soul experiences a series of reincarnations. A person's position in the cosmic scale depends on how well he or she performs duties and rituals. Reincarnation ends only when a soul reaches the highest spiritual level and is reabsorbed in Brahma, the divine power.[11]

Caste system

The four original castes were **Brahmins,** priest-educators; *Kshatriyas,* rulers, judges, and warriors; *Vaishyas,* merchants; and *Shudras,* the farmers. At the bottom of the caste system were the untouchables, who performed the most menial work. There was no social mobility. People stayed in the caste into which they were born. Based on their caste, people learned their duties and roles by imitating parents and other adults. Schooling was reserved for the upper castes, primarily the Brahmins. Outlawing caste-based discrimination, modern India has an "affirmative action" for

[11]James Mulhern, *A History of Education: A Social Interpretation* (New York: Ronald Press, 1959), pp. 80–128; and Mehdi Nakosteen, *The History and Philosophy of Education* (New York: Ronald Press, 1965), pp. 23–40.

lower caste members. However, like racism in the United States, discrimination still exists.

Vedic Education

Vedas

Hinduism's religious texts are the **Vedas,** the *Bhagavad Gita,* and the *Upanishads.* They portray the goal of life as a search for spiritual truths.[12] Like the ancient Greek philosopher Plato, Indian educators see knowledge as innate in a person's mind.[13] They search for truth requires disciplined meditation. Contemporary transcendental meditation and yoga follow these ancient Indian principles for finding inner spiritual truth and peace.

Schools and teaching

Ancient India had different types of schools. Brahminic schools, for the priestly caste, stressed the *Vedas,* religion, and philosophy. *Tols* were one-room schools where a single teacher taught religion and law. Court schools were sponsored by princes. Temple schools, like those in Egypt, emphasized religion and ritual. Hindu educational philosophy, stressing education's religious purposes, prescribed appropriate teacher-student relationships. The teacher, an *ayoha,* was to transmit his wisdom to students. Teachers should refrain from ridiculing or humiliating students.[14]

Mughuls

In the thirteenth century, Islamic tribes, the ancestors of India's Muslim population, invaded India and established the Mughul empire at Delhi. The Mughul dynasty introduced Persian and Arabic art, music, literature, astronomy, mathematics, medicine, philosophy, religion, and architecture.

English entry

By the time the English entered India in the late eighteenth century, India's schools were conducted either by Hindus or Muslims or by smaller sects such as Buddhists, Jains, and Parsis. Only about only 10 percent of India's children, mostly boys, attended. Hindu higher schools, conducted by Brahmins, emphasized religious literature, mathematics, astronomy, and Sanskrit grammar. Muslim schools, called *madrassahs,* were attached to mosques and emphasized grammar and the Koran.[15]

When the English established their colonial rule in India, they encountered an ancient civilization with many languages and religions. Placing a greater value on their own language than on those spoken in India, the English imposed their own language as the official one for government and commerce. Therefore, they established English-language schools to train Indians for positions in the British-controlled civil service.

India's Contribution to World and Western Education

Ancient India's legacy to the world demonstrates how education helped a civilization to endure over the centuries. Through the processes of cultural assimilation and readaptation, Indian civilization has survived to the present. Hinduism bears philosophical similarities to the idealist Platonic philosophy that sees education as a search for internal and eternal truth. Finally, the Indian situation reveals how

---

[12]Percival Spear, *A History of India* (London: Penguin Books, 1990), p. 156.
[13]Mehdi Nakosteen, *The History and Philosophy of Education* (New York: Ronald Press, 1965), p. 25.
[14]Nandish Patel, "A Comparative Exposition of Western and Vedic Theories of the Institution of Education," *International Journal of Educational Management,* 8 (1994), pp. 9–14.
[15]Michael Edwards, *Raj: The Story of British India* (London: Pan Books, 1967), p. 133.

caste, like racism in the United States, was once perpetuated by society and education but is now being corrected through educational processes.

Education in Ancient Egyptian Civilization

An unchanging cosmos

Like other early civilizations, ancient Egypt — one of the world's earliest — developed as a river-valley culture. Because of the Nile River's life-sustaining water, agricultural groups established small village settlements on the Nile's banks that were first organized into tribal kingdoms. About 3000 B.C. these kingdoms consolidated into a large empire, which eventually became a highly organized and centralized political colossus.

An important Egyptian religious and political principle affirmed that the pharaoh, the emperor, was of divine origin. The concept of divine emperorship gave social, cultural, political, and educational stability to the Egyptian empire by endowing it with supernaturally sanctioned foundations. Knowledge and values were seen as reflecting an orderly, unchanging, and eternal cosmos. The concept of a king-priest also gave the priestly elite high status and considerable power in Egyptian society. The educational system reinforced this status and power by making the priestly elite guardians of the state culture.

Religious and Secular Concerns

Educationally, the Egyptians were both otherworldly and this-worldly. Although preoccupied with the supernatural, they were also concerned with the technologies needed to irrigate the Nile Valley and to design and build the massive pyramids and temples in which they entombed the mummies of their pharaohs and other nobility. To administer and defend their vast empire, they studied statecraft, and their concern with mummification led them to study medicine, anatomy, and embalming.

Temple and court schools

The Egyptians developed a system of writing, a hieroglyphic script, that enabled them to create and preserve religious, political, and medical literatures. The empire also required an educated bureaucracy to collect and record taxes. By 2700 B.C. the Egyptians had in place an extensive system of temple and court schools. One of the school system's basic functions was to train scribes, many of whom were priests, in the skills of reading and writing. Schools were often built as part of the temple complex, and there was a close relationship between formal education and religion.[16] After receiving some preliminary education, boys studied the literature appropriate to their future professions. Special advanced schools existed for certain kinds of priests, government officials, and physicians.

Education of scribes

In the scribal schools, students learned to write the hieroglyphic script by copying documents on papyrus, sheets made from reeds growing along the Nile. Their teachers' basic method was dictating to students, who copied what they heard. The goal was to reproduce a correct, exact copy of a text. Often students would chant a short passage until they had memorized it thoroughly. For those who proceeded to advanced studies, the curriculum included mathematics, astronomy, religion, poetry, literature, medicine, and architecture.

---

[16]James Mulhern, *A History of Education: A Social Interpretation,* pp. 55–79.

Historical Controversies About Egypt

Traditional interpretation

Ancient Egypt's role in shaping Western civilization has become controversial. In 332 B.C. Egypt was conquered by Alexander the Great and incorporated into Hellenistic civilization, which in turn had been shaped by ancient Greek culture. The conventional historical interpretation was that ancient Egyptian civilization was a highly static despotism and that its major cultural legacy was its great architectural monuments. This interpretation saw Greek culture, especially Athenian democracy, as the cradle of Western civilization.

Bernal's theory

A highly controversial interpretation by Martin Bernal argues that the Greeks borrowed many of their concepts about government, philosophy, the arts, and sciences from ancient Egypt. Furthermore, the Egyptians, geographically located in North Africa, were an African people, and the origins of Western culture are therefore African.[17] While historians continue to debate the matter, tentative findings indicate that Egyptian-Greek contacts, particularly at Crete, introduced the Greeks to Egyptian knowledge, such as mathematics, and to Egyptian art forms.

The past as a source of power

This intriguing historical controversy has important ideological significance. Whoever interprets the past gains the power of illuminating and shaping the present. In particular, the controversy relates to the current debate about Afrocentrism and the Afrocentric curriculum. It also shows how contemporary multicultural issues are stimulating new historical interpretations.

In the next section we turn to the ancient Greeks. Whether influenced directly or indirectly by the Egyptians, the Greeks continue to hold an important place in the history of education. Keep in mind, however, that most historical cultures have borrowed from one another in many ways, and the roots of Greek thought may indeed be traceable to Egypt or elsewhere.

Education in Ancient Greek and Roman Civilizations

The educational history of ancient Greece and Rome illuminates the origin of many persistent issues that today's teachers face. Among the educational questions the Greeks and Romans debated were: What is the true, the good, and the beautiful? Who are worthy models for children to imitate? How does education shape good citizens? How should education respond to social, economic, and political change?

Homeric education

Generations have thrilled to the dramatic suspense of Homer's epic poems, the *Iliad* and *Odyssey*. Appearing about 1200 B.C., Homer's epics helped Greeks define themselves and their culture. Like ritual ceremonies in preliterate societies, Homer's dramatic portrayal of the Greek warriors' battles against the Trojans served important educational purposes: (1) it preserved the culture by transmitting it from adults to the young; (2) it cultivated Greek cultural identity based on mythic and historical origins; and (3) it shaped the character of the young.[18] Agamemnon, Ulysses, Achilles, and other warriors dramatically personified life's heroic dimensions. By using these heroes as role models, the young Greek learned about the values that made life worth living, the behaviors expected of warrior-knights, and the character defects that led to one's downfall.[19]

---

[17]Martin Bernal, *Black Athena: The Afroasiatic Roots of Classical Civilization: The Fabrication of Ancient Greece 1785–1985* (New Brunswick, N.J.: Rutgers University Press, 1987), pp. 2–3.
[18]Louis Goldman, "Homer, Literacy, and Education," *Educational Theory* (Fall 1989), pp. 391–400.
[19]Robert Holmes Beck, "The *Iliad:* Principles and Lessons," *Educational Theory* (Spring 1986), pp. 179–195.

Education for citizenship

Ancient Greece also illuminates education's role in forming good citizens. Just as Americans are likely to disagree on the precise formula for educating good citizens, so the Greeks debated the issue. Unlike the great empires of China and Egypt, ancient Greece was divided into small and often competing city-states, such as Athens and Sparta, which defined civic responsibilities and rights differently. After experimenting with different forms of government, Athens became a democracy that emphasized the shared public responsibility of its citizens. Sparta, Athens' chief rival, was an authoritarian military dictatorship.[20] To match its distinctive government, each city-state, or *polis,* had its own type of citizenship education.

Acculturation vs. formal education

For the Greeks, acculturation — immersion and participation in the city-state's total culture — was more important than formal schooling. Through acculturation Greek youths were prepared to become a citizens of their society. Formal education, in contrast, was reserved for particular classes of citizens. In Athens, for example, formal education was usually limited to the male children of citizens. The Athenians believed that a free man needed a liberal education to perform his civic duties as well as to develop personally.[21] This assumption did not extend to women, slaves, and resident aliens, all of whom, with a few exceptions, had very little or no opportunity to attend schools. About two-thirds of Athens' population were thus excluded from formal education.

The role of slaves

Greek society, including that of Athens, rested at least partially on slave labor. The vast majority of slaves, including women and children, were people conquered in war or judicially condemned to slavery. In Athens, although there were educated slaves who tutored wealthy children, the majority of slaves were trained to perform specific skills in agriculture or trade. Slaves, the Athenians believed, neither needed nor should have the liberal education suited for free men. This distinction between vocational training for slaves and a general, liberal education for free citizens was typical of ancient Greek society.[22]

Education of women

Although a minority of exceptional women attained education and status, Greek society was dominated by men. Women's status and education reflected the particular Greek city-state's customs. In Athens, where women had no legal or economic rights, the vast majority of women did not receive a formal education. More fortunate young women were educated at home by tutors. Others, such as priestesses of the religious cults, learned religious rituals at special cult schools. In contrast to Athens, Sparta's young women received some schooling that emphasized athletic training to prepare them to be healthy mothers of future Spartan soldiers.

A more structured education began when the Sophists appeared on the scene. They were followed by Socrates and Plato, the moral philosophers; Aristotle, who attempted to formulate rational explanations of natural phenomena; and Isocrates, the rhetorician.

The Sophists

In the fifth century B.C., a changing economy brought new social and educational patterns to Greece, especially Athens. The older landed aristocracy was displaced by

---

[20]Nigel M. Kennell, *The Gymnasium of Virtue: Education and Culture in Ancient Sparta* (Chapel Hill, N.C.: University of North Carolina Press, 1995).
[21]Kevin Robb, *Literacy and Paideia in Ancient Greece* (New York: Oxford University Press, 1994).
[22]Joseph M. Bryant, *Moral Codes and Social Structure in Ancient Greece: A Sociology of Greek Ethics from Homer to the Epicureans and Stoics* (Albany: State University of New York Press, 1995).

new commercial classes, which had profited from Athenian expansion and colonization. This socioeconomic change created the conditions for the Sophists.

Wandering teachers

The **Sophists**, a group of wandering teachers, developed a variety of methods to instruct the new commercial class in rhetoric and the techniques of oratory. Skill in public speaking was important in Athens, where it could be used to persuade the assembly and the courts in one's favor. The Sophists claimed that they could teach any subject or skill to anyone who wished to learn it. Although they exaggerated their teaching skills, the Sophists created educational opportunities for more people.

Grammar, logic, and rhetoric

The Sophists sought to develop their students' communication skills so that the students could become successful advocates and legislators. The most important subjects were grammar, logic, and rhetoric — subjects that developed into the liberal arts. Logic, or the rules of argument, helped students clarify and organize their presentations, and grammar helped them express ideas clearly. Of special importance was **rhetoric**, the power of persuading others through speech. The Sophists generally believed that, with the proper skills, an orator could argue and win any case.

A mixed record

The Sophists had a mixed record as teachers. Some were gifted and well prepared to teach. Others, however, were fakes who promised instant success through tricks and gimmicks. Protagoras (485–415 B.C.), among the most effective Sophists, was highly concerned with developing an effective method of teaching.[23] His first step was to (1) deliver an outstanding speech so students knew their teacher could do what he was attempting to teach them; this speech also gave them a model to follow. Then Protagoras had the students (2) examine the great orations of famous speakers to amplify the available models; (3) study the key subjects of rhetoric, grammar, and logic; and (4) deliver practice orations that he assessed to provide feedback. Finally, (5) the student orators delivered public speeches. Protagoras's method is similar to present teacher-education programs, in which prospective teachers study the liberal arts and professional subjects, learn various teaching strategies, and do practice teaching under the guidance of a cooperating teacher.

Protagoras's method

Knowledge as an instrument

The Sophists did not believe that truth existed as unchanging universal principles. To them, knowledge was not speculation about abstract concepts of truth, beauty, and goodness but rather an instrument to achieve human objectives. Thus the Sophists promised to teach the skills and information that would give their students political power and social prestige. It was not what you said, the Sophists believed, but how you expressed yourself that won the argument.

Democratic and opportunistic

As traveling teachers, the Sophists did not establish schools in an institutional sense — they taught anyone who could pay tuition. Critics such as Socrates and Plato labeled them opportunists who stressed appearance and technique rather than truth and honesty. In some respects, the Sophists resembled modern image-makers who use the media to "package" political candidates and celebrities.

Socrates: Education by Self-Examination

Unlike the Sophists, the Athenian philosopher Socrates (469–399 B.C.) sought to discover the universal principles of truth, beauty, and goodness, which he believed should govern human conduct. Socrates is important in educational history because he firmly defended the academic freedom to think, question, and teach. He

---

[23]L. Glenn Smith, *Lives in Education: People and Ideas in the Development of Teaching* (Ames, Iowa: Educational Studies Press, 1984), pp. 7–9.

Universal principles

Moral excellence

Role of the Socratic teacher

Self-examination, dialogue, and the Socratic method

was also significant as the teacher of Plato, who later systematized many of Socrates' ideas.[24]

Socrates' philosophy stressed the ethical principle that a person should strive for moral excellence, live wisely, and act rationally. A genuine education should cultivate morally excellent people. This generalized moral excellence, Socrates believed, was far superior to the Sophists' technical training.

Socrates' concept of the teacher differed from that of the Sophists. He did not believe that knowledge or wisdom could be transmitted from a teacher to a student because he believed the concepts of true knowledge were present, but buried, within the person's mind. The teacher was to ask the right questions that would make students think critically about important issues. A truly liberal education would stimulate learners to discover ideas by bringing to consciousness the truth that was present but latent in their minds.

Socrates' educational aim was to help individuals define themselves through self-examination. In this way each person could seek the truth that is universally present in all people. As a teacher, Socrates asked leading questions that stimulated students to investigate perennial human concerns about the meaning of life, truth, and justice. The students then became involved in lively but rigorous discussion, or *dialogue,* in which they clarified, criticized, and reconstructed their basic concepts. For Socrates, dialogue did not mean merely sharing opinions; it meant reflecting on and criticizing them to find the underlying truth. This technique is still known as the **Socratic method.**

Frequenting Athens' marketplace, Socrates attracted a group of young men who joined him in critically examining all kinds of issues — religious, political, moral, and aesthetic. But as a social critic, Socrates made powerful enemies. Then as now, some people, including those in high places, feared that critical thinking would challenge the status quo and lead to unrest. In 399 B.C., after being tried on the charge of impiety to the gods and corrupting Athenian youth, Socrates was condemned to death.

Plato: Eternal Truths and Values

Reality as universal, eternal ideas

Reminiscence

Socrates' pupil Plato (427–346 B.C.) continued his mentor's educational tradition. Plato founded the Academy, a philosophical school, in 387 B.C. He wrote *Protagoras,* a discourse on virtue, and the *Republic* and the *Laws,* treatises on politics, law, and education. Rejecting the Sophists' relativism, Plato argued that reality consisted of an unchanging world of perfect ideas — universal concepts such as truth, goodness, justice, and beauty. Individual instances of these concepts, as they appear to our senses, are but imperfect representations of the universal and eternal concepts that reside in an absolute idea, the Form of the Good.

Plato's theory of knowledge is based on **reminiscence**, a process by which individuals recall the ideas present in latent form in their minds. Reminiscence implies that the human soul, before birth, has lived in a spiritual world of ideas, the source of all truth and knowledge. At birth, these ideas are repressed within one's subconscious mind. For Plato, learning means that one rediscovers or recollects these perfect ideas.[25] Because sense impressions distort reality, genuine knowledge is

---

[24]Alven Neiman, "Ironic Schooling: Socrates, Pragmatism and the Higher Learning," *Educational Theory* (Fall 1991), pp. 371–384.
[25]Gerald L. Gutek, *Philosophical and Ideological Perspectives on Education* (Boston: Allyn and Bacon, 1997), pp. 16–18.

intellectual, changeless, and eternal not sensory. There is but one idea of perfection for all human beings regardless of when or where they live. Since what is true is always true, education should also be universal and unchanging.

Universalism vs. relativism

The belief in innate knowledge that was latently present in the mind had a powerful influence on early Western education, as well as on education in India. The theory of innate ideas would be challenged by later educational reformers such as Locke, Pestalozzi, Dewey, and others, whose ideas are described in Chapter 4. Many later educational controversies, even the current interest in Constructivism, can be seen as counterarguments to Plato's theory of ideas.

Innate ideas

Plato's Ideal Society.   In the *Republic,* Plato projected a plan for a perfect society ruled by philosopher-kings, an intellectual elite. Although **Plato's** *Republic* was never implemented, his ideas are useful in portraying an idealized version of a certain kind of education. The Republic's inhabitants were to be divided into three classes: the philosopher-kings, the intellectual rulers; the auxiliaries and military defenders; and the workers, who produced goods and provided services. A person's intellectual capacity would determine his or her class assignment.

The Republic

A parallel exists between the hierarchical societies in Plato's republic and the ancient Indian caste system. At the summit of both societies were intellectuals — Plato's philosopher kings and the Hindus' Brahmins.

Education corresponding to social role

In educational terms, it is possible to think of Plato's Republic as consisting of permanent homogeneous groups. Once assigned to such a group, individuals would receive the education appropriate to their social role. The philosopher-kings, educated for leadership, also were responsible for identifying the intellectually able in the next generation and preparing them for their destined roles. The second class, the warriors, courageous rather than intellectual, would be trained to defend the Republic and to take orders from the philosopher-kings. The third and largest class, the workers, would be trained to be farmers and artisans. With an educational track for each group, the Republic prepared its members for their appropriate functions, which in turn contributed to the community's harmony and efficient functioning.

Women's education

Unlike the Athenians, Plato believed that women should have the privileges and responsibilities accorded men.[26] Women, too, fell within the three classes to which Plato assigned human beings. Women who possessed high-level cognitive powers could become members of the ruling philosophical elite; others of lesser intellect would be assigned to lower ranks. Like men, women would receive the education or training appropriate to their abilities and their destined occupations.

Plato's Curriculum.   Plato's curriculum corresponded to the educational objectives of a hierarchical rather than an egalitarian society. Since he feared parents would pass on their ignorance and prejudices to their children, Plato wanted children reared by experts in child care. Separated from their parents, children would live in state nurseries, prepared environments that would cultivate good habits and purge habits harmful to children's proper development.

State-run nurseries

Plato's basic curriculum

From ages six to eighteen, children would be in schools, where they studied music and gymnastics. "Music," in Plato's definition, was a broad subject that included reading, writing, literature, arithmetic, choral singing, and dancing. After mastering reading and writing, students would read the approved classics. Regarding literature as a powerful force in character formation, Plato believed that children should read only poems and stories that epitomized truthfulness, obedience to

---

[26]Robert S. Brumbaugh, "Plato's Ideal Curriculum and Contemporary Philosophy of Education," *Educational Theory* (Spring 1987), pp. 169–177.

authorities, courage, and control of emotions. After mastering basic arithmetic, students would apply themselves to geometry and astronomy. Gymnastics, which consisted of functional exercises useful for military training, such as fencing, archery, javelin throwing, and horseback riding, was considered essential for character building and for physical development. Plato also included the rules of diet and hygiene in his curriculum.

Higher education

From ages eighteen to twenty, students would pursue intensive physical and military training. At twenty, the future philosopher-kings would be selected for ten years of additional higher education in mathematics, geometry, astronomy, music, and science. At age thirty, the less intellectually capable among this group would become civil servants; the most intellectually capable would continue the higher study of metaphysics. When their studies were completed, the philosopher-kings would begin to direct the Republic's military and political affairs. At age fifty, the philosopher-kings would become the Republic's elder statesmen.

Aristotle: Cultivation of Rationality

Plato's student Aristotle (384–322 B.C.) was the tutor of Alexander the Great. Aristotle founded the Lyceum, an Athenian philosophical school, and wrote extensively on physics, astronomy, zoology, botany, logic, ethics, and metaphysics. His *Nichomachean Ethics* and *Politics* examine education in relation to society and government.[27]

An objective reality

Unlike his mentor Plato, who believed that reality exists in the realm of ideas, Aristotle held that reality exists objectively. For him, objects, composed of form and matter, exist independently of human knowledge of them. Aristotle also saw a basic duality in human nature. Like animals, people have instincts and appetites that satisfy physical needs and enable them to survive. But unlike lower animals, humans also possess intellect — the power to think. As rational beings, humans have the ability to know the natural laws that govern the universe.

Sensation as the root of knowledge

For Aristotle, knowing begins with one's sensation of objects in the environment. From this sensory experience, one forms concepts about objects. The Aristotelian emphasis on sensory experience as the beginning of knowing and of instruction was later stressed by eighteenth- and nineteenth-century educators such as Locke and Pestalozzi. Aristotle's philosophical position was the historical predecessor of realism, discussed in Chapter 12.

Education as cultivation of rationality

Aristotle on Education. In his *Politics*, Aristotle argues that the good community rests on its members' rationality. If education, the cultivation of rationality, is neglected, then the community suffers. Like Plato, Aristotle distinguished between liberal education and technical training. Aristotle saw the liberal arts as enlarging a person's horizons, consciousness, and choices, and he saw vocational training as a servile interference with intellectual development. Contemporary debates between liberal and career educators often reflect the same issues Aristotle and other Greek theorists examined.

Aristotle's curriculum

Aristotle recommended compulsory schooling. Infant schooling was to consist of play, physical activity, and appropriate stories. Children from ages seven to fourteen learned basic numeracy and literacy and proper moral habits to prepare them for future study in liberal arts. Their curriculum also included physical education

---

[27]J. J. Chambliss, *Educational Theory as Theory of Conduct: From Aristotle to Dewey* (Albany: State University of New York Press, 1987), pp. 23–25.

TAKING ISSUE

Universal Truth or Cultural Relativism?

In classical Greece, the question of whether education should reflect universal truth or the beliefs relative to different peoples living at a particular place and time was debated. Plato, who argued that truth was unchanging, debated this issue with the Sophists, who claimed all things were relative to time and circumstances. The issue is debated today by those who want schools to instill basic morality and by others who want students to clarify their values.

Universalists contend that what is true today has always been true. Relativists argue that changing values make life satisfying at a particular place and time.

QUESTION   Should education be based on universal truths or on beliefs and values that are relative to different cultures at different times and places?

Arguments PRO

1 Truth is universal and eternal. As human beings search for truth, their quest will bring them to the same general ideas and values. What is true is true in all places and at all times. It is not based on changing public opinion polls.

2 Although different races and ethnic and language groups inhabit the earth, they are all members of the same human family and thus share common hopes and dreams.

3 Education, as Socrates and Plato argued, should engage students in seeking answers to the great questions, such as What is true, good, and beautiful? Especially in the new computer-driven information age, programs need to be based on enduring truth and value.

4 Schools should emphasize universal truths and value found in religion, philosophy, mathematics, science, and other subjects that transcend particular cultural and political barriers.

Arguments CON

1 What is called "truth" is really a tentative knowledge claim that is relative to different groups living in different places at different times. What is true at a given time is that which solves a problem in living.

2 Society is relative and changing. Human behavior needs to be flexible to adapt to social, economic, political, and technological change.

3 Education is a pragmatic tool, a means of personal and social adaptation. As such, it emphasizes new ways of learning to prepare people to be efficient users of new technologies. It is more important for students to be computer competent than to ponder unanswerable questions about the true, the good, and the beautiful.

4 Schooling, based on people's needs, will be different from culture to culture and from time to time. That is why the Constructivist approach, by which students create their own conceptions of reality, is so useful in today's schools.

and music to cultivate proper emotional dispositions. From age fifteen through twenty-one, youths would study mathematics, geometry, astronomy, grammar, literature, poetry, rhetoric, ethics, and politics. At age twenty-one, students would proceed to more theoretical subjects, such as physics, cosmology, biology, psychology, logic, and metaphysics.

Limited roles for women

Believing women were intellectually inferior to men, Aristotle was concerned only with male education. Girls were to be trained to perform the household and child-rearing duties necessary for their future roles as wives and mothers.

Knowledge as concepts based on objects

Aristotle's Theory of Knowledge.   Aristotle differs from Plato in that his concepts are evident in an object rather than as preexisting ideas in the mind. If a teacher of botany uses the Aristotelian method, he or she can teach about trees as a class, a general category in botanical reality, and also about the particular trees that are members of the class. Since knowledge is always about an object, education and teaching, too, are always about objects. For Aristotelian teachers, instruction focuses on a body of knowledge, a subject matter. Teaching and learning are never merely interpersonal relationships or the expression of feelings.

Aristotle's lasting influence

An Aristotelian school's primary goal is to cultivate each student's rationality. As academic institutions, schools should offer a prescribed subject-matter curriculum based on scholarly and scientific disciplines. Teachers are to possess expert knowledge of their subjects and be skilled in motivating and transmitting knowledge to students. Aristotle's philosophy was very significant in Western education. Along with Christian doctrine, it became the foundation of medieval Scholastic education, discussed later in this chapter.

An illustration of a student learning the alphabet at a school in ancient Greece. From a vase by Duris, 5th Century B.C., Ashmolian Museum, Oxford. (© Corbis-Bettmann)

Isocrates: Oratory and Rhetoric

Emphasis on rhetoric

The Greek rhetorician Isocrates (436–388 B.C.) is significant for his exceptionally well constructed educational theory, which emphasized both knowledge and rhetorical skills.[28] His theory took a middle course between the conflicts of the Sophists and Plato. Isocrates' treatise *Against the Sophists* explained the method used at his school.

For Isocrates, education's primary goal was to prepare clear-thinking, rational, and truthful statesmen. Civic reform, he believed, required educating virtuous leaders who could be effective administrators. Of the liberal studies, Isocrates held that rhetoric, defined as the rational expression of thought, was most important in cultivating morality and political leadership. Rhetorical education should include both the arts and sciences and the skills of effective communication. The worthy orator should argue for honorable causes that advance the public good. Above reproach, the orator would persuade people to follow good policies. Isocrates opposed some of the Sophists who taught rhetoric as merely persuasive routines or public relations techniques.

Isocrates' students, who attended his school for four years, studied rhetoric, politics, history, and ethics. They analyzed and imitated model orations and practiced public speaking. As a model teacher, Isocrates believed that he was responsible for influencing students by his own demonstration of knowledge, skill, and ethical conduct.

Balancing Plato and the Sophists

Although Isocrates opposed the Sophists' crass opportunism, he also rejected Plato's contention that education was purely theoretical and abstract. For Isocrates, education contributed to public service guided by knowledge. Isocrates influenced the rhetorical tradition in education, in particular the Roman educational theorist Quintilian. By recognizing the humanistic dimension of rhetoric, Isocrates also contributed to the ideal of the liberally educated person.

Education in Ancient Rome

While Greek culture and education were developing in the eastern Mediterranean, the Romans were consolidating their political position on the Italian peninsula and throughout the western Mediterranean. In their movement from small republic to great empire, the Romans initially were preoccupied with war and politics. Once they became an imperial power, they concentrated on the administration, law, and diplomacy needed to maintain the empire. Whereas the Greeks were noted for philosophy, the Romans concentrated on educating practical politicians, able administrators, and skilled generals.

Access to education

As in ancient Greece, only a minority of Romans were formally educated. Schooling was reserved for those who had both the money to pay the tuition and the time to attend school.

Primary and secondary schools

Whereas upper-class girls often learned to read and write at home or were taught by tutors, boys from these families attended a *ludus,* a primary school, and then secondary schools taught by Latin and Greek grammar teachers. Boys were escorted to these schools by educated Greek slaves, called *pedagogues,* from which the word *pedagogy,* meaning the art of instruction, is derived.

Ideal of the orator

Rome's educational ideal was exemplified by the orator. The ideal Roman ora-

[28]Gerald L. Gutek, *A History of the Western Educational Experience,* 2nd ed. (Prospect Heights, Ill.: Waveland Press, 1995), pp. 52–54.

tor was the broadly and liberally educated man of public life — the senator, lawyer, teacher, civil servant, and politician. To examine the Roman ideal of oratory, we turn to Quintilian.

Quintilian: Master of Oratory.   Marcus Fabius Quintilianus (A.D. 35–95), or Quintilian, was one of imperial Rome's most highly recognized rhetoricians. The emperor appointed him to the first chair of Latin rhetoric.

Instruction based on stages of growth

Quintilian's *Institutio Oratoria,* a systematic educational treatise, included (1) the education preparatory to studying rhetoric, (2) rhetorical and educational theory, and (3) the practice of public speaking or declamation. Quintilian made the very important educational point that instruction should be based on stages of human growth and development. Anticipating the modern teacher's concern for learners' individual differences, he advised that instruction be appropriate to students' readiness and abilities. He stressed the importance of early childhood in forming behavior, and he recommended that teachers motivate students by making learning interesting and attractive.

For the first stage, from birth until age seven, when the child was impulsive and concerned with immediate needs and desires, he advised parents to select well-trained and well-spoken nurses, pedagogues, and companions for their children.

Reading and writing

In Quintilian's second stage of education, from seven to fourteen, the child was to learn from sense experiences, form clear ideas, and train his memory. He now wrote the languages that he already spoke. The primary teacher, the *litterator,* who taught reading and writing in the *ludas,* was to have a worthy character and teaching competence. Instruction in reading and writing was to be slow and thorough. A set of ivory letters was to aid in learning the alphabet. Like Montessori many centuries later, Quintilian advised that children would learn to write by tracing the letters' outlines. Anticipating modern education, he urged that the school day include breaks for games and recreation so that students could refresh themselves and renew their energy.

Study of liberal arts

For the third stage of education, from fourteen to seventeen, Quintilian emphasized the liberal arts. Both Greek and Latin grammar, literature, history, and mythology were to be studied bilingually and biculturally. Students also studied music, geometry, astronomy, and gymnastics.

Rhetorical studies

The prospective orator undertook rhetorical studies, the fourth stage, from ages seventeen to twenty-one. In rhetorical studies Quintilian included drama, poetry, law, philosophy, public speaking, declamation, and debate.[29] Declamations — systematic speaking exercises — were of great importance. After being properly prepared, the novice orator spoke to a public audience in the Forum and then returned to the master rhetorician for expert criticism. The teacher was to correct the student's mistakes with a sense of authority but also with patience, tact, and consideration.

The Greek and Roman Contributions to Western Education

Liberal arts

Western culture and education inherited a rich legacy from ancient Greece and Rome. Many of the cultural and educational structures that shaped Western civilization developed in classical Greece and Rome. Believing it possible to cultivate human excellence, the Greeks and Romans gave education an important function in society's political well-being. The Greco-Roman distinction between liberal edu-

---

[29]William M. Smail, *Quintilian on Education* (New York: Teachers College Press, 1966).

cation and vocational training has led to curricular controversies throughout Western educational history. The Romans, particularly Quintilian, through cultural and educational borrowing from Greece, readapted Isocrates' rhetorical method to prepare administrators for their vast empire.

Many ideas of the Greeks and Romans influenced Arab scholars, who preserved and interpreted them. As Europeans encountered Arabic scholarship, these ideas were transmitted to European and later American culture.

Arabic Learning and Education

Absorption and transmission of culture

Revolutionizing mathematics

Preservation of Aristotle

Arab scholars Avicenna and Averroës

The Arab legacy

Islamic civilization, originating with the Arabs, became a global cultural and educational force because of its ability to absorb, reinterpret, and transmit knowledge from one world region to another. Arabic scholarship's early impetus came from the Islamic religious movement led by Mohammed (569–632). Spurred by missionary zeal to spread **Islam**, Arabic scholars carried their ideas throughout North Africa, as far east as India and Malaysia, and as far west as Spain. Their extensive conquests brought the Arabs into contact with a wide variety of peoples and cultures — Hindus, Egyptians, Syrians, and others. They incorporated elements from these cultures into their own civilization. Arab scholars encountered and refined elements of mathematics, medicine, astronomy, science, and architecture from the Indians, Persians, and Greeks into their own culture. For example, after learning the technology of paper making from the Chinese, the Arabs carried it to the Europeans. The Arabs developed a new number system, including the concept of zero, that revolutionized arithmetic. Combining Indian arithmetic and Greek geometry, they developed algebra.[30] Arabic scholars established higher schools at Baghdad, Cairo, Cordoba, Grenada, Toledo, and Seville, where they codified and taught their versions of knowledge.

In the tenth and eleventh centuries, Islamic learning had a pronounced influence on Western education, especially on medieval scholasticism (the philosophy underlying medieval thought and higher learning). From contact with Arab scholars in North Africa and Spain, Western educators gained new insights into mathematics, science, medicine, and philosophy. For example, important Arabic advances in medicine were introduced to the medieval university of Salerno in Italy. Arab scholars also translated and preserved the works of such important thinkers as Aristotle, Euclid, Galen, and Ptolemy. Because many of these works had disappeared from Europe by the Middle Ages, they might have been lost to European culture if they had not been preserved by the Arabs.

Arab scholars, such as Avicenna (980–1037) and Averroës (1126–1198), had an impact on Western European education. After encountering Aristotle's texts, Avicenna translated them into Arabic. Although Western European educators were familiar with Aristotle's logic, many of his philosophical texts were presumed lost. When Scholastic educators acquired Avicenna's translations of Aristotle, they rendered them into Latin. Averroës, a physician in Cordoba and also a translator of and commentator on Aristotle, wrote treatises on medicine, astronomy, and philosophy.[31]

The global influence of Arabic scholarship is a prime example of the frequent cross-cultural transference of educational ideas. Through their innovations in

---

[30]Richard M. Eaton, *Islamic History as Global History* (Washington, D.C.: American Historical Association, n.d.), pp. 22–26.
[31]Bernard Lewis, *Islam and the West* (New York: Oxford University Press, 1993).

mathematics and science and their preservation of classical Greek texts, the Arabs not only contributed to their own educational system but also partially shaped the future course of European and American education.[32]

Medieval Culture and Education

Decline, then revival in learning
Institutions of learning

Historians designate the millennium between the fall of Rome and the Renaissance (c. 500–1400) as the Middle Ages, or medieval period. This era of Western culture and education spanned the time between the end of the Greco-Roman classical era and the beginning of what we call the modern period. The medieval period was characterized first by a decline in learning and then by its revival by Scholastic educators. After the Roman empire in the west collapsed, the Catholic Church, headed by the pope in Rome, partially filled the resulting political, cultural, and educational vacuum.

During the medieval period, European formal education at the primary level was conducted by the church in parish, chantry, and monastic schools. At the secondary level, both monastic and cathedral schools offered a general studies curriculum. Higher education was provided in the universities of Paris, Bologna, Salerno, Oxford, and Cambridge.[33] Merchant and craft guilds also established some schools that offered basic education as well as training for a trade. Knights learned military tactics and the chivalric code in the castles.

Access to schooling

As in the earlier Greek and Roman eras, only a small minority of the population attended schools in the medieval period. Schools were attended primarily by men who planned to enter religious vocations as priests, monks, or members of other clerical orders. The vast majority of people were serfs who were required to serve as agricultural workers on the estates of feudal lords. The large class of serfs was generally illiterate.

Education of medieval women

The condition of women in medieval society varied according to their socioeconomic class. Although medieval Christianity stressed the spiritual equality of women and the sacramental nature of marriage, women continued to be consigned to traditional gender-prescribed roles. For the vast serf and peasant classes of the agricultural poor, women's roles involved the traditional household chores and child-rearing. Girls of the peasant classes learned their future roles by imitating their mothers. Women of the noble classes also followed the prescriptions of their class and learned the roles appropriate to the code of chivalry, which often meant managing the domestic life of the castle or manor.[34] The medieval church provided a different educational opportunity for women through religious communities. Convents, like monasteries, had libraries and schools to prepare nuns to follow the religious rules of their communities.

Aquinas: Scholastic Education

Faith and reason combined

By the eleventh century, medieval educators had developed **scholasticism** — a method of inquiry, scholarship, and teaching. The Scholastics, as the teaching clerics were called, relied on faith and reason as complementary sources of truth. They

[32]Daniel G. Bates and Amal Rassam, *Peoples and Cultures of the Middle East* (Englewood Cliffs, N.J.: Prentice-Hall, 1982), pp. 29–57.
[33]C. Stephen Jaeger, *The Envy of Angels: Cathedral Schools and Social Ideals in Medieval Europe, 950–1200* (Philadelphia: University of Pennsylvania Press, 1994), p. 153.
[34]Joel T. Rosenthal, ed., *Medieval Women and the Sources of Medieval History* (Athens: University of Georgia Press, 1990); and Mary Erler and Maryanne Kawsaleski, *Women and Power in the Middle Ages* (Athens: University of Georgia Press, 1988).

OVERVIEW 3.2   Major Educational Theorists, to A.D. 1600

Theorist	Philosophical Orientation	View of Human Nature
Confucius 551–479 B.C. (Chinese)	Developed ethical system based on hierarchical ordering of human relationships and roles; emphasized order and stability through subordination.	Human beings need the order of a highly stable society in which people accept the duties that come with their station in life.
Socrates 469–399 B.C. (Greek)	Social and educational iconoclast; tended toward philosophical idealism and political conservatism.	Human beings can define themselves by rational self-examination.
Plato 427–346 B.C. (Greek)	Philosophical idealist; sociopolitical conservative.	Human beings can be classified on the basis of their intellectual capabilities.
Aristotle 384–322 B.C. (Greek)	Philosophical realist; view of society, politics, and education based on classical realism.	Human beings have the power of rationality, which should guide their conduct.
Isocrates 436–388 B.C. (Greek)	Rhetorician; oratorical education in service of self and society.	Humans have the power of using their speech (discourse) for social and political improvement.
Quintilian A.D. 35–95 (Roman)	Rhetorician; oratory for personal gain and public service.	Certain individuals have the capacity for leadership, based on their disposition, liberal knowledge, and oratorical skill.
Aquinas A.D. 1225–1274 (Italian medieval theologian)	Christian theology and Aristotelian (realist) philosophy.	Human beings possess both a spiritual nature (soul) and a physical nature (body).
Erasmus A.D. 1465–1536 (Dutch Renaissance humanist)	Christian orientation; the educator as social and intellectual critic.	Human beings are capable of great achievements but also of profound stupidity.
Luther A.D. 1483–1546 (German Protestant)	Reformed theology stressing salvation by faith and individual conscience.	Human beings are saved by faith; individual conscience shaped by scripture and Reformed theology.

accepted the sacred scriptures and the writings of the church fathers as sources of God's revealed word, but they also trusted in human reason. The Scholastics believed that the human mind could deduce first principles that, when illuminated by scriptural authority, were a source of truth.

Scholastic philosophy and education reached its zenith in the *Summa Theologiae* of Saint Thomas Aquinas (1225–1274), a Dominican theologian at the University of Paris. Aquinas was primarily concerned with reconciling authorities — that is, linking faith as represented by the scriptures with Greek rationalism as represented by Aristotle. Aquinas used both faith and reason to answer basic questions about the Christian concept of God, the nature of humankind and the universe, and the relationship between God and hu-

Reconciling scriptures with Greek reasoning

Views on Education and Curriculum

Education prepares people for their sociopolitical roles by cultivating reverence for ancestors and traditions; curriculum of ancient Chinese classics and Confucius's *Analects*; highly selective examinations.

Use of a probing intellectual dialogue to answer basic human concerns; education should cultivate moral excellence.

Reminiscence of latent ideas; music, gymnastics, geometry, astronomy, basic literary skills; philosophy for ruling elite of philosopher-kings.

Objective and scientific emphasis; basic literary skills, mathematics, natural and physical sciences, philosophy.

Rhetorical studies; basic literary skills; politics, history, rhetoric, declamation, public speaking.

Basic literary skills; grammar, history, literature, drama, philosophy, public speaking, law.

Education should be based on human nature, with appropriate studies for both spiritual and physical dimensions.

Education for a literary elite that stressed criticism and analysis.

Elementary schools to teach reading, writing, arithmetic, religion; secondary schools to prepare leaders by offering classics, Latin, Greek, and religion; vocational training.

Contribution and Influence

Confucianist ethics shaped Chinese culture for centuries, creating a value system of enduring importance.

Socratic dialogue as a teaching method; teacher as a role model.

Use of schools for sorting students according to intellectual abilities; education tied to civic (political) purposes.

Emphasis on liberally educated, well-rounded person; importance of reason.

Use of knowledge in public affairs and in political leadership; teacher education has both a content and a practice dimension.

Role of motivation in learning; recognition of individual differences.

Teacher as moral agent; education related to universal theological goals; synthesis of the theological and philosophical; basis of philosophy used in Roman Catholic schools.

Role of secondary and higher education in literary and social criticism; emphasis on critical thinking.

Emphasis on universal literacy; schools to stress religious values, vocational skills, knowledge; close relationship of religion, schooling, and the state.

---

mans.[35] For Aquinas, humans possess a physical body and a spiritual soul. Although they live temporarily on earth, their ultimate purpose is to experience eternity with God. Like Aristotle, Aquinas asserted that human knowledge begins in sensation and is completed by conceptualization. (See Overview 3.2 for the ideas of Aquinas and other educators discussed in this chapter.)

The teacher's vocation

In *de Magistro (Concerning the Teacher)*, Aquinas portrayed the teacher's vocation as combining faith, love, and learning. Teachers need to be contemplative scholars,

---

[35]Francis J. Selman, *Saint Thomas Aquinas: Teacher of Truth* (Edinburgh, Scotland: T&T Clark, 1994); and Etienne Gilson, *The Christian Philosophy of St. Thomas Aquinas* (Notre Dame, Ind.: University of Notre Dame Press, 1994).

Forerunners of our modern institutions of higher learning, the medieval universities established specialized professional schools.
(© Corbis/Bettmann)

active agents of learning, experts in their subjects, skillful teachers, and lovers of humanity. Aquinas and the other Scholastic educators saw no conflict between research and teaching. The good teacher needs to do both and do them well so that teaching and scholarship are carefully integrated.

Subject-matter disciplines

Scholastic teachers were clerics, and schools were governed and protected by the church. The curriculum was organized into formal subjects, following the liberal arts tradition; for example, in higher education the subject disciplines were logic, mathematics, natural and moral philosophy, metaphysics, and theology. In their teaching, Scholastics used the syllogism — deductive reasoning — to create organized bodies of knowledge. They emphasized basic principles and their implications. In addition to formal schooling, Aquinas recognized the importance of informal education through family, friends, and environment.[36]

Medieval Universities

Aquinas and other Scholastic educators taught in medieval universities, where the patterns of higher education were established. The universities evolved from students' and teachers' associations called *universitas*. The famous medieval universities of Paris, Salerno, Bologna, Oxford, Cambridge, Padua, Heidelberg, Erfurt, and Prague developed during the intellectual revival of the twelfth and thirteenth centuries.[37]

[36]John W. Donohue, *St. Thomas Aquinas and Education* (New York: Random House, 1968), pp. 76–89.
[37]See the classic work of Hastings Rashdall, *The Universities of Europe in the Middle Ages,* ed. R. M. Powicke and A. B. Emden, 3 vols. (Oxford: Oxford University Press, 1936). See also Stephen C. Ferruolo, *The Origins of the University: The Schools of Paris and Their Critics, 1100–1215* (Stanford, Calif.: Stanford University Press, 1985).

Growth of universities

Some major universities grew out of the expanding enrollments of the cathedral schools, which by the twelfth century had attracted large numbers of students. Enrollment had increased because of improved economic conditions and a more secure political situation. Greater contacts with Byzantine and Arabic scholarship also stimulated the desire for higher learning.

Rediscovery of the classics

As mentioned earlier, medieval educators rediscovered the works of Aristotle, Euclid, Ptolemy, Galen, and Hippocrates through Byzantine and Arab scholars. The interpretation of these rediscovered works was of major interest to the Scholastics.

Professional schools

Although theology was the most important subject in medieval universities, other disciplines were also offered. In addition to the liberal arts, the universities offered professional studies in law, medicine, and theology. The University of Bologna in Italy and the University of Paris in France represented two distinctive patterns of government and control in higher education: Bologna was governed by students; Paris, by faculty.

The Medieval Contribution to Western Education

Preserving and institutionalizing knowledge

The medieval educators contributed to Western education primarily by preserving and institutionalizing knowledge — that is, by presenting it within an organized framework. Parish, monastic, and cathedral schools all transmitted knowledge in this manner. The epitome of this trend was the medieval university, the model for the modern university. Within its walls, medieval educators not only taught but also preserved knowledge by recording and codifying it.

Renaissance Classical Humanism

Reviving humanistic aspects of the classics

The Renaissance, which began in the fourteenth century and reached its zenith in the fifteenth century, saw a marked revival in the humanistic aspects of the Greek and Latin classics. It is considered a period of transition between the medieval and modern ages. Renaissance scholars of **classical humanism**, like medieval Scholastics, found their authorities in the past and stressed classical literature. Unlike the Scholastics, however, classical humanists were interested more in earthly experience than in God-centered theology.[38]

Classical humanism in Italy

The Renaissance was particularly notable in Italy, where commercial revival had generated enough wealth for the patronage of art and literature. Wealth, flowing into the prosperous Italian cities, supported humanist schools. Italian classical humanists, considering themselves a literary elite, were self-proclaimed "custodians of knowledge." It Italy, the works of Dante, Petrarch, and Boccaccio reflected the humanist literary revival. Italian nobles established court schools to prepare their children in the revived classical learning.

The courtier as a model

Rejecting scholasticism, classical humanist educators turned again to Isocrates and Quintilian. In the Greek and Latin classics, they found models of literary excellence and style, the ideal of the educated person, and a view that cherished antiquity's wisdom. For humanist educators, the courtier became the model of the educated person. A person of style and elegance, liberally educated in classical literature, the courtier was a tactful diplomat who could serve his ruler well in affairs of

---

[38]Erika Rummel, *The Humanist-Scholastic Debate in the Renaissance and Reformation* (Cambridge: Harvard University Press, 1995).

During the Renaissance, the curriculum pursued by young women of the upper classes reflected the notion that certain studies—such as art, music, needlework, dancing, and poetry—were appropriate for their gender. *(© Giraudon/Art Resource, NY)*

state. Baldesar Castiglione (1478–1529) described the courtier and his education in a famous work, *The Book of the Courtier.*[39]

Educating the courtier

In northern Europe, classical humanist scholars critically examined medieval theological works. Considering scholastic education to be fossilized, humanist educators developed teaching methods and materials to prepare well-rounded, liberally educated courtiers. Their curriculum featured classical Greek and Latin literature.

The Renaissance humanist educators were literary figures — writers, poets, and translators. Artist-teachers, critics of taste and society, they brought wit, charm, and satire as well as erudition to their work. They sought to educate critical people who could challenge existing customs and mediocrity in literature and life. But Renaissance humanists often kept a distance between themselves and the mass of people, distilling their conception of human nature from a carefully aged literature. As a vintage wine is used to grace an elegant dinner, humanist education was for the connoisseur. It was not provided to everyone but reserved for an elite.

Critical thinking

Limited access to schools

Though there were some increases, the Renaissance did not dramatically expand school attendance. Humanist preparatory and secondary schools were attended by the children of the nobility and upper classes. Elementary schools served the commercial middle classes. Lower-socioeconomic-class children received little, if any, formal schooling.

---

[39]Baldesar Castiglione, *The Book of the Courtier,* trans. C. S. Singleton (New York: Doubleday, 1959). A commentary is Peter Burke, *The Fortunes of the Courtier: The European Reception of Castiglione's Cortegiano* (University Park: Pennsylvania State University Press, 1996).

Erasmus: Critic and Humanist

Erasmus on education

Desiderius Erasmus (1465–1536) was the leading classical scholar of the late Renaissance.[40] His writings demonstrate his concept of the teacher as a critic and cosmopolitan humanist. Concerning the teaching of classical languages, he advised teachers to be well acquainted with archeology, astronomy, etymology, history, and scripture, since these subjects touched on the study of classical literature. Like Quintilian, he saw early childhood as a crucial formative period in human development.[41] The child's education should begin as early as possible, and parents were to take their educational responsibilities seriously. Children should receive gentle instruction in good manners and hear stories that had a beneficial effect on character development.

Early childhood education

Teaching methods

Erasmus believed that understanding the meaning of literature was much more important for students than slavishly imitating the author's style of writing. He especially encouraged teachers to use conversation to explore meaning, and to devise games and other activities that illustrated the meaning of a particular piece of literature. Erasmus developed the following method for teachers to use in studying literature: (1) present the author's biography, (2) identify the type of work, (3) discuss the basic plot, (4) analyze the author's style, (5) consider the moral implications, and (6) explore the work's broader philosophical issues.

The Renaissance Contribution to Western Education

Emphasis on classical languages and literature

Renaissance humanists emphasized knowledge of Latin as the hallmark of the educated person. To be educated meant to have learned classical languages and literature. For centuries, these classical humanist preferences both shaped and confined Western secondary and higher education. In Europe and the United States, knowledge of Latin was required for admission to many colleges and universities until the end of the nineteenth century.

Humanistic (not scientific) knowledge

It is also important to note that Erasmus and other Renaissance educators were moving to a humanistic, or human-centered, conception of knowledge. Rather than approaching their human subject through scientific inquiry, humanist educators explored their concerns through literature. The educated person was defined as one who acquired classical knowledge through books. The later educational reforms of Rousseau, Comenius, Pestalozzi, and Dewey (discussed in Chapter 4) argued against instruction that emphasized literature while neglecting experience.

The printing press

The invention of the printing press in 1423 was a major technological innovation that advanced literacy and schooling. Before the printing press, students painstakingly copied dictation from teachers. The university lecture was essentially an experience in which students recorded their professor's words.

By mid-fifteenth century, experiments were made to print with movable metal type. Johannes Gutenberg, a German jeweler, invented a durable metal alloy that could be used to form the letters of the printing press. His Bible, in 1455, was the first major book to be printed. Printing spread throughout Europe, multiplying the output and cutting the costs of books. It made information accessible to a larger

---

[40]For biographies of Erasmus, see Leon E. Halkin, *Erasmus: A Critical Biography* (Oxford, U.K., and Cambridge, Mass.: Basil Blackwell, 1993); and James McConics, *Erasmus* (New York: Oxford University Press, 1991).
[41]William H. Woodward, *Desiderius Erasmus Concerning the Aim and Method of Education* (New York: Teachers College Press, 1964).

part of the population.[42] The invention of the printing press, inaugurating the "information revolution," was a momentous technological innovation whose consequences were not unlike that of the electronic dissemination of information by computers. (See Overview 3.3 for the invention of the printing press and other significant events in the history of education.)

The Religious Reformation and Education

Freedom from papal authority

The religious reformation of the sixteenth and seventeenth centuries was stimulated by northern European humanist criticism of medieval institutions and authorities. As humanism replaced medieval scholasticism, the Catholic Church's central authority to enforce religious conformity eroded. This paved the way for diverse religious opinions, which ultimately led to disputes about education.[43]

The rise of the commercial middle classes and strong national states contributed to the reformation movements. Primarily, however, Protestant religious reformers — such as John Calvin, Martin Luther, Philip Melanchthon, and Ulrich Zwingli — sought to free themselves and their followers from papal authority and to reinterpret their own religious doctrines and practices. While doing so, the Protestant reformers formulated their own educational theories, established their own schools, structured their own curricula, and reared their children in the reformed creeds.

Extension of popular literacy

Since many reformers insisted that the faithful should read the Bible in their own native tongues, the Reformation extended popular literacy. Protestants established **vernacular schools** to instruct children in their group's own language — for example, German, Swedish, or English rather than Latin. These primary institutions offered a basic curriculum of reading, writing, and arithmetic as well as religion. For Catholics, the Mass and liturgies were still in Latin rather than vernacular languages; to compete with Protestants, however, Catholics also began to teach vernacular languages along with Latin in their schools.

The catechism

To defend the reformed faith, Protestant educators developed the *catechistic method* of religious education. Catechisms were important textbooks in Reformation and post-Reformation schools for both Protestants and Catholics. In question-and-answer form, they summarized the particular denomination's beliefs and practices. Although memorization had always been present in schooling, the catechistic method put particular emphasis on it. The objective was to have children memorize the catechism and internalize the principles of their particular church. The question-answer format gained a powerful hold on teaching and was also used in secular subjects such as history and geography.

Rising literacy

By emphasizing popular literacy and increasing school attendance, the Protestant Reformation inaugurated a major change in education and in literacy rates. For example, only 10 percent of the men and 2 percent of the women in England were literate in 1500; by 1600 the percentages had risen to 28 for men and 9 for women; and by 1700 nearly 40 percent of English men and about 32 percent of English women were literate. Literacy rates were higher in northern than in southern Europe, in urban as opposed to rural areas, and among the upper as compared to the lower classes.[44]

---

[42]Lucien Febvre and Henri-Jean Martin, *The Coming of the Book: The Impact of Printing, 1450–1800* (London: Verso, 1990).

[43]Alister McGrath, *The Intellectual Origins of the European Reformation* (New York: Basil Blackwell, 1987).

[44]Mary Jo Maynes, *Schooling in Western Europe: A Social History* (Albany: State University of New York Press, 1985).

OVERVIEW 3.3	Significant Events in the History of Western Education, to A.D. 1600

Period	Political and Social Events	Significant Educational Events
Greek	1200 B.C. Trojan War	c. 1200 B.C. Homer's *Iliad* and *Odyssey*
	594 B.C. Athenian constitutional reforms	
	479–338 B.C. Golden Age of Greek (Athenian) culture	
	445–431 B.C. Age of Pericles	
	431–404 B.C. Peloponnesian War between Athens and Sparta	
		399 B.C. Trial of Socrates
		395 B.C. Plato's *Republic*
		392 B.C. School established by Isocrates in Athens
		387 B.C. Academy founded by Plato
		330 B.C. Aristotle's *Politics*
	336–323 B.C. Alexander the Great	
Roman	753 B.C. Traditional date of Rome's founding	
	510 B.C. Roman republic established	
	272 B.C. Rome dominates Italian peninsula	449 B.C. References appear to the existence of Latin schools, or *ludi*
	146 B.C. Greece becomes Roman province	
	49–44 B.C. Dictatorship of Julius Caesar	167 B.C. Greek grammar school opened in Rome
	31 B.C. Roman empire begins	
	A.D. 476 Fall of Rome in the West	A.D. 96 Quintilian's *Institutio Oratoria*
Medieval	713 Arab conquest of Spain	
	800 Charlemagne crowned Holy Roman Emperor	
	1096–1291 Crusades to the Holy Land	
	1182–1226 St. Francis of Assisi	1079–1142 Abelard, author of *Sic et Non*
		1180 University of Paris granted papal charter and recognition
		1209 University of Cambridge founded
	1295 Explorations of Marco Polo	1225–1274 Thomas Aquinas, author of *Summa Theologiae*
Renaissance	1304–1374 Petrarch, author of odes and sonnets	
	1313–1375 Boccaccio, founder of Italian vernacular literature	
	1384 Founding of Brethren of the Common Life	
	1393–1464 Cosimo de' Medici encourages revival of art and learning in Florence	1428 Da Feltre, classical humanist educator, established court school at Mantua
	1423 Invention of printing	1507–1589 Sturm, creator of gymnasiums in Germany

<table>
<tr><td colspan="3">**OVERVIEW 3.3**   **Significant Events in the History of Western Education, to A.D. 1600 (cont.)**</td></tr>
</table>

Period	**Political and Social Events**	**Significant Educational Events**
	1455 Bible printed	
	1492 Columbus arrives in America	1509 Erasmus's *Praise of Folly*
Reformation	1517 Luther posts Ninety-five Theses calling for church reform	
	1509–1564 John Calvin, Protestant reformer, founder of Calvinism	1524 Luther's "Letter . . . in Behalf of Christian Schools"
	1509–1547 King Henry VIII of England, founder of the Church of England	1524 Melanchthon, an associate of Luther, organizes Lutheran schools in German states
	1540 Jesuit order founded by Loyola	
	1545 Council of Trent launches Roman Catholic Counter Reformation	1630–1650 Calvinist schools organized in Scotland by John Knox

Increasing school attendance

As these figures suggest, reformers wanted both girls and boys to attend the primary vernacular schools, and their efforts increased school attendance for both sexes. Nevertheless, Protestant reformers continued to reserve the prestigious classical humanist preparatory and secondary schools for upper-class boys. Preparatory and secondary schools such as the German *gymnasium,* the English Latin grammar school, and the French *lycée* prepared upper-class boys in Latin and Greek, the classical languages needed for university entry. This elite was destined for leadership roles in the church and state.

Many strong characters — Calvin, Zwingli, Ignatius Loyola, and Henry VIII among them — made an impact on the Protestant Reformation and the Roman Catholic Counter Reformation. As a significant case study, we examine the impact of Martin Luther.

Luther: Protestant Reformer

Challenges Catholic Church

Martin Luther (1483–1546) stands out as one of the most important religious reformers in shaping Western history and education. An Augustinian monk in Germany, Luther had grown increasingly critical of Catholic practices. In 1517, he posted his famous Ninety-five Theses on the door of the castle church at Wittenberg. With these theses and later writings, Luther challenged the Roman Catholic Church and the pope on issues such as indulgences, the sacraments, papal authority, and freedom of individual conscience. Luther's challenges were a catalyst for the Protestant Reformation, which spread throughout western Europe.

Education as part of religious reform

Luther recognized that education was a potent ally of religious reformation.[45] He saw church, state, family, and school as crucial reform agencies. Believing that

---

[45]Marilyn J. Harran, ed., *Luther and Learning: The Wittenberg University Luther Symposium* (Cranbury, N.J.: Associated University Presses, 1985).

the family had a key role in forming children's character and behavior, Luther encouraged family Bible reading and prayer. He also wanted parents to make sure that children had vocational training so they could support themselves as adults and become productive citizens.

Luther on schooling

Advising public officials to take educational responsibility, Luther's "Letter to the Mayors and Aldermen of All Cities of Germany in Behalf of Christian Schools" emphasized schooling's political and economic as well as spiritual benefits. Schools should be organized and inspected by state officials to train literate, orderly, and productive citizens and members of the church. Advanced education in the *gymnasium* and in universities would prepare well-educated ministers of the Lutheran Church.

Luther on women's education

Luther's views on women's education reflected traditional restrictions but also contained some liberating ideas. Influenced by Saint Paul, he believed that the husband, as the head of the household, had authority over his wife. Domestic duties and child-rearing remained women's appropriate roles. On the other hand, because of Luther's emphasis on reading the Bible in one's own language, girls as well as boys were to attend primary schools. Having received this schooling, women then had a shared, if subordinate, role in educating their own children.

School codes

To design and implement educational reforms, Luther relied heavily on Philip Melanchthon (1497–1560). Seeking to end the Roman Catholic Church's control over schools, Luther and Melanchthon wanted the state to supervise schools and license teachers. In 1559, Melanchthon drafted the School Code of Würtemberg, which became a model for other German states. The code specified that primary vernacular schools should be established in every village to teach religion, reading, writing, arithmetic, and music. Classical secondary schools, *gymnasium*, were to provide Latin and Greek instruction for those select young men expected to attend universities.

Confirming the dual-track system

Even though Luther and Melanchthon wanted primary schools established to teach reading, writing, and religion to the common people, they believed that the Renaissance's classical Latin and Greek curriculum provided the best preparation for leaders of the church and state. Thus one general effect of the Protestant Reformation on educational institutions was to firmly fix the **dual-track system of schools**: primary schools for the common people and classical humanist schools for upper-class boys and men.

Reformation Views on Knowledge and Education

Luther, Melanchthon, Calvin, and other leaders of the Reformation were concerned with questions of knowledge, education, and schooling because they wanted these powerful weapons to advance the Protestant cause. On the question of knowledge, their authority was the Bible. Regarding Bible reading as essential to salvation, the reformers promoted universal primary schooling to advance literacy.

Bible reading

Religious indoctrination

For both Protestants and Catholics, schooling was to indoctrinate children with "correct" religious beliefs. Teachers were hired only if they were members of the officially approved church, and they were carefully supervised to make certain they taught approved doctrines.

The Reformation's Contribution to Western Education

The Protestant Reformation reconfirmed many institutional developments from the Renaissance, especially the dual-track school system. While vernacular schools provided primary instruction to the lower socioeconomic classes, the various classical humanist grammar schools prepared the upper classes for higher education. The colonists who settled in North America were transplanted Europeans who brought this two-track school structure to the New World.

Through their stress on Bible reading, Protestant reformers also bequeathed to later educators the all-important emphasis on literacy. This attitude helped accelerate the movement toward universal schooling.

Religion has had a tremendous impact on education and schooling from ancient times, from India and Egypt through the early twentieth century. Many schools were conducted by the churches. In the United States, too, the early establishment of schools and colleges was closely tied to religion.

In the eighteenth century, however, the influence of religion and the churches over education was challenged by the naturalism and rationalism of the Enlightenment, the Age of Reason.

The Enlightenment's Influence on Education

Reason and the scientific method

Belief in progress

Reducing inequalities in education

As we examine the eighteenth-century Age of Enlightenment (also called the Age of Reason), we should recall that the United States's political institutions are products of that era. Enlightenment ideas influenced such major educational reformers as Rousseau, Pestalozzi, and Froebel, discussed in Chapter 4. The ideas of these European reformers were transplanted to America.

Foremost among the Enlightenment's ideas was the supremacy of reason. The philosophers, scientists, and scholars of the Enlightenment firmly believed that humans could improve their lives and institutions by using reason to solve problems.[46] Stressing the importance of scientific inquiry, these thinkers attempted to discover "natural laws," the orderly processes by which the universe functioned. They also devised theories for social reform. For example, the ideologies underlying the American and French revolutions sought to reconstruct the political order according to reason. The ideologies of the Enlightenment implied that schools should cultivate students' ability to reason and thereby help them free themselves from superstition.

Notable Enlightenment figures, such as Diderot, Rousseau, Franklin, and Jefferson, saw humanity as marching progressively forward to a new and better world. No longer was it necessary to look backward to the "golden age" of Greece or Rome. By using their reason and the scientific method, humans could achieve continual cycles of progress on earth. Schools were to be reshaped into progressive institutions that encouraged students to develop an open-minded, questioning attitude and an eagerness to employ science's empirical method.

As they sought to use social science to reform society, Enlightenment educators attempted to create a new kind of schooling based on equality, individualism, civic responsibility, and scientific reasoning. Enlightenment concepts especially influenced America's revolutionary generation. While much of Europe continued to limit educational opportunities according to social class, the open frontier in America helped to reduce inequalities in access to education.

Enlightenment ideas took root in the United States, where they developed into an optimistic faith in political democracy and universal education. They were behind Benjamin Franklin's emphasis on utilitarian and scientific education and Thomas Jefferson's arguments for state-supported schools. Convinced of

---

[46]Ulrich Im Hoff, *The Enlightenment* (Cambridge, Mass.: Basil Blackwell, 1994).

PROFESSIONAL PLANNING

for your first year

Developing an Ethic of Teaching

The Situation

You have been asked to serve on a team that will present an in-service workshop to teachers in your school district about ethical issues in teaching. The consensus of the team is that professional development should help teachers develop and demonstrate in their behavior a clear commitment to a professional ethic — a knowledge of what is right and wrong. The team believes that the history of education provides many ideas about teachers' ethics that can be applied in the present. It has assigned you the task of presenting a brief historical overview of teaching ethics in Western education, encapsulating the views of some of the great philosophers — ideally in twenty-five words or less. You return to your notes from this class to prepare the following list for use as a one-page handout to spark discussion at the in-service workshop:

The Sophists: Good teaching aims to create effective persons who can organize their ideas and language to meet changing social, economic, and political situations.

Socrates: Good teaching aims to create critical thinkers who are not afraid to challenge current opinions, even if they are popular ones.

Plato: Students have different intellectual capacities. Teachers should divide students into groups based on their intellectual ability and concentrate on the most intellectually gifted, providing experiences that develop their abilities.

Aristotle: Good teaching always requires that teachers know their subject thoroughly and that they know how to teach it.

Isocrates: Good teaching requires knowledge of the liberal arts and sciences and effective communication skills.

Quintilian: Good teaching is based on designing educational experiences appropriate to the stages of human growth and development.

Aquinas: Good teachers should be experts in what they teach, active in teaching it, and love and respect their students.

Erasmus: The good teacher, well-versed in literature and history, should be a social and educational critic.

Luther: The good teacher should educate students who have intellectual, vocational, and religious knowledge and values.

Thought Questions

1. Plan how you would answer teachers at the workshop who request a fuller description of the position of these philosophers.
2. How would you lead a discussion of the importance and applicability in today's classrooms of these historical views on ethics?
3. Which of these principles will you use or reject in your own professional development? Which of the ones you accept seems to have the highest priority?
4. Describe some of the ways you plan to express your commitment to your own ethic of teaching in your everyday activities as a teacher.

their ability to direct their own future, Americans saw education as the key to progress.[47]

In Chapter 4, when we examine the educational contributions of the major pioneers of education, we will begin with those from the Enlightenment era.

Summing Up

1. We have examined in historical context questions about the nature of teaching and learning raised at the beginning of this chapter: What is knowledge? What is education? What is schooling? Who should attend school? How should teaching and learning be carried on? Contemporary educators continue to examine these powerful questions. Some emphasize traditional knowledge and values, as did Confucius in ancient China, or the preservation of the culture, as in Egypt. Some seek to answer in universal terms, as did Plato; others shape their responses according to changing perceptions of knowledge and the role of education.

2. Since we live on an increasingly internationally interdependent planet, it is important to think about the global context of education. By examining education in such culturally diverse societies as ancient China, India, Egypt, and Greece, we explored themes about knowledge, the purpose of education, and who should attend school.

3. Many institutions and processes in American education originated in Europe. As in preliterate societies, schooling continues to involve the transmission of the cultural heritage from one generation to the next. In ancient Greece, the concepts of the educated person, rational inquiry, and freedom of thought were enunciated by Socrates, Plato, and Aristotle. The concept and methods of rhetorical education were devised by the Sophists, refined by Isocrates, and further developed by the Roman rhetorician Quintilian.

4. During the medieval period, the foundations of the university were established. Medieval education was influenced by mathematical and scientific contributions that entered the Western world by way of the Arabs. Renaissance classical humanist educators developed the concept of the well-rounded, liberally educated person. With its emphasis on literacy and vernacular education, the Protestant Reformation directly influenced colonial America's schools. The Enlightenment was especially influential in America.

5. From the classical period of ancient Greece and Rome to the Protestant Reformation in the fifteenth century, only a minority of children attended schools. With the Protestant Reformation, school attendance began to increase.

6. Schools in western European societies developed into a two-track set of institutions based on socioeconomic class differences. While the common people attended primary schools, upper-class males attended preparatory schools that prepared them for university entrance. Girls attended primary schools but were generally excluded from secondary and higher education.

---

[47]Daniel Feller, *The Jacksonian Promise: America, 1815–1840* (Baltimore: Johns Hopkins University Press, 1995), pp. xiii–xiv.

Key Terms

acculturation *(67)*

Confucius *(70)*

caste *(73)*

Brahmins *(73)*

Vedas *(74)*

Sophists *(78)*

rhetoric *(78)*

Socratic method *(79)*

reminiscence *(79)*

Plato's *Republic (80)*

Islam *(86)*

scholasticism *(87)*

classical humanism *(91)*

vernacular schools *(94)*

dual-track system of schools *(97)*

Discussion Questions

1. Examine storytelling and holiday observances as a way of introducing children to their culture. How are these patterns of informal education similar to or unlike education in preliterate societies?

2. Examine the Confucian ethical principle of appropriate behavior. Compare and contrast the concept of Confucianist ethical behavior with that of modern American society.

3. Compare and contrast the effects on education of caste in India with race in the United States.

4. Whereas the Arabic scholars tended to absorb knowledge from other cultures, the ancient Chinese tended to resist cultural borrowing. In your judgment, is the adaptation of "foreign" concepts in American education positive or negative? How has this phenomenon manifested itself in U.S. education in recent years?

5. Compare and contrast the Sophists' educational objectives with those found in modern political and advertising campaigns.

6. Consider who has the greatest opportunities to attend preschools, elementary schools, secondary schools, and colleges and universities in contemporary America. How does the pattern of opportunity vary at each level? How do these educational opportunities compare with the historical patterns discussed in this chapter?

7. Historically, how have changes in women's education reflected changing roles of women in society?

Suggested Projects for Professional Development

1. To gain a global perspective on professional development, interview international students on education in their country, especially on the status of the teacher.

2. To gain a historical perspective on professional development, interview experienced teachers on how the teaching profession has changed since they began teaching.

3. Professional development includes a sense of ethics. To compare and contrast ethics, conduct a survey among students in your course or colleagues to identify the three people in the world who are most worthy of imitation by young people. How do these role models compare with the models of the educated

person in ancient China, India, Egypt, Greece, and in the medieval, Renaissance, and Reformation periods?

4. Professional development includes developing and improving one's teaching style. This chapter discussed teaching styles associated with Sophists, Socrates, Plato, Aquinas, and others. Examine the development of teaching styles and methods. Use this historical background to examine your own teaching style and methods.

Suggested Readings and Resources

Internet Resources

Plato, Aristotle, and other philosophers (**www.georgetown.edu/labyrinth/ subjects/phil.html**) provides information on these important figures in philosophy.

Classics and Mediterranean Archaeology Home Page (**www.rome.classics. lsa.umich.edu/welcome.html**) provides sources on topics related to the classical Mediterranean world.

Diogenes' Links to the Ancient World (**www.snider.net/lyceum/**) provides connections to information about Egypt, Greece, and other ancient civilizations.

Diotima: Materials for the Study of Women and Gender in the Ancient World (**www.uky.edu/Arts Sciences/Classics/gender.html**) provides course descriptions, essays, and images about the topic.

Erasmus (**www.ciger.be/erasmus/index.html**) provides information about the Renaissance scholar Erasmus.

Oral History. "h-oralhist" provides a forum for people interested in oral history. A list of participants in oral history is available on **listserv@h-net.msu.edu/**

History. Information about the American Historical Society is available on **www.chnm.gmu.edu/aha/**

The Perseus Project (**www.perseus.tufts.edu**) is a digital library on ancient Greece and Rome.

Religion: University of Toronto Center for Study of Religion (**www.cir.library.utoronto.ca/MindT**) provides a data base for the study of religion.

World-L: On non-Eurocentric world history (**www.neal.ctstateu.edu/history/ world-history.html**) provides information on world history.

Videos

The Ancient Greeks. VHS, 17 minutes (1988). Insight Media, 2162 Broadway, Box 621, New York, NY 10024-0621. Phone: 212-721-6316. *Discusses Socrates, Plato, and Aristotle and their educational contributions.*

Ancient Lives: Temple Priests and Civil Servants. VHS, 25 minutes (1985). Films for the Humanities and Sciences, P.O. Box 2053, Princeton, NJ 08543. Phone: 800-257-5126. *Excavated temple and palace and other artifacts are used to show the training and careers of priests, scribes, and civil servants in ancient Egypt.*

Ancient Lives: Women's Place. VHS, 35 minutes (1985). Films for the Humanities and Sciences, P.O. Box 2053, Princeton, NJ 08543. Phone: 800-257-5126. *Through artifacts and other archeological sources, the program depicts women's lives and rituals in ancient Egypt.*

Black Athena. VHS, 52 minutes (1991). CA Newsreel, 149 Ninth Street, San Francisco, CA 94103. Phone: 415-621-6196. *Examines the controversy surrounding Professor Martin Bernal's book on the African origins of Greek culture. It also deals with controversies about multiculturalism and the Afrocentric curriculum.*

Civilization: Protest and Communication. VHS, 50 minutes (1970). Public Media, 5547 North Ravenswood Ave., Chicago, IL 60640. Phone: 312-878-2600. *Examines the impact of the printing press during the Reformation.*

Greek Fire: Ideas. VHS, 26 minutes (1990). Mystic Fire Video, P.O. Box 422, Prince Street Station, New York, NY 10012. Phone: 212-941-0999. *This program examines the intellectual impact of ancient Greece on the modern world. It is especially interesting on the development of rhetoric.*

The Humanists, Ancient Greeks. VHS, 20 minutes (1988). Insight Media, 2162 Broadway, Box 621, New York, NY 10024-0621. Phone: 212-721-6316. *Discusses the educational ideas of such Renaissance humanists as Erasmus.*

Publications

Boyd, William, and Edmund J. King. *The History of Western Education.* 12th ed. Lanham, Md.: Barnes and Noble, 1995. *A fine analysis by a distinguished historian and a talented comparative educator.*

Cunningham, Hugh. *Children and Childhood in Western Society Since 1500.* New York: Longman, 1995. This history of childhood is a thoughtful and well-written examination of changing conceptions of child-rearing and education. It is useful in relating important concepts of childhood to education.

Gordon, Edward E., and Elaine H. Gordon. *Centuries of Tutoring: A History of Alternative Education in America and Western Europe.* Lanham, Md.: University Press of America, 1990. *The Gordons provide a historical treatment of leading tutors and their methods of teaching. They suggest that tutors had a significant impact on the development of educational ideas.*

Gutek, Gerald L. *A History of the Western Educational Experience.* 2nd ed. Prospect Heights, Ill.: Waveland Press, 1995. *Describes and analyzes the historical development of educational ideas, institutions, and processes in Western civilization from the classical period to the present.*

Hanawalt, Barbara A. *Growing Up in Medieval London: The Experience of Childhood in History.* New York: Oxford University Press, 1993. *Using extensive primary sources, Hanawalt examines the process of growing up as experienced by men and women and rich and poor.*

Power, Edward J. *A Legacy of Learning: A History of Western Education.* Albany: State University of New York Press, 1991. *Examines the cultural and intellectual contexts of European and American educational history from the classical Greco-Roman eras to the twentieth century.*

Robb, Kevin. *Literacy and Paideia in Ancient Greece.* New York: Oxford University Press, 1994. *Presents an important contribution to the history of literacy by examining the change from an oral to a written tradition in ancient Greece.*

Smith, L. Glenn, and Joan K. Smith. *Lives in Education: A Narrative of People and Ideas.* New York: Lawrence Erlbaum, 1995. *A well-written and highly readable treatment of significant educational theorists.*

CHAPTER FOUR

Pioneers in Education

In this and other chapters, you are posed with the challenge of developing your own philosophy of education. Here, we see how the great educational pioneers created their own educational philosophies.[1]

Despite differences among the educators discussed in this chapter, we can identify certain common patterns. Comenius's theory incorporated a spiritual love of human beings with emphasis on Nature's goodness. He and other naturalistic educators such as Rousseau, Pestalozzi, and Spencer challenged the inherited concept of child depravity and passive learning that had long dominated schooling. The **child depravity theory,** claiming that children are born evil, argued that this inherited weakness could be exorcised by authoritarian teachers.

In contrast, **naturalistic educators** believed children were innately good. The stages of human growth and development, they argued, provided cues for effective teaching. These pioneering educators came to be called *naturalistic* because they believed children learned most effectively and efficiently by examining objects in their immediate natural environment. The environment's educative power was a theme used by such later American progressive educators as Dewey and Counts. As we will see, Froebel's kindergarten and Montessori's prepared environment were deliberate efforts to create learning situations that would respect and utilize the child's own process of development. As you read Chapter 4, consider the following questions:

- Who qualifies as an educational pioneer?
- How did the pioneers develop their own philosophies of education?
- How did they redefine knowledge, education, schooling, teaching, and learning?
- How did they challenge and change traditional concepts of the child and the curriculum?
- What ideas or practices of the pioneers' contributions are present in today's teaching and learning?
- What contributions from the pioneers are useful to you in developing your own philosophy of education?

[1]Gerald L. Gutek, *Historical and Philosophical Foundations of Education: A Biographical Introduction* (Columbus, Ohio: Merrill, 1997), pp. 4–7.

Comenius: The Search for a New Method

Pansophism

Learning language by natural means

Respecting children's needs and development

Principles of teaching

Jan Komensky (1592–1670), known as Comenius, was born in the Moravian town of Nivnitz. He lived during the religious wars in Europe between Catholics and Protestants that followed the Reformation — a time of bitter hatred and discrimination. His family belonged to the Moravian Brethren, a small Protestant church that suffered persecution. Comenius, a bishop and educator of the Brethren, was forced to flee and lived in exile in several European countries. Hoping to end religious intolerance, he created a new educational philosophy, *pansophism,* to cultivate universal understanding. A pioneering peace educator, he believed that universally shared knowledge would stimulate a love of wisdom that would overcome national and religious hatreds and create a peaceful world order.[2]

Comenius occupied a middle position between the Renaissance humanist educators and later naturalistic reformers such as Rousseau, Pestalozzi, and Spencer. Although still emphasizing Latin's importance in the curriculum, Comenius taught it by methods that used the senses rather than passive memorization. In his book *Gates of Tongues Unlocked,* he taught Latin in the learner's own vernacular. Beginning with short, simple phrases, the student gradually progressed to more complicated sentences. Comenius also prepared a picture book for teaching Latin, *The Visible World in Pictures,* consisting of illustrations that designated objects in both their Latin and vernacular names. His approach of using illustrations combined language learning with sense perception.[3] His belief that concept formation began with sensory learning would be developed further by Locke, Rousseau, and Pestalozzi.

Principles of Teaching and Learning.   Comenius, an early pioneer of the permissive classroom environment, respected children's natural needs and development. He rejected the conventional wisdom that children were inherently bad and that teachers needed to use corporal punishment to discipline them. Instead, Comenius sought to attract gentle and loving persons as teachers who would create joyful and pleasant classrooms. By focusing on children's natural growth and development, teachers could develop an efficient teaching method and appropriate materials.[4] Part of their task was to recognize that children learn most efficiently when they are ready for a particular kind of learning; children should not be hurried, coerced, or pressured to learn. Thus Comenius advised teachers to organize lessons into easily assimilated steps to make learning gradual, cumulative, and pleasant.[5]

In building his own philosophy of education, Comenius emphasized the following principles for teachers: (1) use objects or pictures to illustrate concepts; (2) apply lessons to the students' practical life; (3) present lessons directly and simply; (4) emphasize general principles before details; (5) emphasize that all creatures and objects are part of a whole universe; (6) present lessons in sequence, stressing one thing at a time; (7) do not leave a specific subject until students understand it completely.[6]

---

[2]Gerald L. Gutek, "Knowledge: The Road to Peace," *Christian History,* 6 (1987), pp. 29–30.
[3]Edward A. Power, *A Legacy of Learning: A History of Western Education* (Albany: State University of New York Press, 1991), pp. 195–197.
[4]M. W. Keatinge, ed. and trans., *Comenius* (New York: McGraw-Hill, 1931). Jean Piaget, ed., *John Amos Comenius on Education* (New York: Teachers College Press, 1967).
[5]Josef Smolik, "Comenius: A Man of Hope in a Time of Turmoil," *Christian History,* 6 (1987), pp. 15–18.
[6]Edward J. Power, *Evolution of Educational Doctrine: Major Educational Theorists of the Western World* (New York: Appleton-Century-Crofts, 1969), pp. 238–241.

Universal knowledge, a force for peace

Education and Schooling.

In developing his own philosophy of education and school practices, Comenius was a pioneer who honored ethical principles of tolerance for religious differences. He also incorporated the technological changes of his time such as the invention of the printing press by writing widely used textbooks that popularized his new educational ideas and methods. For him, schooling, by cultivating universal knowledge, could promote peace and international understanding. An early proponent of multicultural education, he wanted schools to encourage tolerance and understanding of people of different religions and cultures.

Anticipating progressivism and naturalism

Influence on Educational Practices Today.

Comenius anticipated many practices associated with modern child-centered progressive education. He also developed plans for organizing and administering effective schools. He believed that teaching should build on children's interests and actively involve their senses. The teacher as a patient and permissive person should gently lead children to understand the world in which they live. Such later educational theorists as Rousseau and Pestalozzi would follow Comenius's pioneering work in naturalistic education.

Locke: Empiricist Educator

John Locke (1632–1704), an English physician and philosopher, lived during a time of political change when people in England wanted a more representative government.[7] Contributing to the period's new ways of thinking about philosophy, Locke challenged the older Platonic theory of innate ideas. We shall see how Locke built his own philosophy of education by emphasizing the political principles of inalienable human rights and the educational process of learning through the senses.

Locke opposed King James II, who sought to be England's absolute ruler. James was overthrown in the Glorious Revolution of 1688. In his *Two Treatises of Government,* in 1689, Locke argued against the "divine right of kings" theory, which proclaimed the monarch's right to be absolute ruler over his subjects.[8] Instead, Locke argued that political order should be based on a contract between the people and the government, which ruled by the consent of those who had established it. He asserted that all persons possessed inalienable rights of life, liberty, and property. Locke's philosophy contributed to the concepts of representative government and checks and balances among a government's legislative, executive, and judicial branches. Thomas Jefferson and other founders of the American republic were indebted to Locke's ideas.

Inalienable rights

Education for self-governance

Locke's theory implied that the people of a country were to establish their own government and select their own leaders. To do this intelligently and responsibly, they had to be educated. This idea became a significant principle of the nineteenth-century American common school movement, and remains a major responsibility of public schools. (For Locke's ideas on education as well as those of other pioneers discussed in this chapter, see Overview 4.1.)

The mind as a blank slate

Principles of Teaching and Learning.

Locke's major philosophical contribution, *An Essay Concerning Human Understanding,* published in 1690, examined how we acquire ideas.[9] Locke held that at birth the human mind is a blank slate, a *tabula rasa,* that is empty of ideas. We gradually acquire knowledge from the information about

---

[7]John Dunn, *Locke* (New York: Oxford University Press, 1984).
[8]John Locke, *Second Treatise of Government,* ed. C. B. Macpherson (Indianapolis: Hackett Publishing Co., 1980).
[9]John Locke, *An Essay Concerning Human Understanding,* ed. Alexander Fraser (New York: Dover, 1959).

OVERVIEW 4.1   Educational Pioneers

Pioneer	Historical Context	Purpose of Education	Curriculum
Comenius 1592–1670 (Czech)	17th-century religious war following Protestant Reformation	To relate education to children's natural growth and development; to contribute to peace and understanding	Vernacular language, reading, writing, mathematics, religion, history, Latin; universal knowledge
Locke 1632–1704 (English)	English Glorious Revolution of 1688	To develop ideas in the mind based on sense perception; to educate individuals capable of self-government	Reading, writing, arithmetic, foreign language, mathematics, history, civil government, physical education
Rousseau 1712–1778 (Swiss-French)	18th-century French Enlightenment	To create a learning environment that allows the child's innate, natural goodness to flourish	Nature; the environment
Pestalozzi 1746–1827 (Swiss)	Early-19th-century post-Napoleonic period and beginnings of industrialism	To develop the human being's moral, mental, and physical powers harmoniously; to use sense perception in forming clear ideas	Object lessons; form, number, sound
Froebel 1782–1852 (German)	19th-century resurgence of philosophical idealism and rise of nationalism	To develop the latent spiritual essence of the child in a prepared environment	Songs, stories, games, gifts, occupations
Spencer 1820–1903 (English)	Darwin's theory of evolution in 1859 and rise of 19th-century industrial corporations	To enable human beings to live effectively, economically, and scientifically	Practical, utilitarian, and scientific subjects
Dewey 1859–1952 (American)	Early-20th-century American progressive movement, growth of science, and rise of pragmatic philosophy	To contribute to the individual's personal, social, and intellectual growth	Making and doing; history and geography; science; problems
Montessori 1870–1952 (Italian)	Late-19th- and early-20th-century assertion of feminism; greater attention to early childhood education	To assist children's sensory, muscular, and intellectual development in a prepared environment	Motor and sensory skills; preplanned materials
Piaget 1896–1980 (Swiss)	20th-century developments in psychology by Freud, Hall, Jung, and others	To organize education in terms of children's patterns of growth and development	Concrete and formal operations
Illich 1926–	End of colonialism in 20th century; rise of multinational corporations	To empower human beings by deinstitutionalizing them; to remove education from institutionalized controls of schooling	Skill learning of specific skills by drill and apprenticeship; liberal learning through voluntary groups

Methods of Instruction	Role of the Teacher	Significance	Influence on Today's Schools
Based on readiness and stages of human growth; gradual, cumulative, orderly; use of objects	To be a permissive facilitator of learning, to base instruction on child's stages of development	Developed a more humane view of the child; devised an educational method incorporating sensation	Schools organized according to children's stages of development
Reliance on sensation; slow, gradual, cumulative learning	To encourage sense experience; to base instruction on empirical method	Developed a theory of knowledge based on sensation	Schooling that emphasizes sensory observation
Reliance on sensation; experience with nature	To assist nature; not to impose social conventions on the child	Led a romantic revolt against the doctrine of child depravity; a forerunner of child-centered progressivism	Permissive schooling based on child freedom
Reliance on sensation; object lessons; simple to complex; near to far; concrete to abstract	To act as a loving facilitator of learning by creating a homelike school environment; to be skilled in using the special method	Devised an educational method that changed elementary education	Schooling based on emotional security and object learning
Self-activity; play; imitation	To facilitate children's growth	Created the kindergarten, a special early childhood learning environment	Preschools designed to liberate the child's creativity
Reliance on sensation and the scientific method; activities	To organize instruction in basic activities	A leading curriculum theorist who stressed scientific knowledge	Schooling that stresses scientific knowledge and competitive values
Problem solving according to the scientific method	To create a learning environment based on the shared experience of learners	Developed the pragmatic experimentalist philosophy of education	Schooling that emphasizes problem solving and activities in a context of community
Spontaneous learning; activities; practical, sensory, and formal skills; exercises	To act as a facilitator or director of learning by using didactic materials in a prepared environment	Developed a widely used method and philosophy of early childhood education	Early childhood schooling that is intellectually and developmentally stimulating
Individualized programs; exploration and experimentation with concrete materials	To organize instruction according to stages of cognitive development	Formulated a theory of cognitive development	Schooling organized around cognitive developmental stages
On-the-job skill training or apprenticeship; dialogue and participation in voluntary interest groups	Not certificated schoolteachers; rather friends, peers, experts	Stimulated deschooling movement, which led to other critical analyses of education and schooling	Critical attitude toward schools and toward formal institutionalized learning

the world that our senses bring to us. Simple ideas become compound ideas as we combine them, and these in turn become more complex through comparison, reflection, and generalization.

Empiricism and the scientific method

Although Comenius and others had stressed sensation's role in forming ideas, Locke, because of his systematic writing on the subject, is often acclaimed the pioneer of **empiricism.** According to this theory, human knowledge is acquired by the senses. Because it relies on sensation, empiricism is closely related to **induction,** the process of developing explanations or hypotheses from observed phenomena. In his theory, Locke attacked Plato's belief that ideas are present latently in the mind at birth. Locke's stress on studying objects in the environment was developed further by Rousseau, Franklin, Pestalozzi, and Dewey. It was also used by later educators who advocated the **scientific method** — the testing of hypotheses by experimentation — as the best approach for teaching and learning.

Necessity of a good environment

Education and Schooling. In *Some Thoughts Concerning Education,* in 1697, Locke wrote that a proper education began very early in a child's life. Stressing a sound mind in a strong and healthy body, he called attention to the importance of a child's physical and social environments, diet, and activities. Children should breathe fresh air, have plenty of sleep, eat nourishing and plain food, bathe frequently, exercise regularly, and have time for recreation and play.

Slow and cumulative learning

Learning, Locke said, should be a gradual process in that instruction in reading, writing, and arithmetic should be slow and cumulative. In addition to these basics, Locke's curriculum included conversational learning of foreign languages, especially French; mathematics; and history. Physical education, games, and athletics should be encouraged. He believed that this educational foundation would achieve the educational goal of cultivating ethical individuals who would competently manage their social, business, and political affairs.[10]

Impact on modern pragmatic approaches

Citizenship education

Influence on Educational Practices Today. Locke's emphasis on sensory experience and on civic education shaped the practical and vocational aspects of Benjamin Franklin's plan for an English grammar school in Philadelphia in 1741. Franklin's proposal, in turn, was a forerunner of the modern comprehensive high school. Locke's stress on empirical learning also influenced the pragmatic and experimental views of modern education that emphasize "learning by doing" and interaction with the environment. His political theory of individual freedom shaped the way Americans think about citizenship and civic participation.[11]

Rousseau: Educating the Natural Person

Jean Jacques Rousseau (1712–1778) a Swiss-born French theorist, lived during an era of intellectual ferment that anticipated the American and French Revolutions.[12] He was part of a group of intellectuals in Paris who, through their writings, questioned the status quo of the established church and absolute monarchy. His works

---

[10]Ruth W. Grant and Nathan Tarcov, eds., *John Locke: Some Thoughts Concerning Education and of the Conduct of the Understanding,* Indianapolis: Hackett Publishing Co., 1996, p. 187.
[11]Charles F. Bahmueller, ed., *CIVITAS: A Framework for Civil Education* (Calabasas, Calif.: Center for Civic Education, 1991), p. 384.
[12]For biographies, see Maurice W. Cranston, *Jean-Jacques: The Early Life and Work of Jean-Jacques Rousseau, 1712–1754* (Chicago: University of Chicago Press, 1991); and Maurice W. Cranston, *The Noble Savage: Jean-Jacques Rousseau, 1754–1762* (Chicago: University of Chicago Press, 1991).

Noble savages in the state of nature

On the Origin of the Inequality of Mankind and *The Social Contract* condemn distinctions of wealth, property, and prestige that generate social inequalities.[13] In the original state of nature, according to Rousseau, people were "noble savages," innocent, free, and uncorrupted; it was socioeconomic artificialities that corrupted people.

Emile: a novel of education

Rousseau conveyed his educational philosophy though his famous novel, *Emile,* in 1762, which tells the story of a boy's education from infancy to adulthood.[14] The novel attacks the child depravity theory and an exclusively verbal and literary education, which Rousseau felt ignored the child's natural interests and inclinations. He also believed that the child must be freed from society's imprisoning institutions, of which the school was one of the most coercive.

Although Rousseau's novel was about the education of an upper-class French man, many progressive and child-centered educators have found much in Rousseau's book to liberate both boys and girls from authoritarian educational practices.[15]

Stages of development

Principles of Teaching and Learning.   Like Comenius, Rousseau recognized the crucial importance of stages of human development. In *Emile,* Rousseau identified five developmental stages: infancy, childhood, boyhood, adolescence, and youth. Each stage requires an appropriate education to lead to the next stage.[16] To preserve the child's natural goodness, Rousseau insisted that the early formative stages be free from society's corruption. Thus Emile was to be educated by a tutor on a country estate away from the temptations of a ruinous society.[17]

Infancy: first contacts with environment

Rousseau's first stage, infancy (from birth to five), sees the infant as helpless and dependent on others. Yet freedom to move and exercise his body allows the infant to make his first contacts with the objects of the environment.

Childhood: exploring the world through senses

During childhood (from five to twelve), the child shapes his own personality as he becomes aware that his actions produce either painful or pleasurable consequences. Motivated by curiosity, he actively explores his environment, learning about the world through his senses. Calling the eyes, ears, hands, and feet the first teachers, Rousseau argues that the senses are better and more efficient than the schoolmaster, who teaches words the learner does not understand, and better than the schoolroom's silence and the master's rod. Emile's tutor deliberately refrained from introducing books at this stage to avoid substituting reading for the child's own direct interaction with nature.

Boyhood: natural science

During boyhood (from twelve to fifteen), Emile learned natural science by observing the cycles of growth of plants and animals. By exploring his surroundings, he learned geography far more realistically than from studying maps. In addition, Emile read *Robinson Crusoe,* Defoe's story of a man marooned on an island who had to meet nature on its own terms. Emile also learned a manual trade, carpentry, to make the connection between mental and physical work.

---

[13]Jean Jacques Rousseau, *Discourse on the Origin of Inequality* (Indianapolis: Hackett, 1992); see also Daniel Cullen, *Freedom in Rousseau's Political Philosophy* (DeKalb: Northern Illinois University Press, 1993).

[14]William Boyd, *The Emile of Jean Jacques Rousseau* (New York: Teachers College Press, 1962); and Allan Bloom, *Emile or On Education* (New York: Basic Books, 1979).

[15]Jane Roland Martin, *Reclaiming a Conversation: The Ideal of the Educated Woman* (New Haven, Conn.: Yale University Press, 1985), pp. 361–369. See also Linda M. Zerilli, *Signifying Woman: Culture and Chaos in Rousseau, Burke, and Mill* (Ithaca, N.Y.: Cornell University Press, 1994).

[16]Christopher Winch, "Rousseau on Learning: A Re-Evaluation," *Educational Theory,* 46 (Fall 1996), pp. 424–425.

[17]David B. Owen, "History and the Curriculum in Rousseau's *Emile,*" *Educational Theory,* 32 (1982), pp. 117–130.

GETTING TO THE SOURCE

Rousseau on Natural Education

JEAN JACQUES ROUSSEAU

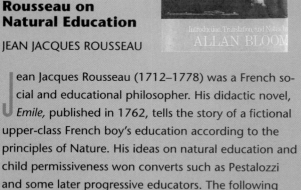

Jean Jacques Rousseau (1712–1778) was a French social and educational philosopher. His didactic novel, *Emile,* published in 1762, tells the story of a fictional upper-class French boy's education according to the principles of Nature. His ideas on natural education and child permissiveness won converts such as Pestalozzi and some later progressive educators. The following excerpt from *Emile* warns educators not to turn children into pseuoadults but to recognize the vital importance of childhood as a natural stage of human development.

Nature wants children to be children before being men. If we want to pervert this order, we shall produce precocious fruits which will be immature and insipid and will not be long in rotting. We shall have young doctors and old children. Childhood has its ways of seeing, thinking, and feeling which are proper to it. Nothing is less sensible than to want to substitute ours for theirs, and I would like as little to insist that a ten-year-old be five feet tall as that he possess judgment. Actually, what would reason do for him at that age? It is the bridle of strength, and the child does not need this bridle.

In trying to persuade your pupils of the duty of obedience, you join to this alleged persuasion force and threats or, what is worse, flattery and promises. In this way, therefore, lured by profit or constrained by force, they pretend to be convinced by reason. They see quite well that obedience is advantageous to them and rebellion harmful when you notice either. But since everything you insist on is unpleasant and, further, it is always irksome to do another's will, they arrange to do their own will convertly. They are persuaded that what they do is right if their disobedience is unknown, but are ready on being caught — in

Adolescence: entering society

Next in Rousseau's developmental schema is adolescence (from fifteen to eighteen). During these years, Emile entered society. As he became aware of and interested in sex, his questions about human sexuality were to be answered honestly and directly. Having benefited from a natural education, Emile was now ready to cope with the outside world, and to learn about society, government, economics, and business. His aesthetic tastes were to be cultivated by visits to museums, art galleries, libraries, and theaters. During the last stage of education (from eighteen to twenty), Emile traveled to Paris and to foreign countries to visit different peoples and societies.

Education and Schooling.   Preferring the natural to the social, Rousseau stressed human instincts as the initial means to knowledge.[18] He believed that the school often interferes with learning. As a social institution, the school conditions children to accept confining traditional customs and institutions. Rousseau sought to liberate the child and adult from such artificial social restrictions. Emile, a child of nature, followed rather than repressed his natural instincts and impulses. If pleasure was the result, then Emile earned his own reward. If his actions caused pain, then Emile brought these consequences upon himself. Either way, he learned from the experience. Rousseau used the following key ideas in formulating his own philosophy of education: (1) childhood is an important foundation of human devel-

Education vs. schooling

[18]J. J. Chambliss, *Educational Theory as Theory of Conduct: From Aristotle to Dewey* (Albany: State University of New York Press, 1987), pp. 101–115.

order to avoid a worse evil — to admit that what they do is wrong. Since the reason for duty cannot be grasped at their age, there is not a man in the world who could succeed in giving duty a truly palpable sense for them. . . . Do not forbid him to do that from which he should abstain; prevent him from doing it without explanations, without reasonings. What you grant him, grant at his first word, without solicitations, without prayers — above all, without conditions. Grant with pleasure; refuse only with repugnance. But let all your refusals be irrevocable; let no importunity shake you; let "no," once pronounced, be a wall of bronze against which the child will have to exhaust his strength at most five or six times in order to abandon any further attempts to overturn it.

It is thus that you will make him patient, steady, resigned, calm, even when he has not got what he wanted, for it is in the nature of man to endure patiently the necessity of things but not the ill will of others. . . .

Questions

1. Why does Rousseau warn against turning children into pseudoadults or adultlike children?
2. Consider contemporary American society. What factors in society tend to turn children into pseudoadults and work to diminish the importance of childhood? What is your opinion of these trends?
3. What does Rousseau consider to be the natural development of moral education? Do you agree or disagree?
4. Do you believe that Rousseau's concepts of natural education and child permissiveness are beneficial or harmful to contemporary education?
5. Why do you think that Rousseau's educational theory enjoyed such popularity and had such influence on other educators?

Source: Jean Jacques Rousseau, *Emile or On Education,* ed. and trans. Allan Bloom (New York: Basic Books, 1979), pp. 90–91.

---

opment; (2) children's natural interests and instincts are valuable beginnings of a more thorough exploration of the environment; (3) human beings, in their life cycles, go through necessary stages of development; (4) adult coercion has a negative impact on children's development. These ideas have had a continuing influence on education and schooling.

Impact on progressive educators

Influence on Educational Practices Today. Rousseau contributed to child-centered progressive education. In the United States, child-centered progressives such as Francis Parker and Marietta Johnson, discussed in Chapter 12, devised a pedagogy based on children's interests and needs. One of Rousseau's significant ideas was that the curriculum should be based on children's interests and needs; it should not force them to conform to adult prescriptions. Thus Rousseau anticipated the view of child development that sees children as interpreting their own reality rather than learning information from indirect sources.

Pestalozzi: Educator of the Senses and Emotions

The life of the Swiss educator, Johann Heinrich Pestalozzi (1746–1827), coincided with important changes in both Europe and America. He lived during the early stages of the industrial revolution when factory-made products were replacing handicrafts made at home. Early industrialization brought changes to family life as women and children entered the work force. Concerned about the impact of this economic change on families and children, Pestalozzi sought to develop schools that, like loving families, would nurture children's development. His ideas about the relationship of families and schools are useful in today's rapidly changing society. Pestalozzi was an attentive reader of Rousseau's *Emile*. He agreed with Rousseau that humans were naturally good but were spoiled by a corrupt society, that traditional schooling was a dull mess of deadening memorization and recitation, and that pedagogical reform could generate social reform.[19]

Group instruction by the object lesson

Acting on his beliefs, Pestalozzi established a school at Burgdorf to educate children and prepare teachers. Here he sought to devise an efficient method of group instruction by which children learned in a loving and nonhurried manner.[20]

Warm, secure school

Principles of Teaching and Learning.   Pestalozzi's approach to teaching can be divided into the "general" and "special" methods. The general method was designed to create a permissive and emotionally healthy homelike learning environment that had to be in place before more specific instruction occurred. Thus the general method required teachers who, emotionally secure themselves, could gain students' trust and affection.

Sensory learning

Once the general method was in place, Pestalozzi implemented his special method. Believing like Locke that thinking began with the senses, he devised the **object lesson** so that instruction would also be sensory. In this approach, children

Johann Pestalozzi believed that teachers should encourage the development of the whole child in a secure, loving, and homelike school environment. *(© Stock Montage, Inc.)*

---

[19]Gerald L. Gutek, *Pestalozzi and Education* (New York: Random House, 1968); and Robert B. Downs, *Heinrich Pestalozzi: Father of Modern Pedagogy* (Boston: Twayne, 1975).
[20]Johann Heinrich Pestalozzi, *How Gertrude Teaches Her Children,* trans. L. E. Holland and F. C. Turner (Syracuse, N.Y.: Bardeen, 1990).

studied the common objects in their environment — the plants, rocks, artifacts, and other objects encountered in daily experience. To determine the form of an object, they drew and traced it. They also counted and then named objects. Thus they learned the form, number, and name or sound related to objects.

From these lessons grew exercises in drawing, writing, counting, adding, subtracting, multiplying, dividing and reading. The first writing exercises consisted of drawing lessons in which the children made a series of rising and falling strokes and open and closed curves. These exercises developed the hand muscles and prepared children for writing. In this method Pestalozzi was following Rousseau's rule that mere verbal learning or abstract lessons are futile. Like Rousseau, he wanted lessons based on sense experiences that originated in the learner's home and family life. This basic innovation became an important part of progressive school reform in the twentieth century.

Instructional strategies

To ensure that instruction followed nature, Pestalozzi developed the following strategies. Instruction should (1) begin with the concrete object before introducing abstract concepts; (2) begin with the learner's immediate environment before dealing with what is distant and remote; (3) begin with easy exercises before introducing complex ones; and (4) always proceed gradually, cumulatively, and slowly.

Naturalistic schooling

Education and Schooling. Like Rousseau, Pestalozzi based learning on natural principles and stressed the importance of human emotions. Unlike Rousseau, however, Pestalozzi did not rely on individual tutoring but sought to incorporate naturalism into schooling. For both Rousseau and Pestalozzi, to "know" meant to understand nature, its patterns, and its laws. Like Locke, Pestalozzi stressed empirical learning, through which people learn about their environment by carefully observing natural phenomena.

Slow, precise learning in a loving environment

Like Comenius, Pestalozzi felt children should learn slowly, understanding thoroughly what they were studying. He was especially dedicated to children who were poor, hungry, and socially or psychologically handicapped. If children were hungry, Pestalozzi fed them before he attempted to teach them. If they were frightened, he comforted them. For him, a teacher was not only skilled in instructional method but also capable of loving all children. In fact, Pestalozzi believed that love of humankind was necessary for successful teaching.

Pestalozzianism brought to United States

Influence on Educational Practices Today. In the early nineteenth century, William Maclure was among the first to import Pestalozzianism to the United States.[21] Through Maclure, a pioneering early-nineteenth-century geologist and natural scientist, Pestalozzian education was linked with scientific discovery and exploration. Basic scientific knowledge was transmitted through practical education based on the object lesson.[22]

Henry Barnard, U.S. commissioner of education in the late nineteenth century, also brought Pestalozzian ideas to the United States. Barnard's *Pestalozzi and Pestalozzianism* introduced American educators to the method's basic principles.[23] These

---

[21]*Partnership for Posterity: The Correspondence of William Maclure and Marie Duclos Fretageot, 1820–1833*, ed. Josephine M. Elliott (Indianapolis: Indiana Historical Society, 1994), pp. 1–17.
[22]Charlotte M. Porter, *The Eagle's Nest: Natural History and American Ideas, 1812–1842* (Tuscaloosa: University of Alabama Press, 1986), pp. 93–95; and George E. DeBoer, *A History of Ideas in Science Education: Implications for Practice* (New York: Teachers College Press, 1991), pp. 21–24.
[23]Thomas A. Barlow, *Pestalozzi and American Education* (Boulder, Colo.: Este Es Press, University of Colorado Libraries, 1977), pp. 35–48, 74–88.

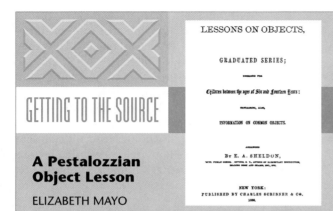

GETTING TO THE SOURCE

A Pestalozzian Object Lesson

ELIZABETH MAYO

LESSONS ON OBJECTS,

GRADUATED SERIES;

designed for

Children between the ages of Six and Fourteen Years:

CONTAINING, ALSO,

INFORMATION ON COMMON OBJECTS.

ARRANGED

By E. A. SHELDON,

WITH PUBLIC SCHOOL, OSWEGO, N. Y., AUTHOR OF ELEMENTARY INSTITUTION,
DRAWING BOOK AND GRADE, ETC., ETC.

NEW YORK:
PUBLISHED BY CHARLES SCRIBNER & CO.
1866.

Johann Heinrich Pestalozzi (1746–1827) was a Swiss educational reformer who emphasized the use of the senses and object teaching in education. His ideas attracted disciples in many countries. In England, Charles and Elizabeth Mayo founded a school that taught future teachers how to use the Pestalozzian method. The following excerpt from Elizabeth Mayo's 1835 text presents a model of the object lesson for a class of children aged six to eight. It should be noted that texts of this sort tended to formalize Pestalozzi's method, making it more rigid than Pestalozzi himself might have desired.

Glass has been selected as the first substance to be presented to the children, because the qualities which characterize it are quite obvious to the senses. The pupils should be arranged before a black board or slate, upon which the result of their observations should be written. The utility of having the lesson presented to the eyes of each child, with the power of thus recalling attention to what has occurred, will very soon be appreciated by the instructor.

The glass should be passed round the party to be examined by each individual.

TEACHER. What is this which I hold in my hand?

CHILDREN. A piece of glass.

TEACHER. Can you spell the word *glass?* (The teacher then writes the word "glass" upon the slate, which is thus presented to the whole class as the subject of the lesson.) You have all examined this glass; what do you observe? What can you say that it is?

CHILDREN. It is bright.

TEACHER. (Teacher having written the word "qualities," writes under it — It is bright.) Take it in your hand and *feel* it.

CHILDREN. It is cold. (Written on the board under the former quality.)

TEACHER. Feel it again, and compare it with the

---

ideas were applied by Edward Sheldon, who integrated the Pestalozzian object lesson into teacher preparation at Oswego Normal School in New York. Some progressive education reforms, such as the emphasis on environment, use of objects, and reliance on sensory experience, reveal the Pestalozzian imprint.

Pestalozzi's ideas developed by Herbart

Another route of Pestalozzian influence was through the German philosopher Johann Herbart (1776–1841) and his followers. Intrigued with Pestalozzi's ideas, Herbart reformulated them into a method of education that included moral development and systematic instruction. Herbart believed that education must include two major classes of interests, knowledge and ethical matters, and that each subject should be taught in relationship to other subjects — an important concept known as **curriculum correlation.** Herbart's followers developed the five-step instructional method that became extremely popular among teachers: (1) *preparation,* which stimulates the learner's readiness for the new lesson by referring to previous learning; (2) *presentation* of the new lesson; (3) *association,* which relates the new lesson to ideas or materials studied earlier; (4) *systematization,* in which examples are used to illustrate important generalizations; and (5) *application,* which tests ideas of the new lesson to demonstrate mastery.[24]

The five-step method of instruction

---

[24]Herbert M. Kliebard, *The Struggle for the American Curriculum, 1893–1958* (Boston: Routledge and Kegan Paul, 1986), pp. 44–45, 56–57.

piece of sponge that is tied to your slate, and then tell me what you perceive in the glass.

CHILDREN. It is smooth — it is hard.

TEACHER. What other glass is there in the room?

CHILDREN. The windows.

TEACHER. Look out at the window and tell me what you see.

CHILDREN. We see the garden.

TEACHER. (Closes the shutter). Look out again, and tell what you observe.

CHILDREN. We cannot see anything.

TEACHER. Why cannot you see anything?

CHILDREN. We cannot see through the shutters.

TEACHER. What difference do you observe between the shutters and the glass?

CHILDREN. We cannot see through the shutters, but we can see through the glass.

TEACHER. Can you tell me any word that will express this quality which you observe in the glass?

CHILDREN. No.

TEACHER. I will tell you then; pay attention, that you may recollect it. It is transparent. What shall you now understand when I tell you that a substance is transparent?

CHILDREN. That you can see through it.

TEACHER. You are right. Try and recollect something that is transparent.

CHILDREN. Water.

Questions

1. How was the Pestalozzian object lesson an improvement over the conventional teaching practices of the early nineteenth century?
2. How did Elizabeth Mayo's object lesson anticipate modern "hands-on" methods of teaching?
3. What are the strengths and weaknesses of object teaching?
4. Do you find any evidence of Pestalozzian object teaching in today's schools?

Source: Elizabeth Mayo, *Lessons on Objects, as Given to Children Between the Ages of Six and Eight, in a Pestalozzian School, at Cheam, Surrey,* 5th ed. (London, 1835), pp. 5–8. Cover from E. A. Sheldon, *Lessons on Objects, Graduated Series; Designed for Children Between the Ages of Six and Fourteen Years: Containing, Also, Information on Common Objects* (New York: Charles Scribner, 1866).

At-risk children

Finally, when American educators came to focus on the education of at-risk children, Pestalozzi's ideas took on a further relevance. His claim that emotional security was a necessary precondition of skill learning strongly parallels the contemporary emphasis on supportive home-school partnerships.

Froebel: The Kindergarten Movement

Idealism and nationalism

The German educator Friedrich Froebel (1782–1852) is renowned for his pioneering work in developing a school for early childhood education — the kindergarten, or child's garden.[25] Froebel was influenced by two trends in the first half of the nineteenth century: (1) a resurgence of philosophical idealism and (2) the rising nationalism of the post-Napoleonic eras. As discussed in Chapter 12, idealism emphasizes a spiritually based reality. Idealists saw the nation as embodying the world spirit on earth. During Froebel's life, there were efforts to unite the various small German kingdoms into one large nation. Froebel believed that an education that emphasized German traditions and folk tales would advance this cause. Froebel's idealism was a reaction against the empiricism of Locke and Rousseau. However, his educa-

---

[25]Norman Brosterman, *Inventing Kindergarten* (New York: Harry N. Abrams, 1997), pp. 14–18, 22–29.

Student of Pestalozzi

tional philosophy emphasized the dignity of child nature as recommended by Rousseau and Pestalozzi. Thus Froebel attempted to weave several threads into his philosophy of education: idealism, nationalism, and child freedom.

Froebel's attraction to teaching led him to Pestalozzi's institute at Yverdon, where he interned from 1808 to 1810. Although he accepted certain aspects of Pestalozzi's method — the emphasis on nature, the permissive school atmosphere, and the object lesson — he believed that Pestalozzi's theory lacked an adequate philosophical foundation. Froebel gave Pestalozzi's object lesson a more symbolic meaning by saying that the concrete object was to stimulate recall of a corresponding idea in the child's mind. He readily accepted Pestalozzi's general method that saw schools as emotionally secure places for children, but he elevated the concept to a highly spiritual level. Like Pestalozzi, he wanted to prepare teachers who would be sensitive to children's readiness and needs rather than be taskmasters who heard preset recitations and who forced children to memorize words they did not understand.

Kindergarten: a prepared, permissive environment

Principles of Teaching and Learning. A philosophical idealist, Froebel believed that every child's inner self contained a spiritual essence that stimulated self-active learning. He therefore designed a kindergarten that would be a prepared environment to externalize children's interior spirituality through self-activity.[26]

Froebel's kindergarten, founded in 1837 in Blankenburg, was a permissive environment featuring games, play, songs, stories, and crafts. The kindergarten's songs, stories, and games, now a standard part of early childhood education, stimulated

This American kindergarten, circa 1900, drew on Froebel's theories that the child's first formal learning should be based on self-activity — in games, play, songs, and crafts — in a prepared, emotionally secure environment. *(© Culver Pictures, Inc.)*

[26]Robert B. Downs, *Friedrich Froebel* (Boston: Twayne, 1978), p. 43.

Gifts and occupations

children's imaginations and introduced them to the culture's folk heroes and heroines and values. The games socialized children and developed their physical and motor skills. As the boys and girls played with other children, they became part of the group and were prepared for further socialized learning activities. The curriculum also included "gifts," objects with fixed form, such as spheres, cubes, and cylinders, which were intended to bring to full consciousness the underlying concept represented by the object. In addition, Froebel's kindergarten featured "occupations," which consisted of materials children could shape and use in design and construction activities. For example, clay, sand, cardboard, and sticks could be manipulated and shaped into castles, cities, and mountains.[27]

Importance of teacher's personality

Education and Schooling.   For many of us, our first impressions of schools and teachers were formed in kindergarten. For Froebel, the kindergarten teacher's personality was of paramount importance. The kindergarten teacher should respect the dignity of human personality and personify the highest cultural values so that children could imitate those values. Above all, the kindergarten teacher should be a sensitive, approachable, and open person.

Spread of the kindergarten movement

Influence on Educational Practices Today.   Froebelianism soon grew into an international education movement. Immigrants who fled Germany after the Revolution of 1848 brought the kindergarten to the United States, where it became part of the American school system. The first U.S. example was the German-language kindergarten established in Wisconsin in 1855 by Margarethe Meyer Schurz, wife of the German American patriot Carl Schurz. Another key person in incorporating the Froebelian kindergarten into American education was Elizabeth Peabody, who founded an English-language kindergarten and a training school for kindergarten teachers in Boston in 1860.[28] Her enthusiasm for Froebel's method took her to Germany in 1867, where she visited kindergartens and interviewed teachers trained by Froebel. Upon returning to the United States, she revised her kindergarten concepts to bring them into greater conformity with Froebel's ideas, and she worked to make the kindergarten part of the American school system.[29] Another key figure was William T. Harris, superintendent of schools in St. Louis, Missouri, and later U.S. commissioner of education, who energetically campaigned for kindergarten education.

Spencer: Social Darwinist and Utilitarian Educator

Theory of evolution

Herbert Spencer (1820–1903) was an English social theorist whose ideas were very popular and influential in the United States in the late nineteenth and early twentieth centuries. His American popularity rested on Spencer's ability to bring the important trends of this period into his educational philosophy. He lived during the time when Charles Darwin was changing the ways people thought about change and progress. According to Darwin's theory of evolution, species evolved naturally and gradually over long periods of time. Members of certain species survived and

[27]Friedrich Froebel, *The Education of Man*, trans. W. Hailmann (New York: Appleton, 1889).
[28]Peabody's contributions to kindergarten education are described in Ruth M. Taylor, *Elizabeth Palmer Peabody: Kindergarten Pioneer* (Philadelphia: University of Pennsylvania Press, 1965); and Evelyn Weber, *The Kindergarten: Its Encounter with Educational Thought in America* (New York: Teachers College Press, 1969).
[29]Caroline Winterer, "Avoiding a 'Hothouse System of Education': Nineteenth-Century Early Childhood Education from the Infant Schools to the Kindergartens," *History of Education Quarterly* (Fall 1992), pp. 310–311.

reproduced themselves by adapting to changes in the environment. As their off-spring inherited these characteristics, they too survived and reproduced themselves and continued the life of the species. Those who were unable to adapt — the unfit — perished.[30]

A social theory based on Darwin

Spencer was a key proponent of **Social Darwinism,** which translated Darwin's evolutionary theory into social, political, economic, and educational relationships. Spencer contended that social development followed a natural evolutionary process by which simple homogeneous societies evolved into more complex, specialized, industrial systems. Spencer's Social Darwinism created a rationale for the last half of the nineteenth century, when industrialization was transforming American and western European societies, creating an economic system characterized by special-ized professions and occupations.

Survival of the fittest

Spencer believed that in a modern industrialized society, as in earlier and sim-pler societies, the "fittest" individuals of each generation would survive because of their skill, intelligence, and adaptability. Competition was a natural ethical force that brought the best in the human species to the top of the socioeconomic order. As winners of the competitive race over slower and duller individuals, the fittest would inherit the earth and populate it with their intelligent and productive chil-dren. Those individuals who were lazy, stupid, or weak would slowly disappear. Ac-cording to Social Darwinism, competition would bring about gradual but inevitable progress.

Opposition to public schools

Spencer argued against public schooling, which he claimed would create a mo-nopoly for mediocrity by catering to the lowest common denominator. Private schools, he thought, should compete with each other for students. Like some con-temporary proponents of a voucher system, Spencer believed the best schools would attract the brightest students and the most capable teachers.

Education for utilitarian purposes

Principles of Teaching and Learning.   In addition to being a staunch Social Dar-winist, Spencer followed the naturalist tradition in education. Rather than a hu-manist classical education, he believed that industrialized society requires a **utilitarian education** based on useful scientific and practical objectives. As a founder of modern curriculum theory, Spencer argued that education should be based on the necessary activities that sustain the survival of the species.

Vocational studies

Stressing empiricism like Locke and Pestalozzi, Spencer advocated sensory learning that involved the learner with the environment. Like them, he opposed rote memorization and recitation and wanted instruction to be gradual, cumula-tive, and unhurried. Since he favored education directed to the marketplace, he strongly advocated vocational and professional preparation that could be applied to science and engineering.[31]

Education and Schooling.   Like such naturalistic educational theorists as Rousseau and Pestalozzi, Spencer opposed the excessively verbal, literary, and clas-sical education associated with traditional schooling. He criticized the traditional grammar schools of England as being outmoded and ornamental. The most valu-able curriculum, in Spencer's view, included the physical, biological, and social sci-ences.

Stress on sciences

Using a rationale that anticipated modern curriculum making, Spencer classi-fied human activities according to their capacities for advancing survival and progress. Science was especially important because it could be applied to the effec-

---

[30]Jonathan Howard, *Darwin* (New York: Oxford University Press, 1982).
[31]R. S. Dreyer, "Take a Tip from Herbert Spencer," *Supervision* (May 1993), pp. 22–23.

tive performance of life activities.[32] Spencer identified five types of activities to include in the curriculum: (1) those needed for self-preservation, which are basic to all other activities; (2) those needed to perform one's occupation or profession, which makes a person economically self-supporting; (3) those needed to rear children properly; (4) those needed for social and political participation; and (5) those needed for leisure and recreation.

Activities-based curriculum

Spencer's arguments for an activities-based curriculum created a major controversy in the late nineteenth century. At that time, secondary and higher education still focused on the Latin and Greek classical languages and literatures, and science was neglected. Those who supported Spencer's curriculum had to wage a concerted struggle to bring about curricular change.

Impact on curriculum design

Influence on Educational Practices Today.   Spencer's ideas on curriculum, which emphasized science and practicality, were readily accepted in the United States, especially by the social efficiency educators. American educators were less resistant to curricular change than those in England. In 1918, a National Education Association committee, in its landmark *Cardinal Principles of Secondary Education,* reiterated Spencer's list of basic life activities. Modern curriculum designers continue to reflect Spencer's influence when they base curriculum on human needs and activities.

After dominating American social science in the late nineteenth century, Social Darwinism was pushed aside by John Dewey's Experimentalism and progressive reform. However, in the 1980s and 1990s, some key Social Darwinist ideas reemerged in the neoconservative agenda of privatizing schools through vouchers, reducing government's regulatory powers, and increasing economic productivity through basic skills that have market value.

Dewey: Learning Through Experience

School and society

Laboratory school

John Dewey (1859–1952) was one of the most important American philosophers.[33] He developed his pioneering Experimentalist philosophy of education against the backdrop of the social, political, scientific, and technological changes taking place in the United States in the first half of the twentieth century. The progressive reform movement in politics stimulated his thinking. He sought to incorporate the concept of relativism current in science. Keenly aware of technology's power to transform society, Dewey wanted it used for democratic purposes. Seeing education as social progress, Dewey envisioned schools as closely connected to society. When he was director of the University of Chicago Laboratory School from 1896 to 1904, he tested his pragmatic educational philosophy by using it as the foundation for children's learning activities and projects.[34] (For a discussion of pragmatism as an educational philosophy, see Chapter 12).

Principles of Teaching and Learning.   Dewey's *The Child and the Curriculum* provides a guide to principles and practices used at the University of Chicago Laboratory School. Children were seen as socially active human beings who are eager to

---

[32]Andreas Kazamias, *Herbert Spencer on Education* (New York: Teachers College Press, 1966); and Valerie A. Haines, "Spencer's Philosophy of Science," *British Journal of Sociology* (June 1992), pp. 155–172.

[33]Robert B. Westbrook, *John Dewey and American Democracy* (Ithaca, N.Y.: Cornell University Press, 1991); for an extensive commentary, see Walter Feinberg, "Dewey and Democracy: At the Dawn of the Twenty-first Century," *Educational Theory* (Spring 1993), pp. 195–216.

[34]John Dewey, *The Child and the Curriculum* (Chicago: University of Chicago Press, 1902). A recent commentary is Laurel N. Tanner, *Dewey's Laboratory School: Lessons for Today* (New York: Teachers College Press, 1997).

Confronting problems

explore and gain control over their environment. By interacting with their world, learners confront both personal and social problems. Such problematic encounters stimulate children to use their intelligence to solve the difficulty — to use their knowledge in an active, instrumental manner.[35]

For Dewey, the scientific method is the most effective process we have to solve problems. When they use the scientific method to solve problems, children learn how to think reflectively and to direct their experiences in ways that lead to personal and social growth. The following steps are extremely important in Dewey's version of the scientific method as a process of teaching and learning:

Steps in learning by the scientific method

1. The learner is involved in a "genuine experience" that truly interests him or her.
2. Within this experience, the learner has a "genuine problem" that stimulates thinking.
3. The learner acquires the information needed to solve the problem.
4. The learner frames possible, tentative solutions that may solve the problem.
5. The learner tests the solutions by applying them to the problem. In this way, the learner validates his or her own knowledge.[36]

Reconstructing knowledge to solve problems

For Dewey, knowledge is not inert information but an instrument to solve problems. The fund of human knowledge — past ideas, discoveries, and inventions — is used to frame the hypothetical solutions to problems. People then test and reconstruct this knowledge in light of present needs. Since people and their environment are constantly changing, knowledge, too, is continually reconfigured or reconstructed. Once a problem has been solved, its solution enters into the knowledge fund.

Education and Schooling. Dewey saw education as a social process by which the group's immature members, especially children, are brought to participate in group life. Through education, children are introduced to their cultural heritage and learn to use it in problem solving. Education's sole purpose is to contribute to a person's personal and social growth. As Dewey put it, education "is that reconstruction or reorganization of experience which adds to the meaning of experience, and which increases ability to direct the course of subsequent experience."[37]

Education for personal and social growth

Schools as miniature societies

In this view, schools used children's interests, needs, and problems to introduce them to society and culture. As miniature societies, they brought children into social participation. They were social laboratories in which children and youth, by using the scientific method, could test their ideas and values.[38]

Activities for the curriculum

Dewey's approach to learning emphasized activities and processes by which children interacted with their environment. He identified three levels of activity in the curriculum. The first level, for preschool children, involved activities to develop sensory abilities and physical coordination. The second level involved using materials and instruments in the environment. Schools were to be well stocked with materials that stimulated children's creative and constructive interests. At the third level, children discovered, examined, and used new ideas. These three curricular

---

[35]For an analysis of Dewey's democratic approach to education, see Sandra Rosenthal, "Democracy and Education: A Deweyan Approach," *Educational Theory* (Fall, 1993), pp. 377–389.
[36]John Dewey, *Democracy and Education* (New York: Macmillan, 1916), p. 192.
[37]Ibid., pp. 89–90.
[38]Kliebard, *The Struggle for the American Curriculum,* pp. 58–88.

levels moved learning from simple impulses to careful observation of the environment, to planning actions, and finally to reflecting on and testing the consequences of action.

Schools as liberating and democratic

As an advocate of democratic education and schooling, Dewey wanted schools to be liberating environments in which students were free to test all ideas, beliefs, and values. Institutions, ideas, customs, and values were all open to critical inquiry, investigation, and reconstruction. As democratic institutions, schools should be open to and used by all. Opposing traditions that separate people from each other because of ethnic origin, race, gender, or economic class, Dewey believed that communities were enriched when people shared their experience to solve their common problems. His ideal school was a place where administrators, teachers, and students planned the curriculum together.

Impact on progressivism

Influence on Educational Practices Today.   John Dewey exercised an enormous influence on American education. By applying pragmatism to education, he helped to open schooling to change and innovation. Dewey's ideas about socially expanding children's experience became associated with progressive education, which emphasized children's interests and needs. Today, educators who relate schooling to social purposes are often following Dewey's pioneering educational concepts.[39]

Dewey's influence can also be seen in teaching that takes a "hands-on" or process-oriented approach. For example, the "whole language" approach, with its emphasis on teaching language arts through the entire educational environment, is a recent development stemming from Dewey's pioneering Experimentalist philosophy.

Montessori: The Prepared Environment

Early childhood and feminism

Maria Montessori (1870–1952), an Italian educator, devised an internationally popular method of early childhood education. In considering Montessori's life and times, we can identify two important trends: emphasis on early childhood and the rise of feminism. Like the early childhood educators Pestalozzi and Froebel, Montessori emphasized the influence of formative experiences on later life. She was also a feminist who challenged traditional beliefs about women's role and education.

Despite parental disapproval, Montessori left the conventional schooling considered appropriate for Italian upper-class young women to attend a technical school, and then became the first woman in Italy to earn the degree of doctor of medicine. As a physician, Montessori worked with children regarded as mentally handicapped and brain damaged. Her work was so effective with these children that she concluded it was useful for all children.

Emphasis on structured work

Principles of Teaching and Learning.   In 1908 Maria Montessori established a children's school, the *Casa dei Bambini,* whose students were impoverished children from the slums of Rome. In this school, Montessori fashioned a "specially prepared environment" that featured methods, materials, and activities based on her observations of children. She also refined her theory by doing extensive reading in the theories of Itard and Sequin, two early pioneers in special education. Children, she found, are capable of sustained concentration and work. Enjoying structure and preferring

---

[39]For analyses of Dewey's work in education, see Jim Garrison, "A Deweyan Theory of Democratic Listening," *Educational Theory,* 46 (Fall 1996), pp. 429–451; and Dee Russell, "Cultivating the Imagination in Music Education: John Dewey's Theory of Imagination and Its Relationship to the Chicago Laboratory School," *Educational Theory,* 48 (Spring 1998), pp. 198–210.

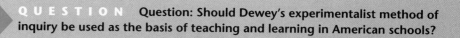

TAKING ISSUE

Dewey's Learning by Experience

Since John Dewey developed his experimentalist or pragmatic philosophy and applied it to education, his approach has been vigorously debated. Proponents of Dewey's method, many of whom are professors of education, emphasize learning by experience through the use of the scientific method. Opponents of Dewey's method claim that it lowers academic standards and achievement by weakening systematic subject-matter learning and encouraging relativistic values.

Arguments PRO

1 Dewey's method provides continuity between children's world of direct experience and a school curriculum that arises from and develops that experience. Because of this continuity, students readily become interested and motivated, eager to pursue their interests into areas of broader educational importance.

2 Free from absolutes based on previous concepts of reality, Dewey's method encourages students to question inherited traditions and values. It fosters an experimental attitude that leads to invention, discovery, and innovation and equips people to use knowledge as an instrument to solve the problems of a changing world.

3 Since Dewey's method of inquiry requires the freedom to think and to question, it encourages a democratic orientation to life and society. Dewey's method is therefore well suited to the American culture's stress on representative institutions and open discussion of issues.

4 Dewey's educational goal — human growth for the sake of further growth — promotes an instructional flexibility in which teachers and students are free to respond to personal and social issues. This type of education encourages the capacity for flexible responses to the environment, a capacity sorely needed in today's technological and interdependent world.

Arguments CON

1 By stressing the interests and needs of children and adolescents, Dewey's method fails to emphasize the important role of adults in transmitting the cultural heritage. It also minimizes the fact that learning often requires the child to apply effort *before* developing interests.

2 Dewey's method falsely assumes that the scientific method can be applied to any problem without a deep knowledge of the problem's context. On the contrary, it is important that students learn subjects systematically, not experimentally. The failure to master subject matter leads to many of the deficiencies of American students, especially in mathematics and science.

3 Dewey's method is highly relativistic and situational, denying the existence of universal truths and values. In order to survive and prosper, American democracy needs to reaffirm certain basic and traditional values, not call all values into question.

4 Dewey's argument that the only goal of education is growth for further growth neglects the need for standards that encourage intellectual achievement and economic productivity. Schools, teachers, and learners need substantive goals to guide the educational process; vague notions about human growth are not sufficient.

work to play, they like to repeat actions until they master a given activity. She argued that children, contrary to the assumptions of conventional schooling, have an inner need to work at what interests them without the prodding of teachers and without being motivated by external rewards and punishments. In fact, children's capacity for spontaneous learning leads them to begin pursuing reading and writing.[40]

Types of activity

Education and Schooling. Montessori's curriculum included three major types of activity and experience: practical, sensory, and formal skills and studies. It was designed to introduce children to such practical activities as setting the table, serving a meal, washing dishes, tying and buttoning clothing, and practicing basic manners and social etiquette. Repetitive exercises developed sensory and muscular coordination. Formal skills and subjects included reading, writing, and arithmetic. Children were introduced to the alphabet by tracing unmounted, movable sandpaper letters. Reading was taught after writing. Colored rods of various sizes were used to teach measuring and counting.

Didactic materials

The Montessori school had preplanned teaching (didactic) materials designed to develop the practical, sensory, and formal skills. Examples included lacing and buttoning frames, weights, and packets to be identified by their sound or smell. Since they direct learning in the prepared environment, Montessori educators are called directresses rather than teachers. Under the guidance of the directress, chil-

Maria Montessori developed an educational method that emphasized a structured and orderly prepared environment. Here, a child is at work on an individual learning activity at the Montessori school he attends. *(© Elizabeth Crews)*

<hr />

[40]Maria Montessori, *The Discovery of the Child* (New York: Ballantine Books, 1972).

dren use materials in a prescribed way to acquire the desired skill mastery, sensory experience, or intellectual outcome.

Montessori movement in United States

Influence on Educational Practices Today.   Montessori education has experienced two periods of popularity in the United States. The first round of enthusiasm occurred just before World War I when Montessori visited the United States and lectured on her method. However, William Kilpatrick and other progressive educators charged that the Montessori method was overly structured and provided insufficiently for children's socialization.[41]

Revival of interest

Today, Montessori education enjoys a marked revival in the United States, coinciding with the growing emphasis on early childhood education. Private **Montessori schools** enroll preschool children throughout the country. Many parents send their children to Montessori schools to enhance the children's intellectual development and to give them an academic head start.

Piaget: Developmental Growth

Jean Piaget (1896–1980), a Swiss psychologist, made significant contributions to educational psychology and early childhood education. His work in the twentieth century coincided with important developments in psychology by Sigmund Freud, G. Stanley Hall, and others. These developments were part of the historical milieu that stimulated research on child psychology. Piaget is especially known for investigating the development of children's thought, cognition, and language. He examined children's conceptions of number, space, logic, geometry, physical reality, and moral judgment.

Investigating children's development

Principles of Teaching and Learning.   Piaget believed that children, as they explore their environments, become creative actors in their own cognitive development. Their complex and continuous environmental interactions shape their conceptions of reality. The environment stimulates their curiosity about the objects they encounter, and as they keep interacting with this environment, they add to their emergent world by assimilating and adapting to their new experiences. Thus through their own exploratory processes, children develop the power to generalize, differentiate, and coordinate their concepts of reality, building concepts based on their experiences of the external world and continually reconceptualizing these ideas with each new experience.

Children interacting with environment

Piaget argued that human intelligence develops sequentially and that children proceed on their own from one developmental stage to the next. Each stage depends on the preceding one and leads to the next. Piaget's four developmental stages are (1) sensorimotor, from eighteen months to two years; (2) preoperational, from two to seven years; (3) concrete operations, from seven to eleven years; and (4) formal operations, from eleven to fifteen years.[42]

Developmental stages

Education and Schooling.   The Piagetian curriculum is guided by these stages of children's cognitive development. However, the stages should not be used in a rigid or doctrinaire way. Each stage is not merely a chronological passage through time; rather, it is an exploratory experience of understanding the world in a qualitatively new and more complex way. Children learn by investigating and probing the ob-

Exploratory learning

---

[41]William H. Kilpatrick, *The Montessori System Examined* (New York: Arno Press and New York Times, 1971).

[42]Jean Piaget, *The Origins of Intelligence in Children,* trans. Margaret Cook (New York: W. W. Norton, 1952), pp. 23–42; William O. Penrose, *A Primer on Piaget* (Bloomington, Ind.: Phi Delta Kappa Educational Foundation, 1979).

jects and social situations that they encounter on these environmental explorations. To enhance the exploratory process, teachers need to ensure that the classroom learning environment is rich enough to stimulate children's curiosity.[43]

Sensorimotor stage

Preoperational stage

Concrete operations

Formal operations

Informal learning situations

In the early **sensorimotor stage**, infants first carry out isolated environmental explorations by using their mouths, eyes, and hands. Later, they coordinate their senses for larger environmental explorations. Through this activity, children construct and organize their view of the world. During the **preoperational stage**, between ages two and seven, children continue to organize their perceptions by classifying objects into groups and naming them. Although their thinking still differs from adult thinking in many respects, the organization and classification begin to approximate those of adults. This marks the beginning of the development of logical relationships. The third stage, **concrete operations**, between ages seven and eleven, occurs as children isolate the general characteristics of objects — size, duration, length, and so on — and use them in more complex mental operations. Although still based on concrete objects, cognition is becoming more abstract. Children can comprehend number signs, processes, and relationships. The stage of **formal operations**, which begins sometime between ages eleven and fifteen, is characterized by the individual's ability to formulate abstract conclusions. Now understanding cause-and-effect relationships, children can use the scientific method to explain reality and can learn complex mathematical, linguistic, mechanical, and scientific processes.[44]

Piaget believed that teachers need to individualize instruction by being sensitive to children's readiness at different stages of development. Effective teaching requires teachers to create informal learning situations in which children can experiment and manipulate objects and thus discover the structures in their environment. It does not mean merely transmitting information. Learning cannot be forced before the individual child is ready. In the Piagetian classroom environment, the following should occur:

1. Teachers should encourage children to explore and experiment.
2. Instruction should be individualized so that children can learn in accordance with their own readiness.
3. Teachers should arrange the classroom so that children have concrete materials to touch, manipulate, and use.

Influence on Educational Practices Today. Although Piaget's cognitive psychology has had its greatest impact on early childhood education, it also has implications for elementary and secondary education. Schools should be informal learning centers where teachers create classrooms that are a rich environment for students. They should be permissively organized so that students' individual differences, readiness, and stage of development guide the educational process.

Illich: Deschooling Society

Ivan Illich (1926–) is an educational pioneer who developed a radical alternative for social and educational change. He developed his theory of education in the second half of the twentieth century at a time of global social, economic, and political change. Important among these changes was the end of colonialism, when people

---

[43]Penrose, *Primer.*
[44]Piaget, *Origins of Intelligence*, pp. 23–42.

in Africa and Asia were freed from political domination by European nations. In this postcolonial era, Illich fears the return of a new kind of domination, neocolonial economic exploitation.

A bold idea: eliminate schools

Unlike educators seeking to promote educational change by reforming schools, Illich boldly wants to reform society by eliminating schools. Schools, he asserts, indoctrinate people to accept existing social, political, and economic conditions that trap them in a spiderlike web of institutions. They also indoctrinate the young to become wasteful consumers who despoil the environment. The pursuit of paper credentials — certificates, diplomas, and degrees — in no way attests to their holders' real competency. Finally, schools condition people to accept institutionally defined, disempowering roles. Thus true reform of society, Illich argues, requires its deinstitutionalization. The elimination of schools, or **deschooling**, is the first step in the process of liberation.[45]

Education and Schooling.   Since Illich's critique of the school is crucial to his argument, we should consider it before his principles of learning. Because he wants to end the school's monopoly over education, Illich's discussion of the school's role differs radically from that of the other educational pioneers described in this chapter. For him, schooling is an "age-specific, teacher-related process requiring full-time attendance at an obligatory curriculum" that makes people dependent rather than independent.[46] Illich believes the schools' educational monopoly has created the myth that education must be highly complicated, expensive, and conducted by certified experts. This monopoly rests on four false assumptions: (1) teacher-dominated behavior is especially valuable to students and society; (2) children and adolescents need to be socialized in schools; (3) learning requires a prestructured, sequential, and cumulative curriculum; and (4) young people should defer efforts to change society until they have completed school.[47] Illich contends that most people acquire their genuine knowledge informally outside of schools rather than in structured programs.

Schools as an educational monopoly

Schools as consumeristic

The school curriculum, Illich argues, reflects a consumer's orientation to reality. Each course is programmed, packaged, and scheduled so that students have to consume additional courses each year. The consequence is a course-taking and credit-accumulating addition, a dependency that requires more schooling.

Exaggeration of teachers' authority

Illich also argues that schools exaggerate the teachers' authority. Not only do teachers correct students' skill and errors, but they also act as therapists who intrude into students' private worlds, persuading them to submit to the teacher's standards of truth, value, and behavior. For Illich, schooling should be replaced by "relational structures" that encourage people to define themselves "by learning and by contributing to the learning of others."[48] Friends, peer group members, and knowledgeable and skilled adults are better educators than teachers.

Principles of Teaching and Learning.   Illich differentiates learning into "drill training" and "liberal education." Drill training is used to learn specific skills that may range from swimming to piano playing to computer programming. For this type of learning, Illich wants to create circumstances outside schools where people can choose from hundreds of definable skills. Skill training can occur as on-the-job training or as apprenticeship in workplaces. In a more general sense, it may also take place through skill banks. Those who have a skill and want to teach it merely

Learning skills outside schools

---

[45]Ivan Illich, *Deschooling Society* (New York: Harper and Row, 1971), pp. 113–114.
[46]Ibid., pp. 25–26.
[47]Ibid., pp. 67–68.
[48]Ibid., pp. 40–71.

advertise, and those who wish to learn the skill can then respond to the advertisement. Arrangements for teaching the skill can be negotiated by the participants. Progress in skill learning is easily verified by performance.

Educational webs

Liberal education, a broad concept that applies to a wide range of human activities, takes place mainly by discussion and dialogue. In Illich's version, interested people form groups to discuss an idea, a book, a play, or a movie; to examine an issue; or to solve a common problem. The main ingredient in this liberal education is interest. People who share common interests can identify each other and get together through educational webs or exchanges. For example, the Internet and its electronic resources can be used to advance Illich's concept of liberal education. Groups also can meet in learning centers, libraries, laboratories, or homes. An important feature of both drill training and liberal education is that they are voluntary and last as long as needed.

Influence on Educational Practices Today.   Illich's theory of deschooling has provoked heated debate. Some educators condemn it as a flight into romantic unreality. Others, attracted to the proposal, have become proponents of deschooling. However, the larger significance has come from Illich's analysis of schooling.[49] His view that schooling, especially in its capitalist version, is a form of coercive expropriation has appealed to certain educators in less technologically developed countries. It has also been used by those who seek to use education as a community-based agency for social change. For example, Paulo Freire developed a theory of liberation pedagogy to raise the consciousness of exploited and landless peasants in Brazil. In Freire's method, people come together at a grass roots level and engage in critical dialogues about how to eliminate oppressive conditions. These dialogues contribute to the forming of literacy circles in which people learn to read about the conditions, issues, and possibilities that really affect their lives.[50]

Heated debate

Creating Your Own Philosophy

One of the criticisms of contemporary professional development is that educators keep reinventing the wheel rather than using the ideas of the past to inform present practice. As you create your own philosophy of education, it is highly instructive to look at how the educator pioneers created their philosophies.

The history of the educational pioneers examined in Chapter 3 reveals that they learned from each other. They did not create their educational philosophies in an intellectual vacuum, but by studying, incorporating, and revising the ideas of their philosophical predecessors. For example, in developing his teaching method, Comenius stressed sensory more than traditional classical study. Locke moved further in that direction by insisting that ideas were based on sensory experience. Rousseau reinforced that idea by emphasizing the importance of giving children the freedom to explore their environments. Pestalozzi, in turn, developed object teaching for use in schools. Spencer, continuing in the naturalist and empiricist tradition, added the new elements of evolution, competition, and specialization. Though he rejected Spencer's Social Darwinian competitive ethic and replaced it with democratic collaboration, Dewey, in emphasizing the scientific method, continued in the empiricist philosophical path. To this stream of educational thought, Piaget added the importance of children exploring their environments.

---

[49]For reactions to Illich's theory, see Alan Gartner, Colin Greer, and Frank Riessman, *After Deschooling, What?* (New York: Harper and Row, 1973).
[50]Paulo Freire, *Pedagogy of the Oppressed,* trans. Myra Bergman Ramos (New York: Continuum, 1984), pp. 72–73, 102–103.

Using the Pioneer Educators to Create Your Own Philosophy

The Situation

You have volunteered to be part of a team putting together an interactive computer-based tutorial for the professional development of teachers in your school district. The topic of the program is "developing and acting on your personal philosophy of education." You are part of a small group that is assigned to create plans for a short historical overview section of the program. You have been told by the programmers that your part of the program can include only ten photo or graphic images. Each one may be accompanied by fifty or fewer words of text. In response to these limitations, your small group has decided to include photos or drawings that illustrate the ideas of ten key educational pioneers. Each image will be accompanied by a one- or two-sentence description of that person's educational philosophy and some questions designed to help teachers link that philosophy to their own concerns in today's world. Here are six of the descriptions, written by a colleague:

Locke: I emphasized the importance of learning by the senses. Do you agree with me that sensory and hands-on learning is important? If so, how would you include more of these kinds of learning activities?

Pestalozzi: I emphasized the importance of transforming schools into homelike, emotionally secure places. I still think that many children are victims of insecure homes and communities. Do you agree with me? If so, what do you think schools should do?

Froebel: I believed that each child has an inner spiritual core that needs to be nurtured by teachers. Do you think that schools pay sufficient attention to a child's spiritual development?

Spencer: I argued that individual competition brings forth a person's best efforts and leads to social and economic progress. I still think that the best and brightest, the gifted students, are held back by the group. Do you agree with me that schools should be challenging arenas of competitive activities?

Montessori: I believed that children prefer learning in an orderly and structured environment. Today, I fear that some schools lack the structure needed for learning. Do you agree with me? If you do, how would you create more orderly learning situations?

Piaget: I believed that children learn by encounters with their environments and that classrooms should be rich in materials that stimulate these learning situations. If you agree with me, how would you create these kinds of classrooms?

Thought Questions

1. Do you believe the descriptions prepared by your colleague accurately capture the essence of each pioneer's view? Would you change any elements of the descriptions? Are there any further questions you believe teachers should ponder, based on these descriptions?
2. Create similar descriptions and questions for four other pioneers described in this chapter: Comenius, Rousseau, Dewey, and Illich.
3. How would you answer each of the questions posed in the above descriptions?
4. Describe photos or images that you think would effectively illustrate each of the descriptions of a pioneering philosophy.

While the pioneer educators constructed their educational philosophies by using and reinterpreting the work of their predecessors, we also can see that they created their philosophies by challenging inherited concepts. For example, Froebel, influenced by idealism, challenged empiricism by looking into the spiritual nature of children. Dewey challenged Spencer's ethic of individual competition by encouraging group solidarity and collaboration. Initially, Montessori challenged traditional views that limited the education of children who had mental handicaps, and then she elaborated her findings into a general philosophy of education. Illich's proposal to deschool society ranks among the most revolutionary attempts to change education and society.

As you proceed to develop your own philosophy of education, consider this legacy of the pioneer educators. Do you find their ideas valuable contributions that you wish to continue by incorporating them into your philosophy? Or do you wish to confront them and possibly discard their ideas as you build your philosophy as an educator?

Summing Up

1. The pioneers discussed in this chapter made distinctive contributions to the development of education in their own countries and throughout the world.

2. In challenging the dogma of child depravity, Comenius, Locke, and Rousseau developed a method of education based on children's natural growth and goodness.

3. Pestalozzi developed teaching methods that used objects in children's immediate environments. Froebel's theory was the basis of the kindergarten. Both Pestalozzi and Froebel liberated early childhood education by encouraging teachers to be sensitive to children's interests and needs.

4. Spencer's development of a sociology of education was a pioneering effort to relate the school to society. His identification of social activities contributed to curriculum development.

5. Dewey's pioneering work at the University of Chicago Laboratory School stimulated progressive educational reform. Montessori's prepared environment is currently popular in early childhood education.

6. Piaget's developmental psychology illuminated thinking on children's cognitive operations.

7. Illich's deschooling theory is a radical departure from existing approaches to reforming schooling.

Key Terms

child depravity theory *(105)*

naturalistic educators *(105)*

empiricism *(110)*

induction *(110)*

scientific method *(110)*

object lesson *(114)*

curriculum correlation *(116)*

Social Darwinism *(120)*

utilitarian education *(120)*

Montessori schools *(126)*

sensorimotor stage *(127)*

preoperational stage *(127)*

concrete operations stage *(127)*

formal operations stage *(127)*

deschooling *(128)*

Discussion Questions

1. How would you define an educational pioneer? Whom would you include in a chapter about educational pioneers?

2. In your personal philosophy of education, how do you define knowledge, education, and schooling? How do your conceptions agree with or differ from those of the pioneer educators in this chapter?

3. Of the educators discussed in this chapter, whose ideas are most relevant to you as a prospective teacher? Whose are least relevant? Why?

4. Identify a current educational trend such as whole-language learning, collaborative learning, constructivism, or portfolio assessment. How might the educators discussed in this chapter react to it?

Suggested Projects for Professional Development

1. Visit a kindergarten, and record your observations. Did you find any evidence of Froebel's method?

2. Visit a Montessori school, and record your observations. What evidence did you find of Montessori's method?

3. Keep a newspaper clippings file and a journal of news telecasts on the social and educational issues being debated in Congress. Do you find any evidence of Spencer's arguments on either Social Darwinism or Dewey's views on democratic education?

4. Develop and present a demonstration of Pestalozzi's object lesson.

5. Survey the bulletin boards in your college or university. Note any examples of advertisements for what Illich called "drill training" or "liberal education."

6. In your fieldwork or classroom observation, see if you find any evidence of the methods devised by the pioneers discussed in this chapter. Discuss your findings with the class.

7. Choose one of the pioneer educators. Prepare some lesson planning notes describing how you would teach an activity or subject according to that educator's principles of teaching and learning.

Suggested Readings and Resources

Internet Resources

Dewey: Information about John Dewey can be found with a general net search using his name. For examples of educational strategies based on Dewey's philosophy, begin the search at the federal government's educational site, **www.ed.gov.**

History of Education and Educational Biographies. The history of education since the 1700s is chronicled on a web site at the University of Nijmegen, The Netherlands. The site features a collection of links to papers, bibliographies, and biographies of noted educators and the home pages of research organizations: **www.socsci.kun.nl/ped/whp/histeduc.**

Montessori: For information about Maria Montessori and educational practices based on her philosophy, search the home page of the Montessori Foundation at its journal, *Tomorrow's Child*.

Piaget: For information on Piaget's educational ideas, see the Jean Piaget Society's Web page at **www.vanbc.wimsey.com/chrisl/JPS/JPS.html.**

Videos

Bridge to Adulthood: A Montessori Middle School Model. VHS, 21 minutes (1988). Insight Media, 2162 Broadway, P.O. Box 621, New York, NY 10024-0621. Phone: 212-721-6316. *Provides scenes from two Montessori middle schools.*

Imagine a School: Montessori for Elementary-Age Children. VHS, 13 minutes (1988). Insight Media, 2162 Broadway, P.O. Box 621, New York, NY 10024-0621. Phone: 212-721-6316. *Provides scenes from Montessori elementary schools.*

The New Educators. VHS, 22 minutes (1988). Insight Media, 2162 Broadway, P.O. Box 621, New York, NY 10024-0621. Phone: 212-721-6316. *Examines the life and work of such pioneer educators as Locke, Rousseau, Froebel, and others.*

Nurturing the Love of Learning: The Montessori Method. VHS, 9 minutes (1994). Insight Media, 2162 Broadway, P.O. Box 621, New York, NY 10024-0621. Phone: 212-721-6316. *Introduces the Montessori method by showing classroom organization.*

Johann Pestalozzi: The First of the New Educators. VHS, 20 minutes (1988). Insight Media, 2162 Broadway, P.O. Box 621, New York, NY 10024-0621. Phone: 212-721-6316. *Discusses Pestalozzi's career and contributions.*

Publications

Bloom, Allan. *Emile or On Education.* New York: Basic Books, 1979. *Bloom's annotated edition of Rousseau's Emile is well translated and includes an introductory essay.*

Brosterman, Norman. *Inventing Kindergarten.* New York: Harry N. Abrams, 1997. *Brosterman's beautifully illustrated book examines Froebel's kindergarten. The images provide excellent illustrations of kindergarten gifts, occupations, and activities in historical perspective.*

Eldridge, Michael. *Transforming Experience: John Dewey's Cultural Instrumentalism.* Nashville, TN: Vanderbilt University Press, 1998. *Eldridge examines Dewey's thought as a philosophy for dealing with life's problems.*

Froebel, Frederich. *The Education of Man.* Translated by W. N. Hailman. New York: Appleton, 1896. *Hailman's translation of Froebel's classic work remains the most useful version of the kindergarten founder's philosophy.*

Gutek, Gerald L. *Historical and Philosophical Foundations of Education: A Biographical Introduction.* Columbus, Ohio: Merrill, 1997. *Placing each educator in historical and cultural context, Gutek examines the educational ideas of Plato, Quintilian, Aquinas, Calvin, Rousseau, Pestalozzi, Froebel, Spencer, Montessori, Addams, Dewey, Du Bois, Gandhi, and Mao.*

Lillard, Paula. *Montessori: A Modern Approach.* New York: Schocken, 1973. *Lillard presents an appraisal of Montessori and her educational method.*

Shapiro, Michael S. *Child's Garden: The Kindergarten Movement from Froebel to Dewey.* University Park: University of Pennsylvania Press, 1983. *An excellently written and carefully researched history of the kindergarten movement in the United States, this book is highly recommended for its treatment of leaders and ideas in early childhood education.*

Smith, L. Glenn, and Joan K. Smith. *Lives in Education: A Narrative of People and Ideas.* New York: Lawrence Erlbaum, 1995. *This book features the biographies and contributions of important American and world educators.*

Tanner, Laurel N. *Dewey's Laboratory School: Lessons for Today.* New York: Teachers College Press, 1997. *Tanner carefully examines the origins of Dewey's curriculum and methods at the University of Chicago Laboratory School and provides ideas of how such practices can be used in today's schools.*

Westbrook, Robert B. *John Dewey and American Democracy.* Ithaca, N.Y.: Cornell University Press, 1991. *Presents a definitive examination of the intellectual origins of John Dewey's thought.*

CHAPTER FIVE

Historical Development of American Education

Chapter 5 traces the evolution of American educational institutions and identifies formative contributions of individuals and groups to American education. The chapter examines (1) the colonial period, when European educational ideas and institutions were transported to America; (2) the creation of a uniquely American educational system during the revolutionary and early national eras; (3) the diffusion of universal education; (4) the development of secondary education from the Latin grammar school, through the academy, to today's comprehensive high school; (5) the development of institutions of higher learning; (6) the education of culturally diverse populations; and (7) trends, such as the development of educational technology, in the recent history of American education. As you read Chapter 5, consider the following questions:

- How did the American environment transform European educational ideas and institutions?

- How did American democratic ideas contribute to public schooling in the United States?

- How does the American educational ladder differ from the European dual system?

- How did the United States become a culturally diverse society?

- How has American education become more inclusive over time?

- What are the recent trends in the history of American education?

The Colonial Period

Many ethnic groups among colonists

The European colonists who settled in North America in the seventeenth and eighteenth centuries represented a variety of ethnic and language backgrounds. The major settlements were established by the French in Canada and the Mississippi Valley; by the Spanish in Mexico, Florida, and the Southwest; by the Dutch in New Netherlands, now New York State; and by the English in the original thirteen colonies that would form the United States after the War of Independence.[1] Other groups of European colonists included the Scots-Irish, German, Scots, Irish, Swedish, and Jewish groups. The English, who defeated the Dutch and the French, had the greatest impact on colonial politics, society, culture, and education.

Effect on Native Americans

The colonization of North America resulted in complex cultural interchanges and often violent encounters between the Europeans and the indigenous peoples. Especially along the Atlantic coast, the Native Americans were decimated by diseases introduced by Europeans, such as smallpox. The English generally considered the Native Americans as savages who were to be dispossessed of their lands and pushed westward in forced resettlement.[2]

Enslaved Africans

Although slavery was practiced throughout the colonies, the largest population of enslaved Africans was located in the southern colonies. The enslaved Africans were seized by force and brutally transported in slave ships to North America to work on the southern plantations. Over time, the African heritage became the genesis of African American culture.

The colonists recreated the socioeconomic class–based **dual-track system** with which they were familiar in Europe. For the lower classes the primary-school curriculum included reading, writing, arithmetic, and religious indoctrination. The language of instruction was the local vernacular — for example, English in English-speaking areas and Dutch in New Amsterdam. Meanwhile, upper-class boys attended the Latin grammar school, a preparatory school that taught the Latin and Greek languages and literature required for admission to colonial colleges. Although girls could attend primary schools as well as dame schools (private schools taught by women), they rarely attended Latin grammar schools during the colonial period. Secondary and higher education was primarily reserved for boys.

The various colonies handled education matters differently. In New England, the governing bodies exerted general authority over education and directly supported schools. In the Middle Atlantic colonies, religious diversity caused the various churches to conduct their own schools. The southern colonies often treated education as a private responsibility; wealthy parents hired tutors or sent their children to private schools.

New England Colonies

The New England colonies of Massachusetts, Connecticut, and New Hampshire were a crucible for the development of American educational ideas and institutions. In fact, Massachusetts enacted the first formal education laws in British North America.

Puritan Schools

The Puritans, who colonized Massachusetts, believed that educated persons who knew God's commandments, as preached by Puritan ministers, could resist the

---

[1]For example, see Roger Magnuson, *Education in New France* (Montreal: McGill-Queens University Press, 1992).

[2]Ronald Takaki, *A Different Mirror: A History of Multicultural America* (Boston: Little, Brown, 1993), pp. 21–24. See also Gregory H. Nobles, *American Frontiers: Cultural Encounters and Continental Conquest* (New York: Hill and Wang, 1997).

In the Colonial period, hornbooks were used by children to learn the alphabet, syllables, and words. *(© The Bettman Archive)*

devil's temptations. Closely tied to the church, schools emphasized obedience to what was preached as divine law.

Schools for economic and social utility

Puritanism also gave education a Calvinist economic rationale. According to the Puritan work ethic, good Puritans, in addition to reading their Bibles, were to be industrious and thrifty businessmen, farmers, and workers. To shape such enterprising individuals, schools stressed values of punctuality, honesty, and hard work. This tendency to relate school to economic productivity remains a strong influence on American education.

Child seen as sinful

Child Depravity.   The Puritan concept of child nature, derived from Calvinist theology, shaped colonial New England's child-rearing and educational beliefs. Children were regarded as depraved or, at least, inclined to evil. Children's play was seen as idleness and children's talk as gibberish. Following on the adage "Spare the rod and spoil the child," Puritan teachers used firm discipline and often corporal punishment. The stories children heard and the books they read stressed an unremitting need for prayer and repentance. To learn the alphabet's first letter, for example, children recited the rhyme "In Adam's fall/we sinned all."[3] When properly educated, childish ways would yield to disciplined behavior, the civility marking the elect. The good child would act like a miniature adult.[4] The Puritan view of children

---

[3]Stanford Fleming, *Children and Puritanism: The Place of Children in the Life and Thought of New England Churches* (New Haven, Conn.: Yale University Press, 1933).

[4]Ross W. Beale, Jr., "In Search of the Historical Child: Miniature Adulthood and Youth in Colonial New England," in N. Ray Hiner and Joseph M. Hawes, eds., *Growing Up in America: Children in Historical Perspective* (Urbana: University of Illinois Press, 1985), pp. 7–24.

dramatically contrasts to the attitudes of Comenius, Rousseau, Pestalozzi, and other educational pioneers discussed in Chapter 4.

"Old Deluder Satan." Even in the first years of settlement in Massachusetts, the Puritans began to establish schools. In 1642, the Massachusetts General Court passed a law making parents and guardians responsible for children in their care being able to read and understand the principles of religion and the commonwealth's laws. In 1647, the General Court enacted the "Old Deluder Satan" Act, a law intended to outwit Satan, who, the Puritans believed, tricked ignorant people into sinning. The law required every town of fifty or more families to appoint a reading and writing teacher. Towns of one hundred or more families were to employ a Latin teacher to prepare young men to enter Harvard College.[5] The New England colonists recreated the dual-track system, mentioned earlier. (See Overview 5.1 for significant events in American Education.)

A teacher for every town

The three Rs, plus religion

The Town School. The New England **town school** was a locally controlled institution attended by both boys and girls, ranging in age from six to thirteen or fourteen. Attendance was irregular, depending on weather conditions and the need for children to work on family farms. The school's curriculum included reading, writing, arithmetic, catechism, and religious hymns. Children learned the alphabet, syllables, words, and sentences by memorizing the **hornbook**, a sheet of parchment covered by transparent material made by flattening cattle horns. The older children read the *New England Primer*, which included religious materials such as the Westminster catechism, the Ten Commandments, the Lord's Prayer, and the Apostle's Creed. Arithmetic was primarily counting, adding, and subtracting.

Atmosphere of the town school

The New England town school was often a simple log structure, dominated by the teacher's pulpitlike desk at the front of the single room. Sitting on wooden benches, pupils memorized their assignments until called before the schoolmaster to recite. The teachers were men, some of whom earned their living in this way while preparing for the ministry. Others took the job to repay the money they owed for their voyage to North America. Some, unfortunately, were incompetents who dominated their pupils by using corporal punishment.

The Latin Grammar School. The sons of the upper classes attended the **Latin grammar school,** which prepared them for college entry. These boys generally had learned to read and write English from private tutors. Entering the Latin grammar school at age eight, the student would complete his studies at fifteen or sixteen.[6] He studied such Latin authors as Cicero, Terence, Caesar, Livy, Vergil, and Horace. More advanced students studied such Greek authors as Isocrates, Hesiod, and Homer. Little attention was given to mathematics, science, or modern languages. The Latin masters who taught in these schools held college degrees and enjoyed higher social status than elementary teachers. As historian Samuel Morrison points out, the Latin grammar school was one of colonial America's closest links to European education, resembling classical humanist schools of the Renaissance.[7]

Classics for upper-class boys

Harvard College

After completing the Latin grammar school, the New England upper-class young man sought admission to Harvard College, established in 1636. Harvard was

---

[5]Nathaniel Schurtleff, ed., *Records of the Governor and Company of the Massachusetts Bay in New England*, vol. 2 (Boston: Order of the Legislature, 1853).
[6]Robert Middlekauff, *Ancients and Axioms: Secondary Education in Eighteenth-Century New England* (New Haven, Conn.: Yale University Press, 1963).
[7]Samuel E. Morrison, *The Intellectual Life of Colonial New England* (New York: New York University Press, 1956).

founded on the Puritan belief that future ministers and other leaders needed a sound classical and theological education. Students had to demonstrate competency in Latin and Greek to be admitted to Harvard, where the curriculum consisted of grammar, logic, rhetoric, arithmetic, geometry, astronomy, ethics, metaphysics, and natural science. In addition, Hebrew, Greek, and ancient history were offered for their usefulness in studying the Bible and other religious works.

Middle Atlantic Colonies

Diverse cultures

The Middle Atlantic colonies — New York, New Jersey, Delaware, and Pennsylvania — differed from New England. Whereas New England had a common language and religion, the Middle Atlantic colonies were characterized by linguistic, religious, and cultural pluralism. Although the majority was English-speaking, there were Dutch in New York, Swedes in Delaware, and Germans in Pennsylvania. In addition to different languages, there was religious diversity. The Dutch, members of the Dutch Reformed Church, the Society of Friends, or Quakers, were located in Pennsylvania, and Germans might be Lutherans or members of small denominations such as the Moravians. There were also Baptists, Roman Catholics, and a small Jewish population. This cultural diversity influenced schooling. Whereas New England created town schools, the churches in the Middle Atlantic colonies established parochial schools.

New York.   In New York, initially a Dutch colony, the Dutch Reformed Church continued to operate schools after the English seized New Netherlands. Dutch parochial schools taught reading, writing, and religion.[8] With English rule, the Church of England established some charity and missionary schools.

Private schools

In New York City, a commercial port, private for-profit schools offered navigation, surveying, bookkeeping, Spanish, French, and geography on a fee-paying basis to students. For-profit private schools also operated in other colonies.

Quaker schools

Pennsylvania.   Pennsylvania, a proprietary colony founded by William Penn, became a haven for the Society of Friends, or Quakers, a religious denomination. As conscientious objectors, Quakers refused to support war efforts or serve in the military. Quaker schools were open to all children, including blacks and Native Americans.[9] (Philadelphia had a small African American community, and some Native Americans remained in the colony.) Quaker schools taught the reading, writing, arithmetic, and religion found in other colonial primary schools but were unique in including vocational training, crafts, and agriculture.[10] Still another difference was that Quaker teachers, rejecting the concept of child depravity, did not use corporal punishment.

Southern Colonies

The southern colonies — Maryland, Virginia, the Carolinas, and Georgia — had still another pattern of education. Except for some flourishing cities in tidewater

---

[8]William H. Kilpatrick, *The Dutch Schools of New Netherlands and Colonial New York* (Washington, D.C.: U.S. Government Printing Office, 1912).
[9]James D. Hendricks, "Be Still and Know: Quaker Silence and Dissenting Educational Ideals, 1740–1812," *Journal of the Midwest History of Education Society* (Annual Proceedings, 1975), pp. 14–40.
[10]Thomas Woody, *Early Quaker Education in Pennsylvania* (New York: Teachers College Press, Columbia University, 1920).

areas, such as Charleston and Williamsburg, the southern population was generally more dispersed than in New England or the Middle Atlantic colonies. In rural areas it was difficult to bring children together at a single location to attend school. Moreover, culture, economics, and politics in the South were profoundly shaped by the use of enslaved Africans as the plantation labor force.[11] Overall, the economic, social, and geographic patterns in the southern colonies retarded the development of school systems.

Private tutors

Because the population was so spread out, the children of privileged white plantation owners were often taught by private tutors who lived in the manor house. Some wealthy families also sent their children to private schools sponsored by the Church of England.[12] By the late colonial period, boarding schools were established, usually in towns such as Williamsburg or Charleston.

Class bias in schooling

Enslaved Africans were trained to be agricultural workers, field hands, craftspeople, or domestic servants, but generally were forbidden to learn reading or writing. Some notable exceptions learned to read secretly. For the poor, non-slave-holding whites, who tilled the infertile back country or the mountainous areas, formal education was very limited. The ideology of white supremacy, used to convince the children of subsistence farmers of their cultural and racial superiority to the enslaved Africans, became a basis for racism.

Colonial Education: A Summary View

Parallels among regions

Despite regional variations, certain educational parallels existed among New England, the Middle Atlantic colonies, and the South. All three were British colonial possessions, and, despite language and religious differences, inherited the Western European educational tradition. Religious belief shaped morality, and the family was a strong force in shaping opinions, values, and skills.[13]

Gender discrimination

In all three regions, educational opportunities were limited by sex. Both girls and boys attended primary schools, but Latin grammar schools and colleges were restricted to boys and men. Since women were not allowed to be ministers or lawyers, there was no need, according to the educational philosophy of the time, for them to follow the curriculum of a Latin grammar school or college. Instead of Greek and Latin, they were trained in the basics (reading and writing) needed to fulfill their family and religious responsibilities. There was also a general opinion, especially among the men who controlled educational institutions, that women were intellectually incapable of higher studies.

Tracking by social class

In their division of schooling into two tracks, colonial schools reflected European class biases. Primary schools, intended for lower-class children, provided basic literacy but discouraged upward social mobility. With some exceptions, pupils who completed primary schools did not advance to Latin grammar schools and colonial colleges. The sons of the upper classes, in contrast, attended the preparatory Latin grammar schools and, if successful, entered college. During the nineteenth century, frontier egalitarianism, political democratization, and economic change would erode these European-based educational structures, creating the American system of universal, public education.

---

[11]For the origins and impact of slavery in the South, see Takaki, *A Different Mirror*, pp. 31–76.
[12]Jane Turner Censer, *North Carolina Planters and Their Children, 1800–1860* (Baton Rouge: Louisiana State University Press, 1984).
[13]Lawrence A. Cremin, *American Education: The Colonial Experience, 1607–1783* (New York: Harper and Row, 1970).

The Early National Period

The American Revolution of 1776 ended British rule in the thirteen colonies. Although the inherited vernacular and denominational elementary schools and Latin grammar schools continued for some time, the new republic's leaders sought to devise educational patterns appropriate to the self-governing citizens of the United States.

Northwest ordinance

The earliest federal educational legislation was incorporated in the Northwest Ordinance of 1785, which required that a section of each thirty-six-square-mile township be used for education. The Northwest Ordinance established the precedent for financing education through **land grants** in the nineteenth century.

Tradition of local control

Although the U.S. Constitution made no mention of education, the Tenth Amendment's "reserved powers" clause (which reserved to the states all powers not specifically delegated to the federal government or prohibited to the states by the Constitution) left responsibility for education with the individual states. The New England tradition of local school control and general opposition to centralized political power contributed to a state rather than a national school system in the United States.

New educational ideas for the new nation

During the early national period, several political and intellectual leaders designed educational proposals for the emergent republic. These plans generally argued that education should prepare people for republican citizenship; (2) should include the utilitarian and scientific emphases to aid in developing the nation's vast expanses of frontier land and abundant natural resources; and (3) should be divested of European cultural residues and create a uniquely American culture.[14] These general goals are evident in the proposals of Benjamin Franklin, Thomas Jefferson, and Noah Webster.

Franklin: The Academy

Franklin's academy

Benjamin Franklin (1706–1790), who founded an **academy,** a private secondary school, described its educational rationale in his "Proposals Relating to the Education of Youth in Pennsylvania."[15] His academy's utilitarian curriculum was notably different from the traditional Latin grammar school. English grammar, composition, rhetoric, and public speaking replaced Latin and Greek as the chief language studies. Students could also choose a second language based on their future careers. For example, prospective clergy could choose Latin and Greek, and those planning on commercial careers could elect French, Spanish, or German. Mathematics was taught for its practical use in bookkeeping, surveying, and engineering rather than as an abstract subject. History and biography supplied ethical study in which students examined the moral decisions made by famous historical personages.

Emphasis on science and practical skills

Prophetically, Franklin recognized the future importance of science, invention, and technology. His curriculum also incorporated utilitarian skills that schools had traditionally ignored, such as carpentry, shipbuilding, engraving, printing, carpentry, and farming.[16]

---

[14]Jacqueline S. Reinier, *From Virtue to Character: American Childhood, 1775–1850* (New York: Twayne of Macmillan, 1996), p. xi.

[15]Esmond Wright, ed., *Benjamin Franklin: His Life As He Wrote It* (Cambridge, Mass.: Harvard University Press, 1990); and Francis Jennings, *Benjamin Franklin: Politician* (New York: W.W. Norton, 1996).

[16]Bernard Cohen, *Benjamin Franklin's Science* (Cambridge, Mass.: Harvard University Press, 1990); and W. J. Rorabaugh, *The Craft Apprentice: From Franklin to the Machine Age in America* (New York: Oxford University Press, 1986).

Expansion of academics

By the mid-nineteenth century, many academies similar to Franklin's had been established. The late nineteenth and early twentieth centuries saw the emergence of high schools and junior high or middle schools that incorporated Franklin's utilitarianism and vocationalism.

Jefferson: Education for Citizenship

Education for citizenship

Thomas Jefferson's (1743–1826) educational philosophy was expressed in his "Bill for the More General Diffusion of Knowledge," which was introduced in the Virginia legislature in 1779. Education's major purpose, Jefferson stated, was to promote a democratic society of literate and well-informed citizens. Committed to separation of church and state, Jefferson believed that the state, not the churches, should exercise the primary educational role. State-sponsored schools would be funded by public taxes.[17]

Jefferson's plan

Jefferson's bill, though not passed, is important for the issues that it sought to resolve in the new nation. For example, it suggested establishing public schools and attempted to resolve conflicts between equity and excellence. It would have subdivided Virginia's counties into wards. Excluding enslaved children, the bill stipulated that free children, both girls and boys, could attend an elementary school in each ward. Here they would study reading, writing, arithmetic, and history. Tuition would be free for the first three years. Jefferson's proposal also would have established twenty grammar schools, located throughout the state, to provide secondary education to boys. In these grammar schools, students would study Latin, Greek, English, geography, and higher mathematics.

Scholarships based on merit

Jefferson's bill anticipated the idea of academic merit scholarships. In each ward school, the most academically able male student who could not afford tuition would receive a scholarship to continue his education at a grammar school. The ten scholarship students of highest achievement would receive additional support to attend the College of William and Mary.

Webster: Schoolmaster of the Republic

Noah Webster (1758–1843) was one of the early republic's leading cultural nationalists.[18] When the Constitution was ratified in 1789, Webster argued that the United States should have its own "language as well as government." The language of Great Britain, he reasoned, "should no longer be our standard; for the taste of her writers is already completed, and her language on the decline."[19] Realizing that a distinctive national language and literature built a sense of national identity, Webster sought to create an American version of the English language.

Rejection of British standards

Learning American culture through language

Webster believed that as children learned Americanized English they would acquire a uniquely American cultural identity. The American version of English that Webster proposed would have to be taught deliberately and systematically to children in the nation's schools. Since teaching would be shaped by textbooks, Webster spent his life writing spelling and reading books. His *Grammatical Institute of the En-*

Webster's texts

---

[17]Thomas Jefferson, "A Bill for the More General Diffusion of Knowledge," in P.L. Ford, ed., *The Writings of Thomas Jefferson*, vol. 2 (New York: Putnam, 1893), p. 211. See also Robert H. Heslep, *Thomas Jefferson and Education* (New York: Random House, 1969).
[18]Harry R. Warfel, *Noah Webster: Schoolmaster to America* (New York: Octagon, 1936); and Ervin C. Shoemaker, *Noah Webster: Pioneer of Learning* (New York: Columbia University Press, 1936).
[19]Noah Webster, *Dissertations on the English Language* (Boston: Isaiah Thomas, 1789).

TAKING ISSUE

Schools and American Culture

A long-standing issue in American education is the degree to which public schools should transmit a distinctively American culture. Some educators believe that all public schools should teach certain key cultural concepts and values. Others contend that schools should promote multi-culturalism and a respect for diversity.

> **QUESTION** Should American public education transmit a distinctively American culture? In other words, should there be a specific cultural core that schools deliberately convey?

Arguments PRO

1 As American leaders since Thomas Jefferson have recognized, a primary purpose of schooling is to educate responsible citizens. Without a basic knowledge of the ideas and values central to our national life, we could not function as citizens.

2 Because the United States has always been a nation of immigrants, it needs a core culture to bind diverse groups together. Noah Webster recognized this point, and it is even more important today. Without a shared culture to unite our different peoples and cultures, our society is in danger of splintering.

3 Because schools bring diverse people together, they can inculcate the basic values of our common culture. By doing so, schools can help solve some of the problems that plague us, including such acknowledged evils as violence and drug abuse.

4 Given the intense economic competition among countries, it is vital that American citizens share certain common purposes. Schools can promote shared goals by transmitting the values and concepts unique to American culture.

Arguments CON

1 From the earliest days of American history, the nation has been characterized by cultural pluralism. Beyond a basic knowledge of how the government works, there is no one set of ideas or values that makes a responsible American citizen.

2 The strength of American society has always stemmed from the creative diversity of its people, not from a core culture that makes everyone think alike. To find real unity, we need to appreciate our diversity and respect what every group brings to American life.

3 If schools try to impose a single set of values, they alienate many students. Instead, schools should help students understand the many different types of values in our society.

4 What the United States needs for success on the world scene is a greater knowledge and appreciation of foreign cultures. Schools should therefore focus on multiculturalism and internationalism, not on a rigidly defined Americanism.

glish Language was published in 1783. The first part, separately published as the *American Spelling Book*, became one of the most popular textbooks in the United States in the nineteenth century. Going through many editions, it sold some 15 million copies by 1837. Webster's greatest work, however, was his *American Dictionary*, completed in 1825 after twenty-five years of intensive research.[20]

---

[20]Henry Steel Commager, ed., *Noah Webster's American Spelling Book* (New York: Teachers College Press, 1962); and Richard M. Rollins, "Words as Social Control: Noah Webster and the Creation of *The American Dictionary,*" *American Quarterly* (Fall 1976), pp. 415–430.

Webster's influence on Americanization

Called the "schoolmaster of the republic," Noah Webster helped to create a sense of American language, identity, and nationality. At the same time he encouraged a monolithic American cultural identity. In future years, immigrants were "Americanized" by learning what had become the standard form of American English. Today, educational efforts for multiculturalism and bilingualism seek to recognize American diversity and mitigate the excesses of cultural nationalism.

The Movement Toward Public Schooling

Sunday schools

Before the movement to public schooling began, several efforts were made to develop nonpublic voluntary alternatives to tax-supported education. Chief among them were the Sunday and monitorial schools. In the early nineteenth century, many children worked in the factories of the industrializing Northeast. To provide a minimal basic education, Sunday schools were opened in larger cities, such as New York and Philadelphia. Meeting on the one day of the week when factories were closed, Sunday schools taught writing, reading, arithmetic, and religion to the children who attended.

Students as assistant teachers

Another voluntary approach to education was provided by monitorialism, a method of instruction that was briefly popular in the early nineteenth century. The **monitorial method** used monitors, older and more experienced pupils trained by a master teacher, to assist in teaching classes, taking attendance, and maintaining order.[21] For example, the master teacher would train monitors in a particular skill, such as adding single-digit numbers. These monitors would then teach that skill to groups of students. Designed to teach masses of students in basic skills, monitorial schools were supported by private philanthropists who wanted to have a large system of education but at very little cost.

Rise and fall of monitorial schools

Initially, monitorial schools were popular in large eastern cities such as New York and Philadelphia. For example, more than 600,000 children attended the monitorial schools conducted by the New York Free School Society.[22] Monitorial schools were replaced by common schools in the 1840s when people realized that they could provide only rudimentary education.

The Common School

A school for all classes

The common school movement of the first half of the nineteenth century is highly significant in American education because it won popular support for publicly financed elementary education. The **common school**, today's public school, may be defined as an elementary educational institution that offered a basic curriculum of reading, writing, and arithmetic. It was called a "common" school because it was open to children of all social and economic classes. Historically, however, enslaved African children in the South did not attend until the Civil War ended slavery.

Differences among regions

Because the Tenth Amendment of the U.S. Constitution reserved education to the individual states, the United States did not create a national school system as did other countries such as France and Japan. Thus the patterns by which common schools were established differed from state to state and even within a given state.

---

[21]William R. Johnson, "Chanting Choristes": Simultaneous Recitation in Baltimore's Nineteenth-Century Primary Schools," *History of Education Quarterly*, 34 (Spring 1994), pp. 1–23.
[22]John Reigart, *The Lancasterian System of Instruction in the Schools of New York City* (New York: Teachers College Press, Columbia University, 1916).

Especially on the western frontier, where many small school districts were created, resources and support for schooling varied from one district to another.

Growth of the common school

The common school movement gained momentum between 1820 and 1850. Common schools were first established in the New England states, where Massachusetts and then Connecticut were leading examples. In 1826 Massachusetts passed a law that required every town to elect a school committee responsible for all the schools in the town. This began the policy of organizing public schools into a school system under a single authority. Ten years later, in 1836, Massachusetts established the first state board of education. Connecticut then followed its neighbor's example.[23] Other northern states generally adopted New England's common school model. As the frontier expanded westward and new states were admitted to the Union, they, too, established a common or public elementary school system. In the South, however, the establishment of common schools was generally delayed until after the Civil War.

Three stages of legislation

Although there were variations from state to state, common schools were usually established in three legislative stages: *permissive, encouraging,* and *compulsory.* In the permissive stage, the state legislature permitted local school districts to organize subject to approval by voters in the district. In the second stage, the state legislature deliberately encouraged but did not compel establishment of school districts, election of school boards, and raising of tax revenues for school support. Finally, in the third stage, the state compelled the establishment of school districts, election of school boards, and taxation for common schools. In its school code, the state also might specify a minimum curriculum and standards for school construction, lighting, and maintenance. Since the revenue generated from taxes varied from one school district to another, educational resources and support were uneven. For a time many districts also charged a tuition payment per child, called a rate bill.

The common schools laid the foundation of the American public school system. Later in the nineteenth century, the public high school would complete the educational ladder that prepared students to enter state colleges and universities. Perhaps the most prominent American educator then in the common school movement was Horace Mann.

Mann: The Struggle for Public Schools

Horace Mann (1796–1859) was a steadfast proponent of common schools. When the Massachusetts legislature established a state board of education in 1837, Mann was appointed its secretary. His *Annual Reports* contained his philosophy of education and opinion on educational issues. As editor of the *Common School Journal,* moreover, Mann won national support for public schools.[24] (For Mann's appointment and other events in American education, see Overview 5.1)

Building support for common schools

Using his political acumen, Mann skillfully mobilized support for public education. First, he had to convince taxpayers that it was in their self-interest to support public schools. To win support from the business community, Mann developed the stewardship theory. He argued that wealthy people had a special responsibility in providing public education. Those who had prospered, Mann asserted, were the guardians or stewards of wealth. In addition, their support of public education

---

[23]Lawrence A. Cremin, *The American Common School: A Historical Conception* (New York: Teachers College Press, 1951).
[24]Jonathan Messerli, *Horace Mann: A Biography* (New York: Knopf, 1972).

OVERVIEW 5.1   Significant Events in the History of American Education

Major Political Events	Significant Educational Events
1630 Settlement of Massachusetts Bay Colony	1636 Harvard College founded, first English-speaking college in Western Hemisphere
	1642 First education law enacted in Massachusetts
	1647 Old Deluder Satan Act enacted in Massachusetts, requiring establishment of schools
	1751 Benjamin Franklin's Academy established in Philadelphia
1775–1783 American Revolution	1783 Noah Webster's *American Spelling Book* published
1788 U.S. Constitution ratified	1785 Northwest Ordinance, first national education law, enacted
	1821 First public high school in the United States opened in Boston
	Emma Willard's Female Seminary, first school of higher education for women, established in Troy, New York
	1823 First private normal school in the United States opened in Concord, Vermont
1824 Bureau of Indian Affairs established	1825 Webster's *American Dictionary* completed
	1827 Massachusetts law requiring public high schools passed
1830 Indian Removal Act	1837 Horace Mann appointed to Massachusetts state board of education
1846–1848 Mexican-American War; U.S. acquisition of southwestern territories	1839 First public normal school opened in Lexington, Massachusetts
	1855 First German-language kindergarten in the United States established
1849 Gold Rush to California	1860 First English-language kindergarten in the United States established
1861–1865 Civil War	1862 Morrill Land Grant College Act passed, establishing in each state a college for agricultural and mechanical instruction
	1865 Freedmen's Bureau established
	1872 *Kalamazoo* decision upheld public taxation for high schools
1887 Dawes Act divides tribal lands into individual plots	1881 Tuskegee Institute established by Booker T. Washington
1898 Spanish-American War; U.S. acquisition of Puerto Rico and the Philippines	1892 Committee of Ten established
	1896 *Plessy* v. *Ferguson* decision used to uphold constitutionality of "separate but equal" schools for white and black students
	1909 First junior high school established in Berkeley, California

Major Political Events

1914–1918   World War I

1929   Beginning of the Great Depression

1939–1945   World War II

1950–1953   Korean War

1965–1973   Vietnam War

1990   End of Cold War
1991   Gulf War

Significant Educational Events

1917   Smith-Hughes Act passed, providing money grants for vocational education, home economics, and agricultural subjects

1918   *Cardinal Principles of Secondary Education* published

1919   Progressive Education Association organized

1930s   New Deal programs during the Great Depression provided federal funds for education of the unemployed and for school construction

1944   G.I. Bill passed, providing federal funds for continuing education of veterans

1954   *Brown v. Board of Education of Topeka* decision required racial desegregation of public schools

1957   Soviet Union launched *Sputnik*, leading to criticism and reevaluation of American public education

1958   National Defense Education Act passed, providing federal funds to improve science, math, and modern foreign language instruction and guidance services

1964   Civil Rights Act authorizes federal lawsuits for school desegregation

1965   Elementary and Secondary Education Act passed, providing federal funds to public schools, especially for compensatory education

1968   Bilingual Education Act

1972   Title IX Education Amendment passed, outlawing sex discrimination in schools receiving federal financial assistance

1975   Education for All Handicapped Children (Public Law 94-142) passed

1980   Department of Education established in federal government with cabinet status

1983   Publication and dissemination of *A Nation at Risk* stimulated national movement to reform education

1994   Goals 2000: The Educate America Act outlines national education goals

would create industrious men and women who would obey the law, be diligent in their work, and add to the state's economy. Thus tax support of public education was actually an investment that would yield high dividends in the form of public safety, progress, and prosperity. To the workers and farmers of Massachusetts, Mann argued that the common school would be a great social equalizer, enabling children from lower socioeconomic classes to gain the skills and knowledge to acquire better jobs and upward mobility.

Public schools as vital to democratic society

Mann, like Jefferson, saw a crucial relationship between public schooling and a democratic society. Fearing that illiteracy would lead to mob action, Mann argued that literacy was necessary for citizens to participate intelligently in representative political processes. Like Noah Webster, Mann also believed that public education could create a unique American identity. For him, the United States, a nation of immigrants, differed from the homogeneous western European nations. To develop a unifying common culture, the country needed a common elementary education that would promote a sense of national identity and purpose.[25] Mann took a definite assimilationist stance on public schooling's cultural role.

School taxes

According to Mann, the common, or public, school was to be financed by state and local taxes. The public, which paid for the schools, was to govern them. Following the New England tradition of local control, popularly elected officials would exercise ultimate authority. The common schools were also to be nonsectarian and free of church control.[26]

Normal Schools and the Education of Women

In addition to providing publicly supported elementary education for the majority of American children, the common school movement had two important complementary consequences: (1) it contributed to establishing normal schools as teacher-preparation institutions, and (2) it helped make elementary school teaching an important career path for women.

Rise of normal schools

Normal schools took their name from the French *école normale* on which they were modeled. First established in New England in 1823 and encouraged by Horace Mann, normal schools were two-year institutions that provided courses in history and philosophy of education, methods of teaching, and practice or demonstration teaching for prospective teachers. By the end of the nineteenth century, however, many normal schools had become four-year teacher-education colleges.[27]

Expanding opportunities for women

The establishment of common schools created a demand for trained teachers, and many women were attracted to teaching careers in the expanding elementary school system. The normal schools prepared women for these careers and at the same time provided opportunities for higher education that hitherto had been denied to them. Although salaries were low and conditions demanding, teaching gave middle-class women a rare opportunity for a career outside the home.

Until the Civil War the majority of rural schoolteachers were men. By 1900, however, partly as a result of the growth of normal schools, 71 percent of the rural teachers were women. Among the leaders of this dramatic change in women's roles was Catharine Beecher.

---

[25]Lawrence A. Cremin, ed., *The Republic and the School: Horace Mann on the Education of Free Men* (New York: Teachers College Press, 1957).
[26]Horace Mann, *Lectures and Annual Reports on Education* (Cambridge, Mass.: Cornhill Press, 1867).
[27]For the history of American teacher education, see Jurgen Herbst, *And Sadly Teach: Teacher Education and Professionalization in American Culture* (Madison: University of Wisconsin Press, 1989).

Catharine Beecher: Preparing Women as Teachers

Reform and women's rights

The first half of the nineteenth century was a time of general social reform movements that included public schooling, women's rights, and abolition of slavery. Feminist leaders such as Elizabeth Cady Stanton, Emma Willard, Susan B. Anthony, and Catharine Beecher spoke out for women's educational and political equality.

A key role for women

Catharine Beecher (1800–1878) founded the Hartford Female Seminary in 1828 to prepare women for teaching careers. She also organized and led the American Women's Educational Association. Believing the United States had a moral mission, she also believed that women had a key role to play in the nation's development. Beecher advocated establishing special teacher-education institutions, or seminaries, for women's professional development as teachers.[28] Like normal schools, each seminary would have a demonstration school where future teachers, supervised by experienced master teachers, did practice teaching. Professionally educated women, Beecher reasoned, could contribute to national development by bringing literacy, civility, and morality to the American frontier, where there was an acute need for prepared teachers to staff the many one-room schools.[29]

The One-Room School

The local school district with its one-room school was almost a direct democracy in which an elected school board set the tax rate and hired and supervised the teacher.[30] Teacher certification was simple but chaotic as each board issued its own certificates to its teachers; however, in many cases these were not recognized in other districts. Today's more uniform state certification is a step toward greater professionalization for teachers.

The typical schoolhouse

On the western frontier, the one-room log school was often the first community building constructed.[31] By the 1870s, wood frame schoolhouses, painted white or red, replaced the crude log structures. These improved buildings, heated by wood-burning stoves, had slate blackboards and cloakrooms. At the front of the room was the raised teacher's desk. Many classrooms had large double desks which seated two pupils. Later, these were often replaced with single desks, each with a desktop attached to its back. The single desks had to be arranged in straight rows, one behind the other, so that a seat was behind each desktop.[32]

Basic curriculum

The pupils, who ranged in age from five to seventeen, studied a basic curriculum of reading, writing, grammar, spelling, arithmetic, history, geography, and hygiene. Teachers used the recitation method in which each pupil stood and recited a previously assigned lesson. The values stressed were punctuality, honesty, and hard work. The rural one-room schoolteachers, expected to be disciplinarians as well as instructors, had "to be their own janitors, record keepers, and school administrators."[33]

---

[28]Barbara M. Cross, ed., *The Educated Woman in America: Selected Writings of Catharine Beecher, Margaret Fuller, and M. Carey Thomas* (New York: Teachers College Press, Columbia University, 1965), pp. 73–75.

[29]Polly Welts Kaufman, *Women Teachers on the Frontier* (New Haven, Conn.: Yale University Press, 1984).

[30]For the one-room country school, see Andrew Gulliford, *America's Country Schools* (Washington, D.C.: Preservation Press, 1984); and Wayne E. Fuller, *The Old Country School: The Story of Rural Education in the Middle West* (Chicago: University of Chicago Press, 1982).

[31]Wayne E. Fuller, *One-Room Schools of the Middle West: An Illustrated History* (University Press of Kansas, 1994), pp. 7–17.

[32]Ibid., pp. 18–27, 30–40.

[33]Ibid., p. 61.

In its approach to school government, the one-room school represented a form of direct democracy: the elected school board set the tax rate and hired and supervised the teacher. The small rural school also served as a cultural center for the community. *(© Art Resource)*

District consolidation

In the early twentieth century, many small districts were consolidated into larger ones. Administrators, leading the consolidation movement, claimed that larger districts and schools could provide more student services, reduce duplication, and offer an enriched curriculum.

The McGuffey Readers

120 million copies

The ideals of literacy, hard work, diligence, and virtuous living that characterized nineteenth-century American public schools were epitomized by *McGuffey readers.* William Holmes McGuffey (1800–1873), clergyman, professor, and college president, is best known for the series of readers that bears his name. It is estimated that more than 120 million copies of McGuffey's readers were sold between 1836 and 1920. McGuffey himself was nurtured in the theology and values of Scotch Presbyterianism, and his books emphasized the importance of individual virtue and goodness.[34]

Patriotism and moral values

Stressing the moral values of white Anglo-Saxon Protestant rural America, the McGuffey readers also emphasized patriotism and heroism. Among the selections included were the orations of Patrick Henry, Daniel Webster, and George Washington. Through his readers, McGuffey was a teacher to several generations of Ameri-

---

[34]John H. Westerhoff, *McGuffey and His Readers: Piety, Morality, and Education in Nineteenth Century America* (Nashville: Abingdon, 1978). See also James M. Lower, "William Holmes McGuffey: A Book or a Man? Or More?" *Vitae Scholasticae* (Fall 1984), pp. 311–320.

cans. He also provided the first graded readers for our school systems and paved the way for a totally graded system, which had its beginnings in the 1840s.

The Development of American Secondary Schools

Completing the educational ladder

Common schools created the foundation for tax-supported and locally controlled public elementary education in the United States. Upon this base were erected public high schools — institutions that linked elementary schools with state colleges and universities. Public secondary schooling completed the institutional rungs of the American **educational ladder.** Unlike Europe's dual-track system, which limited the education of students from lower socioeconomic classes, America's single educational ladder created the opportunity for students to progress to higher education.

The Academy: Forerunner of the High School

Academy replaces grammar school

The Latin grammar school of the colonial period was replaced by the academy, the dominant secondary school during the first half of the nineteenth century. Serving middle-class educational needs, it offered a wide range of curricula and subjects.[35] By 1855, the more than 6,000 academies in the United States enrolled 263,000 students.

Broader curriculum and student body

Unlike the Latin grammar schools, academies did not limit their enrollment to students preparing for college; they also served students planning to complete their formal education at the academy. The academies' curriculum also included more than Latin and Greek. Programs varied considerably in quality and quantity but usually followed three patterns: (1) the traditional college preparatory curriculum with emphasis on Latin and Greek; (2) the English-language program, a general curriculum for those planning to end formal education with completion of secondary school; and (3) the normal course, for prospective common school teachers. There were, in addition, some specialized military academies.

Academies for women

In contrast to the Latin grammar schools, some academies were coeducational, enrolling women as well as men. Others were founded expressly for young women. Among the academies founded for women was the Troy Female Seminary, established in 1821 in New York by Emma Willard, a leader in the women's rights movement. Along with the conventional domestic science program, women's academies offered classical and modern languages, science, mathematics, art, and music. The teacher-preparation, or normal, curriculum was also a popular course.

The academies were generally controlled by private boards of trustees or governing bodies. Occasionally, they might be semipublic and receive some funding from cities or states. The era of the academies extended to the 1870s, when they declined and were replaced by public high schools. However, some private academies still provide secondary education for a small percentage of the population.

The High School

Taxes for public high schools

Although a small number of high schools had existed in the United States since the founding of the English Classical School of Boston in 1821, the **high school** did not become the dominant institution of American secondary education until the sec-

---

[35]Theodore R. Sizer, *The Age of Academies* (New York: Teachers College Press, 1964).

ond half of the nineteenth century, when it gradually replaced the academy.[36] In the 1870s the courts ruled in a series of cases (especially the *Kalamazoo*, Michigan, case in 1874) that the people of the states could establish and support public high schools with tax funds if they desired. After that, the public high school movement spread rapidly. By 1890 the 2,526 public high schools in the United States were enrolling more than 200,000 students. In contrast, the 1,600 private academies at that time were enrolling fewer than 95,000 students.[37]

Compulsory attendance

Eventually the states passed compulsory school attendance laws. Provision of public secondary schools thereafter became a state obligation, rather than a voluntary matter. Students were permitted to attend approved nonpublic schools, but the states had the right to set minimum standards for *all* schools.

Urbanization and the High School.   The rise of the high school resulted from a variety of socioeconomic forces. The United States in the mid-nineteenth century experienced a dramatic transition from an agricultural and rural society to an industrial and urban nation. For example, New York City's population grew from 1,174,779 in 1860 to 4,766,833 in 1910. By 1930, more than 25 percent of all Americans lived in seven great urban areas: New York, Chicago, Philadelphia, Boston, Detroit, Los Angeles, and Cleveland. Rapid urbanization also generated a need for more specialized occupations, professions, and services, a need to which high schools responded.[38]

Reshaping the High-School Curriculum.   In the high school's early years, educators sought to define its purpose and curriculum. Traditionalists saw it as a college preparatory school, but others wanted more immediately practical vocational and career programs. In some large cities, high schools, known as "people's colleges," offered liberal arts and science programs.[39] To resolve these issues, the National Education Association (NEA) in 1892 established the **Committee of Ten**, chaired by Charles Eliot, Harvard University's president. The committee made two important recommendations: (1) uniform teaching of subjects for both students continuing on to college and terminal students planning to end formal education upon graduation; (2) eight years of elementary and four years of secondary education.[40] It identified four curricula as appropriate for the high school: classical, Latin-scientific, modern language, and English. However, each curriculum included foreign languages, mathematics, sciences, English, and history — courses found in college preparatory programs. Although the committee suggested alternatives to the dominant Latin and Greek classical curriculum, its recommendations were still oriented to college preparatory rather than terminal students.

Effort to standardize curriculum

Rising diversity

By 1918, thirty states required full-time school attendance until age sixteen.[41] Increasing enrollments made high school students more representative of the general population and more culturally varied than in the past. No longer only the

---

[36]For recent histories of the high school, see Jergen Herbst, *The Once and Future School: Three Hundred and Fifty Years of American Secondary Education* (New York: Routledge, 1996); and William J. Reese, *The Origins of the American High School* (New Haven: Yale University Press, 1995).

[37]Edward A. Krug, *The Shaping of the American High School, 1880–1920* (New York: Harper and Row, 1964).

[38]Edward A. Krug, *The Shaping of the American High School, 1920–1941* (Madison: University of Wisconsin Press, 1972).

[39]For the high school as a people's college, see Jurgen Herbst, *The Once and Future School: Three Hundred and Fifty Years of American Secondary Education*, pp. 95–106.

[40]National Education Association, *Report of the Committee on Secondary School Studies* (Washington, D.C.: U.S. Government Printing Office, 1893).

[41]Krug, *The Shaping of the American High School, 1920–1941*, p. 7.

children of the professional and business classes, high school students came from the nation's adolescent population at large.

A comprehensive orientation

The high school population's changing characteristics were recognized by the NEA's **Commission on the Reorganization of Secondary Education** in its 1918 report, *Cardinal Principles of Secondary Education*. Recognizing the needs of an urban and industrial society, the commission redefined the high school as a comprehensive institution serving the country's various social, cultural, and economic groups.[42] The curriculum should be differentiated to meet agricultural, commercial, industrial, and domestic as well as college preparatory needs without sacrificing its integrative and comprehensive social character.[43]

Secondary School Organization

Varied programs for varied students

By the 1920s, there were four curricular patterns in high schools: (1) the college preparatory program, which included English language and literature, foreign languages, mathematics, natural and physical sciences, and history and social studies; (2) the commercial or business program with courses in bookkeeping, shorthand, and typing; (3) industrial, vocational, home economics, and agricultural programs; and (4) a general academic program for students whose formal education would end with graduation.

A four-year sequence

Despite some variations, the typical high-school pattern followed a four-year sequence encompassing grades nine, ten, eleven, and twelve and generally including the age group from fourteen to eighteen.[44] There were exceptions, however. In some reorganized six-year schools, students attended a combined junior-senior high school after completing a six-year elementary school. There were also three-year junior high schools, which comprised seventh, eighth, and ninth grades, and three-year senior high schools for tenth, eleventh, and twelfth grades.

Junior high schools

The **junior high school** was developed by educators who wanted a transitional institution between elementary and secondary education. As they developed in the 1920s and 1930s, junior high schools were sometimes two-year institutions encompassing grades seven and eight, or three-year institutions that also included ninth grade. Today, junior high schools are part of the pattern of organization in many districts.

Middle schools

In the 1960s, **middle schools** were developed as another type of transitional institution between elementary and high school. Generally including grades six, seven, and eight (ages eleven through thirteen), they facilitate a gradual transition from childhood to adolescence by emphasizing programs suited for preadolescents.[45]

Frequent efforts to redefine the high school

There have been frequent efforts to redefine the high school's purpose and curriculum. One such scenario occurred in 1957, when the Soviet Union, the Cold War adversary of the United States, successfully orbited *Sputnik*, a space satellite. The Soviet success and well-publicized American space failures generated a national crisis. Attempting to explain U.S. slippage in the space race, critics alleged that American

---

[42]A recent historical analysis of the impact of the Cardinal Principles can be found in William G. Wraga, *Democracy's High School: The Comprehensive High School and Education Reform in the United States* (Lanham, Md.: University Press of America, 1994).

[43]Commission on the Reorganization of Secondary Education, *Cardinal Principles of American Secondary Education*, Bulletin no. 35 (Washington, D.C.: U.S. Government Printing Office, 1918).

[44]Robert L. Hampel, *The Last Little Citadel: American High Schools Since 1940* (Boston: Houghton Mifflin, 1986).

[45]Judith L. Irvin, ed., *Transforming Middle Level Education: Perspectives and Possibilities* (Needham Heights, Mass.: Allyn and Bacon, 1992).

students were deficient in mathematics and science in comparison with Soviet students. Congress responded by passing the National Defense Education Act (NDEA) in 1958, which provided federal funds to improve curricula and instruction in areas considered crucial to national defense: mathematics, science, and foreign languages. The NDEA illustrates how high schools are affected by external forces. Later chapters in this book discuss more recent attempts to redefine high schools' organization and curriculum in response to perceived social and economic crises.

The Development of Educational Technology

Early technologies

In the 1930s, educational radio and motion pictures entered the schools. Although these innovations were often add-ons rather than integrated into the curriculum, they infused instruction with dynamic audio and visual elements. A major development in educational technology, the advent of television, followed World War II. In the early 1950s, educators began experimenting with educational television. In 1957, Alexander J. Stoddard initiated the National Program in the Use of Television in the Schools.

Educational television

The 1960s, called a time of educational revolution, saw further developments in instructional technologies such as educational television, programmed learning, and computer-assisted instruction. In 1961, the six-state Midwest Program on Airborne Television Instruction began telecasting lessons to schools. Indiana University, in 1965, established a National Center for School and College Television.[46] Since these early developments, educational television has had a major and continuing impact on instruction. Today, many high schools have their own television studio and channel. In the classroom, the videotape has tended to replace the motion picture. Closed-circuit television is frequently used in teacher education, providing prospective teachers with an instant videotaped critique of their teaching.

Cultural impact of television

Although television has important educational possibilities, it also needs to be considered in terms of its total cultural impact. Many U.S. children and adolescents spend hours viewing commercial television, which carries many mixed messages about such issues as sex, violence, and other social mores. Network television and CNN can bring events to viewers in a rapid-fire and dynamic way. The television image, however, lacks the reflective element of the printed page.

Teaching machines and programmed instruction

The educational revolution also included "teaching machines" that used programmed and computer-assisted instruction. Programmed instruction was aimed at forming concepts through carefully graduated steps that provided students with instant self-evaluation. Since students could recognize their successes and mistakes as quickly as they made them, they could proceed at their own learning rate. Programmed instruction was especially adaptable to subjects such as grammar, foreign languages, logic, and mathematics, which could be reduced to elemental steps.

Computers

In the 1990s, computers and computer-assisted instruction, the Internet, the World Wide Web, and CD-ROMs were important additions to the ongoing technological revolution. Having a major impact on education, they provide teachers and students with up-to-date information. Computers represent both continuity and change in education. While they are extensions of such historical technological breakthroughs as writing and the printing press, they represent a new technological dynamic that has dramatically increased the storage of information in readily accessible form. In his 1997 State of the Union Message, President Clinton proposed

---

[46]Gerald L. Gutek, *An Historical Introduction to American Education* (Prospect Heights, Ill.: Waveland Press, 1991), pp. 206–207.

legislation to provide free access for public schools to the Internet to ensure that "every 12-year old" is able to "log on. . . ;" as described in Chapter 1, knowledge and skill in the new educational technology, especially in using computers, is regarded as so essential to teachers that it is required in many teacher-education programs and in teachers' professional development.

The American College and University

Colleges of the colonial period

The colonial colleges were established under religious auspices. Believing that an educated ministry was needed to establish Christianity in the New World, the Massachusetts General Court created Harvard College in 1636. By 1754 Yale, William and Mary, Princeton, and King's College (later Columbia University) had also been established by various denominations. Other colonial colleges were the University of Pennsylvania, Dartmouth, Brown, and Rutgers. Although there were curricular variations, the general colonial college curriculum included (1) Latin, Greek, Hebrew, rhetoric, and logic during the first year; (2) Greek, Hebrew, logic, and natural philosophy during the second year; (3) natural philosophy, metaphysics, and ethics during the third year; and (4) mathematics and a review in Greek, Latin, logic, and natural philosophy during the fourth year.[47]

Morrill Act and land-grant colleges

During the first half of the nineteenth century, states established colleges and universities. Many religious denominations also founded their own private colleges as revivalism swept the country. By the early 1850s, critics of traditional liberal arts colleges were arguing that colleges for agriculture and mechanical science should be established with support from federal land grants. Such institutions, they claimed, were essential for national development. They got their wish when the Morrill Act of 1862 granted each state 30,000 acres of public land for each senator and representative in Congress. The income from this grant was to support state colleges for agricultural and mechanical instruction.[48] The general impact of **land-grant colleges)** was to further agricultural education, engineering, and other applied sciences as well as liberal arts and professional education. Many leading state universities originated as land-grant colleges.

Community colleges

Today, one of the largest and most popular higher-education institutions is the two-year community college. Many two-year institutions originated as junior colleges in the late nineteenth and early twentieth centuries when several university presidents recommended that the first two years of undergraduate education take place at another institution rather than at a four-year college. After World War II, many junior colleges were reorganized into community colleges and numerous new community colleges were established with the broader function of serving their communities' educational needs. Important constituents in statewide higher-education systems, community colleges are exceptionally responsive in providing training for technological change, especially those related to the communications and electronic data revolutions.[49]

G.I. Bill

The greatest growth in American higher education came after World War II with the 1944 passage of the Servicemen's Readjustment Act, known as the G.I. Bill. To help readjust society to peacetime and reintegrate returning service people into

---

[47]Frederick Rudolph, *The American College and University: A History* (Athens: University of Georgia Press, 1990).
[48]Benjamin E. Andrews, *The Land Grand of 1862 and the Land-Grant College* (Washington, D.C.: U.S. Government Printing Office, 1918).
[49]Judy Temkin, "Community Colleges Can Help Pros Build on Experience," *Chicago Tribune*, Section 19 (November 16, 1997), p. 9.

Rising enrollments

domestic life, the G.I. Bill provided federal funds for veterans for education. Tuition, fees, books, and living expenses were subsidized, and between 1944 and 1951, 7,800,000 veterans used the bill's assistance to attend technical schools, colleges, and universities. The effect was to double the nation's population of college students and usher in an era of rapid growth of higher education.[50] The following statistics illustrate this phenomenal growth in student enrollments:

1950 — 2,400,000

1965 — 4,900,000

1975 — 9,000,000

1980 — 12,000,000

1994 — 14,278,790[51]

2004 — 16,000,000 (projected)[52]

Rising cost of college

Since the 1980s, the cost of attending colleges and universities has steadily increased. Because of rising costs for medicare, highways, and prisons, many states have reduced the percentage of their budgets for higher education. To meet increased expenditures for faculty and staff salaries, construction, and operations, institutions have raised tuition. Private institutions have made even larger increases than public ones in student tuition and fees.

Challenges facing colleges

Colleges and universities face a number of serious challenges. Among them are the need to do the following:

- Contain escalating costs so that higher education is affordable for most people
- Maintain high standards of instruction while educating larger numbers of students
- Train faculty in the new modes of technology to improve instruction

Colleges and universities are making progress in using the new electronic information technology — computers and the Internet — to make instruction more interactive and up to date. Distance education is being used to reach students who cannot be present on campuses. Although there has been progress in effectively using the new technology, a continuing challenge remains at all levels of American education — the need to provide equitable and excellent education to an ethnically and racially diverse population.

Education in a Culturally Diverse Society

A history of diversity

Historically, the United States has been, just as it is today, a racially and ethnically diverse nation. With the exception of the Native Americans, the roots of Americans can be traced to other continents, especially to Europe, Africa, and Asia. So far, this chapter has concentrated mainly on the European heritage; this section examines other groups that have contributed to the United States.

---

[50]Diane Ravitch, *The Troubled Crusade: American Education, 1945–1980* (New York: Basic Books, 1983), pp. 3–14.

[51]*Digest of Education Statistics, 1980*, Table 94, p. 102; *Projections of Educational Statistics, 1986–87* (Washington, D.C.: U.S. Government Printing Office, 1978), Table 2, p. 14; Table 5, p. 20.

[52]*The Chronicle of Higher Education Almanac* (September 2, 1996), pp. 9, 18.

African Americans

The Civil War, Reconstruction, and the Thirteenth Amendment ended slavery in the United States. Although free blacks had attended schools in some northern states before the Civil War, southern states had prohibited the teaching of African American children, whether slave or free. Emancipation brought with it the challenge of providing education for the freed men and women and their children, particularly in the defeated Confederate states.

Freedmen's Bureau

In 1865, Congress established the Freedmen's Bureau to assist in the economic and educational transition of African Americans from bondage to freedom in the South. Under the leadership of General O. O. Howard, the bureau established schools throughout the South. In 1869, its schools enrolled 114,000 students. The schools followed a New England common school curriculum of reading, writing, grammar, geography, arithmetic, and music, especially singing. LIke their nothern counterparts, the Freedman's Bureau schools used standard textbooks, including Webster's spellers and McGuffey's readers. Many of the schools functioned until 1872, when bureau operations ended.[53]

Stereotypes limited teaching

Although a small number of African American teachers were trained by the Freedmen's Bureau, most schools were staffed by northern schoolteachers, who brought with them their educational philosophies and teaching methods. These northern white teachers had stereotypic notions about the education African Americans should receive. Rather than encouraging educational self-determination,

Under the leadership of Booker T. Washington, the Tuskegee Institute emphasized agricultural and vocational training. These students were learning scientific analysis of soil. (© UPI/Corbis–Bettmann)

---

[53]Paul A. Cimbala, *Under the Guardianship of the Nation: The Freedmen's Bureau and the Reconstruction of Georgia, 1865–1870* (Athens: University of Georgia Press, 1997).

GETTING TO THE SOURCE

The Education of W. E. B. Du Bois

DUSK OF DAWN

AN ESSAY TOWARD
AN AUTOBIOGRAPHY
OF A RACE CONCEPT

BY

W. E. Burghardt Du Bois

HARCOURT, BRACE AND COMPANY, NEW YORK

William E. B. Du Bois (1868–1963) was a leader in the civil rights movement and the campaign to achieve equality of educational opportunity for African Americans. Du Bois was born in and received his elementary and secondary education in Great Barrington, Massachusetts. From 1885 to 1890, he attended Fisk University, an historically black institution in Tennessee. The following reading describes reactions that Du Bois, a northern African American, had to racism and segregation in the South. Du Bois would later earn his doctorate from Harvard University and devote his life to writing, teaching, and advocating equality for all races and peoples.

[My] three years at Fisk [University] were years of growth and development. I learned new things about the world. My knowledge of the race problem became more definite. I saw discrimination in ways of which I had never dreamed: the separation of passengers on the railways of the South was just beginning; the race separation in living quarters throughout the cities and towns was manifest; the public disdain and even insult in race contact on the street continually took my breath; I came in contact for the first time with a sort of violence that I had never realized in New England; I remember going down and looking wide-eyed at the door of a public building, filled with buck-shot, where the editor of the leading daily paper had been publicly murdered the day before. I was astonished to find many of my fellow students carrying fire-arms and to hear their stories of adventure. On the other hand my personal contact with my teachers was inspiring and beneficial as indeed I suppose all personal contacts between human beings must be. Adam Spence of Fisk first taught me to know what the Greek language meant. In a funny little basement room crowded with apparatus, Frederick Chase gave me insight into natural science and talked with me about future study. I knew the President, Erastus Cravath, to be honest and sincere.

educators such as Samuel C. Armstrong, the mentor of Booker T. Washington, emphasized the industrial training and social control that kept African Americans in a subordinate economic and social position.[54]

Washington: From Slavery to Freedom. Booker T. Washington (1856–1915) was the leading educational spokesperson for African Americans in the half century after the Civil War. As illustrated in his autobiography, *Up from Slavery*, Washington was a transitional figure who was born a slave, experienced the hectic years of Reconstruction, and cautiously developed a compromise with the white establishment.[55]

As a student at Hampton Institute, Washington learned the educational philosophy of General Samuel Armstrong, who established the institute to prepare African American youth for teaching, agriculture, and industry. Armstrong argued that industrial education would prepare African Americans to be competent work-

"Uplift" through work

---

[54]James D. Anderson, *The Education of Blacks in the South, 1860–1935* (Chapel Hill: University of North Carolina Press, 1988).
[55]Booker T. Washington, *Up from Slavery* (New York: Doubleday, 1938).

I determined to know something of the Negro in the country districts; to go out and teach during the summer vacation. I was not compelled to do this, for my scholarship was sufficient to support me, but that was not the point. I had heard about the country in the South as the real seat of slavery. I wanted to know it. I walked out into east Tennessee ten or more miles a day until at last in a little valley near Alexandria I found a place where there had been a Negro public school only once since the Civil War; and there for two successive terms during the summer I taught at $28 and $30 a month. It was an enthralling experience. I met new and intricate and unconscious discrimination. I was pleasantly surprised when the white school superintendent, on whom I had made a business call, invited me to stay for dinner; and he would have been astonished if he had dreamed that I expected to eat at the table with him and not after he was through. All the appointments of my school were primitive: a windowless log cabin; hastily manufactured benches; no blackboard; almost no books; long, long distances to walk. And on the other hand, I heard the sorrow songs sung with primitive beauty and grandeur. I saw the hard, ugly drudgery of country life and the writhing of landless, ignorant peasants. I saw the race problem at nearly its lowest terms.

Questions

1. How did the problem of racial discrimination become a reality for Du Bois?
2. How was Du Bois's education different from that which Booker T. Washington had prescribed for African Americans?
3. Based on Du Bois's narrative, describe the conditions of African American education in the rural South at the turn of the century.
4. After reflecting on how higher education changed Du Bois's views of racism in America, consider if and how it has changed your thinking of racial, ethnic, and gender relationships.
5. After reflecting on Du Bois's summer teaching experiences while a Fisk University student, consider if and how clinical experiences have either confirmed or changed your opinions about teaching.

Source: W. E. Burghardt Du Bois, *Dusk of Dawn: An Essay Toward an Autobiography of a Race Concept* (New York: Schocken, 1968), pp. 30–31. Copyright © 1983 Transaction Publishers. Reprinted with permission; all rights reserved.

ers. Washington subscribed to Armstrong's philosophy of moral and economic "uplift" through work.[56]

Washington's influence at Tuskegee

In 1881, Washington was appointed principal of the educational institute that the Alabama legislature had established for African Americans at Tuskegee. Washington shaped the Tuskegee curriculum according to his perceptions of the living and working conditions of southern African Americans. Feeling that they faced the problem of being a landless agricultural class, he created an economic base — primarily in farming but also in occupational trades — that would provide economic security. Thus Tuskeegee's curriculum stressed basic academic, agricultural, and occupational skills and emphasized the values of hard work and the dignity of labor. While it encouraged students to become elementary school teachers, farmers, and artisans, it discouraged involvement in law and politics. Professional education and political action, Washington believed, were premature and would cause conflict with the dominant white power structure in the South.

---

[56]Raymond W. Smock, ed., *Booker T. Washington in Perspective: Essays of Louis R. Harlan* (Jackson: University Press of Mississippi, 1988).

Theory of social separation

Washington, a dynamic and popular platform speaker, developed the theory that blacks and whites were mutually dependent economically but could remain separate socially. In 1885, Washington summed up his philosophy in an address at the Cotton Exposition in Atlanta, Georgia, when he said, "In all things that are purely social, we can be as separate as the fingers, yet one as the hand in all things essential to mutual progress."[57]

Controversy about Washington

Today, Washington is a controversial figure in history. Defenders say he made the best of a bad situation and that, although he compromised on racial issues, he preserved and slowly advanced African Americans' educational opportunities. Critics see Washington as the head of a large educational network that he operated to advance his own power rather than to improve the situation of African Americans in the United States. One of Washington's critics was W. E. B. Du Bois.

Du Bois: Challenger to the System.   W. E. B. Du Bois (1868–1963) was a sociological and educational pioneer who challenged the segregated system that severely limited the educational opportunities of African Americans.[58] Questioning Booker T. Washington's leadership, Du Bois urged a more determined stand against segregation and racism.

Du Bois as a scholar

Unlike Washington, whose roots were in southern agriculture, Du Bois's career spanned both sides of the Mason-Dixon Line. Born in Massachusetts, he attended Fisk University in Nashville, did graduate work in Germany, earned his doctorate at Harvard University, and directed the Atlanta University Studies of Black American Life. His important book, *The Philadelphia Negro: A Social Study*, examined the social, economic, and educational problems of an urban African American community.[59] An academic sociologist and historian, he was also a determined civil rights activist.

Du Bois as a civil rights leader

In 1909 Du Bois helped organize the National Association for the Advancement of Colored People (NAACP). His editorials in *The Crisis*, the NAACP's major publication, argued that *all* American children and youth, including African Americans, should have genuine equality of educational opportunity.[60] Du Bois and the NAACP were persistent adversaries of racially segregated schools, and his dedicated efforts helped outlaw racial segregation in public schools. (The progress of desegregation is discussed in Chapter 11.)

Promoting social and educational change

Unlike Booker T. Washington, who took a compromising and accommodationist path on racial relations, Du Bois worked for deliberate social change. He believed that African Americans needed well-educated leaders, especially in the professions, and he articulated the concept of the "talented tenth," according to which 10 percent of the African American population would receive a higher education. Both Washington and Du Bois believed strongly in the dignity of work, but Du Bois was adamant that a person's occupation should be determined by ability and choice, not by racial stereotyping. A prophetic leader, Du Bois set the stage for the significant changes in American race relations that have taken place since the mid-1950s.

Bethune: Educational Activist.   Mary McLeod Bethune (1875–1955) was a distinguished African American educator. The daughter of a South Carolina sharecropper, Bethune attended Scotia Seminary in Concord, North Carolina, and the Moody

---

[57]Booker T. Washington, *Selected Speeches of Booker T. Washington* (New York: Doubleday, 1932).
[58]David Levering Lewis, *W. E. B. Du Bois: Biography of a Race, 1868–1919* (New York: Henry Holt, 1973).
[59]W. E. B. Du Bois, *The Philadelphia Negro: A Social Study* (Philadelphia: University of Pennsylvania Press, 1899).
[60]W. E. B. Du Bois, *Dusk of Dawn: An Essay Toward an Autobiography of a Race Concept* (New York: Harcourt, Brace & World, 1940).

Bible Institute in Chicago. In 1904, she founded the Daytona Normal and Industrial School, now Bethune-Cookman College.

Education as means to upward mobility

Bethune was convinced that education was the surest means of winning equality of opportunity and upward social and economic mobility for African Americans. She combined certain aspects of Booker T. Washington's program of academic, vocational, and religious education with a more activist civil rights stance that resembled Du Bois's strategy. Working within rather than outside the political system, she became an adviser to President Franklin D. Roosevelt during the New Deal era of the 1930s and early 1940s. President Roosevelt appointed her director of the Negro Affairs Division of the National Youth Administration.[61] Bethune was appointed to the United Nations as a delegate by President Truman when World War II ended.

Human rights and women's rights

Bethune was not only active in educational affairs; she was also an able advocate for women's and human rights. For example, she organized the National Council of Negro Women and the Southern Conference on Human Rights and was an important spokesperson for human rights and racial and gender equality.[62]

The more recent history of the movements for civil rights and racial integration, especially after the Supreme Court decision in the Brown Case in 1954, is discussed in Chapter 11.

Native Americans

Traditional tribal education

The education of Native Americans before the encounter with Europeans was largely informal. Children learned skills, social roles, and cultural patterns from their direct experience with tribal life and the traditions of their own society. Tribal education involved vocational training: young men learned to hunt, fish, or trap, and young women learned to weave, prepare food, and care for children. Religious rituals also helped children become participants in tribal life.

Marked by suspicion and violence, the encounters of Native Americans and European colonists changed both cultures. While the colonists attempted to recreate European culture in North America and Native Americans sought to preserve their culture, both were changed.[63]

Missionary educational efforts

Efforts by the European colonists in North America to "civilize" the indigenous Native Americans rested on the Europeans' sense of their own cultural superiority. In the Mississippi Valley, French missionaries, seeking to convert the Native Americans to Catholicism as well as educate the children of French colonists, established schools that introduced the French language and culture.

In the Southwest, controlled by Spain, Jesuit and Franciscan priests sought to alleviate the exploitation of Native Americans by Spanish landlords. Priests established missions to protect, control, and convert the tribes to Catholicism. In mission schools, some children learned religion, reading, and writing. The end result was often an unusual mixture of Native American and Spanish culture and religion. Often it produced two cultures — one Native American and the other Spanish — standing side by side.[64]

---

[61]Mary Frances Berry and John W. Blassingame, *Long Memory: The Black Experience in America* (New York: Oxford University Press, 1982).

[62]Harvard Sitkoff, *A New Deal for Blacks: The Emergence of Civil Rights as a National Issue,* vol. 1, *The Depression Decade* (New York: Oxford University Press, 1978).

[63]Colin G. Calloway, *New Worlds for All: Indians, Europeans, and the Remaking of Early America* (Baltimore: Johns Hopkins University Press, 1997), p. 42.

[64]For a discussion of mission culture, see Christopher Vecsey, *On the Padres' Trail* (Notre Dame, Ind.: University of Notre Dame Press, 1996).

Moravians

In the English colonies, Church of England missionary and educational activities among the Native Americans were sporadic and conducted on a small scale. Noteworthy educational efforts were also made by Moravians, a German religious group who were followers of the Bohemian bishop and educational reformer John Amos Comenius. The Moravians, who saw education as a means for bringing peace to the world, went out to teach the Native American tribes and translated the Bible and religious tracts into Indian languages. Among the early Native American educators was Sequoyah, a Cherokee, who devised an alphabet in his native language. His alphabet, completed in 1832, made the Cherokees the first Native American tribe to have a written language.

Cherokee alphabet

Assimilationist education

In the nineteenth century, the U.S. government forcibly relocated the majority of Native Americans on reservations in remote areas of the Great Plains and Southwest in territory west of the Mississippi River. After 1870, the federal Bureau of Indian Affairs (BIA), encouraged by well-intentioned but misguided reformers, again attempted to "civilize" Native Americans by assimilating them into white society. These "reformers" sought to eradicate tribal cultures and instill "white" values through industrial training.[65]

Boarding schools

From 1890 to the 1930s, the BIA used **boarding schools** to implement the assimilationist educational policy. Boarding schools emphasized a basic curriculum of reading, writing, arithmetic, and vocational training. In these schools, Native American youngsters were ruled by military discipline, forbidden to speak their own native languages, and forced to use English.[66]

Students' reactions

Native American younsters either resisted, passively accepted, or accommodated to the boarding schools' regimen. Active resisters repeatedly ran away from the boarding schools. Accommodationists were often encouraged by their parents to accept the boarding schools' program as a way to learn a trade in order to earn a living.[67] Many students suffered a loss of cultural identity, feeling trapped in a never-never land between two different cultures.

Contemporary schooling

After the boarding-school concept was discontinued in the 1930s, Native American education experienced significant change. The population of Native Americans increased slowly, from an estimated 248,000 in 1890 to 357,000 in 1950, and then grew rapidly to 2,000,000 in the 1990s.[68] Many Native Americans left reservations to live in urban centers, particularly inner cities. Children living on reservations attended a variety of schools: schools maintained by the Bureau of Indian Affairs, tribal schools, and public and private institutions. Those living in cities usually attended public schools.

---

[65]David W. Adams, "Fundamental Considerations: The Deep Meaning of Native American Schooling, 1880–1900," *Harvard Educational Review*, 58 (February 1988), pp. 1–28; see also Robert M. Utley, *The Indian Frontier of the American West, 1846–1890* (Albuquerque, N.M.: University of New Mexico Press, 1984).

[66]Robert A. Trennert, Jr., "Corporal Punishment and the Politics of Indian Reform," *History of Education Quarterly* (Winter 1989), pp. 595–617; see also Robert A. Trennert, Jr., *The Phoenix Indian School: Forced Assimilation in Arizona, 1891–1975* (Norman, Ok.: University of Oklahoma Press, 1988).

[67]David W. Adams, "From Bullets to Boarding Schools: The Educational Assault on Native American Identity, 1878–1928," in Philip Weeks, ed., *The American Indian Experience* (Arlington Heights, Ill.: Forum Press, 1988), pp. 218–239; see also K. Tsianina Lomawaima, *They Called it Prairie Light: The Story of Chilocco Indian School* (Lincoln, Neb.: University of Nebraska Press, 1994).

[68]U.S. Department of Commerce, Bureau of the Census, *We the First Americans* (Washington, D.C.: U.S. Government Printing Office, n.d.), p. 3; U.S. Bureau of the Census, *Statistical Abstract of the United States, 1991* (Washington, D.C.: U.S. Government Printing Office, 1991), p. 22.

Alienation from the system

Although assimilation is no longer an official government policy, Native Americans still suffer from a discrimination that alienates many youngsters from the educational system. Although more Native Americans are under twenty years of age — in comparison to the national population — their participation in schooling is far lower than average. Because of a very high dropout rate, the level of Native American high-school completion is far below that of the U.S. population at large.

Hispanic Americans

Hispanic peoples and cultures

Hispanic Americans comprise the fastest-growing ethnic group in the United States. *Hispanic* is a collective term used to identify Spanish-speaking people whose ethnic origins can be traced to Mexico, Puerto Rico, Cuba, or other Latin American countries. Although Hispanic Americans may speak Spanish as a common language and may share many general Spanish traditions, each national group has its own distinctive culture.

Assimilation in the Southwest

Mexican Americans are the largest Hispanic American ethnic group. Many Mexican Americans are descendants of people forcibly joined to the U.S. as a result of the Mexican-American War, when Mexico in 1848 ceded to the United States territory now included in California, Arizona, Texas, Colorado, and New Mexico.[69] In these states, public schools followed the assimilationist policy, known as **Americanization,** then used throughout the United States. Mexican American children were taught in English, rather than their vernacular Spanish, and their own Hispanic cultural heritage was ignored. Consequently, schooling imposed a negative self-image, often portraying Mexican Americans as the conquered people of an inferior culture. Today, bilingual and multicultural education, replacing Americanization, contributes to developing a Mexican American historical consciousness.[70] (For more on bilingual and multicultural education, see Chapter 11.)

Few educational opportunities

In later years, the Mexican American population increased as migrant workers crossed the U.S.-Mexican border to work in the United States. Since Mexicans provided cheap labor on ranches, on railroad crews, and especially as farm workers, employers encouraged their entry. Wages were low, housing frequently squalid, and working conditions harsh. Children of the migrant workers, even if not working in the fields with their parents, had few or no educational opportunities. Although many migrant workers returned to Mexico, others remained in the United States, either legally or illegally.

Chicano movement

Since World War II the Mexican American population has expanded from the Southwest to other states, often to the large Northeastern and Midwestern cities. Today, approximately 90 percent of Mexican Americans live in urban areas. In the 1960s a Chicano movement, similar to the African American civil rights crusade, was organized to improve Mexican American social, economic, and educational conditions.[71] However, Mexican Americans still seek greater access and participation in higher education, where their enrollments fall below the national average.

---

[69]Leonard Dinnerstein and David M. Reimers, *Ethnic Americans; A History of Immigration and Assimilation* (New York: Harper and Row, 1972), pp. 88–89; and Julian Neva, *Mexican Americans: A Brief Look at Their History* (New York: Anti-Defamation League of B'nai B'rith, 1970), p. 31.
[70]Lisbeth Haas, *Conquests and Historical Identities in California, 1769–1930* (Berkeley and Los Angeles: University of California Press, 1995), p. 151.
[71]For the Mexican American urban experience, see George J. Sanchez, *Becoming Mexican American: Ethnicity, Culture, and Identity for Chicano Los Angeles, 1900–1945* (New York: Oxford University Press, 1993). Mexican American social and political consciousness is treated in David G. Gutierrez, *Walls and Mirrors: Mexican Americans, Mexican Immigrants, and the Politics of Ethnicity* (Berkeley and Los Angeles: University of California Press, 1995).

Americanization of Puerto Ricans

The history of Puerto Rican Americans, another large Hispanic group, dates from the Spanish-American War of 1898, when the United States acquired the island of Puerto Rico. U.S. officials replaced the Spanish colonial education system with American public schools. Although some classes continued to be taught in Spanish, English was made compulsory to promote Americanization. American educators also trained Puerto Rican teachers in U.S. teaching methods. The result was a kind of dual cultural identity in students — their island's Hispanic culture and the English-speaking American culture.

Dropout rates

Since the early twentieth century, there has been continuous Puerto Rican immigration to the U.S. mainland. Today, more than two million Puerto Rican Americans live in the large urban centers, such as New York, Chicago, and Philadelphia.[72] Puerto Rican Americans have had to struggle against economic and educational disadvantagement. Historically, their high-school dropout rates have been high and college attendance rates low. In recent years, however, Puerto Rican Americans have become more politically active, especially in New York and Chicago, and have improved their economic and educational position. Programs such as ASPIRA encourage Puerto Rican American and Latino youth to complete high school and attend college.[73]

Varied educational backgrounds

The Cuban American experience in the United States represents a different pattern from that of other Hispanic groups in that its origins were those of a community in political exile from its native land. Several waves of immigration from Cuba combined to form the Cuban American community in the United States. The first exiles, fleeing Fidel Castro's repressive Communist regime, came from 1959 to 1973. Many exiles were upper- and middle-class Cubans who brought with them the political, economic, and educational background and organizations needed to create a distinctive Cuban American cultural community. The Mariel immigrants of the 1980s came from Cuba's disadvantaged underclass. The Cuban American community, mirroring some aspects of the Cuba they left, has created a unique but adaptive culture.[74]

Bilingual education

The enactment of the Bilingual Education Act in 1968 was a watershed for Hispanic Americans. That act, along with the 1974 Supreme Court decision in *Lau* v. *Nichols*, led to the establishment of bilingual education programs (see Chapter 11). Public schools have now abandoned the old assimilationist and Americanization policies. Recently, however, bilingual education has become politically controversial. Some of its opponents want to make English the official language. California, in a statewide referendum in 1998, voted to end bilingual education programs. The impact of this referendum and the future of bilingual education remain in question.

Asian Americans

Whereas European immigrants entered the United States by way of the East Coast, principally New York City, Asian Americans generally came by way of the West Coast, especially the cities of Los Angeles and San Francisco. For these geographical reasons, the Asian American population was concentrated historically in the west-

---

[72]Dinnerstein and Reimers, *Ethnic Americans*, p. 102.
[73]ASPIRA, a national organization with local branches, encourages access of Latinos and Latinas to higher education. Information is available from ASPIRA, 1112 16th Street, Washington, D.C. 20036.
[74]Maria Cristina Garcia, *Havana USA: Cuban Exiles and Cuban Americans in South Florida, 1959–1994* (Berkeley and Los Angeles: University of California Press, 1996), pp. 111–118.

Even though interned during World War II, Japanese American children still attended school. Here, a group of students is being taught by white teachers in an internment center in Idaho in 1943.
(© Corbis–Bettmann)

Early Chinese immigrants

Japanese immigrants

ern states bordering the Pacific Ocean. From there Asian Americans moved eastward. The first Asian people to settle in the United States were Chinese and Japanese. More recent Asian immigrants include Filipinos, Indians, Thais, Koreans, Vietnamese, Laotians, and Cambodians.

Chinese immigration began in California during the gold rush of 1848–49 and then reached its peak between 1848 and 1882, when 228,945 Chinese were admitted to the United States.[75] The early Chinese immigrants worked as miners, farm workers, and railroad construction workers. Enterprising Chinese merchants operated small businesses, grocery stores, and laundries in the cities of the West Coast. In San Francisco and Los Angeles, Chinese enclaves developed with social, religious, cultural, and educational societies.[76]

Japanese immigration, beginning later than Chinese, occurred between 1885 and 1924. Japanese immigrants came primarily from the agricultural area of southwestern Japan where labor contractors recruited workers for the sugar and pineapple plantations of Hawaii and the farms of California. There was a steady immigration of Japanese. From 1871 to 1880, there were 149 Japanese immigrants; from 1881 to 1890, there were 2,270 Japanese immigrants; from 1891 to 1900, 25,942; and from 1901 to 1910, 129,797.[77] After 1910, the number of immigrants declined because of economic and political issues between Japan and the United States.

---

[75]David J. O'Brien and Stephen S. Fugita, *The Japanese American Experience* (Bloomington, Ind.: Indiana University Press, 1991), p. 17.
[76]Shih-Shan Henry Tsai, *The Chinese Experience in America* (Bloomington, Ind.: Indiana University Press, 1986), pp. 1–20.
[77]David J. O'Brien and Stephen S. Fugita, *The Japanese American Experience* pp. 14–17. For the Japanese American experience in Hawaii, see Eileen H. Tamura, *Americanization, Acculturation, and Ethnic Identity: The Nisei Generation in Hawaii* (Urbana: University of Illinois Press, 1994).

PROFESSIONAL PLANNING

for your first year

Determining What Kind of Teacher You Will Be

The Situation

Many issues in American education have their roots in history. The study of American educational history illuminates the context of these issues. Among the current issues is the continuation of bilingual education programs. Assume that the principal at your school argues that bilingual education provides a necessary transition for pupils who are not English speakers. Recently, however, opponents of your district's bilingual program have become very vocal. They contend that these programs threaten America's cultural identity. You are uncertain. You know, however, that your core beliefs about this important issue will shape your personal philosophy of education and your professional development. Consider the following questions and reflect on how your answers will contribute to your professional development.

Thought Questions

1. Has American cultural identity, historically, been based on a common core of values, or is it a composite of many different cultures?
2. Do you think the United States should have an official language? If not, why not? If so, which language should it be?
3. Do you favor the replacement of assimilationist policy in schools by multiculturalism? Why or why not?

Excluding Asian immigrants

Limited educational opportunity

Between 1882 and 1924, the U.S. Congress enacted laws to prohibit further Chinese and Japanese immigration and to prevent Chinese and Japanese from becoming U.S. citizens. The Chinese Exclusion Act in 1882 made Chinese the first group to be officially excluded from immigrating to the United States. For immigrants who had arrived before these laws took effect, educational and economic opportunities were often limited by racial discrimination. In 1906, for example, the San Francisco Board of Education began segregating students of Asian ethnicity from other pupils. Diplomatic protests from the Japanese government persuaded the board to rescind its segregationist policy.[78] Before World War II, few Chinese or Japanese Americans attained sufficient levels of education to enter the professions.

Japanese American internment

For Japanese Americans, World War II brought racial prejudice to the surface. Responding to fears that Japanese in the United States would aid the enemy, the U.S. government interned 110,00 people of Japanese heritage, many of whom were American citizens, in relocation camps. Located in remote areas, the camps lacked basic services and amenities. Although camp schools were eventually established for the young people, the internment experience produced both physical hardship and psychological alienation. The government's repressive action was based on unfounded fears, since not a single act of sabotage was committed by a Japanese American. Not until the 1980s did the federal government admit its wartime violation of civil liberties and compensate those interned.[79]

---

[78]David J. O'Brien and Stephen S. Fugita, *The Japanese American Experience,* p. 17.
[79]Dinnerstein and Reimers, *Ethnic Americans,* p. 52; Roger Daniels, Sandra C. Taylor, and Harry H. L. Kitano, *Japanese Americans: From Relocation to Redress* (Seattle: University of Washington Press, 1991).

Filipino migration

A substantial number of Filipinos had also migrated to the mainland United States by the start of World War II. Because the Philippines was a U.S. commonwealth, Filipinos did not experience the immigration restrictions applied to other Asians. Many Filipino men served in the U.S. Navy and afterwards settled with their families on the West Coast. Others, especially in the 1930s, came to the mainland as farm workers.

Improvement after World War II

After World War II the economic and educational status of Chinese, Japanese, and Filipino Americans improved substantially. The McCarran-Walter Act of 1952, while retaining limited quotas, repealed the ban on Asian immigration and citizenship. Asian immigration then increased dramatically, and many newcomers were professionals with advanced education. Their arrival sparked a rise in higher education among Asian Americans generally. The change has been particularly notable for Japanese Americans, whose participation in postsecondary education is higher than either the white majority or any other minority group. Nearly 90 percent of third-generation Japanese Americans attend colleges or universities.

New Asian immigrants

Since the 1960s, immigration by other Asian groups, especially Koreans and Indians, increased. Following the collapse of American-supported governments in Southeast Asia in the 1970s, Vietnamese, Cambodians, Laotians, and Hmongs arrived. These newest Asian immigrants have differing educational backgrounds. For example, among the South Vietnamese are former military officers, government officials, businessmen, and professionals. The Hmongs, by contrast, come from a rural culture that does not have a written language.

Multiculturalism in Historical Perspective

Debate on multiculturalism

An important debate in American education focuses on the question of whether public schools should cultivate a common national character or encourage greater cultural diversity. This question is significant for educational policy and is highly relevant to teachers as they create their own personal philosophy of education.[80]

Common culture or forced dominance?

Ronald Takaki, author of *A Different Mirror: A History of Multicultural America*, employs a multiculturalist interpretation of U.S. history.[81] He sees racism running through much of American history as the dominant white group has imposed its culture and values, often ruthlessly, upon dominated minority groups. Arthur M. Schlesinger, Jr., in *The Disuniting of America*, disagrees, arguing that some multiculturalist trends are eroding a shared American culture by requiring "ethnic and racial criteria" that fragment a "unifying American identity."[82]

Recent Historical Trends

Though it is difficult to assess which trends in contemporary education will be long-lasting and historically significant, this section identifies some that seem important. (An in-depth discussion of these trends is provided throughout the book, especially in Chapters 6, 11, and 12).

[80]For multiculturalism, see James Davison Hunter, *Culture Wars: The Struggle to Define America* (New York: Basic Books/Harper Collins, 1991); Michael Kammen, *Contested Values: Democracy and Diversity in American Culture* (New York: St. Martin's Press, 1995); and James A. Banks, *Multiethnic Education: Theory and Practice* (Boston: Allyn and Bacon, 1994).
[81]Ronald Takaki, *A Different Mirror: A History of Multicultural America* (Boston: Little, Brown, 1993).
[82]Arthur M. Schlesinger, Jr., *The Disuniting of America* (New York: W.W. Norton, 1992), pp. 16–17.

Title IX

Title IX of the 1972 Education Amendments to the Civil Rights Act prohibited discrimination against women in federally aided education programs. This legislation, as well as the Women's Educational Equity Act of 1974, evolved as an extension of the civil rights movement to incorporate women's rights and concerns. Recent developments occurred when the U.S. Supreme Court, in 1996, ruled the Virginia Military Institute's all-male enrollment policy unconstitutional. Following this decision, the Citadel in Charleston, South Carolina, began admitting women cadets. This ended the all-male policy at the only two public institutions of higher education that did not admit women.

Education for All Handicapped Children Act

In 1975, Congress passed the Education for All Handicapped Children Act (PL 94-142), which improved opportunities for a group of children who had previously lacked full access to a quality education. The law established a national mandate that children with disabilities would receive an "appropriate public education." (Again, a full discussion about educating children with disabilities is found in Chapter 11).

U.S. Department of Education

In 1979, Congress enacted legislation, promoted by President Carter, to establish a U.S. Department of Education whose secretary would be a member of the president's cabinet. Prior to this legislation, the Office of Education was part of other federal agencies, such as the Department of Interior or Department of Health, Education, and Welfare. Proponents of a separate Department of Education had argued that education as a vital national interest should be represented by a cabinet-level department. Opponents contended that the proposed department would involve the federal government in what historically were states' and local school districts' prerogatives. (See Chapter 6 for more on educational governance.)

National reports and education reforms

Throughout the 1980s, the condition of American education became, once again, a hotly debated topic. A series of national reports, especially *A Nation at Risk*, spotlighted alleged deficiencies in American schooling.[83] (Chapter 16 examines school reform issues and the development of charter schools.)

The trends highlighted in this section, when tested over time, are likely to be the next chapters in American education's ongoing history.

Summing Up

1. The origins of American schooling in the colonial era were based on elitist and religiously oriented European antecedents. When the English colonists settled in North America, they imported conventional European educational institutions based on a social-class pattern. Primary or vernacular schools for the lower socioeconomic strata of society provided a basic curriculum of reading, writing, arithmetic, and religion. Preparatory schools, such as the Latin grammar school and the colonial colleges, were reserved for upper-class boys and men, offering a classical curriculum to prepare them for leadership roles in church, state, and society. Although girls could attend the elementary vernacular schools, their formal educational opportunities were limited to the basic skills taught there.

2. After the United States won its independence, the forces of democracy, social mobility, and frontier egalitarianism eroded the elitist educational structures imported from Europe. The American common school was created to develop basic literacy, numeracy, and civic competencies. The common or public

---

[83]National Commission on Excellence in Education, *A Nation at Risk: The Imperative for Educational Reform* (Washington, D.C.: U.S. Department of Education, 1983), p. 14.

school movement led to the establishment of elementary schools throughout the country.

3. The emergence of the public high school in the nineteenth century contributed to the growing inclusiveness of public schooling in the United States. The rise of state colleges and universities and the enactment of the Morrill Act in 1862 created the final step of an educational ladder that replaced the vestiges of the exclusive European dual-track system. By the beginning of the twentieth century, the American public school system embraced elementary, secondary, and higher institutions. At mid-twentieth century, the infusion of educational technology began to transform teaching and learning.

4. By the mid-twentieth century, concerted efforts were being made to bring equality of educational opportunity to the children of minority groups, especially African Americans, Native Americans, and Hispanic Americans. The major educational problem of the present lies in reforming schools into genuinely multicultural institutions that serve all Americans equally well, regardless of race, sex, or socioeconomic class.

5. The Americanization ideology of the late nineteenth and early twentieth centuries stressed assimilation into a homogeneous cultural pattern. This idea was replaced, beginning in the mid-1960s, by a pluralistic philosophy that values multicultural contributions of all American people, including those of hitherto neglected minority groups.

6. Recent trends in American education have included more groups in the mainstream of American schooling and have emphasized greater academic achievement.

Key Terms

dual-track system *(136)*

town school *(138)*

hornbook *(138)*

Latin grammar school *(138)*

land grants *(141)*

academy *(141)*

monitorial method *(144)*

common school *(144)*

normal schools *(148)*

McGuffey readers *(150)*

educational ladder *(151)*

high school *(151)*

Committee of Ten *(152)*

Commission on the Reorganization of Secondary Education *(153)*

junior high school *(153)*

middle school *(153)*

land-grant colleges *(155)*

boarding schools *(162)*

Americanization *(163)*

Discussion Questions

1. In what ways has American education become more inclusive over time? In what way does it still fall short of complete inclusiveness? What do you believe you can do, as a teacher, to foster inclusiveness? How do your beliefs about inclusiveness reflect your professional development as a teacher and your personal philosophy of education?

2. What has been the influence of the Puritan ethic on American culture and education? What place does the Puritan ethic hold in your own philosophy of education?

3. Is Jefferson's concept of civic education adequate for the needs of contemporary American society? What place does citizenship education have in your philosophy of education?

4. In terms of the history of American secondary education, why is the purpose of the high school often so controversial? What do you believe should be the purpose of secondary education?

5. Establish a rationale that supports your opinion on "Americanization" and cultural pluralism. Examine this rationale in terms of your professional development as a teacher and in your personal philosophy of education.

6. Is it possible for schools to cultivate both a common and a culturally pluralistic culture?

7. Reflect on the extent to which the history of American education shows continuity and change. How has U.S. schooling stayed the same and how has it changed?

Projects for Professional Development

1. Reflect on the major historical developments treated in Chapter 5. Then develop a class project using oral interviews with experienced K–12 school administrators and classroom teachers that focus on the major changes that have occurred in their professional work. For example, what was the school situation and environment like when you began your work as an administrator or teacher? What changes have occurred? How significant have these changes been? How have you adapted to or worked to create change?

2. Review and reflect on the sections of the chapter dealing with racial and ethnic groups. Many teacher-education programs and state requirements contain multicultural standards. See if your teacher-education program has such a standard. Then arrange a class discussion that focuses on multicultural standards as part of a teacher's professional development.

3. Review the sections dealing with common, normal, and high schools in the chapter. Then examine the professional teacher-education programs that prepare elementary and secondary teachers at your institution. How has their historical origin and development shaped these programs?

4. Conduct oral history interviews about the school experience of senior members of your family or relatives. Work out some common questions that will be asked the interviewees. After the oral interviews have been completed and analyzed, prepare an interpretive history of your family's education.

5. Organize a group research project in which the students will examine representative books and materials that have been used to teach reading in elementary school. Identify key periods such as the 1840s, 1850s, 1860s, and so on. You might begin with the McGuffey readers. Using historical research and interpretation, try to determine how the nature of the stories, the characters, and the values in the books have changed over time.

6. Organize a panel discussion in which each presenter reads an autobiography and analyzes a particular author's educational experiences based on his or her autobiography. For example, autobiographies might be those that include themes such as a Native American's experience at a boarding school, an African American's experience in segregated schools, a woman's experience in

entering a male-dominated profession, a Christian fundamentalist's rejection of cultural relativism, and so forth.

Suggested Readings and Resources

Internet Resources

The Education Alliance for Equity and Excellence on the Nation's Schools at Brown University examines the theme of culture and diversity at **www.brown.edu/Research/The_Education_Alliance/.**

Information about educational technology, especially distance learning, is available on WestEd's Distance Learning Resource Network: **www.wested.org/tie/dirn.**

Information about Native American education is available through Yahoo: **www.yahoo.com** by choosing the subject Education K–12 and then Indian Education.

For information about Native Americans, especially laws and treaties, consult Oklahoma State University's **www.library.okstate.edu/kappler.**

Education is one of the topics dealt with at the sites: "African American Webliography" or the "African American Haven."

For information, essays, and bibliographies on early American history, especially the Revolutionary era, consult Michigan State University and the Omohundro Institute of Early American History and Culture: **www.revolution.h-net.msu.edu.**

For information on Asia and Asian Americans, consult the Asia Society site: **www.asiasociety.org.**

For information about the women's rights movement, consult the National Women's History Project: **www.nwhp.org.**

Groups devoted to Asian Americans and other racial and ethnic groups are listed on the "pfish" submenu at **www.metscape.org.**

The Public Broadcasting Service provides information about the documentary "The Two Nations of Black America" at **www.pbs.org/wgbh/pages/frontline/shows/race/main.html.**

The University of California at Los Angeles's Center for African American Studies provides access to "Though My Eyes," a project that examines how African Americans cope with and react to racism at **www.thinklink.net/thrumyeyes.**

David Phillips, an associate professor of American history at Bennington College, has developed a collection of on-line resources on American social and cultural history that deal with immigration, women's rights, and other topics at **www.bennington.edu/courses/history.**

A hypertext edition of Jacob Riis's *How the Other Half Lives: Studies Among the Tenements of New York* is available at **www.cis.yale.edu/amstud/inforev/riis/title.html.**

Videos

American Decades, for Windows, an interactive program that allows users to explore significant periods in U.S. history, unloads from a CD-ROM. Contact Gale Research Inc., 7625 Empire Drive, Florence, KY 41041. Phone: 800-865-5840.

Common Threads. VHS, 20 minutes (1995). Insight Media, 2162 Broadway, P.O. Box 621, New York, NY 10024-0621. Phone: 212-721-6316. *Chronicles the history of education in the U.S. from the colonial period to the present.*

A Day in the Life of the One-Room School. VHS, 16 minutes (1988). Insight Media, 2162 Broadway, P.O. Box 621, New York, NY 10024-0621. Phone: 212-721-6316. *Provides an overview of daily life in a one-room school at the turn of the twentieth century.*

Education in America: The 17th and 18th Centuries. VHS, 16 minutes (1958). Insight Media, 2162 Broadway, P.O. Box 621, New York, NY 10024-0621. Phone: 212-721-6316. *Examines the history of American education from the early New England school laws to the Northwest Ordinance.*

Education (Gender and Education). VHS, 60 minutes (1994). Insight Media, 2162 Broadway, P.O. Box 621, New York, NY 10024-0621. Phone: 212-721-6316. *Focuses on goals of education for women and men during various historical periods.*

Publications

Adams, David W. *Education for Extinction: American Indians and the Boarding School Experience, 1875–1928*. Lawrence: University Press of Kansas, 1995. *In a comprehensive examination of federal Indian boarding schools, Adams analyzes their policies, curriculum, and environments. The title refers to so-called reformers' efforts to assimilate Native American children into white culture by eradicating their tribal cultures.*

Anderson, James D. *The Education of Blacks in the South, 1860–1935*. Chapel Hill: University of North Carolina Press, 1988. *A leading historian of the African American educational experience documents the role that stereotypic thinking played in the model of schooling imposed on African Americans in the South.*

Beatty, Barbara A. *Preschool Education in America: The Culture of Young Children from the Colonial Era to the Present*. New Haven: Yale University Press, 1995. *Beatty provides a very useful history of such early childhood institutions as infant schools, kindergartens, and nursery schools in the United States.*

Cohen, Ronald D. *Children of the Mill: Schooling and Society in Gary, Indiana, 1906–1960*. Bloomington: Indiana University Press, 1990. *Cohen's book offers much information about the impact of schooling on southern and eastern European ethnics and African Americans in a northern industrial city.*

Herbst, Jurgen. *And Sadly Teach: Teacher Education and Professionalization in American Culture*. Madison: University of Wisconsin Press, 1989. *This book examines the history of U.S. teacher education as it relates to efforts to create a teaching profession.*

Herbst, Jurgen. *The Once and Future School: Three Hundred and Fifty Years of American Secondary Education*. New York: Routledge, 1996. *Herbst provides a thorough examination of the history of secondary education in the United States, focusing on the phases of development of the high school with a special emphasis on its one-time role as a "people's college."*

Kaestle, Carl, et al. *Literacy in the United States: Readers and Reading since 1880*. New Haven, Conn.: Yale University Press, 1991. *This book provides a historical perspective on the reading habits and literacy rates of Americans.*

Reese, William J. *The Origins of the American High School*. New Haven: Yale University Press, 1995. *Contextualizing the history of the American high school in terms of significant cultural, economic, and political developments, Reese uses examples of high schools across the nation.*

Reinier, Jacqueline S. *From Virtue to Character: American Childhood, 1775–1850.* New York: Twayne of Macmillan, 1996. *The author analyzes adult beliefs and children's experience in the perspective of American history. The book is useful in developing insights into American conceptions of childhood.*

Rippa, S. Alexander. *Education in a Free Society: An American History.* New York: Longman, 1992. *Rippa's history of American education has gone through many editions. It is a well-done general history of American education and schooling.*

Schlesinger, Arthur M. *The Disuniting of America.* New York: W.W. Norton & Co., 1992. *Schlesinger argues against the current trends in multiculturalism as being potentially divisive and threatening to erode American consensus and identity.*

Takaki, Ronald. *A Different Mirror: A History of Multicultural America.* Boston: Little, Brown, and Co., 1993. *In this history of the United States, Takaki argues for a comparative treatment of the racial and ethnic groups who are part of American culture. He argues that racism and discrimination against these groups should be examined as a part of American history.*

Tyack, David, and Elisabeth Hansot. *Learning Together: A History of Coeducation in American Public Schools.* New Haven, Conn.: Yale University Press, 1990. *This book gives a comprehensive history of the policies and practices of gender in American public schools and examines the factors that have shaped coeducation.*

Vinovskis, Maris A. *Education, Society, and Economic Opportunity: A Historical Perspective on Persistent Issues.* New Haven: Yale University Press, 1995. *Vinovskis, a respected historian of education, examines such issues as the changing role of families, early childhood education, and secondary education in their relationship to socioeconomic participation and mobility.*

PART THREE

Political, Economic, and Legal Foundations

CHAPTER SIX

Governing and Administering Public Education

This chapter was revised by Dr. James Lawlor, Towson University

Education in the United States is organized on four governmental levels — local, intermediate (in some states), state, and federal. Knowledge of the formal organization of schools and how they are governed puts teachers, or prospective teachers, in a better position to make wise choices and realistic decisions about schools and to take appropriate political action. In this chapter, we examine the various governmental levels and how they affect education.

A national system of education does not exist in this country in the same sense that it does in Great Britain, France, or Japan. Education here is considered a state and/or local function; we have fifty different state educational systems and many differences among local school systems even within the same state. Moreover, various reform movements have been altering traditional structures of school governance in many areas of the country. For example, because of school-based management, some school boards and administrators are sharing their responsibilities with teachers, parents, and community members. This chapter concentrates primarily on the standard forms of local, state, and federal responsibility.

The U.S. Constitution makes no mention of public education, but the Tenth Amendment to the Constitution reserves to the states all powers not specifically delegated to the federal government or prohibited to the states by the Constitution. This amendment is the basis for allocating to the states primary legal responsibility for public education. However, responsibility for the practical day-to-day operation of school systems has been delegated by the states to local districts. So we begin our discussion of how schools are governed and administered at the local level. As you read Chapter 6, think about the following questions:

■ How do local, state, and federal governments influence education?

■ How does the local school board work with the district superintendent in formulating school policy?

■ Why have many school districts consolidated or decentralized?

■ What are the different roles and responsibilities of the governor, state legislature, state board of education, state department of education, and chief state school officer in determining school policy?

■ How has the federal role in education changed in recent years?

Local Responsibilities and Activities

Every public school in the United States is part of a local school district. The district is created by the state. The state legislature, subject to the restrictions of the state constitution, can modify a local district's jurisdiction, change its boundaries and powers, or even eliminate it altogether. The local district encompasses a relatively small geographical area and operates the schools for children within a specific community. However, because a school district operates to carry out a state function, not a local function, local policies must be consistent with policies set forth in the state school code. The local district can be compared to a limited corporation whose powers are granted by state laws; it has only those powers expressly granted to it and those discretionary powers essential to its operation.

Local School Boards

Responsibilities of local boards

Despite the fact that the state limits their prerogatives, **local school boards** have assumed significant decision-making responsibility. Many school boards have the power to raise money through taxes. They exercise power over personnel and school property. Some states leave curriculum and student policy very much in the hands of the local school board, but others, by law, impose specific requirements or limitations.

Methods of selecting board members are prescribed by state law. The two standard methods are election and appointment. Election is thought to make for greater accountability to the public, but some people argue that appointment leads to greater competence and less politics. Election is by far the most common practice, accounting for about 95 percent of school board members nationwide.[1] A few states specify a standard number of board members, still others specify a permissible range, and a few have no requirements. Most school boards fall within a seven-to-nine-member range, with the largest school board having nineteen members.

Most school boards elected

School board diversity: a continuing concern

Many educators are concerned about whether school boards adequately reflect the diversity of the communities they serve. Recent nationwide surveys indicate that the number of women on school boards has increased, from about 33 percent in 1981 to over 44 percent in 1997 (see Figure 6.1). Minority representation has remained stationary over the same period at 8.5 percent, even though the proportion of minority students in U.S. public schools continues to rise (29.6 percent in 1995).[2] The largest one hundred school systems (those enrolling 35,000 or more students) tend to have more heterogeneous boards. A 1991 survey indicated that minority members constituted 28 percent of the school board membership in these systems; women made up 42 percent.[3]

School board members tend to be older than the general population (almost 85 percent are over forty); more educated (75 percent have had four or more years of college); wealthier (80 percent have family incomes of $40,000 or more, and 38 percent earn more than $80,000 annually); and more likely to be professionals or managers (44 percent) or owners of their own businesses (13 percent). Interestingly, only 57 percent are parents, and almost 47 percent have no children in school. Most board members see their political affiliation as conservative (55 percent), and

---

[1]Donna Harrington-Leuker, "School Boards at Bay," *American School Board Journal* (May 1996), pp. 18–22.
[2]*Digest of Education Statistics, 1997,* Table 45, p. 60.
[3]*Education Vital Signs, 1997* (Alexandria, Va.: National School Boards Association, 1997), p. 15; and Allan C. Ornstein, "School Superintendents and School Board Members: Who They Are," *Contemporary Education* (Winter 1992), pp. 157–159.

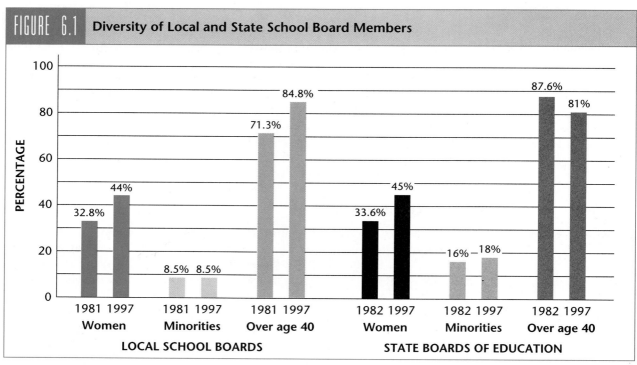

FIGURE 6.1 Diversity of Local and State School Board Members

Source: "Leadership," *Education Vital Signs, 1997* (Alexandria, Va.: National School Boards Association, 1997), pp. A15–A20; telephone interview with Brenda Welburn, Director, National Association of State Boards of Education, December 13, 1995; Dinah Wiley, *State Boards of Education* (Arlington, Va.: National Association of State Boards of Education, 1983), Tables 1–2, pp. 15–16; and National Association of State Boards of Education, *Gender, Age, and Racial Demographics of the State Board Members* (Alexandria, Va.: Author, 1998), pp. 2, 4, 8.

38 percent are liberal. Thirty-four percent of school board members live in small towns, and an almost equal number live in suburban areas. Twenty-two percent live in rural communities, and almost 12 percent live in urban areas.[4]

Types of board meetings

There are three types of board meetings: regular, special, and executive. The first two are usually open meetings and the public is invited. The third type, usually closed to the public, deals with personnel issues or serious problems. Open board meetings obviously enhance school-community relations and allow parents and other citizens to understand the problems of education as well as to air their concerns. The use of closed board meetings to reach major policy decisions is often criticized and is illegal in many states.

Pressure on school boards

There is considerable pressure on school board members as they listen to and weigh the competing demands of citizen advisory groups, the business community, parents with special concerns (such as students with disabilities, gifted and talented programs, school-based management committees), the teachers' association, and local and state politicians, whose support is often needed to fund their decisions. Sometimes there are winners and at other times losers; high priorities take precedence over lower ones, and funding constraints frequently mean difficult (and sometimes unpopular) decisions.

---

[4]*Education Vital Signs*, p. A15.

School Board Responsibilities

Schools are big business

The administration and management of schools is big business, and school board members must understand good business practices. Overall, school boards have fiscal responsibility for $314 billion each year and employ almost 5 million teachers, administrators, and support staff (such as guidance counselors, librarians, and nurses)[5]; this makes them the largest nationwide employer. Board members must be fair and mindful of the law when dealing with students, teachers, administrators, parents, and other community residents.

Authority of board members

Board members are expected to govern the school system without encroaching on the authority of the superintendent. Members, in theory, have no authority except during a board meeting and while acting as a collective group or board. Board members must be politically prudent because eventually someone will ask for a favor, and members must be able to resist this pressure.

More divisive school boards

The quality of local schools is an important factor in determining a community's reputation, the value of property, and the willingness of businesses to locate nearby. Yet according to a recent survey of sixty-six Illinois school superintendents, school boards have become more political and divisive in recent years; newer board members seem more interested in the views of their electors than in the views of other board members or professional educators. This has caused some educators and citizens to question the value of elected school boards and the politicization they often bring.[6]

The powers and responsibilities of school boards may be classified as follows:

Responsibilities of school board members

1. *Policy.* School boards set the general rules about what will be done in the schools, who will do it, and how. The shift to school-based management recently has changed the complexion of the "what," "who," and the "how," permitting greater involvement of teachers, school-based administrators, and parent groups in the day-to-day operation and direction of the school.

2. *Staffing.* Technically the board is responsible for hiring all the employees of the school district. In practice, however, school boards usually confine themselves to recruiting and selecting the school superintendent (the district's chief executive officer) and high-ranking members of the central office staff. Decisions on the hiring and retention of principals and teachers are usually made at lower levels of the hierarchy.

3. *Employee relations.* School board members are responsible for all aspects of employee relations, including collective bargaining with teacher unions. Large school districts rely on consultants or attorneys to negotiate with teachers; small school districts may use the superintendent or a school board committee to negotiate.

4. *Fiscal matters.* The board must keep the school district solvent and get the most out of every tax dollar. The school district usually has a larger budget than any other local government.

---

[5]*Digest of Education Statistics, 1997* (Washington, D.C.: U.S. Government Printing Office, 1997), Table 82, p. 89; Table 32, p. 35.
[6]David Eisner, "School Boards More Political," *Chicago Tribune,* January 22, 1990, sect. 2, p. 4; Mel Heller and Edward Ransic, "Are We Turning Superintendents into Politicians?" *Illinois School Board Journal* (May–June 1992), pp. 12–13; and Thomas A. Shannon, "The Changing Local Community School Board," *Phi Delta Kappan* (January 1994), special edition.

5. *Students.* The board addresses questions of student rights and responsibilities, requirements for promotion and graduation, extracurricular activities, and attendance.

6. *Curriculum and assessment.* The school board is in charge of developing curriculum — especially as it relates to state law and guidelines — and approving the textbooks to be used. Likewise, the board must implement state requirements for assessing student performance.

7. *Community relations.* The school board must be responsive not only to parents but also to other members of the community.

8. *Intergovernmental requirements.* Federal and state agencies establish a variety of requirements for local schools, and the school board is responsible for seeing that these mandates are carried out.[7]

The School Superintendent and Central Office Staff

Executive officer of school system

One of the board's most important responsibilities is to appoint a competent **superintendent of schools**. The superintendent is the executive officer of the school system, whereas the board is the legislative policy-making body. Since the school board consists of laypeople who are not experts in school affairs, it is their responsibility to see that the work of the school is properly performed by professional personnel. The board of education often delegates many of its own legal powers to the superintendent and staff, although the superintendent's policies are subject to board approval.

One of the major functions of the school superintendent is to gather and present data so that school board members can make intelligent policy decisions. *(© Bob Daemmrich/Stock Boston)*

[7]"NSBA and AASA Sketch Your Roles," *American School Board Journal* (June 1994), pp. 20–21; Paul Houston and Anne Bryant, "The Roles of Superintendents and School Boards in Engaging the Public with the Public Schools," *Phi Delta Kappan* (June 1997), pp. 756–759; and Michael W. Kirst, "Recent Research on Intergovernmental Relations in Education Policy," *Educational Researcher* (December 1995), pp. 18–22.

Board reliance on superintendent

One of the major functions of the school superintendent is to gather and present data so that school board members can make intelligent policy decisions. As school systems grow in size, the board relies increasingly on the superintendent and staff. The superintendent advises the school board and keeps members abreast of problems; generally, the school board refuses to enact legislation or make policy without the recommendation of the school superintendent. However, if there is continual disagreement or a major conflict over policy between the school board and the superintendent, the latter is usually replaced. The average tenure of superintendents is only about three to four years.[8] One survey in the early 1990s reported that 24 percent of the superintendents in the largest one hundred school districts had served in their current positions for one year or less.[9]

Duties of the superintendent

Besides being an adviser to the board of education, the superintendent is usually responsible for many other functions, including the following:

1. Supervising professional and nonteaching personnel (for example, janitors and engineers)
2. Making recommendations regarding the employment, promotion, and dismissal of personnel
3. Ensuring compliance with directives of higher authority
4. Preparing the school budget for board review and administering the adopted budget
5. Serving as leader of long-range planning
6. Developing and evaluating curriculum and instructional programs
7. Determining the internal organization of the school district
8. Making recommendations regarding school building needs and maintenance

In addition, the superintendent is responsible for the day-to-day operation of the schools within the district and serves as the major public spokesperson for the schools.

Community pressure on superintendents

Superintendents are often under strong pressure from various segments of the community, such as disgruntled parents or organized community groups with their own agendas (sometimes overt, sometimes covert). Much of the superintendent's effectiveness will depend on his or her ability to deal with such pressure groups. Only a confident school leader can balance the demands and expectations of parents and community groups with the needs of the students. Experts agree that the key to success as a superintendent is communication — with school board members, citizen groups, teachers, parents, unions, and elected officials. Failure to build citizen, legislative, and political support will quickly lead to the downfall of a superintendent.[10]

Central office organization

A **central office staff** assists the superintendent. In large districts of 25,000 or more students, there may be many levels in the staff hierarchy: a deputy superintendent, associate superintendents, assistant superintendents, directors, department heads, and a number of coordinators and supervisors, each with their own

---

[8]William E. Eaton, *Shaping the Superintendency* (New York: Teachers College Press, Columbia University, 1990); and Ralph B. Kimbrough and Michael Y. Nunnery, *Educational Administration*, 3rd ed. (New York: Macmillan, 1988).
[9]Ornstein, "School Superintendents and School Board Members."
[10]Thomas Shannon, "The Trouble with Generalizations," *American School Board Journal* (February 1994), pp. 60–62; and Thomas Shannon, "The People's Choice: A Blueprint for Involving the Community in Superintendent Selection," *American School Board Journal* (March 1997), pp. 29–32.

support staffs. In small school districts, the operation of the central office is less bureaucratic simply because there are fewer layers. Figure 6.2 shows a larger organizational chart of a medium-sized school district with 5,000 to 25,000 students; this is representative of almost 12 percent of the school districts nationwide.[11] Small school districts, ranging in size from 1,000 to 5,000 students and representing 38 percent of all districts nationally, have an organizational structure much simpler than Figure 6.2. The organizational hierarchy of larger school districts is even more cumbersome, and a chart of those with 100,000 or more students would extend off the page.

Critique of bureaucracy

Critics charge that the many-layered bureaucracies of large school districts are inefficient — a waste of the taxpayers' money. Actually, in terms of administrator-to-student ratios, the largest districts are not necessarily the least efficient. Nevertheless, like large corporations, many school districts are considering the benefits of streamlining in this era of limited resources and school reform.

The Principal and the School

Usually, each school has a single administrative officer, a **principal**, who is responsible for school operations. In small schools, the principal may teach part time as well; in large schools, there may be one or more assistant or vice principals. The administrative hierarchy may also consist of a number of department chairpersons, discipline officers (for instance, a dean of students), and guidance counselors. Each of these individuals works closely with the school principal and under his or her direction. Furthermore, it is common practice for the principal to work with some type of community group for the improvement of the school, often a parent-teacher association or, more recently, a school-based management team.

The principal's role

Probably the most important aspect of the principal's job is the role of manager: dealing with the day-to-day operation of the school, the meetings, paperwork, phone calls, and other everyday tasks. However, principals are also expected to exert leadership in curriculum and instruction. Some authorities recommend that principals spend from 50 to 75 percent of their time focusing on curriculum and instruction (e.g., math, English, social studies, art, and music).[12] However, as principals point out, their numerous managerial tasks often make this impossible. In general, secondary school principals tend to see themselves primarily as general managers, whereas elementary school principals view themselves as leaders in curriculum and instruction.[13] The reason for this difference may be that the larger size of secondary schools creates more managerial work for the principal. Moreover, secondary school principals are usually assisted by chairpersons in various subject areas who handle curriculum and instructional activities, whereas elementary school principals rarely have such assistance.

Influence of school-based management

Traditionally, authority concerning school policies has proceeded in a top-down fashion, from the school board through the superintendent and central office staff to the principal. In some districts, however, as explained in Chapter 2, the practice of *school-based management* has brought more decision-making power to

---

[11]*Digest of Education Statistics, 1997,* Table 90, p. 96.
[12]Daniel L. Duke, *School Leadership and Instructional Improvement* (New York: Random House, 1987); and Thomas J. Sergiovanni, *The Principalship: A Reflective Practice Perspective,* 2nd ed. (Needham Heights, Mass.: Allyn and Bacon, 1991).
[13]Laura A. Cooper, "The Principal as Instructional Leader," *Principal* (January 1989), pp. 13–16; and Allan C. Ornstein, "Leaders and Losers," *Executive Educator* (August 1993), pp. 28–30.

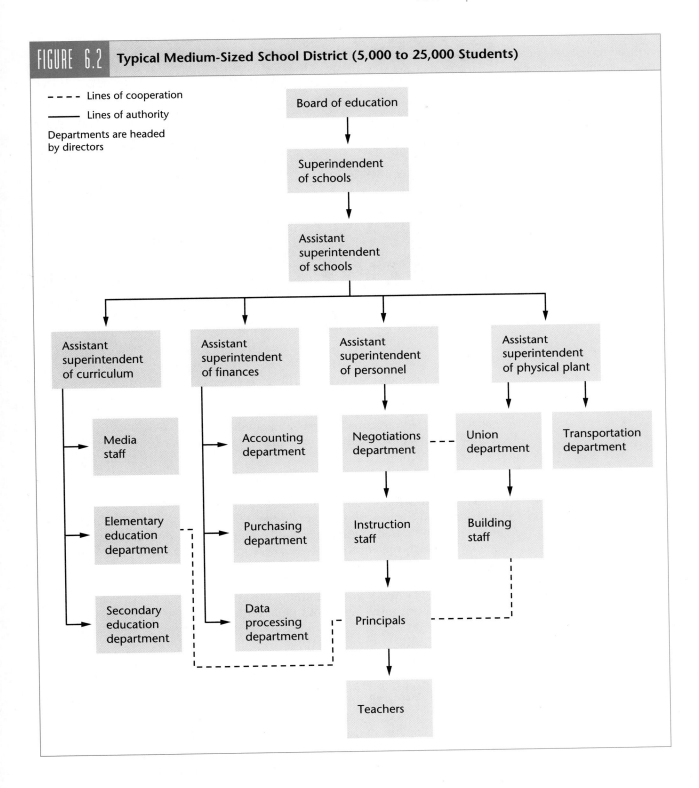

FIGURE 6.2   **Typical Medium-Sized School District (5,000 to 25,000 Students)**

- - - - Lines of cooperation
———— Lines of authority

Departments are headed
by directors

Board of education

Superindendent of schools

Assistant superintendent of schools

Assistant superintendent of curriculum

Assistant superintendent of finances

Assistant superintendent of personnel

Assistant superintendent of physical plant

Media staff

Accounting department

Negotiations department

Union department

Transportation department

Elementary education department

Purchasing department

Instruction staff

Building staff

Secondary education department

Data processing department

Principals

Teachers

In general, secondary school principals tend to see themselves primarily as general managers, whereas elementary school principals view themselves as leaders in curriculum and instruction. *(© Michael Grecco/Stock Boston)*

the level of the individual school. This gives principals and teachers increased responsibility for such matters as curriculum, staff development, teaching assignments, and even hiring and budgeting. This arrangement, which involves collaborating with teachers and other school staff to create school policies, calls for a more participatory governance style than is traditional for school principals.[14]

Parent and Community Involvement

Many programs for school-based management go beyond collaboration among principals and teachers by giving important roles to parents and other community members as well. In doing so, they build on a movement for increased parent and community involvement that has been evident since the 1970s.

Reasons for parent involvement

Many educators have promoted parent involvement for the most basic of reasons: research indicates that it pays off in higher student test scores, better grades, and improved attitudes toward learning,[15] particularly for inner-city and minority students.[16] Across the nation, polls indicate that the public overwhelmingly sup-

[14]Larry E. Frase and R. Gerald Melton, "Manager or Participatory Leader? What Does It Take?" *NASSP Bulletin* (January 1992), pp. 17–25; Larry E. Sackney and Dennis J. Dibski, "School-Based Management: A Critical Perspective," *Educational Management and Administration* (April 1994), pp. 104–112; and Jerome Delaney, "Principal Leadership: A Primary Factor in School-Based Management and School Improvement," *NASSP Bulletin* (February 1997), pp. 107–111.

[15]Lloyd Campbell, "Parents and Schools Working for Student Success," *NASSP Bulletin* (April 1992), pp. 1–4; and David A. Squires and Robert D. Kranyik, "The Comer Program," *Educational Leadership* (December 1995–January 1996), pp. 29–33.

[16]James P. Comer, "Empowering Black Children's Educational Environment," in H. P. McAdoo and J. L. McAdoo, eds., *Black Children* (Beverly Hills, Calif.: Sage, 1985), pp. 114–139; James Comer, *Waiting for a Miracle* (New York: Penguin, 1998). pp. 442–446; Barbara L. Jackson and Bruce S. Cooper, "Involving Parents in Urban Schools," *NASSP Bulletin* (April 1992), pp. 30–38; and Christina Ramirez-Smith, "Stopping the Cycle of Failure," *Educational Leadership* (February 1995), pp. 14–19.

Community members, and students themselves, are taking advantage of what school systems have to offer. Community involvement is key to achieving quality education. *(© Spencer Grant/ Stock Boston)*

ports the idea of parent involvement and believes that parents play a major role in children's education.[17]

Uninvolved parents

Nevertheless, relatively few parents take full advantage of existing opportunities to involve themselves with their children's schooling. In a Department of Education survey of parents, only 32 percent of parents with eighth-grade children reported that they belonged to a parent-teacher organization, and only 36 percent had attended one or more school meetings.[18] According to another survey, most parents had neither the time nor the inclination to participate deeply in school matters. More than 75 percent never helped teachers in the classroom or participated in school functions. Many parents, according to recent research, are deterred from involvement in the schools because of feelings of inadequacy, negative experiences in schools as students, and negative perceptions of administrator and teacher attitudes.[19]

Types of community involvement

Despite such lack of participation from individual parents, the pressure for reform has produced formal arrangements that give parents and other community members a voice in local educational decisions. Usually the community members merely offer advice, but in a few cases they have been granted substantial control over the schools. For purposes of discussion, we can divide the types of community involvement into three broad categories: community participation, community control, and community education.

---

[17]Vivian R. Johnson, "Parent Centers Send a Clear Message," *Equity and Choice* (Winter 1994), pp. 42–44; and Rob McPhee, "Orchestrating Community Involvement," *Educational Leadership* (December 1995–January 1996), pp. 71–75; Debbie Price, "Students Who Succeed Have Parents Who Care," *The Sun*, May 20, 1998, pp. A1,12.

[18]*Digest of Education Statistics, 1997*, Table 25, p. 30; and "Parent Involvement," *NEA Today* (March 1991), p. 12.

[19]Kristy Sasser, "Parental Involvement in Schools: Reluctant Participants [Do Not Equal] Uninterested Parents" (Paper presented at annual meeting of the Mid-South Educational Research Association, Lexington, Ky., November 13, 1991); and Julie Z. Aranson, "How Schools Can Recruit Hard-to-Reach Parents," *Educational Leadership* (April 1996), pp. 58–60.

GETTING TO THE SOURCE

PHI DELTA KAPPAN MAY 1995

A Kappan Special Section On
Youth and Caring

Robert J. Chaskin and
Diana Mendley Rauner,
Guest Editors

Partnerships Among School, Family, and Community: What the Research Says

JOYCE L. EPSTEIN

The term *partnership* comes up again and again in recent publications about school governance. Many educators think that schools cannot be effectively reformed until parents and community members become involved in school decision making. However, research shows that it is much easier to talk about partnership than to implement it. Joyce Epstein, codirector of the Schools, Family, and Community Partnerships Program at Johns Hopkins University, has drawn up a point-by-point summary of impediments to true partnerships — and steps that can be taken to remove them.

In surveys and field studies involving teachers, parents, and students at the elementary, middle, and high school levels, some important patterns relating to partnerships have emerged.

■ Partnerships tend to decline across the grades, *unless* schools and teachers work to develop and implement appropriate practices of partnership at each grade level.

■ Affluent communities currently have more positive family involvement, on average, *unless* schools and teachers in economically distressed communities work to build positive partnerships with their students' families.

■ Schools in more economically depressed communities make more contacts with families about the problems and difficulties their children are having, *unless* they work at developing balanced partnership programs that include contacts about positive accomplishments of students.

■ Single parents, parents who are employed outside the home, parents who live far from the school, and fathers are less involved, on average, at the school building, *unless* the school organizes opportunities for families to volunteer at various times and in various places to support the school and their children.

Researchers have also drawn the following conclusions.

Areas of community participation

Community Participation. The usual form of **community participation** involves advisory committees at either the neighborhood school or central board level. These committees are commonly appointed by school officials and generally offer the school board help and advice. Citizen groups provide advice and assistance in many areas: (1) identification of goals, priorities, and needs; (2) selection and evaluation of teachers and principals; (3) development of curricula and extracurricular programs; (4) support for financing schools; (5) recruitment of volunteers; and (6) assistance to students in school and in "homework hotline" programs.[20]

Shared power

Community Control. In a system of **community control**, an elected community council or board does more than offer advice — it shares decision-making power

---

[20]Department of Education, *Strong Families, Strong Schools: Building Community Partnerships for Learning* (Washington, D.C.: U.S. Government Printing Office, 1994); Debbie Beardsley and Carol Erickson, "Building on Trust: A Parent's Perspective on School-Based Management," *Schools in the Middle* (September 1994), pp. 29–32; and Izona Warner, "Parents in Touch: District Leadership for Parent Involvement," *Phi Delta Kappan* (January 1991), pp. 372–375.

- Just about all families care about their children, want them to succeed, and are eager to obtain better information from schools and communities so as to remain good partners in their children's education.

- Just about all teachers and administrators would like to involve families, but many do not know how to go about building positive and productive programs and are consequently fearful about trying. This creates a "rhetoric rut" in which educators are stuck, expressing support for partnerships without taking any action.

- Just about all students at all levels — elementary, middle, and high school — want their families to be more knowledgeable partners about schooling and are willing to take active roles in assisting communications between home and school. However, students need much better information and guidance than most now receive about how their schools view partnerships and about how they can conduct important exchanges with their families about school activities, homework, and school decisions.

Questions

1. Looking back over the schools you have attended, do you see any of the "patterns" of interaction that Epstein describes?

2. In the school district with which you are most familiar, what steps are the schools taking to involve families and parents? What steps would you suggest they take?

3. What could you do, as a teacher, to involve parents in their children's education, both in the classroom and in the school community as a whole?

Source: Joyce L. Epstein, "School/Family/Community Partnerships: Caring for the Children We Share," *Phi Delta Kappan* (May 1995), p. 703. Reprinted by permission.

with the central school board. Systems of this sort evolved in New York City and Detroit in the 1970s, but bitter disputes soon erupted between African American and white members and between militant community representatives and professional educators.[21] Detroit ultimately rescinded the powers of the community school boards in the early 1980s. In New York City, community control has persisted, but disputes about exactly who represents the community are frequent.

Experience in Chicago

In 1990 Chicago instituted a form of community control as part of local educational reform. Parent and community groups were given significant input regarding matters such as recruitment and retention of school principals, curriculum, and budgets. Yet a recent examination showed that on three important reform indicators — student achievement, attendance, and dropout rate — Chicago public

---

[21]Bernard Bell, "The Battle for School Jobs: New York's Newest Agony," *Phi Delta Kappan* (May 1972), pp. 553–558; Martin Schiff, "The Educational Failure of Community Control in Inner-City New York," *Phi Delta Kappan* (February 1976), pp. 375–378; and telephone conversation with Anthony Alvarado, Superintendent of District #2, New York City Board of Education, August 9, 1991.

TAKING ISSUE

The Politics of Community Control

In the 1960s and 1970s, community control became a catchword of the Black Power movement and was seen as one way for African Americans to exert some influence over the neighborhood schools their children attended. By the 1980s this idea had lost ground as the less radical alternative of community participation in schools gained momentum. Recently, however, under the heading of "school reform," the idea of community control has resurfaced as a thorny political issue.

Arguments PRO

1 Community control will make teachers and administrators accountable to parents and community residents, where the authority truly belongs.

2 Community control will lead to greater educational innovation and help streamline existing school bureaucracies.

3 Community control will lead to greater public participation in the schools, especially from the parents of children who are failing.

4 Only strict community control will compel local school boards to hire principals and superintendents who can relate to the diverse backgrounds of the children they are serving.

5 Under community control, schools will develop instructional programs that raise student achievement and increase cultural pride among minority groups.

6 Community control will increase participatory democracy and the power of the people.

Arguments CON

1 It is questionable whether community groups, who often have their own hidden agendas, can objectively assess the performance of teachers and administrators.

2 Community school boards are too focused on politics and self-interest to take the necessary steps required for educational innovation.

3 Most people, including parents, have little time as it is to participate in school affairs. The increased responsibility demanded by community control will discourage parental involvement.

4 Community control will result in hiring and promotion patterns based on race and ethnicity rather than on merit.

5 Community control may actually hinder student achievement by favoring cultural programs over academic programs.

6 Community control leads to extremism, vigilantism, and separatism among people.

schools have either remained the same or declined. Though Chicago teachers, administrators, and local school councils generally felt positive about the administrative changes, the larger community of businesspeople, citizens, parents, and legislators did not.[22]

---

[22]Herbert J. Walberg and Richard P. Niemiec, "Is Chicago School Reform Working?" *Phi Delta Kappan* (May 1994), pp. 713–715; and Thomas E. Hogueisson, "Chicago Public School Teachers' Opinions of the Reform School Board of Trustees," ERIC Document Number ED 398332, 1996.

School system serving all ages

Community Education. Since the early 1980s, the school has come to be seen as one, but only one, of the educational agencies within the community. Under this concept — called **community education** — the school serves as a partner, or coordinating agency, in providing educational, health, social, legal, recreational, and cultural activities to the community.[23] In Baltimore, Maryland, for example, schools offer a variety of services to local citizens, such as preschool programs for three- and four-year-olds and their parents, as well as adult sports and drama, exercise, recreational, and vocational programs. Child psychologist David Elkind believes that the American public school has undergone a major transformation in recent years, providing health services, vocational training, child care, child support services, sex education, drug education, parent education, and education for special-needs students. All of this has occurred in response to changes in society.[24]

Schools sharing with other agencies

As part of the community education plan, schools share their personnel and facilities with other community agencies or even businesses. In return, schools may expect to share in the facilities, equipment, and personnel of other community agencies, local businesses, and area universities. This type of sharing is especially important in a period of retrenchment and school budget pressures.

Operation of charter schools

Perhaps the newest major development in community education is the establishment of **charter schools** (discussed in Chapter 7). In this arrangement, the local school board or state board of education grants a community group a "charter" (a contract listing specific rights, privileges, and expectations) that permits the group to establish and operate a public school. Specific arrangements about finance, school operation, student enrollment, and accountability are negotiated. If the charter school does not meet prescribed accountability standards, its charter is revoked and the school is closed. Charter schools are an opportunity for both community involvement in local schools and community control over the fate of those schools.[25]

Size of Schools and School Districts

Debate about school size

Educators have long debated the question of size: How large should a school be? How many students should be enrolled in a single district? Four decades ago, James Conant argued that the most effective high schools were the ones large enough to offer comprehensive and diversified facilities.[26] More recently, however, other educators have contended that small schools are more effective.

Problems of large schools

In 1987, after reviewing several studies, two researchers concluded that high schools should have no more than 250 students. Larger enrollments, according to this analysis, result in a preoccupation with control and order, and the anonymity of a large school makes it harder to establish a sense of community among students,

---

[23]Mario D. Fantini, Elizabeth L. Loughren, and Horace B. Reed, "Toward a Definition of Community Education," *Community Education Journal* (April 1980), pp. 11–33; and S. Hoover and C. M. Achilles, "What Does One Look Like: A School and Community Approach," ERIC Document Number ED 366065, 1994.

[24]Dan Conrad and Diane Hedin, "School-Based Community Service: What We Know from Research and Theory," *Phi Delta Kappan* (June 1991), pp. 743–749; David Elkind, "School and Family in the Postmodern World," *Phi Delta Kappan* (September 1995), pp. 8–14; and George Jeffers and Margaret Olebe, "One Step Family Service Center: The Community School," *Community Education Journal* (Spring 1994), pp. 4–7.

[25]Judith Saks, *The Basics of Charter Schools: A School Board Primer* (Alexandria: National School Boards Association, 1997); Bob Stein, "O'Farrell Community School: Center for Advanced Academic Studies; A Charter School Prototype," *Phi Delta Kappan* (September 1996), pp. 28–29; and Louann A. Bierlein, "Catching On, but the Jury's Still Out," *Educational Leadership* (December 1995–January 1996), pp. 90–91.

[26]James B. Conant, *The American High School Today* (New York: McGraw-Hill, 1959).

GETTING TO THE SOURCE

The Problems of Small Schools

JAMES CONANT

THE AMERICAN HIGH SCHOOL TODAY

A First Report to Interested Citizens
James Bryant Conant

McGraw-Hill Company
New York Toronto

Probably the most influential educator of the mid-twentieth century, James Conant rose to the presidency of Harvard University by age forty. His history-making studies of American schools and teachers have helped to shape educational policy for over a quarter century. In the following selection, he sets forth the basis of his argument for consolidating or reorganizing school districts in order to eliminate small high schools. Some of these ideas are controversial today.

The enrollment of many American public high schools is too small to allow a diversified curriculum except at exorbitant expense. The prevalence of such high schools — those with graduating classes of less than one hundred students — constitutes one of the serious obstacles to good secondary education throughout most of the United States. I believe such schools are not in a position to provide a satisfactory education for any group of their students — the academically talented, the vocationally oriented, or the slow reader. The instructional program is neither sufficiently broad nor sufficiently challenging. A small high school cannot by its very nature offer a comprehensive curriculum. Furthermore, such a school uses uneconomically the time and efforts of administrators, teachers, and specialists, the shortage of whom is a serious national problem.

Financial considerations restrict the course offerings of the small high schools. As the curriculum is narrowed, so is the opportunity for a meaningful program. Unless a graduating class contains at least one hundred students, classes in advanced subjects and separate sections within all classes become impossible except with extravagantly high costs. . . . The normal pattern of distribution of academic talent is such that a class of one hundred will have between fifteen and twenty academically talented

teachers, and parents.[27] More recent studies indicate that learning is best in high schools of 600 to 900 students; learning declines as school size grows and is considerably less in high schools over 2,100 students. Not surprisingly, studies showed that more affluent communities had larger schools and effective student learning, whereas low socioeconomic neighborhoods, or schools with high concentrations of minority students, needed small schools for students to learn.[28] For example, a 1994 study of thirty-four large high schools in New York City showed that when students were organized into "houses" of approximately 250 students, attendance improved, student responsiveness in school increased, and grades went up.[29]

Ideal size of districts

The debate about school size parallels similar disputes about the optimum size of school districts. Larger school districts, according to their proponents, offer a

---

[27]Thomas B. Gregory and Gerald R. Smith, *High Schools as Communities: The Small School Reconsidered* (Bloomington, Ind.: Phi Delta Kappa, 1987); see also Ann Bradley, "Thinking Small," *Education Week,* March 22, 1995, pp. 37–41.

[28]Valerie Lee and Julia Smith, "High School Size: Which Works Best, And for Whom?" *Educational Evaluation and Policy Analysis* (Fall 1997), pp. 205–227.

[29]Rosalind Eichenstein et al., *Project Achieve, Part I: Qualitative Findings, 1993–94* (Brooklyn: New York City Board of Education, 1994); and Craig Howley, "Ongoing Dilemmas of School Size: A Short Story," *Eric Digest* (1996).

students — those who can and should study effectively and rewardingly advanced courses in mathematics, science, and foreign languages as well as general education courses in English and social studies. A slightly smaller number of less bright students will, if they work hard, be able to study a somewhat less intensive program. In a class of one hundred, these two groups together will barely provide sufficient enrollment to justify the school's offering advanced academic courses. If the graduating class were much smaller, these two groups together would be too small to warrant a properly organized sequential program in mathematics, science, and foreign languages. The reluctance of academically talented girls to study advanced science and mathematics courses exists also in small high schools and adds to the financial difficulty of offering such courses. . . .

In many of the really small high schools there are only a few teachers. The scope even of the academic program is correspondingly limited. Courses are often not offered in advanced mathematics, physics or chemistry, and foreign languages, or are offered only every other year. Where there are such courses, they are often taught by teachers whose training in the subject-matter area is inadequate and insufficient. Personnel services such as guidance also tend to be nonexistent or to become the additional responsibilities of the administrator or teachers who lack professional training in these fields. To the extent that there are trained specialists, there is waste. There are not enough students to warrant the full-time services of such specialists.

The same waste occurs in the case of teachers in some fields. A properly qualified physics or mathematics teacher has only limited opportunities in a small high school. He is obliged to teach such subjects as general science and biology on the one hand, or general mathematics and business arithmetic on the other, in addition to his field of special competence. Thus a very scarce national asset is squandered.

Questions

1. Do you agree with Conant's description of the disadvantages of small schools? Why or why not?
2. Can modern communications technology help to alleviate some of the problems Conant identifies? How?
3. On the basis of your own experiences in high school, what would you say is the ideal size for a comprehensive high school? Why?

Source: James Bryant Conant, *The American High School Today: A First Report to Interested Citizens* (New York: McGraw-Hill, 1959), pp. 77–79.

broader tax base and reduce the educational cost per student; consequently, these districts are better able to afford high-quality personnel, a wide range of educational programs and special services, and good transportation facilities. Most studies of this subject over the last sixty years have placed the most effective school district size between 10,000 and 50,000 students,[30] although one classic study by Paul Mort considered the optimum to be 100,000 students per district.[31]

Advantages of small districts

Today, however, small is often considered better, in school districts as well as in individual schools. In a 1993 study of school board members, 78 percent of those surveyed felt that smaller districts were more manageable and promoted citizen involvement, whereas large systems were seen as administrative nightmares.[32]

---

[30]Howard A. Dawson, *Satisfactory Local School Units*, Field Study no. 7 (Nashville, Tenn.: George Peabody College for Teachers, 1934); Mario D. Fantini, Marilyn Gittell, and Richard Magat, *Community Control and the Urban School* (New York: Praeger, 1970); A. Harry Passow, *Toward Creating a Model Urban School System* (New York: Teachers College Press, 1967).
[31]Paul R. Mort and Francis G. Cornell, *American Schools in Transition* (New York: Teachers College Press, 1941); Paul R. Mort, William S. Vincent, and Clarence Newell, *The Growing Edge: An Instrument for Measuring the Adaptability of School Systems,* 2 vols. (New York: Teachers College Press, 1955); and Herbert J. Walberg, "Losing Local Control," *Educational Researcher* (June–July 1994), pp. 19–26.
[32]"Break Up Large School Districts," *American School Board Journal* (May 1993), p. 48.

Trend toward larger districts

Arguments and counterarguments aside, the trend in American education has been toward larger school districts. By 1996 one-third of all public school students were in 295 districts containing 20,000 or more students.[33] In most cases, the larger school systems are located in or near cities, the largest being the New York City system with approximately 1,049,000 students, followed by Los Angeles with 647,000 students and Chicago with 413,000. Two other large school systems, Puerto Rico and Hawaii, span an entire territory and state, respectively.[34]

Combining school districts

Consolidation. The increased size of school districts results both from population growth and from **consolidation**, the combination of a number of smaller school districts into one or two larger ones. As Figure 6.3 illustrates, consolidation has produced a dramatic decline in the overall number of districts, from more than 130,000 in 1930 to slightly less than 15,000 in 1996, with the bulk of the decline taking place in the thirty-year period between 1930 and 1960.[35]

School districts consolidate for a variety of reasons, chief among them being the following:

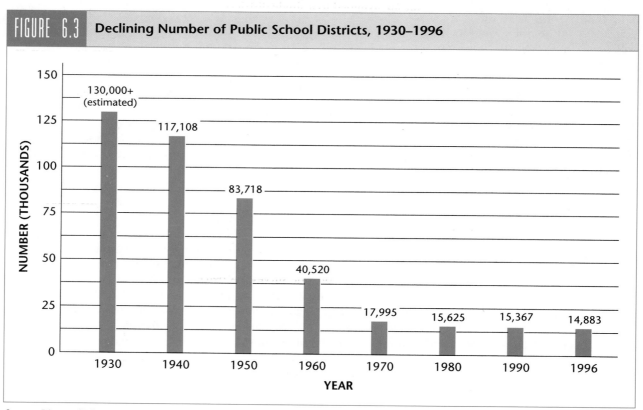

FIGURE 6.3 **Declining Number of Public School Districts, 1930–1996**

Source: Digest of Education Statistics, 1997 (Washington, D.C.: U.S. Government Printing Office, 1997), Table 89, p. 96.

---

[33]*Digest of Education Statistics, 1997*, Table 92, pp. 98–102.
[34]The reader may find a list of the largest school systems in *Digest of Education Statistics, 1994*, Table 93, pp. 98–102. Varied information regarding big-city districts can be obtained by searching the Internet for "Great Cities Schools."
[35]*Digest of Education Statistics, 1997*, Table 89, p. 96.

Reasons for consolidation

- Size. Larger schools, especially high schools, permit broader curriculum offerings and the hiring of specialized faculty.
- Services. Larger schools justify the hiring of counselors, deans of students, assistant principals, team leaders, and specialists normally not found in smaller schools.
- Economics. Purchasing decisions (for example, books, ditto and xerox paper, art supplies, etc.) yield significant cost savings when ordered in bulk. Consolidation also permits older buildings to be retired at considerable cost savings. The elimination of high-salaried, central office positions also occurs when school districts combine.

Options for consolidation

Consolidating districts usually means closing some schools, and this has proved to be a serious and emotional matter, especially in small and rural districts where the local school may be a focal point of the community's identity. A less drastic method of consolidation is for neighboring districts to share programs and personnel. For example, in 1995, 67 Iowa school districts were sharing superintendents, 71 were involved in *whole-grade sharing* (programs in which all students in a certain grade are assigned to a single district).[36]

Dividing districts into smaller units

Decentralization.   Ironically, even as consolidation was taking place, the 1960s saw the advent of a countervailing trend, **decentralization**. Decentralization divides a school system into smaller administrative units, often referred to as zones, areas, or regions. Like the various forms of community involvement discussed earlier, decentralization was seen as a way to bring school issues and control closer to the local community.

Role of ethnicity

In the decades after the Second World War, middle-class and white populations migrated from the cities to the suburbs — in what became known as *white flight* — and the percentages of low-income and minority residents increased in the cities. By the 1960s, members of many inner-city ethnic groups, especially African Americans, began to feel that the schools did not serve their needs. Decentralization, they argued, would give the people more opportunity to be involved in the schools and thereby make the educational system more responsive to their multiethnic student body.

Extent of decentralization

Consequently, while small and rural school districts continued the process of consolidation in the 1960s and 1970s, many large urban districts decentralized. By 1980, according to a nationwide survey, 64 percent of school systems with 50,000 or more students reported that they were decentralized.[37] By the late 1980s, however, the proportion reporting decentralization dropped to 31 percent; many of the large districts had halted decentralization to reduce bureaucracy and to save money. In fact, decentralization did not address the need for responsiveness to the community; in most large urban school districts, decisions continued to be made at the central level — the "downtown office" — rather than at local branch offices.[38]

---

[36]Telephone conversation with Sharon Slezak, Communications Consultant, Iowa State Department of Education, September 12, 1995; and Mary Anne Raywid and Thomas Shaheen, "In Search of Cost Effective Schools," *Theory Into Practice* (Spring 1994), pp. 67–74.

[37]Allan C. Ornstein, "School Consolidation vs. Decentralization: Trends, Issues and Questions," *Urban Review* (June 1993), pp. 167–174.

[38]Allan C. Ornstein, "Centralization and Decentralization of Large Public School Districts," *Urban Education* (July 1989), pp. 233–235; Dan Lewis and Kathryn Nakagawa, *Race and Educational Reform in the American Metropolis: A Study of School Decentralization*, (Albany: State University of New York Press, 1995); and "Southern Regional Education Board: Legislative Update," available by searching the Internet for "Daily Report Card" and clicking to obtain December 15, 1995.

Perhaps this is one reason behind the growth of charter schools and the revival of interest in community control.

Intermediate Units

Coordination and supplementary services

Services provided

The term **intermediate unit** or **regional educational service agency** (RESA) refers to an office or agency in a middle position between the state department of education and local school districts. This agency provides coordination and supplementary services to local districts and links local and state educational authorities. The intermediate unit is usually a legal and political extension of the state department of education created by the state legislature. By 1996 twenty-nine states had some form of intermediate unit. The average intermediate unit comprises twenty to thirty school districts and covers about 50 square miles. In total there are some 1,185 intermediate or regional agencies.[39] In recent years, the intermediate unit has provided school districts with a wide range of consulting services and resource personnel in such general areas of education as curriculum, instruction, evaluation, and in-service training. Intermediate units have also provided services in more specialized areas, such as bilingual education, prekindergarten education, vocational education, education of the gifted and talented and children with disabilities, and data processing and computer education. Many educators believe that an intermediate unit covering several districts can economically provide services that many small or financially strapped school districts could not afford on their own.

State Responsibilities and Activities

Legal responsibility of state

State laws

Every state, by constitution, statute, and practice, assumes that education is one of its primary functions, and federal and state court decisions have supported this interpretation. Each state has legal responsibility for the support and maintenance of the public schools within its borders. The state enacts legislation; determines state school taxes and financial aid to local school districts; sets minimum standards for the training and recruitment of personnel; provides curriculum guidelines (some states also establish "approved" textbook lists); makes provisions for accrediting schools; and provides special services, such as student transportation and free textbooks.

The **state school code** is the collection of laws that establish ways and means of operating schools and conducting education in the state. The state, of course, cannot enact legislation that conflicts with the federal Constitution. In many states the laws are quite detailed concerning methods of operating the schools. The typical organizational hierarchy, from the state level down to the local level, is shown in Figure 6.4.

The Governor and State Legislature

Powers of the governor

Although the powers of governors vary widely, their authority on educational matters is spelled out in law. Usually a governor is charged with making educational budget recommendations to the legislature. In many states, the governor has legal access to any accumulated balances in the state treasury, and these monies can be used for school purposes. The governor can generally appoint or remove school personnel at the state level. But these powers often carry restrictions, such as approval

---

[39]*Digest of Education Statistics, 1997,* Table 91, p. 97.

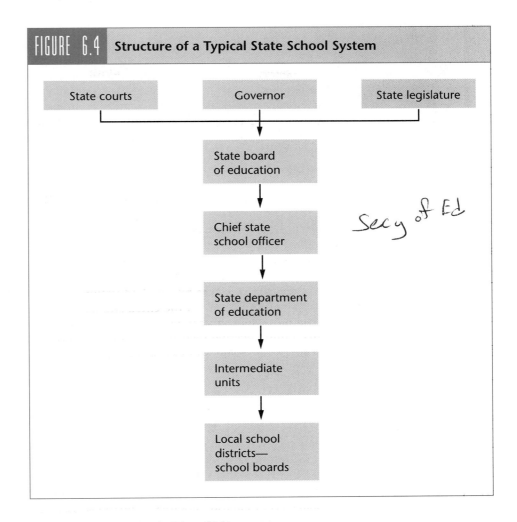

FIGURE 6.4 **Structure of a Typical State School System**

State courts | Governor | State legislature

State board of education

Chief state school officer

Secy of Ed

State department of education

Intermediate units

Local school districts— school boards

by the legislature. In most states, the governor can appoint members of the state board of education and, in a few states, the chief state school officer. A governor can cancel educational measures through his or her veto powers or threaten to use the veto to discourage the legislature from enacting educational laws he or she opposes.

Powers of the legislature

In most states, the legislature is primarily responsible for establishing and maintaining the public schools and has broad powers to enact laws pertaining to education. These powers are limited by restrictions in the form of federal and state constitutions and court decisions. In terms of the basic structure and functions of the educational system, the state legislature usually determines the following:

- The selection process for, and duties of, the state boards of education and the chief state school officer
- The functions of the state department of education
- The types of local and regional school districts
- Whether the state will provide community colleges, adult schools, and vocational schools
- The selection methods and powers of local school boards

The legislature also usually decides on major financial matters, including the nature and level of state taxes for schools and the taxing powers of local school districts. It may also determine basic parameters of teaching and instruction, including (1) what may or may not be taught, (2) how many years of compulsory education will be required, and (3) the length of the school day and school year. In addition, the legislature may establish testing and evaluation procedures, authorize school programs, and set standards for building construction. Where the legislature does not enact these policies, they are usually the responsibility of the state board of education.

New state legislation

Legislative powers over education have been particularly evident during the reform movement that began in the 1980s. Nationwide, more than 1,200 state statutes pertaining to school reform were enacted between 1983 and 1990 alone.[40] The new statutes have addressed matters ranging from curriculum to teaching qualifications, from class size to graduation requirements. Not since the wave of school reform that followed the Soviet launch of *Sputnik* in 1957 have state legislatures played such a prominent role in educational policy. A recent study of seven states (Alabama, Florida, Georgia, Mississippi, North Carolina, South Carolina, and Texas) revealed that the normal turnover of governors and state legislators, each often having his or her own education reform plan, resulted in an on-again, off-again approach to reform. Researchers concluded that the time necessary to initiate positive change in the schools (about ten years) is longer than the tenure of most elected officials.[41]

Time needed for educational reform

The State Board of Education

The **state board of education** is usually the most influential and important state education agency. With the exception of Wisconsin, all states have some sort of state board of education, which depends on the state legislature for appropriations and authority and serves an advisory function for the legislature. (New York's Board of Regents is perhaps the strongest and most respected state board of education.) In addition, most states have a separate governing board for state colleges and universities. The precise duties and functions of state boards of education vary, but Table 6.1 lists duties common to most state boards.

Selection of state board members

In thirty-one states, as of 1998, the board members were appointed by the governor. In three states the state legislature appointed board members, and in ten states the members were elected by popular vote (a method that has become more prevalent in recent decades). The remaining states used either legislative appointment or a combination of appointed members and elected members. The number of members on state boards ranges from seven to nineteen, with an eleven-member board occurring most frequently.[42] (An odd number of members eliminates tie votes.)

Increasing diversity of board members

As with local boards, a recent increase in women is evident, and the proportion of minority members is also rising. By 1982, about 34 percent of board members

[40]Linda Darling-Hammond and Barnett Berry, *The Evolution of Teacher Policy* (Santa Monica, Calif.: Rand Corporation, 1988); Allan C. Ornstein, "Reforming American Schools: The Role of the States," *NASSP Bulletin* (October 1991), pp. 46–55; and Thomas B. Timar and David Kirp, *Managing Educational Excellence* (New York: Falmer Press, 1988).
[41]Richard P. McAdams, "The Systems Approach to School Reform," *Phi Delta Kappan* (October 1997), pp. 138–142.
[42]"State Education Governance at a Glance," (Alexandria, Va.: National Association of State Boards of Education, 1995).

TABLE 6.1 Duties and Responsibilities of State Boards of Education and Chief State School Officers	
State Board of Education	**Chief State School Officer**
1. Adopting and enforcing policies, rules, and regulations necessary to implement legislative acts related to education	1. Serving as the chief administrator of the state department of education and of the state board of education
2. Establishing qualifications and appointing personnel to the state department of education	2. Selecting personnel for the state department of education
3. Setting standards for teaching and administrative certificates	3. Recommending improvements in educational legislation and in educational budgets
4. Establishing standards for accrediting schools	4. Ensuring compliance with state educational laws and regulations
5. Managing state funds earmarked for education	5. Explaining and interpreting the state's school laws
6. Keeping records and collecting data needed for reporting and evaluating	6. Impartially settling controversies involving the administration of the schools within the state
7. Adopting long-range plans for the development and improvement of schools	7. Arranging studies, committees, and task forces as deemed necessary to identify problems and recommend solutions
8. Creating advisory bodies as required by law	8. Reporting on the status of education within the state to the governor, legislature, state board of education, and the public
9. Acting as a judicial body in hearing disputes arising from state policies	
10. Representing the state in determining policies on all matters pertaining to education that involve relationships with other agencies (including the federal government)	
11. Advising the governor or legislature on educational matters	
12. In some states, appointing the chief state school officer, setting minimum salary schedules for teachers and administrators, and adopting policies for the operation of institutions of higher learning	

were women, and 16 percent were members of minority groups; by 1998 the corresponding percentages had risen to 45 percent and 18 percent.[43] (See Figure 6.1 on page 178.) This trend is important because heterogeneity broadens the perspectives of board members and increases the likelihood that boards reflect a wide range of social and educational concerns.

The State Department of Education – *usually appointed*

Functions of state education departments

The **state department of education** usually operates under the direction of the state board of education and is administered by the chief state school officer. Traditionally, the primary function of state departments of education was to collect and disseminate statistics about the status of education within the state. Since the

---

[43]Telephone interview with Brenda Welburn, Director, National Association of State Boards of Education, July 15, 1998; and Dinah Wiley, *State Boards of Education* (Arlington, Va.: National Association of State Boards of Education, 1983), Tables 1–2, pp. 15–16.

includes higher ed

Recent issues

1950s, however, state departments have taken on many other functions. For example, they certify teachers, oversee student transportation and safety, monitor compliance with federal regulations, develop programs to meet the needs of special students (such as bilingual students and students with disabilities), evaluate existing programs, and issue reports.[44] In short, they carry out the laws of the state legislature and the regulations of the state board.

During recent decades, the state departments have had to grapple with controversial issues such as desegregation, compensatory education, student rights and unrest, school finance reform and fiscal crisis, aid to minority groups, collective bargaining, accountability, student assessment, and competency testing. Accordingly, the state departments of education, once nearly invisible, have grown significantly in size. By 1997, five states (California, Michigan, New Jersey, New York, and Texas) had professional staffs approaching 1,000.[45]

The Chief State School Officer

Chief executive

The **chief state school officer** (sometimes known as the state superintendent or commissioner of education) serves as the head of the state department of education and is also the chief executive of the state school board. He or she is usually a professional educator.

Increasing numbers of women

The office is filled in one of three ways: in 1998, ten states filled the position through appointment by the governor, twenty-five states through appointment by the state board of education, and fourteen states by popular election.[46] As of 1998, only one chief state school officer was African American; however, there were fifteen female chief officers (29 percent) — a notable increase from earlier decades and almost double the figure in 1990.[47] The greater number of women in the position represents a departure from the "good old-boy network" that once dominated the upper echelons of educational administration.

Duties of the chief state school officer

The duties of the chief state school officer and the relationship between that position and the state board and state department vary widely. Generally an elected chief officer has more independence than one who is appointed. See Table 6.1 for the basic responsibilities of chief state school officers.

The Federal Role in Education

The role of the federal government will be considered in four parts: (1) the federal agencies that promote educational policies and programs; (2) the trend that has moved many educational decisions from the federal government to the state governments; (3) federal financing of education; and (4) the Supreme Court's decisions concerning education. In this chapter we focus on the first two parts. Federal spending is examined in Chapter 7, and court decisions are discussed in Chapter 8.

---

[44]Fred C. Lunenburg and Allan C. Ornstein, *Educational Administration: Concepts and Practices* (Belmont, Calif.: Wadsworth, 1991).

[45]Fenwick W. English, *Educational Administration: The Human Science* (New York: Harper-Collins, 1992); Thomas J. Sergiovanni et al., *Educational Governance and Administration,* 2nd ed. (Needham Heights, Mass.: Allyn and Bacon, 1992); and telephone conversation with Barbara Clements, Staff Specialist in Statistics, Council of Chief State School Officers, July 16, 1998.

[46]*State Education Governance at a Glance* (Alexandria, Va.: National Association of State Boards of Education, 1998).

[47]*The Council, 1995* (Washington, D.C.: Council of Chief State School Officers, 1998), pp. 2–3.

PROFESSIONAL PLANNING

for your first year

Who Are These People?

The Situation

Richard is a beginning teacher in a large, suburban school district of 90,000 students. Having been raised in a less populated area, he is somewhat overwhelmed by the size and complexity of the school district. It has taken him months to discover that when people referred to "the board" some meant the local school board made up of citizens; others meant the professional board (superintendent and staff); and still others meant the state department of education. He finds frequent references to "the state," which on some days, he discovers, means the state legislature, while on other occasions it means the state department of education. All very confusing! Further complicating things are frequent references to "the central office," those ubiquitous people who seem to be everywhere when they want something done and nowhere when a beginning teacher needs help. Today, Richard found a notice in his mailbox about a "citizen's advisory committee" meeting this evening at the school. Who are all these people and what do they do? How do they help shape education policy in the school district?

Thought Questions

1. How would your philosophy of education be positively and negatively affected by teaching in a large school district like Richard's?
2. As you prepare to interview for a teaching position, what questions do you have for the interviewer about school district organization and management? What is really important for you to know?
3. How would you feel about teaching in a school district as large and potentially as confusing as Richard's? List pros and cons.
4. Contact your state department of education and ask for information on the location, size, and organization of public school districts in the area in which you are interested in teaching. What specific information causes you to select some school districts over others?
5. As a beginning teacher, what will you do to discover how your district is organized, who the important "players" and "stakeholders" are, and how these competing groups shape policy for the school district?

Federal Educational Agencies

For the first 150 years of the nation's history, between 1787 and 1937, Congress enacted only fourteen significant educational laws. In the last six decades, however, more than 160 significant laws have been passed.[48] Traditionally, the major organizations of teachers and administrators, such as the American Federation of Teachers, the National Education Association, and the National School Boards Association, have preferred that the federal government offer financial aid and special services but refrain from interfering in educational policy. But many educators now believe that the federal government should provide a clear statement of mission and

Desire for federal leadership

---

[48]*Digest of Education Statistics, 1997* (Washington, D.C.: U.S. Government Printing Office, 1997), pp. 375–384.

specific kinds of guidance — curriculum frameworks as well as funds — to state and local agencies that are struggling to improve the schools.[49]

Evolution of the department

The U.S. Department of Education.
Although many different federal agencies are now involved in some type of educational program or activity, the **U.S. Department of Education** is the primary federal educational agency. From very humble beginnings in 1867 the Office of Education has grown to about 4,800 employees, and in 1997 its annual expenditures were over $31.1 billion.[50] The department currently administers over 120 separate programs.[51]

Over time, the Office of Education assumed the responsibilities of (1) administering grant funds and contracting with state departments of education, school districts, and colleges and universities; (2) engaging in educational innovation and research; and (3) providing leadership, consultative, and clearing-house services related to education.

Cabinet-level status

In 1979, after much congressional debate and controversy, the Office of Education was changed to the Department of Education. A secretary of education was named, with full cabinet-level status, and the department officially opened in 1980.

Role of the secretary of education

The secretary of education has widespread visibility and influence. Besides managing educational policies and promoting programs to carry out those policies, the secretary can exert persuasion and pressure in political and educational circles. Recent heads of the department, including William Bennett, Lamar Alexander, and Richard Riley, have been in the limelight, pushing their own brands of reform. However, many conservatives have argued for a cutback in the department's activities and elimination of its cabinet-level status.

Federal Retrenchment: Returning Responsibility to the States

Shift in federal policy

Although the federal role in education has expanded dramatically since the 1930s, the 1980s and 1990s brought an era of retrenchment. In what was known as a "new federalism," funds for education were slashed by 16 percent in the 1980s, and more monetary and program responsibilities were shifted to state (and local) agencies. Federal rules and regulations governing education were revoked or more loosely enforced. The powers of the Department of Education were restricted, and the overall scope of the federal role in education was narrowed.[52]

Changes in federal spending

President Bush, who took office in 1989 with the pledge to become the "Education President," outlined a number of national programs to boost achievement in education, promoting such ideas as magnet schools, alternative certification of teachers, and teacher excellence awards. However, these programs continued the Reagan administration's tendency to minimize federal spending and shift responsibilities to the local schools.[53] Moreover, the budget for the Department of Educa-

---

[49]*A National Imperative: Educating for the 21st Century* (Washington, D.C.: National School Boards Association, 1989); Allan C. Ornstein, "The National Reform of Education: Overview and Outlook," *NASSP Bulletin* (September 1992), pp. 89–101; and Ronald Anderson, "Curriculum Reform: Dilemmas and Promise," *Phi Delta Kappan* (September 1995), p. 35.
[50]*Digest of Education Statistics, 1997*, Figure 20, p. 385.
[51]*Digest of Education Statistics, 1994*, Table 349, pp. 370–373.
[52]David L. Clark, Terry A. Astuto, and Paula M. Rooney, "The Changing Structure of Federal Education Policy in the 1980s," *Phi Delta Kappan* (November 1983), pp. 188–193; and Larry Cuban, "Four Stories About National Goals for American Education," *Phi Delta Kappan* (December 1990), pp. 265–271.
[53]Bruce Joyce, "The Doors to School Improvement," *Educational Leadership* (May 1991), pp. 59–62; Joe Nathan and Jim Kiesmeier, "The Sleeping Giant of School Reform," *Phi Delta Kappan* (June 1991), pp. 738–742; and *Digest of Education Statistics, 1997*, p. 375.

tion, though increasing, did not keep up with inflation. Thus it actually declined. In 1993 and 1994 the Clinton administration reversed this trend and increased the department's funding, and has continued these increases through 1998 even with a Republican-controlled Congress.[54]

Less stress on equalitarianism

Along with the reluctance to spend federal funds for education, federal retrenchment generally means less emphasis on equalitarianism as a national policy. For example, in the late 1980s the government cut back programs for big-city schools, especially those for minority and low-income groups.[55] As a result, many people became concerned that urban schools, which educate the children of most of the nation's low-income families, were being shortchanged. Many liberal and equalitarian groups would like the federal government to return to the activism in educational matters that it demonstrated in the 1960s and 1970s. Conservative groups contend that such federal involvement is neither appropriate nor affordable. These debates about the proper federal role in education promise to continue for some time.

Nonpublic Schools

State aid for nonpublic schools

Although this chapter has focused on public education, nonpublic schools are not exempt from some governmental influences. In particular, education laws passed by state legislatures often apply to private and parochial schools as well as to public institutions — laws pertaining to health standards, building codes, welfare of children, student codes, and so forth. In addition, legislative bodies in many states have passed laws to help private schools and, using public funds, to provide aid in such areas as student transportation, health services, dual enrollment or shared-time plans, school lunch services, purchasing of books and supplies, student testing services, teacher salary supplements, student tuition, and student loans.

Enrollment in nonpublic schools

As indicated in Chapter 1, nonpublic schools now account for over 11 percent of total enrollments in U.S. elementary and secondary schools. Catholic schools still enroll the greatest number of private-school students, although their enrollment has declined from 85 percent of all private-school students in 1969 to 50 percent in 1997. Nonreligious, independent schools have increased their share of students from 8 percent of private-school enrollments in 1969 to 15.5 percent by 1997. Evangelical and fundamentalist Christian schools have also grown dramatically in number and student population, reflecting the increased influence of conservative Protestants who seek schools that emphasize God, discipline, and faith in community and country.[56]

Private schools are not typically organized and run in the same manner as public schools. They have a principal or headmaster, but generally do not have the cadre of support people mentioned earlier in this chapter. They usually derive their authority from a board of directors or school committee, which, unlike a public school board, is concerned only with the operation of one particular private school.

Competition or cooperation?

Many commentators see the relationship between the public and private sectors as one of competition for students and for funds. Other educators, however, prefer to think in terms of potential cooperation between public and private

---

[54]*Digest of Education Statistics, 1997*, Table 33, p. 36.
[55]*Digest of Education Statistics, 1990*, Table 329, p. 345. See also Nancy A. Madden et al., "Success for All," *Phi Delta Kappan* (April 1991), pp. 593–599.
[56]*Digest of Education Statistics, 1997*, Table 61, p. 72; Allan C. Ornstein, "The Growing Popularity of Private Schools," *Clearing House* (January 1990), pp. 210–213; and Charles Park, "The Religious Right and Public Education," *Educational Leadership* (May 1987), pp. 5–11.

schools. In some ways, in fact, the distinction between public and private schools is becoming blurred.[57] For example, programs of *school choice* sometimes blend the public and private by allowing students to apply public funds to a private education. (Privatization is discussed in detail in Chapter 16 and school choice in Chapter 7.).

Summing Up

1. The governance of education is organized on four governmental levels: local, intermediate (in some states), state, and federal.

2. Schools are organized into school districts; today there are approximately 15,000 public school systems operating in the United States.

3. At the local level, the school board, the school superintendent, the central office staff, and school principals all take part in governing and administering the schools.

4. Educators have made a number of efforts to increase the involvement of parents and community members in the schools. Programs for school-based management often include a greater role for parents and community members. Other forms of public involvement include community participation, community control, community education, and charter schools.

5. Educators have long debated the optimum size for schools and school districts. Many have come to believe that increases in size do not necessarily mean increases in efficiency or effectiveness and may result in the opposite.

6. Whereas small and rural school districts have undergone a great deal of consolidation since the 1930s, many large urban districts have followed the contrary trend of decentralization.

7. More than half of the states have one or more intermediate units that support local school districts and exercise limited regulatory powers.

8. In most states, the legislature is primarily responsible for establishing and maintaining public schools and has broad powers to enact laws pertaining to school education.

9. With the exception of Wisconsin, all states have state boards of education. Operating under the state boards are the state departments of education, headed by the chief state school officer.

10. Overall, the federal role in education has dramatically expanded since the 1930s. The last two decades, however, have witnessed a movement toward reduced federal involvement.

11. Nonpublic schools account for over 11 percent of total enrollments in U.S. elementary and secondary schools, with Catholic schools comprising 50 percent of these enrollments and nonreligious, independent schools 15.5 percent.

---

[57]Arthur G. Powell, "A Glimpse at Teaching Conditions in Top Private Schools," *American Educator* (Winter 1990), pp. 28–34; Dennis P. Doyle, "The Role of Private Sector Management in Public Education," *Phi Delta Kappan* (October 1994), pp. 128–132; and Paul D. Houston, "Making Watches or Making Music?" *Phi Delta Kappan* (October 1994), pp. 133–135.

Key Terms

local school boards *(177)*

superintendent of schools *(180)*

central office staff *(181)*

principal *(182)*

community participation *(186)*

community control *(186)*

community education *(189)*

charter schools *(189)*

consolidation *(192)*

decentralization *(193)*

intermediate unit *(194)*

regional educational service
  agency *(194)*

state school code *(194)*

state board of education *(196)*

state department of education *(197)*

chief state school officer *(198)*

U.S. Department of Education *(200)*

Discussion Questions

1. What do you think are the advantages and disadvantages of elected, rather than appointed, local school boards? Do the same arguments apply to state boards of education? Where would you rather work — where school boards are elected or appointed? Explain.

2. React to the following statement made by Ernest Boyer, president of the Carnegie Foundation, when critiquing the 1983 presidential report *A Nation at Risk:* "If indeed the nation is at risk, then where is the federal government's effort to address the problem?"

3. What are some reasons for and against shifting educational responsibilities from the federal government to the states?

4. How, as a teacher, can you influence educational change at the local level? At the state level?

Projects for Professional Development

1. Interview classmates who went to large high schools (over 1,000 students) and those who went to smaller high schools (under 1,000 students). Where would you rather teach and why?

2. Write a statement addressing the following questions: (a) Why have many small school districts consolidated? (b) Why have many urban systems decentralized? (c) What are the advantages and disadvantages of consolidation and decentralization, and what can you conclude about these contrary trends? Talk to a classmate about your conclusions.

3. Interview teachers and administrators in local schools regarding issues of teacher empowerment and school governance. You might ask the following questions: (a) To what extent are teachers involved in school governance and management? Is true school-based management in operation in the school? If so, how? (b) How do teachers feel about their involvement in running the school? (c) How do principals and other administrators feel about teacher involvement in school governance? Analyze your interview responses. What can you conclude about teacher involvement in school governance? Is school-based management worthwhile or is it just another educational fad?

4. Talk with teachers and administrators in local schools about ways in which parents and the school community are involved in the schools. Prepare a plan

that would reach out to and/or involve students' parents in meaningful ways in your classroom and in the school community.

5. Attend a local school board meeting. Note who is present, both on the school board and in the audience. Examine the meeting agenda. Then answer the following questions: (a) What topics and issues were discussed? (b) What individuals or community groups were present, and what views did they express? (c) Did any individuals or groups express differing or alternative views? How did the school board respond to these different viewpoints? (d) What decisions were made by the school board, and how were they reached? (e) What did you learn about school district governance from your attendance at the meeting?

Suggested Readings and Resources

Internet Resources

If you have not yet visited the U.S. Department of Education's home page on the World Wide Web (**www.ed.gov**), you may wish to do so for a glance at the scope of the federal government's involvement in education. The subsidiary page "Educational Resources by State" (**/programs.html**) lists Department of Education offices and programs in each state. For on-line sites of individual school districts, a good starting point is the Education K–12 category on the Yahoo home page (**www.yahoo.com**). In addition, useful information on topics addressed in this chapter can be accessed by starting with a general net search for NCREL (the North Central Regional Educational Laboratory), CPRE (the Center for Policy Research in Education), AERA (the American Educational Research Association), or other education-related organizations such as the American Federation of Teachers and the National Education Association.

Publications

Campbell, Roald F., Luvern L. Cunningham, Raphael O. Nystrand, and Michael D. Usdan. *The Organization and Control of American Schools,* 6th ed. Columbus, Ohio: Merrill, 1990. *An important work on the organization of American schools, including a detailed discussion of the federal, state, and local governments' impact on school districts.*

Donmoyer, Robert, Michael Imber, and James J. Scheurich, eds. *The Knowledge Base in Educational Administration.* Albany: State University of New York Press, 1995. *An excellent book on school organization and management, particularly concerning interactions with the community.*

Gregory, Thomas B., and Gerald R. Smith. *High Schools as Communities: The Small School Reconsidered.* Bloomington, Ind.: Phi Delta Kappa, 1987. *A powerful discussion of the need for small schools and the importance of school ethos and school-community relations.*

Lunenburg, Fred C., and Allan C. Ornstein. *Educational Administration: Concepts and Practices.* Belmont, Calif.: Wadsworth, 1991. *A discussion of how to improve schools in the context of the political structure.*

Poston, William K. *Making Governance Work.* Thousand Oaks, Calif.: Corwin Press, 1994. *An excellent discussion of school boards, school leadership, school-based management, and total quality management.*

Ravitch, Diane. "Different Drummers: The Role of Nonpublic Schools in America Today." *Teachers' College Record* (Spring 1991), pp. 409–414. An excellent essay on the role of and growth of nonpublic schools in America, particularly in response to growing dissatisfaction with public schools.

Sarason, Seymour B. *Parental Involvement and the Political Principle.* San Francisco: Jossey-Bass, 1995. *An excellent book focusing on school management and organization, parental involvement, the politics of education, school boards, and educational change.*

Sergiovanni, Thomas. *Leadership for the Schoolhouse: How Is It Different?* San Francisco, Calif.: Jossey-Bass, 1996. *A fresh look at the importance of principal leadership behavior and management.*

Spring, Joel. *Conflict of Interests: The Politics of American Education.* New York: Longman, 1993. *An essay on the politics of education at the national, state, and local levels.*

CHAPTER SEVEN

Financing Public Education

Education in the United States is big business. By 1997, more than $339 billion was being spent annually for public education (K–12), and elementary and secondary education represented 4.5 percent of the nation's annual gross national product.[1] Because most school-related costs have increased more rapidly than inflation in recent years, the business of schooling is in deep financial trouble. Since the mid-1980s, school board members have consistently ranked "lack of financial support" as the number one challenge they face.[2]

There are three major sources of revenue for public schools: local, state, and federal governments. As Figure 7.1 shows, revenues from federal sources have increased from less than half a percent in 1929–30 to 7 percent currently (achieving a high of almost 10 percent in 1979–80). State contributions have also risen from less than 17 percent in 1929–30 to over 45 percent by the 1980s. With the state and federal contributions rising, local revenues have fallen in proportion, from over 80 percent to less than 50 percent.[3]

This chapter explores the reasons for both the overall changes in school financing and the current climate of uncertainty. Today's educators must deal with budget constraints, equity in school financing, taxpayer resistance, and various plans to restructure the system of financial support. As you read, think about the following questions:

- What proportion of school revenues do the local, state, and federal governments contribute?

- What is wrong with relying on property taxes as revenue sources for schools?

- What particular fiscal problems characterize urban schools?

- Why are there significant differences among and within states in spending for education? How does public opinion affect spending?

- What major steps have been taken to reform school finance?

- What financial considerations will most affect school management?

This chapter was revised by Dr. James Lawlor, Towson University

[1]*Digest of Education Statistics, 1997* (Washington, D.C.: U.S. Government Printing Office, 1997), Tables 31 and 32, pp. 34–35.
[2]*Education Vital Signs, 1994* (Alexandria, Va.: National School Boards Association, 1994), p. A-20; Rebecca Jones, "The Kids are Coming," *American School Board Journal* (April, 1997), pp. 20–25. See also Daniel M. Seaton, "The Burden School Board Presidents Bear," *American School Board Journal* (January 1992), pp. 32–36.
[3]*Vital Signs, 1994,* p. A-25; and *Digest of Education Statistics, 1997,* Figure 11, p. 49.

Tax Sources of School Revenues

Criteria for evaluating taxes

Progressive vs. regressive

Elastic vs. inelastic

The operation of public schools relies primarily on revenues generated from taxes, especially the property tax at the local level and sales and income taxes at the state level. Some kinds of taxes are considered better than others. Most people today accept the following criteria for evaluating taxes:

1. *A tax should not cause unintended economic distortions.* It should not change consumer spending patterns or cause the relocation of business, industry, or people.

2. *A tax should be equitable.* It should be based on the taxpayer's ability to pay. Those with greater incomes or with property worth more money should pay more taxes. Taxes of this sort are called **progressive taxes**. Taxes that are not equitable and that require lower-income groups to pay a higher proportion of their income than higher-income groups are called **regressive taxes**.

3. *A tax should be easily collected.*

4. *The tax should be responsive to changing economic conditions, rising* during inflation and decreasing in a recession.[4] Responsive taxes are *elastic;* those that are not responsive are *inelastic.*

Local Financing of Public Schools

Although education is the responsibility of the states, traditionally the states have delegated much of this responsibility to local school districts. As indicated earlier, the local contribution to school financing has decreased over the last several decades, but it still amounts to well over 40 percent of the total.

Property Tax

How property tax is calculated

Problems with property tax

The **property tax** is the main source of revenue for local school districts, accounting for 76 percent of local funding nationwide. In eleven states, including all six of the New England states, property taxes make up more than 98 percent of local school revenues.[5] The property tax has been used to support education in this country ever since the colonial period.

Property taxes are determined by first arriving at the *market value* of a property — the amount the property would probably sell for if it were sold. Then the market value is converted to an *assessed value* using a predetermined index or ratio, such as one-fourth or one-third; for example, a property with a market value of $80,000 might have an assessed value of only $20,000. The assessed value is always less than the market value. Finally, the local tax rate, expressed in mills, is applied to the assessed value. A **mill** represents one-thousandth of a dollar; thus a tax rate of 25 mills amounts to $25 for each $1,000 of assessed value (or $25 x 20 = $500 tax).

The property tax is not an equitable tax. Because of different assessment practices and lack of uniform valuation, people owning equivalent properties may pay different taxes. Also, the property tax does not always distribute the tax burden according to the ability to pay. A retired couple may have a home whose market value has increased substantially, along with their taxes, but because they live on a fixed income they cannot afford the increasing taxes. In this respect, the property tax is regressive.

---

[4]James Guthrie and Rodney J. Reed, *Education Administration and Policy,* 2nd ed. (Needham Heights, Mass.: Allyn and Bacon, 1991); and Donald E. Orlosky et al., *Educational Administration Today* (Columbus, Ohio: Merrill, 1984).
[5]*Significant Features of Fiscal Federalism, 1995* (Washington, D.C.: U.S. Advisory Commission on Intergovernmental Relations, 1995), Table 13, pp. 34–35.

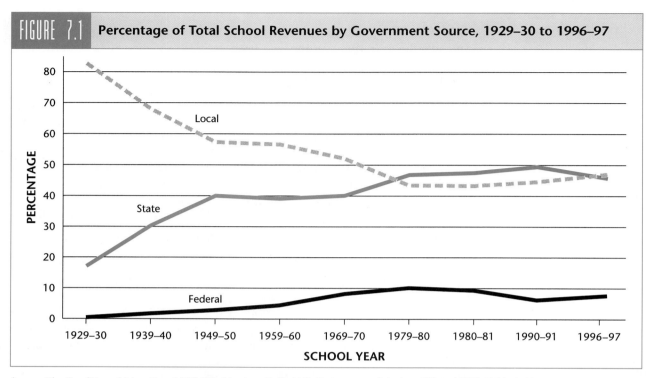

FIGURE 7.1 Percentage of Total School Revenues by Government Source, 1929–30 to 1996–97

Source: The Condition of Education, 1987 (Washington, D.C.: U.S. Government Printing Office, 1987), Table 1.13, p. 36; *Digest of Education Statistics, 1982* (Washington, D.C.: National Center for Education Statistics, 1982), Table 66, p. 75; *Digest of Education Statistics, 1997*), Table 159, p. 158; and *Estimates of School Statistics, 1994–95* (Washington, D.C.: National Education Association, 1995), Table 9, p. 39.

In addition, the property tax is not immediately responsive to changing economic conditions. In some states properties are reassessed every one to two years, but in others reassessments occur only every three to four years. Thus a property's assessed value and actual tax are often based on out-dated market conditions.

Other Local Taxes and Fees

In addition to the property tax, school districts can gather revenues through special income taxes and other taxes or fees. Some municipalities, especially small villages and towns, depend on such sources as traffic fines and building permits to help raise money for schools.

Rise in user fees

User fees, which are fees charged specifically to the people who use a certain facility or service, are the most common type of special assessment. User fees can be levied on bus service, textbooks, athletic and recreational activities, nursery classes, and after-school centers. By the mid-1990s, more than thirty states permitted schools to assess user fees on students, and many of the school districts in these states imposed such fees.[6] Because they are not based on ability to pay, user fees are considered a regressive tax.

---

[6]Jay Goldman, "User Fees to the Rescue?" *School Administrator* (October 1991), pp. 30–32, 34; Richard Ducker, "Using Impact Fees for Public Schools," *School Law Bulletin* (Spring 1994), pp. 1–14; and Claudette Bauman and David Brown, "Public School Fees as Hidden Taxation," *Educational Administration Quarterly* (December 1996), pp. 665–685.

Exclusive product rights

Recently some school boards have signed lucrative contracts with corporations for **exclusive product rights**. For example, Jefferson County (Colorado) schools signed an exclusive product contract with Pepsi estimated to bring 7.3 million in revenue over seven years. Other school districts have developed multimillion-dollar fund-raising campaigns with corporate sponsors, generating everything from cash donations to new stadiums, auditoriums, scoreboards, and equipment purchases. Nevertheless, these contracts are negotiated on a district-by-district basis, with some districts benefiting handsomely while others struggle to fund their school district budgets.[7]

Local Resources and Disparities

Wealthy vs. poor districts

Despite state and federal aid, some school districts are much less able than others to support education. A school district located in a wealthy area or an area with a broad **tax base** (for example, residential neighborhoods, shopping centers, businesses, and industry) can obviously generate more revenue than a poor school district. As a result, in most states today, total expenditures per student are frequently two to four times greater in the five wealthiest school districts than in the five poorest school districts.[8] As we discuss later in this chapter, state courts and legislatures have attempted to reduce these disparities through reforms in the system of educational finance. In most states, however, substantial disparities in funding persist.

Municipal overburden

Although financial problems affect many rural and suburban districts, the greatest financial troubles are usually found in large cities. Cities are plagued by what is commonly called **municipal overburden**, a severe financial crunch caused

Considerable federal and state aid is being made available to support the upgrading of computer technology in schools as well as the repair and modernization of schools themselves. (© Julie Houck/Stock Boston)

[7]Chris Pipho, "The Selling of Public Education," *Phi Delta Kappan* (October, 1997), pp. 101–102.
[8]Allan Odden and Lori Kim, "Finance Reform Topples Old Structures," *School Administrator* (October 1991), pp. 8–12; Robert E. Slavin, "After the Victory: Making Funding Equity Make a Difference," *Theory into Practice* (Spring 1994), pp. 98–103; and Howard Wainer, "Does Spending Money on Education Help?" *Educational Researcher* (December 1993), pp. 22–24.

Educational overburden

by population density and a high proportion of disadvantaged and low-income groups. The result is that large cities cannot devote as great a percentage of their total tax revenues to the schools as suburban and rural districts can.

Then there is the issue of educational overburden. A large percentage of the student population in city schools is in technical, vocational, and trade programs, which cost more per student than the regular academic high-school program. Similarly, there is a greater proportion of special-needs students — namely, bilingual and low-income students and students with disabilities. These students require remedial programs and services, which cost 50 to 100 percent more per student than basic programs.[9] City schools also have higher vandalism, lunch, desegregation, insurance, transportation, and maintenance costs (their buildings are older than suburban buildings).

Urban cycle of financial strain

Finally, despite their dire need for more revenues, cities often cannot realistically raise taxes. In many cities, the property taxes are already 30 percent higher per capita than in adjacent suburbs.[10] Ironically, tax increases can contribute to the decline of urban schools because they cause businesses and middle-income residents to depart for the suburbs. The city's tax base is thus undermined, which forces the local government to cut city services, including education, to balance the budget. These cuts, in turn, drive away middle-class families and businesses and negatively affect tax revenues.

State Financing of Public Schools

Although the states have delegated many of their educational powers and responsibilities to local school districts, each state remains legally responsible for educating its children and youth, and the proportion of funding supplied by the states has increased steadily until the 1990s (see Figure 7.1). In this section we look at the principal types of state taxes used to finance education, the variations in school funding from state to state, the methods by which state aid is apportioned among local districts, and the role of state courts in promoting school finance reform.

State Revenue Sources

The **sales tax** and **personal income tax** are the two major sources of revenue for states. Since states currently pay over 45 percent of the cost of public elementary and secondary education (see Figure 7.1), these two taxes are important elements in the overall support of public schools.

Sales Tax. As of 1995, forty-five states had statewide sales taxes, with such taxes making up 33 percent of state revenues. The median rate was 5.12 percent, and seventeen states had rates of 6 percent or higher.[11]

---

[9]Harold Hodgkinson, "Reform Versus Reality," *Phi Delta Kappan* (September 1991), pp. 8–16; and Mary Jean LeTendre, "Improving Chapter 1 Programs: We Can Do Better," *Phi Delta Kappan* (April 1991), pp. 576–581; and "Poverty in Public Schools: Chicago Students Suffer," available by searching the Internet for "Daily Report Card" and clicking on December 1, 1995.

[10]Rudolph Ponner, "Fiscal Policy in the Short and Long Run," *Urban Institute Research Papers* (January 1991), pp. 1–15; and Commentary, "Tales from the City," *Education Week*, September 27, 1995, pp. 33–36.

[11]*Significant Features in Fiscal Federalism, 1995,* Table 25, pp. 89–91; Table 13, pp. 34–35; *Recent Changes in State, Local, and State-Local Tax Levels* (Denver: National Conference of State Legislatures, 1991); and "End of Segregation: Panel Says No to Separate Special Ed," available by searching the Internet for "Daily Report Card" and clicking on December 15, 1995.

Sales tax evaluated

Measured against the criteria for evaluating taxes, the sales tax rates high. For example, the sales tax meets the criterion of equity if food and medical prescriptions are removed from the tax base. (If not, however, low-income groups are penalized since they spend a large portion of their incomes on basic goods such as food and medicine.) The sales tax is easy to administer and collect; it does not require periodic valuations or entail legal appeals (as the property tax does). The sales tax is also elastic, because the revenue derived from it tends to parallel the economy. The trouble is that when the state is in a recession, as happened in the early-mid 1990s, sales tax revenues decrease sufficiently to reduce the state's income. But the tax is useful because relatively small increases in the rate result in large amounts of revenue.

Personal Income Tax. The personal income tax is the second largest source of tax revenue for the states, representing about 32 percent of state revenues. Only six states do not levy a personal state income tax.[12] Just as the sales tax rate varies among states, from 3 to 7 percent, so the state income tax (based on a percentage of personal income) also varies.

Income tax evaluated

A properly designed income tax should cause no economic distortions. Assuming no loopholes, it rates very high in terms of equity, reflecting the taxpayer's income and ability to pay. The income tax is also more equitable than other taxes since it usually considers special circumstances of the taxpayer, such as dependents, illness, moving expenses, and the like. In general, state income taxes have become more progressive because of increased standard deductions and personal exemptions, and fifteen states have eliminated taxes on poor families altogether.[13]

The personal income tax is easy to collect and usually is collected through payroll deductions. It is also very elastic, allowing the state government to vary rates according to the economy. However, the elasticity of the income tax makes it vulnerable to recession because the revenue derived from it declines.

Other State Taxes. Other state taxes contribute limited amounts to education. These taxes include (1) excise taxes on motor fuel, liquor, and tobacco products; (2) estate and gift taxes; (3) severance taxes (on the output of minerals and oils); and (4) corporate income taxes.

State lotteries

There has also been a trend to establish state lotteries to support education. Although this was a major purpose of the early lotteries, funds have been diverted to meet other social priorities, such as health care, social welfare agencies, and road construction. The result, in most of the thirty-six states where lotteries currently exist, is that the lottery contributes less than 2 percent of the state's total revenue for education.[14] Lotteries are somewhat regressive because low-income individuals play the lottery in a greater proportion than high-income individuals and spend larger percentages of their annual income on it.

The Ability of States to Finance Education

State variations in spending

Some students are more fortunate than others, simply by geographic accident. State residence has a lot to do with the type and quality of education a child receives. In

---

[12]*Significant Features of Fiscal Federalism, 1994,* Table 55, pp. 100–101; *Significant Features, 1995,* Table 13, pp. 34–35.
[13]*State Deficit Management Strategies; State Fiscal Conditions,* Legislative Finance Paper No. 55 (Denver: National Conference of State Legislators, 1986); and Jerry L. Patterson, *Leadership for Tomorrow's Schools* (Alexandria, Va.: Association for Supervision and Curriculum Development, 1993).
[14]*Significant Features of Fiscal Federalism, 1994,* Table 58, pp. 106–107.

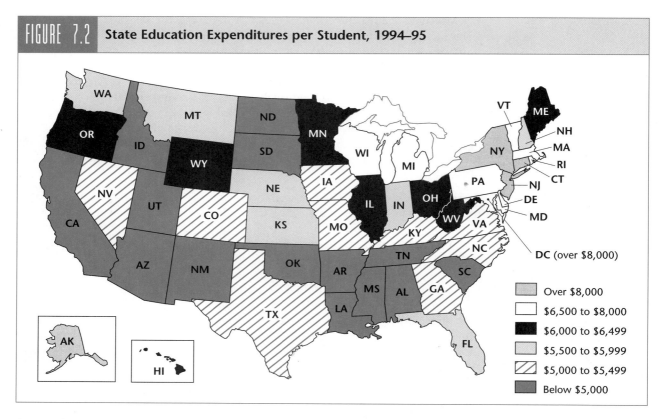

FIGURE 7.2 **State Education Expenditures per Student, 1994–95**

Legend:
- Over $8,000
- $6,500 to $8,000
- $6,000 to $6,499
- $5,500 to $5,999
- $5,000 to $5,499
- Below $5,000

DC (over $8,000)

Source: Adapted from *Digest of Education Statistics, 1997* (Washington, D.C.: National Center for Education Statistics, 1997), Table 168, p. 17. State expenditures are based on average daily attendance and include federal, state, and local revenues.

What can states afford?

1994–95, New Jersey, New York, and the District of Columbia spent more than $9,000 per student. In contrast, Arkansas, Idaho, Mississippi, Utah, and Tennessee spent less than $4,500 per student (Figure 7.2.).

It is incorrect to assume from these figures that the education priorities of some states are more than twice as high as the priorities of other states. We must ask what the states can afford, and this has a lot to do with the personal incomes of the states' inhabitants; then we must ask what the states spend on all other services and functions, such as housing, transportation, and medical care.

For example, in 1995, Mississippi spent $4,080 per student — the second-lowest figure nationwide and far short of the national average of $5,988 — yet this amount represented 3.8 percent of Mississippi's per capita income (average income for each person living in the state). The national average was 2.9 percent of per capita income, which made Mississippi's percentage higher than the percentages of twenty-six other states. The wealthier states of California, Washington, and Virginia each spent between $4,992 and $5,906 per student, but in percentage terms the expenditures in these states fell between 2.3 and 2.7 percent of per capita income — less than in Mississippi.[15]

---

[15]*Estimates of School Statistics, 1994–95* (West Haven, Conn.: National Education Association, 1995), Table 11, p. 41.

Aging population

Educational Support and the Graying of America.   Another factor negatively influencing states' abilities to finance public education is the aging of the population. The median age of the U.S. population has risen steadily since 1900. The proportion of people over 65, which increased from 4.1 percent in 1900 to 12.7 percent by the mid-1990s, is expected to reach 13.2 percent or more by 2010.[16] Correspondingly, the proportion of households without children has increased in recent decades, from 21 percent in 1970 to 30 percent by 1997.[17] Older people who no longer have children in school are generally more resistant to increased taxes for schools. They

Effect on school budgets

are less likely than younger people to vote for expanding school budgets; and in areas where they form a major segment of the population, their influence will be felt on the priorities of state and local officials. This effect can be seen in recent changes in government spending patterns. Through the 1980s educational spending per student outpaced inflation by about 30 percent; yet by the late 1980s it began to decline. At the same time, government medical and health expenditures — a large proportion of which go to older people — increased.[18]

Graying of the Frostbelt

The increase in average age is a nationwide trend; however, some parts of the country are "graying" faster than others. In the 1970s and 1980s Frostbelt states, such as New York, Pennsylvania, Illinois, and Michigan, lost sizable numbers of young people to the Sunbelt. The effects were especially noticeable in large cities, where much of the young middle-class population was already migrating to the suburbs. Elderly, less affluent people left behind in the cities were neither able nor very willing to support urban school systems. Although parts of the Frostbelt have revived with the influx of new industries, and Sunbelt states such as California and Texas are now experiencing an out-migration in population, in many areas of the Northeast and Midwest the graying population is increasingly reluctant to provide financial and political support for schools.[19] In contrast, areas with a boom in student enrollments can offset the growing influence of older age groups.

State Aid to Local School Districts

States use four basic methods to finance public education. Some states have financial strategies that combine methods.

The oldest, most unequal method

1. *Flat grant model.* This is the oldest and most unequal method of financing schools. State aid to local school districts is based on a fixed amount multiplied by the number of students in attendance. It does not consider the special needs of students (bilingual students are more expensive to educate than are native English speakers), special programs (vocational and special education) or the wealth of the school districts.

The remaining three methods each seek to bring about greater equality of educational opportunity by allocating more funds to the school districts in greatest need of assistance.

A minimum per student

2. *Foundation plan.* This is the most common approach. A foundation, or minimum annual expenditure per student, is guaranteed to all school districts in the

---

[16]Harold G. Shane, "Improving Education for the Twenty-first Century," *Educational Horizons* (Fall 1990), pp. 11–15; *Rankings of the States, 1993* (West Haven, Conn.: NEA Professional Library, 1993), Table A–9, p. 8; and U.S. Bureau of the Census, *Statistical Abstract of the United States, 1997* (Washington, D.C.: U.S. Government Printing Office, 1997), Table 35, p. 35 and Table 36, p. 36.
[17]*Statistical Abstract, 1997*, Table 67, p. 59 and Table 68, p. 60.
[18]*Digest of Education Statistics, 1997*, Table 34, p. 37.
[19]Albert R. Crenshaw, "So Long Sunbelt," *Philadelphia Inquirer*, March 4, 1994, p. A-2.

state, irrespective of local taxable wealth. However, the minimum level is usually considered too low by reformers, and wealthy school districts easily exceed it. School districts with a high percentage of children from low-income families suffer with this plan.

Inverse ratio to wealth

3. *Power-equalizing plan.* Many states have adopted some form of this more recent plan. The state pays a percentage of the local school expenditures in inverse ratio to the wealth of the district. Although the school district has the right to establish its own expenditure levels, wealthier school districts are given fewer matching state dollars and poorer districts more.

Students weighted by characteristics

4. *Weighted student plan.* Students are weighted in proportion to their special characteristics (that is, disabled, disadvantaged, and so forth) or special programs (for example, vocational or bilingual) to determine the cost of instruction per student. For example, a state may provide $4,000 for each regular student, 1.5 times that amount ($6,000) for vocational students, and 2 times that amount ($8,000) for students with disabilities.

The Courts and School Finance Reform

Serrano

Efforts to equalize educational opportunities among school districts within a state have been spurred by a series of court decisions that have fundamentally changed the financing of public education in most states. The 1971 landmark decision in *Serrano* v. *Priest* radically altered the way California allocated education funds. California, like nearly all the states, depended on local property taxes to support the schools, and plaintiffs argued that this system of financing resulted in unconstitutional disparities in expenditures between wealthy and poor school districts. The California Supreme Court agreed.

Rodriguez

After the *Serrano* decision, the Supreme Court ruled in 1973 in *San Antonio* v. *Rodriguez* that expenditure disparities based on differences in local property taxes between school districts in a state were not unconstitutional under the federal constitution but might be unconstitutional under state constitutions. The *Rodriguez* decision placed the issue of inequities in school finance in the hands of the state courts and legislatures, where many felt it belonged.

The Kentucky plan

Since *Rodriguez* a number of state courts have ruled that school financing arrangements are unconstitutional if they result in large disparities in per-pupil expenditures based on wealth differences among school districts. For example, in *Rose* v. *Council for Better Education* (1989), the Kentucky Supreme Court declared the entire state educational system, including the method of funding schools with property taxes, unconstitutional. This decision prompted the legislature to hike average education spending some 30 percent and to undertake an extensive plan of educational reform (described in Chapter 16).[20] Similarly, in a New Jersey case, *Abbott* v. *Burke* (1990), after examining the poorest twenty-eight school districts (mainly city districts), the state court found the state's system of school finance unconstitutional

New Jersey reforms

and required that spending be equalized at the level of the highest-spending dis-

[20]Ronald Henkoff, "Four States: Reform Turns Radical," *Fortune,* October 21, 1991, pp. 137–144; Robert Rothman, "KERA: A Tale of One School," *Phi Delta Kappan* (December, 1997), pp. 272–275; and Jane C. Lindle, "Lessons from Kentucky About School-Based Decision Making," *Educational Leadership* (December 1995–January 1996), pp. 20–23.

tricts. The outcome of the decision moved more than $100 million annually from wealthy districts to poor districts to help address funding inequities.[21]

In all, thirteen states have reformed their school finance laws since the *Rodriguez* case in 1973. In these states the state share of public-school revenues has increased, and poorer school districts are receiving substantially more money.[22] In nineteen other states plaintiffs have been unsuccessful in their suits and disparities remain, and the litigation will undoubtedly continue. As of 1997, suits similar to the ones in Kentucky and New Jersey had been filed in thirty states, and it appears that the problem of unequal funding is being revisited again and again in state legislatures.[23]

Disparities remain

Does money alone make a difference?

Recent court decisions have focused on both adequacy, a minimum state contribution, and equity, the belief that students in poor school districts "have the right to the same educational opportunity that money buys for others."[24] In short, states need to close the gap between the best- and worst-financed education systems.[25] Yet some critics of school finance reform have argued that money alone makes little difference in the quality of education.[26] They contend that educational improvement demands commitment and responsibility on the part of students, teachers, and parents. Moreover, a variety of social and cognitive factors, especially family structure, must be addressed, or reform efforts may be useless. With all of these issues unresolved, school finance reform will continue to be a hotly debated topic for years to come.

Federal Education Funding

The changing federal role

Until the middle of the twentieth century, the federal government gave very little financial assistance to the states (or local schools) for the education of American students. This attitude was in line with the majority belief that the federal government should have little to do with education and that education is a state responsibility. One might characterize federal programs and activities as passive and uncoordinated during this period. This is not to say that the federal government had no influence on American education. National laws and federal programs had a significant impact on the way education developed in the United States. However, these programs and acts were unsystematic and not part of a broadly conceived national plan for education. After the Soviet Union launched the *Sputnik* satellite in 1957, national policy became more closely linked to education; as a result, federal funding dramatically increased and focused on specific, targeted areas.

---

[21]Robert Hanley, "New Jersey Shifts Approach in Helping 'At Risk' Students," *New York Times*, October 6, 1990, p. 9; and Michael Newman, "Finance System for N.J. Schools Is Struck Down," *Education Week*, June 13, 1990, pp. 1, 18.

[22]*Estimates of School Statistics 1990–91* (Washington, D.C.: National Education Association, 1991), pp. 6–7; Louis Fischer, David Schimmel, and Cynthia Kelly, *Teachers and the Law*, 5th ed. (White Plains, N.Y.: Longman, 1998), p. 483; and Fabio Silva and Jon Sonstelie, "Did 'Serrano' Cause a Decline in School Spending?" *National Tax Journal* (June 1995), pp. 199–215.

[23]Deborah A. Verstegen, "The New Wave of School Finance Litigation," *Phi Delta Kappan* (November 1994), pp. 243–250; and Rothman, "KERA," p. 273.

[24]Newman, "Finance System for N.J. Schools Is Struck Down," p. 18.

[25]Verstegen, "New Wave," pp. 243–250; Chris Pipho, "The Scent of the Future," *Phi Delta Kappan* (September 1994), pp. 10–11.

[26]Gerald W. Bracey, "The Seventh Bracey Report on the Condition of Public Education," *Phi Delta Kappan* (October 1997), pp. 120-136; and Eric A. Hanushek, "Moving Beyond Spending Fetishes," *Educational Leadership* (November 1995), pp. 60–64.

TAKING ISSUE

Expanding State Funding for Education

Education is in deep financial trouble for many reasons. Not only are new taxes, such as user fees, being levied in many areas, but the argument about the proper level of funding from state and federal sources has taken on new urgency. Embattled local districts look to higher levels of government to help them out; but states have their own financial difficulties, and the federal role in education remains a thorny political issue.

QUESTION   Should state contributions to educational funding be substantially increased to make up for federal shortfalls and thus reduce the percentage of funds derived from local sources?

Arguments PRO

1 The federal government has shifted much of the responsibility for educational funding to the states. The states must accept this responsibility and raise their contributions accordingly.

2 State funding can be used to reduce or eliminate the discrepancies between poor and wealthy districts. Such discrepancies are unfair to students in poorer areas. In fact, in many state court decisions, financing systems that foster inequalities in funding have been ruled unconstitutional.

3 State financing will be free of the parochial judgments and petty politics that often plague local decision making. Higher levels of government are better equipped to solve financing problems professionally.

4 A common obstacle in local funding is the need for voters to approve any substantial change in the way schools are financed. State governments can levy taxes, such as income and sales taxes, that do not require public referenda.

5 State governments do not need to ask for large tax hikes for education. They can raise sufficient amounts through the combined total of numerous small taxes. Thus their taxing will not be seen as excessive.

Arguments CON

1 The federal government needs to restore its financial commitment of the late 1970s and early 1980s to education. Most states are financially burdened, unable to tax their residents further without squeezing the middle class or inciting tax rebellion.

2 More money for poorer districts will not necessarily improve educational performance; the problems are not mainly financial. Moreover, more state money will bring more state regulations, and educational priorities will be set at the state level. Ordinary people will have little influence on the schools their children attend.

3 State governments are no strangers to favoritism and pork barreling. Politics will be just as evident at the state level, and there will be less accountability to the local taxpayer and little concern for local interests.

4 The solution to financial problems lies not in easier ways to tax but in reducing the schools' burden of responsibilities. We must decide which responsibilities can be returned to other social institutions, such as the family, the church, and community agencies.

5 Taxpayer revolts derive from feelings that citizens no longer control their own financial fate. People cannot be fooled for long. State tax hikes, even if spread over many varieties of tax, will eventually provoke resistance.

History of Federal Aid to Education

During the first one hundred and seventy-five years of our nation's history (1783–1958), the federal government's most notable efforts to assist education were as follows:

Morrill Act and land-grant colleges

- ■ ***Grants for Schools and Colleges.***   The Northwest Ordinances of 1785 and 1787 were the first instances of federal assistance to education. As a result of these ordinances, thirty-nine states received land from the federal government for public schools.[27] Seventy-five years later, in the Morrill Act of 1862, more federally owned lands were set aside for each state to establish colleges for the study of agriculture and mechanical arts. These "people's colleges" or *land-grant* institutions were to become the great multipurpose state universities.

Smith-Hughes Act

- ■ ***Vocational Education Acts.***   The Smith-Hughes Act in 1917 provided money grants for vocational education, home economics, and agricultural subjects. More recent acts have extended such funding to people with disabilities, single parents, homemakers, and the incarcerated.

G.I. Bill

- ■ ***War Acts.***   The Servicemen's Readjustment Act (1944), commonly called the *G.I. Bill,* provided funds for the education of veterans and enabled hundreds of thousands of Americans to attend institutions of higher learning or special training schools. The benefits of the G.I. Bill were later extended to veterans of the Korean and Vietnam conflicts. The G.I. Bill, along with the baby boom, was a major factor in the growth and expansion of American colleges, including community colleges.

Education for national defense

- ■ ***Recent Trends.***   With the Soviet Union's launch of *Sputnik* in 1957, pressure for better schools underscored the importance of education to the national defense. Increased federal monies were allocated for improvement of science, mathematics, foreign language instruction, and for teacher education.[28] The 1960s and 1970s brought a new emphasis on equality in education. With the War on Poverty and the spread of the civil rights movement, national policy became linked to education. The federal government targeted specific groups — minorities, the poor, and individuals with disabilities — and created specific policies to improve their educational opportunities.

Targeting federal funds

Civil Rights Act

From the mid-1960s through the 1970s, the full force of the federal government came into play to enforce U.S. Supreme Court decisions on school desegregation. The impetus came from the Civil Rights Act of 1964, which provided that all programs supported by federal funds must be administered and operated without discrimination, or all federal funds were to be withheld.

Programs for diverse groups

In addition to these desegregation efforts, the educational needs of minority groups and women received considerable attention and funding from the mid-1960s to the late 1970s. Diverse groups such as bilingual students, African Americans, Native Americans, low-income students, and students with disabilities were targeted for special programs.

---

[27]Ellwood P. Cubberley, *Public Education in the United States,* rev. ed. (Boston: Houghton Mifflin, 1934).

[28]S. Alexander Rippa, *Education in a Free Society,* 6th ed. (New York: Longman, 1988); and Paul Woodring, *The Persistent Problems of Education* (Bloomington, Ind.: Phi Delta Kappa, 1983).

GETTING TO THE SOURCE

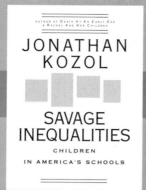

Savage Inequalities

JONATHAN KOZOL

Since his first book in 1969, *Death at an Early Age,* Jonathan Kozol has been an eloquent and unrelenting advocate of equal educational opportunity for poor and disadvantaged students, particularly those in America's inner cities. In *Savage Inequalities* he again attempts to raise the nation's social and political consciousness, focusing on the unequal funding that, in his view, lies behind unequal opportunities. In the following passage he argues against the skeptics who claim that increased funding for impoverished inner-city schools would make little difference.

The point is often made that, even with a genuine equality of schooling for poor children, other forces still would militate against their school performance. Cultural and economic factors and the flight of middle-income blacks from inner cities still would have their consequences in the heightened concentration of the poorest children in the poorest neighborhoods. Teen-age pregnancy, drug use and other problems still would render many families in these neighborhoods all but dysfunctional. Nothing I have said within this book should leave the misimpression that I do not think these factors are enormously important. A polarization of this issue, whereby some insist upon the primacy of school, others upon the primacy of family and neighborhood, obscures the fact that both are elemental forces in the lives of children.

The family, however, differs from the school in the significant respect that government is not responsible, or at least not directly, for the inequalities of family background. It *is* responsible for inequalities in public education. The school is the creature of the state; the family is not. To the degree, moreover, that destructive family situations may be bettered by the future acts of government, no one expects that this could happen in the years immediately ahead.

Current Trends in Federal Aid to Education

The 1980s brought a new conservatism at the federal level, and federal spending for education decreased in the early years of the decade, taking inflation into consideration (Table 7.1). By mid-decade federal spending began rising again in absolute dollars, although the federal contribution since then has represented a smaller percentage of total school financing (compare Table 7.1 with Figure 7.1).

During the 1980s the method of school funding also changed. **Categorical grants** (funds for specific groups and designated purposes) gave way to **block grants** (funds for a general purpose without precise categories). Categorical grants had been an important feature of federal involvement in education during the 1970s. But Chapter 2 of the federal Education Consolidation and Improvement Act (ECIA) of 1981 replaced categorical grants for twenty-eight separate education programs with one block grant that state and local education agencies could use for broadly defined educational purposes. This move was part of a "new federalism," which, as we saw in Chapter 6, shifted responsibility for many federal social and educational programs from the national to the state governments.

ECIA and block grants

In the first years of the new century, the role of the federal government will probably increase in the area of technology (specifically computers) as well as in

Schools, on the other hand, could make dramatic changes almost overnight if fiscal equity were a reality. . . .

It is obvious that urban schools have other problems in addition to their insufficient funding. Administrative chaos is endemic in some urban systems. (The fact that this in itself is a reflection of our low regard for children who depend upon these systems is a separate matter.) Greater funding, if it were intelligently applied, could partially correct these problems — by making possible, for instance, the employment of some very gifted, high-paid fiscal managers who could assure that money is well used — but it probably is also true that major structural reforms would still be needed. To polarize these points, however, and to argue, as the White House has been claiming for a decade, that administrative changes are a "better" answer to the problem than equality of funding and real efforts at desegregation is dishonest and simplistic. The suburbs have better administrations (sometimes, but not always), and they also have a lot more money in proportion to their children's needs. To speak of the former and evade the latter is a formula that guarantees that nothing will be done *today* for children who have no responsibility for either problem.

To be in favor of "good families" or of "good administration" does not take much courage or originality. It is hard to think of anyone who is opposed to either. To be in favor of redistribution of resources and of racial integration would require a great deal of courage — and a soaring sense of vision — in a president or any other politician. Whether such courage or such vision will someday become transcendent forces in our nation is by no means clear.

Questions

1. How are the needs of poor and disadvantaged children, especially those in inner cities, different from those of children in suburban school districts?

2. Do you agree or disagree with Kozol that suburban districts have "a lot more money in proportion to their children's needs"? If so, how should government officials address this disparity?

3. What constituencies might argue against Kozol, and what would their reasoning be?

Source: Jonathan Kozol, *Savage Inequalities: Children in America's Schools*, pp. 123–124. Copyright © 1991 by Jonathan Kozol. Reprinted by permission of Crown Publishers, Inc.

Predictions for federal funding

support for the infrastructure necessary to upgrade aging and deteriorating schools. There is increased congressional support, along with that of President Clinton, for national achievement tests in content disciplines, which, if enacted, may drive national curriculum standards. Pre-K education for disadvantaged and at-risk students is also a priority of the Clinton administration. Additionally, President Clinton has expressed concern for the need to prepare 100,000 teachers by 2007 to replace retiring veterans, meet the increasing number of "mini-baby boom" students, and lower swelling class size. His "Teacher Quality Act of 1998" calls for spending 20.8 billion by 2005 to support this effort.[29]

Federal grants funding magnet schools will continue as a way to address racial imbalance within school districts. There is increasing concern at the local, state, and federal levels regarding school violence and how to restore moral authority to America's public schools. Finally, school choice and vouchers remain popular alternative funding concepts with legislators, the public, and increasingly the courts.

[29]American School Board Journal, "Clinton Congress at Odds Over Testing." *American School Board Journal* (November, 1997), pp. 20–24; Teacher Education Reports, "President Clinton Sends Congress His Proposal to Provide 20.8 Billion in Federal Aid to Prepare and Hire New Teachers," *Teacher Education Reports*, May 14, 1998, p. 2.

TABLE 7.1	Federal Funds for Elementary, Secondary, and Higher Education, 1970–1997	
Year	**Amount (billions)**	**Amount adjusted for Inflation (billions)**
1970	$ 9.2	$ 6.8
1972	11.9	7.7
1974	13.1	8.7
1976	19.6	11.8
1978	21.6	12.0
1980	27.5	13.1
1982	26.8	11.6
1984	30.5	12.3
1986	33.7	13.9
1988	37.5	14.4
1990	45.3	15.3
1994	64.0	16.7
1997	73.0	17.4

Note: As a result of the Education Consolidation and Improvement Act in 1981, many programs and funds were shifted among various federal departments; the base of comparison has not been exactly the same since then.

Source: Digest of Education Statistics, 1980 (Washington, D.C.: National Center for Education Statistics, 1980), Table 160, pp. 184–186; *Digest of Education Statistics, 1982* (Washington, D.C.: National Center for Education Statistics, 1982), Tables 153–154, pp. 171–172; and *Digest of Education Statistics, 1990* (Washington, D.C.: National Center for Education Statistics, 1990), Table 327, p. 343. Amounts adjusted for inflation have been calculated by the authors on the basis of *Consumer Price Index: 1913–1990* (Washington, D.C.: Bureau of Labor Statistics, U.S. Department of Labor, 1990), pp. 1–3. See also *Digest of Education Statistics, 1994,* Table 349, pp. 370–373; and *Digest of Education Statistics, 1997,* Table 360, p. 402.

There will probably be increased pressure for "choice" in either public education or private school alternatives by parents dissatisfied with public schools and by economically disadvantaged students living in subpar (often urban) school districts (as in Milwaukee, Wisconsin, where public money is used to pay parochial school tuition for low-income students).[30]

School Finance Trends

Financial crises in education sometimes make the headlines. For example, a national recession in the early 1990s triggered state revenue shortfalls and, coupled with rising costs and other budgetary problems, placed many school districts in a bleak fiscal situation. Such crises may come and go with changes in the economy and in federal and state budgets. However, a number of long-lasting concerns about school finance remain. As we examine the current trends, keep in mind that educators today are being asked to show proof that they are spending public money wisely.

[30]Ronald Stephens, "Ten Steps to Safer Schools," *American School Board Journal* (March, 1998), p. 30; Pete DuPont, "Wisconsin Ruling Gives Poor Students a Victory," *The Sun,* July 6, 1998, p. A9.

PROFESSIONAL PLANNING

for your first year

Money Woes

The Situation

It is that time of year again — budget hearings for your school district. As a promising new teacher, your principal as asked you to serve as one of two faculty representatives who attend the hearings and report back to the PTA executive board and the faculty. This could be a tedious evening! Yet your colleague, Ernestine Garcia, an experienced teacher, urges you to keep your ears open, suggesting you will learn a lot tonight about the school system and the community.

To your surprise, the discussion is fairly lively and full of controversy. The first speaker, the president of the local teacher's union, hints that the union will soon be seeking a higher salary scale and more preparation time for teachers; as a fledgling union member, you find it easy to agree with his premises. The next speaker, however, the head of Taxpayers United Against Tax Increases, bluntly argues that the community will not stand for tax increases, regardless of what the schools or teachers may need. She presents statistics showing that the local tax burden is among the highest in the state (so much for the pay raise). Next a representative of the Committee for Safe Schools deplores the leaking roofs, dilapidated school buildings, and (worst of all) the asbestos problem in several district schools. These matters must be addressed immediately, she contends, and they involve "big money." Then the chairperson of the Ad Hoc Citizen's Council rises to demand that the school district apply the principles of effective business management: less spending, less waste, more efficiency, and more accountability for results.

What, you wonder, should you and Ernestine say to the PTA board and the faculty? And where do you stand on these issues?

Thought Questions

1. Based on what you have read about the different tax sources for school revenue, what is your evaluation of the position stated by the head of Taxpayers United? How would you respond to her?
2. What do you believe would be a fair and effective way to fund schools?
3. How would you react if your school district needed to replace your school building but wasn't sure how to obtain the money?

Taxpayer Resistance

Taxpayer initiatives

Beginning in the late 1970s, a tax revolt swept the country, putting a damper on the movement for school finance reform. In California a taxpayer initiative called Proposition 13, passed in 1978, set a maximum tax of 1 percent on the fair market value of a property and limited increases in assessed valuation to 2 percent a year. Similar measures were passed in Idaho in 1978 and Massachusetts in 1980, and by the 1990s forty-five more states had imposed property tax limitations or direct controls on school spending.[31]

---

[31]John Augenblick, *School Finance: A Primer* (Denver: Education Commission of the States, 1991); and Richard McAdams, "Mark, Yen, Buck, Pound: Money Talks," *American School Board Journal* (July 1994), pp. 35–36.

Results of taxpayer resistance

As a result of this **taxpayer resistance**, average property taxes declined from $4.17 per $100 of personal income in 1977 to $3.38 in 1989. In addition, thirty-five states have introduced *circuitbreaker* programs that give selected populations (such as older persons and first-time homeowners) a credit for property taxes paid.[32]

The current climate

The educational reform movement of the 1980s and 1990s has emphasized the need to improve the quality of education, and the public seems willing to support increased education spending for that purpose. Yet taxpayers remain wary. There is much interest in results: what are we getting for the dollars we spend? This concern has led to increased educator accountability for the use of public funds.

The Accountability Movement

Responsibility for results

Although definitions of **accountability** vary, the term generally refers to the notion that teachers, administrators, school board members, and even students themselves must be held responsible for the results of their efforts. Teachers must meet some standard of competency, and schools must devise methods of relating expenditures to outcomes.

Reasons for accountability movement

The accountability movement stems from a number of factors. In recent years, more parents have realized that schooling is important for success and that their children are not learning sufficiently well. Because the cost of education has increased, parents demand to know what they are paying for. Taxpayers, who want to keep the lid on school spending, wish to hold educators responsible for the outcomes of instruction.[33]

State measures

Most states have taken the position that accountability should be mandatory, leaving the specifics to the discretion of local school districts. Statewide and national assessment programs have been introduced to measure students' performance and the cost-effectiveness of teaching.[34] Some states have passed laws calling for the unseating of school board members and the replacement of school administrators if test scores and other achievement indicators do not measure up. Other states are comparing school district test scores and using the results to cut funding or reward districts with additional monies.[35]

Focus on teachers

Often, the main focus is on teachers. The trend toward testing of teachers and prospective teachers, described in Chapter 1, is part of this movement. Some states issue initial certificates for three to five years, and the teacher must present positive evaluations or proof of further university work to receive permanent certification. Educators agree that all people, in education as in other fields, should be held accountable for producing work that justifies their salaries. What many educators fear is a simplified concept of accountability that places responsibility solely on the teacher or principal, ignoring the roles of parents, community residents, school board members, taxpayers, and the students themselves.

---

[32]*Recent Changes in State, Local, and State-Local Tax Levels* (Denver: National Conference of State Legislatures, 1991), Tables 5–6, pp. 12–13; and *Rankings of the States, 1993* (Washington D.C.: National Education Association, 1993), Table E6, p. 38.

[33]Liz Bowie and Stephen Henderson, "Pupils Lose Ground in City Schools," *The Sun*, November 12, 1997, p. A1,12.

[34]Telephone conversation with Steven Gorman, Project Director, National Assessment of Educational Progress, November 7, 1991; Joe B. Hanson, "Is Educational Reform Through Mandated Accountability an Oxymoron?" *Measurement and Evaluation in Counseling and Development* (April 1993), pp. 11–21; and Robert Rothman, "The Certificate of Initial Mastery," *Educational Leadership* (May 1995), pp. 41–45.

[35]Stephen Henderson and Liz Bowie, "Weakest Schools' Principals Losing Jobs," *The Sun*, June 9, 1998, p. A1,4.

Tuition Tax Credits and Educational Vouchers

Tuition tax credits

Tuition tax credits allow parents to claim a tax reduction for part of the tuition fees they pay to send their children to private schools. In the early 1990s Minnesota became the first state to employ tuition tax credits; other states now have tax credits or tax deductions under consideration.[36] The tax-credit movement reflects the public's desire for increased choice in schools as well as the continuing quest of nonpublic schools for support. The issue has been brought to the fore, however, by the wavering faith in the public schools.

Educational vouchers

Use of **educational vouchers** is another trend in school finance reform. Under a voucher system, parents of school-age children are given a voucher or flat grant representing their children's estimated educational cost. Children then use this voucher to attend any school, public or private, that they and their parents choose.

Arguments against

Debates over tuition tax credits and voucher programs have been vigorous and emotional. The NEA, the AFT, and other educational organizations contend that vouchers or tax credits increase segregation, split the public along socioeconomic lines, and reduce financial support for the public schools.[37] Opponents have also argued that such programs provide unconstitutional support for church-related schools, undermine the public school system by supporting and encouraging the movement of students to nonpublic schools, and result in a large drain on public school budgets or state treasuries.[38]

Arguments in favor

Supporters of tuition tax credits and voucher programs argue that such credits are not unconstitutional and do not seriously reduce federal revenues or hamper public-school tax levy efforts. They also argue that these programs provide wider opportunity for students to attend schools outside the inner city; thus tax credits or vouchers do not contribute to, and might even reduce, racial and socioeconomic isolation. In addition, many supporters believe that tax credits or vouchers, besides providing parents with a choice in selecting schools, stimulate improvement in the public school, particularly when there is a choice within the public school district, as the Clinton administration favors.[39]

School Choice

Choice and the "marketplace"

Proponents of tuition tax credits and vouchers generally link the issue with the concept of **school choice**, which is discussed in detail in Chapter 16. By widening the average person's choices for schooling, the supporters contend, we can increase competition among schools and raise the overall level of educational quality. The idea is to depend on education to follow the laws of the marketplace: if students

---

[36]Fischer, Schimmel, and Kelly, *Teachers and the Law*, p. 474.

[37]"Deleterious Programs," *NEA Handbook, 1994–95* (Washington, D.C.: National Education Association, 1994), p. 247; Joanna Richardson, "Order Blocks Nonsectarian Expansion of Voucher Program," *Education Week*, September 13, 1995, p. 3; and Judith Saks, "The Voucher Debate: Should Public Money Follow Kids to Private Schools," *American School Board Journal* (March, 1997), pp. 24–28.

[38]Daniel U. Levine and Rayna F. Levine, *Society and Education*, 9th ed. (Needham Heights, Mass.: Allyn and Bacon, 1996); Carol A. Langdon, "The Third Phi Delta Kappa Poll of Teachers' Attitudes Toward the Public Schools," *Phi Delta Kappan* (November, 1996), pp. 244–250; and K. L. Billingsley, *Voices on Choice: The Education Reform Debate* (San Francisco: Pacific Research Institute for Public Policy, 1994).

[39]Joe Nathan and James Ysseldyke, "What Minnesota Has Learned About School Choice," *Phi Delta Kappan* (May 1994), pp. 682–688; and John Weisman, "Revolutionary Steps to Better Education," *Fortune*, October 21, 1991, pp. 128–129.

Types of school choice

and parents can choose schools, the effective schools will stay in operation and the less desirable ones will either go out of business or improve.[40]

Some plans allow choice only within the public school system, as is currently the case in Minnesota, Wisconsin, California, Massachusetts, and ten other states.[41] Other choice plans also permit the use of vouchers in private schools.[42] One of the most controversial of these is the Milwaukee Parental Choice Program, which permits 15,000 children from low-income families to attend either public or private schools at no cost to the students. This controversial plan gives poor children the opportunity to escape unsatisfactory inner-city public schools. In November 1998, the U.S. Supreme Court opted not to become involved in this issue and let a Wisconsin Supreme Court decision stand, thereby permitting public monies to benefit over 4,000 poor children attending private, religious schools.[43]

Charter schools

A variation on the school choice theme is the concept of *charter schools,* discussed in Chapter 6. Vested authorities, such as local school boards or the state department of education, issue charters to groups of teachers, parents, or community members who want to operate schools independent of the school district. In exchange for freedom from hundreds of rules and regulations, charter schools are held accountable for specific academic results and risk revocation of their charter if they do not attain their academic goals.[44] As of 1998, twenty-nine states had passed charter school legislation, and a total of almost 800 charter schools were in operation nationally.[45] Interestingly, while President Clinton endorsed the idea of charter schools, a 1994 survey of school board members showed that 84 percent were opposed to the idea, fearing its negative impact on available monies to fund school board budgets.[46]

Streamlining School Budgets

Scrutiny of school budgets

In an era of taxpayer wariness, accountability demands, and strain on state budgets, school boards are being pressed to eliminate unnecessary spending before recommending tax increases. Not only must school outcomes measure up to expected standards, but the budget must stand up to close scrutiny. Corporate leaders often serve on school boards, and the gospel of streamlining and efficiency — so preva-

---

[40]See, for instance, William L. Boyd and Herbert J. Walberg, eds., *Choice in Education* (Berkeley, Calif.: McCutchan, 1990); Joseph Murphy, ed., *The Educational Reform Movement of the 1980s* (Berkeley, Calif.: McCutchan, 1990); and David Osborne, "Schools Got Scary," *Mother Jones* (January–February 1996), pp. 47–48.

[41]Nathan and Ysseldyke, "What Minnesota Has Learned," pp. 682–688; U.S. Department of Education, National Center for Educational Statistics, *State Indicators in Education, 1997,* Washington, D.C.: National Center for Educational Statistics, 1997, p. 40.

[42]Fischer, Schimmel, and Kelly, *Teachers and the Law,* pp. 474–475.

[43]Thomas Fowler-Finn, "Why Have They Chosen Another School System?" *Educational Leadership* (December 1993–January 1994), pp. 60–62; Lyle Denniston, "Religious School Aid Upheld by Wis. Court," *The Sun,* June 11, 1998, p. A1,8; David Reunzel, "A Choice in the Matter," *Education Week,* September 27, 1995, pp. 23–28; Lyle Denniston, "Justices Allow Student Vouchers," *The Sun,* November 10, 1998, p. A1,11.

[44]Lori A. Mulholland and Luann A. Bierlein, *Understanding Charter Schools* (Bloomington, Ind.: Phi Delta Kappa Educational Foundation, 1995), pp. 7–11.

[45]Donna Harrington-Leuker, "Charter Schools," *American School Board Journal* (September 1994), pp. 22–25; Bruno Manno, "How Charter Schools Are Different," *Phi Delta Kappan* (March, 1998), pp. 489–498; and "Charter Schools: Gaining Momentum," available by searching the Internet for "Daily Report Card" and clicking for December 8, 1995.

[46]Joe Nathan and James Ysseldyke, "A Big No to Charter Schools," *American School Board Journal* (September 1994), p. 56; and Louann A. Bierlin, "Catching On but the Jury's Still Out," *Educational Leadership* (December 1995–January 1996), pp. 90–91.

Competing demands for public money coupled with the reduced number of households with children in school have led educators to reduce their budget expectations and do more with less money. (© Jeffrey W. Myers/ Stock Boston)

lent in the business community — has had considerable impact on American education. We should continue to see the following significant trends.

New research on class size

1. *Class size.* For the first time in decdes new research on class size, conducted by the Department of Education's Office of Educational Research and Improvement, shows that "smaller is better," and that smaller classes in the early grades lead to higher student achievement. These significant effects on achievement occur when class size is reduced to a point between fifteen and twenty students. This may lead to a concerted effort nationally to reduce class size.[47]

Maintaining old facilities

2. *Modernization of older buildings.* Rather than build new schools, many districts are choosing to save money by maintaining and modernizing their older buildings. As we will see, however, in the next section, old buildings can cause budgetary strains of their own.

Smaller, more efficient buildings

3. *Smaller schools.* In many areas the trend is toward smaller school buildings, which make more efficient use of space, require less fuel and lighting, are easier to maintain, and require fewer administrators.[48]

Adding more teachers

4. *Need for teachers.* Whereas selected areas of the country may be laying off teachers because of population decline, other areas, particularly suburban areas and Sunbelt states, are experiencing a population boom in the schools. Add to this an aging teaching corps, and projections are that over 2 million new teachers will be needed by 2010.

[47]Teacher Education Reports. "Released to Bolster Clinton Teaching Bill, New Study Concludes Smaller Classes Enhance Achievement," *Teacher Education Reports,* May 14, 1998, p. 5.
[48]Allan C. Ornstein, "Trimming the Fat, Stretching the Meat for 1990 Budgets," *School Administrator* (October 1989), pp. 20–21; and Thomas Sergiovanni, "Small Schools, Great Expectations," *Educational Leadership* (November 1995), pp. 48–52.

Streamlining central staffs

5. *Administrative reductions.* Many districts are finding it possible to operate with smaller central office staffs. These reductions cause much less public outcry than when the teaching force is cut.

Reducing energy costs

6. *Energy economies.* Some schools dial down temperatures, delay warming up the school each morning, reduce heat in the hallways, and buy energy directly from gas and oil distributors.

School Infrastructure and Environmental Problems

Deteriorating facilities

The nation's **school infrastructure** is in a state of critical disrepair. By infrastructure, we mean the basic physical facilities of the school plant (plumbing, sewer, heat, electric, roof, carpentry, and so on). Building experts estimate that schools in the United States are deteriorating at a faster rate than they can be repaired, and faster than most other public facilities. Plumbing, electrical wiring, and heating systems in many schools are dangerously out of date; roofing is below code; and exterior brickwork, stone, and wood are in serious disrepair. The cost of deferred expenditures runs to over $100 million each in Los Angeles, Detroit, Chicago, Seattle, and Miami's Dade County, with an enormous bill of $680 million for the New York City schools. The accumulated cost to repair the public schools was recently estimated by the Government Accounting Office at $112 billion, a staggering increase over earlier projections.[49] A 1996 Government Accounting Office study showed that in the home states of the five school districts mentioned above (California, Michigan, Illinois, Washington, and New York) each reported that an average of 85 percent of their schools needed repairs to bring them up to "good condition."[50]

Asbestos cleanup

Environmental hazards in school buildings are a special problem. For example, the Environmental Protection Agency (EPA) has ordered government and commercial property owners, including school districts, to clean up buildings laden with asbestos. Although the costs are hard to calculate, one estimate placed the bill for schools at $3.1 billion, which would cover some 45,000 schools in 3,100 districts.[51]

Radon

Radon gas is another environmental concern and is costly to eliminate. Preliminary EPA tests found that radon, now considered the second-leading cause of lung cancer, was present at dangerously high levels in 54 percent of the 130 schools randomly checked.[52]

More classrooms will be needed

Even as school boards struggle to meet the needs of an aging infrastructure, the U.S. Census Bureau has increased its projections for the growth of the school-age population. Using 1990 census figures as a baseline, the bureau now expects the school-age population to have grown 19 percent by 2005 and 33 percent by 2025. This prediction is based on increases in fertility rates and in the immigrant population. Repairs aside, there is much concern about where the money will come from to build the additional classrooms that will soon be needed.[53]

---

[49]Allan C. Ornstein, "School Finance and the Condition of Schools," *Theory into Practice* (Spring, 1994), pp. 118–125; and Anne Lewis, "Fixing the Nation's Schoolhouses," *Phi Delta Kappan* (April 1995), pp. 580–581.

[50]Government Accounting Office, *School Facilities: Profiles of School Condition by State,* Washington, D.C.: U.S. Government Printing Office, 1996.

[51]Lewis, "Fixing," pp. 580–581.

[52]Allan C. Ornstein. "School Finance and the Conditions of Schools," *Theory into Practice* (Spring 1994), pp. 118–125; and Hugh Wright, "Radon Gas New Threat in Schools," *USA Today,* April 21, 1989, p. 1A.

[53]Lewis, "Fixing," p. 581.

Summing Up

1. Schools are financially supported by the state and local governments and to a lesser extent by the federal government. Overall, since the early twentieth century, state support has increased dramatically and local support has declined; the percentage of federal support grew until the 1980s and then declined.

2. Although the property tax is the main local source of school revenue, it is considered a regressive tax.

3. There is wide variation in the financial ability among states and within states (at the local district level) to support education. Poorer school districts tend to receive more money from the states than do wealthier school districts, but the amount rarely makes up for the total difference in expenditures.

4. School finance reform, initiated by the courts and carried forward by state legislatures, has attempted to reduce or eliminate funding disparities between poorer and wealthier districts. The basic goal is to equalize educational opportunities and give poorer districts the means to improve their performance.

5. Since the *Sputnik* era, federal funding of education has become increasingly linked to national policy. But since the 1980s, some responsibility for educational funding has shifted from the federal government back to the individual states.

6. Controversies over accountability, tuition tax credits, educational vouchers, charter schools, and school choice reflect increasing public dissatisfaction with the educational system.

7. Taxpayer resistance, especially to increases in property taxes, results in strong pressure to streamline school budgets.

8. Deteriorating school infrastructure and environmental dangers pose significant problems for many schools.

Key Terms

progressive taxes *(207)*

regressive taxes *(207)*

property tax *(207)*

mill *(207)*

user fees *(208)*

exclusive product rights *(209)*

tax base *(209)*

municipal overburden *(209)*

sales tax *(210)*

personal income tax *(210)*

categorical grants *(218)*

block grants *(218)*

taxpayer resistance *(222)*

accountability *(222)*

tuition tax credits *(223)*

educational vouchers *(223)*

school choice *(223)*

school infrastructure *(226)*

Discussion Questions

1. How do school boards and local elected officials design a tax structure that is fair and equitable and capable of keeping abreast of changing economic conditions? What specific elements would make up this tax code?

2. If the federal government would carry through a plan to balance the federal budget in the next decade, what impact do you think this would have on public-school funding?

3. State your reasons for or against the following types of financial support for school choice:

(a) Government vouchers that any student can use to pay tuition in any accredited school, public or private.

(b) Vouchers as in (a), but issued only to students whose families demonstrate financial need.

(c) No vouchers for private or parochial schools, though students are free to choose any *public* schools they like.

Suggested Projects for Professional Development

1. Survey a number of taxpayers (parents, neighbors, classmates, coworkers) about their attitudes toward school taxes. To what extent do they resist such taxes? For what reasons, or under what conditions, might they be willing to pay more? Do you notice any differences of opinion among various age groups, ethnic groups, income groups, or social classes? Summarize your findings for the class.

2. In your visits to schools this term, be alert to infrastructure concerns. What specific problems do you see, and what do the students and faculty complain about? Are things significantly better or worse in neighboring districts? If so, how do people account for these differences? Keep notes on your findings in a journal.

3. Over a period of several weeks, examine the state and local news section of your daily paper for articles relating to school finance. Are these articles supportive or critical of the current system? Do they agree with any of the points of view presented in this chapter, or do they take a different approach? Share your findings with the class.

4. Call or write the public information office of the state department of education to discover how public education is financed in your state. Ask for brochures or charts that specify local, state, and federal contributions. Does your state have a school assessment plan based on student performance outcomes? Does it have a means for taking control of districts that fail to meet state standards?

5. Gather position papers and policy statements from several agencies concerned with school finance: for instance, the local teacher's association or union, the state department of education, and local citizens' organizations. Supplement the written materials by interviewing representatives from at least two of the groups. List the main themes that emerge.

6. Interview a local school board member regarding the following:

   ■ Concerns about funding and the budget process

   ■ His or her most important budget priorities

   ■ Creative ways to address budget problems

   ■ How public support for the budget is built, once the budget is established

Suggested Readings and Resources

Internet Resources

Many up-to-date statistics on school finance are available in the yearly federal publications *The Condition of Education* and *Digest of Education Statistics,* both of which are available through the U.S. Department of Education's Gopher (**gopher:// gopher.ed.gov**). In addition, several of the topics in this chapter, such as "education vouchers," "school choice," and "tuition tax credits," can be researched by conducting searches at federal government Internet sites, particularly **www.ed.gov** and **www.inet.gov**. Recent articles and papers dealing with topics in this and other chapters in the text are tracked in the "current awareness" submenu at **www.dpi.state.nc.us/**.

Publications

Augenblick, John. *School Finance: A Primer.* Denver: Education Commission of the States, 1991. *Examines various existing approaches to financing schools and proposes alternatives.*

Boyd, William L., and Herbert J. Walberg. *Choice in Education.* Berkeley, Calif.: McCutchan, 1990. *Discusses the advantages and disadvantages of school choice, as well as various choice plans in major cities.*

Guthrie, James W., Walter I. Garms, and Lawrence C. Pierce. *School Finance and Education Policy.* Englewood Cliffs, N.J.: Prentice-Hall, 1988. *A comprehensive examination of various methods for distributing resources and services for public schools.*

Mulholland, Lori A., and Louann A Bierlein. *Understanding Charter Schools.* Bloomington, Ind.: Phi Delta Kappa Educational Foundation, 1995. *An excellent book on the emerging concept of charter schools in the United States.*

Odden, Allen R., and Lawrence O. Picus. *School Finance: A Policy Perspective.* New York: McGraw-Hill, 1992. *An examination of school productivity formulas, fiscal policy, and fiscal federalism.*

Rotberg, Iris C., James J. Harvey, Kelly E. Wormer, and Nancy Rizor. *Federal Policy Options for Improving the Education of Low-Income Students.* Santa Monica, Calif.: The Rand Corporation, 1994. *Examines the inequalities in school finance and their impact on poor children in public school districts.*

Swanson, Austin D., and Richard A. King. *School Finance: Its Economics and Politics.* New York: Longman, 1991. *Discusses the hows and whys of school finance decisions.*

Uchitelle, Susan. *School Choice: Issues and Answers.* Bloomington, Ind.: Phi Delta Kappa Educational Foundation, 1994. *Features many of the arguments behind school choice and such issues as vouchers and tuition tax credits.*

Ward, James G., and Patricia Anthony. *Who Pays for Student Diversity?* Newbury, Calif.: Sage/Corwin Press, 1992. *Argues that school finance policy can be a source of social justice and equity funding for students at risk.*

CHAPTER EIGHT

Legal Aspects of Education

During the past fifty years, the courts have increasingly been asked to resolve issues relating to public education in the United States. This rise in educational litigation reflects the fact that education has assumed an importance in our society that it did not have a few decades ago. The growth in litigation has been paralleled, and to some extent spurred on, by an enormous increase in state and federal legislation affecting education.[1]

This chapter presents a general overview of the U.S. court system and examines the legal topics and court decisions that have had the most important effects on today's schools and teachers. The major topics considered are the rights and responsibilities of both teachers and students, religion and the schools, and affirmative action and educational equity.[2] Questions to consider as you read this chapter include the following:

- What legal rights and responsibilities do teachers have?
- What are the legal rights of students?
- Can religious activities be conducted in the public schools?
- Can the government assist nonpublic schools?
- Must the public schools accept students with AIDS?
- How does affirmative action influence education?

[1]David Tyack, Thomas James, and Aaron Benavot, *The Law and the Shaping of Public Education, 1785–1954* (Madison: University of Wisconsin Press, 1987); Michael Imber and Gary Thompson, "Developing a Typology of Litigation in Education," *Educational Administration Quarterly* (May 1991), pp. 225–244; and Michael Imber and Tyll Van Geel, *A Teacher's Guide to Education Law* (New York: McGraw-Hill, 1995).

[2]Other chapters of this book also discuss selected legal issues in education. For court decisions regarding school finance, see Chapter 7; desegregation law is explained in Chapter 11.

The Court System

Most education cases filed in state courts

Cases involving education-related issues can be heard either in federal or state courts, depending on the allegations of the **plaintiffs** (the persons who sue). Federal courts decide cases that involve federal laws and regulations or constitutional issues. State courts adjudicate cases that involve state laws, state constitutional provisions, school board policies, or other nonfederal problems. Most cases pertaining to elementary and secondary education are filed in state courts. However, to keep from overburdening court calendars, both federal and state courts usually require that prospective **litigants** (the parties in a lawsuit) exhaust all administrative avenues available for resolution before involving the court system.

State Courts

Types of state courts

There is no national uniformity in state court organization. The details of each state's judicial system are found in its constitution. At the lowest level, most states have a court of original jurisdiction (often called a municipal or superior court) where cases are tried. The facts are established, evidence is presented, witnesses testify and are cross-examined, and appropriate legal principles are applied in rendering a verdict. The losing side may appeal the decision to the next higher level, usually an intermediate appellate court. This court reviews the trial record from the lower court and additional written materials submitted by both sides. The goals of the appellate court are to ensure that appropriate laws were properly applied, that they fit with the facts presented, and that there was no deprivation of constitutional rights.

If one side is still not satisfied, another appeal may be made to the state's highest court, often called its supreme court. A state supreme court decision is final unless a question involving the U.S. Constitution has been raised. The side wishing to appeal further may then petition the U.S. Supreme Court to consider the case.

Federal Courts

Three tiers of federal courts

Federal courts are organized into a three-tiered system: district courts, circuit courts of appeals, and the Supreme Court. The jurisdiction and powers of these courts are set forth in the Constitution and are subject to congressional restrictions. The lowest level, the district court, holds trials. For appeals at the next federal level, the nation is divided into twelve regions called circuits. Each circuit court handles appeals only from district courts within its particular geographic area. Unsuccessful litigants may request that the U.S. Supreme Court review their case. If four of the nine justices agree, the Supreme Court will take the case; if not, the appellate court ruling stands.[3]

Conflicting rulings

Decisions of a court below the U.S. Supreme Court have force only in the geographic area served by that particular court. For this reason, it is possible to find conflicting rulings in different circuits. Judges often look to previous case law for guidance in rendering decisions, and they may find precedent for a variety of legally defensible positions on a single issue.

First Amendment

The First and the Fourteenth Amendments. Although education is considered a responsibility of the states, it has produced an abundance of federal litigation, particularly in connection with the First and Fourteenth Amendments to the U.S. Con-

---

[3]Some case citations in this chapter include the term *cert. denied.* This means that the losing parties petitioned the U.S. Supreme Court for review, but their request was denied.

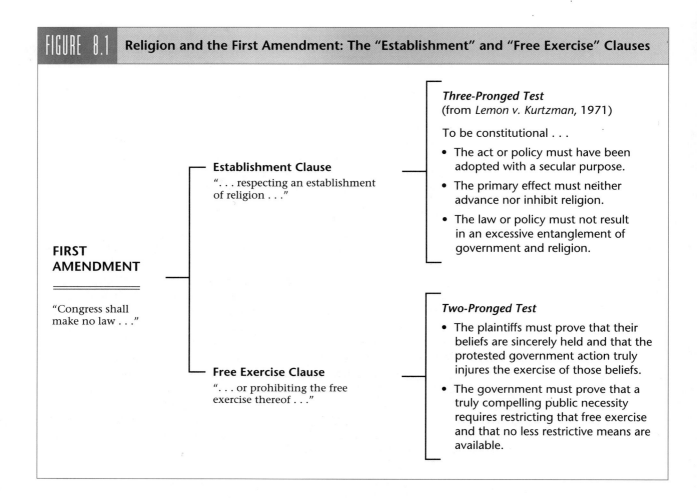

FIGURE 8.1   Religion and the First Amendment: The "Establishment" and "Free Exercise" Clauses

FIRST AMENDMENT

"Congress shall make no law . . ."

Establishment Clause
". . . respecting an establishment of religion . . ."

Three-Pronged Test
(from *Lemon v. Kurtzman*, 1971)

To be constitutional . . .

- The act or policy must have been adopted with a secular purpose.
- The primary effect must neither advance nor inhibit religion.
- The law or policy must not result in an excessive entanglement of government and religion.

Free Exercise Clause
". . . or prohibiting the free exercise thereof . . ."

Two-Pronged Test

- The plaintiffs must prove that their beliefs are sincerely held and that the protested government action truly injures the exercise of those beliefs.
- The government must prove that a truly compelling public necessity requires restricting that free exercise and that no less restrictive means are available.

stitution. The First Amendment concerns freedom of religion, speech, press, and assembly and the right "to petition the government for redress of grievances." Many First Amendment cases have dealt with the role of religion in public education and with the extent of protection guaranteed to freedom of expression by students and teachers. The First Amendment has two clauses that are often cited in lawsuits: the **establishment clause**, which prohibits the establishment of a nationally sanctioned religion, and the **free exercise clause**, which protects rights of free speech and expression. To interpret these clauses, the courts generally use the criteria or "tests" shown in Figure 8.1.

Fourteenth Amendment

Court cases involving the Fourteenth Amendment often focus on the section declaring that no state shall "deprive any person of life, liberty, or property, without due process of law; nor deny to any person within its jurisdiction the equal protection of the law." The first part of this passage is known as the **due process clause**, and the second part as the **equal protection clause**. Fourteenth Amendment cases have addressed the issue of school desegregation as well as the suspension and expulsion of students. Litigants citing the Fourteenth Amendment must show that a "liberty" or a "property" interest is a major element in the case. A liberty interest is

Liberty and property interests

involved if "a person's good name, reputation, honor or integrity is at stake." A property interest may arise from legal guarantees granted to tenured employees; for instance, teachers beyond the probationary period have a property interest in continued employment. Similarly, students have a property interest in their education. If either a liberty or a property interest is claimed, a school district must provide due process to the people involved. The rest of this chapter will explore the use of these and other legal concepts in actual school settings.[4]

Teachers' Rights and Responsibilities

As pointed out in Chapter 2, teachers historically were vulnerable to dismissal by local boards of education for virtually any reason and without recourse. Collective negotiation statutes, tenure laws, mandatory due process procedures, and the like have been established to curb such abuses and to guarantee teachers certain rights. Along with rights come responsibilities, and many of these, too, have been written into law.

Testing and Investigation of Applicants for Certification or Employment

Background checks

Almost everywhere in the United States, individuals who wish employment as teachers must possess teaching certificates, which are usually granted by the state. In recent years many states have passed legislation requiring thorough background checks of prospective teachers, and some extend this requirement to currently employed teachers seeking recertification. This trend has been fueled by two complementary developments. On the one hand, technology has made it more feasible to use fingerprints and other information sources in checking with local, state, and federal law enforcement agencies. On the other hand, the public has become increasingly concerned about dangers posed by child molesters and other potential school employees with criminal records. These checks have generally gone unchallenged.[5]

Nearly all the states require prospective teachers to pass one or more competency tests for certification and, in some cases, for continued employment. In states where minority passing rates are considerably lower than those for nonminority candidates, several lawsuits have been filed charging that specific tests discriminate against minority applicants. To answer such a lawsuit, employers must be able to specify the characteristics that a test is being used to measure, establish that these characteristics are necessary in carrying out the job, and demonstrate that the test correlates with the work behavior in question.

Nondiscrimination requirements

Most lawsuits charging that teacher tests are discriminatory either have not been successful or have been withdrawn because the available data did not demonstrate a clear pattern of discrimination. On the other hand, there is no doubt that worries about possible legal challenges, particularly from minority candidates, sometimes have led states to keep passing scores low. In Massachusetts, for example, concerns regarding a legal challenge alleging discrimination were one of the considerations that led the State Board of Education to substantially reduce the minimum score required for passing a proposed test for certificates in that state.[6]

---

[4]*Goss* v. *Lopez,* 419 U.S. 565 (1975). See also Perry A. Zirkel, *A Digest of Supreme Court Decisions Affecting Education,* 3rd ed. (Bloomington, Ind.: Phi Delta Kappa, 1995); and David Hill, "Tenure on Trial," *Education Week,* January 31, 1996, pp. 22–26.

[5]Linda Jacobson, "Miller Wants to Shake Up Teacher-Investigation Agency," *Education Week,* February 18, 1998; and Teresa Talerico," Fingerprinting Takes Toll on School Workers," *Seattle Post-Intelligences,* January 15, 1998.

[6]Blake Rodman, "Arkansas Union Drops Suit over Teacher Tests," *Education Week,* November 25, 1987, p. 10; Larry D. Bartlett and Lelia B. Helsm, *Recent Developments in Public Education Law* (Washington, D.C.: American Bar Association, 1995); and David J. Hoff, "Federal Court Blocks Alabama Teacher Test," *Education Week,* January 27, 1999.

Employment Contracts and Tenure

In choosing which teachers to hire, local school boards must comply with laws that prohibit discrimination with respect to age, sex, race, religion, or national origin. Upon appointment, the teacher receives a written contract to sign. The contract may specify that the teacher adhere to school board policies and regulations. If the school district has negotiated with a teacher organization, the provisions of that agreement apply as well.

Breach of contract

Contracts are binding on both parties. When one side fails to perform as agreed — called a **breach of contract** — the contract is broken. In such instances, the party that breached the contract may be sued for damages. Some states permit a teacher's certificate to be revoked if the teacher breaches the contract. On the other hand, if a school district breaks a contract, teachers may be awarded damages or be reinstated to their former positions.

Terms of tenure

Nearly every state also has some type of tenure law. **Tenure** provides job security for teachers by preventing their dismissal without cause. What constitutes "cause" is defined by each state; the usual reasons include incompetency, immorality, insubordination, and unprofessional conduct. In addition, as explained in the next section, the school district must follow due process if it wishes to dismiss a tenured teacher.

History of tenure

From its inception, the notion of tenure has been controversial. Arguments for and against tenure are presented in this chapter's Taking Issue box.

Continuing employment

Once tenure has been granted, many teachers do not sign a contract annually. Instead, they are said to be employed under a **continuing contract.** The term means that their reemployment for the next year is guaranteed unless school officials give notice by a specific date that the contract will not be renewed.

Probationary period

Most states have a probationary period before teachers achieve tenure. Moreover, many tenured teachers who change districts lose their tenure and must serve another period of probation. The probationary period often consists of three years of consecutive, satisfactory service, but some states have been moving to establish much shorter periods, at the end of which new teachers can be quickly removed from their jobs. In particular, Florida has legislation allowing for the release of new teachers at the conclusion of a 97-day probationary period.[7]

Probationary contracts in some states allow the teacher to be discharged at the end of the contract term for any reason and without explanation — no due process is required, unless the teacher can demonstrate that his or her dismissal involves a constitutionally guaranteed liberty or property interest. (See the next section for information on the meaning of due process.) In other states probationary teachers have general due process rights, but sometimes the process is streamlined to expedite dismissal of candidates rated as incompetent.[8]

Due Process in Dismissal of Teachers

Due process refers to the use of legal rules and principles that have been established to protect the rights of the accused. For a teacher, these principles are especially im-

---

[7]Jodi M. Farrell, "303 Teachers Let Go Under New State Law," *Miami Herald,* July 15, 1998.
[8]Allan S. Vann, "Preparing Probationary Teachers for Tenure," *Principal* (March 1992), pp. 42–44; David A. Splitt, "On Probation," *The Executive Educator* (July 1995), pp. 13, 39; Andrea H. La Rue, *The Changing Face of Teacher Tenure* (Washington, D.C.: American Federation of Teachers, 1996), available at **www.aft.org**; and Perry A. Zirkel, "Old-Fashioned Teaching," *Phi Delta Kappan* (February 1996), pp. 449–451.

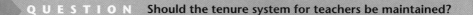

TAKING ISSUE

Tenure for Teachers

At one time, many teaching positions in large cities were controlled by political patronage. In some cities, principalships were available for a certain price at the ward committeeman's office, and teaching jobs were won or lost on the basis of precinct work. In general, teachers were afraid to contradict an administrator or an influential parent. Tenure was introduced partly to stop these abuses and to give teachers independence in and out of the classroom. However, some educators now contend that the tenure system has outlived its usefulness.

Arguments PRO

1 Teaching is, by its nature, controversial. A good teacher cannot help but offend someone at some level. Without the academic freedom that tenure helps to protect, teachers could not do their jobs properly.

2 A tenure system does not protect incompetence. There are procedures for removing a teacher who is clearly ineffective. The responsibility for teacher incompetence lies with lax state licensing procedures and with administrators who are too reluctant to dismiss teachers during probationary periods.

3 Teachers must cope with pressure from a bewildering array of sources: parents, other community members, administrators, and legislators, among others. A complaint from any one of these parties might lead to a teacher's dismissal. For this reason, teachers need — and deserve — the special protection offered by tenure.

4 Tenure was originally a response to serious political and administrative abuses, especially in large cities. The same forces that caused these problems still exist, and they will create similar abuses if the protection of tenure is ever removed.

Arguments CON

1 Some teachers use their positions to advance personal, social, or political views under the guise of controversial discussion. Other teachers are simply lazy or incompetent. Often it is these marginal teachers — not the good teachers — whom the tenure system protects.

2 The procedures for removing a tenured teacher are often so complex and arouse so much resentment among other teachers that administrators are discouraged from trying. Furthermore, even if screening methods are upgraded, many ineffective teachers will continue to slip through. The only solution is to give school officials, like private employers, the right to fire an unproductive employee.

3 The many sources of pressure actually enhance a teacher's security. Active parents and community members often use their influence to protect good teachers. The layers of school administration offer avenues of appeal if a teacher's position is threatened. Thus, even without a tenure system, competent teachers will be secure in their jobs.

4 Teachers now have powerful professional organizations that shield them from undue political and administrative interference. With these organizations looking after teachers' rights, the tenure system has become an anachronism.

TABLE 8.1	Due Process Rules for Dismissing a Teacher

1. The teacher must be given timely, detailed, written notice of the charges.
2. The teacher must be accorded a hearing and sufficient time to prepare.
3. The teacher has a right to be represented by legal counsel.
4. The teacher may present written and oral evidence, including witnesses.
5. The teacher may cross-examine witnesses and challenge evidence.
6. The hearing is to be conducted before an impartial body. The U.S. Supreme Court has ruled (in *Hortonville District* v. *Hortonville Education Association*) that under the U.S. Constitution a school board may be that impartial body unless bias can be proven.
7. The teacher is entitled to a written transcript of the proceedings.
8. The teacher has the right to appeal an adverse ruling to a higher legal authority, usually the state court system.

Source: See *Hortonville District* v. *Hortonville Education Association*, 426 U.S. 482 (1976); and Janine M. Bernard, "Ethical and Legal Dimensions of Supervision," *ERIC Digest* (April 1994), pp. 1–4, accessible on the Internet via ERIC at **www.ed.gov.**

"Fairness" in teacher dismissal

portant if he or she is being dismissed from the job. The core element of due process is "fairness." Although the requirements vary from state to state, the rules shown in Table 8.1 are generally recognized in cases of teacher dismissal.

Firing a teacher for incompetence requires documentation of efforts to help that person improve. Obtaining this documentation can be very burdensome for everyone involved.

Assistance for struggling teachers

Other procedures for removing teachers

Administrators sometimes use less formal procedures for excluding incompetent teachers from their school districts. Some of these procedures include counseling incompetent teachers out of the profession, suggesting and financing early retirement, and allowing the teacher to resign. Nevertheless, it is still true that few tenured teachers are forced out of their jobs.[9]

Negotiation and Strikes

Teachers have the right to form and belong to unions and other professional organizations. Since the 1960s, such teacher groups have lobbied for state legislation to permit school boards to negotiate agreements with them. This effort has been successful in most states; however, a few continue to prohibit negotiations between teachers and school boards. Although the laws enacted vary widely, they usually allow the two sides to bargain collectively or at least to "meet and confer." Some states specify the procedure that must be followed if the two sides fail to agree (for example, fact-finding in Kansas; binding arbitration in Maryland).[10]

Most states allow negotiation

Because education is considered a vital public service, the law generally prohibits strikes by employees. (A few states condone the withholding of services by teachers under specific conditions written into state law.) However, teachers sometimes do strike despite the legal prohibitions. In such instances, school officials can seek court injunctions ordering teachers to return to their classrooms. Defiance of a

Penalties for striking

[9]Edwin M. Bridges, *Managing the Incompetent Teacher,* 2nd ed. (Eugene, Oreg.: ERIC Clearinghouse on Educational Management, 1990); and *Teacher Dismissal Survey* (Washington, D.C.: American Federation of Teachers, 1996), available at **www.aft.org.**

[10]Adrienne D. Coles, "Tepid Season of Teachers' Strikes Exhibits Evidence of Heating Up," *Education Week,* September 7, 1997, p. 6; and Richard C. Seder, "Organizing Principals," *Reason* (January 1998), available at **www.reasonmag.com.**

court order can result in penalties. Florida and Minnesota, for example, prohibit striking teachers from receiving salary increases for one year after a strike; New York law allows striking teachers to be penalized two days' pay for each day on strike; and Michigan permits dismissal of striking teachers.

Protection Against Assault

Physical assault

In recent decades, physical assault on teachers and administrators has become an important problem at some schools, particularly secondary schools in big cities. In such cases, courts generally have convicted defendants who violated either educational statutes or state criminal codes. Some analysts have concluded that educators can help protect themselves and their fellow employees by vigorously pressing criminal charges and initiating civil suits for assault and battery.[11] In addition, many school districts have developed policies that stress punishment of students who assault teachers and also assist teachers in pursuing legal responses. For example, the Cincinnati Board of Education has incorporated the following provisions in its contractual agreement with the district's teachers:

Contractual protection

- A teacher may use such force as shall be reasonable and necessary to protect himself/herself from attack, to prevent school property from damage and/or destruction and/or to prevent injury to another person.
- A student who physically assaults a teacher who is performing a duty in the line of employment, including extracurricular activities, shall be immediately suspended.

Freedom of Expression

Courts have tended to uphold teachers' rights to express themselves in public or in school (see Overview 8.1). However, in determining whether the expression is "protected" under the First Amendment, the court considers the effects on the operation of the school, on the teacher's performance, on teacher-superior relationships, and on coworkers, as well as the appropriateness of the time, place, and manner of the teacher's remarks.

Pickering: protection of free expression

An example is the case of Marvin Pickering, a tenured high-school teacher who published a letter to the editor of the local newspaper criticizing the board and superintendent about bond proposals and expenditures. The letter resulted in his termination. In *Pickering* v. *Board of Education*, the U.S. Supreme Court held that publication of the letter did not impede the "proper performance of his daily duties in the classroom or . . . [interfere] with the regular operation of schools generally." For this reason, Pickering's dismissal was found to be improper.[12]

Impaired teacher effectiveness

On the other hand, two teachers in Alaska were dismissed for writing a letter that was highly critical of their superintendent and contained many false allegations. Reaction to the letter was immediate and prolonged. The Alaska Supreme

---

[11]Perry A. Zirkel and Ivan B. Gluckman, "Assaults on School Personnel," *NASSP Bulletin* (March 1991), p. 10; Fred Hartmeister, *Surviving as a Teacher: The Legal Dimension* (Chicago: Precept Press, 1995); Lolly Bowean, "Teachers Report Fear of Students," *Boston Globe,* June 26, 1998; and "Student Discipline and Teacher Assault" (1998 Internet posting by the American Federation of Teachers), available at **www.aft.org/research.**

[12]*Pickering* v. *Board of Education*, 391 U.S. 563 (1968). See also Linda Greenhouse, "Justices, in Ruling on Free Speech, Put Limits on Government," *New York Times*, June 1, 1995, p. A18; and Benjamin Sendor, "How Free Is Teachers' Speech?" *American School Board Journal* (August 1996), pp. 16–17.

OVERVIEW 8.1   **Selected U.S. Supreme Court Decisions Affecting Teachers' Rights and Responsibilities**

Case	Summary of Decision
Pickering v. *Board of Education* (1968)	Teachers may speak their opinions as long as the school's regular operation is not disrupted.
Board of Regents of State Colleges v. *Roth* (1972)	After the probationary period, teachers have a property interest in continued employment.
Cleveland Board of Education v. *LeFleur* (1974)	Boards of education may establish leave policies for pregnant teachers, but these policies may not contain arbitrary leave and return dates.
Hortonville District v. *Hortonville Education Association* (1976)	In a due process hearing a school board may be the impartial body conducting the hearing.
Washington v. *Davis* (1976)	Underrepresentation of a group in the work force does not, in itself, prove unconstitutional employment discrimination, but the employer in this situation must prove that hiring has not been discriminatory.
Steelworkers v. *Weber* (1979)	Employers (including school districts) may use affirmative action plans to increase the number of minority employees.
Firefighters v. *Stotts* (1984)	In affirmative action programs, government units may not ignore seniority unless the minority candidates who benefit have personally experienced discrimination.
School Board of Nassau County v. *Arline* (1987)	Dismissing a teacher because of a physical impairment or contagious disease is unconstitutional.
Lehnert v. *Ferris Faculty Association* (1991)	Employees who are not union members cannot be required to pay dues used for political purposes unrelated to collective bargaining agreements.

Court held that the teachers' effectiveness had been impaired by their remarks and that their ability to work closely with colleagues had been diminished.[13]

Three-step analysis

A comparison of these cases shows that the decision rested not just on the behavior itself but also on what happened as a result. The courts have developed a three-step analysis for assessing teachers' rights to freedom of expression: (1) Did the teacher's expression of opinion involve a public matter of political, social, or other concern to the community? (2) If yes, courts still must weigh First Amendment rights against the employer's responsibility to promote a productive and harmonious climate for the delivery of education. Finally, (3) the teacher is entitled to judicial relief only if his or her expression of opinion can be shown to be a motivating factor in dismissal or other punitive action.[14]

Nonpublic teachers not necessarily protected

Pickering and similar decisions would not be applicable to private- or parochial-school teachers because those schools are not publicly funded. Private- and parochial-

---

[13]*Watts* v. *Seward School Board*, 454 P. 2d 732 (Alaska 1969), cert. denied, 397 U.S. 921 (1970).
[14]Benjamin Sendor, "Is Speaking Out Cause for Dismissal?" *American School Board Journal* (March 1990), pp. 8, 46; David A. Splitt, "Swatting Gadflies," *The Executive Educator* (January 1995), pp. 14–15; and Dana L. Long, "Freedom of Speech of Teachers" (Paper posted at **http://ideanet.doe.state.in.us/legal**, 1997).

school teachers do not necessarily have the civil rights protections guaranteed to public-school teachers (tenure, freedom of expression, due process, and the like). Their rights depend primarily on the terms of their individual contracts with the school.

Verbal abuse not condoned

Verbal and Emotional Abuse of Students.   Teachers' rights to freedom of expression do not extend, of course, to verbal or emotional abuse of students. Teachers can be sued and/or suspended or dismissed for engaging in such behavior. A teacher who also served as a basketball and football coach was accused of using terms such as "Tontos" in dealing with Native American students and "jungle bunnies" in referring to African American students. Although allowed to continue teaching science and physical education, he was suspended from coaching for unprofessional conduct. Other teachers have had their employment terminated or interrupted for directing obscene curses at students they perceived as troublesome, for persistently using sarcasm and ridicule to pressure or embarrass students, and for allegedly placing students in a shower stall smeared with feces as part of a lesson dealing with slave ships. In the latter case, parents sued the school district for inflicting emotional distress on their children and received a cash settlement before the case was heard in court. Teachers also can be sued personally under civil liability or criminal statutes by parents who believe their children have been injured by verbal or emotional abuse.[15]

Academic Freedom

Challenges to books and other materials

Academic freedom refers to the teacher's freedom to choose subject matter and instructional materials relevant to the course without interference from administrators or outsiders. Recent years have witnessed hundreds of incidents in which parents or others have tried to remove or restrict use of public-school materials, including allegedly immoral or unwholesome works such as *Little Red Riding Hood*, *Snow White*, *Huckleberry Finn*, and the *Goosebumps* fiction series. Several courts have ruled that materials can be eliminated on the basis of vulgarity but not on censorship of ideas. Although the U.S. Supreme Court has not provided definitive rulings, it has emphasized that school officials must take account of the First Amendment. Teachers should consider the objections of parents who do not want their children to study specific materials, but they also must work with administrators to ensure that legitimate materials are not removed entirely from classrooms and libraries.[16]

Teachers upheld

Appeals courts have upheld a high-school teacher's right to assign a magazine article containing "a vulgar term for an incestuous son"; another teacher's use of a film in which citizens of a small town randomly killed one person each year; and elementary teachers' use of a literary anthology in which students were instructed to pretend they were witches and write poetic chants.[17]

---

[15]Jane Gross, "High School Coach Is Suspended over Slurs," *New York Times*, September 30, 1991, p. A11; Perry A. Zirkel and Ivan B. Gluckman, "Verbal Abuse of Students," *Principal* (May 1991), pp. 51–52; and Mark Walsh, "'Slave Ship' Case Settled," *Education Week*, July 8, 1998.

[16]*Board of Education* v. *Pico*, 102 S. Ct. 2799 (1982). David A. Splitt, "Respecting a Review Process," *The Executive Educator* (January 1996), pp. 9, 31; Howard Pankratz, "Court: Teacher's Firing OK," *Denver Post*, June 30, 1998; and "'Censorship' Charges About 'Goosebumps' Intimidate Parents," *Education Reporter* (January 1998), available at **www.basenet.net/~eagle/educate**. Report of censorship incidents nationwide can be tracked on the Internet at **www.pfaw.org/aflo**.

[17]*Keefe* v. *Geanakos*, 418 F. 2d 359 (1st Cir. 1969); *Pratt* v. *Independent School District No. 831*, 670 F. 2d 771 (8th Cir. 1982); and *Brown* v. *Joint Unified School District*, 42-15772 (9th Cir. 1994). See also David A. Splitt, "Respecting a Review Process," *The Executive Educator* (January 1996), pp. 9, 31; and Barbara Miner, "Reading, Writing, and Censorship," *Rethinking Schools* (Spring 1998), available at **www.rethinkingschools.org**.

PROFESSIONAL PLANNING

for your first year

Dealing with a Parent Who Wants an "Obscene" Assignment Eliminated

The Situation

Suppose a parent of a child in your class phones you one day demanding to know why you have assigned such an "obscene, nasty" book. You are taken aback, in part because you cannot imagine which book the parent is talking about. After listening to the explanation, you understand the parent's point of view, but you believe it is misguided. You argue that, given a reasonable interpretation — as you certainly will provide in class — the book is not offensive and is an excellent learning resource. The parent, not at all appeased, demands to know what right you have to use that book in class or to force children to read it.

Thought Questions

1. What are your legal rights in such a situation? Can you stick to your position? Should you? Must you at least exempt that one parent's child from the assignment?
2. By changing your stance, would you be abandoning your professional commitments and beliefs or your responsibility to provide the best possible education to all your students?
3. Who could you turn to for advice? Where might you obtain, on your own, useful legal information related to the situation?
4. What actual book do you think might have generated this scenario? Would you try to avoid using this book or similar books in the future? What modifications would you consider making in how you plan to use them?
5. What steps might you have taken in advance to make it easier to respond to this parent? What steps could have taken, short of not assigning the book, to prevent such a scene from occurring in the first place?

Restrictions upheld

On the other hand, decisions of school officials to restrict teachers' academic freedom have sometimes been upheld. For example, a West Virginia art teacher was suspended for (unwittingly) distributing sexually explicit cartoons, an Ohio English teacher was prohibited from assigning the books *One Flew over the Cuckoo's Nest* and *Manchild in the Promised Land* to juvenile students unless their parents consented, and a North Carolina teacher was disciplined after her students performed an adult-language play in a state drama competition. In general, courts have considered the

Issues courts consider

following issues: (1) the age and grade level of the students, (2) the relevancy of the questioned material to the curriculum, (3) the duration of the material's use, (4) the general acceptance of a disputed teaching method within the profession, (5) the prior existence of board policy governing selection of materials and teaching techniques, and (6) whether the materials are required or optional.[18]

---

[18]*DeVito* v. *Board of Education,* 317 S.E. 2d 159 (W. Va. 1984). See also Jack L. Nelson, Kenneth Carlson, and Stuart B. Palonsy, *Critical Issues in Education* (New York: MGraw-Hill, 1996); and Brooke A. Masters, "Ruling Limits Speech Rights for Teachers," *Washington Post,* February 24, 1998, p. B3.

Teacher as Exemplar or Role Model

Morality standards

Chapter 2 quoted a number of rules governing teacher conduct in Wisconsin in 1922. Teachers' lives were regulated because communities believed they should be exemplars — that is, examples to their students of high moral standards and impeccable character, conservative dress and grooming, and polished manners. Although these standards have relaxed, in some places teachers may still be dismissed under immorality statutes for a drunk-driving incident, homosexuality, or for living unmarried with a member of the opposite sex. Seemingly less weighty behaviors have also been used as grounds for dismissal, such as engaging in a water fight in which a student suffered mild skin irritations, or joking about testes and menstrual periods when these topics were not part of the curriculum being taught by a science teacher.[19]

Since the Supreme Court also has declined to review other cases involving dismissal of teachers for homosexuality, many legal issues involving this topic remain to be resolved.

Renewed emphasis on "role model" responsibilities

In recent years there has been a movement toward reemphasizing the teachers' responsibilities as a "moral exemplar" both inside and outside the school. Many parents have been demanding that the schools reinforce traditional values among students, and "character education" programs have been introduced in many schools. School district policies generally still require that teachers serve as "positive role models." Based in part on such requirements, Indiana courts upheld the dismissal of a teacher who drank beer in the presence of students at a local restaurant and then drove them home. According to attorneys for the National School Boards Association, misbehavior outside the school that reduces teachers' capacity to serve as positive role models can justify reprimands or dismissals as long as rights to free speech and free association (with friends or acquaintances of one's choice) are not violated.[20]

Dress and grooming cases

Courts also have decided a number of cases in which teachers' dress and grooming conflicted with school district policies or traditions. One California court ruled that women teaching at "back-to-basics" schools in Pomona could not be required to wear dresses if they preferred to wear outfits with pants. Another California court ruled that Paul Finot's wearing of a beard was symbolic expression protected by the First Amendment as well as a liberty right protected under the Fourteenth Amendment.[21]

On the other hand, when Max Miller's contract was not renewed because of his beard and long sideburns, the circuit court upheld the dismissal. "As public servants in a special position of trust," the judges stated, "teachers may properly be subjected to many restrictions in their professional lives which would be invalid if generally applied."[22]

---

[19]*Everett Area Sch. Dist.* v. *Ault,* 548 A. 2d 1341 (Pa. Cmwlth. 1988); Perry A. Zirkel, "Weeding Out Bad Teachers," *Phi Delta Kappan* (January 1992), pp. 418–421; *Baldrige* v. *Board of Trustees,* No. 97-230 (Wash., 1997); and R. Joseph Gelarden, "IPS Suspends Teacher Charged with Shooting Pups," *Indianapolis StarNews,* August 8, 1998.

[20]Laurel S. Walters, "Value Ed Also Tests Teachers," *Christian Science Monitor,* November 5, 1997.

[21]*Finot* v. *Pasadena City Board of Education,* 58 Cal. Rptr. 520 (1976); and Bess Keller, "Keep Your Pants On," *Teacher Magazine* (April 1997).

[22]*Miller* v. *School District No. 167 of Cook County, Illinois,* 495 F. 2d 65 (7th Cir. 1974); *Tardif* v. *Quinn,* 545 F. 2d 761 (1st Cir. 1976); and *East Hartford Education Association* v. *Board of Education,* 562 F. 2d 838 (1977).

In summary, restraints on teachers' behavior and attire are not as stringent as in earlier times, but teachers are still expected to behave in exemplary ways and serve as role models for their students. When the issue is raised in court, a major concern is whether the behavior in question seriously impairs the teacher's classroom effectiveness.

Tort Liability and Negligence

Student injuries

Torts are civil wrongs. Under tort law, individuals who have suffered because of the improper conduct of others may sue for damages. For example, educators may be found guilty of negligence when students are injured during classes, on the playground, or elsewhere if the injury resulted from failure to take appropriate preventive action. This does not mean that a case will be filed every time a child is accidentally injured. But when injury results from negligent or intentional action, legal remedies can be pursued if state law permits.

Decline of immunity

A generation ago, nearly every school district was immune from tort liability. This immunity had its origins in English common law, under which the king, as sovereign, could not be sued. Since 1960, more than half the states have eliminated or modified this view of governmental immunity. In states where suits are permitted, the parties sued may include the school district as well as specific school administrators, teachers, and other staff. For example, school districts can be held liable for the negligent or malicious action of their employees (such as sexual abuse or harassment or failure to report students' suicidal intentions) if school officials have provided little or no supervision or ignored persistent complaints. These responsibilities even extend to malicious or neglectful action or inaction by volunteers who donate time to work with a school.[23]

Standards of proper care

Teachers are required by law to protect their students from injury or harm. In nearly all states, the traditional standard of care is what a reasonable and prudent person would do under similar circumstances. In one case, a kindergarten teacher was charged with negligence when a child fell from a playground structure while the teacher was attending to other children. The court ruled that the teacher was not required to have all children in sight at all times. Her presence in the immediate area was sufficient to establish that the teacher was fulfilling her duty. The New York State Supreme Court reached a similar conclusion in overturning a jury award to an injured high-school athlete, on grounds that school officials had exercised "reasonable care" in operating their school's football program. In some other cases, however, school districts or their employees have been found to be partially or wholly responsible for students' injuries that a reasonable person should have been able to forsee.[24]

Can danger be foreseen?

An important principle is whether the injury could have been foreseen and thus prevented. An overweight student expressed concern to her physical education teacher about a class requirement to perform a back somersault. The teacher insisted the somersault be done, and the student's neck snapped in the attempt.

---

[23]David A. Splitt, "Drawing a Line on Liability," *The Executive Educator* (March 1992), pp. 13, 42; Perry A. Zirkel, "Student Suicide," *Principal* (May 1996), pp. 45–46; and Valerie Hall, "Volunteers in Public Schools" (Posting at the Internet site of the Indiana Department of Education Legal Section, 1998), available at **ideanet.doe.state.in.us**.

[24]*Clark v. Furch,* 567 S.W. 2d 457 (Mo. App. 1978); "School Sports-Injury Award Upset," *New York Times,* June 9, 1989, p. 18; and "Ellipses," *The Executive Educator* (May 1995), p. 13.

The court said the teacher showed utter indifference to the student's safety, and the jury awarded $77,000 in damages.[25]

Parental consent forms

School districts require parents to sign consent forms when students are involved in activities such as field trips or athletic competition. The form generally has two purposes: to inform parents of their children's whereabouts and to release school personnel from liability in case of injury. However, since parents cannot waive a child's right to sue for damages if an injury occurs, these forms actually serve only the first purpose. Obtaining a parental waiver does *not* release teachers from their legal obligations to protect the safety and welfare of students.

Rise of strict liability

Recent years have brought what some observers describe as an "explosion" in litigation related to liability and negligence. In addition, rather than accepting the exercise of reasonable precautions as a defense against negligence, recent judicial decisions have frequently emphasized "strict liability." In this situation, teachers cannot be too careful, for there are numerous places in the school setting where negligence might occur. Physical education instructors, sponsors of extracurricular activities, and shop and laboratory teachers must take special care. Prudent safeguards include a clear set of written rules, verbal warnings to students, regular inspection of equipment, adherence to state laws and district policies regarding hazardous activities, thoughtful planning, and diligent supervision.[26]

Liability insurance

As educators' immunity has waned and the number of lawsuits has increased, teacher and school administrator organizations have moved to offer liability insurance to their members. These organizations also may provide legal assistance to members who are sued.

Reporting Child Abuse

Laws require reporting

During recent years, child abuse has become a national issue. Increased media attention has prompted state legislatures to review and stiffen abuse laws. Because a high percentage of abuse is directed at school-age children, schools play an important role in protecting them. In most states, educators are required by law to report suspected cases of child abuse to authorities or designated social service agencies. As a result, increasing numbers of school districts have written policies describing how teachers should proceed when they suspect abuse. Warning signs that may indicate a child is being abused are shown in Table 8.2.

Copyright Laws

Fair use guidelines

A *copyright* gives authors and artists control over the reproduction and distribution of works they create; consequently, permission for reproduction usually must be obtained from the owner. The widespread use of copying machines has bred serious and regular violations of copyright laws. To address this problem, in 1976 Congress amended the original 1909 copyright laws to include photocopying and the educa-

---

[25]*Landers* v. *School District No. 203, O'Fallon,* 383 N.E. 2d 645 (Ill. App. Ct. 1978); and Brian Dudley, "Verdict Causes County to Ban School Swim Teams from Poools," *Seattle Times,* October 6, 1998; Michael D. Richardson et al., "Science Lab Liability for Teachers," *Journal of Chemical Education* (August 1994), pp. 689–690; and *Richardson* v. *Corvallis Public School District No. 1,* No. 96–497 (Wash. 1997).

[26]Perry A. Zirkel, "Negligence Is a Two-Way Street," *Phi Delta Kappan* (November 1995), pp. 259–260; Jonathan Schorr, "A Trust Betrayed," *Teacher Magazine* (February 1996), pp. 37–41; and Julie Rasciot, "Trouble on Wheels," *American School Board Journal* (November 1998), pp. 34–38.

| TABLE 8.2 | Selected Physical and Behavioral Indicators of Physical Abuse and Neglect, Sexual Abuse, and Emotional Abuse |

Physical Indicators	**Behavioral Indicators**

Physical Abuse — nonaccidental injury to a child that may involve some beatings, burns, strangulation, or human bites

• Unexplained bruises, swollen areas	• Self-destructive
• Welts, bite marks, bald spots	• Withdrawn and/or aggressive extremes
• Unexplained burns, fractures, abrasions	• Complaints of soreness or discomfort
• Evidence of inappropriate treatment of injuries	• Bizarre explanation of injuries

Physical Neglect — failure to provide a child with basic necessities

• Unattended medical need, lice, poor hygiene	• Regularly displays fatigue, listlessness
• Consistent lack of supervision	• Steals food, begs from classmates
• Consistent hunger, inadequate nutrition	• Frequently absent or tardy
• Consistent inappropriate clothing	• Reports there is no caretaker at home

Sexual Abuse — sexual exploitation, including rape, incest, fondling, and pornography

• Torn, stained or bloody underclothing	• Withdrawal, chronic depression
• Pain, swelling, or itching in genital area	• Hysteria, lack of emotional control
• Venereal disease	• Inappropriate sex play, premature sex knowledge
• Frequent urinary or yeast infections	• Excessive seductiveness

Emotional Abuse — a pattern of behavior that attacks a child's emotional development, i.e., name calling, put-downs, terrorization, isolation

• Speech disorders	• Habit disorders (sucking, rocking, biting)
• Delayed physical development	• Emotional disturbance
• Substance abuse	• Neurotic traits (sleep disorders, play inhibition)
• Ulcer, asthma, severe allergy	• Antisocial, destructive, delinquent

Note: SOC-UM emphasizes the following advice: "Symptoms, or indications of abuse, vary greatly form child to child. . . . Possibly only one or a few, or none of these symptoms . . . will be readily apparent in a child who IS being abused. Absence of any or all . . . does NOT mean that a child is NOT being abused. If you suspect there is a problem, do NOT try to diagnose or determine the extent of the problem on your own; please contact a professional immediately."

Source: Adapted from guidelines posted by Safeguarding Our Children-United Mothers (SOC-UM), at **www.soc-um.org.** Reprinted with permission. Also see Jane Gross, "Warning Signs of Child Abuse," *New York Times,* July 3, 1998.

tional use of copyrighted materials. In addition, a committee of librarians, publishers, authors, and educators developed "fair use" guidelines. **Fair use** is a legal principle that allows use of copyrighted materials without permission from the author under specific, limited conditions. Table 8.3 summarizes fair use restrictions on copying for classroom use or other educational purposes.[27]

Plays and musicals

Since plays and musical productions usually are copyrighted by their authors, school presentation of such works requires permission from the author or the au-

---

[27]Association of American Publishers, "How to Request Copyright Permissions," *Chronicle of Higher Education,* September 4, 1991, p. R23; Kenneth T. Murray, "Copyright and the Educator," *Phi Delta Kappan* (March 1994), pp. 552–555; and Lesley E. Harns, "Finding Your Way Out of the Copyright Maze," *Computers in Libraries* (June 1998), pp. 20–24.

TABLE 8.3	Restrictions on Copying Materials for Educational Use

- Copying of prose is limited to excerpts of no more than 1,000 words.
- Copies from an anthology or encyclopedia cannot exceed one story or entry, or 2,500 words.
- A poem may be copied if it is less than 250 words, and an excerpt of no more than 250 words may be copied from a longer poem.
- Distribution of copies from the same author more than once a semester or copying from the same work or anthology more than three times during the semester is prohibited.
- Teachers may make one copy per student for class distribution; if charges are made, they may not exceed actual copying costs.
- It is illegal to create anthologies or compilations by using photocopies as a substitute for purchasing the same or similar materials.
- Consumable materials, such as workbooks, may not be copied.
- Under the fair use doctrine, single copies of printed materials may be made for personal study, lesson planning, research, criticism, comment, and news reporting.
- Most magazine and newspaper articles may be copied freely. However, items in weekly newspapers and magazines designed for classroom use by students may not be copied without permission.
- Individual teachers must decide, independently, to copy material; they may not be directed to do so by higher authorities.
- There are three categories of material for which copies may be freely made: writings published before 1978 that have never been copyrighted, published works for which copyrights are more than seventy-five years old, and U.S. government publications.
- New restrictions on use of copyrighted materials are emerging in connection with the Internet and other digital media.

thor's agent. Payment of a royalty is often necessary to secure permission, sometimes with the amount depending on whether or not admission is charged.

Videos

Videotapes also fall within the fair use guidelines of the copyright laws. These guidelines specify that educational institutions may not keep the tapes they make of copyrighted television programs for more than forty-five days without a license. During the first ten days, an individual teacher may use the tape once, and may show it once again after that period when "instructional reinforcement is necessary." After forty-five days the tape must be erased. Videotaping may occur only when a faculty member requests it in advance; thus it may not be done on a regular basis in anticipation of faculty requests.

Anthologies

One touchy copyright issue involves the practice of preparing, duplicating, and distributing anthologies of material without obtaining copyright owners' permission. A major legal challenge to this practice occurred when a group of publishers sued a chain of stores (Kinko's) that frequently duplicated such anthologies. In 1991 a U.S. district court judge determined that the company's practice violated fair use standards. The company — as well as other "anthologizers" — now has to obtain permission to use any copyrighted material included in a duplicated collection.[28]

---

[28]Debra E. Blum, "Copyright Ruling on Anthologies May Spur Vigilance," *Chronicle of Higher Education,* April 10, 1991, p. A14; Richard B. Schockmel, "The Premise of Copyright," *Journal of Academic Librarianship* (January 1996), pp. 15–25; and Patricia Failing, "Scholars Face Hefty Fees and Elaborate Contracts When They Use Digital Images," *Chronicle of Higher Education,* May 29, 1998, pp. B4–B5.

Software

Computer software is subject to the same fair use restrictions as other copyrighted materials. For example, teachers may not copy protected computer programs and distribute them for use on school computers. For computer files downloaded from another source, teachers and students may be required to obtain permission and/or pay fees.[29]

Internet

Copyright issues involving the Internet also are becoming an important concern for teachers, students, and administrators. In some cases, copyright holders have taken action to prohibit unauthorized use of text or images, to correct or restrict posting of incomplete or erroneous materials, or otherwise to reduce or eliminate potentially illegal publication of their materials on the World Wide Web and other platforms. For example after the Business Software Alliance conducted an audit at one Los Angeles school that allegedly possessed pirated copies of hundreds of software programs, district officials agreed to pay $300,000 to rectify this infringement and to develop a multimillion-dollar plan to pay for violations at other schools.

Business and commercial groups led by the entertainment and software industries worked with federal legislators to develop the No Electronic Theft Act of 1997, which provides hefty penalties for possessing or distributing illegal electronic copies, and the Digital Millennium Copyright Act of 1998. This law, which specifies how the United States will comply with two international treaties, includes provisions that make it possible for copyright owners to prevent downloading of their material without permission and/or to require payment of a fee by the recipient. However, because associations representing schools and universities complained vigorously that provisions of the digital millennium law will greatly narrow or eliminate current fair use practices (see above), it also includes a two-year moratorium on actions that cut off access to copyrighted materials by users who have not obtained prior permission or paid a required fee.[30]

Digital Millenium Act

Students' Rights and Responsibilities

Decline of in loco parentis

During the 1960s, students increasingly began to challenge the authority of school officials to control student behavior. Before these challenges, students' rights were considered to be limited by their status as minors and by the concept of ***in loco parentis,*** according to which school authorities assumed the powers of the child's parents during the hours the child was under the school's supervision. Use of this concept has declined, however, and the courts have become more active in identifying and upholding students' constitutional rights. There has also been progress toward recognizing student responsibilities — that is, toward understanding that the educational rights of students are tied in with responsibilities on the part of both students and educators to ensure effective operation of the school.

Nonpublic students not necessarily protected

The following sections summarize some of the most important court decisions involving students' rights and responsibilities. These apply primarily to public

---

[29]David L. Wilson, "U. of Oregon Pays $130,000 to Settle Software-Copying Suit," *Chronicle of Higher Education,* September 4, 1991, pp. A27–A30; Kenneth Frazier, "Protecting Copyright—and Preserving Fair Use—in the Electronic Future," *Chronicle of Higher Education,* June 30, 1995, p. A40; and "Software Piracy," *T.H.E. Journal* (April 1998), pp. 66–67.

[30]Goldie Blumenstyk, "Academic Groups Say Copyright Legislation in Congress would Impede Scholarship," *Chronicle of Higher Education,* May 29, 1998; Wendy A. Grossman, "Downloading as a Crime," *Scientific American* (March 1998); and Charles A. Mann, "Who Will Own Your Next Good Idea?" *Atlantic* (September 1998), pp. 57–82.

Students enjoy constitutional guarantees of freedom of speech, but conduct that "materially disrupts classwork or involves substantial disorder or invasion of the rights of others" can be prohibited by school officials. *(© Michael Newmann/Photo Edit)*

schools. As with teachers, students in nonpublic schools may not enjoy all the constitutional guarantees discussed in this chapter. Unless a substantial relationship between the school and the government can be demonstrated, private-school activity is not considered action by the state and therefore does not trigger state constitutional obligations. However, the movement toward voucher plans (see Chapter 7) and other school choice arrangements (discussed in chapter 16) that provide public funds for students attending nonpublic schools has begun to blur this distinction.[31]

Freedom of Expression

In 1965, John Tinker, fifteen, his sister Mary Beth, thirteen, and friend Dennis Eckhardt, sixteen, were part of a small group planning to wear black armbands to school as a silent, symbolic protest against the war in Vietnam. Hearing of this plan and fearing problems, administrators responded by adopting a policy prohibiting the wearing of armbands; the penalty was suspension until the armbands were removed. The Tinkers and Eckhardt wore the armbands as planned, refused to remove them, and were suspended. Their parents filed suit. In finding for the

Tinker: guarantees of free speech

---

[31]Richard D. Strahan and L. Charles Turner, *The Courts and the Schools* (New York: Longman, 1988); Frank R. Kemerer, "The Constitutionality of School Vouchers," *West's Education Law Quarterly* (October 1995), pp. 646–665; and Pam Belluck, "Voucher Ruling Greeted with Excitement and Alarm," *New York Times,* June 15, 1998.

plaintiffs, the U.S. Supreme Court outlined the scope of student rights, so that this case, *Tinker* v. *Des Moines Independent Community School District,* became the standard for examining students' freedom of speech guarantees (see Overview 8.2 on page 254 for a summary of court decisions affecting students' rights).

To justify prohibition of a particular expression of opinion, the Court ruled, school officials must be able to show that their actions were caused by "something more than a mere desire to avoid the discomfort and unpleasantness that always accompany an unpopular viewpoint." Student conduct that "materially disrupts classwork or involves substantial disorder or invasion of the rights of others" could be prohibited. In the absence of such good reasons for restraint, the students' constitutional guarantees of free speech would apply. This last generalization was reinforced in a 1998 decision in which a Wyoming judge refused to uphold punishment of a high-school student who published an underground newspaper asserting that the principal was a cross-dresser who knew that some teachers in the school were selling drugs illegally.[32]

Bethel/Fraser: limits of free speech

As the preceding statement suggests, there are limits to free expression in public schools. In *Bethel School District No. 403* v. *Fraser,* the U.S. Supreme Court confirmed that students may be punished for offensive or disruptive speech.[33]

Regulation of student publications is often a sore point between school officials and students, especially when policies require administrative review and approval prior to publication or distribution. In these "prior restraint" cases the burden of proof is on the district to show that its actions are fair and that regulation is necessary to maintain order.

Hazelwood/Kuhlmeier: regulating student publications

For example, in one case school policy required the principal to review each proposed issue of *The Spectrum,* the school newspaper written by journalism students at Hazelwood East High School in St. Louis County, Missouri. The principal objected to two articles scheduled to appear in one issue. The principal claimed the articles were deleted not because of the subject matter but because he did not consider them well written and there was not enough time to rewrite them before the publication deadline.

Three student journalists sued, contending that their freedom of speech had been violated. This case, *Hazelwood School District* v. *Kuhlmeier,* reached the U.S. Supreme Court, which upheld the principal's action. The justices found that *The Spectrum* was not a public forum but rather a supervised learning experience for journalism students. As long as educators' actions were related to "legitimate pedagogical concerns," they could regulate the newspaper's contents in any reasonable manner. The ruling further stated that a school could disassociate itself not only from speech that directly interfered with school activities but also from speech that was "ungrammatical, poorly written, inadequately researched, biased, prejudiced, vulgar or profane, or unsuitable for immature audiences." This decision was a clear restriction on student rights as previously understood.

Legitimate regulation

The controversies concerning publications written or distributed by students

[32]*Tinker* v. *Des Moines Independent Community School District,* 393 U.S. 503 (1969). See also Lillian Lodge Kopenhaver, "Toward a Freer Student Press," *Education Week,* January 12, 1994, p. 58; Dorianne Beyer, "School Safety and the Legal Rights of Students," *ERIC Clearinghouse on Urban Education Digest* (May 1997), pp. 1–4; and Coleman Cornelius, "Gross Teen Protected by 1st Amendment," *Detroit Post,* July 28, 1998.
[33]*Bethel School District No. 403* v. *Fraser,* 106 S. Ct. 3159 (1986). See also Michael Levin, *United States School Laws and Rules* (St. Paul: West, 1997); and Clara G. Hoover, "The Hazelwood Decision," *NASSP Bulletin* (October 1998).

have prompted many school boards to develop written regulations that can withstand judicial scrutiny. Generally, these rules specify a time, place, and manner of distribution; a method of advertising the rules to students; a prompt review process; and speedy appeal procedures. Students may not distribute literature that is obscene by legal definition, that is libelous, or that is likely to cause the substantial disruption specified in *Tinker*. School boards also have considerable leeway in determining whether nondisruptive material will be published in school newspapers and yearbooks.[34]

"Acceptable use" policies for internet use

Student Use of the Internet. Although still relatively young, the Internet already has generated legal issues that educators will be contending with for a long time to come. Like businesses and other organizations, schools have been developing "acceptable use policies" that govern the on-line behavior of students and staff provided that statutory and constitutional requirements protecting free speech and other rights are not thereby violated. Developments include the following:[35]

- Many schools have installed software to inhibit access to Internet sites that programmers have classified as pornographic, obscene, or otherwise undesirable for children or youth.

- Some students have been punished for sending e-mail or posting Web pages that school officials considered threatening, defamatory, obscene, or potentially disruptive or destructive. Electronic materials that might fit in these categories have the same legal standing as printed documents, which may require finding a delicate balance between legally protected individual rights on the one hand, and prohibitions on harming individuals and institutions on the other. For example, an Ohio school district had to pay $30,000 to a high-school student after it lost a court case in which he challenged its right to suspend him because he had posted material that ridiculed his band teacher.

Suspensioin for digital ridicule

- Some libraries, including school libraries, have been sued for using filtering software to screen out sexually oriented Internet sites. Other libraries have been sued for not using such software. It is unclear how courts will resolve this issue.

Dress Codes and Regulations. Many courts have had to determine whether dress codes and regulations constitute an unconstitutional restriction on students' rights to free expression. In some instances, as in a Louisiana case dealing with requirements that football team members shave their mustaches, judges have ruled that the Constitution allows school boards to impose dress and grooming codes to advance their educational goals. Similarly, a U.S. district court upheld a ban on boys' earrings as part of a policy prohibiting display of gang emblems. In other cases, however, judges have ruled that prohibitions against long hair were arbitrary and unreasonable, and that girls' wearing of pantsuits or slacks could not be prohibited. Much depends on the arguments and evidence regarding the educational purposes served by such restrictions, the likelihood that violations will be disruptive, and the

Mixed rulings

---

[34]*Hazelwood School District* v. *Kuhlmeier*, 86-836 S. Ct. (1988). See also Winifred Conkling, "The Big Chill," *Teacher Magazine* (November–December 1991), pp. 47–53; and Perry A. Zirkel, "Boring or Bunkum?" *Phi Delta Kappan* (June 1998), pp. 791–792.
[35]Linda Lindroth, "How to improve Online Safety," *Teaching PreK–8* (April 1998); and Andrew Trotter, "High Tech High Jinks," *Teacher Magazine* (August/September 1998). Information and illustrations regarding school "acceptable use policies" can be found easily by using this term to search the Internet.

extent to which dress codes and restrictions are intended to accomplish a valid constitutional goal.[36]

A "rational basis"

In general, school officials must demonstrate a "rational basis" for prohibiting language or symbols they think may contribute to school problems. Applying this test, several courts also have ruled that public schools can require students to wear a designated uniform if school officials present evidence indicating that uniforms could help make schools safer or more productive. In several cases dress codes have been upheld under this standard, but in some cases dress codes have been challenged successfully on the grounds that they were arbitrary or capricious.[37]

Suspension and Expulsion

The issue of expulsion is illustrated in the case of nine students who received ten-day suspensions from their Columbus, Ohio, secondary schools for various alleged acts of misconduct. The suspensions were imposed without hearings but in accordance with state law; the school board had no written procedure covering suspensions. The students filed suit, claiming deprivation of their constitutional rights. In defense, school officials argued that since there is no constitutional right to education at public expense, the due process clause of the Fourteenth Amendment did not apply.

Minimum due process

When this case, *Goss* v. *Lopez,* reached the Supreme Court in 1975, a majority of the Court disagreed with the school officials, reasoning that students had a legal right to public education. In other words, students had a property interest in their education that could not be taken away "without adherence to the minimum procedures" required by the due process clause. Further, the justices said that students facing suspension "must be given some kind of notice and afforded some kind of hearing," including "an opportunity to explain [their] version of the facts." Also, "as a general rule notice and hearing should precede removal of the student from school." Applying these principles to suspensions of up to ten days, the Court added that longer suspensions or expulsions might require more elaborate due process procedures.[38]

School boards potentially liable

In addition, in 1975 the justices ruled in *Wood* v. *Strickland* that ignorance of the law is no excuse and that school board members could be liable for monetary damages if they knew or should have known that their actions would deprive a student of constitutional rights.[39]

Written policies

In response to such court decisions, most school districts have developed written policies governing suspensions and expulsions. These policies usually distinguish between short- and long-term suspensions. Short-term suspension rights typically include oral or written notice describing the misconduct, the evidence on which the accusation is based, a statement of the planned punishment, and an opportu-

---

[36]Benjamin Dowling-Sendor, "A Matter of Disruption, Not Dress," *American School Board Journal* (August 1998), available at **www.asbj.com.**

[37]Perry A. Zirkel and Ivan Gluckman, "Regulating Offensive T-Shirts," *Principal* (May 1995), pp. 46–48; Amy M. Wilson, "Public School Dress Codes," *Brigham Young University Education and Law Journal* (Spring 1998), pp. 147–176; and Perry A. Zirkel, "A Uniform Policy," *Phi Delta Kappan* (March 1998), pp. 550–551.

[38]*Goss* v. *Lopez,* 419 U.S. 565 (1975). See also Perry A. Zirkel, "Supporting Suspenders," *Phi Delta Kappan* (November 1994), pp. 256–257; and Perry A. Zirkel and Ivan B. Gluckman, "Due Process in Student Suspensions and Expulsions," *Principal* (March 1997), pp. 62–63.

[39]*Wood* v. *Strickland,* 420 U.S. 308 (1975). See also Perry A. Zirkel, "Courtside. The Midol Case," *Phi Delta Kappan* (June 1997), pp. 803–804.

nity for the student to explain his or her version or refute the stated facts before an impartial person. Expulsions require full procedural due process similar to that necessary for teacher terminations.[40]

Controversy Regarding Students with Disabilities. Recent court decisions have limited school officials' authority to suspend or expel disabled students who are disruptive or violent. In the case of *Honig* v. *Doe,* the Supreme Court ruled that such students must be retained in their current placement pending the completion of lengthy official hearings. The Individuals with Disabilities Education Act (IDEA) of 1990 specified additional rights that make it difficult to suspend or expel students with disabilities, including those who may be severely disruptive or prone to violence. As a result, educators are seeking new ways to guarantee the rights of students while dealing with disruptive pupils who are classified as disabled. In 1997 Congress passed legislation aimed at making it less cumbersome for administrators to suspend disabled students who violate school discipline rules, but a year later educators reported that practical issues were still murky.[41]

Rights of students with disabilities

Protection from Violence

Schools may be liable for violence

Educators have a duty to protect students against violent actions that occur at school or at school-sponsored events. Frequently this duty extends to off-campus events such as graduation proms and parties. Depending on the circumstances, the courts may find school districts or their employees legally liable for failing in this duty. For example, a Louisiana court held a school district partly responsible for the gunshot wound suffered by a student after a school security guard warned him of trouble but refused to escort him to his car. By contrast, an Illinois appellate court ruled that Chicago high-school officials were not liable for the shooting of a student because they did not know that the weapon had been brought into school. Of course, regardless of questions involving legal culpability, educators should do everything possible to protect their students from violence.[42]

Although school laws and policies dealing with school safety are primarily the responsibility of state and local governments (including public school districts), growing national concern with violence in and around schools helped stimulate passage of the federal Gun-Free Schools Act of 1994. This legislation prohibits districts from receiving federal grants to improve the performance of disadvantaged students unless their respective state governments have legislated "zero tolerance" of guns and other potentially dangerous weapons. (A kitchen knife in a lunch box, a belt buckle with a sharp edge, even a strong rubber band that could make a powerful sling shot may be considered dangerous.) By 1995, all fifty states had introduced

Gun-Free Schools Act

"Zero tolerance"

---

[40]Perry A. Zirkel and Ivan B. Gluckman, "Due Process for Student Suspensions," *NASSP Bulletin* (March 1990), pp. 95–98; Del C. Litke, "When Violence Came to Our Rural School," *Educational Leadership* (September 1996), pp. 77–80; "Due Process," *Teacher Magazine* (May/June 1997); and Paul E. Barton, Richard J. Coley, and Harold Wezlinsky, *Order in the Classroom* (Princeton, N.J.: Educational Testing Service, 1998), available at **www.ets.org.**

[41]Mitchell L. Yell, "*Honig* v. *Doe,*" *Exceptional Children* (September 1989), pp. 60–69; Perry A. Zirkel, "Disabling Discipline?" *Phi Delta Kappan* (March 1995); p. 569; "Draft Rules Still Prompt IDEA Discipline Questions," *Special Education Report,* October 29, 1997, pp. 1–2; and "Schools Face Disability Confusion," *Associated Press Online,* July 4, 1998, available at **www.nytimes.com.**

[42]Mark Walsh, "La. District Shares Liability for Shooting, Court Rules," *Education Week,* February 1, 1995, p. 5; and Tamar Lewin, "Nation's Schools Policing—And Punishing—Off-Campus Behavior," *New York Times,* February 6, 1998.

or expanded such legislation, which generally provides for automatic suspension of students who possess objects that school officials decide are dangerous. Most districts have policies specifying how the legislation will be implemented and whether there are additional grounds, such as possession of drugs, for automatic suspension.[43]

Search and Seizure

Fourth Amendment rights

Lawfully issued search warrants are usually required to conduct searches. But because of rising drug use in schools and accompanying acts of violence, school officials at some locations (particularly big-city high schools) have installed metal detectors or x-ray machines to search for weapons. They have banned beepers (frequently used in drug sales), required students to breathe into alcohol-analysis machines, searched students' book bags, and systematically examined lockers. When such practices have been challenged in court, the issue usually has centered on the Fourth Amendment, which states: "The right of the people to be secure in their persons, houses, papers, and effects, against unreasonable searches and seizures, shall not be violated, and no warrants shall issue, but upon probable cause, supported by oath or affirmation, and particularly describing the place to be searched, and the person or things to be seized."

Reasonable cause

Searches usually are conducted because administrators have reason to suspect that illegal or dangerous items are on the premises. For legal purposes, suspicion exists in differing degrees. Where searches have been upheld, courts have said "reasonable" cause was sufficient for school officials to act. By way of contrast, police are held to the higher standard of "probable" cause mentioned in the Fourth Amendment — that is, some reason for believing it is more probable than not that evidence of illegal activity will be found.

T.L.O.: searching a purse

These principles were considered in a case involving a teacher who discovered two girls in a school restroom smoking cigarettes. This was a violation of school rules, and the students were taken to the vice principal's office and questioned. One of the girls admitted smoking, but T.L.O., age fourteen, denied all charges. The vice principal opened T.L.O.'s purse and found a pack of cigarettes. While reaching for the cigarettes he noticed some rolling papers and decided to empty the purse. The search revealed marijuana, a pipe, some empty plastic bags, a large number of dollar bills, and a list entitled, "People who owe me money." T.L.O.'s mother was called, and the evidence was turned over to the police. T.L.O. confessed to the police that she had been selling marijuana at school.

Two-pronged standard

After she was sentenced to one year's probation by the juvenile court, T.L.O. appealed, claiming the vice principal's search of her purse was illegal under the Fourth Amendment. In finding for school authorities in *New Jersey* v. *T.L.O.,* the U.S. Supreme Court set up a two-pronged standard to be met for constitutionally sanctioned searches: (1) whether the search is justified at its inception, and (2) whether the search, when actually conducted, is "reasonably related in scope to the circumstances which justified the interference in the first place." Using these criteria, the Court found the search of T.L.O.'s purse justified because of the teacher's report of smoking in the restroom. This information gave the vice principal reason to believe that the purse contained cigarettes. Since T.L.O. denied smoking, a search of her

[43]Caroline Hendrie, "One Strike, You're Out," *Teacher Magazine* (February 1998); Chris Pipho, "Living with Zero Tolerance," *Phi Delta Kappan* (June 1998), pp. 725–726; and Adrienne D. Coles, "Tenn. Suspension Reversed," *Education Week,* January 27, 1999.

purse was needed to determine her veracity. When the vice principal saw the cigarettes and came across the rolling papers, he had reasonable suspicion to search her purse more thoroughly.[44]

Drug-sniffing dogs

In some cases, courts have ruled that suspicions expressed or perceived by school officials were not sufficiently reasonable to justify the searches that followed. In Highland, Indiana, 2,780 junior and senior high-school students waited for hours in their seats while six officials using trained dogs searched for drugs. A school official, police officer, dog handler, and German shepherd entered the classroom where Diane Doe, thirteen, was a student. The dog went up and down the aisles sniffing students, reached Diane, sniffed her body, and repeatedly pushed its nose on and between her legs. The officer interpreted this behavior as an "alert" signaling the presence of drugs. Diane emptied her pockets as requested, but no drugs were found. Finally, Diane was taken to the nurse's office and strip-searched. No drugs were found. Before school, Diane had played with her own dog, which was in heat, and this smell remaining on her body had alerted the police dog.

Strip-search unconstitutional

The Does filed suit. Both the district court and the appeals court concluded that although the initial procedures were appropriate, the strip-search of Diane was unconstitutional. The court of appeals said, "It does not require a constitutional scholar to conclude that a nude search of a thirteen-year-old child is an invasion of constitutional rights of some magnitude. More than that: It is a violation of any known principle of human decency." Diane was awarded $7,500 damages. But the sniffing of student lockers and cars was not considered a search because it occurred when the lockers and cars were unattended and in public view.[45]

Guidelines for searches

In sum, when searches are conducted without a specific warrant, the following guidelines seem appropriate:[46]

1. Searches must be particularized. There should be reasonable suspicion that *each student* being searched possesses specific contraband or evidence of a particular crime.

2. Lockers are considered school property and may be searched if reasonable cause exists. Dogs may be used to sniff lockers and cars.

3. Generalized canine sniffing of students is permitted only when the dogs do not touch them.

4. Strip-searches are unconstitutional and should never be conducted.

5. School officials may perform a "pat-down" search for weapons if they have a reasonable suspicion that some students are bringing dangerous weapons to school.

Drug Testing as a Form of Search.   Some school board members and other policy makers have urged administrators to introduce random testing of student athletes'

---

[44]*New Jersey* v. *T.L.O.*, 105 S. Ct. 733 (1985). Similar reasoning and conclusions are reported in *Wynn* v. *Board of Education*, 508 So. 2d 1170 (Ala. 1987). See Perry A. Zirkel and Ivan B. Gluckman, "Search of Student Automobiles," *NASSP Bulletin* (November 1991), pp. 116–120; Andrew Trotter, "The Perils of Strip Searches," *The Executive Educator* (June 1995), pp. 29–30; and Mark Walsh, "Unreasonable Search Disallowed," *Education Week*, June 11, 1997.
[45]*Doe* v. *Renfrou*, 635 F. 2d 582 (7th Cir. 1980), cert. denied, 101 U.S. 3015 (1981).
[46]"Don't Search That Locker Without Good Reason," *The Executive Educator* (September 1991), pp. 16–17; Perry A. Zirkel and Ivan B. Gluckman, "Search of Student Automobiles Revisited," *NASSP Bulletin* (November 1993), pp. 101–104; *Thompson* v. *Carthage School District*, 87 E3d 979 (8th Cir. 1996); and "Sample Policy: School Search and Seizure" (1998 Internet posting at **www.keepschoolsafe.org**).

OVERVIEW 8.2	Selected U.S. Supreme Court Decisions Affecting Students' Rights and Responsibilities

Case	Summary of Decision
Tinker v. Des Moines Independent Community School District (1969)	Students are free to express their views except when such conduct disrupts class work, causes disorder, or invades the rights of others.
Goss v. Lopez (1975)	Suspension from school requires some form of due process for students.
Wood v. Strickland (1975)	A school board's ignorance of the law regarding due process is no excuse for not following it.
Ingraham v. Wright (1977)	Corporal punishment is not cruel or unusual punishment and is permitted where allowed by state law.
New Jersey v. T.L.O. (1985)	To be constitutional, searches of students and students' property must meet a two-pronged test.
Bethel School District No. 403 v. Fraser (1986)	Schools do not have to permit offensive or disruptive speech.
Hazelwood School District v. Kuhlmeier (1988)	A school newspaper is not a public forum and can be regulated by school officials.
Honig v. Doe (1988)	Disabled students who are disruptive must be retained in their current placement until official hearings are completed.
Gebser v. Lago Vista Independent School District (1998)	School districts are not legally at fault when a teacher sexually harasses a student unless the school acted with "deliberate indifference" in failing to stop it.

Testing athletes for drugs

urine to detect marijuana, steroids, and other illegal substances. Such testing generally has been viewed as a potentially unconstitutional search. However, in 1995 the U.S. Supreme Court ruled that this type of drug search is not unconstitutional even though there is no specific reason to suspect a particular individual. A majority of the justices concluded that school officials have reasonable grounds to be specially concerned with drug use among athletes, who presumably set an example for other students and whose participation in athletic programs is on a voluntary basis. On the other hand, several justices emphasized that their decision did not necessarily support drug testing in other school contexts, and it is not clear whether testing of athletes or other students will be used in a significant number of schools in the future.[47]

Classroom Discipline and Corporal Punishment

"Time out" arrangements

Classroom discipline was the issue in a case involving a sixth grader who was placed in a "time out" area of the classroom whenever his behavior became disruptive. The

---

[47]Samatha Shutler, "Random, Suspicionless Drug Testing of High School Athletes," *Journal of Criminal Law and Behavior* (Summer 1996), pp. 1265–1304; and *Todd* v. *Rush County Schools,* No. 97-1548 (7th Cir. 1998).

student had a history of behavioral problems, and the teacher had tried other methods of discipline without success. While in "time out" the boy was allowed to use the restroom, eat in the cafeteria, and attend other classes. His parents sued, charging that the teacher's actions (1) deprived their son of his property interest in receiving a public education; (2) meted out punishment disproportionate to his offense, in violation of his due process rights; and (3) inflicted emotional distress.[48]

The district court said that school officials possess broad authority to prescribe and enforce standards of conduct in the schools, but this authority is limited by the Fourteenth Amendment. In this case the student remained in school and thus was not deprived of a public education. "Time out" was declared to be a minimal interference with the student's property rights. The court noted that the purpose of "time out" is to modify the behavior of disruptive students and to preserve the right to an education for other students in the classroom. All of the student's charges were dismissed.

Use of corporal punishment

A particularly controversial method of classroom discipline is corporal punishment, which has a long history in American education dating back to the colonial period. It is unacceptable to many educators, although it enjoys considerable support within some segments of the community and is administered more frequently than educators like to admit. Recent surveys indicate that nearly half a million children are spanked or paddled each school year, and thousands sustain injuries that require medical attention.[49]

Variations in state law and local policies

A number of state legislatures have prohibited all corporal punishment in public schools. Where state law is silent on this issue, local boards have wide latitude, and they may ban physical punishment if they choose. However, where a state statute explicitly permits corporal punishment, local boards may regulate but not prohibit its use. In this context, many school boards have developed detailed policies restricting the use of corporal punishment. Violations of policy can lead to dismissal, and legal charges are possible for excessive force, punishment based on personal malice toward the student, or unreasonable use of punishment.[50]

Florida is an example of a state that allows corporal punishment. In 1977 the U.S. Supreme Court, in *Ingraham* v. *Wright,* ruled on the constitutionality of this law from two federal perspectives: (1) whether use of corporal punishment was a violation of the Eighth Amendment barring cruel and unusual punishment, and (2) whether prior notice and some form of due process were required before administering punishment.

Paddling of students

In this case, James Ingraham and Roosevelt Andrews were junior high school students in Dade County, Florida. Because Ingraham had been slow to respond to the teacher's instructions, he received twenty paddle swats administered in the principal's office. As a consequence, he needed medical treatment and missed a few days of school. Andrews was also paddled, but less severely. Finding that the intent

---

[48]*Dickens* v. *Johnson County Board of Education,* 661 F. Supp. 155 (E.D. Tenn. 1987). See also Maureen Harrison and Steve Gilbert, eds., *Schoolhouse Decisions of the United States Supreme Court* (San Diego: Excellent Books, 1997).

[49]Daniel Gursky, "Spare the Child?" *Teacher Magazine* (February 1992), pp. 17–19; Perry A. Zirkel and David W. Van Cleaf, "Is Corporal Punishment Child Abuse?" *Principal* (January 1996), pp. 60–61; and "Facts about Corporal Punishment," an Internet compilation available at **www.stophitting.com.**

[50]Irwin A. Hyman, *Reading, Writing, and the Hickory Stick* (Lexington, Mass.: Lexington Books, 1990); William Celis III, "Michigan Eases Ban on Punishment," *New York Times,* March 11, 1992, p. A16; and Pamela Stock, "Can a Teacher Hit Your Child?" *Parenting* (April 1998), p. 25.

UNITED STATES REPORTS
VOLUME 430

CASES ADJUDGED
IN
THE SUPREME COURT
AT
OCTOBER TERM, 1976
Opinion of February 23 Through (in part) April 27, 1977
Orders of February 23 Through April 25, 1977

HENRY PUTZEL, Jr.
REPORTER OF DECISIONS

UNITED STATES
GOVERNMENT PRINTING OFFICE
WASHINGTON : 1979

GETTING TO THE SOURCE

Corporal Punishment/ *Ingraham* v. *Wright*

In a Florida junior high school James Ingraham was paddled for not responding to a teacher's instructions. His parents sued school officials on the grounds that paddling violated the Eighth Amendment's constitutional prohibition of "cruel and unusual punishment." In the opinion excerpted below, the U.S. Supreme Court ruled that corporal punishment in schools is not automatically unconstitutional because the Eighth Amendment was constructed to protect the rights of incarcerated prisoners, not school-age children who can be protected by other means. The *Ingraham* decision means that in states that allow corporal punishment, it is not unconstitutional for teachers to use physical punishment "reasonably necessary" to discipline a student; complaining students or parents have the burden to demonstrate that the teacher's actions went beyond reasonable necessity.

Petitioners acknowledge that the original design of the Cruel and Unusual Punishments Clause was to limit criminal punishments, but urge nonetheless that the prohibition should be extended to ban the paddling of school children. Observing that the Framers of the Eighth Amendment could not have envisioned our present system of public and compulsory education, with its opportunities for noncriminal punishments, petitioners contend that extension of the prohibition against cruel punishments is necessary lest we afford greater protection to criminals than to schoolchildren. It would be anomalous, they say, if schoolchildren could be beaten without constitutional redress, while hardened criminals suffering the same beatings at the hands of their jailors might have a valid claim under the Eighth Amendment. . . .

Whatever force this logic may have in other settings, we find it an inadequate basis for wrenching the Eighth Amendment from its historical context and extending it to traditional disciplinary practices in the public schools.

The prisoner and the schoolchild stand in wholly different circumstances, separated by the harsh facts of criminal conviction and incarceration. The prisoner's conviction entitles the State to classify him as a "criminal," and his incarceration deprives him of the freedom "to be with family and friends and to form the other enduring attachments of normal life." . . .

The schoolchild has little need for the protection

Eighth Amendment not applicable

of the Eighth Amendment was to protect those convicted of crimes, the justices said it did not apply to corporal punishment of schoolchildren. As to due process, the Court said, "We conclude that the Due Process clause does not require notice and a hearing prior to the imposition of corporal punishment in the public schools, as that practice is authorized and limited by common law."[51]

Possible liability

Despite this ruling, the Court also commented on the severity of the paddlings. In such instances, the justices stated, school authorities might be held liable for damages to the child. Moreover, if malice is shown, the officials might be subject to prosecution under criminal statutes. In a later action the Court also indicated a role

---

[51]*Ingraham* v. *Wright,* 430 U.S. (1977). See also Perry A. Zirkel, "You Bruise, You Lose," *Phi Delta Kappan* (January 1990), pp. 410–411; and Perry Zirkel and Ivan B. Gluckman, "Is Corporal Punishment Child Abuse?" *Principal* (January 1996), pp. 60–61.

of the Eighth Amendment. Though attendance may not always be voluntary, the public school remains an open institution. Except perhaps when very young, the child is not physically restrained from leaving school during school hours; and at the end of the school day, the child is invariably free to return home. Even while at school, the child brings with him the support of family and friends and is rarely apart from teachers and other pupils who may witness and protest any instances of mistreatment.

The openness of the public school and its supervision by the community afford significant safeguards against the kinds of abuses from which the Eighth Amendment protects the prisoner. In virtually every community where corporal punishment is permitted in the schools, these safeguards are reinforced by the legal constraints of the common law. Public school teachers and administrators are privileged at common law to inflict only such corporal punishment as is reasonably necessary for the proper education and discipline of the child; any punishment going beyond the privilege may result in both civil and criminal liability. As long as the schools are open to public scrutiny, there is no reason to believe that the common law constraints will not effectively remedy and deter excesses such as those alleged in this case.

We conclude that when public school teachers or administrators impose disciplinary corporal punishment, the Eighth Amendment is inapplicable.

Questions

1. Assuming corporal punishment is desirable in a particular situation, how does one determine whether a given punishment may be reasonably necessary and thus not excessive?

2. How is it possible for the Supreme Court to decide that the First Amendment applies to elementary and secondary students (as in *Tinker* v. *Des Moines*) but the Eighth Amendment does not?

3. Could or should a student who is to be paddled demand the right to "return home" to escape this punishment?

Source: Ingraham v. *Wright, 97 S. Ct. 1401 (1977).*

No excessive force

for the due process clause discussed earlier in this chapter. By declining to hear *Miera* v. *Garcia*, the Court let stand lower court rulings that "grossly excessive" corporal punishment may constitute a violation of students' due process rights. Thus teachers can be prosecuted in the courts for using excessive force and violating students' rights.[52]

Indeed, lower courts have ruled against teachers or administrators who have used cattle prods to discipline students, slammed students' heads against the walls, or spanked students so hard they needed medical attention, and the Supreme Court

---

[52]*Miera* v. *Garcia*, 56 USLW 3390 (1987); Christopher Grasso, "Court Lets Corporal Punishment Stand, Accepts Child Abuse Case," *Education Daily*, March 22, 1988, pp. 3–4; and Mitchell L. Yell and Reece L. Peterson, "Disciplining Students with Disabilities and Those at Risk for School Failure," *Clearing House* (July–August 1996), pp. 365–370.

will probably continue to uphold such rulings. Overall, recent judicial decisions, together with the ever-present possibility of a lawsuit, have made educators cautious in using corporal punishment.[53]

Sexual Harassment or Molestation of Students

Unwelcome sexual advances

The Supreme Court's decision in *Ingraham* v. *Wright* regarding physical punishment and a later decision in *Franklin* v. *Gwinnett* strengthened prohibitions against sexual harassment and sexual molestation. Definitions of these terms vary, but for interactions between students and teachers the terms generally include not only sexual contact that calls into question the teacher's role as exemplar but also unwelcome sexual advances or requests for favors, particularly when the recipient may believe that refusal will affect his or her academic standing. In recent years there has been a dramatic increase in court cases involving school employees accused of sexually harassing students. Although the courts have not been clear on what constitutes illegal sexual harassment of students, it is clear that both staff members and the districts that employ them can be severely punished if found guilty in court.[54]

Proactive action against sexual harassment

School officials' legal responsibilities regarding teachers' sexual harassment of students were clarified in a 1998 Supreme Court decision (*Gebser* v. *Lago Vista Independent School District*) that involved a ninth grader who was seduced by a science teacher but never informed administrators about this sexual relationship. Her parents sued for damages from the school district using the argument that Title IX of the Education Amendments of 1972 requires schools to proactively take action to identify and eliminate sexual harassment. The Supreme Court ruled that school officials are not legally liable unless they know of the harassment and then proceed with "deliberate indifference." Some analysts were unhappy because they believed this decision allowed officials to avoid acting to identify and combat harassment, but others believed it reinforced administrators' resolve to implement policies that demonstrate they are not indifferent to harassment.[55]

Touching students unlawful?

Despite the relief from liability that *Gebser* provides for school officials, individual staff members still must be very wary of any action that a student or parent might interpret as sexual harassment or assault. Given the large number of allegations that have been brought against teachers in recent years, many teacher organizations have been advising their members to avoid touching students unnecessarily. They also recommend that teachers make sure that doors are open and/or that other persons are present when they meet with a student. Legal advisors recognize that it sometimes is necessary or very desirable to touch or even hug a student, as when a kindergarten teacher helps students put on coats or comforts a distressed pupil, but many advise teachers to avoid physical contact as much as possible, particularly with older students.[56]

---

[53]William Celis III, "Debate over School Paddling Grows amid Rising Concerns," *New York Times*, August 16, 1990, pp. A1, A12. See also Alan L. Barbee, "My Child Was Abused," *Executive Educator* (January 1996), pp. 25–27.

[54]*Franklin* v. *Gwinett County Public Schools,* 112 S. Ct. 1028 (1992). See also Mark Walsh, "Unwelcome Advances," *Teacher Magazine* (February 1992), pp. 12–13; Carol Shakeshaft and Audrey Cohan, "Sexual Abuse of Students by School Personnel," *Phi Delta Kappan* (March 1995), pp. 513–519; and Martha M. McCarthy, "The Law Governing Sexual Harassment in Public Schools," *Phi Delta Kappa Research Bulletin* (May 1998), pp. 15–18.

[55]*Gebser* v. *Lago Vista Independent School District,* 98-1866 S. Ct. (1998). See Linda Greenhouse, "School Districts Are Given Shield in Sexual Harassment," *New York Times*, June 23, 1998.

[56]Maria Newman, "Teachers More Reluctant to Touch Children," *New York Times*, June 24, 1998.

Guidelines for dealing with
potential harassment

Sexual abuse or harassment of one student by another is also a serious problem.[57] As in the case of students allegedly harassed by teachers, the law regarding harassment by other students is poorly defined and murky. In some situations, name-calling and teasing with sexual overtones have been interpreted as illegal harassment that educators have a legal obligation to suppress, but in other situations school staff have been absolved of legal responsibility. The following guidelines have been suggested for educators who think such harassment may be occurring:[58]

1. Don't ignore the situation or let it pass unchallenged.
2. Don't overreact; find out exactly what happened.
3. Don't embarrass or humiliate any party to an incident.
4. Initiate steps to support the victim.
5. Apply consequences in accordance with school behavior codes.
6. Don't assume that the incident is an isolated occurrence.

Student Records and Privacy Rights

FERPA curbs abuses

Until 1974, although most student records kept by schools were closed to examination by students or their parents, prospective employers, government agencies, and credit bureaus were allowed access. As might be guessed, abuses occurred. The **Family Educational Rights and Privacy Act** (also called either FERPA or the **Buckley amendment**) was passed by Congress in 1974 to curb possible abuses in institutions receiving federal funds.

Parents' rights

The Buckley amendment requires public school districts to develop policies allowing parents access to their children's official school records. The act prohibits disclosure of these records to most third parties without prior parental consent (in cases of students under eighteen years of age). Districts must have procedures to amend records if parents challenge the accuracy or completeness of the information they contain. Hearing and appeal mechanisms regarding disputed information must also be available. Parents retain rights of access to their child's school records until the child reaches the age of eighteen or is enrolled in a postsecondary institution.

Certain records exempt

However, the Buckley amendment allows several exceptions. Private notes and memoranda of teachers and administrators (including grade books) are exempt from view. In addition, records kept separate from official files and maintained for law enforcement purposes (for example, information about criminal behavior) cannot be disclosed. Nothing may be revealed that would jeopardize the privacy rights of other pupils. Last, schools may disclose directory-type information without prior consent; however, students or their families may request that even this information be withheld.[59]

---

[57]Neil Gilbert, "Touch and Stop," *Reason* (March 1994), pp. 52–53; Perry A. Zirkel, "Student-to-Student Sexual Harassment," *Phi Delta Kappan* (April 1995), pp. 448–450; Andrew Trotter, "Union: Respect All Parties," *Executive Educator* (January 1996), p. 27; and Mark Walsh, "Calif. District to Pay $250,000 in Student Sex-Harassment Suit," *Education Week*, January 15, 1997.
[58]Dan H. Wishnietsky, *Establishing School Policies on Sexual Harassment* (Bloomington, Ind.: Phi Delta Kappa, 1994); Ivan Gluckman, "Administrator Liability for Student Harm," *Cases in Point* (March 1997), pp. 1–2; and Verna L. Williams and Deborah L. Brake, *Do the Right Thing* (Washington, D.C.: National Women's Law Center, 1998).
[59]Lisa Jennings, "Privacy Rights and Public-Safety Concerns," *Education Week,* June 21, 1989, pp. 1, 8–9; P. Tyson Bennett, "Student Records and Privacy Rights" (Paper prepared for the National Association of Secondary School Principals, Washington, D.C. December 1996); and Peter A. Walker and Sara J. Steinberg, "Confidentiality of Educational Records," *Journal of Law and Education* (July 1997), pp. 11–27.

Hatch Amendment

Student privacy policies also are affected by the Hatch Amendment to the federal General Education Provisions Act of 1978. The Hatch Amendment specified that instructional materials used in connection with "any research or experimentation program or project" are to be "available for inspection" by participating students' parents and guardians, and that no student shall be required to participate in testing, psychological examination, or treatments in which "the primary purpose is to reveal information" concerning political affiliations, sexual behaviors or attitudes, psychological or mental problems, income, and other personal matters. It has been difficult to define terms such as "instructional materials" and "research program," and many parents have used the Hatch Act to object to school activities that probe students' feelings or beliefs. Consequently, teachers must consider carefully whether collecting information on students' background or beliefs serves a legitimate goal.[60]

Compulsory Attendance and Home Schooling

Every state has a law requiring children to attend school, usually from age six or seven to age sixteen or seventeen. In the past two decades these compulsory attendance laws have received increased attention because of a revival of interest in home schooling. A growing number of parents who object to some subject matter

Most states allow home schooling subject to various restrictions on subject matter covered, adequacy of texts used, and number of hours of daily instruction provided; parents also must show through standardized test scores that the education provided their children is comparable to that of school-educated peers. *(© Bob Crandell/ Stock Boston)*

---

[60]Edward B. Jenkinson, *Student Privacy in the Classroom* (Bloomington, Ind.: Phi Delta Kappa, 1990); and *Protecting the Privacy of Student Education Records* (Washington, D.C.: National Center for Education Statistics, 1996), available at **www.ed.gov**.

taught in public schools, the teaching methods used, or the absence of religious activities have chosen to teach their children at home. State governments allow for home schooling, but depending on state legislation, they impose regulations dealing with hours of study, testing, whether home-schooled children can participate in extracurricular activities at nearby public schools, and other matters.[61]

Requirements for home schooling

When home-schooling parents have been brought to court for violating compulsory attendance laws, they usually must demonstrate that the home program is essentially equivalent to that offered in public schools with respect to subject matter covered, the adequacy of the texts used, and the number of hours of daily instruction. In some states, they also must show test results indicating that their children's education is comparable to that of school-educated peers. Parents have often prevailed in such cases, but courts have consistently upheld the right of state legislatures to impose restrictions and requirements.[62]

Need for Balance Between Rights and Responsibilities

Critique of courts

During the past several decades, as courts have upheld the constitutional rights of students and placed restrictions on school officials, many educators and parents have decided that the legal process is out of balance. They believe that the courts place too much emphasis on student rights and too little on the need for school discipline. The result, said AFT president Albert Shanker, "is schools where little or no learning goes on because teachers have to assume the role of warden."[63]

Focus on reasonableness

However, some scholars believe that since the mid-1980s the Supreme Court has begun to redress the balance. In this view, the Court's decisions in *T.L.O.* (1985), *Bethel/Fraser* (1986), and *Hazelwood/Kuhlmeier* (1988) place less burden on school officials than the 1969 *Tinker* decision. Rather than demonstrating that certain rules are necessary, school officials now need to show only that the rules are reasonable. This new emphasis on reasonableness indicates that the Court "is placing considerable confidence in school officials," trusting those officials to maintain a proper balance between student rights and the school's needs.[64]

Religion and the Schools

The framers of our Constitution were acutely aware of religious persecution and sought to prevent the United States from experiencing the serious and often bloody conflicts that had occurred in Europe. As noted at the beginning of this chapter, the First Amendment, adopted in 1791, prohibits the establishment of a nationally sanctioned religion (the establishment clause) and government interference with individuals' rights to hold and freely practice their religious beliefs (the free exercise

---

[61]J. Gary Knowles, Stacey E. Marlow, and James Muchmore, "From Pedagogy to Ideology," *American Journal of Education* (March 1991); and Isabel Lyman, *Homeschooling* (Washington, D.C.: CATO Institute 1998), available at **www.cato.org.**

[62]Naomi Gitins, ed., *Religion, Education, and the U.S. Constitution* (Alexandria, Va.: National School Boards Association, 1990); Perry A. Zirkel, "Home Sweet . . . School," *Phi Delta Kappan* (December 1994), pp. 332–333; and Brian D. Ray, *Strengths of Their Own* (Salem, Oreg.: National Home Education Research Institute, 1998).

[63]Albert Shanker, "Discipline in Our Schools," *New York Times,* May 19, 1991, p. E7. See also Stephen B. Thomas, ed., *The Yearbook of Education Law 1994* (Topeka, Kans.: NOLPE, 1994), pp. 74–77; and Perry A. Zirkel, "The Right Stuff," *Phi Delta Kappan* (February 1998), pp. 473–474.

[64]Lowell C. Rose, "Reasonableness—The Court's New Standard for Cases Involving Student Rights," *Phi Delta Kappan* (April 1988), pp. 589–592. See also Lawrence F. Rossow and Janice A. Hiniger, *Students and the Law* (Bloomington, Ind.: Phi Delta Kappa, 1991); and Chastity Platt and Bill Graves, "Strip Search Grows From Zero Tolerance," *Oregonian,* July 1, 1998.

Government "neutral"

clause). The position of government toward religion was succinctly stated by Judge Alphonso Taft over one hundred years ago: "The government is neutral, and while protecting all, it prefers none, and it disparages none."[65]

Prayer, Bible Reading, and Religious Blessings and Displays

State-written prayer unconstitutional

Students in New Hyde Park were required to recite daily this nondenominational prayer composed by the New York State Board of Regents: "Almighty God, we acknowledge our dependence upon thee, and we beg thy blessings upon us, our parents, our teachers and our Country." Although exemption was possible upon written parental request, the U.S. Supreme Court in *Engle* v. *Vitale* (1962) ruled the state-written prayer unconstitutional. According to the Court, "Neither the fact that the prayer may be denominationally neutral nor the fact that its observance on the part of students is voluntary can serve to free it from the limitations of the Establishment Clause."[66]

The decision created a storm of protest that has not subsided to this day. A year later the Court again prohibited religious exercises in public schools. This time, the issue involved oral reading of Bible verses and recitation of the Lord's Prayer. These were clearly religious ceremonies and "intended by the State to be so," even when student participation was voluntary. On the other hand, the courts have ruled that students can lead or participate in prayers at commencement ceremonies, as long as decisions to do so are made by students without the involvement of clergy.[67]

Invocations and benedictions

The Supreme Court also has ruled against invocations and benedictions in which a clergyman opens or closes a public-school ceremony by invoking blessings from a deity. In a 1992 decision, the Court concluded that such blessings violate the standards established in *Lemon* v. *Kurtzman* (see Figure 8.1), which prohibit the government from advancing religion. However, Justice Anthony Kennedy's majority opinion noted that state actions implicating religion are not necessarily unconstitutional because some citizens may object to them, and that the decision was not meant to require a "relentless and pervasive attempt to exclude religion from every aspect of public life."

"Moment of silence" policies

One effect of the decision was to postpone full constitutional review of several important questions, such as whether schools can implement "moment of silence" policies that allow silent prayer on a voluntary basis, whether schools can allow religiously oriented invocations that are conducted by students or spoken by a layperson and are not addressed to a deity, whether a school choir can perform clearly Christian songs at a graduation ceremony, and whether private groups can distribute free Bibles on school premises.[68]

---

[65]Quoted by Justice Tom Clark in *School District of Abington Township* v. *Schempp,* 374 U.S. 203 (1963). See also "Religious Liberty, Public Education, and the Future of American Democracy," *Educational Leadership* (May 1995), pp. 92–93; and Ralph Mawdsley, "Religion in the Schools," *School Business Affairs* (May 1997), pp. 5–10.

[66]*Engle* v. *Vitale,* 370 U.S. 421 (1962). See also "A Matter of Conscience," *Church and State* (March 1995), pp. 10–12; and Associated Press, "Supreme Court Rejects Alabama Appeal on School Prayer," *Los Angeles Times,* June 23, 1998.

[67]*School District of Abington Township* v. *Schempp* and *Murray* v. *Curlett,* 374 U.S. 203 (1963). See also Robert S. Alley, *School Prayer* (New York: Prometheus, 1994), and Mark Walsh, "Appeals Court Allows Student-Led Graduation Prayers," *Education Week,* June 3, 1998.

[68]Perry A. Zirkel and Ivan B. Gluckman, "Invocations and Benedictions at School Events," *NASSP Bulletin* (January 1991), pp. 105–109; Linda Greenhouse, "Justices Affirm Ban on Prayers in Public School," *New York Times,* June 25, 1992, pp. A1, A16; "School Prayer," *Cases in Point* (January 1997), p. 1; and Mark Walsh, "Court Allows Bible Handouts," *Education Week,* September 9, 1998.

A "secular" atmosphere

Display in public schools of religious symbols (such as a cross or a menorah) in a manner that promotes a particular religion is clearly unconstitutional. However, the Supreme Court has ruled that such religiously oriented artifacts as a Nativity scene can be displayed in public settings if the overall atmosphere is largely secular. The interpretation of this ruling is very controversial. In one nonschool case, the Court banned a Nativity scene in front of the Allegheny County (Pa.) Courthouse because it had not been "junked up" (in the words of a county official) with Santa Claus figures or other secular symbols. After that decision, a federal judge required the removal of a crucifixion painting from the Schuylerville (N.Y.) School District, on the grounds that the painting lacked any "meaningful" secular features.[69]

Access to Public Schools for Religious Groups

School meetings of religious groups

Bridget Mergens, a high-school senior in Omaha, organized a group of about twenty-five students who requested permission to meet on campus before school every week or so to read and discuss the Bible. Although similar Bible clubs were allowed to meet at other schools, administrators refused the request, partly to avoid setting a precedent for clubs of Satanists, Ku Klux Klanists, or other groups the school would find undesirable. Bridget's mother brought suit, and in 1990 the U.S. Supreme Court found in her favor. Public high schools, the Court ruled, must allow students' religious, philosophical, and political groups to meet on campus on the same basis as other extracurricular groups. Permitting such meetings, the Court stated, does not mean that the school endorses or supports them.[70]

Options for schools

There has been a great deal of uncertainty about the implications of the *Mergens* case. Schools apparently have to choose between allowing practically any student group to meet and dropping all extracurricular activities. A third option would be to permit meetings only by groups whose activities are related directly to the curriculum, but difficult problems then arise in defining such activities. Recent Supreme Court cases have not greatly clarified the issue.[71]

Pledge of Allegiance

Religious objections to pledge

The separation of church and state also applies to statements of allegiance to the state. In one case, several Jehovah's Witnesses went to court over a West Virginia requirement that their children recite the pledge of allegiance at school each morning. The parents' objection was based on religious doctrine. The court ruled that the children could be exempted from this requirement because it conflicted with their religious beliefs. Using this ruling as precedent, federal judges have concluded that students who refuse to stand and recite the pledge cannot be compelled to do so if

---

[69]Michael McGough, "Menorah Wars," *New Republic,* February 5, 1990, pp. 12–13; Rob Boston, "The Klan, a Cross, and the Constitution," *Church and State* (March 1995), pp. 7–9; "City-Sponsored Religious Display Struck Down by Court," *Church and State* (April 1997), p. 3; and John Leo, "Playing Reindeer Games," *U.S. News and World Report* January 4, 1999, p. 14.

[70]*Board of Education of the Westside Community Schools* v. *Mergens,* 88 S. Ct. 1597 (1990). See also Kern Alexander and M. David Alexander, *American Public School Law,* 4th ed. (Belmont, Calif.: Wadsworth, 1998).

[71]Mark Walsh, "Church Group's Access to Public Schools Upheld," *Education Week,* August 1, 1990, p. 9; Linda Greenhouse, "Church-State Ties," *New York Times,* June 30, 1995, pp. A1, A14; and Benjamin Sendor, "When May Student Clubs Meet?" *American School Board Journal* (August 1997), pp. 14–15.

Federal judges have concluded that students who refuse to stand and recite the pledge of allegiance cannot be compelled to do so if participation violates their religious or other personal beliefs. (© Kenneth Murray/Photo Researchers)

participation violates their religious or other personal beliefs. Recent decisions have provided further support for this conclusion.[72]

Religious Objections Regarding Curriculum

Basal readers challenged

In Tennessee, fundamentalist Christian parents brought suit against the Hawkins County School District charging that exposure of their children to the Holt, Rinehart and Winston basal reading series was offensive to their religious beliefs. The parents believed that "after reading the entire Holt series, a child might adopt the views of a feminist, a humanist, a pacifist, an anti-Christian, a vegetarian, or an advocate of a one-world government." The district court held for the parents, reasoning that the state could satisfy its compelling interest in the literacy of Tennessee schoolchildren through less restrictive means than compulsory use of the Holt series. However, an appellate court reversed this decision, stating that no evidence had been produced to show that students were required to affirm their belief or disbelief in any idea mentioned in the Holt books. The textbook series, the court said, "merely requires recognition that in a pluralistic society we must 'live and let live.'"[73]

In a similar case in Alabama, a district judge upheld a group of parents who contended that school textbooks advanced the religion of secular humanism[74] and

[72]*West Virginia State Board of Education* v. *Barnette,* 319 U.S. 624 (1943); *Lipp* v. *Morris,* 579 F. 2d 834 (3rd Cir. 1978); Perry A. Zirkel and Ivan B. Gluckman, "Pledge of Allegiance," *NASSP Bulletin* (September 1990), pp. 115–117; and Mark Walsh, "Sitting for the Pledge," *Education Week,* June 10, 1998.

[73]*Mozert* v. *Hawkins County Board of Education,* 86-6144 (E.D. Tenn. 1986); *Mozert* v. *Hawkins County Board of Education,* 87-5024 (6th Cir. 1987). See also Michael P. Farris, "A Point-by-Point Analysis of the Claims Made by RLPA Supporters" (1998 posting at the Internet site of Home School Legal Defense), available at **www.hslda.org/nationalcenter.**

[74]Secular humanism is a philosophy that deemphasizes religious doctrines and instead stresses the human capacity for self-realization through reason. See "Teaching Secular Humanism," undated paper available at **www.execpc.com/~dcoy/PEDS.**

Secular humanism

excluded the history of Christianity.[75] This decision was reversed by a federal appeals court, which held that the textbooks did not endorse secular humanism or any other religion, but rather attempted to instill such values as independent thought and tolerance of diverse views. The appeals court noted that if the First Amendment prohibited mere "inconsistency with the beliefs of a particular religion there would be very little that could be taught in the public schools." Similar conclusions have been reached by courts in California and several other states.[76]

The evolution controversy

In 1987 the U.S. Supreme Court considered *Edwards* v. *Aguillard,* a case that challenged Louisiana's Balanced Treatment for Creation-Science and Evolution-Science Act. Creation science, or creationism, is the belief that the development of life has proceeded from divine intervention or creation rather than by biological evolution. The Louisiana act required that creation science be taught wherever evolution was taught, and that appropriate curriculum guides and materials be developed. The Supreme Court ruled this law unconstitutional. By requiring "either the banishment of the theory of evolution . . . or the presentation of a religious viewpoint that rejects evolution in its entirety," the Court reasoned, the Louisiana act advanced a religious doctrine and violated the establishment clause of the First Amendment.[77]

School-district responses

The controversy has continued. The California board of education tried to compromise by referring to evolution as a "theory" rather than a "fact." In line with creationist beliefs, some school districts have introduced books that assert life is too complex to be formed through evolution, but avoid explicit references to divine creation. In other districts, comparable controversies have arisen when parents have objected to certain materials designed to improve students' thinking skills, contending that the materials reflected "New Age" religious practices. Some school districts have responded by eliminating such materials.[78]

Teaching About Religion

Promoting understanding of religious traditions

Guarantees of separation between church and state do not mean that public schools are prohibited from teaching *about* religion. A number of states and school districts have been strengthening approaches for developing an understanding of religious traditions and values while neither promoting nor detracting from any

---

[75]*Smith* v. *Board of School Commissioners of Mobile County,* 87-7216 (11th Cir. 1987); Kenneth R. Miller, "Life's Grand Design," *Technology Review* (March 1994), pp. 25–32; and Perry A. Zirkel, "A Doomed Prayer for Relief," *Phi Delta Kappan* (February 1995), pp. 496–497.

[76]Eugene F. Provenzo, Jr., *Religious Fundamentalism and American Education* (Albany: State University of New York Press, 1990); and David A. Splitt, "Sorting Out What Is and Isn't Religious," *The Executive Educator* (March 1995), pp. 13, 47; and "Science Disclaimer Unconstitutional" (undated paper posting at the Internet site of Parents for Excellence in School Districts), available at **www.execpc.com/~dcoy/PEDS.**

[77]*Edwards* v. *Aguillard,* 197 S. Ct. 2573 (1987); Eugene C. Scott, "Monkey Business," *Policy Review* (January–February 1996), pp. 20–25; "An NSTA Position Paper on the Teaching of Evolution," *Science Scope* (October 1997), pp. 26–27; and Daniel J. Kelves, "Darwin in Dayton," *New York Review of Books,* November 19, 1998, pp. 61–63.

[78]Seth Mydans, "Correction: California Calls Evolution 'a Fact and a Theory,'" *New York Times,* November 14, 1989, p. 12; Tim Beardsley, "Darwin Denied," *Scientific American* (July 1995), pp. 12–13; and Leon Lynn, "The Evolution of Creationism," *Rethinking Schools* (Winter 1997/1998), available at **www.rethinkingschools.org.** See also "Evolution and Creationism," *Education Week on the Web,* at **www.edweek.org/context.** Internet sites dealing with creationism and evolution are easily found by searching **www.yahoo.com** for "creationism."

Federal guidelines

particular religious or nonreligious ideology. In addition, many scholars have been preparing materials for such constitutionally acceptable instruction.[79]

According to guidelines issued in 1995 and reissued in 1998 by the U.S. Department of Education, schools are permitted to teach such subjects as "the history of religion, comparative religion, the Bible (or other scripture) as literature, and the role of religion in the history of the United States and other countries." These federal guidelines, which also touched on many of the other controversies concerning religion and the schools, are summarized in Overview 8.3. However, courts may not necessarily support what the executive branch deems correct.[80]

Government Regulation and Support of Nonpublic Schools

In 1925 *Pierce* v. *Society of Sisters* established that a state's compulsory school attendance laws could be satisfied through enrollment in a private or parochial school.[81] Attention then turned to the question of how much control a state could exercise over the education offered in nonpublic schools. A 1926 case, *Farrington* v. *Tokushige,* gave nonpublic schools "reasonable choice and discretion in respect of teachers, curriculum and textbooks." Within that framework, however, states have passed various kinds of legislation to regulate nonpublic schools. Some states have few regulations; others require the employment of certified teachers, specify the number of days or hours the school must be in session, or insist that state accreditation standards be met. One current controversy involves the application of state standards for special education.[82]

States can regulate

On the other side of the coin, states have offered many types of support for nonpublic schools, including transportation, books, and health services. In the 1947 case *Everson* v. *Board of Education of Erving Township,* the Supreme Court considered a provision in the New Jersey Constitution that allowed state aid for transportation of private and parochial students. The Court held that where state constitutions permitted such assistance, there was no violation of the U.S. Constitution. (Transportation aid for private-school students has been ruled unconstitutional only in Idaho and Hawaii.) Since then, the distinction between permissible and impermissible state aid to nonpublic schools has usually been based on the **child benefit theory:** aid that directly benefits the child is permissible, whereas aid that primarily benefits the nonpublic institution is not.[83]

State aid for transportation

[79]For example, see Charles C. Haynes, Oliver Thomas, John B. Leach, and Alyssa Kendall, eds., *Finding Common Ground* (Nashville, Tenn.: Freedom Forum First Amendment Center, 1994); Robert Dole, "The Establishment Clause," *Policy Review* (January–February 1996), available at Internet site **www.townhall.com;** and Graham Langtree, *At the Heart* (Philadelphia: Trans-Atlantic, 1997).

[80]Richard W. Riley, "Secretary's Statement on Religious Expression" (Statement released by the U.S. Department of Education, Washington D.C. 1998), available at **www.ed.gov.** See also Charles C. Hayne, "Religion in the Public Schools," *School Administrator* (January 1999).

[81]*Pierce* v. *Society of Sisters, 268 U.S. 510 (1925).* See also L. Particia Williams, "The Regulation of Private Schools in America." (Paper prepared for the U.S. Department of Education, February 1996), available at **www.isacs.org.**

[82]*Farrington* v. *Tokushige, 273 U.S. 284 (1926).* See also Millicent Lawton, "Atlanta School Drops Ban on Non-Christian Teachers," *Education Week,* March 10, 1993, p. 16; E. Vance Randall, "The State and Religious Schools in America," *Journal of Research on Christian Education* (Autumn 1994), pp. 175–198; and Mark Walsh, "N.H. Church School Banned," *Education Week* (June 10, 1998).

[83]*Everson* v. *Board of Education of Erving Township, 330 U.S. (1947);* "From Courthouse to Schoolhouse," *Daily Report Card* (February 5, 1996), p. 4; and Ethan Bronner, "Church State, and Schools," *New York Times,* June 28, 1998.

OVERVIEW 8.3 Guidelines on Religion in the Schools, from the U.S. Department of Education

Student prayer and religious discussion: [The U.S. Constitution] does not prohibit purely private religious speech by students. Students therefore have the same right to engage in individual or group prayer and religious discussion during the school day as they do to engage in other comparable activity.

Generally, students may pray in a nondisruptive manner when not engaged in school activities or instruction, and subject to the rules that normally pertain in the applicable setting.

The right to engage in voluntary prayer or religious discussion free from discrimination does not include the right to have a captive audience listen, or to compel other students to participate.

Graduation prayer: Under current [U.S.] Supreme Court decisions, school officials may not mandate or organize prayer at graduation nor organize religious baccalaureate ceremonies. If a school generally opens its facilities to private groups, it must make its facilities open on the same terms to organizers of privately sponsored religious baccalaureate services.

Official neutrality: Teachers and school administrators . . . are prohibited by the [Constitution] from soliciting or encouraging religious activity and from participating in such activity with students. Teachers and administrators also are prohibited from discouraging activity because of its religious content and from soliciting or encouraging anti-religious activity.

Teaching about religion: Public schools may not provide religious instruction, but they may teach about religion . . . the history of religion, comparative religion, the Bible (or other scripture) as literature, and the role of religion in the history of the United States and other countries are all permissible public school subjects.

Although public schools may teach about religious holidays . . . and may celebrate the secular aspects of holidays, schools may not observe holidays as religious events or promote such observance by students.

Student assignments: Students may express their beliefs about religion in the form of homework, artwork, and other written and oral assignments. . . . Such home and classroom work should be judged by ordinary academic standards.

Religious literature: Students have a right to distribute religious literature to their schoolmates on the same terms as they are permitted to distribute other literature that is unrelated to school curriculum or activities.

Religious exemptions: Schools enjoy substantial discretion to excuse individual students from lessons that are objectionable to the student or the student's parents on religious or other conscientious grounds.

Released time: Schools have the discretion to dismiss students to off-premises religious instruction, provided that schools do not encourage or discourage participation. . . . Schools may not allow religious instruction by outsiders on school premises during the school day.

Teaching values: Though schools must be neutral with respect to religion, they may plan an active role with respect to teaching civic values and virtue.

Student garb: Students may display religious messages on items of clothing to the same extent that they are permitted to display other comparable messages.

The Equal Access Act: Student religious groups have the same right of access to school facilities as is enjoyed by other comparable student groups. A school receiving federal funds must allow student groups meeting under the act to use the school media . . . to announce their meetings on the same terms as other noncurriculum-related student groups.

A school . . . trigger[s] equal-access rights for religious groups when it allows students to meet during their lunch periods or other noninstructional time during the school day, as well as when it allows students to meet before and after the school day.

Source: Richard W. Riley, "Secretary's Statement on Religious Expression" (Statement released by the U.S. Department of Education, Washington, D.C., 1998).

In *Wolman* v. *Walter* (1977) and *Agostini* v. *Felton* (1997), the Supreme Court went further. Addressing state support for nonpublic schools permitted by the Ohio and New York constitutions, the Court decided each specific question by applying the three-pronged *Lemon* v. *Kurtzman* test illustrated in Figure 8.1. The Court's decisions were as follows:[84]

1. Providing for the purchase or loan of secular textbooks and standardized tests is constitutional.

2. Providing speech, hearing, and psychological diagnostic services at the nonpublic school site is constitutional.

3. Providing for the purchase and loan of other instructional materials and equipment, such as projectors, science kits, maps and globes, charts, record players, and so on, was ruled unconstitutional because this involves excessive government entanglement with religion.

4. Providing funds for field trips is unconstitutional because "where the teacher works within and for a sectarian institution, an unacceptable risk of fostering religion is an inevitable byproduct."

5. Providing Title 1 remedial services from public-school staff located at nonpublic facilities does not constitute excessive entanglement of church and state.

A legal muddle

The conclusions in *Wolman* v. *Walter* and *Agostini* v. *Felton* show why many legal scholars believe that constitutional law regarding religion and the schools is something of a muddle. Why should government purchase of textbooks and tests for nonpublic schools be constitutional but not purchase of maps, globes, charts, and record players? Why can government-supported psychological services be provided at nonpublic schools, whereas remedial services must be provided at a neutral site? With issues as convoluted as these, the recent administration efforts at clarification are not much help, nor are the subsequent Supreme Court cases.[85]

Affirmative Action and Educational Equity

Laws prohibiting discrimination

Affirmative action generally refers to active steps intended to ensure that disadvantaged individuals receive equal opportunity in employment and education. In general, affirmative action requirements are associated with the Fourteenth Amendment, which guarantees all citizens equal protection under the law. Titles VI and VII of the Civil Rights Act of 1964 and the Civil Rights Restoration Act of 1987 specifically prohibit discrimination in federally assisted educational programs on the basis of race, color, religion, national origin, or sex. These laws also prohibit employment discrimination on the basis of any of these criteria. The Rehabilitation

---

[84]*Wolman* v. *Walter,* 433 U.S. 229 (1977); and *Agostini* v. *Felton,* 96 S. Ct. 552 (1997). See also Jennifer Bradley, "Fighting the Establishment (Clause)," *American Prospect* (Number 28, 1996), pp. 57–60; Benjamin Sendor, "A Change of Heart—And Law," *American School Board Journal* (October 1997), pp. 16, 18; and Mark Walsh, "Ruling in La. Limits Aid For Religious Schools," *Education Week,* September 9, 1998.

[85]"Federal Court Upholds Chapter One Aid to Parochial Schools," *Church and State* (March 1995), pp. 17–18; Joe Loconte, "Making Public Schools Safe for Religion," *Policy Review* (July–August, 1996), available at **www.heritage.org**; and Clint Bolick, "Blocking the Exits," *Policy Review* (May–June 1998), also available at **www.heritage.org**.

Act (1973) and the Americans with Disabilities Act (1991) extend similar protection to persons with disabilities (see Chapter 11).[86]

Disproportionate impact

A large amount of litigation has involved the definition of discrimination and the obligation to overcome past discrimination. The U.S. Supreme Court ruled in *Washington* v. *Davis* (1976) that "disproportionate impact" alone does not prove the existence of unconstitutional discrimination. For example, the fact that minority groups or women are underrepresented among employees in a school district is not by itself sufficient to prove an equal protection violation. However, the Court also ruled that such disproportionate impact is enough to shift the burden of justification to the defendant. Thus if a school-district test for teacher hiring disproportionately eliminates minority candidates, the district must prove that the test has some valid relationship to performance on the job.[87]

Quotas ruled unconstitutional

Affirmative action encouraged

During the 1970s, educational institutions that received federal funds were required to set and meet specific targets for hiring minority applicants and women. Similar policies were being developed for admission of minority students to colleges. However, in 1978 the Supreme Court prohibited this approach. In *Regents of the University of California* v. *Alan Bakke,* the Court ruled that setting aside a specific number of places for minority applicants to a medical school was unconstitutional. On the other hand, the Court encouraged affirmative action policies that were *not* based on firm quotas — for example, a general preference for applicants whose background (such as membership in a minority group) reflected qualities that the institution wished to have more fully represented. The next year, in *Steelworkers* v. *Weber,* the Court upheld such affirmative action plans that offered minorities preferential treatment in employment.[88]

Shifting the burden of proof

However, the legal basis for affirmative action became more tenuous in 1989 and 1995, when the Supreme Court issued several rulings that seemed to reopen issues previously thought to be settled. For example, in *Wards Cove Packing* v. *Antonio,* a case involving the disproportionate impact of employment testing, the Court shifted the burden of proof. Rather than requiring the employer to demonstrate that a test was necessary, the Court said the plaintiffs who alleged discrimination must prove the test unnecessary. Although the Court claimed it was not retreating from Congress's intent to forbid discrimination, many observers were not so sure. A subsequent ruling of the Supreme Court specified that government agencies must show "compelling" reasons that can survive "strict scrutiny" of the courts before they can implement policies that give preferences to minority groups or women.[89]

---

[86]Ward Weldon, "Effects of the 1987 Civil Rights Restoration Act on Educational Policy and Practice," *Journal of Negro Education* (Spring 1990), pp. 155–163; William G. Tierney, "The Parameters of Affirmative Action," *Review of Educational Research* (Summer 1997), pp. 165–196; and William Bowen and Derek Bok, *The Shape of the River* (Princeton, N.J.: Princeton University Press, 1998).

[87]*Washington* v. *Davis,* 426 U.S. 229 (1976). See also Peter Schrag, "So You Want to Be Color-Blind," *The American Prospect* (Summer 1995), pp. 38–43; and Richard D. Kahlenberg, *The Remedy: Class, Race, and Affirmative Action* (New York: Basic Books, 1996).

[88]*Regents of the University of California* v. *Alan Bakke,* 438 U.S. 265 (1978); *Steelworkers* v. *Weber,* 443 U.S. 193 (1979). See also Stephen L. Carter, *Reflections of an Affirmative Action Baby* (New York: Basic Books, 1991); and Perry A. Zirkel, "Affirmative Action? It's a Tossup," *Phi Delta Kappan* (December 1996), pp. 332–333.

[89]Linda Greenhouse, "A Changed Court Revises Rules on Civil Rights," *New York Times,* June 18, 1989, p. E2; and Michael Barone, "What Comes Next?" *The American Enterprise* (January–February 1997), pp. 37–38.

Rejection of preferential admissions

Following directions thus set by the Supreme Court, the U.S. Fifth Circuit Court of Appeals ruled in 1996 that the University of Texas Law School could no longer give minority candidates preference for admission based on race or ethnicity. In addition, voters in California and Washington supported legislation instructing higher education institutions there to eliminate policies and practices that similarly provided for preferential admissions as a form of affirmative action. These two developments in effect made affirmative action of this kind questionable everywhere, in the absence of indications that the U.S. Supreme Court might overrule them in the future.[90]

Political and educational leaders in Texas responded by introducing new policies that provided automatic admission to public postsecondary institutions for all high-school seniors who graduate in the top 10 percent of their class. Because there is so much segregation in the Texas high-school system, this approach makes it likely that colleges and universities will continue to have some racial and ethnic diversity in their student bodies, without preferential admissions based on race or ethnicity. Decision makers in other states undoubtedly will consider possibilities for introducing similar policies, particularly if they currently use preferential admissions practices based on race and ethnicity that are challenged or struck down in the courts.[91]

Magnet schools also affected

Concern with racial and ethnic preference in admission decisions also has been widespread with regard to magnet schools (see Chapter 11) in public school districts. As part of desegregation plans in their districts, many magnet schools have used racial and ethnic preferences or admission quotas specifying the maximum percentage that applicants from a given racial or ethnic group could constitute in enrollment. Following the developments described above in California, Texas, and Washington, legal suits and the threat of court challenges resulted in the abolition of preferences and quotas based on race and ethnicity at Latin High School and other magnet schools in Boston and at some other magnet schools in other locations.[92]

Gender equity

Chapter 11 will discuss desegregation law and other issues of educational equity for minority and non-English-speaking students and children with disabilities. Before leaving the subject of legal guarantees, however, we should consider the impact of federal laws and regulations on educational opportunities for women. As the next chapter points out, opportunities for women have been limited in part by socialization practices in the home and the larger society. Some of these limitations, however, can be reduced through appropriate actions within the educational system. Such actions have been stimulated by Title IX of the 1972 Education Amendments to the Civil Rights Act and by the **Women's Educational Equity Act** (WEEA) of 1974. Among the most important activities conducted under Title IX and the WEEA are the following:[93]

---

[90]*Hopwood* v. *Texas,* 78 F3d. 932 (5th Cir. 1996). See also Peter Schrag, "When Preferences Disappear," *American Prospect* (February 1997), pp. 38–41; and Ronald Dworkin, "Affirming Affirmative Action," *New York Review of Books,* October 23, 1998, pp. 91–102.

[91]Peter Applebome, "Seeking New Approaches to Diversity," *New York Times,* April 23, 1997.

[92]Caroline Hendrie, "New Magnet School Policies Sidestep an Old Issue: Race," *Education Week,* June 10, 1998.

[93]Stan Crock and Michele Galen, "A Thunderous Impact on Equal Opportunity," *Business Week,* June 26, 1995, p. 37; and Daniel E. Tungate and Daniel P. Orie, "Title IX Lawsuits," *Phi Delta Kappan* (April 1998), pp. 603–604.

Effects of the WEEA

- Opening math, science, and technology courses and careers to women
- Reducing sex stereotyping in curriculum materials
- Removing admission restraints and encouraging women to enroll in "nontraditional" vocational education courses, as well as lowering barriers to entry into apprenticeship training
- Increasing the number of women in school administration
- Encouraging greater participation by women in athletics

Athletic participation improved

Federal regulations now require that secondary and postsecondary schools provide equitable opportunities for athletic participation by women. As a result, more than 1 million young women take part annually in secondary school athletics, compared with only 295,000 in 1970–71. However, educators disagree on whether significant progress continues to occur and how much additional change should take place in the future.[94]

Summing Up

1. Education-related court cases have significantly increased in the last few decades. Such cases can be heard in both federal and state courts, depending on the issues involved. Only decisions of the U.S. Supreme Court apply nationally.

2. Tenure protects teachers from dismissal except on such specified grounds as incompetency, immorality, insubordination, and unprofessional conduct. Teachers accused of such conduct are entitled to due process protections.

3. Teachers have the right to form and belong to unions and other professional organizations, but most states prohibit teachers from striking.

4. Teachers' rights regarding freedom of expression and academic freedom depend on a balance between individual and governmental interests. Teachers have rights guaranteed to individuals under the Constitution, but school boards have obligations to ensure the "proper" and "regular" operation of the schools, taking into account the rights of parents, teachers, and students.

5. Restraints on teachers' behavior outside school and on their dress and grooming are not as stringent as they once were in the United States, but teachers still are expected to serve as role models and to behave in an exemplary manner.

6. Schools must uphold definite standards to avoid legal suits charging negligence when students are injured. In addition, teachers must obey copyright laws.

7. The courts have clarified and expanded such students' rights as freedom of expression, due process in the case of suspension or expulsion, prohibition against bodily searches in the absence of specific grounds, limitations on corporal punishment, and privacy of records.

---

[94]David Roach "Compliance and Quotas Don't Mix," *New York Times,* September 17, 1995, p. 22; Debra E. Blum "Measuring Equity," *Chronicle of Higher Education,* January 26, 1996, pp. A33–34; and Jim Naughton, "Focus of Title IX Debate Shifts from Teams to Scholarships," *Chronicle of Higher Education,* May 29, 1998, pp. A45–A46.

8. Organized and mandated prayer and Bible reading are not allowed in public schools. School curricula do not automatically constitute unconstitutional discrimination against religion when they ignore religious points of view or explanations.

9. The legal basis for government support for nonpublic schools is mixed. For example, government may provide textbooks, tests, and psychological services for students at nonpublic schools, but it may not provide funds for field trips, projectors, science kits, or maps. Providing the latter is thought to entangle church and state.

10. Federal laws prohibit discrimination in educational employment and programming on the grounds of race, color, religion, national origin, and sex. School districts and teachers have an obligation to act affirmatively in providing equal opportunity for minorities and women. Preferential admission to educational institutions on the basis of race or ethnicity has been ruled unconstitutional in some courts and is being reduced or eliminated in some states.

Key Terms

plaintiffs *(231)*

litigants *(231)*

establishment clause *(232)*

free exercise clause *(232)*

due process clause *(232)*

equal protection clause *(232)*

breach of contract *(234)*

tenure *(234)*

continuing contract *(234)*

academic freedom *(239)*

torts *(242)*

fair use *(244)*

in loco parentis (246)

Family Educational Rights and Privacy Act (Buckley amendment) *(259)*

child benefit theory *(266)*

affirmative action *(268)*

Women's Educational Equity Act *(270)*

Discussion Questions

1. Should teachers be required to meet higher or different standards of personal morality than other citizens? Why or why not?

2. Debate the pros and cons of prayer, Bible reading, and religious observances in public schools. Should changes be made in current laws regarding these activities?

3. Should the due process rights of students differ from those of adults outside the school? Why or why not? What differences may be most justifiable?

4. To what extent are academic freedom issues different in elementary schools than in secondary schools? How might this distinction be important for you as a teacher?

5. Think of a situation in which your personal views might conflict with your school's policies regarding corporal punishment, student dress codes, or some other legal issue. To what extent would you find it difficult to comply with official policies?

Suggested Projects for Professional Development

1. Find out the teacher tenure regulations in your state and in one or two nearby states. Do the states differ with respect to probationary period, cause for dismissal, or other matters? Are teachers in your community aware of these policies?

2. From a nearby school district, collect and analyze information about teachers' responsibilities for identifying and reporting child abuse. What are the district's explicit policies? Have any teachers been released or otherwise disciplined for failure to meet these responsibilities?

3. Survey several nearby school districts regarding their policies on student and teacher dress codes. Find out whether and how these policies have changed in the past ten or fifteen years. Do you expect to see further changes in the near future?

4. For your portfolio, prepare a lesson plan dealing with religious holidays in a manner that does not unconstitutionally promote or inhibit religion.

Suggested Readings and Resources

Internet Resources

Useful sources dealing with material in this chapter — particularly with major Supreme Court and federal court decisions — can be found by going to the Web page of the Emory University School of Law at **www.law.emory.edu**. Any relevant ERIC digest is quickly and easily downloadable using the search procedure at **www.ed.gov**. The American Civil Liberties Union at **www.aclu.org**, also gives considerable attention to education-related cases. A wealth of law-related material involving school safety and student discipline is available at **www.keepschoolsafe.org**. You can take a virtual tour of the U.S. Supreme Court and listen to the statements and arguments of plaintiffs and defendants in some of the Court's major cases at **court.it-services. nwv.edu/oyez**.

Publications

Alexander, Kern, and David M. Alexander. *American Public School Law*. 4th ed. Belmont, Calif.: Wadsworth, 1998. *This venerable text has been providing solid and reliable information and analysis regarding school law for decades.*

LaMorte, Michael W. *School Law: Cases and Concepts*. 4th ed. Needham Heights, Mass.: Allyn and Bacon, 1995. *A comprehensive text that uses excerpts from judicial opinions to convey important legal principles.*

Provenzo, Eugene F., Jr. *Religious Fundamentalism and American Education*. Albany: State University of New York Press, 1990. *Describes and analyzes major Supreme Court decisions dealing with church and state censorship, family rights and education, and related issues.*

Rossow, Lawrence F., and Janice A. Hiniger. *Students and the Law*. Bloomington, Ind.: Phi Delta Kappa, 1991. *This slim "Fastback" includes chapters on freedom of speech, student publications, search and seizure, drug testing, religious activity, discipline in special education, and expulsions and suspensions.*

Wills, Garry. "H. R. Clinton's Case." *New York Review of Books*, March 5, 1992, pp. 3–5. *This article describes legal theories developed by attorney Hillary Rodham Clinton with respect to protecting the rights of children and adolescents in schools and other institutions.*

PART FOUR

Social Foundations

CHAPTER NINE

Culture, Socialization, and Education

We are all aware that the world is changing rapidly. Communications and the economy are being globalized, advanced skills increasingly are required to succeed at work, immigration has accelerated in the United States and many other countries, and family patterns are much different today than they were thirty years ago. Each such change is having a major impact on education at all levels from elementary school through the university.

Nevertheless, certain underlying imperatives and influences regarding the upbringing of children and youth necessarily continue to be important. Students' development still is strongly influenced by their families, their neighborhoods, and their friends, and by wider cultural and social forces such as the mass media, just as was true thirty or sixty or ninety years ago.

On the other hand, the specific ways in which such forces exert their influence on children and youth change over time. For example, it may be more difficult for teachers to capture students' attention in a digitized world that offers myriads of competing stimuli than it was years ago before video games, cable television, and multiplex cinemas. To respond adequately, educators must understand what is happening with respect to other institutions such as the family, the mass media, and the peer group, and how cultural and social trends are influencing the behaviors and ideas that students bring to the classroom.

As you read the chapter, keep these questions in mind:

- What cultural patterns influence instruction in schools?
- Do sex roles and sex differences influence learning and achievement? If so, how?
- How does the culture of the schools socialize the young?
- How have television and other mass media affected students?
- How do aspects of youth culture affect the schools?

A society ensures its unity and survival by means of culture. The attitudes, behaviors, and understandings that individuals learn in groups — the culture of a large group or society and the subcultures of smaller groups — are what enable people to communicate with one another and to function within a set of common rules. To provide for the transmission of culture and to allow society to function satisfactorily, children must be *acculturated* (taught the concepts, values, and behavior patterns of individuals sharing a common culture) and *socialized* (prepared to function first as young people and then as adults).

Many individuals and institutions play a part in acculturating and socializing children and youth. The family, of course, is most important for young children, but in modern societies formal institutions also help determine what a child learns and how well he or she is prepared to function in society.

This chapter provides an overview of the twin concepts, the **acculturation** and **socialization** of children and youth in our complex, technological society. It emphasizes how the culture of socializing institutions affects young people's development and achievement. It also considers how schools are influenced by the conditions and problems created by other social institutions.

Aspects of culture

The term **culture** has been broadly defined to encompass all the continually changing patterns of acquired behavior and attitudes transmitted among the members of a society. Culture is a way of thinking and behaving; it is a group's knowledge and customs, its traditions, memories, and written records, its shared rules and ideas, its accumulated beliefs, habits, and values. Neither a single individual, nor a group, nor an entire society can be understood without reference to culture. Habits of dress, of diet, of daily routine — the countless small details of ordinary life that seem to require little reflection — all this constitutes cultural identity.[1]

School as cultural agent

In modern societies, the school serves as perhaps the major institution (other than the family) devised by the adult generation for maintaining and perpetuating the culture. It supplies the tools necessary for survival and ensures the transmission of knowledge and values to future generations. It is a highly formal system for educating the young. In school the values, beliefs, and **norms** (rules of behavior) of the society are upheld and passed on, not only in the subject matter of lessons but also through the very structure and operation of the educational system.

In a diverse society such as our own, schools are responsible for helping young people learn to participate in a national culture, but they also must be sensitive to cultural differences and make sure that students from minority groups have equal opportunities to succeed in education. The challenges posed by this imperative are discussed in the sections of Chapter 11 on multicultural education.

A number of social institutions help to transmit culture to children and youth. For many societies, the most important historically have been the church, the peer group, the school, and of course the family. Some of these institutions, such as the

---

[1]Harry F. Wolcott, "Propriospect and the Acquisition of Culture," *Anthropology and Education Quarterly* (September 1991), pp. 251–273. See also Clifford Geertz, *After the Fact* (Cambridge, Mass.: Harvard University Press, 1995); Barbara J. Shade, Cynthia Kelly, Mary Oberg, *Creating Culturally Responsive Classrooms* (Washington, D.C.: American Psychological Association, 1997); and Bruce D. Perry, "Gray Matter," *Forbes ASAP,* November 30, 1998, p. 163.

Major socializing institutions

church, have become less influential in Western societies, while others, such as the mass media, have emerged as a socializing force. In this section we discuss several issues concerning the influence of family patterns on education. We then go on to consider the socializing role and educational implications of the peer group, the culture of the school, and the influence of television and other mass media.

The Family

Early influence of family

Although its organization varies, the family is the major early socializing agent in every society. As such, it is the first medium for transmitting culture to children. Because the family is the whole world to very young children, its members teach a child what matters in life, often without realizing the enormous influence they wield. Desires to achieve popularity, expectations about how boys and girls should behave, motivations to excel scholastically — these and other beliefs and values are passed from parent to child. The behaviors adults encourage and discourage and the ways in which they provide discipline also affect a child's orientation toward the world.

Home environment and preparation for school

Many children do well in school because their family environment has provided them with good preparation for succeeding in the traditional classroom. Others do poorly in part because they have not been well prepared and the schools generally have not made successful adjustments to overcome this disadvantage. (Possibilities for modifying instruction and other ways of helping unsuccessful students are described in later chapters.) Today, changes in the nature of the family have important implications for children's educational development and success in school. This section discusses several of the most important of these changes.[2]

Mothers who work

Increase in Working Mothers and Latchkey Children. The percentage of working mothers with children under eighteen has been increasing steadily in the United States since 1950. In that year, 18 percent of women with children were working; by 1994, 69 percent were working. There are several reasons for this increase in the percentage of mothers in the work force: better employment opportunities for women, rising divorce rates, family financial pressures that require a second income, increase in the age of the first marriage, and changes in traditional cultural attitudes dictating that mothers stay home.[3]

Child-care arrangements

As mothers have gone to work, changes have occurred in child-care arrangements. Today, only about one-fourth of the young children of working mothers are cared for in their homes, as compared with 57 percent in 1958. Researchers do not yet have a complete picture of the average quality of day-care and preschool arrangements for young children, but, as we point out later in this chapter, it is certain that such arrangements are less than satisfactory for many children.

The situation of **latchkey children** who return to unsupervised homes after school is particularly problematic because many of these children spend much of their time watching television or roaming the streets. National data indicate that

---

[2]Earl S. Schaefer, "Goals for Parent and Future-Parent Education: Research on Parental Beliefs and Behavior," *Elementary School Journal* (January 1991), pp. 239–248; and Elaine Woo, "Home Life Plays a Crucial Role in Students' Success or Failure," *Los Angeles Times,* May 18, 1998.

[3]Sally B. Kammerman, "What We Owe to Children Under Three," *The American Prospect* (Winter 1991), pp. 64–73; and Peter Brimelow, "Marriage Rings and Nose Rings," *Forbes,* February 10, 1997, pp. 140–141.

there may be as many as 6 million latchkey children who return to empty homes.[4] Partly for this reason, many school officials as well as civic and political leaders have taken action to expand opportunities that enable children and youth to participate in extended-day programs at school or recreational and learning activities at community centers after school.[5]

School and community responses

Single-Parent Families.   Recent decades also have seen a rapid increase in the percentage of households with a single parent, usually a never-married, divorced, or separated woman. Overall, single-parent families now constitute close to one-third of all households with children under 18. Much of the increase in these households results from the growing divorce rate, which has almost quadrupled in the United States since 1960.[6]

Some observers conclude that modern marriage is a roulette game, as likely as not to leave children at some point in single-parent families. For example, of all white children under six years of age, only 75 percent were living in two-parent households in 1996, compared with 95 percent in 1960. The figures for African American children and youth are even more startling: only 33 percent were living in two-parent households in 1996. Overall, about half of all young people under eighteen have been in a single-parent family for some part of their childhood.[7]

Impact on children

Much research has concentrated on the specific effects of growing up in a home where the father is absent. A few studies conclude that there is little measurable impact on children,[8] but most others find a variety of negative effects, including a greater likelihood that families will fall into poverty and that children will suffer serious emotional and academic problems. Several studies have also concluded that negative effects on children are weakest when adults in their home report that there is relatively little conflict in the home regardless of the marital status of their parent or parents.[9] The major reason this research has not been more conclusive is that it is so difficult to control for the effects of social class. A large percentage of families that "lost" a father also declined in social class, and this change in status makes it difficult to identify the separate effects of each factor.[10]

---

[4]Penelope Leach, *Children First* (New York: Viking, 1995); and Debbie Reese, "Latchkey Children," *Parent News* (May 1997), available at **ericps.crc.uiuc.edu/npin.**
[5]Wendy Schwartz, "After-School Programs for Urban Youth," *ERIC Clearinghouse on Urban Education Digests* (October 1996), available at **www.ed.gov;** and Marian F. Edelman, "Casting a Safety Net for School-Age Children," *CDF Reports* (September 1998), available at **www.childrensdefense.org.**
[6]D. Stanley Eitzen, "Problem Students: The Sociocultural Roots," *Phi Delta Kappan* (April 1992), pp. 584–590; Matthus Kalmun, "Mother's Occupational Status and Children's Schooling," *American Sociological Review* (April 1994), pp. 257–275; and Beth A. Young and Thomas M. Smith, *The Social Context of Education* (Washington, D.C.: National Center for Education Statistics, 1997).
[7]Linda J. Rubin and Sherry B. Borgers, "The Changing Family: Implications for Education," *Principal* (September 1991), pp. 11–13; *America's Children* (Washington, D.C.: Federal Interagency Forum, 1997), available at **www.cdc.gov;** and Westat, "Snapshots of America's families" (1999 posting at the Internet site of the Urban Institute), available at **www.urban.org.**
[8]Sonalde Desai, P. Lindsay Chase-Lansdale, and Robert T. Michael, "Mother or Market?" *Demography* (November 1989), pp. 545–561; Stephanie Coontz, "The American Family and the Nostalgia Trap," *Phi Delta Kappan* (March 1995), pp. K1–K10; and Lynn Smith, "Giving Context to Issues '90s Families Face," *Los Angeles Times,* November 12, 1997.
[9]Elaine C. Kamarck and William Galston, *Putting Children First* (Washington, D.C.: Progressive Policy Institute, 1990); and Maggie Gallagher and David Blankenhorn, "Family Feud," *American Prospect* (July–August, 1997), pp. 12–15.
[10]Alan C. Acock and K. Jill Kiecolt, "Is It Family Structure or Socioeconomic Status?" *Social Forces* (December 1989), pp. 553–571; and Margaret Talbot, "Love, American Style," *New Republic,* April 14, 1997, pp. 30–38.

Contemporary changes in the nature of the family—more working mothers, single-parent families, and children and women living in poverty—have important implications for children's educational development and success in school. *(© Francine Kenny/ Stock Boston)*

Recent studies have tried to adjust for such complexities. Teams of researchers in the United States and Great Britain concluded that divorce or separation has little independent effect on either boys or girls. Children whose parents reported marital problems but remained together subsequently experienced emotional and academic problems about as frequently as children whose parents divorced or separated. The researchers therefore concluded, "At least as much attention needs to be paid to the processes that occur in troubled, intact families as to the trauma that children suffer after their parents separate." However, Judith Wallerstein and her colleagues, who have been periodically interviewing a group of people whose parents divorced, found that serious problems such as depression, low academic performance, and negative interpersonal relationships frequently did not become apparent until ten or more years later.[11]

To help educators respond to the trend toward single-parent families, analysts have recommended steps like the following:[12]

---

[11]Andrew J. Cherlin et al., "Longitudinal Studies of Effects of Divorce on Children in Great Britain and the United States," *Science* (June 7, 1991), p. 1388; Judith S. Wallerstein, "The Long-Term Effects of Divorce on Children: A Review," *Journal of the American Academy of Child and Adolescent Psychiatry* (May 1991), pp. 349–360; and Teresa Moore, "Long-Term Diversified Performance," *San Francisco Chronicle,* June 3, 1997.

[12]P. A. Clay, *Single Parents and the Public Schools* (Columbia, Md.: National Committee for Citizens in Education, 1981); Adele M. Brodkin and Melba Coleman, "Teachers Can't Do It Alone," *Instructor* (May–June 1995), pp. 25–26; and Margaret C. Wang, Geneva D. Haertel, and Herbert J. Walberg, "What We Know About Coordinated School-Linked Services" (Paper prepared for Publication Series No. 1, Philadelphia, 1997), available at **www.temple.edu.**

Recommendations for schools

- Send copies of report cards and other communications to the noncustody parent.
- Include representation of single-parent families in the curriculum.
- Add library materials that show varied lifestyles and help children cope with divorce.
- Cooperate with other agencies in improving child-care arrangements before and after school.
- Conduct workshops to help teachers avoid any negative expectations they may have developed for children from single-parent families.
- Serve as advocates in providing appropriate help for individual students.

Rising child poverty rates

Children in Poverty.   Because of the substantial increase in single-parent families, which typically have much lower income than those with two or more employed adults, the percentage of children and youth growing up below the poverty line also has increased. The poverty rate among children and youth under age eighteen, which fluctuated around 15 percent in the late 1960s, has increased to more than 20 percent since the second half of the 1980s. Poverty rates are particularly high for children from minority groups, who are disproportionately likely to be in single-parent families: more than 40 percent of African American and Hispanic children and youth are growing up in families below the poverty line. The rising poverty rates among children and youth are also connected with what many observers have called the **feminization of poverty**. More than 60 percent of families headed by a single female parent are below the poverty line, compared to only about 10 percent of families with two parents.[13]

Day Care and the Public Schools.   In light of the large increase in maternal employment, provision of day-care arrangements for preschool children has become an important issue in U.S. society. Concerned with the inadequacy of day care, many state governments have acted to limit child-adult ratios, require more training for staff, and otherwise tighten requirements for licensing of day-care centers. In addition, an increasing number of employers have begun to sponsor or subsidize day-care services for the children of their employees.[14]

Attempts to improve day care

Controversies

Controversies over day care focus on a few major questions: whether government should encourage maternal employment by providing or subsidizing services; whether day care — even high-quality day care — has a positive or negative effect on children; whether day care should be provided through the public schools; and what types of programs should be offered. As for the first question, some "pro-family" groups oppose government support because they believe that maternal employment and day care are undermining the responsibility of the family and subjecting very young children to negative social influences. Some observers believe that, compared to children cared for at home, children who attend day care develop less secure and more aggressive personalities and are more likely to acquire severe communicable diseases.

---

[13]Mary Jo Bane and David T. Ellwood, "One Fifth of the Nation's Children: Why Are They Poor?" *Science*, September 8, 1989, pp. 1047–1053; and Elia Kacapyr, "How Hard Are Hard Times?" *American Demographics* (February 1998), pp. 30–31.
[14]Jane L. Ross, "Recipients Face Service Gaps and Supply Shortages," *GAO Testimony*, March 1, 1995; and "The Facts About Child Care," a 1998 posting at **www.childrensdefense.org**. This Web site regularly reports on issues and developments involving arrangements for caring for young children.

PROFESSIONAL PLANNING

for your first year

How Much Can You Help?

The Situation

Suppose that you are attending a conference designed to help educators deal with students who have serious difficulties outside school as well as inside — a vital subject, you think, because helping such students was one of your foremost goals in deciding to become a teacher. At the first session you attend, the primary speaker talks about households with severe problems: for example, homes where the parents neglect their children; families in which the parents are physically or psychologically abusive; and situations where the parents are unable or unwilling to provide the children with adequate food, clothing, shelter, or medical care. Not surprisingly, the speaker says, children from families such as these find it difficult to concentrate on learning. To help these students become productive adults, the speaker concludes, educators must take the lead in working with other institutions — social, psychological, and medical, among others — to help students overcome their multitude of problems.

You leave the session convinced that the speaker is correct. At the next session, however, another speaker argues that diverting significant attention and resources to activities outside the school will detract from instructional programming. This speaker contends that schools are organized primarily to advance academic learning and that teachers are trained in providing instruction, not in social work or psychology. Therefore, schools should remain schools, the speaker concludes; they should not try to take on the roles of families or social agencies. Now you are confused, because this speaker also sounds reasonable.

Thought Questions

1. What are some of the advantages and disadvantages involved in providing social services in the schools?
2. What are some of the obstacles that might need to be overcome in providing social services such as those advocated by the first speaker?
3. Which historical trend described in Chapter 5 does each of the viewpoints described above most closely resemble?
4. What is your personal viewpoint — which of the two speakers do you think has the more valid conclusion?
5. To what extent would a school's policies regarding provision of social services influence your decision to work there or not? How might you find out about its policies and ways in which they affect you as a teacher?

Research on the subject has been mixed. Early research tended to find that day care's effects on children were positive, but recent research has raised concerns that infant day care frequently may reduce children's sense of orderliness in the world while increasing hyperactivity and peer aggression. However, research also suggests that the quality of specific day-care programs may be more important than whether or not a child participated in day care.[15]

---

[15]J. Craig Peery, "Children at Risk: The Case Against Day Care," *The Family in America* (February 1991), pp. 1–10; and Lisbeth B. Schorr, "Helping Kids When It Counts," *Washington Post,* April 30, 1997, p. A21.

Concern for children at risk

Despite the controversies, support for the expansion and improvement of day care has been growing. So, too, has a concern for the welfare of low-income children whose parents cannot afford good nursery schools and who are "at risk" because they are poorly prepared for school. For example, the Committee for Economic Development's major reports (*Children in Need* and *The Unfinished Agenda*) have recommended that the federal government fund preschool education and assistance for all at-risk children through the age of five. This initiative would involve not just day care but a large expansion of preschool programs such as Head Start (see Chapter 11).[16]

"Superbabies"

Pressures on Children.   Awareness of the growing importance of education in contemporary society has stimulated many parents to overemphasize early learning. The desire to raise so-called superbabies appears to be particularly prevalent among middle-class parents, for whom the "ABCs" of childhood frequently center on "Anxiety, Betterment, [and] Competition." To meet the demands of such parents, many preschool and primary classrooms may be focusing so systematically on formal instruction that they are harming children in a misplaced effort to mass-produce "little Einsteins." The concern that many youngsters feel too much pressure to excel at an early age also extends to art, music, and other educational areas. Some developmental psychologists characterize such parental pressure as a type of "miseducation" that creates **hurried children** and deprives young people of childhood. Some responses to this problem include raising the age for enrolling in kindergarten and retaining five-year-olds who are not ready to advance to first grade for an additional year in kindergarten.[17]

School responses to "hurried" children

An "epidemic" of overindulgence?

Overindulged Children.   Whereas many children may be pressured to meet parental demands for early learning, others are overindulged by parents who provide them with too many material goods or protect them from challenges that would foster emotional growth. (Of course, some children may be simultaneously overpressured and overindulged.) Many observers believe that overindulgence is a growing tendency, particularly among young middle-class parents who are trying to provide their children with an abundance of advantages. Some psychologists argue that overindulgence is an "epidemic" afflicting as many as 20 percent of the children in the United States. These "cornucopia kids" may find it hard to endure frustration, and thus may present special problems for their teachers and classmates.[18]

Reports of abuse and neglect increasing

Child Abuse.   As we noted in Chapter 8, educators have a major responsibility to report any evidence that a student has been abused. Our society has become more aware of the extent and consequences of child abuse; the number of children reported as victims of abuse and neglect increased by nearly 90 percent since 1980. More than half these cases involved neglect of such needs as food, clothing, or

---

[16]Committee for Economic Development, *Children in Need: Investment Strategies for the Educationally Disadvantaged* (New York: Committee for Economic Development, 1987); Committee for Economic Development, *The Unfinished Agenda* (New York: Committee for Economic Development, 1991); and Kristin E. Smith, Loretta E. Bass, and Jason M. Fields, *Child Well-Being Indicators from the SIPP* (Washington, D.C.: U.S. Bureau of the Census, 1998).
[17]David Elkind, *The Hurried Child: Growing Up Too Fast* (New York: Addison-Wesley, 1981); David Elkind, *Miseducation: Preschoolers at Risk* (New York: Knopf, 1987); Nick Gillespie, "Child-Proofing the World," *Reason* (June 1997), pp. 20–27; and Linda Jacobson, "Reading Group NAEYC Issue Literacy Recommendations," *Education Week*, July 8, 1998.
[18]Bruce A. Baldwin, *Beyond the Cornucopia Kids* (New York: Direction Dynamics, 1988); Andree Brooks, *Children of Fast-Track Parents* (New York: Viking Penguin, 1989); and Susan Kristol, "Unfulfilled Expectations," *The Public Interest* (Summer 1995), pp. 111–115.

Subsequent problems of abused children

medical treatment; about one-seventh involved sexual mistreatment; and approximately one-fourth involved beatings or other physical violence. Many child-welfare agencies have been overburdened by the extent of the problem.[19]

Research on child abuse indicates that its victims tend to experience serious problems in emotional, intellectual, and social development. When they become adults, they have relatively high rates of alcohol and drug abuse, criminal behavior, learning disorders, and psychiatric disturbance. However, this research is difficult to interpret because a relatively high proportion of abuse victims are low-income children. Since poverty also is linked with developmental problems and delinquent or criminal behavior, it is not easy to separate out the influence of abuse. The relationship is by no means simple, since many abused children manage to avoid serious emotional and behavioral problems.[20]

School and teacher responses

In any case, educators must recognize that students who are abused or seriously neglected not only may have a difficult time learning but also may behave in ways that interfere with other students' learning. For this reason, organizations such as the Children's Television Workshop and the National Education Association have developed materials to help teachers deal with abused children, and they are working with other agencies to alleviate abuse and neglect.[21]

Homelessness and Runaways.   Periods of economic recession, rising real estate values and prices, "deinstitutionalization" of mentally ill persons, and other factors have led to a significant increase in the homeless population in the United States. In particular, more families and children are homeless now than in the past. In fact, in some smaller metropolitan areas, families with children may constitute one-third of the homeless population.

More children homeless

Several studies indicate that homeless children disproportionately suffer from child abuse and physical ill health. As we would expect, they also are relatively low in school attendance and achievement. The federal government, confronted with a severe budget deficit, has done relatively little to provide for homeless adults and children, and many local governments have been unwilling or unable to provide much assistance. However, many schools are striving to provide appropriate help. Some districts and schools, for instance, hire additional counselors, sponsor after-school programs, employ a full-time person to coordinate services with shelters for homeless families, or try to avoid transferring homeless children from one school to another.[22]

Implications for the schools

Runaways

A special category of homelessness applies to young people who flee from intolerable family situations. Frequently they wind up in temporary accommodations

[19]Enrique Garcia, "Visible but Unreported," *Child Abuse and Neglect* (September 1995), pp. 1083–1094; Patrick F. Fagan and Dorothy B. Hanks, "The Child Abuse Crisis" (Paper prepared for the Heritage Foundation, Washington, D.C., 1997), available at **www.heritage.org**; and Diana J. English, "The Extent and Consequences of Child Maltreatmnent," *The Future of Children* (Spring 1998), pp. 39–53, available at **epn.org**.
[20]Tamar Lewin, "Extent of the Physical Abuse of Children Outlined by Two Studies," *New York Times,* December 7, 1995; and Mary P. Larner, Carol S. Stevenson, and Richard E. Behrman, "Protecting Children from Abuse and Neglect," *The Future of Children* (Spring 1998), pp. 4–22, available at **epn.org**.
[21]Lisa Feder-Feitel, "Teachers Against Child Abuse," *Creative Classroom* (January–February 1992), pp. 55–62; and Chandra Muller and Michelle Frisco, "Social Institutions Serving Adolescents," in Kathryn Borman and Barbara Schneider, eds., *The Adolescent Years* (Chicago: University of Chicago Press, 1998), pp. 142–159.
[22]Yvonne Rafferty, "Meeting the Educational Needs of Homeless Children," *Educational Leadership* (January 1998), pp. 48–52; Ernest W. Brewer and Connie Hollingsworth, *Promising Practices* (Scottsdale, Ariz.: Holcomb, Hathaway, 1999); and Ruth Coniff, "Revolving Schools," *Rethinking Schools* (Winter 1998–1999), pp. 16–17.

or on the streets in big cities. The numbers are difficult to estimate, but some observers believe that a million or more teenagers run away from their homes in any given year. Not surprisingly, runaways are at risk for drug abuse and AIDS infection, are very likely to be the victims or instigators of crime, and rarely complete high school.[23]

Over one-third million in foster care

Children in Foster Care. Among the fallout associated with single-parent families, homelessness, child abuse, and the feminization of poverty has been a rapid increase in the number of children in foster-care homes and institutions. By the late 1980s a congressional committee reported that more than one-third of a million children were in foster care. Since the achievement level of children in foster care is far below average even after they have been in care for several years, it is apparent that the guardians and teachers of many of these children are not providing adequate preparation to succeed in school and in adult careers.[24]

Overall effects on children

Assessment of Trends Related to the Family. The various interrelated trends we have been discussing have produced a significant change in the structure and function of families in the United States. Research does not conclusively establish that all the results are damaging to children; in some respects, trends like maternal employment lead to gains for children. However, many studies indicate that maternal employment and life in a single-parent or divorced family have detrimental effects for many children. Trends such as the rise in homelessness and poverty are obviously even more damaging.

Decline of the nuclear family

Difficulties for schools magnified

Historically, according to many analysts, our system of universal education drew support from the development of the **nuclear family** (two parents living with their children), which grew to prominence in Western societies during the last two centuries. The nuclear family has been described as highly child centered, devoting many of its resources to preparing children for success in school and later in life. With the decline of the nuclear family since World War II, the tasks confronting educators appear to have grown more difficult.[25]

The "postnuclear" family

David Popenoe, examining family trends in highly industrialized countries such as Sweden and the United States, concluded that these trends are creating a "postnuclear" family in which the emphasis is on "individualism" (individual self-fulfillment, pleasure, self-expression, and spontaneity), as contrasted with the child-centered "familism" of the nuclear family. Adults, Popenoe further concluded, "no longer need children in their lives, at least not in economic terms. The problem is that children . . . still need adults . . . who are motivated to provide them with . . . an abundance of time, patience, and love." Many social scientists also worry about the "total contact time" between parents and children. Some

[23]Mark D. Janus et al., *Adolescent Runaways: Causes and Consequences* (New York: Lexington, 1987); and Nathaniel E. Terrell, "Street Life," *Youth and Society* (March 1997), pp. 267–290.
[24]Jane Gross, "Collapse of Inner-City Families Creates America's New Orphans," *New York Times,* March 29, 1992, pp. 1, 20; Mary-Lou Weisman, "When Parents Are Not in the Best Interests of the Child," *Atlantic Monthly* (July 1994), pp. 42–63; and Laura Effel, "Foster Care Reform," 1997 posting at **www.fostercare.org/FPHP**. This Web site provides a wealth of information on various aspects of foster care.
[25]Edward Shorter, *The Making of the Modern Family* (New York: Basic Books, 1975). See also Lawrence Stone, *Road to Divorce: England 1537–1987* (New York: Oxford University Press, 1991); Diana Schaub, "Marriage Envy," *The Public Interest* (Winter 1996), pp. 99–102; and Marge Scherer, "On Our Changing Family Values," *Educational Leadership* (April 1996), pp. 61–64.

GETTING TO THE SOURCE

La Ciutat Educadora
The Educating City

Ajuntament de Barcelona

The Problems of Modern Families

URIE BRONFENBRENNER

Problems in raising children and maintaining supportive family arrangements are apparent throughout the world. Urie Bronfenbrenner reviewed many of these problems as part of an address given at an international conference on "The Educating City." Bronfenbrenner is perhaps best known for his analysis of results of preschool programs for poverty children in the United States and his comparisons of child-raising institutions in the United States and the former Soviet Union.

It is not only the poor . . . for whom developmental processes are now at risk. In today's world, the well-educated and the well-to-do are no longer protected; in the past other highly vulnerable contexts have evolved that cut across the domains of class and culture. Recent studies reveal that a major disruptive factor in the lives of families and their children is the increasing instability, inconsistency, and hecticness of daily family life. This growing trend is found in both developed and developing countries, but has somewhat different origins in these two worlds. Yet the debilitating effect on child rearing processes and outcomes is much the same. I begin with an example from my own society, since, in this respect, the United States is probably — and regrettably — a world leader.

In a world in which both parents usually have to work, often at a considerable distance from home, every family member, through the waking hours from morning till night, is "on the run." The need to coordinate conflicting demands of job and child care, often involving varied arrangements that shift from day to day, can produce a situation in which everyone has to be transported several times a day in different directions, usually at the same time — a state of affairs research indicates that this time has declined as much as 40 percent during the past few decades.[26]

In the context of these family changes and the problems they create, social agencies established to help children and youth are often too overloaded to provide services effectively. William Zinsmeister has described how "many child-protection agencies are now doing little more than preventing murder, and sometimes they fail even to do that." For example, one Maryland social worker, when asked why a six-year-old had not been removed from a known crack house run by his mother, responded that there were "twenty similar cases on his desk, and that he didn't have time to go through the time-consuming process of taking a child from a parent" unless there was an immediate emergency.[27]

In the words of the National Commission on Children, though most American children remain "healthy, happy, and secure," many are now "in jeopardy." Even

Agencies overloaded

Many children in jeopardy

---

[26]David Popenoe, *Disturbing the Nest* (New York: Aldine de Gruyter, 1988), pp. 329–330; and David Popenoe, "Where's Papa?" *Utne Reader* (September–October 1997), pp. 68–71, 104–106. See also David Blankenhorn, *Fatherless America* (New York: Basic Books, 1995); and Eric P. Olsen, "Heart of Darkness," *The World and I* (May 1997), available at **www.worldandi.com.**
[27]William Zinsmeister, "Growing Up Scared," *Atlantic Monthly* (June 1990), p. 67; Allan Wolfe, "The New American Dilemma," *New Republic*, April 13, 1992, pp. 30–37; and G. Thomas Kingsley, Joseph B. McNeely, and James O. Gibson, *Community Building Coming of Age* (Washington, D.C.: Urban Institute, 1998).

that prompted a foreign colleague to comment, "It seems to me that, in your country, most children are being brought up in moving vehicles."

Other factors contributing to the disruption of daily family life include long "commutes" to and from work; jobs that require one or the other parent to be away for extended periods of time; the frequent changes in employment; the associated moves for the whole family or those that leave the rest of the family behind waiting till the school term ends, or adequate housing can be found; and, last but far from least, the increasing number of divorces, remarriages, and redivorces. (Incidentally, the most recent evidence suggests that the disruptive effects of remarriage on children may be even greater than those of divorce.)

What are the developmental consequences of family hecticness? Once again, the observed outcomes are educational impairment and behaviour problems, including long-term effects that now also encompass children of the well-educated and the well-to-do.

Questions

1. What is "family hecticness"? What changes in policies or customs might reduce its negative effects?
2. In what ways were children in earlier generations better off than they may be today?
3. Who or what is most responsible for overcoming contemporary problems that make it difficult to raise children?
4. What, if anything, can or should a classroom teacher do to take account of family "hecticness," instability in family life, or other problems that may be important in students' home environment?

Source: Urie Bronfenbrenner, "Cities Are for Families," in *La Ciutat Educadora* (Barcelona: Ajuntament de Barcelona, 1990), cover, pp. 545–546. Reprinted with permission of the author.

those children who are free from extreme misfortune may confront difficult conditions. "They too attend troubled schools and frequent dangerous streets. The adults in their lives are often equally hurried and distracted. . . . The combined effects are that too many children enter adulthood without the skills or motivation to contribute to society."[28]

The Peer Group

Influence of peer groups

Whereas family relationships may constitute a child's first experience of group life, peer-group interactions soon begin to make their powerful socializing effects felt. From play group to teenage clique, the peer group affords young people many significant learning experiences — how to interact with others, how to be accepted by others, and how to achieve status in a circle of friends. Peers are equals in a way parents and their children or teachers and their students are not. A parent or a teacher sometimes can force young children to obey rules they neither understand nor like,

[28]National Commission on Children, *Beyond Rhetoric: A New American Agenda for Children and Families* (Washington, D.C.: U.S. Government Printing Office, 1991), pp. xvii–xviii. See also Anne J. Spencer and Robert B. Shapiro, *Helping Students Cope with Divorce* (West Nyack, N.Y.: Center for Applied Research in Education, 1995); and David Johnson, et al., *America's Children 1998* (Washington, D.C.: U.S. Office of Management and Budget Interagency Forum on Child and Family Statistics, 1998), available at **www.childstats.gov**.

To overcome "peer suppression of academic activity," specialists in cooperative learning recommend that teachers help students develop positive peer relationships conducive to learning. *(© Tony Velez/Photo Edit)*

but peers do not have formal authority to do this; thus the true meaning of exchange, cooperation, and equity can be learned more easily in the peer setting.

Peer groups increase in importance as the child grows up and reach maximum influence in adolescence, by which time they sometimes dictate much of a young person's behavior both in and out of school. Some researchers believe that peer groups are more important now than in earlier periods — partly because some children have little close contact with their parents and few strong linkages with the larger society.[29]

Peer Culture and the School.   Educators are particularly concerned with the peer group and with the associated characteristics of student culture within the school. A landmark 1961 study by James Coleman found that high-school students gained the esteem of their peers by a combination of friendliness and popularity, athletic prowess, an attractive appearance and personality, or possession of valued skills and objects (cars, clothes, records). In other words, scholastic success was not among the favored characteristics; in general, the peer culture hindered rather than reinforced the school's academic goals. Thirty years later, Coleman still believed that peer "suppression of academic activity" had a negative effect in many schools.[30]

Qualities that students esteem

---

[29]Janis B. Kupersmidt et al., "Childhood Aggression and Peer Relations in the Context of Family and Neighborhood Factors," *Child Development* (April 1995), pp. 361–375; Lawrence Steinberg, *Adolescence,* 4th ed. (New York: McGraw-Hill, 1996); and Malcolm Gladwell, "Do Parents Matter?" *New Yorker,* August 17, 1998, pp. 56–65.
[30]James S. Coleman, *The Adolescent Society* (New York: Free Press, 1961); and James S. Coleman, "Reflections on Schools and Adolescents," in Derek L. Burleson, ed., *Reflections* (Bloomington, Ind.: Phi Delta Kappa, 1991), p. 64. See also John W. Maag et al., "Social and Behavioral Predictors of Popular, Rejected, and Average Children," *Educational and Psychological Measurement* (April 1995), pp. 196–205; and Stanford T. Gotto, "Nerds, Normal People, and Homeboys," *Anthropology and Education Quarterly* (March 1997), pp. 70–84.

TABLE 9.1	Secondary Students' Responses to the Question "What Is the *One* Best Thing About This School?"

	My Friends	**Sports**	**Good Student Attitudes**	**Nothing**	**Classes I'm Taking**	**Teachers**	**Other**
Junior high respondents	37%	15%	10%	8%	7%	5%	18%
Senior high respondents	34	12	12	8	7	3	24

Source: Compiled from data in John I. Goodlad, *A Place Called School* (New York: McGraw-Hill, 1984), pp. 76–77.

Importance of friends, looks, athletics

More recent research has continued to support the conclusion that **peer culture** is a major socialization experience.[31] For example, Bradford Brown and Wendy Theobald surveyed ninth and tenth graders and found that 72 percent said the "best thing about school" is either one's friends or extracurricular activities. Similarly, John Goodlad and his colleagues asked more than seventeen thousand students, "What is the one best thing about this school?"; as shown in Table 9.1, "my friends" was by far the most frequent response. Respondents also were asked to identify the types of students they perceived to be most popular. Only 10 percent of respondents in junior and senior high schools selected "smart students"; instead, 70 percent of students selected either "good looking students" or "athletes." Pondering these data, Goodlad concluded that "physical appearance, peer relationships, and games and sports" are not just concerns carried into the school; these phenomena "appear to prevail" there. Noting that Coleman and others reported similar findings in earlier decades, he further wondered "why we have taken so little practical account of them in schools."[32]

Suggestions for teachers

To foster peer relationships that support rather than impede learning, some educators recommend conducting activities that encourage students to learn cooperatively. In addition, teachers should promote children's interaction with peers, teach interpersonal and small-group skills, assign children responsibility for the welfare of their peers, and encourage older children to interact with younger children. Such steps may help counteract peer pressure for antisocial behavior.[33]

Participation in Extracurricular Activities. Polls continually show that students consider their cooperation and interaction with peers in extracurricular activities to

[31]B. Bradford Brown and Wendy Theobald, "Learning Contexts Beyond the Classroom," in Kathryn Bowman and Wendy Theobald, eds., *The Adolescent Years* (Chicago: University of Chicago Press, 1998), p. 109.

[32]John I. Goodlad, *A Place Called School* (New York: McGraw-Hill, 1984), p. 75; John Goodlad, *Educational Renewal* (San Francisco: Jossey-Bass, 1994); and Mark F. Goldberg, "A Portrait of John Goodlad," *Educational Leadership* (March 1995), pp. 82–85. See also Robert Feirsen, "From Elementary to Middle School," *Middle School Journal* (January 1997), pp. 10–15; and Mara Sapon-Shevin et al., "Everyone Here Can Play," *Educational Leadership* (September 1998), pp. 42–45.

[33]David W. Johnson, Roger T. Johnson, and Edythe J. Holubec, *The New Circles of Learning* (Alexandria, Va.: Association for Supervision and Curriculum Development, 1994); and Lora L. Qualey and Cynthia A. Erdley, "Sociometrically Neglected Children" (Paper presented at the annual meeting of the American Educational Research Association, San Diego, April 1998).

be a highlight of their school experience. Many educators believe this participation is a positive force in the lives of students, but the effect has been difficult to measure. The difficulty lies in determining whether participation in extracurricular activities is a cause or an effect of other aspects of students' development. It is known, for example, that students who participate in many extracurricular activities generally have higher grades, other things being equal, than those who do not participate. It may also be true, however, that students with higher grades are more likely to participate than are those with lower grades.

Positive impact on educational aspirations

Despite these difficulties, research does tend to support the conclusion that participation — especially in athletics, service, leadership activities, and music — fosters students' aspirations to higher educational and occupational attainment (for example, more years of school completed later). The research also suggests that positive effects are more likely in small schools than in large schools.[34]

Importance for teachers

These conclusions have great significance for educators. Participation outside the academic curriculum probably is more "manipulable" (alterable by the school) than most other factors related to educational outcomes. For example, home environments may cause problems, but educators can rarely change a student's home environment. But teachers and administrators can promote student participation in extracurricular activities, and this may be one of the most effective ways to improve students' performance.

Causes and prevention of bullying

Research on Bullies.   In recent years, research has begun to address the problems caused by "bullies" — antisocial youngsters who severely harass their peers either inside or outside the school. Factors frequently cited as causing some children to behave as bullies include neglect and abuse in their homes, the influence of television, and a lack of social skills that leads to a cycle of aggressive behavior and dislike by peers. Educators are concerned about not only the harm bullies do to others but also the tendency of bullies to exhibit criminal behavior as adults. Some approaches for modifying the behavior of bullies include behavioral contracts, instruction in peaceful conflict resolution, classroom activities designed to reduce teasing, and parental involvement in supervising behavior.[35]

The Culture of the School

Aspects of school culture

Education in school, compared with learning experiences in the family or peer-group context, is carried on in relatively formal ways. Group membership is not voluntary but is determined by age, aptitudes, and frequently gender. Students are tested and evaluated; they are told when to sit, when to stand, how to walk through hallways, and so on. The rituals of school assemblies, athletic events, and graduation ceremonies — as well as the school insignia, songs, and cheers — all convey the culture of the school and socialize students. A number of scholars have focused

---

[34]Luther B. Otto, "Extracurricular Activities," in H. Walberg, ed., *Improving Educational Standards and Productivity* (Berkeley, Calif.: McCutchan, 1982), pp. 217–227; Alyce Holland and Thomas Andre, "Participation in Extracurricular Activities in Secondary Schools," *Review of Educational Research* (Winter 1987), pp. 437–466; and Alex Poinsett, *The Role of Sports in Youth Development* (New York: Carnegie Corporation, 1996).

[35]Peter Smith and Sonia Sharp, *School Bullying* (New York: Routledge, 1995); Mary Jordan, "When Schoolyard Pranks Become Deadly," *Washington Post National Weekly Edition*, January 22–28, 1996, p. 17; and Derek Glover and Netta Cartwright with Denis Gleeson, *Towards Bully-Free Schools* (London: Open University Press, 1998).

on school culture in the United States and what it means for both students and teachers.[36]

Institutionalizing Disadvantages.   In a study of working-class adolescents, Ellen Brantlinger found that their disadvantages of background were often compounded by the social and organizational aspects of their schools. School practices like special education and tracking — designed to address differences among students — reinforced "attitudes that high-income students are talented and worthy and low-income students are inferior." The low-income adolescents in this study seldom were successful academically, and they acquired negative self-concepts. "There is widespread acknowledgement," Brantlinger concluded, "that students from various social, ethnic, and racial backgrounds differ in the extent to which their performance meets school standards, but accepted school practices meant to address such differences result in segregation, differentiation, and humiliation for many children."[37]

Practices that backfire

Student Roles and the Hidden Curriculum.   Gita Kedar-Voivodas has examined teacher expectations for student roles — that is, desired student behaviors and characteristics — in the elementary classroom. She identified three main types of expected student role: the pupil role, the receptive learner role, and the active learner role.

The *pupil role* is one in which teachers expect students to be "patient, docile, passive, orderly, conforming, obedient and acquiescent to rules and regulations, respectful to authority, easily controllable, and socially adept." The *receptive learner role* requires students to be "motivated, task-oriented, . . . good achievers, and as such, receptive to the institutional demands of the academic curriculum." This role also requires that students work independently and efficiently despite distractions and that they adequately perform homework and class assignments. In the *active learner role*, according to Kedar-Voivodas, students go "beyond the established academic curriculum both in terms of the content to be mastered and in the processes" of learning. Traits of the active learner include "curiosity, active probing and exploring, challenging authority, an independent and questioning mind, and insistence on explanations." She noted that many educational philosophers, among them John Dewey and Maria Montessori, have stressed the value of active learning.[38]

Three major student roles

Kedar-Voivodas also found, however, that students exemplifying the active learner role sometimes are rejected by teachers. That is, many teachers are negative about children who are active, independent, and assertive. There is a large difference, Kedar-Voivodas said, between the school's "academic" curriculum, which

Rejecting the active learner

[36]Edgar Z. Friedenberg, *Coming of Age in America* (New York: Random House, 1965); Edward Wynne, *Growing Up Suburban* (Austin: University of Texas Press, 1977); Peter Schrag, "Reform School Politics," *The Nation,* October 9, 1995, pp. 397–399; and Ralph Parish and Frank Aquila, "Cultural Ways of Working and Believing in School," *Educational Leadership* (December 1996), pp. 298–305.

[37]Ellen Brantlinger, "Social Class in School: Students' Perspectives," *Phi Delta Kappa Research Bulletin* (March 1995), p. 4. See also Ricardo D. Stanton-Salazer, "A Social Capital Framework for Understanding the Socialization of Racial Minority Children and Youth," *Harvard Educational Review* (Spring 1997), pp. 1–40.

[38]Gita Kedar-Voivodas, "The Impact of Elementary Children's School Roles and Sex Roles on Teacher Attitudes: An Interactional Analysis," *Review of Educational Research* (Fall 1983), p. 417.

demands successful mastery of cognitive material, and its "hidden" curriculum, which demands "institutional conformity."[39]

Effects of the hidden curriculum

The **hidden curriculum** — a term used by many critics of contemporary schools — is what students learn, other than academic content, from what they do or are expected to do in school. In addition to teaching children to conform passively in the classroom, the hidden curriculum may be preparing students with economic disadvantages to be docile workers later in life. It can communicate negative racial and sexual stereotypes through material included in (or omitted from) textbooks. By putting too much emphasis on the competition for grades, the hidden curriculum may also teach students that "beating the system" is more important than anything else.[40]

Culture of the Classroom. In his study of classroom processes in elementary schools, Philip Jackson found a diversity of specific subjects but few different types of classroom activity. The terms *seatwork, group discussion, teacher demonstration,* and *question-and-answer period* described most of what happened in the classroom. Further, these activities were performed according to well-defined rules, such as "no loud talking during seatwork" and "raise your hand if you have a question." The teacher served as a "combination traffic cop, judge, supply sergeant, and timekeeper." In this cultural system, the classroom often becomes a place where things happen "not because students want them to, but because it is time for them to occur."[41]

Routine classroom activities

Stress on order, obedience

The "rules of order" that characterize most elementary school classrooms, Jackson concluded, focus on prevention of disturbances. Thus the prevailing socialization pattern in the culture of the school and classroom places its greatest emphasis on what Kedar-Voivodas called the obedient "pupil" role. Other studies have reached essentially the same conclusion. For example, "A Study of Schooling" conducted by John Goodlad and his colleagues described the following widespread patterns:[42]

1. The classroom is generally organized as a group that the teacher treats as a whole. This pattern seems to arise from the need to maintain "orderly relationships" among twenty to thirty people in a small space. Socialization into this pattern is "rather thoroughly achieved" by the end of the primary grades.

Enthusiasm controlled

2. "Enthusiasm and joy and anger are kept under control." As a result, the general emotional tone is "flat" or "neutral."

3. Most student work involves "listening to teachers, writing answers to questions, and taking tests and quizzes." Students rarely learn from one another.

---

[39]Ibid., p. 418. See also Michael Apple, *Education and Power,* 2nd ed. (New York: Routledge, 1995); and Chris Richards, "Popular Culture, Politics, and the Curriculum," *Educational Researcher* (June–July 1998), pp. 32–34.

[40]William Bigelow, "Inside the Classroom: Social Vision and Critical Pedagogy," *Teachers College Record* (Spring 1990), pp. 437–448; Maggie Rosen, "The Hidden Curriculum," *Principal* (September 1995), p. 60; and Patricia Burdell, "Young Mothers As High School Students," *Education and Urban Society* (February 1998), pp. 207–223.

[41]Philip W. Jackson, *Life in Classrooms* (New York: Holt, 1968), pp. 8–9, 13. See also Philip W. Jackson, *The Practice of Teaching* (New York: Teachers College Press, 1986); and Fritz K. Oser, "Ethnographic Inquiries into the Moral Complexity of Classroom Interaction," *Educational Researcher* (April 1995), pp. 33–34.

[42]Goodlad, *A Place Called School,* pp. 123–124, 236, 246. See also Donald J. Willower and William L. Boyd, *Willard Waller on Education and Schools* (Berkeley, Calif.: McCutchan, 1989); Erwin Flaxman and A. Harry Passow, eds., *Changing Populations Changing Schools* (Chicago: University of Chicago Press, 1995); and Thomas Armstrong, *Awakening Genius in the Classroom* (Alexandria, Va.: Association for Supervision and Curriculum Development, 1998).

Little use is made of audiovisual equipment, guest lecturers, or field trips. Except in physical education, vocational education, and the arts, there is little "hands-on activity." Textbooks and workbooks generally constitute the "media of instruction."

4. These patterns become increasingly rigid and predominant as students proceed through the grades.

Curiosity not encouraged

5. Instruction seldom goes beyond "mere possession of information." Little effort is made to arouse students' curiosity or to emphasize rational thinking.

In summary, Goodlad wrote, students "rarely planned or initiated anything, read or wrote anything of some length, or created their own products. And they scarcely ever speculated on meanings."[43]

Why so much passive learning?

As we discuss elsewhere in this book, such systematic emphasis on passive learning by rote is in opposition to most contemporary ideas of what education should accomplish. Why, then, do so many classrooms so often function in this way? This is a very important question, and many analysts have addressed it.[44] Some of the reasons they have offered are as follows:

1. *Institutional requirements to maintain order* As Jackson points out, a multitude of routines are devised to govern the interactions between twenty or thirty students and a teacher. Researchers use terms like *institutional realities* and *organizational dynamics* to describe the forces that translate a need for order into an emphasis on passive learning.[45]

Institutional realities

2. *Student preferences for passive learning.* The degree to which many students resist active learning should not be underestimated. As Walter Doyle writes, students may "restrict the amount of output they give to a teacher to minimize the risk of exposing a mistake." By holding back, students can also get other students or the teacher to help them. As one older student said, "Yeah, I hardly do nothing. All you gotta do is act dumb and Mr. Y will tell you the right answer. You just gotta wait, you know, and he'll tell you."[46]

Students hold back

3. *Accommodations, bargains, and compromises between students and teachers.* In a context that combines institutional requirements for order with student preference for passive learning, the teacher and students may reach an *accommodation* or *bargain* by which they *compromise* on a set of minimal standards. For example, Martin Haberman has observed what he calls "the Deal" that is present in many urban classrooms: students are nondisruptive as long as the teacher ignores the

Making a deal for low standards

---

[43]John I. Goodlad, "A Study of Schooling: Some Findings and Hypotheses," *Phi Delta Kappan* (March 1983), p. 468. See also Anna Maria Villegas, *Culturally Responsive Teaching* (Princeton, N.J.: Educational Testing Service, 1991); Bill Bigelow et al., *Rethinking Our Classrooms* (Milwaukee: Rethinking Schools, 1994); and Ronald E. Comfort and Jacqueline Giorgi, "In a Different Voice," *High School Journal* (February/March 1997), pp. 178–183.

[44]Larry Cuban, "A Fundamental Puzzle of School Reform," *Phi Delta Kappan* (January 1988), pp. 341–344; Gerald W. Bracey, "Change and Continuity in Elementary Education," *Principal* (January 1996), pp. 17–21; and Max Angus, *The Ruler of School Reform* (London: Falmer, 1998).

[45]Goodlad, "A Study of Schooling," pp. 469–470; Barbara B. Tye, "The Deep Structure of Schooling," *Phi Delta Kappan* (November 1987), pp. 281–284; and Daniel U. Levine and Rayna F. Levine, *Society and Education,* 9th ed. (Needham Heights, Mass.: Allyn and Bacon, 1996.)

[46]Walter Doyle, "Academic Work," *Review of Educational Research* (Summer 1983), pp. 184–185. See also David Tyack and William Tobin, "The 'Grammar' of Schooling," *American Educational Research Journal* (Fall 1994), pp. 453–479; and David Tyack and Larry Cuban, *Tinkering Toward Utopia* (Cambridge, Mass.: Harvard University Press, 1995).

GETTING TO THE SOURCE

Authority and Subversion

WILLARD WALLER

illard Waller (1899–1946) is remembered mostly for essays examining the balance of freedom and order in the classroom. Published originally in 1932, his *Sociology of Teaching* was an influential work that helped create a new field of study — the sociology of education. Waller believed it desirable to emphasize active participation and creativity in the learning process, but he was pessimistic about the prospects for doing this. In his view, the culture of classrooms and school tends to encourage teacher domination that in turn produces alienation among students.

THE SOCIOLOGY OF TEACHING

BY
WILLARD WALLER, Ph.D.

NEW YORK
RUSSELL & RUSSELL

The teacher-pupil relationship is a form of institutionalized dominance and subordination. Teacher and pupil confront each other in the school with an original conflict of desires, and however much that conflict may be reduced in amount, or however much it may be hidden, it still remains. The teacher represents the adult group, ever the enemy of the spontaneous life of groups of children. The teacher represents the formal curriculum, and his interest is in imposing that curriculum upon the children in the form of tasks; pupils are much more interested in life in their own world than in the desiccated bits of adult life which teachers have to offer. The teacher represents the established social order in the school, and his interest is in maintaining that order, whereas pupils have only a negative interest in that feudal superstructure. Teacher and pupil confront each other with attitudes from which the underlying hostility can never be altogether removed. Pupils are the material in which teachers are supposed to produce results. Pupils are human beings striving to realize themselves in their own spontaneous manner, striving to produce their own results in their own way. Each of these hostile parties stands in the way of the other; in so far as the aims of either are realized, it is at the sacrifice of the aims of the other.

fact that they are not diligent in their classwork. The widespread existence of such "ABCs" has been documented in a number of major studies.[47] Michael Sedlak and his colleagues called such an arrangement "a complex, tacit conspiracy to avoid rigorous, demanding academic inquiry."[48]

Which students get attention?

4. *Teachers' allocation of attention.* Many teachers feel compelled to give the largest share of their time and attention to a limited number of students. In some cases, these will be the slowest students — whomever the teacher perceives as most in need of help. In many other cases, however, attention goes primarily to the brightest students, who frequently are perceived to benefit the most from extra attention. This attitude is particularly prevalent if there are so many "slow" students that the task of helping all of them seems almost impossible.

Helen Gouldner and her colleagues found these dynamics in an inner-city, all-black elementary school with a large proportion of students from low-income

[47]For examples, see Theodore R. Sizer, *Horace's Compromise* (Boston: Houghton Mifflin, 1984); Arthur Powell, Eleanor Farrar, and David Cohen, *The Shopping Mall High School* (Boston: Houghton Mifflin, 1985); Robert I. Hampel, *The Last Little Citadel* (Boston: Houghton Mifflin, 1986); and Martin Haberman, "The Ideology of Nonwork in Urban Schools," *Phi Delta Kappan* (March 1997), pp. 499–503.
[48]Michael W. Sedlak et al., *Selling Students Short* (New York: Teachers College Press, 1986), p. 13. See also Dennis Sparks, "A 'Friendly Conversation' with Ted Sizer," *Journal of Staff Development* (Winter 1991), pp. 42–46; and M. Lee Manning and Leroy G. Baruth, *Students at Risk* (Boston: Allyn and Bacon, 1995).

Authority is on the side of the teacher. The teacher nearly always wins. In fact, he must win, or he cannot remain a teacher. Children, after all, are usually docile, and they certainly are defenseless against the machinery with which the adult world is able to enforce its decisions; the result of the battle is foreordained. Conflict between teachers and students therefore passes to the second level. All the externals of conflict and of authority having been settled, the matter chiefly at issue is the meaning of those externals. Whatever the rules that the teacher lays down, the tendency of the pupils is to empty them of meaning. By mechanization of conformity, by "laughing off" the teacher or hating him out of all existence as a person, by taking refuge in self-initiated activities that are always just beyond the teacher's reach, students attempt to neutralize teacher control. The teacher, however, is striving to read meaning into the rules and regulations, to make standards really standards, to force students really to conform. This is a battle which is not unequal. The power of the teacher to pass rules is not limited, but his power to enforce rules is, and so is his power to control attitudes toward rules.

Questions

1. Are students today more or less interested than their counterparts sixty years ago in "life in their own world," as contrasted with "desiccated bits of adult life" offered by teachers?
2. Is it still true that children "are usually docile" and are "defenseless against the machinery with which the adult world is able to enforce its decisions"? Has anything happened that might suggest a modification in this observation?
3. Have you ever participated in an activity undertaken to "neutralize teacher control"? What will you do if your own students some day initiate similar activities?

Source: Willard Waller, *The Sociology of Teaching* (New York: Russell & Russell, 1961), cover, pp. 195–196. Copyright © by Russell & Russell. Reprinted by permission of John Wiley & Sons.

home environments that did not prepare them to function well in the classroom. The few students who were well prepared (and who generally came from families with relatively high status) were the "pets" — those whom teachers helped throughout their school careers. The largest group of students (the "nobodies") received relatively little teacher attention and generally were neither disruptive nor particularly successful. The remaining students, a small group of "troublemakers," were unable or unwilling to conform to the routine demands of the classroom. These patterns were well in line with the school's "sorting and selecting" function because the teachers, most of whom were African American, could feel they were promoting success for at least some black students in a difficult learning environment.[49]

Conformity as a social demand

5. *Society's requirement that students learn to conform.* Underlying schools' emphasis on passive learning is the reality that young people must learn to function in other social institutions outside the school. Since most people in contemporary society must cope with large economic, political, and social institutions, children must be socialized to follow appropriate routines and regulations. Philip Jackson

---

[49]Helen Gouldner, *Teachers' Pets, Troublemakers, and Nobodies* (Westport, Conn.: Greenwood, 1978), pp. 133–134. This self-fulfilling prophecy and the way it operated at the school studied by Gouldner and her colleagues are described at greater length in Ray C. Rist, *The Urban School: A Factory for Failure* (Cambridge, Mass.: MIT Press, 1973). See also Alfred L. Joseph and C. Anne Brossard, "Tracking," *Social Work in Education* (April 1998), pp. 110–120.

summarizes this part of a school's socialization mission as follows: "It is expected that children will adapt to the teacher's authority by becoming 'good workers' and 'model students.' The transition from classroom to factory or office is made easily by those who have developed 'good work habits' in their early years." This goal of schooling is part of the "hidden curriculum" mentioned earlier.[50]

Burdens on teachers

6. *Teacher overload.* It is difficult for teachers to provide active, meaningful learning experiences when they must cope with the demands of large classes and class loads, a variety of duties and tasks outside their classrooms, pressures to "cover" a very wide range of material and skills, and other such responsibilities.[51] As we document elsewhere in this book, there is growing recognition of the heavy burdens on teachers, and many reformers are working to reduce teacher overload.

Many additional reasons could be offered to explain why instructional patterns in the classroom have been relatively unaffected by contemporary learning theory, but most of them in some way involve institutional constraints that favor passive, rote learning.[52] Overcoming such constraints requires significant innovations in school organization and pedagogy, as we will see in Chapter 16.

Passive learning in working-class schools

Before concluding this discussion, we should mention that research indicates that passive, rote learning is more likely to be emphasized in schools with low-achieving, working-class students than in schools with high-achieving, middle-class students. To study this topic, Jean Anyon examined five elementary schools that differed markedly in social class. In the two predominantly working-class schools, Anyon found that instruction emphasized mostly mechanical skills such as punctuation and capitalization. In contrast, instruction in the schools she categorized as predominantly middle-class or "affluent professional" emphasized working independently and developing analytical and conceptual skills. Similar patterns have been reported by other researchers.[53]

Positive aspects

Since much of this section has focused on negative aspects of school culture, we should emphasize that many positive statements can be made about elementary and secondary schools in the United States. Most schools provide an orderly learning environment, and most students learn to read and compute at a level required to function in our society. Relationships among teachers, students, and parents generally are positive. The large majority of students receive a high-school diploma, and many proceed to some form of postsecondary education. Successful aspects of the U.S. system of education are described in Chapters 5, 10, 15, 16, and elsewhere in this book.

---

[50]Jackson, *Life in Classrooms,* p. 32. See also Jack L. Nelson, Kenneth Carlson, and Stuart B. Palonsky, *Critical Issues in Education* (New York: McGraw-Hill, 1996).

[51]Linda M. McNeil, *Contradictions of Control* (New York: Routledge and Kegan Paul, 1986); and Stuart B. Palonsky, *900 Shows a Year* (New York: Random House, 1986). See also Kenneth G. Wilson and Bennett Davis, *Redesigning Education* (New York: Henry Holt, 1994); and Dick Lilly, "In Education, Size Seems to Count," *Seattle Times,* July 1, 1998.

[52]Other frequently cited reasons include the tendency for teachers to teach the way they were taught, and lack of adequate preservice and in-service training. See Leon Lederman, "Blackboard Bungle," *The Sciences* (January–February 1995), pp. 16–20; and Marc S. Tucker and Charles S. Clark, "The New Accountability," *American School Board Journal* (January 1999).

[53]Jean Anyon, "Social Class and the Hidden Curriculum of Work," *Journal of Education* (Winter 1980), pp. 67–92, reprinted in Gerald Handel, ed., *Childhood Socialization* (New York: Aldine de Gruyter, 1990); Barbara Means, Kerry Olson, and Joan Ruskus, *Orchestrating Innovative Uses of Technology* (Menlo Park, Calif.: SRI, 1995); and Linda D. Hammond, *The Right to Learn* (San Francisco: Jossey Bass, 1997).

Television and Emerging Digital Media

More TV time than school time

Some social scientists refer to television as the "first curriculum" because it appears to affect the way children develop learning skills and orient themselves toward the acquisition of knowledge and understanding.[54] Because watching television requires little of the viewer in the way of effort and skills, educators face a formidable challenge in maintaining students' interest and motivation in schoolwork. This task is particularly daunting because many children spend more time watching television than they do in school. The average eighth grader spends nearly three times as much time viewing television as doing homework and reading outside school. In addition, a large proportion of children and youth believe that the values of their peers are significantly influenced by what they see on television.[55]

Television and school achievement

Although research shows a relationship between school achievement and television viewing, the nature of this relationship is not entirely clear. Some studies suggest that viewing television may reduce students' reading activities, but this conclusion is not well documented, and international studies show that students in some countries that rank high on TV viewing among children also have relatively high achievement scores. It is difficult to separate cases in which television "causes" reduced attention to reading from those in which low-performing students turn to television for escape. Nevertheless, many educators are very concerned that watching television may lower achievement for large numbers of students, particularly since surveys indicate that millions of children watch TV late into the night and then yawn their way through school the next day.[56]

General mass media effects

Apart from their possibly negative effects on school achievement, television and other mass media, such as the movies and the music industry, deeply influence the acculturation and socialization of children and youth. The mass media both stimulate and reflect fundamental changes in the attitudes and behaviors that prevail in our society, from recreation and career choices to sexual relationships and drug use. Unfortunately, there are no conclusive data to determine just how much the media affect children and youth or whether overall effects are positive or negative (depending, of course, on what one values as positive or negative). For example, twenty-four-hour-a-day rock-music programming on cable television has been viewed both as a means to keep young people off the streets and as the beginning of the end of Western civilization. Although most observers would agree on the vast influence of the mass media, data to assess their effects are limited.[57]

Many adults are particularly worried that television and other media may encourage aggressive or violent behavior. The average child now witnesses thousands

---

[54]Neil Postman, *Teaching as a Conserving Activity* (New York: Delacorte, 1979); Carolyn A. Stroman, "Television's Role in the Socialization of African American Children and Adolescents," *Journal of Negro Education* (Summer 1991), pp. 314–326; and Rachel Taylor, "Media 101," *Brill's Content* (July–August, 1998), pp. 78–79.

[55]Jane M. Healy, "Chaos on Sesame Street," *American Educator* (Winter 1990), pp. 22–27, 39; Robert D. Putnam, "The Strange Disappearance of Civic America," *The American Prospect* (Winter 1996), pp. 34–49; and Judith Tamas, "Do You Know What Children Are Watching?" *Childhood Education* (Summer 1998), p. 224.

[56]*Survey of Sixth Grade School Achievement and Television Viewing Habits* (Sacramento: California State Department of Education, 1982); Barbara F. Mates and Linda Strommen, "Why Ernie Can't Read: Sesame Street and Literacy," *The Reading Teacher* (December 1995–January 1996), pp. 300–307; and Angela T. Clark and Beth Kurtz-Costes, "Television Viewing, Educational Quality of the Home Environment, and School Readiness," *Journal of Educational Research* (May–June 1997), pp. 279–286.

[57]Leo N. Miletich, "Rock Me with a Steady Roll," *Reason* (March 1987), pp. 20–27; David Watson, "Against Forgetting," *Utne Reader* (March–April 1994), pp. 112–115; Robert Hughes, "Why Watch It, Anyway?" *New York Review of Books*, February 16, 1995, pp. 37–42; and Alexandra Marks, "What Children See and Do," *Christian Science Monitor*, April 17, 1998.

TAKING ISSUE

The Influence of Television

Television is a fixture in almost every home; its influence is so pervasive that it has been called another parent. Because most children spend more time watching television than attending school, there is a continuing debate about television's effect on student learning and behavior.

Arguments PRO

1 Television enriches the background knowledge of students so that they can understand much instruction more readily. By taking advantage of what students already have learned from TV, teachers can accelerate the presentation of subject matter.

2 In addition to providing useful information, television awakens interest in a wide range of topics. Drawing on the interests that television arouses, teachers can involve students more deeply in many parts of the curriculum.

3 Television assists teachers by making learning palatable at an early age. Programs such as *Sesame Street* have increased student achievement in the early years by showing children that learning can be fun.

4 Television provides a catharsis for feelings of hostility and anger. By watching television dramas, children can work out potentially violent impulses that might otherwise be directed at classmates, parents, or teachers.

5 Television can provide a good socializing experience. Research has shown that programs like *Sesame Street* can increase cooperative behavior among children. Furthermore, many children's shows offer their viewers a welcome relief from the world of adults.

Arguments CON

1 Most often, the information students gain from television is a superficial collection of facts, not useful background knowledge. Moreover, TV may delude students into thinking that these scattered facts represent genuine understanding.

2 Although television may provoke a fleeting interest in a topic, it accustoms students to learning through passive impressions rather than thoughtful analysis. Thus it creates mental habits that teachers must try to counteract.

3 Early exposure to "fun" learning often raises false expectations about school. The teacher cannot be as entertaining as Big Bird. The need to compete with such TV shows makes the teacher's job more difficult.

4 Research on modeling indicates that many children, confronted with a situation parallel to one they have seen on TV, respond with the same behavior used by the television characters. In other words, violent TV programs often encourage violent behavior.

5 For every *Sesame Street,* there are dozens of TV programs that tend to alienate children from the values of the school and the wider society. For example, some programs reinforce negative peer attitudes toward social institutions; some present simplistic or distorted notions of right and wrong; and many encourage dangerous fantasies.

of simulated murders and tens of thousands of other violent acts by the time he or she completes elementary school. The effects depend in part on situational factors: for example, the child's degree of frustration or anger, similarities between the available target and the target in the television or movie, potential consequences such as pain or punishment, and opportunity to perform an act of violence. Overall, however, according to a committee of behavioral scientists, "television violence is as strongly correlated with aggressive behavior as any other behavioral variable that has been measured." The American Academy of Pediatrics and the American Psychological Association also have concluded that repeated exposure to violence on TV promotes violent behavior.[58]

Correlation with aggression

It also is true, however, that television can be an important force for positive socialization. For example, research shows that the program *Sesame Street* has helped both middle-class and working-class youth academically, and that children can become more cooperative and nurturant after viewing programs emphasizing these behaviors. Research also indicates that programs like *Square One TV* can help elementary students improve in mathematics.[59]

Positive uses of television

Recognizing both the good and the damaging effects that the media can have on children and youth, many people are working for improvements. The Parent-Teacher Association has made reform of television — particularly reduction in sex, commercialism, and violence during prime time — one of its major national goals, and organizations such as the National Citizens Committee for Broadcasting have lobbied for change.

Reform efforts

Despite these efforts, the situation in recent years appears to have grown worse: A typical afternoon of "kidvid" these days can be a mind-numbing march of cartoon superheroes, and many programs insistently instruct children to demand another trip to the nearest toy store. (Critics classify some popular children's shows as little more than extended commercials.) In 1996 the federal government introduced a requirement that television stations broadcast at least three hours per week of "educational and informational" programs for children, but much of this programming has few viewers, and programs emphasizing sex and/or violence continue unabated.[60]

The Net Generation in the Digital Age.   Some analysts have begun to examine the effects and implications of socialization and educational changes that may be occurring as children and youth grow up in an environment permeated by digital communications and information sources such as interactive video, digitized gadgets of all kinds, and, above all, the increasingly ubiquitous Internet. One of the first books to address these developments is Don Tapscott's *Growing Up Digital.*

[58]U.S. Department of Health and Human Services, *Television and Human Behavior: Ten Years of Scientific Progress and Implications for the Eighties,* Vol. 1, Summary Report (Washington, D.C.: U.S. Government Printing Office, 1982), pp. 6, 38–39; *Big World, Small Screen* (Washington, D.C.: American Psychological Association, 1992); Scott Stossel, "The Man Who Counts the Killings," *Atlantic* (May 1997), pp. 86–104; and Ed Donnerstein et al., *National Television Violence Study* (Santa Barbara, Calif.: University of California at Santa Barbara, 1998).

[59]David A. England, *Television and Children* (Bloomington, Ind.: Phi Delta Kappa, 1984); John C. Wright and Aletha C. Huston, *Effects of Educational TV Viewing of Lower Income Preschoolers on Academic Skills, School Readiness, and School Adjustment One to Three Years Later* (New York: Children's Television Workshop, 1995); and Daniel R. Anderson, "Educational Television Is Not an Oxymoron," *Annals of the American Academy of Political and Social Science* (May 1998), pp. 24–38.

[60]Nancy Carlsson-Paige and Diane E. Levin, "Saturday Morning Pushers," *Utne Reader* (January–February 1992), pp. 68–70; Charles Krauthammer, "A Social Conservative Credo," *The Public Interest* (Fall 1995), pp. 15–22; and Paul Farhi, "Flunking the Ratings Test," *Washington Post,* January 9, 1998, p. A01.

Different from television

Tapscott, who refers to young people growing up in the emerging digital age as the "net generation," believes the Internet is quite different from television — it stimulates interactive participation rather than passive viewing, and thereby helps children develop qualities opposite to those engendered by "couch potato" media that were available to their parents:

> On the net there is great diversity of opinion regarding all things. . . . [a situation that is creating] a generation which increasingly questions the implicit values contained in information . . . [and in so doing forces children] to exercise not only their critical thinking but their judgment . . . [and thus contributes] to the relentless breakdown of the notion of authority.[61]

Liberating and productive

Concern for have-nots

Tapscott believes that the primary effect of the digital revolution will be liberating for individuals and productive for society. For individuals, information and knowledge will be easily accessible, while opportunities and experiences available to the net generation will be vastly expanded. For society, a knowledge-based economy will improve efficiency and productivity, and technology will enable the educational system to function successfully in preparing young persons for skilled employment. Like other analysts, however, Tapscott is concerned that digital media and learning will increase the already troublesome gap between the haves and the have-nots, that is, between middle-class youth who have good access to new technologies and low-income youth who have relatively poor access and thus may be further disadvantaged.

Questions and Implications for Educators.   Many observers are more cautious than Tapscott in assessing socialization problems that may be associated with emerging digital media. For example, educators and media specialists at the Center for Media Education have identified a series of questions that should be attended to if emerging technologies are to be a positive force in children's development:

■ What are the unique characteristics of new interactive technologies, and how can they be integrated with the child's development?

■ Are there applications that can become successful models for enhancing children's "natural eagerness to learn, to create, and to communicate"?

What role for educators?

■ What roles should educators, parents, and technology advocates play in shaping evolution of the interactive media market?

Positive interactive learning

Staff of the Center for Media Education have described their investigations involving these and related questions in their online publication titled *InfoActive Kids*. One recent issue reviewed projects under way at media labs where developers are devising interactive learning experiences that can foster students' skills in constructing meaning, solving problems, and generally learning to learn. Projects described in such publications have great potential for shaping children's growth in a positive direction.[62]

---

[61]Don Tapscott, *Growing Up Digital* (New York: McGraw-Hill, 1998), p. 26. See also **www.growingupdigital.com.**
[62]"Out of the Lab and Into the Market," *InfoActive Kids* (Winter 1997), available at **www.tap.epn.org/cme.**

Sex Roles and Sex Differences

Early reinforcement of sex roles

Not only does society demand conformity to its fundamental values and norms; it also assigns specific roles to each of its members, expecting them to conform to certain established behavioral patterns. Socialization is particularly forceful regarding **sex roles** — ideas about the ways boys and girls and men and women are "supposed" to act. Sex roles vary from culture to culture, but within a given culture they are rather well defined and are developed through an elaborate schedule of selective reinforcement. For example, a preschool boy may be ridiculed for playing with dolls, and young girls may be steered away from activities considered too physically rough. By age three, as Robert Havighurst has remarked, there is already a "noticeable difference in behavior between boys and girls." Even at such an early age, boys are more "active," girls more "dependent" and "nurturant."[63]

Sex roles and school problems for boys

When children go to school, they discover that it is dominated by traditional norms of politeness, cleanliness, and obedience. Teachers generally suppress fighting and aggressive behavior. This can be a problem for boys because, as research indicates, on the average they are more aggressive than girls almost from the time they are born, probably because of hormone differences.[64] Some scholars believe that teachers' tendency to reward passive behavior and discourage aggressiveness helps account for boys' relatively high rates of failure and violation of school rules. Boys receive many more reprimands from teachers than do girls, and by the time students enter the secondary grades, boys greatly outnumber girls in remedial classes and in classes for those with emotional disturbances.[65]

Sex roles and school problems for girls

By way of contrast, the problems that girls encounter in the educational system generally reflect their socialization for dependence rather than assertiveness. Until recently, most girls were not encouraged to prepare for high-status fields such as law or medicine or high-paying technical occupations. Instead they were expected to prepare for roles as wives and homemakers. The few occupations women were encouraged to consider, such as elementary teacher, social worker, and nurse, tended to have relatively low pay and low status. This type of socialization did not motivate girls to acquire skills useful for later economic success. Furthermore, verbal skills of the kind in which girls tend to excel did not prepare them for success in mathematics and science. The result was that girls were excluded from many educational opportunities.[66]

Girls not encouraged in competition or leadership

Although socialization in the elementary school frequently is intended to make boys obedient and cooperative, in high school the emphasis placed on athletics means that boys have received more opportunities than girls to learn leadership

---

[63]Robert J. Havighurst, "Sex Role Development," *Journal of Research and Development in Education* (Winter 1983), p. 61. See also Timothy J. Lensmire, "Learning Gender," *Educational Researcher* (June–July 1995), pp. 31–32; and Giovanna Tomada and Barry H. Schneider, "Relational Aggression, Gender, and Peer Acceptance," *Developmental Psychology* (July 1997), pp. 601–610.

[64]Diane McGuiness, "How Schools Discriminate Against Boys," *Human Nature* (February 1979), pp. 87–88; Susan F. Chipman, "Far Too Sexy a Topic," *Educational Researcher* (April 1988), pp. 46–49; and Megan Rosenfeld, "Little Boys Blue," *Washington Post*, March 26, 1998, p. A01.

[65]Kedar-Voivodas, "The Impact of Elementary Children's School Roles and Sex Roles"; Jeff Jacoby, "Alarming Facts About Boys, Girls," *Boston Globe*, February 6, 1995, p. 15; and Debra Viadero, "For Better or Worse, Girls Catching Up to Boys," *Education Week*, June 24, 1998, p. 5.

[66]Susan L. Gabriel and Isaiah Smithson, eds., *Gender in the Classroom* (Urbana: University of Illinois Press, 1990); Susan F. Klein, ed., *Handbook for Achieving Sex Equity Through Education*, 2nd ed. (Baltimore, Md.: Johns Hopkins University Press, 1990); *Growing Smart: What's Working for Girls in School* (Washington D.C.: American Association of University Women, 1995); and Gayle V. Melvin, "Girls Still Cast in Stereotype," *Detroit Free Press*, May 1, 1997.

and competitive skills that may be useful in later life. Girls, expected to be cooperative and even docile, traditionally have had relatively little encouragement to learn the skills of leadership or competition, and those who did were perceived as violating "proper" norms for female behavior in American society.

Boys' vs. girls' peer groups

Raphaela Best found that peer groups in the schools also help communicate traditional expectations for boys and girls. Best reported that boys' peer groups stress "canons" such as "always be first" and "don't hang out with a loser," whereas girls' peer groups place relatively more emphasis on having fun rather than winning and on cooperation rather than competition. Best also reported that as the students she studied grew older, they made some progress in overcoming stereotypes that limited the aspirations of girls and restricted the emotional growth of boys. Similarly, Barrie Thorne studied elementary-school students and concluded that gender roles are "socially constructed" at an early age. She also concluded that teachers should try to counteract gender stereotypes by facilitating cooperative behaviors and enhancing opportunities to participate in diverse activities.[67]

Sex Differences in Achievement and Ability

Reading and mathematics

Recent studies in the United States indicate that sex differences in achievement are relatively small. For example, data on the reading performance of nine-, thirteen-, and seventeen-year-olds indicate that girls score only a little higher than boys. Conversely, among seventeen-year-olds, boys score higher than girls in higher-order mathematics achievement, but this difference is smaller than it was in 1970; among nine- and thirteen-year-olds, there is little meaningful difference in mathematics scores for girls and boys. Research also indicates that female gains in mathematics probably are partly due to greater participation in math courses during the past few decades.[68]

Innate differences?

Though sex differences in achievement are narrowing, there is still much controversy about possible differences in innate ability. These arguments often focus on whether a larger proportion of boys than girls have unusually strong innate ability for higher-order mathematics or abstract thinking in general. Research on this topic shows more variability in ability among boys than among girls: boys are more likely to be either very high or very low in ability.[69]

Different brain functioning

Those who believe that ability differences between the sexes are present at birth point to differences in the brain functioning of boys and girls. For most people, the left hemisphere of the brain specializes in verbal tasks, whereas the right hemisphere specializes in nonverbal ones, including the spatial functions that are important in mathematics. In this respect brain research suggests some differences

---

[67]Raphaela Best, *We've All Got Scars: What Boys and Girls Learn in Elementary School* (Bloomington: Indiana University Press, 1983); and Barrie Thorne, *Gender Play* (New Brunswick, N.J.: Rutgers University Press, 1993). See also Judith S. Kleinfeld and Suzanne Yerian, eds., *Gender Tales* (Mahwah, N.J.: Erlbaum, 1995), and Cathrine E. Matthews et al., "Challenging Gender Bias in Fifth Grade," *Educational Leadership* (January 1998), pp. 54–57.

[68]Nancy Cole, *The ETS Gender Study* (Princeton: Educational Testing Service, 1997), available at **www.ets.org.**; and Alan Vanneman and Sheida White, *Long-Term Trends in Student Reading Performance* (Washington, D.C.: National Center for Education Statistics, 1998), available at **www.nces.gov.**

[69]Doreen Kimura, "Kimura Replies," *Scientific American* (February 1993), p. 15; Elizabeth Fennema et al., "New Perspectives on Gender Differences in Mathematics," *Educational Researcher* (June–July, 1998), pp. 19–21; and Eleanor E. Maccoby, *The Two Sexes* (Cambridge, Mass.: Harvard University Press, 1998).

between men and women. Among right-handed people (the majority), women handle spatial functions more with the *left* hemisphere than do men. Women also use the *right* hemisphere more in verbal functions.[70]

"Math anxiety" and fear of success

Other observers, however, argue that differences in experience and expectations account for most or all of the learning differences between boys and girls.[71] Particular attention has been paid to "math anxiety" among women — the possibility that the relatively poor performance of some women in math (and therefore in science and other fields dependent on math) stems from socialization practices that make them anxious and fearful about mathematical analysis. A related line of argument is that women fear success in traditionally male activities and occupations because succeeding would violate sex stereotypes, thereby inviting ridicule. Still other analysts believe that girls tend to divert their attention more toward social relationships as they enter adolescence. But the situation is complex, and few large-scale generalizations can be made.[72]

Educational and Occupational Attainment of Women

Attitudes regarding sex roles have changed substantially in the United States since the 1960s. Women's attitudes in particular have become much less traditional as they have developed more favorable views toward equal home and work roles for

Educational gains for women

both sexes. Throughout most of U.S. history, women completed fewer years of schooling than did men. By 1977, however, that difference was erased. In 1979, women for the first time outnumbered men among college freshmen. By 1992, more than half of all bachelor's and master's degrees were awarded to women, compared with 40 percent in 1962; and 38 percent of all doctoral degrees were earned by women, compared with 11 percent in 1962. Women have continued to increase their proportions in higher education in the 1990s.[73]

Occupational gains

Related gains have also been registered in the occupational status of women. For example, in 1950 only 15 percent of accountants were women, compared to 56 percent in 1996; the comparable percentages for female lawyers were 4 percent in 1950 and 30 percent in 1996. Very large recent increases in the percentages of female students in medicine, business administration, and other professional fields should increase the number of women employed in high-status positions in the future. Affirmative action in employment and education (see Chapter 8), encouragement of girls to attend college and prepare for the professions, efforts to eliminate

---

[70]Richard M. Restak, "The Other Difference Between Boys and Girls," *Educational Leadership* (December 1979), pp. 232–235; Doreen Kimura, "Male Brain, Female Brain: The Hidden Difference," *Psychology Monthly* (March 1988), pp. 77–82; Natalie Angier, "Gene May Account for Social Skills in Girls," *New York Times*, June 12, 1997; and Jill Ross, "Examining Male and Female Cognitive Processes May Lead to New Kinds of Tests," *ETS Developments* (Spring–Summer 1998), p. 7.

[71]Lynn Friedman, "The Space Factor in Mathematics: Gender Differences," *Review of Educational Research* (Spring 1995), pp. 22–50; Kim Strosnider, "A Controversial Study of Testing Finds the Gap Between Boys and Girls Is Shrinking," *Chronicle of Higher Education*, May 16, 1997, p. A34; and Karen W. Arenson, "A Revamped Student Test Reduces Gap Between Sexes," *New York Times*, January 14, 1998.

[72]Shelia Tobias and Carol S. Weissbrod, "Anxiety and Mathematics: An Update," *Harvard Educational Review* (February 1980), pp. 63–70; Jacquelynne S. Eccles, "Gender-Roles and Women's Achievement," *Educational Researcher* (June–July 1986), pp. 15–19; and Andrew S. Latham, "Gender Differences on Assessments," *Educational Leadership* (January 1998), pp. 88–89.

[73]"Fact File," *Chronicle of Higher Education*, July 2, 1998, p. A28.

Much to be accomplished

sexism from school curricula, support for girls and women to enter scientific fields and computing, and other actions to equalize opportunity are having an impact in the schools and in the wider society.[74]

Nevertheless, much remains to be achieved, and improvements of various kinds should continue to occur. Despite recent gains, women still tend to be concentrated in low-paying, low-status occupations, and there is a higher proportion of women in clerical and service jobs now than in 1910. Although the number of female scientists and engineers with doctoral degrees more than doubled between 1973 and 1995, they still constitute less than one-quarter of the total. In 1995 the average female worker earned only 76 percent of the annual income of the average male. (This gap is substantially less when experience and number of hours worked are taken into account.)

The increase in educational and occupational attainment of women is associated with growth in the percentage of working mothers and single-parent families. As we saw earlier, these trends may have a negative impact on children and the schools. Nevertheless, they signify greater equalization of opportunity, and they may improve the social class and income of many families. Researchers' suggestions for further improving educational opportunities and equity for girls and women include the following:[75]

Ways to improve gender equity in education

- Provide increased teacher training dealing with gender issues
- Attend more closely to gender equity in vocational education
- Eliminate any remaining bias in standardized tests, and reduce the role of these tests in college admissions
- Ensure a central role for women and girls in school reform efforts
- Improve educational programs dealing with health and sexuality
- Reduce sex stereotyping and further increase the representation of females in instructional materials
- Protect the rights of pregnant girls and teenage parents
- Introduce "gender-fair" multicultural curricula that accommodate differences in learning styles
- Increase the number of girls who take advanced courses in computing
- Encourage girls to participate in math and science programs and to interview women scientists in the community
- Introduce and expand programs that can improve girls' performance in science and math
- Work to counteract the decline in self-esteem that many girls experience as they grow older and become increasingly concerned with their physical appearance and social relationships

---

[74]"Contrasting Wage Gaps by Gender and Race," *The Urban Institute Policy and Research Report* (Winter–Spring 1992), pp. 7–8; Pamela Mendels, "Who's Managing Now?" *Working Woman* (October 1995), pp. 44–45; and Pamela Mendels, "New Efforts Seek to Help Girls with Computer Education," *New York Times,* July 8, 1998.
[75]*How Schools Shortchange Women: The A.A.U.W. Report* (Washington, D.C.: American Association of University Women, 1992); Eileen V. Hilke and Carol Conway-Gerhardt, *Gender Equity in Education* (Bloomington, Ind.: Phi Delta Kappa, 1994); and Linda Phillips, *The Girls Report. What We Know and Need to Know About Growing Up Female* (New York: National Council for Research on Women, 1998).

Adolescent and Youth Problems

Adolescence as a modern phenomenon

In many traditional, nonindustrialized cultures, the young are initiated into adult life after puberty. This initiation sometimes takes place through special rituals designed to prove the young person's worthiness to assume adult roles. In such societies one is either a child or an adult; there is only a brief gap between the two — if there is any gap at all.

In modern technological societies the young are forced to postpone their adulthood for a period of time called adolescence or youth. A major reason is that modern society no longer has an economic need for young people in this age group. One unfortunate result is that youth have become more and more isolated from the rest of society. In recent decades, this isolation has intensified many youth-centered problems, such as drug use, drinking, suicide, early pregnancy, and delinquency. At the same time, the isolation of youth hampers efforts by the schools and other social institutions to prepare young people for adulthood.[76]

Drugs and Drinking

Patterns of use

General usage of drugs and alcohol among youth has grown markedly over the past half-century, and recently, after a decade or more of decline, the use of some drugs has begun to rise again. Parents, educators, and others who work with youth remain deeply concerned with the effects of drug use and abuse. The following list summarizes some recent patterns:[77]

Cigarettes. The percentage of high-school seniors who smoked cigarettes daily declined from 21 percent in 1980 to 19 percent in 1992 but then increased to more than 23 percent in 1996.

Marijuana. The percentage of high-school seniors who had used marijuana during the previous year declined from 50 percent in 1978 to 26 percent in 1992, but then increased to 39 percent in 1997.

Heroin. Less than 2 percent of seniors had used heroin or other opiates within the previous month in 1997.

Cocaine. Annual use of cocaine increased from 6 percent in 1975 to 12 percent in 1981, but then declined to less than 6 percent in 1997.

Methamphetamine (Crank). During the past few years the increase in the use of methamphetamines has been so explosive that an analyst for *Time* magazine described the scene as follows: "In cities large and small [and in] towns where the drug is known as the poor man's cocaine . . . the drug arrives nonstop from every direction and by every imaginable route." Although precise information is not available regarding rates of use among various population subgroups, there is no doubt that many of those experiencing serious negative effects from using Crank are adolescents and young adults.

Alcohol. Regular use of alcohol has remained fairly stable, with less than 5 percent of seniors reporting *daily* use. The percentage reporting that they drank alcohol

---

[76]James S. Coleman, "Families and Schools," *Educational Researcher* (August–September 1987), pp. 32–38; Carnegie Council on Adolescent Development, *Great Transitions* (New York: Carnegie Corporation, 1995); and Rachael Kessler, "Passages" (1997 posting at the Internet site of New Horizons for Learning), available at **www.newhorizons.org.**

[77]Data are summarized largely from annual surveys conducted by the University of Michigan Institute for Survey Research. For information on organized efforts to deal with youth substance abuse problems, visit Internet site **www.jointogether.org.**

during the previous year has declined significantly, but research indicates that use of alcohol has been increasing among students less than fifteen years old, that many teenagers have driven an automobile while intoxicated, that an alarming number of teenagers frequently drink alone when they are bored or upset, and that laws prohibiting the sale of alcohol to minors are widely violated.[78]

Implications of drug and alcohol use

Educators worry that young people's use of alcohol, marijuana, and other relatively mild drugs may reinforce or stimulate alienation from social institutions or otherwise impede the transition to adulthood. This is not to say that problems like low academic performance, rebelliousness, and criminal activity are *caused* by drug use; just as often, it may be that the problems arise first and then lead to the drug use. Many young people are using drugs and alcohol to escape from difficulties they encounter in preparing for adult life. But whatever the sequence of causation, usage rates among U.S. youth remain higher than in any other industrialized nation. Moreover, contrary to much earlier opinion, some authorities now believe that mild drugs such as marijuana are often a steppingstone to stronger drugs such as cocaine and heroin. Young people themselves believe that drugs and alcohol are a negative influence in their lives. National surveys consistently show that most high-school students cite either drugs or alcohol as the "single worst influence" in their lives.[79]

Suicide

Rise in suicide rate

Educators have become increasingly concerned about suicide among young people. The suicide rate among children and youth has nearly quadrupled since 1950, and some surveys suggest that as many as one in ten school-age youth may attempt suicide. Reasons for this increase appear to include a decline in religious values that inhibit suicide, influence of the mass media, perceived pressures to excel in school, failed relationships with peers, and pressures or despondency associated with divorce or other problems in the family.[80]

Teachers should learn warning signs

Teachers and other school personnel need to be alert to the problem. As Deborah Strother has remarked, "Young people who are deeply troubled will show it, and observers who notice the symptoms can direct such young people to appropriate sources of help." Warning signs include the following: withdrawal from friends, family, and regular activities; violent or rebellious behavior; running away; alcohol or drug abuse; unusual neglect of personal appearance; radical change in personality; persistent boredom; difficulty in concentrating; decline in the quality of schoolwork; and emotional or physical symptoms such as headaches and stomachaches. Teachers also should keep in mind a U.S. District Court ruling that found school of-

[78]Jacqueline Jones, "Lessons from the Past About Preventing Alcohol and Drug Use," *Join Together Strategies* (Spring 1995), pp. 1,4; Walter Kirk, "Crank," *Time*, June 22, 1998, p. 27; and Jessica Portner, "Survey Finds Slowdown of Students' Drug Use," *Education Week*, January 13, 1999.

[79]Carol J. Mills and Harvey I. Noyes, "Patterns and Correlates of Initial and Subsequent Drug Use Among Adolescents," *Journal of Consulting and Clinical Psychology* (April 1984), pp. 231–243; and Adrienne D. Coles, "Proms, Graduations Spur Schools to Redouble Anti-Drinking Efforts," *Education Week*, June 10, 1998.

[80]*Suicide* (Eugene, Oreg.: ERIC Clearinghouse on Educational Management, 1991); Steven Stack, Jim Gundlach, and Jimmie L. Reeves, "The Heavy Metal Culture and Suicide," *Suicide and Life-Threatening Behavior* (Spring 1994), pp. 15–23; and Janice Arenofsky, "Teen Suicide," *Current Health* (December 1997), pp. 16–18.

ficials partly responsible for a student's suicide when they failed to provide "reasonable" care and help for a young man who had displayed suicidal symptoms.[81]

Teenage Pregnancy

Rise in births out of wedlock

Among teenagers as a whole, the number and rate of births have fallen substantially during the past half-century, partly because of the availability of contraceptives and abortion and the success of abstinence campaigns in some communities. On the other hand, the percentage of births to teenage mothers that occur out of wedlock has skyrocketed from 15 percent in 1960 to more than 90 percent in the 1990s. Researchers have linked this trend to a number of social problems. For example, families headed by young mothers are much more likely than other families to live below the poverty line, and teenage mothers are much less likely to receive prenatal care than are older mothers. Not surprisingly, then, children of teenage mothers tend to have poor health and to perform poorly in school. Moreover, society spends billions of dollars each year to support the children of teenage mothers.[82]

Associated problems

Reasons for increase

Teenage births constitute a substantially higher percentage of births in the United States than in most other industrialized nations. According to social scientists who have analyzed fertility data, the increase in out-of-wedlock births among teenagers results from such interrelated factors as a greater social acceptance of teenage sexuality and illegitimacy, earlier and more frequent sexual intercourse, a decrease in early marriages, a decline in community and parental influence over the young, and the assumption by social agencies of responsibility for helping younger mothers. After carefully analyzing thirty years of data, two analysts encapsulated their conclusion as follows: "the increased availability of contraception and abortion made shotgun weddings a thing of the past."[83]

School responses

Many schools have responded by establishing school-based clinics for pregnant teenagers and new mothers, and expanding courses that focus on sex education, health, personal development, and family life. Although early data on these activities were generally negative, recent studies indicate that they can be effective in preventing or at least alleviating problems associated with teenage pregnancy. Positive results also have been reported for a variety of approaches that have been implemented since 1996 as part of the federally sponsored National Campaign to Prevent Teen Pregnancy.[84] In addition, organizations such as Girls, Inc. have conducted

---

[81]Deborah Strother, "Suicide Among the Young," *Phi Delta Kappan* (June 1986), p. 759. See also Melissa Etlin, "How to Help a Suicidal Student," *NEA Today* (May–June 1990), p. 6; and "Adults May Prevent Teen Suicide," *Brown University Child and Adolescent Behavior Newsletter* (June 1997), p. 3.

[82]Janet B. Hardy and Laurie S. Zabin, *Adolescent Pregnancy in an Urban Environment* (Washington, D.C.: Urban Institute Press, 1991); Jane Mauldron and Kristin Luker, "Does Liberalism Cause Sex?" *The American Prospect* (Winter 1996), pp. 80–85; Kathryn Borman and Barbara Schneider, eds. *The Adolescent Years* (Chicago: University of Chicago Press, 1998); and Steven A. Holmes, "Birth Rate for Unmarried Black Mothers Is at 40-Year Low," *New York Times,* July 1, 1998.

[83]Kingsley Davis, "A Theory of Teenage Pregnancy in the United States," in Catherine S. Chilman, ed., *Adolescent Pregnancy and Childbearing* (Washington, D.C.: U.S. Government Printing Office, 1980); Andrew Hacker, *Two Nations* (New York: Ballantine, 1995); Julia Henly, "Comparative Research on Adolescent Childbearing," *African American Research Perspectives* (Spring 1995), pp. 70–81; Douglas A. Besharov and Karen N. Gardner, "Paternalism and Welfare Reform," *The Public Interest* (Winter 1996), pp.70–84; and George A. Akerlof and Janet L. Yellen, "An Analysis of Out-of-Wedlock Births in the United States," *Brookings Policy Brief No. 5* (September 1998).

[84]Joy G. Dryfoos, *Safe Passage* (New York: Oxford University Press, 1998).

projects that provide girls with a combination of assertiveness training, health services, communications skills, personal counseling, and information about sexuality. Recent data show that these efforts appear to have substantially reduced the incidence of teenage pregnancies.[85]

Delinquency and Violence

Overall trends

Juvenile delinquency has increased in recent decades, paralleled by related increases in the size of the youth group, the influence of peer culture, the use of drugs and alcohol, and the growth of low-income neighborhoods in big cities. Problems connected with violence and delinquency are particularly acute among young African American males, whose rate of death from homicide has more than tripled since 1985. Even among young white males, however, homicide rates are more than twice as high as in any other industrialized country.[86]

Research on delinquency and violence among youth supports a number of generalizations:

- Significant delinquency rates are found among youth of all social classes. However, violent delinquency is much more frequent among working-class than among middle-class youth.[87]

- Although a large proportion of crimes are committed by people under twenty-five, most delinquents settle down to a productive adult life.[88]

- An increase in gangs has helped generate greater violence among youth in the past two decades.[89]

Unemployment

- Delinquency is associated with unemployment. As Daniel Glaser has observed, "To combat youth crime is largely futile unless an effort is also made to assure legitimate employment for youths." From this point of view, delinquency is a partial response to the restricted opportunity available to some young people in modern society.[90]

- Family characteristics related to delinquency include lack of effective parental supervision and lack of community cohesiveness.[91]

Delinquency among girls

- Delinquency and violent crime rates for girls have been increasing much more rapidly than those for boys. However, community delinquency rates for

---

[85]Dean F. Miller, *The Case for School-Based Health Clinics* (Bloomington, Ind.: Phi Delta Kappa, 1990); and "Teen Birth Rates Down in All States" (Bulletin released by the U.S. Department of Health and Human Services, Washington, D.C., April 1998), available at **www.hhs.gov.**

[86]Edward Wynne and Marcia Hess, "Long-term Trends in Youth Conduct and Revival of Traditional Value Patterns," *Educational Evaluation and Policy Analysis* (Fall 1986), pp. 294–308; John J. DiIulio, Jr., "Liberalism's Last Stand?" *The Public Interest* (Winter 1995), pp. 119–124; and John Hagan, "Defiance and Despair," *Social Forces* (September 1997), pp. 119–134.

[87]"Youth Violence," *Rand Research Brief #RB4517*, no date, available at **www.rand.org.**

[88]Christopher Jencks, *Rethinking Social Policy* (Cambridge, Mass.: Harvard University Press, 1992).

[89]Marshall Croddy, "Violence Redux," *Social Education* (September 1997), pp. 258–265.

[90]Daniel Glaser, "Economic and Sociocultural Variables Affecting Rates of Youth Unemployment," *Youth and Society* (September 1979), p. 79; and Jeff Grogger, "Market Wages and Youth Crime" (NBER Working Paper No. 5983, Cambridge, Mass.), available at **www.nber.org.**

[91]James Q. Wilson, *Thinking About Crime* (New York: Basic Books, 1983); Dale A. Blyth and Nancy Leffert, "Communities as Contexts for Adolescent Development," *Journal of Adolescent Research* (January 1995), pp. 64–87; and Fox Butterworth, "Study Links Violence Rate to Cohesion in Community," *New York Times*, August 17, 1997.

females and males are highly correlated: communities that have high rates for one sex also tend to have high rates for the other.[92]

School performance

- Delinquency is related to learning disabilities and associated low levels of school performance.[93]

- When punishment is perceived as more certain, delinquency tends to decline. However, other considerations such as peer influence frequently outweigh deterrent effects of perceived likelihood of punishment.[94]

- Crime and delinquency may reflect genetic dispositions, such as high aggressiveness, that culture channels into antisocial outlets.[95]

Influence of peers

- One of the strongest predictors of delinquency is influence of peers, but this influence interacts with the family, the school, the neighborhood, and other causal factors.[96]

- Violent crime among youth in suburban and rural areas has been increasing rapidly.[97]

Effects on the Schools

Major consequences for schools

As we have seen, young people do not simply leave larger cultural patterns behind when they enter the schoolhouse door. Like the other topics discussed in this chapter, the characteristics of youth culture have enormous consequences for the U.S. educational system. The most direct problems are drugs and alcohol in the schools, and violence, theft, and disorder on school grounds. Indicators of antisocial behavior in and around the schools have been a continuing topic of debate during the past thirty years. In almost all the annual Gallup Polls of public opinion on education conducted since 1968, "discipline" and "drugs" have been most frequently cited as the most serious problems in the schools.[98]

Although violence and vandalism are most common at low-income schools in big cities, they are serious problems at many schools outside the inner city,

[92]Felicia R. Lee, "For Gold Earrings and Protection, More Girls Take Road to Violence," *New York Times,* November 25, 1991, pp. A1, A16; "Female Gangs Are Growing in Numbers," *Law and Order* (March 1996), pp. 87–90; and Abigail Zuger, "A Fistful of Hostility Is Found in Women," *New York Times,* July 28, 1998.

[93]Delbert S. Elliott, David Huizinga, and Suzanne S. Ageton, *Explaining Delinquency and Drug Use* (Newbury Park, Calif.: Sage, 1985); Peter E. Leone, ed., *Understanding Troubled and Troubling Youth* (Newbury Park, Calif.: Sage, 1990); and Alexander T. Vazsonyi, "Early Adolescent Delinquent Behaviors," *Journal of Early Adolescence* (August 1997), pp. 271–293.

[94]Paul J. McNulty, "Natural Born Killers," *Policy Review* (Winter 1995), pp. 84–87; and Wanda D. Foglia, "Perceptual Deterrence and the Mediating Effects of Internalized Norms," *Journal of Research in Crime and Delinquency* (November 1997), pp. 414–443.

[95]Christopher Jencks, "Genes and Crime," *New York Review of Books,* February 12, 1987, pp. 33–41; W. Wayt Gibbs, "Seeking the Criminal Element," *Scientific American* (March 1995), pp. 99–107; and J. Philippe Rushton, "The Mismeasures of Gould," *National Review,* September 15, 1997).

[96]LeGrande Gardner and Donald J. Shoemaker, "Social Bonding and Delinquency," *Sociological Quarterly* (Fall 1989), pp. 481–500; Roberto Rodriguez, "Understanding the Pathology of Inner-City Violence," *Black Issues in Higher Education,* April 23, 1992, pp. 18–20; and Jerome H. Skolnick, "Tough Guys," *American Prospect* (January–February, 1997), pp. 86–91.

[97]Dan Korem, *Suburban Gangs* (Richardson, Tex.: International Focus Press, 1994); Mark Pitsch, "My Town," *Teacher Magazine* (January 1996), pp. 38–43; and Kathleen B. Powell, "Correlates of Violent and Nonviolent Behavior Among Vulnerable Inner-City Youths," *Family and Community Health* (July 1997), pp. 38–47.

[98]Lowell C. Rose and Alec M. Gallup, "The 30th Annual Phi Delta Kappa Gallup Poll," *Phi Delta Kappan* (September 1998), pp. 41–56.

especially when the schools are afflicted by teenage and young-adult gangs, by crime connected with substance abuse and drug sales, and by infiltration of school buildings by trespassers. Nearly one-third of teachers at nonurban schools report that physical conflict among their students constitutes a moderate or serious problem.[99]

Social service personnel in schools

In response to youth problems, schools now employ many more counselors, social workers, and other social service personnel than they did in earlier decades. Urban high schools, for example, use the services of such specialized personnel as guidance and career counselors, psychologists, security workers, nurses, truant officers, and home-school coordinators. Many of these specialists help conduct programs that target alcohol and drug abuse, teenage sex, school dropout, suicide, intergroup relations, and parenting skills.

In addition, many schools are cooperating with other institutions in operating school-based health clinics and/or in providing coordinated services which help students and their families receive assistance with respect to mental and physical health problems, preparation for employment, and other preoccupations that detract from students' performance in school. Thousands of schools also are implementing programs to improve discipline on a schoolwide basis, teach students conflict resolution skills, develop peer-mediation mechanisms, and control the activities of gangs. Later chapters of this book provide additional information on efforts to improve school climates and environments.[100]

1. Changes in the family may be having a detrimental influence on children's behavior and performance in school. Although the situation is complicated, increases in single-parent families and in the number of working mothers appear to be having a negative effect for many students.

2. The peer culture becomes more important as children proceed through school, but it has an important influence on education at all levels of schooling. Educators should be aware of the potentially positive effects of participation in extracurricular activities.

3. The culture of the school (that is, "regularities" in school practice) appears to stress passive, rote learning in many elementary and secondary schools, particularly in working-class schools and mixed-class schools with relatively large numbers of low-achieving students. This happens in part because schools are institutions that must maintain orderly environments; because many students prefer passive learning; because teachers generally cannot adequately attend to the learning needs of all students; and because society requires that students learn to function within institutions.

4. Television probably increases aggressiveness and violent behavior among some children and youth, and it may tend to detract from achievement, par-

---

[99]Gary Burnett and Garry Walz, "Gangs in the Schools," *ERIC Clearinghouse on Urban Education Digest* (July 1994), pp. 1–2; Linda Lantieri, "Waging Peace in Our Schools," *Phi Delta Kappan* (January 1995), pp. 386–388; and Rene Sanchez, "Educators Pursue Solutions to Violence Crisis," *Washington Post,* May 23, 1998.
[100]Grace Pung Guthrie and Larry F. Guthrie, "Streamlining Interagency Collaboration for Youth at Risk," *Educational Leadership* (September 1991), pp. 17–22; R. Craig Sauter, "Standing Up to Violence," *Phi Delta Kappan* (January 1995), pp. K1–K12; "School-Based Care Management," *Addressing Barriers to Learning* (Summer 1997); and Shelley Blum, *Violence and Discipline Problems in U.S. Public Schools* (Washington, D.C.: National Center for Education Statistics, 1998), available at **www.nces.ed.gov.**

ticularly in reading. Some analysts have also begun studying the social and cultural effects of digital technologies.

5. Girls traditionally have not been encouraged to seek education that prepares them for full participation in the larger society, and both girls and boys have experienced sex-role pressures in the school. Even so, educational and occupational opportunities for women have been improving rapidly. Although sex differences in school achievement have been declining, some differences in ability may persist in verbal skills (favoring females) and advanced mathematics (favoring males).

6. In some ways, youth has become a separate stage of life marked by immersion in a number of subcultures. Teenage drug use and drinking, suicide, pregnancy, delinquency, and violence raise serious concerns about the development of adolescents and youth both inside and outside the school.

acculturation *(277)*

socialization *(277)*

culture *(277)*

norms *(277)*

latchkey children *(278)*

feminization of poverty *(281)*

hurried children *(283)*

nuclear family *(285)*

peer culture *(289)*

hidden curriculum *(292)*

sex roles *(301)*

1. How do the socialization experiences of adolescents differ in urban and rural communities? Are such differences declining over time, and if so, why?

2. How does "schooling" differ from "education"? As a prospective teacher, what implications do you see in this line of analysis?

3. In your experience, which types of students are most popular? Do you believe that popularity patterns have changed much in recent decades? If so, why?

4. What might the schools do to alleviate the problems of drug use, violence, and teenage pregnancy? What *should* they do? If you believe the "might" and "should" are different, why?

1. Write a description of the "regularities" of schooling as you remember them at the high school you attended. Compare your description with those of your classmates. Do these patterns seem to vary much from one school to another? If so, how?

2. Contact local government officials in a nearby city to obtain data on changes that have been occurring in family life and family composition. Does the city have any data showing how such changes have affected the schools? What can you learn or predict from the data?

3. Interview local school district officials to determine what their schools are doing to reduce drug use and abuse. Is there any evidence that these efforts have been effective? What might be done to make them more effective?

4. Based on library and Internet sources cited in this chapter, develop a plan that could help a school or a teacher respond effectively and appropriately to challenges posed by students who have difficult home situations. Consider including this plan in your personal portfolio.

Suggested Readings and Resources

Internet Resources

Internet sites that are particularly useful in finding basic sources and keeping current on topics introduced in this chapter include the following World Wide Web locations (each prefaced by **www.**): **childrensdefense.org**; **census.gov**; **epn.org**; **frc.org**; and **townhall.com**. Many relevant documents also can be found by starting with a search at **www.ed.gov**.

Video

Learning to Change. VHS, 29 minutes (1990). Southern Regional Council, 134 Peachtree St., N.W., Suite 1900, Atlanta, GA 30303-1825. Phone: 404-522-8764. *This video describes how some schools are working to overcome barriers to change in school cultures and practices, particularly to improve the performance of at-risk students.*

Publications

Best, Raphaela. *We've All Got Scars: What Boys and Girls Learn in Elementary School.* Bloomington: Indiana University Press, 1983. *Gives detailed observations of gender-related behaviors in the elementary grades, analyzes why relatively more boys than girls are poor readers, and examines the differences in boys' and girls' participation in the academic curriculum and the hidden curriculum.*

Borman, Kathryn, and Barbara Schneider, eds. *The Adolescent Years.* Chicago: University of Chicago Press, 1998. *Chapters in this wide-ranging volume focus on the problems of adolescence, socialization of girls, extracurriculuar activities, and other related topics and issues.*

Burleson, Derek L., ed. *Reflections.* Bloomington, Ind.: Phi Delta Kappa, 1991. *Many of the thirty-three distinguished educators who describe their careers in this book of essays focus on changes they have seen in the family, peer groups, the media, and other social institutions.*

Helgesen, Sally. *Everyday Revolutionaries.* New York: Doubleday, 1998. *Subtitled "Working Women in the Transformation of American Life," this book examines the positives and some negatives that developed as the percentage of women working outside the home increased greatly in the second half of the twentieth century.*

Lortie, Dan C. *Schoolteacher.* Chicago: University of Chicago Press, 1975. *A seminal analysis of the role and functioning of teachers within the culture of elementary and secondary schools.*

Sedlak, Michael W., Christopher W. Wheeler, Diana C. Pullin, and Philip Cusick. *Selling Students Short.* New York: Teachers College Press, 1986. *Evaluates classroom "bargains" that result in low-level learning and analyzes the weaknesses of bureaucratic school reform that takes little account of these classroom realities.*

Spindler, George, and Louise Spindler. *The American Cultural Dialogue and Its Transmission.* New York: Falmer, 1990. *The authors summarize decades of their observation and analysis on topics relating to culture and education.*

CHAPTER TEN

Social Class, Race, and School Achievement

This chapter begins by briefly explaining social class and examining relationships among students' social class, racial and ethnic background, and performance in the educational system. It then discusses why students with low social status, particularly disadvantaged minority students, typically rank low in educational achievement and attainment. The chapter concludes by examining the implications of these relationships in the context of our nation's historic commitment to equal educational opportunity.

This chapter, like the preceding one, offers no easy answers; but it provides, we hope, a deeper understanding. We will show how inadequate achievement patterns have become most prevalent among students with socioeconomic disadvantages, especially if those students also belong to minority groups that have experienced widespread discrimination. Later chapters will look at efforts to change the prevailing patterns and improve the performance of disadvantaged students. First, however, we need to focus on the multiple root causes of the problem and their implications for teaching and learning. As you read this chapter, think about these questions:

- What is the relationship between social class and success in the educational system?

- After accounting for social class, are race and ethnicity associated with school achievement?

- What are the major reasons for low achievement among students with low socioeconomic status?

- What is the role of home and family environment in encouraging or discouraging high achievement?

- Do environment and heredity interact to cause low achievement?

- How does the relationship between social class and school achievement affect the national goal of providing equal educational opportunities for all students?

Social Class and Success in School

Know This

American society is generally understood to consist of three broad classes: working, middle, and upper. It is well known that there is a strong relationship between social class and educational achievement. Traditionally, working-class students have not performed as well as middle- and upper-class students. As you read the analysis in this section, you should ask yourself why it has been so difficult to improve the achievement of working-class students and what can be done to improve their achievement in the future.

Categories of Social Class

Class and SES

In the 1940s W. Lloyd Warner and his colleagues used four main variables — occupation, education, income, and housing value — to classify Americans and their families into five groups: upper class, upper middle class, lower middle class, upper lower class, and lower lower class. Individuals high in occupational prestige, amount of education, income, and housing value ranked in the higher classes. Such people are also said to be high in **socioeconomic status (SES)**; that is, they are viewed by others as upper-class persons and are influential and powerful in their communities. Conversely, people low in socioeconomic status are viewed as low in prestige and power.[1]

Social classes defined

Today, the term *working class* is more widely used than *lower class,* but social scientists still identify three to six levels of SES, ranging from upper class at the top to lower working class at the bottom. The **upper class** is usually defined as including very wealthy persons with substantial property and investments. The **middle class** includes professionals, managers, and small-business owners (upper middle) as well as technical workers, technicians, sales personnel, and clerical workers (lower middle). The **working class** is generally divided into upper working class (including skilled crafts workers) and lower working class (unskilled manual workers). Skilled workers may be either middle class or working class, depending on their education, income, and other considerations such as the community in which they live.

Historically researchers commonly used a two-factor, social-class index devised by August Hollingshead, who assigned individuals a score based on years of education and on occupation using categories similar to those illustrated in the preceding paragraph, and then multiplied the scores together and classified the result in five social-class categories. However, over the years his categories became outdated as educational attainment increased in the population and socioeconomic changes produced new occupations and changed the status of some old ones. Although no one has created an index that is as widely used as was the two-factor index, various researchers have devised indices that designate social-class categories in terms of occupation and/or scores given for education. Income categories are less commonly used because an individual's income tends to fluctuate much more than his or her occupation and education, but for various reasons some analysts continue to use in-

[1]W. Lloyd Warner, Marcia Meeker, and Kenneth Eells, *Social Class in America* (Chicago: Science Research Associates, 1949). See also Delbert C. Miller, *Handbook of Research Design and Social Measurement,* 5th ed. (Newbury Park, Calif.: Sage, 1991); S. M. Miller and Karen M. Ferroggiaro, "Class Dismissed?" *The American Prospect* (Spring 1995), pp. 100–104; and Rebecca P. Heath, "The New Working Class," *American Demographics* (January 1998), available at **www.demographics.com.**

Intergenerational poverty

come categories such as the $25,000–$75,000 annual income category to distinguish the middle class from the upper class and the working class.[2]

In recent years, a number of observers have identified an **underclass** group within the working class. The underclass generally resembles the lower working class, but many of its members are the third or fourth generation to live in poverty and are dependent on public assistance to sustain a relatively meager existence. Usually concentrated in the inner slums of cities or in deteriorated areas of rural poverty, many members of the underclass frequently have little hope of improving their economic and social situation.[3]

Recently some analysts have gone still further and have identified an *overclass* that they believe is prospering in a competitive international economy at the same time that much of our population is stagnating economically. Like observers who have been studying the development of the underclass, these analysts generally emphasize the importance of education in determining one's social status and income.[4]

Research on Social Class and School Success

"Middletown" study

One of the first systematic studies investigating the relationship between social class and achievement in school was Robert and Helen Lynd's study of "Middletown" (a small midwestern city) in the 1920s. The Lynds concluded that parents, regardless of social class, recognize the importance of education for their children; however, many working-class children do not come to school equipped to acquire the verbal skills and behavioral traits required for success in the classroom. The Lynds' observations of social class and the schools were repeated by W. Lloyd Warner and his associates in a series of studies of towns and small cities in New England, the Deep South, and the Midwest. Hundreds of studies have since documented the close relationship between social class and education in the United States and, indeed, throughout the world.[5]

NAEP

For example, a clear picture of this relationship has been provided by the **National Assessment of Educational Progress** (NAEP) and other agencies that collect achievement information from nationally representative samples of students. As shown in Table 10.1, mathematics and reading proficiency scores of groups of students vary directly with their social class. Students whose parents are well educated (one primary measure of social class) score much higher than students whose

---

[2]August B. Hollingshead, "Cultural Factors in the Selection of Marriage Mates," *American Sociological Review* (October 1950), pp. 619–627; and William A. Galston and Elaine C. Kamarck, "Five Realities That Will Shape 21st Century Politics," *Blueprint* (Fall 1998), available at **www.dlc.org/blueprint.**

[3]Ken Auletta, *The Underclass* (New York: Random House, 1982); Christopher Jencks and Paul E. Peterson, eds., *The Urban Underclass* (Washington, D.C.: The Brookings Institution, 1991); and Martin M. Wooster, "Inside the Underclass," *American Enterprise* (May–June 1998), pp. 83–84.

[4]Jerry Adler, "The Rise of the Overclass," *Newsweek,* July 31, 1995, pp. 32–46; Michael Lind, *The Next American Nation* (New York: Free Press, 1995); and Peter Beinart, "Dollar Democrats," *New Republic,* May 11, 1998, pp. 23–27.

[5]Robert S. Lynd and Helen M. Lynd, *Middletown: A Study in American Culture* (New York: Harcourt, Brace and World, 1929); Doris R. Entwisle and Nan M. Astone, "Some Practical Guidelines for Measuring Youth's Race/Ethnicity and Socioeconomic Status," *Child Development* (December 1994), pp. 1521–1540; and John Ralph, "First-Graders' Achievement in Top and Bottom Schools," *National Center for Education Statistics Issue Brief* (January 1998), pp. 1–2, available at **nces.ed.gov.**

TABLE 10.1	Average Mathematics and Reading Proficiency Scores of Nine- and Thirteen-Year-Olds, by Parental Education and Type of Community		
	Thirteen-Year-Olds, Mathematics	**Thirteen-Year-Olds, Reading**	**Nine-Year-Olds, Reading**
Parental Education			
Not graduated high school	254	241	197
Graduated high school	267	252	207
At least some college	281	270	220
Type of Community			
Disadvantaged urban	251	231	184
Rural	272	257	206
Advantaged Urban	292	281	234

Note: The National Assessment of Educational Progress defines community type as follows: *advantaged urban,* communities located in or around cities with a population of 200,000 or more, and a "high proportion of the residents are in professional or managerial positions"; *rural,* communities located in areas with population below 10,000, and many of the residents are farmers or farm workers; *disadvantaged urban,* communities located in or around cities of 200,000 or more, and a "high proportion of the residents are on welfare or are not regularly employed." Parental education data are for 1996; type of community data are for 1994.

Source: Jay R. Campbell, Kristin E. Voekel, and Patricia L. Donahue, *NAEP Trends in Academic Progress* (Washington, D.C.: U.S. Department of Education, 1998); and Thomas D. Snyder et al., *The Condition of Education 1998* (Washington, D.C.: U.S. Government Printing Office, 1998), available at **www.nces.gov.**

parents have less education. This holds to such an extent that average scores for nine-year-olds whose parents had at least some college are not far below those for thirteen-year-olds whose parents did not complete high school.

Achievement correlated with community

School achievement is also correlated with type of community, which reflects the social class of people who reside there. As shown in Table 10.1, the average mathematics and reading scores of students in "advantaged" urban areas (with a high proportion of residents in professional or managerial occupations) are much higher than those of students in "disadvantaged" areas (with a high proportion of residents who receive public assistance or are unemployed). Nine-year-olds in the advantaged communities perform as well as thirteen-year-olds in disadvantaged areas.

Concentrated poverty schools

Further evidence of the relationship between social class and school achievement can be found in studies of poverty neighborhoods in very large cities. For example, Levine and his colleagues examined sixth-grade achievement patterns at more than a thousand predominantly low-income schools (which they called concentrated poverty schools) in seven big cities and reported that all but a few had average reading scores more than two years below the national average. They also pointed out that at least one-fourth of the students at these schools cannot read well enough to be considered functionally literate when they enter high school. This pattern can be found at concentrated poverty schools in big cities throughout the United States.[6]

---

[6]Daniel U. Levine and Rayna F. Levine, *Society and Education,* 9th ed. (Needham Heights, Mass.: Allyn and Bacon, 1996). See also Richard D. Kahlenberg, "Equal Opportunity Critics," *New Republic,* July 17 and 24, 1995, pp. 20–25; and Stephen J. Schellenberg, "Does It Matter Where Poor Kids Live?" (Paper presented at the annual meeting of the American Educational Research Association, San Diego, April 1998).

Rural poverty

Many educators also are concerned about the achievement of rural students, especially those who live in low-income regions and pockets of rural poverty. Although the average achievement of rural students is generally at about the national average, research indicates that poverty and inequality hamper their achievement, and that two-thirds of rural educators believe the academic performance of their low-income students is in either "great need" or "fairly strong need" of improvement.[7]

Effective schools

We also should emphasize, however, that there are methods for improving the achievement of students with low socioeconomic status. In particular, the "effective schools" movement that came to prominence in the 1980s showed that appropriate schoolwide efforts to enhance instruction can produce sizable gains in the performance of disadvantaged students, even in concentrated poverty schools in big cities and rural schools in poor areas. It is easier today than only ten or fifteen years ago to find schools that have improved the achievement of low-income students. The effective schools movement and other efforts to improve the performance of disadvantaged students are described in subsequent chapters, particularly Chapter 16.

Social Class and College Attendance.   Social class is associated with many educational outcomes in addition to achievement in reading, math, and other subjects. On the average, working-class students not only have lower achievement scores, but also are less likely than middle-class students to complete high school or to enroll in and complete college. Only about 7 percent of high-school students from the lowest socioeconomic quartile (the lowest 25 percent of students measured in terms of family income) enter college and attain a postsecondary degree, compared with more than 50 percent of high-school graduates in the highest quartile. (Each "quartile" contains one-quarter of the population.)[8]

Percentages attending college

However, social class is correlated with test scores, and one would not expect students with low test scores to succeed in college to the same extent as those with high scores. For that reason, assessments of the relationship between social class and college attendance should take account of test scores. Data from studies that do this demonstrate that social class is related to college attendance and graduation even after one controls for achievement level. For example, one study showed that low-status high-school seniors were nearly 50 percent less likely to enter a postsecondary institution than were high-status seniors with similar reading achievement scores. Because of limitations in federal financial aid, among other causes, this discrepancy has been growing in recent years.[9]

---

[7]Joyce D. Stern, ed., *The Condition of Education in Rural Schools* (Washington, D.C.: U.S. Department of Education, 1994); Alan J. DeYoung and Barbara K. Lawrence, "On Hoosiers, Yankees, and Mountaineers," *Phi Delta Kappan* (October 1995), pp. 104–112; and Charles D. Manges and Daryl J. Wilcox, "The Role of the Principal in Rural School Reform," *Rural Educator* (Spring 1997), pp. 21–23.

[8]Thomas G. Mortenson, *Equity of Higher Educational Opportunity for Women, Black, Hispanic, and Low-Income Students* (Iowa City: American College Testing Program, 1991); and Stephanie Cuccaro-Alamin, *Postsecondary Persistence and Attainment* (Washington, D.C.: U.S. Department of Education, 1997).

[9]Thomas G. Mortenson, *The Impact of Increased Loan Utilization Among Low Family Income Students* (Iowa City: American College Testing Program, 1990); Jack McCurdy, *Broken Promises* (San Jose: California Higher Education Policy Center, 1994); and Stephen Martin, "An Outspoken Expert Tries to Influence the Debate on Student Aid," *Chronicle of Higher Education,* May 16, 1997, p. A27.

| TABLE 10.2 | Indicators of School Performance, Attainment, and Socioeconomic Background, by Racial and Ethnic Group |

Racial/Ethnic Group	Average Mathematics Scores of Public-School Eighth Graders, 1996	Eighth Graders Below Basic Reading Level, 1994 (Percent)	Poverty Rate, 1997 (Percent)
African American	255	57	27
Asian American/Pacific	280	20	14
Hispanic	268	51	27
Non-Hispanic White	284	22	11

Note: The "basic reading level" is defined in terms of literal comprehension.

Source: The Nation's Report Card (Washington, D.C.: National Assessment of Educational Progress, 1998), available at **nces.ed.gov;** *Statistical Abstract of the United States 1997* (Washington, D.C.: U.S. Government Printing Office, 1997), available at **www.census.gov;** and *Poverty in the United States: 1997* (Washington, D.C.: U.S. Bureau of the Census, 1998).

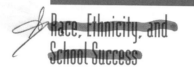

Race, Ethnicity, and School Success

Race and ethnicity defined

Status of minority groups

Eighth-grade samples

Patterns of social class and educational achievement in the United States are further complicated by the additional factors of race and ethnicity. The term **race** identifies groups of people with common ancestry and physical characteristics. The term **ethnicity** identifies people who have a shared culture. Members of an **ethnic group** usually have common ancestry and share language, religion, and other cultural traits. Since there are no "pure" races, some scholars prefer to avoid referring to race and instead discuss group characteristics under the heading of ethnicity.

As we saw in Chapter 5, the population of the United States is a mix of many races and ethnicities. It is well established that most racial and ethnic minority groups in this country have experienced social and economic oppression *as a group* despite the accomplishments of certain individuals. The nation's largest racial minority group — African Americans — is, on the whole, much lower in socioeconomic status than is the white majority. Some other major ethnic minority groups, such as Mexican Americans and Puerto Ricans, are also disproportionately low in socioeconomic status. (These two groups, combined with Cuban Americans and citizens with Central and South American ancestors, constitute the Hispanic/Latino population, which is growing rapidly and will soon outnumber the African American population.) An ongoing concern for educators is the fact that these racial and ethnic minority groups are correspondingly low in academic achievement, high-school and college graduation rates, and other measures of educational attainment.[10]

The close association among social class, race or ethnicity, and school performance is shown in Table 10.2, which presents average math and reading scores attained by nationally representative samples of eighth graders. As shown in the table, African American students have the lowest SES scores (as measured by per

[10]Robin M. Williams, Jr., and Gerald D. Jaynes, *A Common Destiny* (Washington, D.C.: National Academy Press, 1989); Nicholas Lemann, *The Promised Land* (New York: Knopf, 1991); Larry H. Shinagawa and Michael Jang, *Atlas of American Diversity* (Walnut Creek, Calif.: Altamira, 1998); and Roberto Suro, *America's Racial Divide and the Latino Challenge* (New York: Knopf, 1998).

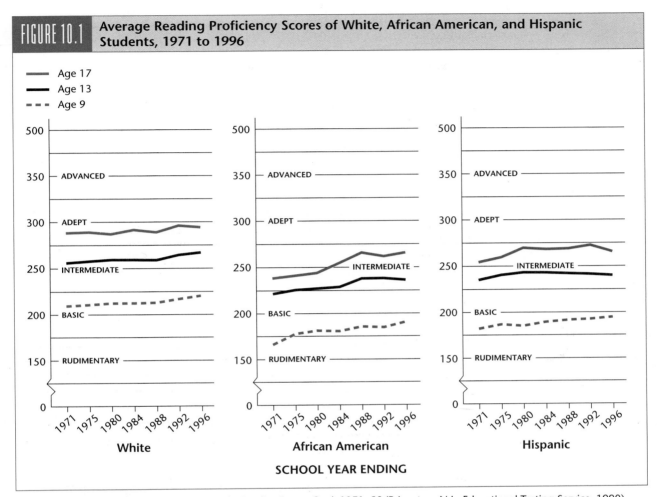

FIGURE 10.1 **Average Reading Proficiency Scores of White, African American, and Hispanic Students, 1971 to 1996**

- Age 17
- Age 13
- Age 9

White

African American

Hispanic

SCHOOL YEAR ENDING

Source: Ina V. S. Mullis and Lynn B. Jenkins, *The Reading Report Card, 1971–88* (Princeton, N.J.: Educational Testing Service, 1990), pp. 54, 58, 62; Ina V. S. Mullis et al., *NAEP 1992 Trends in Academic Progress* (Princeton, N.J.: Educational Testing Service, 1993), p. 17; and Alan Vanneman, "Long-Term Trends in Student Reading Performance," *NAEP Facts* (January 1998), Table 1, available at **nces.ed.gov/pubs98.**

Gains by minorities

capita income), the lowest math scores, and the lowest reading scores. In contrast, non-Hispanic whites are highest in SES and math and second highest in reading scores. In general, school achievement scores roughly parallel scores on socioeconomic status; the higher the SES score, the higher the achievement scores.[11]

However, data collected by the NAEP also indicate that African American and Hispanic students have registered gains in reading, math, and other subjects. As shown in Figure 10.1, gains in reading have narrowed the gap between white students on the one hand and African American and Hispanic students on the other.

[11]Further analysis of these and other data also indicates considerable variation within broad racial and ethnic classifications. For example, among Hispanics, Cuban Americans have much higher SES and achievement scores than do Mexican American and Puerto Rican students. Among Asian American subgroups, Hmong and Vietnamese students tend to be low in status and achievement.

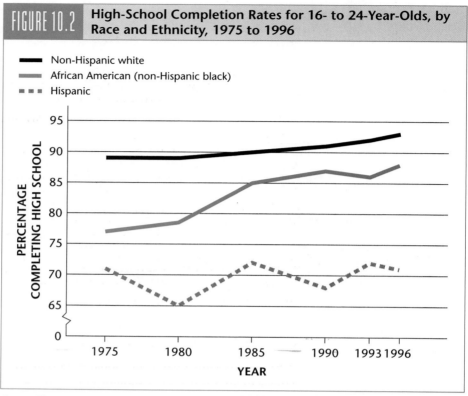

FIGURE 10.2   High-School Completion Rates for 16- to 24-Year-Olds, by Race and Ethnicity, 1975 to 1996

Source: The National Educational Goals Report (Washington, D.C.: National Education Goals Panel, 1991), p. 8; and Pascal D. Forgione, Jr., *Achievement in the United States* (Washington, D.C.: National Center for Education Statistics, 1998), Table M.

Some observers attribute these improvements partly to the effects of the federal Title 1 program and/or to some increase in desegregation. (See Chapter 11 for discussions of Title 1 and desegregation.) On the other hand, African American and Hispanic students still score far below whites in reading and other subjects, and black and Hispanic seventeen-year-olds still have approximately the same average reading scores as white thirteen-year-olds.[12]

Dropout rates

As one would expect from the data shown in Table 10.2, non-Hispanic white and Asian students (other than Vietnamese Americans) are more likely to complete high school than are African American students. As Figure 10.2 shows, the high-school completion rate for African American students has been rising since 1975, but it is still significantly below the rate for whites, and the rate for Hispanics has remained so low that national leaders are gravely concerned about the future of Hispanic youth. In addition, high-school dropout rates are still extremely high among African American and Hispanic students in big-city poverty areas. Knowledgeable observers estimate that dropout rates range from 40 to 60 percent in some big cities

---

[12]Samuel S. Peng, DeeAnn Wright, and Susan T. Hill, *Understanding Racial-Ethnic Differences in Secondary School Science and Mathematics Achievement* (Washington, D.C.: U.S. Department of Education, 1995); and Annie Nakao, "How Race Colors Learning," *San Francisco Examiner,* June 6, 1998.

and sometimes exceed 75 or 80 percent at schools enrolling mostly underclass students. Inasmuch as high-school dropouts have rapidly diminishing opportunities to succeed in the economy, the high dropout rate of urban schools has become a major problem for American society.[13]

College attendance

African American and Hispanic students are also less likely to enter and complete college and other postsecondary institutions. Postsecondary enrollment rates for African American and Hispanic high-school graduates rose substantially in the 1960s and early 1970s but have increased only slightly since then. As a result, African American and Hispanic students constitute less than 20 percent of enrollment in higher education, well below their percentage in the college-age population. The causes cited for these patterns include rising tuition, reductions in federal funds, and cuts in special recruiting and assistance programs. Some educators also note that participation in drug cultures may have disabled many minority youth. Finally, many students may have concluded that higher education will not help them obtain better employment.[14]

Calls for improvement

Reports from major educational agencies have referred to the rate of minority enrollment in higher education as "shockingly low" and "intolerable." Some reports have pointed out that the nation's self-interest demands attention to the matter. The reports generally conclude that colleges, universities, and government officials should take various steps to increase minority enrollment.[15]

The Effect of Minority Status Plus Poverty

Segregated inner cities

As we have documented, educational achievement generally is distressingly low at schools in poor inner-city neighborhoods. We have also pointed out that although high-school completion rates for African American students have been rising nationally, the dropout problem is still severe in big cities. These problems reflect the fact that the inner cores of large urban areas in the United States have increasingly become segregated communities populated by working-class and underclass African American and Hispanic residents. Some of the causes and results of this socioeconomic and racial/ethnic stratification include the following:

Polarization among African Americans

1. *The African American population of the United States has become more economically polarized.* The overall socioeconomic status and income of this population have increased substantially since 1950: opportunities for African Americans have improved, and many have joined the middle class. For example, the average income of married couples among African Americans has approximately doubled (in real dollars) since 1950, and the number of black families earning $50,000 or more has nearly quadrupled. However, many other African Americans still live in urban

[13] Richard Riley, "American Education Has 'Turned a Corner' Reaching for Excellence," *Goals 2000 Community Update,* March 22, 1995. This online source is published monthly. It can be reached by accessing Internet site **www.ed.gov** and selecting "News and Events." See also *The State of the Cities — 1998* (Washington, D.C.: U.S. Department of Housing and Urban Development, 1998, available at **www.huduser.org.**

[14] Richard C. Richardson, Jr., "Promoting Fair College Outcomes," *Policy Perspectives* (May 1991), pp. 7B–8B; and Sonia M. Perez, *Latino Education: Status and Prospects* (Washington, D.C.: National Council of La Raza, 1998).

[15] The agencies mentioned include the Education Commission of the States, the State Higher Education Executive Officers, the United States Commission on Civil Rights, and the American Council on Education. See, for example, Richard C. Richardson, Jr., *Promoting Fair College Outcomes* (Denver: Education Commission of the States, 1991); and *Equal Educational Opportunity and Nondiscrimination for Students with Limited English Proficiency* (Washington, D.C.: United States Commission on Civil Rights, 1997).

poverty, in neighborhoods where most families are headed by single women and where rates of crime, delinquency, drug abuse, teenage pregnancy, and other indicators of social disorganization are all very high.[16]

Somewhat similar statements can be made concerning the Hispanic or Latino population. There is a substantial split between a growing middle-class segment and a large segment residing in big-city poverty neighborhoods. Rates of social disorganization in these latter neighborhoods are very high.[17]

Increasing concentration in urban poverty areas

2. *Both the number and the percentage of low-income minority people living in urban poverty areas have increased substantially.* Although the overall population of the fifty largest cities in the United States has declined since 1970, the number of low-income African Americans living in poverty areas has increased by more than one-third. In addition, low-income people in these areas are further below the poverty line than they were in the 1960s. In a related trend, more than two-thirds of the students in many big-city school districts, such as Chicago, Detroit, and New York, are now from low-income families, and more than 80 percent are minority students.[18]

Dysfunctional institutions

3. *Social institutions such as the family, the school, and the law enforcement system often appear to have collapsed in the inner city.* Parents find it increasingly difficult to control their children, and law enforcement agencies are unable to cope with rising rates of juvenile delinquency and adult crime.[19]

Rising social isolation

4. *The concentration of low-income minority populations in big-city poverty areas has increased their isolation from the larger society.* In contrast to the urban slums and ghettos of fifty or one hundred years ago, today's concentrated poverty areas are larger geographically, and in many cases their residents are more homogeneous in (low) socioeconomic status. Unskilled and semiskilled jobs are more difficult to obtain, and many jobs have moved to the suburbs, where they are practically inaccessible to central-city residents. Andrew Hacker observed that the contemporary "mode of segregation, combining poverty and race, is relatively new. To reside amid so many people leading desultory lives makes it all the harder to break away."[20]

Problems for young black males

5. *The problems experienced by young black males have escalated enormously.* Some knowledgeable observers believe that the plight of young males in inner-city poverty areas is at the root of a series of other serious problems: very high rates of out-of-wedlock births, the persistence of welfare dependency, and violent crime and delinquency. The growth in female-headed families in urban poverty areas is directly related to the high rates at which young African American men drop out

---

[16]Bart Landry, *The New Black Middle Class* (Berkeley: University of California Press, 1987); William J. Wilson, *The Truly Disadvantaged: The Inner City, the Underclass, and Public Policy* (Chicago: University of Chicago Press, 1987); Henry L. Gates, Jr., "The Two Nations of Black America," *Brookings Review* (Spring 1998), pp. 4–7, available at **www.brook.edu;** and Gregg Easterbrook, "America the O.k." *New Republic,* January 6 and 11, 1999, pp. 19–25.

[17]"Latino Neighborhoods and Poverty," *The Urban Institute Policy and Research Report* (Winter–Spring 1995), p. 12; Peter Dreier and David Moberg, "Moving from the 'Hood,'" *The American Prospect* (Winter 1996), pp. 75–79; and Michael B. Teitz and Karen Chapple, "The Causes of Urban Poverty," *Cityscape* (Vol. 3, No. 3, 1998) available at **www.huduser.org.**

[18] Alan Wolfe, "The New American Dilemma," *New Republic,* April 13, 1992, pp. 30–37; Craig St. John, "Interclass Segregation, Poverty, and Poverty Concentration," *American Journal of Sociology* (March 1995), pp. 1325–1333; and "Minorities in Public Schools," *Education Digest* (February 1998), pp. 4–11.

[19]Karl Zinsmeister, "Growing Up Scared," *The Atlantic* (June 1990), pp. 49–66; and Carl L. Bankston and Stephen J. Caldas, "Race, Poverty, Family Structure and the Inequality of Schools," *Sociological Spectrum* (January–March, 1998), pp. 55–74.

[20]Andrew Hacker, "American Apartheid," *New York Review of Books,* December 3, 1987, pp. 32–33; Andrew Hacker, *Two Nations* (New York: Ballantine, 1995); and Andrew Hacker, "Grand Illusion," *New York Review of Books,* June 11, 1998, pp. 26–29.

of the labor force, are incarcerated in prisons, enter the military, or otherwise are excluded or exclude themselves from mainstream institutions. The result is a great reduction in the pool of men available to participate in stable families and accumulate resources for upward mobility.[21]

City vs. suburban schools

Aggravating all these conditions is the fact that poverty schools in big cities are usually overloaded with problems that make them dysfunctional and ineffective for many students. The extent of this ineffectiveness has been underlined by comparisons of achievement data at city and suburban schools in the same metropolitan area. In a study of the Milwaukee area, for example, the city high schools enrolled many more low-income and minority students than the suburban schools. At the city high schools, an average of only 40 percent of tenth graders had reading and math scores above the national average, whereas the average for the eleven suburban high schools was 64 percent. Since Milwaukee has less segregation in its city schools than do many other urban communities, the achievement disparity in this study may represent only the tip of the iceberg.[22]

The Influence of Social Class

Social class as the primary factor

Because social class, race and ethnicity, and school achievement are so closely interrelated, researchers frequently ask whether race and ethnicity are associated with performance in the educational system even after one takes into account the low socioeconomic status of African Americans and other disadvantaged minority groups. In general, the answer has been that social class accounts for most of the variation in educational achievement by race and ethnicity. That is, if one knows the social class of a group of students, one can predict with a good deal of accuracy whether their achievement, ability scores, and college attendance rates are high or low. Information about their racial or ethnic group does relatively little to improve such a prediction. This also means that working-class white students as a group are low in achievement and college attainment, whereas the average middle-class minority student ranks relatively high on these variables.[23]

One of the central problems faced by disadvantaged minorities in the United States, therefore, is that they are still disproportionately working class and underclass and that their children are much less successful in the educational system than are the children of the middle class. Moreover, because education is an important channel for gaining access to the job market, minority students with low socioeconomic status have relatively less opportunity for economic success later in their lives. From this point of view, the ineffectiveness of the schools in educating students from working-class homes helps to perpetuate the current class system — and the burden of poverty and low achievement falls disproportionately on the nation's racial and ethnic minority groups.

---

[21]Ronald B. Mincy, "No Underclass Solution Can Ignore Young Males," *The Urban Institute Policy and Research Report* (Fall 1990), p. 28; Glenn Loury, "The Impossible Dilemma," *New Republic,* January 1, 1996, pp. 21–25; and Melanie Eversly, "Rising Tide of Young Blacks Behind Bars," *Detroit Free Press,* February 21, 1998.

[22]Levine and Levine, *Society and Education;* John Witte and Daniel J. Walsh, "A Systematic Test of the Effective Schools Model," *Educational Evaluation and Policy Analysis* (February 1990), pp. 188–218; and *The State of the Cities — 1997* (Washington, D.C.: U.S. Department of Housing and Urban Development, 1997), available at **www.huduser.org.**

[23]Sandra Graham, "How Causal Beliefs Influence the Academic and Social Motivation of African-American Children," in Gary G. Branigan, ed., *The Enlightened Educator* (New York: McGraw-Hill,1996), pp. 110–125; and Paul A. Barton, *Toward Inequality: Disturbing Trends in Higher Education* (Princeton, N.J.: Educational Testing Service, 1997), available at **www.ets.org.**

The Situation

Suppose you are assigned as a student teacher to a school in a low-income neighborhood. Most of the students are from minority groups, and their backgrounds often include one or more of the social disadvantages identified in Chapter 9. In your first class, you give your best lesson: challenging, upbeat, informative, imaginative. The students pay attention and several participate, responding to questions and asking their own. You feel you've done a good job. But as the students leave the room, one of them — a quiet, rather thoughtful young person — stops to say this to you: "I can see you're tryin'. But pretty soon you'll quit on us like others do. We're the wrong type or the wrong color, and some of us don't talk your language. Everybody knows we ain't going anywhere but out on the streets."

The comment upsets you. You want to respond that it's not true: these students *can* go somewhere. You feel challenged by the student's bleak outlook.

Thought Questions

The following questions should be useful to keep in mind as you read not just this chapter but subsequent chapters in this book.

1. To what extent is it true that middle-class student teachers do not "speak the same language" as students from low-income families? Should teachers try to do this? How might doing so affect the teacher's relationships with his or her students?
2. If you were to face a situation like this, what would you say or do to reassure the student?
3. What would your reaction be if most of the students in the class indicated they were not interested in the lesson you had worked so hard to prepare? Who might you turn to for help?
4. How might the teacher in this latter situation (question 3) try to modify his or her lesson to stimulate more interest among students?
5. What are some of the things you might do to ensure that all the students in your classroom have an equal opportunity to achieve?

A divided population

For educators, the challenge is to improve the performance of all low-status students, from whatever ethnic group. The U.S. population as a whole has become more divided, with a growing high-income segment, a growing low-income segment, and a shrinking middle segment. Many commentators share the alarm of Secretary of Labor Robert Reich: "If we lose our middle class and become a two-tiered society, we not only risk the nation's future prosperity but also its social coherence and stability. As the economy grows, people who work the machines and clean the offices and provide the basic goods and services are supposed to share in the gains, but that hasn't been happening."[24]

---

[24]Quoted in Keith Bradsher, "Productivity Is All, But It Doesn't Pay Well," *New York Times,* June 25, 1995, p. 4E. See also Keith Bradsher, "America's Opportunity Gap," *New York Times,* June 4, 1995, p. E4; and Peter Passell, "Benefits Dwindle for the Unskilled Along with Wages," *New York Times,* June 14, 1998.

Reasons for Low Achievement Among Low-Status Students

Over the past forty years, much research has been aimed at understanding and overcoming the academic deficiencies of low-achieving students in general and low-achieving students from working-class or poor families in particular. Although the explanations are not necessarily mutually exclusive, we will group them under the following major factors: home environment, heredity versus environment, and obstacles in the classroom.

Know This

Home Environment

Chapter 9 pointed out that the family and home environment is the most important agent in the early socialization and education of the child. We also noted that characteristics of the home environment closely reflect the family's social class. Thus social-class differences in home environment are associated with the level of educational performance and attainment that students achieve. Many working-class students grow up in homes that do not prepare them well for school. Thus even though their parents may stress the importance of education, they tend to function poorly in the typical classroom.

One way to categorize the home environment is to look at differences in knowledge and understandings, cognitive and verbal skills, and values and attitudes. Regarding *knowledge and understandings,* middle-class children are more likely than working-class children to acquire a wide knowledge of the world outside the home through access to books and cultural institutions (for example, museums), parental teaching, and exploration of diverse environments. Knowledge and understandings acquired through exposure to the wider world are helpful to children when they enter school. Working-class students today may experience even greater disadvantages than in earlier eras because they tend to have much less access to computers at home than do middle-class students.[25]

Cognitive and verbal skills

Students' *cognitive and verbal skills* also reflect social-class differences in family language environments. Basil Bernstein has found that both middle- and working-class children develop adequate skills with respect to "ordinary" or "restricted" language, but middle-class children are superior in the use of "formal" or "elaborated" language. Ordinary, restricted language is grammatically simple, relying on gestures and further explanations to clarify meaning. Elaborated, formal language is grammatically complex and provides greater potential for organizing experience within an abstract meaning system.[26] Many scholars believe that facility in using elaborated language helps middle-class children excel in cognitive development. Other researchers also have reported that working-class mothers are less likely than middle-class mothers to establish productive conversational

Knowledge and understandings

---

[25]Annette Lareau, "Social Class Differences in Family-School Relationships: The Importance of Cultural Capital," *Sociology of Education* (April 1987), pp. 73–85; Sheila White and Peter Dewitz, "Reading Proficiency and Home Support for Literacy," *NAEP Facts* (October 1996), pp. 1–4; Thomas D. Snyder et al., *The Condition of Education 1998* (Washington, D.C.: U.S. Government Printing Office, 1998); and Ernest W. Brewer and Connie Hollingsworth, *Promising Practices* (Scottsdale, Ariz.: Holcomb Hathaway, 1999).
[26]Basil Bernstein, *Class, Codes, and Control* (London and Boston: Routledge and Kegan Paul, 1975); Basil Bernstein, *The Structuring of Pedagogic Discourse* (New York: Routledge, 1990); and Betty Hart and Todd R. Risley, *Meaningful Differences in the Everyday Experience of Young American Children* (Baltimore: Brookes, 1995).

Middle-class children are more likely than working-class children to acquire a wide knowledge of the world outside the home through access to books and cultural institutions. *(© Elizabeth Crews)*

routines and to provide responsive talk that helps children improve in abstract language.[27]

Values and attitudes

Regarding *values and attitudes,* many children from lower socioeconomic backgrounds are at a disadvantage because their socialization appears to emphasize obedience and conformity, whereas middle-class families tend to stress independent learning and self-directed thinking. Differences along these lines undoubtedly reflect the fact that many working-class environments are relatively dangerous for children; other differences arise from parents' education, resources, and knowledge of what practices help children develop intellectually. Although the child-raising methods of working-class families probably are becoming more like those of middle-class families, and although they may be superior in preparing children to function in a hostile environment, socialization practices in many working-class homes do not prepare children to function independently in the school and classroom. After an intensive study of 700 families in Nottingham, England, John and Elizabeth Newson summarized these different socialization patterns as follows:[28]

> Parents at the upper end of the social scale are more inclined on principle to use democratically based, highly verbal means of control, and this kind of discipline

[27]Catherine E. Snow, Clara Dubber, and Akke De Blauw, "Routines in Mother-Child Interaction," in Lynne Feagans and Dale Clark Farran, eds., *The Language of Children Reared in Poverty* (New York: Academic Press, 1982); Erwin Flaxman and A. Harry Passow, eds., *Changing Populations Changing Schools* (Chicago: University of Chicago Press, 1995); and Catherine E. Snow, M. Susan Burns, and Peg Griffin, eds., *Preventing Reading Difficulties in Young Children* (Washington, D.C.: National Academy of Sciences, 1998).

[28]Duane F. Alwin, "Changes in Qualities in Children Valued in the United States," *Social Science Research* (September 1989), pp. 195–236; and John Newson and Elizabeth Newson, *Seven Years Old in the Home Environment* (London: Allen and Unwin, 1976), p. 406. Chapter 3 in *Society and Education* by Levine and Levine describes in detail the advantages of emphasizing obedience in a working-class environment, particularly in the inner city. See also Robin L. Jarrett, "Growing Up Poor," *Journal of Adolescent Research* (January 1995), pp. 111–135; and Thomas J. Gorman, "Social Class and Parental Attitudes Toward Education," *Journal of Contemporary Ethnography* (April 1998), pp. 60–74.

The most rapid development of many human characteristics — including cognitive skills — occurs during the preschool years; home environment therefore is crucial to cognitive development. *(© Elizabeth Crews/The Image Works)*

is likely to produce personalities who can both identify successfully with the system and use it for their own ends later on. At the bottom end of the scale . . . parents choose on principle to use a highly authoritarian, mainly non-verbal means of control, in which words are used more to threaten and bamboozle the child into obedience than to make him understand the rationale behind social behavior. . . . Thus the child born into the lowest social bracket has everything stacked against him including his parents' principles of child upbringing.

Stimulation by home environment

The importance of the home and family environment for general intellectual development has also been documented in studies by J. McVicker Hunt, Martin Deutsch, and other researchers. These studies generally indicate that environmental stimulation in working-class homes is less conducive to intellectual development, on the average, than it is in middle-class homes. Deutsch outlined a number of factors, such as lack of productive visual and tactile stimulation, that detract from readiness to learn among many disadvantaged children. Deutsch and others have developed indexes of environmental disadvantage that correlate more closely with IQ scores and school success than do social-class indicators.[29]

[29]Martin Deutsch, "The Role of Social Class in Language Development and Cognition," in A. H. Passow, M. I. Goldbery, and A. J. Tannenbaum, eds., *Education of the Disadvantaged* (New York: Holt, 1967), pp. 214–224; J. McVicker Hunt, *Intelligence and Experience* (New York: Ronald Press, 1961); and Jane E. Miller and Diane Davis, "Poverty History, Family History, and Quality of Children's Home Environment," *Journal of Marriage and the Family* (November 1997), pp. 996–1008.

Early cognitive development

The environmental disadvantage theory holds that early years of development are more important than later years. As pointed out by Benjamin Bloom, David Hamburg, and others, the most rapid development of many human characteristics, including cognitive skills, occurs during the preschool years. Furthermore, the child's intellectual development is affected even during the prenatal stages by the mother's general health, her diet, her alcohol intake and drug usage, and stress and other emotional factors. This does not mean that it is impossible to remedy learning deficits that arise from disadvantaged home environments, but it does imply that it is more difficult to produce changes for older children; that a more powerful environment is needed to bring about these changes; and that, as a society, we should use more of our resources to address early environmental problems and disadvantages. These understandings helped lead to the development of *compensatory education,* which, as described in the next chapter, tries to remedy the effects of environmental disadvantages by providing preschool education and improved instruction in elementary and secondary schools.[30]

Early brain development

Negative effects on cognitive performance from impoverished environments have become of increasing concern as scientists have learned more about how the brain develops and what this knowledge may mean for educators. In general, neurologists and other investigators have reinforced Bloom's conclusions about the importance of a positive home environment in the first two or three years of life, when the brain is growing rapidly and establishing billions of neural connections. In addition to emphasizing the value of good preschools, many educators are exploring the implications for devising instructional methods and environments that take into account how the brain works and thereby may stimulate cognitive development. However, it may be some time before enough is known to anticipate that substantial improvements in curriculum and instruction will occur based on an understanding of how the brain functions and develops.[31]

Average differences are not universal patterns

Socialization differentials like those we have been discussing in this section reflect average differences across social-class groups, not universal patterns that distinguish all middle-class families from all working-class families. Many families with low socioeconomic status do provide a home environment conducive to achievement, and the great majority of low-income parents try to offer their children a positive learning environment. Similarly, many children from working-class families do well in school, and many middle-class children do not. Nevertheless, children from low-income, working-class homes are disproportionately likely to grow up in an environment that does not adequately prepare them to succeed in contemporary schools.

The Heredity Versus Environment Debate

Early IQ tests

During the past century, there has been heated controversy about whether intelligence is determined primarily by heredity or by environment. When IQ tests were

---

[30]Benjamin S. Bloom, *Stability and Change in Human Characteristics* (New York: Wiley, 1964); Benjamin S. Bloom, *Human Characteristics and School Learning* (New York: McGraw-Hill, 1976); Benjamin S. Bloom, *All Our Children Learning* (New York: McGraw-Hill, 1981); J. Larry Brown and Ernesto Pollitt, "Malnutrition, Poverty, and Intellectual Development," *Scientific American* (February 1996), pp. 38–43; and B. Devlin and Michael Daniels, "The Heritability of IQ," *Nature* (July 1997), pp. 468–471.
[31]Justine C. Baker and Frances G. Martin, *A Neural Network Guide to Teaching* (Bloomington, Ind.: Phi Delta Kappan, 1998); Janelle Miller, *Brain Research and Education* (Denver Education Commission of the States, 1998), available at **www.ecs.org**; and Judith Blake, "Building Your Baby's Brain Power," *Seattle Times,* January 5, 1999.

undergoing rapid development early in the twentieth century, many psychologists believed that intelligence was determined primarily by heredity. These *hereditarians* thought that IQ tests and similar instruments measured innate differences in people's capacity. When economically disadvantaged groups and some minority groups, such as African Americans, scored considerably below other groups, the hereditarians believed that the groups with the lower scores were innately inferior in intellectual capacity.

Stress on compensatory help

Environmentalist View. By the middle of the twentieth century, numerous studies had counteracted the hereditarian view, and most social scientists took the position that environment is as important as or even more important than heredity in determining intelligence. The preceding section mentioned the work of some noted proponents of the **environmentalist view of intelligence** — J. McVicker Hunt, Martin Deutsch, and Benjamin Bloom. Environmentalists generally stress the need for compensatory programs on a continual basis beginning in infancy. Many also criticize the use of IQ tests on the grounds that these tests are culturally biased. Many attribute the differences in IQ scores between African Americans and whites, for example, to differences in social class and family environment and to systematic racial discrimination.

IQ gains

Sandra Scarr and Richard Weinberg studied differences between African American children growing up in biological families and those growing up in adopted families. They concluded that the effects of environment outweigh the effects of heredity. Thomas Sowell, after examining IQ scores collected for various ethnic groups between 1920 and 1970, found that the scores of some groups such as Italian Americans and Polish Americans have substantially improved. Other studies indicate that the test scores of African Americans and Puerto Ricans have risen more rapidly than scores in the general population in response to improvements in teaching and living conditions.[32]

Cause of IQ gains

Similar data on other countries have been collected by James Flynn, who found that "massive" gains have occurred during the twentieth century in the IQ scores of the population in fourteen nations. The major cause of these improvements, according to Flynn's analysis, is not genetic improvement in the populations but environmental changes that led to gains in the kinds of skills assessed by IQ tests. Torsten Husen and his colleagues also have concluded, after reviewing large amounts of data, that improvements in economic and social conditions, and particularly in the availability of schooling, can produce substantial gains in average IQ from one generation to the next. In general, educators committed to improving the performance of low-achieving students are encouraged by these studies.[33]

Hereditarian View. The **hereditarian view of intelligence** underwent a major revival in the 1970s and 1980s, based particularly on the writings of Arthur Jensen, Richard Herrnstein, and a group of researchers who have been conducting the Minnesota Study of Twins. Summarizing previous research as well as their own studies,

---

[32]Sandra Scarr and Richard A. Weinberg, "I.Q. Test Performance of Black Children Adopted by White Families," *American Psychologist* (July 1976), pp. 726–739; Thomas Sowell, *Race and Culture* (New York: Basic Books, 1994); and James J. Heckman, "Cracked Bell," *Reason* (March 1995), pp. 49–56. See also Trish Hall, "IQ Scores Are Up, and Psychologists Wonder Why," *New York Times,* February 24, 1998.

[33]James R. Flynn, *Asian Americans: Achievement Beyond IQ* (Hillsdale, N.J.: Erlbaum, 1991); John Horgan, "Get Smart, Take a Test," *Scientific American* (November 1995), pp. 12, 14; Wendy M. Williams, "Democratizing Our Concept of Human Intelligence," *The Chronicle of Higher Education,* May 15, 1998, p. A60; and Marguerite Holloway, "Flynn's Effect," *Scientific American* (January 1999).

these researchers concluded that heredity is the major factor in determining intelligence — accounting for up to 80 percent of the variation in IQ scores.[34]

Jensen and his critics

One very controversial study was published by Jensen in the *Harvard Educational Review* in 1969. Pointing out that African Americans averaged about 15 points below whites on IQ tests, Jensen attributed this gap to a genetic difference between the two races in learning abilities and patterns. Critics countered Jensen's arguments by contending that IQ is affected by a host of environmental factors, such as malnutrition and prenatal care, that are difficult to measure and impossible to separate from hereditary factors. IQ tests are biased, they said, and do not necessarily even measure intelligence. Moreover, institutionalized racial discrimination could account for differences in IQ that might exist between African Americans and whites.[35]

Since his 1969 article, Jensen has continued to cite data that he believes link intelligence primarily to heredity. His critics continue to respond with evidence that environmental factors, and schooling in particular, have a major influence on IQ.[36]

A middle position

Synthesizers' View. A number of social scientists have taken a middle, or "synthesizing," position in this controversy. The **synthesizers' view of intelligence** holds that both heredity and environment contribute to differences in measured intelligence. For example, Christopher Jencks, after reviewing a large amount of data, divided the IQ variance into 0.45 due to heredity, 0.35 due to environment, and 0.20 due to interaction between the two ("interaction" meaning that particular abilities thrive or wither in specific environments). Robert Nichols reviewed all these and other data and concluded that the true value for heredity may be anywhere between 0.40 and 0.80 but that the exact value has little importance for policy. In general, Nichols and other synthesizers maintain that heredity determines the fixed limits of a range; within those limits, the interaction between environment and heredity yields the individual's intelligence. In this view, even if we cannot specify exactly how much of a child's intelligence is the result of environmental factors, teachers (and parents) should provide each child with a productive environment in which to realize her or his maximum potential.[37]

Interaction of heredity and environment

----

[34]Arthur R. Jensen, "How Much Can We Boost IQ and Scholastic Achievement?" *Harvard Educational Review* (Winter 1969), pp. 1–123; Arthur R. Jensen, *Bias in Mental Testing* (New York: Free Press, 1980); Richard J. Herrnstein and Charles Murray, *The Bell Curve* (New York: Free Press, 1994); Linda S. Gottfredson, "What Do We Know About IQ?" *American Scholar* (Winter 1996), pp. 15–30; J. Philippe Rushton, "The Mismeasures of Gould," *Personnel Psychology* (Summer 1997), pp. 485–490; and J. Philippe Rushton, "The New Enemies of Evolutionary Science," *Liberty* (March 1998), pp. 31–35.

[35]"How Much Can We Boost IQ and Scholastic Achievement: A Discussion," *Harvard Educational Review* (Spring 1969), pp. 273–356; and Howard Gardner, "Cracking Open the IQ Box," *The American Prospect* (Winter 1995), pp. 71–80. Part of the criticism of Jensen focused on his use of data on twins, which had been collected by a distinguished British psychologist (Sir Cyril Burt). Many scholars now believe that these data were fabricated to support hereditarian conclusions. See also Leon J. Kamin, *The Science and Politics of IQ* (Potomac, Md.: Erlbaum, 1974); Arthur R. Jensen, "IQ and Science," *The Public Interest* (Fall 1991), pp. 93–106; J. Phillippe Rushton, "Victim of Scientific Hoax," *Society* (March 1994), pp. 40–44; and APA Task Force on Intelligence, "Intelligence: Knowns and Unknowns" (Paper prepared for the American Psychological Association, Washington, D.C., 1997), summary available at **www.apa.org.**

[36]Arthur R. Jensen, "g: Artifact or Reality?" *Journal of Vocational Behavior* (December 1986), pp. 330–331; Elaine Mensh and Harry Mensh, *The IQ Mythology* (Carbondale: Southern Illinois University Press, 1991); Stephen J. Gould, "Curveball," *New Yorker,* November 28, 1994, pp. 139–149; and Arthur R. Jensen, *The g Factor* (Westport, Conn.: Praeger, 1998).

[37]Robert C. Nichols, "Policy Implications of the IQ Controversy," in Lee S. Shulman, ed., *Review of Research in Education* (Itasca, Ill.: Peacock, 1978); Robert Plonim, *Genetics and Experience* (Thousand Oaks, Calif.: Sage, 1994); B. Devlin, Michael Daniels and Kathryn Roeder, "The Heritability of IQ," *Nature* (July 1997), pp. 468–469; and John Rennie, "Outsmarting Our Genes," *Scientific American* (May 1998).

Obstacles in the Classroom

We have noted that the home and family environment of many working-class students lacks the kind of educational stimulation needed to prepare students for success in the classroom. However, certain school and classroom dynamics also help foster low achievement. The following list highlights some of the most important classroom obstacles to better achievement by working-class students.[38]

Concepts increasingly abstract

1. *Inappropriate curriculum and instruction.* Curriculum materials and instructional approaches in the primary grades frequently assume that students are familiar with vocabulary and concepts to which working-class students have had little or no exposure. As students proceed through school, terminology and concepts become increasingly abstract, and many students fall further behind because their level of mastery is too rudimentary to allow for fluent learning. After grade three, much of the curriculum requires advanced skills that many working-class students have not yet acquired; hence they fall further behind in other subject areas.[39]

Students' perceptions of inadequacy

2. *Lack of previous success in school.* Lack of academic success in the early grades not only detracts from learning more difficult material later; it also damages a student's perception that he or she is a capable learner who has a chance to succeed in school and in later life. Once students believe that they are inadequate as learners and lack control over their future, they are less likely to work vigorously at overcoming learning deficiencies.[40]

Insufficient higher-order instruction

3. *Ineffective fixation on low-level learning.* When a student or group of students is functioning far below grade level, teachers tend to concentrate on remediating basic skills in reading, math, and other subjects. This reaction is appropriate for some low achievers, who need intensive help in acquiring initial skills, but it is damaging for those who could benefit from more challenging learning experiences and assignments. Although helping low-achieving students master higher-order learning skills is a difficult challenge for teachers, instructional strategies have been devised that make it possible to move successfully in this direction. Unfortunately, various problems (such as difficult teaching conditions and large class size) discussed in the remainder of this section have inhibited efforts to introduce such strategies, which we illustrate and discuss in some detail in Chapter 16.[41]

Problems for teachers

4. *Difficulty of teaching conditions in working-class schools.* As students fall further behind academically and as both teachers and students experience frustration and discouragement, behavior problems increase in the classroom. Teachers then find it still more difficult to provide a productive learning environment. One frequent result is that some teachers give up trying to teach low achievers or leave the school to seek less frustrating employment elsewhere.[42]

---

[38]The discussion in this section is based in part on material in Levine and Levine, *Society and Education,* Chapter 8.

[39]Michael S. Knapp and Patrick M. Shields, eds., *Better Schooling for the Children of Poverty* (Berkeley, Calif.: McCutchan, 1991); and Gerald N. Tirozi, "It's About Teaching and Learning, Not Testing," *Education Week,* August 5, 1998.

[40]Bernard Weiner, "Integrating Social and Personal Theories of Achievement Striving," *Review of Educational Research* (Winter 1994), pp. 557–563; and "School Climate," in *Quality Counts* (Washington, D.C.: Editorial Projects in Education, 1998), pp. 18–19.

[41]Miriam Alfassi, "Reading for Meaning," *American Educational Research Journal* (Summer 1998), pp. 309–332.

[42]Reba Page and Linda Valli, eds., *Curriculum Differentiation* (Albany: State University of New York Press, 1990); Stanley Pogrow, "Making Reform Work for the Educationally Disadvantaged," *Educational Leadership* (February 1995), pp. 20–24; and Lynn Olson and Craig D. Gerald, "The Teaching Challenge," in *Quality Counts* (Washington, D.C.: Editorial Projects in Education, 1998), pp. 16–17.

Gaps in language and culture

5. *Differences in teacher and student backgrounds.* Teachers from middle-class backgrounds may have difficulty understanding and motivating disadvantaged pupils. Particularly in the case of white teachers working with disadvantaged minority students, differences in dialect, language, or cultural background may make it difficult for the teachers to communicate effectively with their students.[43]

Self-fulfilling prophecy

6. *Teacher perceptions of student inadequacy.* Many teachers in working-class schools may see low achievement in their classrooms and conclude that large numbers of their students cannot learn. This view easily becomes a self-fulfilling prophecy because teachers who question their students' learning potential are less likely to work hard to improve academic performance, particularly since improvement requires an intense effort that consumes almost all of a teacher's energy.[44]

Separate groups for "slow" learners

7. *Ineffective homogeneous grouping.* Educators faced with large groups of low achievers frequently address the problem by setting them apart in separate classes or subgroups in which instruction can proceed at a slower pace without detracting from the performance of high achievers. Unfortunately, both teachers and the students themselves tend to view concentrations of low achievers as "slow" groups for whom learning expectations are low or nonexistent.

Ray Rist studied this type of arrangement, called **homogeneous grouping**, at a working-class school in St. Louis. A kindergarten class was divided into groups, the "fast learners" and the "slow learners." The "fast" group received "the most teaching time, rewards, and attention from the teacher." The "slow" group was *Less support for the "slow"* "taught infrequently, subjected to more control, and received little if any support from the teacher." Naturally, by the end of the year, there were differences in how these children were prepared for first grade, and the first grade teacher grouped the students on the basis of their "readiness."[45]

Instructional alternatives

In situations like the one Rist described, it might be preferable to keep the students in heterogeneous classes (i.e., classes very diverse in terms of students' previous achievement) but give them individualized instruction so that each can progress at his or her own rate. However, individualization is extremely difficult to implement, and it often requires such systematic change in school practices that it becomes almost an economic impossibility. Thus teachers confronted with heterogeneous classes in schools with mostly low-income students generally have not been able to work effectively with the large numbers of low achievers in their classrooms. One solution is to group low achievers homogeneously for blocks of reading and language instruction but to make sure that the groups are small and are taught by highly skilled teachers who work well with such students. This alter-

[43]Jacqueline J. Irvine, "Teacher Race as a Factor in Black Student Achievement" (Paper presented at the annual meeting of the American Educational Research Association, New Orleans, April 1988); and Ricardo D. Stanton-Salazar, "A Social Capital Framework for Understanding the Socialization of Racial Minority Children and Youth," *Harvard Educational Review* (Spring 1997), pp. 1–40.

[44]Charles M. Payne, *Getting What We Ask For* (Westwood, Conn.: Greenwood, 1984); Lisa Delpit, *Other People's Children* (New York: New Press, 1995), pp. 173–174; Stephanie Madon, Lee Jussim, and Jacqueline Eccles, "In Search of the Powerful Self-Fulfilling Prophecy," *Journal of Personality and Social Psychology* (April 1997), pp. 791–809; and "What Makes the Difference?" *Cityschools* (Spring 1998), pp. 7–10.

[45]Ray C. Rist, *The Urban School: A Factory for Failure* (Cambridge, Mass.: MIT Press, 1973), p. 91. See also Daniel L. Duke and Robert L. Canaday, *School Policy* (New York: McGraw-Hill, 1991; Richard McAdams, "Improving America's Schools," *Principal* (November 1994), pp. 34–35; Elizabeth G. Cohen and Rachel A. Lotan, *Working for Equity in Heterogeneous Classrooms* (New York: Teachers College Press, 1997); and Anne Wheelock, "Keeping Schools on Track," (Winter 1998–1999), p. 22.

TAKING ISSUE

Homogeneous Grouping

Many schools and classrooms group students by ability in specific subjects, separating the slower from the faster learners or the more advanced from the less advanced. Advocates of homogeneous grouping argue that it is both fair and effective, but critics have charged that it harms students, particularly low achievers.

QUESTION Is homogeneous grouping of students by ability a generally effective approach for classroom instruction?

Arguments PRO

1 In a large, heterogeneous class with students at many different levels, the teacher cannot give the slowest learners the special attention they need. In fact, students who struggle to master the lesson may come to be seen as "problems," and quicker students may become favorites. Therefore, it makes sense to separate students into ability groups for specific subjects.

2 For high-achieving students who are capable of learning quickly, it is unfair to slow the pace of instruction to meet the needs of the average student. The high achievers may become bored and discouraged unless they are separated into groups that can proceed at a faster rate.

3 Homogeneous grouping encourages the growth of an esprit de corps among group members. With cooperation and friendly competition, students at similar levels can spur each other forward.

4 Many teachers are more effective with certain kinds of students than with others. Homogeneous grouping allows teachers to spend more time with groups they enjoy teaching and are best suited to teach.

5 Homogeneous grouping indicates to parents that the school recognizes differences in learning styles. The school is seen as making a commitment to each child's individual needs.

Arguments CON

1 Research has shown that ability grouping tends to stereotype slower learners and hamper their progress. The instruction offered to such groups is often inferior. Because little is expected of them, they are seldom challenged, and thus they fall further behind the more advanced students. In general, slower learners will do better in heterogeneous classes.

2 Although high-achieving students may be hindered somewhat in a heterogeneous setting, they will remain motivated as long as they sense that the teacher appreciates their talents. Moreover, it is important for them to learn that students of all academic levels have something of value to contribute.

3 A group spirit may develop among high achievers who feel a special honor in being placed together. But low achievers will feel stigmatized, and their attitudes as a group will often be negative. They may become increasingly alienated from school and society.

4 Only a few very special teachers have the skill, patience, and enthusiasm needed to work effectively with an entire group of low achievers. Teachers assigned to such groups may become frustrated and demoralized.

5 Parents of low achievers are rarely pleased at seeing their children separated from others. A heterogeneous setting is the best indication that the school cares about all its students.

native is in line with research indicating that "restrictive" settings (that is, separate arrangements for low achievers) may have either positive or negative outcomes, depending on what one does to make instruction effective.[46] The issue of homogeneous grouping is discussed further in Chapter 16.

Overload on teachers and schools

8. *Delivery-of-service problems.* The problems we have described suggest that it is very difficult to deliver educational services effectively in classes or schools with a high percentage of low achievers. If, for example, a teacher in a working-class school has ten or twelve very low achieving students in a class of twenty-five, the task of providing effective instruction is many times more difficult than that of a teacher who has only four or five low achievers in a middle-class school. Not only may teachers in the former situation need to spend virtually all their time overcoming low achievers' learning problems, but the negative dynamics that result from students' frustration and misbehavior make the task much more demanding.[47] Administrators, counselors, and other specialized personnel in working-class schools experience the same predicament: so much time is taken up with addressing learning and behavior problems that little may be left for improving services for all students. In such **overloaded schools** the high incidence of serious problems makes it very difficult for educators to function effectively.

Benefits of small classes

9. *Overly large classes.* As suggested above, one reason instruction is ineffective for many low-achieving students is that classes often are too large for teachers to provide sufficient help to overcome learning problems. This is particularly true with respect to critical thinking, reading comprehension, mathematics problem solving, and other higher-order skills. Acquisition of complex skills among low achievers appears to require systematic "mediated" assistance to individuals or small groups.[48]

This conclusion has been supported by a major study of primary-grade students in Project STAR classes in eighty schools in Tennessee. Students were assigned randomly to classes respectively classified as "small" (13 to 17), "regular" (22 to 25), or "regular plus a full-time teacher aide." Contrasting their results with earlier studies, which frequently reached ambiguous conclusions, researchers assessing Project STAR found that students in small classes scored substantially higher in reading and math in kindergarten and first grade than did students in regular classes, and then maintained their advantage in later grades. Effects were particularly impressive at schools that enrolled large proportions of students from

---

[46]Michael Scriven, "Problems and Prospects for Individualization," in Harriet Talmage, ed., *Systems of Individualized Education* (Berkeley, Calif.: McCutchan, 1975), pp. 199–210; Gaea Leinhardt and Allan Pallay, "Restrictive Educational Settings: Exile or Haven?" *Review of Educational Research* (December 1982), pp. 557–558; Elizabeth G. Cohen, "Restructuring the Classroom: Conditions for Productive Small Groups," *Review of Educational Research* (Spring 1994), pp. 1–35; Michael F. Giangreco, "What Do I Do Now?" *Educational Leadership* (February 1996), pp. 56–59; Yiping Lou et al., "Within-Class Grouping," *Review of Educational Research* (Winter 1996), pp. 423–458; and Tom Rudin and LaRima Lane, *A Review of the Literature on Middle-Grades Schools* (New York: College Board, 1998).
[47]Eugene E. Eubanks and Daniel U. Levine, "Administrative and Organizational Arrangements and Considerations," in Dorothy S. Strickland and Eric J. Cooper, eds., *Educating Black Children* (Washington, D.C.: Howard University, 1987), pp. 19–32; and Stephen J. Schellenberg, "Does It Matter Where Poor Kids Live?" (Paper presented at the annual meeting of the American Educational Research Association, San Diego, April 1998).
[48]Lorna Idol and Beau Fly Jones, eds., *Educational Values and Cognitive Instruction* (Hillsdale, N.J.: Erlbaum, 1991); and Linda Darling-Hammond, *The Right to Learn* (San Francisco: Jossey-Bass, 1997).

low-income minority backgrounds. Several other smaller studies in the 1990s have arrived at similar conclusions.[49]

10. *Teacher preparation and experience.* In the case of high-poverty schools in big cities, research indicates that students from low-income families tend to have teachers who are less well prepared for teaching their subjects and less experienced than are teachers whose students are mostly middle class. Research also indicates that teachers who are well prepared and experienced in their subjects produce higher achievement among their students than do inexperienced teachers with less preparation. For these reasons, many analysts believe that upgrading the teaching force with respect to training, preparation, and appropriate experience should be a priority goal in efforts to improve the achievement of low-income and working-class students.[50]

11. *Negative peer pressure.* Several researchers have reported that academically oriented students in predominantly working-class schools are often ridiculed and rejected for accepting school norms. Paul Willis and Robert Everhardt found this pattern prominent among working-class students in England and the United States, respectively. John Ogbu and Signithia Fordham, among others, have described negative peer influences as being particularly strong among working-class African American students. At some inner-city schools where significant numbers of students react in this way, high achievers who work hard are labeled as "brainiacs" and accused of "acting white."[51] (Some researchers have reported that such attitudes appear to be much less prevalent or nonexistent among black students who are middle class or who attend desegregated schools.[52]) Commenting on these phenomena, an African American professor concluded that the "notion that someone with a hunger for knowledge would be regarded as a 'traitor to his race' . . . would seem like some kind of sinister white plot. In a society where blacks had to endure jailings, shootings, and lynchings to get an education, it seems utterly unbelievable that some black youngsters now regard . . . academic failure as a sign of pride."[53]

Ridiculing high achievers

[49]Jeremy D. Finn and Charles M. Achilles, "Answers and Questions About Class Size: A Statewide Experiment," *American Educational Research Journal* (Fall 1990), pp. 557–577; Jeremy D. Finn and Charles M. Achilles, "Class Size and Students at Risk" (Paper prepared for the U.S. Department of Education, Washington, D.C., 1998); David J. Hoff, "Federal Class-Size Reports Do an About-Face," *Education Week,* June 10, 1998; and Alan B. Krueger, "Reassessing the View That American Schools Are Broken," *Economic Policy Review* (March 1998), pp. 29–43.

[50]William J. Bennett et al., "A Nation Still at Risk," *Policy Review* (July–August, 1998), available at **www.heritage.org.**

[51]Paul Willis, *Learning to Labour* (Westmead, England: Saxon House, 1977); Robert Everhardt, *Reading, Writing and Resistance* (Boston: Routledge and Kegan Paul, 1983); Signithia Fordham, "Racelessness as a Factor in Black Students' School Success: Pragmatic Strategy or Pyrrhic Victory?" *Harvard Educational Review* (February 1988), pp. 54–84; and Stephanie U. Spina and Robert H. Tai, "The Politics of Racial Identity," *Educational Researcher* (January–February 1998), pp. 36–40.

[52]Alan Peshkin and Carolyne J. White, "Four Black American Students: Coming of Age in a Multiethnic High School," *Teachers College Record* (Fall 1990), pp. 21–39; Peter Schmidt, "Anti-Achievement Attitude Among African-Americans Challenged," *Education Week,* May 11, 1994, p. 10; and Louis F. Mirón and Mickey Lauria, "Student Voice as Agency," *Anthropology and Education Quarterly* (June 1998), pp. 155–188.

[53]Mark Naison, "Blacks Blocking the School Door," *Newsday* (April 2, 1990), pp. 40, 42. See also Roslyn A. Mickelson, "The Attitude-Achievement Paradox Among Black Adolescents," *Sociology of Education* (January 1990), pp. 48–61; Albert Shanker, "The Crab Bucket Syndrome," *New York Times,* June 19, 1994, p. E7; and Tamar Jacoby, "Whatever Became of Integration?" *Washington Post,* June 28, 1998, p. C2.

Recognizing education's importance

However, research by Lois Weis and her colleagues suggests that antischool peer pressures among working-class students lessen as they realize that education is important for future success. Although working-class adolescents historically tended to view academic learning as irrelevant to their future employment, the high-school boys in her study perceived schooling as offering "utilitarian opportunities" for acquiring skilled jobs and thus were willing to "put in their time" in school and even go to college. She also found that girls were more likely than earlier studies suggested to reject the traditional "patriarchal premise" that "woman's primary place is in the home-family sphere."[54]

➤ 12. *Incompatibility between classroom expectations and students' behavioral patterns and learning styles.* Numerous analysts have concluded that the behavioral patterns and learning styles of many working-class students and some groups of minority students are different from those of middle-class or nonminority students, and that these differences frequently lead to school failure. Traditional class-room expectations may be geared to high-achieving, middle-class students. For example, some research has suggested that many African American students tend to be very energetic (i.e., have high "activation" levels) and do not perform well if teachers require them to sit in one place for extended periods of time or prohibit impulsive responses; that some low-income African American students tend to become confused when teachers do not act forcefully and "authoritatively"; and that African American and Hispanic students may tend to be "field dependent" — that is, they do not learn well when instruction begins with abstract, "decontextualized" concepts. Various observers have therefore recommended that teachers should allow more physical movement, present concrete material before moving to abstract analysis, avoid treating students as "buddies," provide opportunities for students to learn in pairs or cooperative groups, and take other steps that accommodate different behavioral patterns and learning styles.[55]

Middle-class expectations for behavior

It should be emphasized that research has not conclusively established the existence of such distinctive behavioral patterns or learning styles among working-class or minority students. To the extent that some low-income African American, Hispanic, or other minority students do learn differently than nonminority students, the differences may stem mostly from socioeconomic status, rather than from race or ethnicity. Nevertheless, numerous studies do support the conclusion that teachers who adjust for different learning styles can help improve the performance of their low-achieving students. Such alternative teaching practices are discussed in the next chapter's section on multicultural education.[56]

Our analysis so far makes it clear that many students are not only economically disadvantaged but also experience educational disadvantages in schools and class-

---

[54]Lois Weis, "The 1980s: De-Industrialization and Change in White Working Class Male and Female Youth Cultural Forms," *Metropolitan Education* (Fall 1987), pp. 93, 114; Lois Weis, *Working Class Without Work* (New York: Routledge, 1990); and Maxine Seller and Lois Weis, *Beyond Black and White* (Albany: State University of New York Press, 1997).

[55]Jacqueline J. Irvine, *Black Students and School Failure* (Westport, Conn.: Greenwood, 1990); Diana T. Slaughter-Defoe, "Revisiting the Concept of Socialization," *American Psychologist* (April 1995), pp. 276–286; and A. Wade Boykin and Caryn T. Bailey, "Cultural Factors in School-Relevant Cognitive Functioning" (Undated paper available at **crespar.law.howard.edu**).

[56]Madge G. Willis, "Learning Styles of African American Children: A Review of the Literature and Interventions," *Journal of Black Psychology* (Fall 1989), pp. 47–65; Gregory J. Cizek, "On the Limited Presence of African American Teachers," *Review of Educational Research* (Spring 1995), pp. 78–92; and Ronnie Hopkins, *Educating Black Males* (Stony Brook, N.Y.: SUNY Press, 1997).

rooms. Recent research indicates that disadvantaged students can be much more successful in the educational system than they are now if they are given outstanding teachers and the right instructional strategies.[57] But the discouraging facts of achievement and social class have led some to question whether schools do indeed make a difference — whether they help in any significant way in counteracting the disadvantages students experience. The rest of this chapter confronts this issue. Later chapters, particularly Chapter 16, will discuss ways to bolster student achievement by improving the organization and delivery of instruction.

Do Schools Equalize Opportunity?

Coleman's study

Influence of school spending vs. social class

The research discussed in the preceding sections indicates that disproportionate numbers of students from low-income backgrounds enter school poorly prepared to succeed in traditional classrooms, and in later years rank relatively low in school achievement and other indicators of success. If equal opportunity is defined in terms of overcoming the disadvantages associated with family background so that students on the average perform equally well regardless of socioeconomic status, one must conclude that the educational system has not been very successful in equalizing opportunity.

The issue of equal educational opportunity has received considerable attention since the publication in 1966 of a massive national study conducted by James Coleman and his colleagues. Titled *Equality of Educational Opportunity,* this federally supported study collected data on approximately 600,000 students at more than 4,000 schools. Its congressional sponsors expected it to show that low achievement among students with low socioeconomic status was due to low expenditures on their education, thus providing a basis for increased funding of the schools they attended.

As expected, Coleman and his colleagues reported that achievement was highly related to students' socioeconomic background and that schools with high proportions of working-class and underclass students generally were not as well funded as middle-class schools. However, they also found that expenditures for reduced class size, laboratories, libraries, and other aspects of school operation were fundamentally unrelated to achievement after one took into account (1) a student's personal socioeconomic background and (2) the social-class status of other students in the school. Many readers incorrectly interpreted the data to mean that schools cannot improve the performance of economically disadvantaged students. In reality, the results supported two conclusions: (1) simply spending more on education for disadvantaged students should not be expected to improve their achievement substantially, and (2) placing students who previously attended mostly working-class schools in schools with middle-class students *could* improve achievement.[58]

---

[57]Daniel U. Levine and Beau Fly Jones, "Mastery Learning," in Richard Gorton, Gail Schneider, and James Fischer, eds., *Encyclopedia of School Administration and Supervision* (Phoenix: Oryx, 1988); Daniel U. Levine, "Instructional Approaches and Interventions That Can Improve the Academic Performance of African American Students," *Journal of Negro Education,* Winter 1994, pp. 46–63; and Barnett Berry, "Who Is Teaching Your Child?" *Changing Schools in Long Beach* (Spring 1998), available at **www.middleweb.com.**

[58]James S. Coleman et al., *Equality of Educational Opportunity* (Washington, D.C.: U.S. Government Printing Office, 1966); Frederick Mosteller and Daniel P. Moynihan, eds., *On Equality of Educational Opportunity* (New York: Random House, 1972); and James S. Coleman, *Equality and Achievement in Education* (Boulder, Colo.: Westview, 1990). See also Ronald G. Ehrenberg, "Did Teachers' Verbal Ability and Race Matter in the 1960s? 'Coleman' Revisited," *Economics of Education Review* (Spring 1995), pp. 1–21; and Marc H. Walker, "What Research Really Says," *Principal* (March 1996), pp. 41–43.

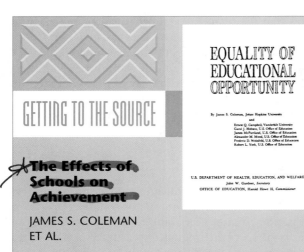

EQUALITY OF
EDUCATIONAL
OPPORTUNITY

By James S. Coleman, Johns Hopkins University
and
Ernest Q. Campbell, Vanderbilt University
Carol J. Hobson, U.S. Office of Education
James McPartland, U.S. Office of Education
Alexander M. Mood, U.S. Office of Education
Frederic D. Weinfeld, U.S. Office of Education
Robert L. York, U.S. Office of Education

U.S. DEPARTMENT OF HEALTH, EDUCATION, AND WELFARE
John W. Gardner, Secretary
OFFICE OF EDUCATION, Harold Howe II, Commissioner

GETTING TO THE SOURCE

The Effects of Schools on Achievement

JAMES S. COLEMAN ET AL.

James S. Coleman is a sociologist who has devoted much of his research to issues involving the behavior and achievement of students in different types of schools. In the 1960s he led a team of researchers who conducted a massive study of achievement in public elementary and secondary schools. The resulting report, *Equality of Educational Opportunity*, is still cited widely in discussions on how to improve our schools.

✶ Know This also

Of the many implications of this study of school effects on achievement, one appears to be of overriding importance. This is the implication that stems from the following results taken together:

1. The great importance of family background for achievement;
2. The fact that the relation of family background to achievement does not diminish over the years of school;
3. The relatively small amount of school-to-school variation that is not accounted for by differences in family background, indicating the small independent effect of variations in school facilities, curriculum, and staff upon achievement;
4. The small amount of variance in achievement explicitly accounted for by variations in facilities and curriculum;
5. Given the fact that no school factors* account for much variation in achievement, teachers' characteristics account for more than any other — [but] teachers tend to be socially and racially similar to the students they teach;
6. The fact that the social composition of the student body is more highly related to achievement, inde-

Jencks's conclusions

In the next decade, two influential books by Christopher Jencks and his colleagues bolstered this analysis. After examining a great deal of data, Jencks and his colleagues reached the following conclusions:[59]

1. School achievement depends substantially on students' family characteristics.

2. The schools accomplish relatively little in terms of reducing the achievement gap between students with higher and lower socioeconomic status.

3. Family background accounts for nearly half the variation in adult occupational status and between 15 percent and 35 percent of the variation in adult earnings. Individuals from families with high status are relatively successful economically in part because they acquire more education and skills than individuals from families with low status.

International parallels

Studies from other countries support similar conclusions. For example, scholars at the World Bank, after reviewing several decades of international research, reported that family background has an "early and apparently lasting influence" on achievement. Likewise, a review of studies in Great Britain concluded that schools there have served as "mechanisms for the transmission of privileges from one gen-

[59]Christopher Jencks et al., *Inequality* (New York: Basic Books, 1972); and Christopher Jencks et al., *Who Gets Ahead?* (New York: Basic Books, 1979). See also Daniel P. McMurrer and Isabel V. Sawhill, *Getting Ahead* (Washington, D.C.: Urban Institute, 1998).

pendently of the student's own social background, than is any school factor;

7. The fact that attitudes such as a sense of control of the environment, or a belief in the responsiveness of the environment, are extremely highly related to achievement, but appear to be little influenced by variations in school characteristics.

Taking all these results together, one implication stands out above all: That schools bring little influence to bear on a child's achievement that is independent of his background and general social context; and that this very lack of an independent effect means that the inequalities imposed on children by their home, neighborhood, and peer environment are carried along to become the inequalities with which they confront adult life at the end of school. For equality of educational opportunity through the schools must imply a strong effect of schools that is independent of the child's immediate social environment, and that strong independent effort is not present in American schools.

Questions

1. What are some of the reasons why the relationship between family background and achievement

does not diminish as a group of low-income students proceeds through the grades?

2. In what ways might the socioeconomic composition of the student body as a whole influence a student's achievement level?

3. In what way can findings from *Equality of Educational Opportunity* be used to support the conclusion that low-income students attending inner-city poverty schools should be transferred to predominantly middle-class schools?

4. If you were employed in a school with many students from low-income homes, what might you do to help improve their achievement? How might a teacher or a school faculty work to help low-status students become more positive about their chances for succeeding in school and later in life?

*School factors analyzed in the study included facilities and instructional materials, class size, expenditures per student, curricula, characteristics of the teachers, and the social and educational backgrounds of the other students.

Source: James S. Coleman et al., *Equality of Educational Opportunity* (Washington, D.C.: U.S. Government Printing Office, 1966), cover, p. 325.

eration of middle-class citizens to the next." Analyses of data from France, Germany, India, Ireland, Poland, Scotland, Sweden, and elsewhere also suggest that education helps children from middle-class families attain financially rewarding employment more frequently than it helps children from working-class families.[60]

This does not mean, however, that all or even most students from low-income families will be unsuccessful as adults or that the schools should be viewed as mostly unsuccessful in helping provide opportunities for students with diverse socioeconomic backgrounds. Research supports the following general conclusions:

1. *Although students with low socioeconomic status tend to perform poorly in school and later have restricted employment opportunities, a substantial proportion of working-class children and some from families living in poverty do eventually attain middle-class status.* For example, although nearly two-thirds of men in the U.S. labor force grew up in working-class families or on a farm, more than 50 percent are in middle- or high-status jobs; nearly 40 percent are in upper-middle-class jobs even though less

Significant socioeconomic mobility

[60]Marlaine E. Lockheed, Bruce Fuller, and Ronald Nyirongo, *Family Background and School Achievement* (Washington, D.C.: The World Bank, 1988), p. 23; Alan C. Kerckhoff, *Diverging Pathways* (New York: Cambridge University Press, 1993); Yossi Shavit and Hans-Peter Blossfeld, eds., *Persistent Inequality* (Boulder, Colo.: Westview, 1993); Daniele Cheechi, "Education and Intergenerational Mobility in Occupations," *American Journal of Economics and Sociology* (July 1997), pp. 331–350; and Richard Hatcher, "Class Differentiation in Education," *British Journal of Sociology of Education* (March 1998), pp. 5–24.

than 25 percent were raised in upper-middle-class families. Socioeconomic mobility of this kind has been present throughout U.S. history. It appears to have increased somewhat in recent decades because technological and economic change has been creating high-status jobs and eliminating unskilled jobs.[61]

Role of education

2. *The educational system has helped many people rise higher in status than their parents.* Its role in promoting socioeconomic mobility has grown more central as middle- and high-status jobs have become more complex and dependent on specialized educational skills and credentials.[62]

College as the dividing line

3. *As education increasingly determines socioeconomic status and mobility, college attendance and graduation constitute a kind of "dividing line" between those who are likely to attain high socioeconomic status and those who are not.* Enrollment in high school probably was the best educational indicator of socioeconomic status one hundred years ago. As of fifty or sixty years ago, high-school graduation was the clearest dividing line. Today postsecondary education is almost a prerequisite for middle- or high-status jobs.[63]

Continuing disadvantages of underclass

4. *Despite the success of many working-class students, there are not enough available opportunities — either educational, social, or economic — to overcome the disadvantages of the underclass.* Children who attend low-achieving poverty schools are still disproportionately likely to remain very low in socioeconomic status.

Traditional Versus Revisionist Interpretations

Opposite views of U.S. schools

Growing recognition of the strong relationship between social class and school achievement has led to a fundamental disagreement between two groups of observers of education in the United States. Briefly, according to the **traditional view of schools**, the educational system succeeds in providing economically disadvantaged students with meaningful opportunities for social and economic advancement. The **revisionist view of schools**, in contrast, holds that the schools fail to provide most disadvantaged students with a meaningful chance to succeed in society. Many revisionists also believe that schools are not even designed to accomplish this purpose, but instead are operated to perpetuate the disadvantages experienced by working-class students.[64] The term **critical theory** or **critical pedagogy** is often used as a synonym for the revisionist view. The following sections explore the ramifications of these two arguments.

The Revisionist View and Critical Pedagogy

Education as maintaining elite dominance

Revisionists contend that, through control of the schools, elite groups have channeled disadvantaged students into second-rate secondary schools and programs,

[61]David L. Featherman and Robert M. Hauser, *Opportunity and Change* (New York: Academic Press, 1978); Michael Hout, "More Universalism, Less Structural Mobility: The American Occupational Structure in the 1980s," *American Journal of Sociology* (May 1988), pp. 1358–1400; and Daniel P. McMurrer and Isabel V. Sawhill, "The Declining Importance of Class," *Opportunity in America* (April 1997), pp. 1–3.

[62]Hout, "More Universalism"; and Daniel P. McMurrer, Mark Condon, and Isabel V. Sawhill, "Intergenerational Mobility in the United States" (Paper prepared at the Urban Institute, Washington, D.C., 1997).

[63]Frank Levy and Robert C. Michel, *The Economic Future of American Families* (Washington, D.C.: The Urban Institute, 1991); and John S. Barry, "Rigging the Price for Higher Education," *Academic Questions* (Winter 1997–98), pp. 84–89.

[64]Some of the revisionists are often referred to as neo-Marxists because they believe that the capitalist system must be abolished or fundamentally changed if schools are to provide truly equal opportunity for all students.

third-rate community colleges, and fourth-rate jobs. Many critical pedagogists also believe that the educational system has been set up specifically to produce disciplined workers at the bottom of the class structure. This is accomplished in part by emphasizing discipline in working-class schools, just as the working-class family and the factory labor system emphasize discipline.[65]

Why students "resist"

Much recent analysis in critical pedagogy has been referred to as **resistance theory**, which attempts to explain why some students with low socioeconomic status refuse to conform to school expectations and do not comply with the demands of their teachers. The students' resistance, in this view, arises partly because school norms and expectations contradict the traditional definitions of masculinity and femininity these students hold. In addition, an "oppositional peer life" stimulates students to resist what they perceive as the irrelevant middle-class values of their teachers. Resistance theorists have further concluded that the traditional curriculum marginalizes the everyday knowledge of such students, thereby reinforcing anti-intellectual tendencies in working-class cultures.[66]

What teachers should do

Critical theorists have been devoting considerable attention to what educators can do to improve the situation. Using a variety of related terms such as *critical discourse, critical engagement,* and *critical literacy,* they have emphasized the goal of teachers becoming "transformative intellectuals" who work to broaden the role that schools play in contributing to the attainment of a democratic society. For example, Pauline Lipman believes that teachers should promote not just the "personal efficacy" but also the "social efficacy" of working-class and minority students, and should help them prepare to become leaders in their local communities. She also believes that teachers should pursue this type of goal as part of a larger effort to reform public schools.[67]

The Traditional View

Proponents of the traditional view acknowledge the relationships among social class, educational achievement, and economic success, but they emphasize the opportunities that exist and the data indicating that many working-class youth do experience social mobility through the schools and other social institutions. Most traditionalists believe that our educational and economic institutions balance a requirement for excellence with provision of opportunity. From this perspective, each individual who works hard, no matter how socially or economically disadvantaged,

Education as balancing excellence with opportunity

[65]Major writings of the revisionist scholars and critical pedagogists include the following: Martin Carnoy, ed., *Schooling in a Corporate Society* (New York: McKay, 1975); Joel H. Spring, *The Sorting Machine* (New York: McKay, 1976); Samuel Bowles and Herbert Gintis, *Schooling in Capitalist America* (New York: Basic Books, 1976); Michael W. Apple and Lois Weis, eds., *Ideology and Practice in Schooling* (Philadelphia: Temple University, 1983); Henry A. Giroux, *Cultural Workers and the Politics of Education* (New York: Routledge, 1991); Barry Kanpol, *Critical Pedagogy* (Westport, Conn.: Bergin and Garvey, 1994); Michael Apple, *Education and Power,* 2nd ed. (New York: Routledge, 1995); and Henry A. Giroux, *Channel Surfing* (New York: St. Martin's Press, 1997).

[66]Robert W. Connell et al., *Making the Difference* (Boston: George Allen and Unwin, 1982); Henry A. Giroux and Roger I. Simon, eds., *Popular Culture, Schooling and Everyday Life* (Granby, Mass.: Bergin and Garvey, 1989); Scott Davis, "Leaps of Faith: Shifting Currents in Sociology of Education," *American Journal of Sociology* (May 1995), pp. 1448–1478; and Henry A. Giroux, "Youth and the Politics of Representation," *Educational Researcher* (May 1997), pp. 27–30.

[67]Henry A. Giroux, *Teachers as Intellectuals* (Granby, Mass.: Bergin and Garvey, 1988); Judith Goleman, *Working Theory* (Westport, Conn.: Greenwood, 1995); and Pauline Lipman, *Race, Class, and Power in School Restructuring* (Albany: State University of New York Press, 1998).

is afforded the opportunity to succeed in elementary and secondary schools and to go to college.

Multiple chances

Traditionalists point out that the U.S. educational system gives the individual more chances to attend college than do the educational systems of most other countries (see Chapter 15). Students in this country are not confronted with an examination at age eleven or twelve that shunts them into an educational track that is almost impossible to escape. Even if American students do poorly in high school, they can go to a community college and then transfer to a university. Furthermore, admission standards at many four-year colleges permit enrollment of all but the lowest-achieving high-school graduates.

Schools as screening devices

Traditionalists admit that schools serve as a screening device to sort different individuals into different jobs, but they do not believe that this screening is as systematically based on race ethnicity, or income as the revisionists contend. Instead, they believe, the better educated get the better jobs primarily because they have been made more productive by the schools. Additional years of schooling are an indication of this greater productivity. The employer has to use some criteria to decide whom to hire, and in a democratic society that values mobility and opportunity, it is largely the quality of education that counts — not the applicant's family connections, race ethnic origin, or social class.

An Intermediate Viewpoint

This chapter began by providing data indicating that working-class students as a group perform more poorly in the educational system than do middle-class students. After examining some of the reasons that have been offered to account for this difference, we summarized several decades of research concluding that elementary and secondary schools frequently fail to overcome the disadvantages that working-class students bring to school. Although recent studies have pointed to some schools that are more successful, the overall pattern offers support for some of the revisionists' conclusions.

Schools' failures vs. successes

On the other hand, it is not true that all working-class students or all minority students fail in the schools or that all middle-class students succeed. An accurate portrayal of the relationships between social class and achievement lies somewhere between the revisionist and the traditional views. Schools do not totally perpetuate the existing social-class structure into the next generation; but schools also do not provide sufficient opportunity to break the general pattern in which a great many working-class students perform at a predictably low level. Levine and Levine, reviewing the research on each side of the debate, have offered an intermediate view that stresses the following:[68]

Schools promote mobility

■ Although we cannot pinpoint the exact percentage of working-class students who succeed in the schools or who use their education to advance in social status, the schools do serve as an important route to mobility for many economically disadvantaged children.

■ Although many working-class students attend predominantly working-class schools in which their initial disadvantages are reinforced through ineffective delivery of instruction, many others attend mixed-status schools in which

---

[68]Levine and Levine, *Society and Education*. See also George F. Kneller, *Educationists and Their Vanities* (San Francisco: Caddo Gap, 1994); and Michael W. Apple, "Are Markets and Standards Democratic?" *Educational Researcher* (August–September 1998), pp. 24–27.

teaching and learning conditions are somewhat more conducive to high performance.

Lowest class positions most "frozen"

■ Research on mobility in the United States indicates that it is mainly at the bottom level that people tend to be "frozen" into the status of their parents. Whereas there is considerable intergenerational movement up the socioeconomic ladder and some movement down, large proportions of Americans with the lowest social-class backgrounds do not progress beyond the status of their parents.

Minorities and concentrated poverty schools

■ Social and demographic trends have concentrated many children in low-income urban and rural communities whose schools are very low on achievement measures. A disproportionately high percentage of students in these schools are from racial or ethnic minority groups.

Equal opportunity, past and present

Historically, educational leaders such as Horace Mann worked to establish and expand the public school system partly because they felt this would help give all American children an equal chance to succeed in life, regardless of the circumstances of their birth. The data cited in this chapter suggest that the traditional public-school function of providing equal educational opportunity has taken on a more charged meaning. Provision of equal opportunity now depends on improving the effectiveness of instruction for children — particularly those from minority backgrounds — who attend predominantly poverty schools. This issue will be discussed further in succeeding chapters.

Summing Up

1. Social class is related both to achievement in elementary and secondary schools and to entry into and graduation from college. Students with low socioeconomic status tend to rank low in educational attainment; middle-class students tend to rank high. Low achievement is particularly a problem in poverty areas of large cities.

2. Low-income minority groups generally are low in educational achievement, but there is little or no independent relationship between race or ethnicity and achievement after taking account of social class.

3. Major reasons for low achievement include the following: (a) students' home and family environments do not prepare them well for success in the traditional school; (b) genetic considerations (that is, heredity) may interact with environment in some cases to further hamper achievement; and (c) traditionally organized and operated schools have not provided effective education for economically disadvantaged students.

4. Many problems in the schools tend to limit achievement: inappropriate curriculum and instruction, lack of previous success in school, difficult teaching conditions, differences in teacher and student backgrounds, teacher perceptions of student inadequacy, ineffective homogeneous grouping, delivery-of-service problems, overly large classes, negative peer pressures, and incompatibility between classroom expectations and students' behavioral patterns.

5. To some extent, research on social class and education has supported the revisionist view that schools help perpetuate the existing social-class system. This contrasts with the traditional view that U.S. society and its educational system provide children and youth with equal opportunity to succeed regardless of their social-class background.

6. Because recent research indicates that the schools can be much more effective, the ideal of equal opportunity may be attained more fully in the future.

Key Terms

socioeconomic status (SES) *(314)*

upper class *(314)*

middle class *(314)*

working class *(314)*

underclass *(315)*

National Assessment of Educational Progress *(315)*

race *(318)*

ethnicity *(318)*

ethnic group *(318)*

environmentalist view of intelligence *(329)*

hereditarian view of intelligence *(329)*

synthesizers' view of intelligence *(330)*

homogeneous grouping *(332)*

overloaded schools *(334)*

traditional view of schools *(340)*

revisionist view of schools *(340)*

critical theory (critical pedagogy) *(340)*

resistance theory *(341)*

Discussion Questions

1. What can teachers and schools do to overcome each of the school-related obstacles and problems that contribute to low achievement among economically disadvantaged students? What do you think you might be able to accomplish personally in working to overcome these obstacles and solve these problems?

2. Which revisionist arguments are the most persuasive? Which are most vulnerable to criticism?

3. Imagine that you have been hired as a new teacher in a school with a racial, economic, and linguistic composition very different from your own background. What can you do to improve your chances to succeed, and whom might you ask for assistance?

4. What was your own experience with homogeneous and heterogeneous grouping in high school? Were these arrangements beneficial for both high- and low-achieving students? What might or should have been done to make them more effective?

5. To what extent would you be willing to contact parents of low-achieving students when you become a teacher? Do you think this should be part of the responsibilities of a classroom teacher?

Suggested Projects for Professional Development

1. For your portfolio, prepare an analysis of schools that are unusually effective in that their students achieve more than students with similar social background at most other schools. What are the characteristics or "correlates" of these unusually effective schools? Searching the Internet for "effective schools" will give you access to sites that focus on effective schools.

2. Contact a nearby elementary school to determine what steps teachers are taking to improve the achievement of low-income and/or minority students. Compare your findings with those of your classmates. You may wish to work with some of them in identifying ideas and approaches that may be useful in your own classroom.

3. Interview someone from a low-income background who has been successful in the educational system. To what does he or she attribute this success? What special obstacles did the person encounter, and how were they overcome?

4. Compile newspaper and magazine articles discussing low achievement in the public schools. Do these sources consider the kinds of material presented in this chapter? How? What solutions do the authors propose? What is your assessment of the likely effectiveness of these solutions?

Suggested Readings and Resources

Internet Resources

Useful sites to explore regarding topics in this chapter include home pages of professional organizations such as the American Psychological Association (**www.apa.org**) and the National Education Association (**www.nea.org**). Sites sponsored by the Brookings Institution (**www.brook.edu**), the Institute for Research on Poverty (**ssc.wisc.edu/irp**) the Rand Organization (**www.rand.org**), and other organizations concerned with public policy also provide information on relevant topics. Many can be accessed quickly by going first to **epn.org**.

Publications

Flaxman, Erwin, and A. Harry Parsow, eds. *Changing Populations Changing Schools.* Chicago: University of Chicago Press, 1995. *Noting that population changes have been increasing the problems involved in educating disadvantaged students, the contributors examine issues related to low achievement patterns and high dropout rates.*

Gould, Stephen Jay. *The Mismeasure of Man.* New York: Norton, 1981. *A relatively nontechnical discussion of material on the hereditarian-environmentalist controversy.*

Herndon, James. *The Way It Spozed to Be.* New York: Bantam, 1968. *A classic account of the way education works, or doesn't work, in inner-city schools.*

Levine, Daniel U., and Rayna F. Levine. *Society and Education,* 9th ed. Needham Heights, Mass.: Allyn and Bacon, 1996. *A text on the sociology of education, this book pays special attention to issues of social class, race and ethnicity, and school achievement.*

McQuilan, Patrick J. *Educational Opportunity in an Urban American High School.* Albany: State University of New York Press, 1998. *Much of the analysis in this book, which describes a project to improve instruction for low-achieving high school students, illustrates teaching and learning problems discussed in this chapter and in Chapter 16.*

Ogbu, John U. *Minority Education and Caste.* New York: Academic Press, 1978. *A detailed description and analysis of how minority racial status interacts with social class to affect opportunities in education and society.*

Payne, Charles M. *Getting What We Ask For.* Westport, Conn.: Greenwood, 1984. *An outstanding case study of an inner-city high school and the forces that generate low expectations and performance among students and teachers.*

Presseisen, Barbara Z., ed. *Teaching for Intelligence I: A Collection of Articles.* Arlington Heights, Ill.: Skylight, 1999. *Chapters in this collection analyze and provide suggestions for possible solutions of problems involved in teaching low-income students whose academic achievement is unsatisfactory.*

CHAPTER ELEVEN

Providing Equal Educational Opportunity

Our schools became the first in the world to aim at providing all students with educational opportunity through high school and postsecondary levels. Nonetheless, as Chapter 10 indicated, in all too many cases effective education is not being extended to economically disadvantaged and minority students. Stimulated by the civil rights movement, many people have recognized that educational opportunity should be improved not just for disadvantaged students but also for students with disabilities.

In this chapter, we examine desegregation, compensatory education for economically disadvantaged students, multicultural education (including bilingual education), and education for students with disabilities. These topics reflect four significant movements that have attempted to enlarge and equalize educational opportunities for our students. Certainly, you may think, our schools should provide equal opportunity, but that is a matter for the government, the school board, and civil rights groups. How would it affect me in the classroom?

First, wherever you teach, you will find yourself professionally and morally obligated to furnish specific help for low-achieving students.

Second, because student populations are becoming increasingly diverse, racially and ethnically, you will probably need to accommodate different ethnic groups, different cultural backgrounds, and perhaps different languages.

Third, more students than ever before are being classified as having disabilities, and increasingly these students are included in regular classrooms. As a teacher, you will be at least partly responsible for addressing their special needs. To begin formulating your own philosophy and approach to equal educational opportunity, think about the following questions as you read this chapter:

- What are the rationales for desegregation, compensatory education, multicultural education, and education of children with disabilities?

- What are the major obstacles and approaches in desegregating the schools?

- What are the major approaches to compensatory education?

- What is multicultural education? What forms does it take in elementary and secondary schools? What are its major benefits and dangers?

- What does the law say about providing education for students with disabilities? What are the major issues in their education?

Desegregation

Desegregation and integration

Desegregation of schools is the practice of enrolling students of different racial groups in the same schools. **Integration** generally means more: not only that students of different racial groups attend schools together, but also that effective steps are taken to accomplish two of the underlying purposes of desegregation: (1) overcoming the achievement deficit and other disadvantages of minority students and (2) developing positive interracial relationships. During the past four decades attention has turned increasingly from mere desegregation to integration, with the goal of providing equal and effective educational opportunity for students of all backgrounds. However, much remains to be done to fully achieve either of these goals.

A Brief History of Segregation in American Education

Slavery and the Constitution

Discrimination and oppression by race were deeply embedded in our national institutions from their very beginning. The U.S. Constitution, for example, provided for representation of the free population but allowed only three-fifths representation for "all other persons," generally meaning slaves. ("Representation" refers to distribution of seats in the U.S. House of Representatives.) In most of the South before the Civil War, it was a crime to teach a slave to read and write.

After the Civil War, the Thirteenth, Fourteenth, and Fifteenth Amendments to the Constitution attempted to extend rights of citizenship irrespective of race. During Reconstruction, some gains were made by African Americans, but after 1877 blacks throughout the South and in some other parts of the country were segregated by legislative action. They were required to attend separate schools, were barred from competing with whites for good employment, and were denied the right to vote.[1] Victimized by "Jim Crow" laws, African Americans were required to use separate public services and facilities (for instance, transportation, recreation, restrooms, drinking fountains) and frequently had no access at all to private facilities such as hotels, restaurants, and theaters. Many were lynched or severely beaten by members of the Ku Klux Klan and other extremist associations. Similar though

Segregated facilities

generally less virulent discriminatory practices were carried out against Asian Americans, Hispanics, Native Americans, and other minority groups. For example, in some states Chinese Americans were excluded by law from many well-paid jobs, and their children were required to attend separate schools.[2]

Separate, unequal schools

On any measure of equality, schools provided for African Americans were seldom equal to schools attended by whites. As an example, in the early 1940s school officials in Mississippi spent $52.01 annually per student in white schools but only $7.36 per student in black schools. In many cases, African American students had to travel long distances at their own expense to attend the nearest black school, and often there was no black senior high school within a hundred miles or more.[3]

---

[1] In this chapter the term *whites* is used to refer to non-Hispanic whites, that is, citizens who are not classified as members of a racial or ethnic minority group for the purposes of school desegregation.

[2] Gwen Kin Kead, "Chinatown-1," *New Yorker,* June 10, 1991, pp. 45–83; Christopher Vasillopulos, "Prevailing upon the American Dream," *Journal of Negro Education* (Summer 1994), pp. 289–298; Dennis E. Gale, *Understanding Urban Unrest* (Thousand Oaks, Calif.: Sage, 1996); and Norman R. Yetman, ed., *Majority and Minority,* 6th ed. (Boston: Allyn and Bacon, 1999).

[3] U.S. Commission on Civil Rights, *Fulfilling the Letter and Spirit of the Law: Desegregation of the Nation's Public Schools* (Washington, D.C.: U.S. Government Printing Office, 1976); National Research Council, *Common Destiny* (Washington, D.C.: National Academy Press, 1989); and William T. Trent, "The Continuing Effects of the Dual System of Education in St. Louis," *Journal of Negro Education* (Summer 1997), pp. 336–340.

The Brown case

A number of legal suits challenging segregation in elementary and secondary schools were filed in the early 1950s. The first to be decided by the U.S. Supreme Court was a case in which lawyers for Linda Brown asked that she be allowed to attend white schools in Topeka, Kansas. Attacking the legal doctrine that schools could be "separate but equal," the plaintiffs argued that segregated schools were inherently inferior, even if they provided equal expenditures, because forced attendance at a separate school automatically informed African American students that they were second-class citizens and thus destroyed many students' motivation to succeed in school and in society. In May 1954, in a unanimous decision that forever changed U.S. history, the Supreme Court ruled in *Brown* v. *Board of Education* that "the doctrine of separate but equal has no place" in public education. Such segregation, the Court said, deprived people of the equal protection of the laws guaranteed by the Fourteenth Amendment.[4]

Civil rights movement

Effects of the *Brown* decision soon were apparent in many areas of U.S. society, including employment, voting, and all publicly supported services. After Mrs. Rosa Parks refused in December 1955 to sit at the back of a bus in Montgomery, Alabama, protests against segregation were launched in many parts of the country. Dr. Martin Luther King, Jr., and other civil rights leaders emerged to challenge deep-seated patterns of racial discrimination. Fierce opposition to civil rights demonstrations made the headlines in the late 1950s and early 1960s as dogs and fire hoses were sometimes used to disperse peaceful demonstrators. After three civil rights workers were murdered in Mississippi, the U.S. Congress passed the 1964 Civil Rights Act and other legislation that attempted to guarantee equal protection of the laws for minority citizens.[5]

Resistance to desegregation

Initial reaction among local government officials to the *Brown* decision was often negative. Although the Supreme Court ruled in 1955 (*Brown II*) that school desegregation should proceed with "all deliberate speed," there was massive resistance. This resistance took such forms as delaying reassignment of African American students to white schools, opening private schools with tuition paid by public funds, gerrymandering school boundary lines to increase segregation, suspending or repealing compulsory attendance laws, and closing desegregated schools. In 1957, Arkansas governor Orval Faubus refused to allow school officials at Central High in Little Rock to admit five African American students, and President Dwight Eisenhower called out the National Guard to escort the students to school. As of 1963, only 2 percent of African American students in the South were attending school with whites.

The Progress of Desegregation Efforts

Reducing desegregation for African Americans

Since the early 1960s, considerable progress has been made in desegregating the country's public schools in medium-sized cities and towns and in rural areas. In response to court orders, school officials have been able to reduce African American attendance in racially isolated minority schools (often defined as either 50 percent

[4]John U. Ogbu, *Minority Education and Caste* (New York: Academic Press, 1978); and William L. Taylor, "The Role of Social Science in School Desegregation Efforts," *Journal of Negro Education* (Summer 1998), pp. 196–203.
[5]Frank Brown, "*Brown* and Educational Policy Making at 40," *Journal of Negro Education* (Summer 1994), pp. 336–348; Clayborne Carson, "The Boycott That Changed Dr. King's Life," *New York Times Magazine,* January 7, 1996, p. 38; and John R. Wachtal, "We'll Never Turn Back," *American Educational Research Journal* (Summer 1998), pp. 167–198.

Since 1957, when the National Guard escorted African American students to a formerly all-white public high school in Little Rock, Arkansas, considerable progress has been made in desegregating the country's public schools in medium-sized cities and towns in rural areas. *(© UPI/Corbis-Bettmann)*

or more minority, or 90 percent or more minority).[6] As shown in Figure 11.1, the national percentage of African American students attending schools 90 percent or more minority decreased from 64 percent in 1969 to 34 percent by 1995. Progress has been greatest in the South, where the percentage of African American students in schools 90 percent or more minority decreased from 78 percent in 1969 to less than 30 percent in the 1980s and 1990s. The South is now the most integrated region of the United States.[7]

In many instances, predominantly minority neighborhoods also have high poverty rates and rank very low in socioeconomic status. As noted in Chapter 10, schools in these neighborhoods struggle with the effects of concentrated poverty, and most have not functioned very well in trying to provide effective education.

Types of segregation

In sum, progress seems to have occurred in small and medium-sized communities in combating both **de jure segregation** (segregation resulting from laws, government actions, or school policies specifically designed to bring about separation) and **de facto segregation** (segregation resulting from housing patterns rather than from laws or policies). At the same time, segregation in large metropolitan regions has increased as housing segregation has become more pronounced. Today, the large majority of public-school students in big cities such as Atlanta, Chicago,

---

[6]The term *minority* in this context refers to African Americans, Asians, Hispanics, Native Americans, and several other smaller racial or ethnic groups as defined by the federal government.

[7]Gary Orfield and Franklin Monfort, *Status of School Desegregation: The Next Generation* (Washington, D.C.: National School Boards Association, 1992); William M. Gordon, "The Implementation of Desegregation Plans Since Brown," *Journal of Negro Education* (Summer 1994), pp. 310–322; and Gary Orfield, Mark D. Bachmeier, David R. James, and Tamela Eitle, *Deepening Desegregation in American Public Schools* (Cambridge, Mass.: Harvard Project on School Desegregation, 1997).

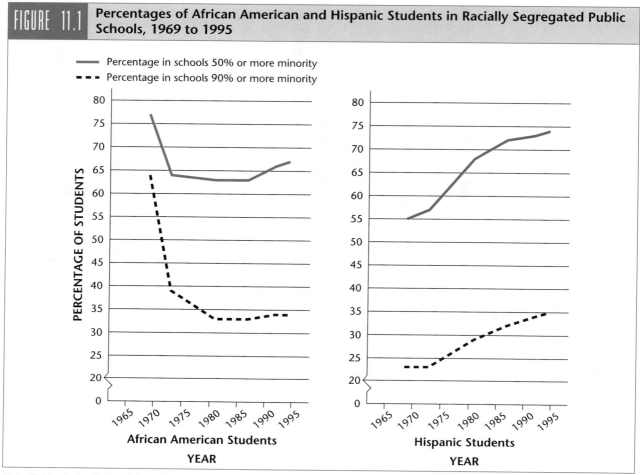

FIGURE 11.1 Percentages of African American and Hispanic Students in Racially Segregated Public Schools, 1969 to 1995

— Percentage in schools 50% or more minority
- - - Percentage in schools 90% or more minority

African American Students
YEAR

Hispanic Students
YEAR

Note: "Minority" refers to Asian, African American, Hispanic, and other racial and ethnic minority groups as defined by the federal government.

Source: Data from Gary Orfield, Sara Schley, Diane Glass, and Sean Reardon, "The Growth of Segregation in American Schools," *Equity and Excellence in Education* (April 1994), pp. 5–8; and Gary Orfield, Mark D. Bachmeier, David R. James and Tamela Eitle, *Deepening Segregation in American Public Schools* (Cambridge, Mass.: Harvard Project on School Desegregation, 1997).

Detroit, New York, and Philadelphia are minority students, and most attend predominantly minority schools.[8]

For Hispanic students, moreover, there has been little increase in desegregation; in fact, the reverse appears to be true. The percentage of Hispanic students attending predominantly minority schools has actually increased since 1969 (see Figure 11.1). In that year, 55 percent of Hispanics attended schools more than 50 percent minority; by 1995, 74 percent of Hispanic students attended such schools.

Increasing segregation for Hispanics

[8]Karl Taeuber, "Desegregation of Public School Districts," *Phi Delta Kappan* (September 1990), pp. 18–24; Peter Dreier and David Moberg, "Moving from the 'Hood,'" *The American Prospect* (Winter 1996), pp. 75–79; and Robert W. Peebles, "Inherently Unequal?" *Education Week,* February 12, 1997.

By 1987, nearly 80 percent of Hispanic students in six states (California, Illinois, New Jersey, New York, New Mexico, and Texas), representing more than four-fifths of U.S. Hispanic enrollment, were in predominantly minority schools. This trend toward greater segregation among Hispanic students reflects the movement of Hispanic people into inner-city communities in large urban areas, particularly the migration of Mexicans into cities in California and Texas and of Puerto Ricans into New York, Chicago, and other eastern and midwestern cities.[9]

Evolving Desegregation Law

Important court cases

Desegregation was greatly accelerated by the Supreme Court's 1968 decision in *Green* v. *County School Board of New Kent County,* in which the Court required segregated districts to devise a desegregation plan that "promises realistically to work now." Its 1971 decision in *Swann* v. *Charlotte-Mecklenberg* supported busing of students, revision of attendance zones, or other actions to remove the "vestiges" of state-imposed segregation, as long as a desegregation plan is workable. In 1974 in *Keyes,* which involved the Denver schools, the Court concluded that if a portion of a school district is segregated as a result of official government action, the entire district may have to be desegregated. This decision laid the basis for court orders aimed at districtwide desegregation in Boston, Dallas, Cleveland, San Francisco, and several other large cities.

Metropolitan desegregation

A series of important Supreme Court decisions also formed the basis for some movement toward metropolitan or regional desegregation, allowing for solutions that cross school district boundary lines.[10] For example, metropolitan desegregation has come about as a result of the *Liddell* case in St. Louis, twice upheld after appeals to the Supreme Court. In this case, federal judges stimulated a 1983 plan to encourage suburban districts to accept African American students transferring from city schools. The plan included provisions for improving segregated city schools. By 1998, nearly 13,000 African American students from the city were attending suburban schools, and approximately 1,400 suburban white students were attending city schools.[11]

Trend toward cessation

The major school desegregation trend of the 1990s has been the cessation of all or part of many of the desegregation plans that school districts had introduced in previous decades. This trend has been particularly apparent in urban school districts that have become predominantly minority in enrollment and hence find it difficult to maintain desegregated schools even with substantial busing of students. Other, related reasons for this trend include judicial rulings that districts had accomplished enough to overcome discriminatory effects attributable to the original

---

[9]Gary Orfield, Franklin Monfort, and Melissa Aaron, *Status of School Desegregation 1968–1986* (Washington, D.C.: National School Boards Association, 1989); Gary Orfield, Sara Schley, Diane Glass, and Sean Reardon, "The Growth of Segregation in American Schools," *Equity and Excellence in Education* (April 1994), pp. 5–8; and Beverly McLeod, *School Reform and Student Diversity* (Washington, D.C.: National Clearinghouse for Bilingual Education, 1996), available at **www.ncbe.gwu.edu.**

[10]David S. Tatel, Kevin J. Lanigan, and Maree F. Sneed, "The Fourth Decade of *Brown*: Metropolitan Desegregation and Quality Education," *Metropolitan Education* (Spring 1986), pp. 15–35; James Traub, "Can Separate Be Equal?" *Harper's* (June 1994), pp. 36–47; and Gary Orfield and Susan E. Eaton, "Dismantling Desegregation," *Michigan Law Review* (May 1997), pp. 1715–1737.

[11]Gerald Vance, "Reflections," *Compact Connection* (Spring 1993), p. 11; and Celeste Smith, "St. Louis Transfer Plan Faces Uncertain Future," *Charlotte Observer,* April 7, 1997.

constitutional violations, and public perceptions that desegregation activities were not helping minority students very much in some communities. By 1998 school officials in Boston, Indianapolis, Kansas City, Little Rock, Seattle, and numerous other districts had eliminated or were considering eliminating desegregation plan components that had been in place for twenty to twenty-five years — particularly with respect to busing arrangements that required many students to attend schools far from their homes and neighborhoods.[12]

Obstacles to Desegregation

Middle-class withdrawal

Given the fact that residential patterns in most metropolitan areas are so highly segregated, a major stumbling block to desegregation of schools has been the desire of most whites, and of many minority parents, to maintain neighborhood schools. In addition, opposition to desegregation has increased in school districts where a high percentage of minority students are from low-income families. Middle-class parents, whether nonminority or minority, are reluctant to send their children to schools with a high proportion of students from low-income families. They generally are quick to withdraw their children from schools in which desegregation has substantially increased the proportion of such students. Involuntary busing of students, a highly emotional issue, has also generated substantial white withdrawal from many school districts. The net result is that city school districts and schools have become increasingly low income and minority in their student composition.[13]

Suburban resegregation

In addition, some suburban public schools have become resegregated as middle-class minority families have moved to the suburbs only to find white enrollment falling as the white population declines or withdraws. The situation in the Cleveland metropolitan area illustrates the growing segregation of minority students in the suburbs: the East Cleveland suburban school district has become nearly all African American. In the Los Angeles metropolitan area, a number of suburban school districts have enrollments that are more than half minority.

Desegregation Plans

Characteristics of desegregation plans

Plans to accomplish desegregation usually involve one or more of the following actions:[14]

1. Alter attendance areas to include a more desegregated population.

2. Establish **magnet schools** — schools that use specialized programs and personnel to attract students throughout a school district.

3. Bus students involuntarily to desegregated schools.

---

[12]Caroline Hendrie, "Plan for Little Rock Would Shift Away From Busing," *Education Week,* April 29, 1998; Carey Goldberg, "Boston Mulls Return to School Plan That Ignited Busing Conflict," *New York Times,* June 26, 1998; and Kelley D. Carey and Bonnie A. Lesley, "Planning Your Exit," *American School Board Journal* (January 1999).

[13]Daniel U. Levine and Eugene E. Eubanks, "The Promise and Limits of Regional Desegregation Plans for Central City School Districts," *Metropolitan Education* (Spring 1986), pp. 36–51; Karen Avenoso, "Report Finds Safety Is Concern of 40% Who Leave City Schools," *Boston Globe,* January 11, 1996, p. 1; and Lynn Olson and Craig D. Jerald, "Concentrated Poverty," in *Quality Counts 98* (Washington, D.C.: Editorial Projects in Education, 1998), available at **www.edweek.org.**

[14]Charles V. Wille, "Controlled Choice Avoids the Pitfalls of Choice Plans," *Educational Leadership* (January 1991), pp. 62–64; and Jerome Weiler, "Recent Changes in School Desegregation" (Paper prepared for the ERIC Clearinghouse on Urban Education, New York, 1998).

4. Pair schools, bringing two schools in adjacent areas together in one larger zone. For example, School A enrolls all students from grades one through four; School B enrolls all students from grades five through eight.

5. Allow **controlled choice**, a system in which students can select the school they wish to attend as long as such choice does not result in segregation.

6. Provide voluntary transfer of city students to suburban schools.

Milwaukee as an example

Means such as these have led to the substantial desegregation of schools in many small or medium-sized cities. A good example is Milwaukee. At a time when African American students made up approximately 40 percent of the city's school population, Milwaukee increased the number of its desegregated schools (defined as 25 to 50 percent black) from 14 in 1976 to 101 in 1978. Most of this increase was achieved through (1) establishing magnet schools, (2) implementing a voluntary city-suburban transfer plan, and (3) redrawing school boundaries. By 1995, nearly 6,000 minority students from the city were attending suburban schools. This progress illustrates what can be accomplished through voluntary desegregation in all but the largest, most segregated cities.[15]

Big-city obstacles

In large, central-city districts, however — especially those with 50 percent or higher minority enrollment — desegregated schooling is difficult to attain. For example, in a big city with 80 percent minority students, action to eliminate predominantly single-race schools may involve hour-long bus rides and the transportation of students from one largely minority school to another. Middle-class and/or nonminority students may leave in the process. Many educators do not believe that this type of "desegregation" is very meaningful.[16]

Emphasizing quality of instruction

For these and similar reasons, desegregation plans in some big cities include little, if any, student reassignment and leave most minority students in predominantly minority schools. Instead of aiming for full desegregation, such plans generally concentrate on trying to improve the quality of instruction. Plans of this type have been approved by courts in such cities as Detroit and Chicago, and the Supreme Court has approved lower court rulings that require state governments to pay half or more of the cost of instructional improvements.[17]

Magnet schools

According to research, even large and very segregated cities can benefit from the expansion of magnet schools and other voluntary means of desegregation — more so than from large-scale, involuntary busing that transports students to predominantly minority schools. Districts that have operated or still operate a substantial number of magnet schools include Boston, Buffalo, Cincinnati, Dallas, Houston, Minneapolis, and San Diego. The magnet plan in Kansas City, Missouri, for example, used a variety of themes (shown in Table 11.1) to draw nonminority students to schools that had been largely minority and minority students to schools that had been largely nonminority. To improve the quality and effectiveness of all the district's schools and so make the district more attractive for desegregation, the

[15]Robert S. Peterkin, "What's Happening in Milwaukee?" *Educational Leadership* (January 1991), pp. 50–52; Barbara Miner, "Which Way for Chapter 220?" *Rethinking Schools* (Spring 1995), pp. 5, 26; and Peter W. Cookson, Jr., and Sonali M. Shroff, "Recent Experience with Urban School Choice Plans," *ERIC Clearinghouse on Urban Education Digest* (No. 127, 1997), available at **eric-website.columbia.edu.**

[16]Caroline Hendrie, "Pressure for Community Schools Grows As Court Oversight Wanes," *Education Week*, June 17, 1998.

[17]John A. Murphy, "After Forty Years: The Other Half of the Puzzle," *Teachers College Record* (Summer 1995), pp. 743–750; and "Local Comprehensive Schools" (Undated posting at the Internet site of the Prince George's County Public Schools) available at **www.princegeorges.com.**

| **TABLE 11.1** | Selected Magnet Themes and Subthemes in the Kansas City, Missouri, Public Schools, by Level of School |

Senior High	**Middle School**	**Elementary**
Agribusiness	College prep	Applied learning
Business/communications	Communications	Communications
Engineering	Computers	Computers
Environmental science	Environmental science	Environmental science
Health professions	Foreign language	French/German/Spanish
International studies/languages	Global studies	Latin grammar/traditional*
Law and public service	Latin grammar/traditional*	Montessori
Military science	Olympic sports	Olympic sports
Olympic sports	Performing and visual arts	Performing and visual arts
Performing and visual arts	Science/math	Science/math
Science/math/technology		

Questions for your consideration:

1. Would you like to teach at one of these schools? 2. How would you prepare yourself? 3. What particular challenges might you expect?

---

*"Traditional" refers to schools with strict policies regarding discipline, dress, homework, and other matters.

Source: Phale D. Hale and Daniel U. Levine, *Kansas City, Missouri School District Long-Range Magnet School Plan* (Kansas City: Kansas City Public Schools, 1986), pp. 15–16; Phale D. Hale, "Kansas City, Missouri: A Comprehensive Magnet Plan," in Nolan Estes, Daniel U. Levine, and Donald R. Waldrip, eds., *Magnet Schools* (Austin, Tex.: Morgan, 1990), pp. 143–160, and *Magnet Schools of Choice* (Kansas City: Kansas City, Missouri, School District, 1996).

Kansas City plan also provided for reducing class size, enhancing libraries, expanding preschool education, renovating all school buildings, and other improvements.[18]

Nonblack Minorities

What is a minority group?

Another aspect of desegregation that deserves special attention is the status of nonblack minority groups. Depending on regional and local circumstances and court precedents, some racial minority groups may or may not be counted as minority for the purposes of school desegregation. For example, in the 1970s, the courts determined that Mexican American students in the Southwest were victims of the same kinds of discrimination as were African American students. However, in some northern cities, the courts have not explicitly designated Mexican American and other Hispanic students to participate as minorities in a desegregation plan, even though many or most attend predominantly minority schools.[19]

---

[18]Pedro A. Noguera, "A Tale of Two Cities: School Desegregation and Racialized Discourse in Berkeley and Kansas City" (Paper presented at the annual meeting of the American Educational Research Association, San Francisco, April 1995); and Caroline Hendrie, "Falling Stars," *Education Week,* February 28, 1998.

[19]However, federal data collection activities are standardized and have required that student enrollments be reported separately for the following groups: "Black," "American Indian," "Spanish-Surnamed American," "Portuguese," "Asian," "Alaskan Natives," "Hawaiian Natives," and "Non-Minority."

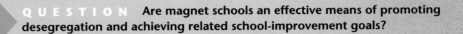

TAKING ISSUE

Magnet Schools and Desegregation

In recent years, many city school districts have established desegregation plans that rely in part on magnet schools. By offering a specialized program in a particular field of interest, a magnet school can attract students from all parts of a city or region, thereby creating a mix of ethnic and racial groups. Critics have argued, however, that magnet schools often cause more problems than they solve.

Arguments PRO

1 Research in a number of cities has shown that a coordinated plan involving magnet schools can lead to substantial gains in desegregation. Milwaukee and Buffalo, for example, are using magnet schools effectively.

2 Through their specialized, high-level programs, magnet schools attract middle-class and college-bound students to the public school system. In this way, they help to reverse the white, middle-class exodus that has long plagued desegregation efforts.

3 In addition to attracting various ethnic and racial groups, magnet schools create a mixture of socioeconomic classes. Working-class and middle-class students are brought together in a setting that encourages beneficial socialization.

4 Because of their concentration of resources, magnet schools can offer a better education than a system of nonspecialized schools. Most important, they make this high-quality education available to everyone, regardless of racial, social, or cultural background.

5 As students gain recognition for academic excellence at the magnet schools, community pride will grow. The schools will become a means of promoting community identity, bringing together all races and classes in a common endeavor.

Arguments CON

1 Only limited evidence supports the idea that magnet schools make a significant contribution to desegregation. Because magnets frequently are expensive to develop and maintain, they may well become unjustifiable financial burdens for school districts.

2 Magnets often "drain away" the best students, leaving other public schools in the district with high concentrations of low achievers. These other schools find it increasingly difficult to maintain teacher and student morale and deliver a good education.

3 In some areas, the conversion of a local school into a magnet has led to increased tension between socioeconomic groups. Local students distrust the "outsiders" (generally of a different social class) who come into the neighborhood to attend the school.

4 Many magnet schools are not really for everyone. Instead, they are selective: students must meet certain achievement standards to be admitted. Thus low-achieving students — the ones most in need of help — are not as likely to benefit from magnet schools as are other students.

5 Because of their elitist nature, magnet schools will not foster a sense of community. More likely, they will provoke resentment among parents whose children are excluded — especially when taxes are raised to support the magnet program.

The situation is further complicated by the relatively large number of Asian American groups in some big cities. With a rapidly growing population of Filipino, Korean, and Vietnamese students added to the many students of Chinese and Japanese ancestry, city school districts face considerable uncertainty in devising multiethnic desegregation plans. The court order for San Francisco, for example, has required multiethnic enrollment and busing of four groups: Asian American, African American, Hispanic, and non-Hispanic white.

Difficult issues

Questions regarding the desegregation of nonblack minority groups will multiply in the future because of the continuing in-migration of Asian and Hispanic students to many localities. Resolution of these issues will be difficult because bilingual services that tend to require a concentration of these students will conflict with desegregation goals emphasizing dispersal and multiethnic enrollment. Many educators and lay leaders also are uncertain about whether or how to include middle-class Asian American and Hispanic students in desegregation plans. Most of these students perform well academically, and many seem to be well integrated into U.S. schools and society.[20]

Effects on Student Performance and Attitudes

Inconsistent data

To what extent do students benefit from integrated schools? The voluminous research on this subject is somewhat contradictory. Some studies show a positive relationship between desegregation and academic achievement, but other studies show little or no relationship. Several analysts have concluded that desegregation seldom detracts from the performance of white students and frequently contributes to achievement among minority students. The latter results are most likely to occur when low-income minority students attend schools with middle-income nonminority students, but only if desegregation plans are well implemented (see below) and substantial action is taken to improve the effectiveness of instruction.[21]

Importance of implementation

Similarly, whereas some data show that desegregation has positive effects on interracial attitudes, other studies indicate no effect or even a negative effect. Positive intergroup relationships develop only if desegregation is implemented well and if educators promote equal-status contact between minority and nonminority students. Studies on students' aspirations are much more consistent, indicating that desegregation frequently improves the educational aspirations and college enrollment of minority students by making those aspirations more realistic and better informed. Several studies also indicate that desegregated schooling helps minority students enter the mainstream "network" of social and cultural contacts needed for success in later life.[22]

---

[20]Peter Schmidt, "Calif. District Strives to Mix Blacks, Hispanics," *Education Week,* April 18, 1995, p. 3; and Leonard A. Valverde, "Latino Communities: 1998 Perspectives on School Desegregation" (Paper presented at the Annual Meeting of the American Educational Research Association, San Diego, April 1998).

[21]Ronald A. Krol, "A Meta Analysis of the Effects of Desegregation on Academic Achievement," *Urban Review* (December 1980), pp. 211–224; Daniel U. Levine, "Desegregation," in Torsten Husen and T. Neville Postlethwaite, eds., *International Encyclopedia of Education,* 3rd ed. (Oxford: Pergamon, 1994), pp. 1483–1486; and Gary Orfield, "Does Desegregation Help Close the Gap?" *Journal of Negro Education* (Summer 1997), pp. 241–254.

[22]Janet Schofield, "School Desegregation and Intergroup Relations: A Review of the Literature," in Gerald Grant, ed., *Review of Research in Education 17* (Washington, D.C.: American Education Research Association, 1991), pp. 335–412; Amy Stuart Wells, "Re-examining Social Science Research on School Desegregation," *Teachers College Record* (Summer 1995), pp. 691–706; William T. Trent, "Outcomes of School Desegregation," *Journal of Negro Education* (Summer 1997), pp. 255–257; and Thomas F. Pettigrew, "Intergroup Contact Theory," in *Annual Review of Psychology* (Palo Alto, Calif.: Annual Reviews, 1998), pp. 65–85.

Implications for minority students at poverty schools

Given the complexities involved in desegregation and its effects on achievement and attitudes, many people are perplexed and confused regarding implications for minority students who attend predominantly minority, low-achieving schools in high-poverty neighborhoods. As suggested in research discussed in Chapter 10, assigning such students to a desegregated school with a substantially lower percentage of low-achieving students places them in a potentially much less dysfunctional educational environment. Provided that they receive appropriate support and teaching, their academic performance then can be substantially improved. We emphasize elsewhere — particularly in Chapter 16 — that some high-poverty schools are unusually successful and that many more should be equally successful. Until that happens, effective implementation of instruction at desegregated schools is an important alternative for helping low-achieving minority students.

Characteristics of well-desegregated schools

Unfortunately, only a few studies focus on schools in which desegregation seems to have been carried out effectively. One of the most comprehensive of such studies is a report evaluating the Emergency School Aid Act, which provided hundreds of millions of dollars between 1972 and 1982 to facilitate desegregation. This study indicated that desegregation had a favorable impact on the achievement of African American students in schools in which (1) resources were focused on attaining goals, (2) administrative leadership was outstanding, (3) parents were more heavily involved in the classroom, and (4) staff systematically promoted positive interracial attitudes.[23]

Moral and political imperatives

Despite the mixed evidence, perhaps the most compelling reasons for integration are moral and political. Morally, our national education policy must reflect a commitment to American ideals of equality. Politically, two separate societies, separately educated, cannot continue to exist in America without serious harm to the body politic. In the words of Federal Appeals Court Judge Gerald Heaney, because minority students will have to "compete in an integrated society, they must, to the extent possible, be educated in an integrated school system."[24]

Compensatory Education

Another aspect of our nation's commitment to equal educational opportunity is the compensatory education movement, which has sought to overcome (that is, "compensate" for) disadvantaged background and thereby improve the performance of low-achieving students, particularly those from low-income families. Stimulated in part by the civil rights movement in the 1960s, compensatory education was expanded and institutionalized as part of President Lyndon Johnson's War on Poverty. Although it has been funded largely by the federal government, some states and local school districts also have set aside funds for this purpose.

ESEA

The Elementary and Secondary Education Act (ESEA), passed in 1965, immediately provided $1 billion in Title I funds to improve the education of economically disadvantaged children. (A disadvantaged student was defined as a student from a family below the government's official poverty line.) In 1981, Title I of ESEA was revised and became known as Chapter 1 until 1995, when Congress reauthorized it

---

[23]J. E. Coulson, *National Evaluation of the Emergency School Aid Act* (Washington, D.C.: System Development Corporation, 1976). See also Daniel U. Levine and Rayna F. Levine, *Society and Education*, 9th ed. (Needham Heights, Mass.: Allyn and Bacon, 1996); and Marjorie Coeyman, "Backing Busing," *Christian Science Monitor*, September 29, 1998, p. B1.
[24]Gerald W. Heaney, "School Desegregation: Results and Prospects," *Metropolitan Education* (Spring 1987), pp. 79–85; David L. Kirp, "Following the Color Line," *The Nation*, April 24, 1995, pp. 567–572; and Caroline Hendrie, "Without Court Orders, Schools Ponder How to Pursue Diversity," *Education Week*, April 30, 1997.

Title 1

and renamed it Title 1. By 1999, Title 1 funding amounted to more than $8 billion to provide assistance to more than 5 million students, and many additional students participated in other compensatory programs. Substantial compensatory education programs dealing with early childhood education, bilingual education, and other services also have been put in place. Some of the important services of compensatory education include the following:

Services provided by compensatory education

1. *Parental involvement and support.* Programs emphasizing parental involvement and support have ranged from helping parents learn to teach their children to improving family functioning and employability.

 2. *Early childhood education.* **Head Start** and **Follow Through** have been the largest programs of this kind. Head Start generally attempts to help disadvantaged four- and five-year-olds achieve "readiness" for the first grade. Since Head Start was initiated in 1965, more than 16 million children have participated, at a cost of more than $35 billion. Follow Through has concentrated on sustaining this readiness and improving achievement in the primary grades.

3. *Reading, language, and math instruction.* Most Title 1 projects have concentrated on improvement in reading, language, and math.

4. *Bilingual education.* Hispanic children constitute the largest group in bilingual programs, but nationwide, bilingual programs have been provided in more than sixty languages. Bilingual programs are discussed in the following section on multicultural education.

5. *Guidance, counseling, and social services.* Various psychological and social services have been provided for disadvantaged students, and social workers have been employed to help bridge gaps between school and home.

6. *Dropout prevention.* Along with vocational and career education, a number of services have aimed at preventing students from dropping out of school, usually by offering work-study programs or on-the-job training.

7. *Personnel training.* Many preservice and in-service training programs have been funded to help teachers improve instruction.

8. *Additional school personnel.* Recruitment and training of teacher aides and paraprofessionals have increased, and instructional specialists have been employed.

9. *After-school programs.* These provide academic-improvement services or general enrichment activities, or both.

10. *Computer laboratories and networks.* In recent years Title 1 and other compensatory education funds have made it possible for many schools to establish computer laboratories and in-school networks that provide and link computers in individual classrooms.

Evaluation of Programs

Discouraging early results

During the first decade of compensatory education, most interventions appeared to be relatively ineffective in raising student achievement levels and cognitive development. Despite the expenditure of billions of dollars per year, students generally were not making long-range academic gains.

Improved procedures and funding

After this discouraging start, corrections were made. The federal and state governments improved monitoring procedures, required more adequate evaluation, and sponsored studies to improve compensatory education. Some states also began to provide additional money for compensatory programs. By the early 1980s, research suggested that compensatory education in preschool and primary grades could indeed improve the cognitive development and performance of disadvantaged students.[25]

Exemplary early childhood programs

In particular, several studies of outstanding early childhood education programs demonstrated that such efforts can have a long-lasting effect if they are well conceived and effectively implemented. Positive long-range achievement results also have been reported for disadvantaged students in outstanding preschool programs in Ypsilanti, Michigan; Syracuse, New York; and several other locations. Compared with nonparticipants, students who participate in such programs are less likely to be later placed in special education or to repeat grades (both of which are very expensive). Participants are also more likely to graduate from high school and to acquire the skills and motivation needed for rewarding employment, thereby increasing tax revenues and reducing the reliance on public assistance.[26]

Overall pluses and minuses

These impressive results, however, come from programs that researchers consider exemplary. The vast majority of preschool programs have not been as well funded or well implemented and have not produced such compelling gains. In addition, Title 1 programs in elementary and secondary schools still do not ensure that most low-achieving students will acquire the academic and intellectual skills necessary to obtain good jobs in a modern economy. On the one hand, Title 1 students typically gain about a year in reading and math achievement for each year of participation in the elementary grades, and thus they no longer fall further behind their more advantaged peers. On the other hand, various problems persist: many disadvantaged students receive only one or two years of compensatory services and then frequently decline in relative achievement; comparatively few disadvantaged students are served above the sixth grade; and participants who start out far behind national achievement averages usually remain there.[27]

Comprehensive Ecological Intervention

For some students who grow up in particularly harmful environments, such as concentrated poverty neighborhoods, improvement in school programs cannot be expected to overcome their extreme disadvantages. For this reason, policy makers and

[25]Thomas W. Fagan and Camilla A. Heid, "Chapter 1 Program Improvement: Opportunity and Practice," *Phi Delta Kappan* (April 1991), pp. 582–585; Robert E. Slavin, "Making Money Make a Difference," *Rethinking Schools* (Summer 1995), pp. 10, 23; and Kenneth K. Wong, Gail L. Sunderman, and Jaekyung Lee, "Redesigning the Federal Compensatory Education Program," *CEIC Review* (August 1997), available at **www.temple.edu.**
[26]Irving Lazar et al., "Lasting Effects of Early Education," *Monographs of the Society for Research in Child Development* (Nos. 2–3, 1982); W. Steven Barnett and Colette M. Escobar, "The Economics of Early Educational Intervention: A Review," *Review of Educational Research* (Winter 1987), pp. 387–414; Betty Hart and Todd R. Risley, *Meaningful Differences in the Everyday Experience of Young American Children* (Baltimore: Brookes, 1995); "Long-Term Outcomes of Early Childhood Programs," *The Future of Children* (Winter 1995), available at **www.futureofchildren.org;** and Rebecca Jones, "What Works," *American School Board Journal* (April 1998), available at **www.asbj.org.**
[27]Lorin W. Anderson and Leonard O. Pellicer, "Synthesis of Research on Compensatory and Remedial Education," *Educational Leadership* (September 1990), pp. 10–16; Virginia R. L. Plunkett and Benjamin D. Stickney, "Most Assuredly an Achievement Program," *Educational Leadership* (May 1991), pp. 87–89; and Nina S. Rees, "The Real Divide on Education," *New York Times* (October 8, 1998).

Importance of early family environment

Features of successful programs

Examples of comprehensive intervention

educators increasingly support **ecological intervention** — comprehensive efforts to improve the family environment of very young children.[28]

Advocates of ecological intervention point to research on the important cognitive development that occurs during infancy, as well as to the frequently disappointing results of Head Start interventions that do not begin until age four or five. Comprehensive psychological, social, and economic support can be successful, the research indicates, if it begins when children are less than two or three years old. In some effective programs of this type, very young children are enrolled in educationally oriented day care or preschool classes. The successful programs also typically include nutrition and health care, and capable staff members often provide individualized guidance on parenting. Among the best-known efforts that have begun to report promising outcomes are the following:[29]

- The Beethoven Project, which provides coordinated services focused on health, adult education, employment training, parent education, and children's intellectual and psychological development. It is available for all members of families with very young children at a large public-housing project in Chicago.

- The Parents as Teachers approach, which operates in several states. Specially trained teachers visit the homes of preschool children to help parents learn how to provide supportive learning environments.

- Early Head Start programs, which enroll children from birth to age three, and address not just child development but also family and community development.

Obstacles to helpful intervention

Unfortunately, analysts report that most efforts have not been as comprehensive and intensive as these successful programs. Moreover, increases in crime, delinquency, and other aspects of social disorganization in poverty neighborhoods appear to be making it more difficult to implement comprehensive ecological intervention. For example, drug addiction among women in inner cities is relatively frequent, and many babies born to addicted mothers are likely to suffer from long-term intellectual and emotional retardation. Hospitals and social agencies in many poverty neighborhoods are overwhelmed with problems that limit their capacity to improve the prospects of severely disadvantaged children.

Coordinated Human Services

Collaboration to integrate services

Comprehensive types of intervention — including education, health care, economic assistance, and social and psychological support — are also increasingly being extended to older disadvantaged children and youth. Such coordinated-service approaches are often referred to as "coordination of human services," "collaboration among schools and social service agencies," and "integration of social and educa-

---

[28]Lizbeth Schorr, *Within Our Reach* (New York: Anchor Doubleday, 1989); and Edna W. Comes and Mark W. Fraser, "Evaluation of Six-Family-Support Programs," *Families in Society* (March–April, 1998), pp. 134–148.

[29]Michael F. Kelley and Elaine Surbeck, *Restructuring Early Childhood Education* (Bloomington, Ind.: Phi Delta Kappa, 1991); National Commission on Children, *Beyond Rhetoric* (Washington, D.C.: U.S. Government Printing Office, 1991); "Early Head Start (Birth to Three) Research Projects" (Undated paper posted by the Catholic University of America) available at **www.campus.cua.edu;** and Ernest W. Brewer and Connie Hollingsworth, *Promising Practices* (Scottsdale, Ariz.: Holcomb Hathaway, 1999).

tional services." These approaches have been endorsed by innumerable groups of educators and civic leaders.[30]

Mobilizing many types of help

Advocates of **coordinated human services** aim to reach all young people who have problems growing up in modern society, especially those for whom school-based efforts probably will not be sufficient to counteract the effects of severely damaging environments. Coordination is necessary because numerous forms of help often must be mobilized. Fortunately, in many communities, city, county, or regional agreements and taxes make coordinated services possible. Political leaders are exploring ways to enhance collaboration through youth-service coordinating boards, interagency compacts with schools, and other mechanisms. Scholars report that successful collaborative programs share the following characteristics:[31]

Characteristics of successful collaboration

- They offer a wide array of services and provide an easy entry point.
- They cross bureaucratic and organizational boundaries to provide services coherently, often at nontraditional hours in nontraditional settings.
- They provide staff with the necessary time and training.
- They view the child as part of the family, and the family as part of the community.

Questions About Compensatory Education

Although data collected since the 1980s suggest that compensatory education can be successful for disadvantaged students, there still are many questions about its nature and effectiveness.

Ineffective "pullout"

1. *How can Title 1 be made more effective?* Research indicates that Title 1 has been relatively ineffective in many schools partly because most programs use a **pullout approach** — that is, they take low achievers out of regular classes for supplementary reading or math instruction. With some exceptions, pullout approaches generally have not worked well because they tend to generate much movement of students and therefore confusion throughout the school. In addition, they usually have overemphasized the acquisition of "mechanical" subskills, such as word recognition in reading and simple computation in math, rather than broader and more functional skills, such as reading comprehension, math problem solving, and "learning-to-learn" strategies.[32]

Recent improvements

In recent years, federal legislation has made it much easier to replace Title 1 pullout with schoolwide approaches that allow for coordinated, in-class assistance for low achievers. In addition, expanded staff development has helped teachers learn how to broaden compensatory instruction beyond mechanical subskills.

---

[30]See, for example, Anne C. Lewis, "All Together Now: Building Collaboration," *Phi Delta Kappan* (January 1992), pp. 348–349; and *Head Start Programs* (Washington, D.C.: U.S. General Accounting Office, 1998), available at **www.gao.gov.**
[31]Grace P. Guthrie and Larry F. Guthrie, "Streamlining Interagency Collaboration for Youth at Risk," *Educational Leadership* (September 1991), pp. 17–22; Calvin R. Stone, "School/Community Collaboration," *Phi Delta Kappan* (June 1995), pp. 794–800; and Sharon L. Kagan and Nancy E. Cohen, *Not By Chance* (Washington, D.C.: The Quality 2000 Initiative, 1997).
[32]Michael S. Knapp and Patrick M. Shields, eds., *Better Schooling for the Children of Poverty* (Berkeley, Calif.: McCutchan, 1991); Kathleen Cotton, *Effective Schooling Practices: A Research Synthesis 1995 Update* (Portland, Oreg.: Northwest Regional Educational Laboratory, 1995); and Stanley Pogrow, "What Is an Exemplary Program, and Why Should Anyone Care?" *Educational Researcher* (October 1998), pp. 22–30.

GETTING TO THE SOURCE

Know this

Comprehensive Social Services

RICHARD WEISSBOURD

MAKING THE SYSTEM WORK FOR POOR CHILDREN

by

Richard Weissbourd

for the
Executive Session on Making the System Work
for Poor Children

HARVARD UNIVERSITY
JOHN F. KENNEDY SCHOOL OF GOVERNMENT
Malcolm Wiener Center for Social Policy

I n line with many major policy reports and recommendations, numerous projects have been initiated to coordinate the work of social agencies and schools to provide comprehensive social services for young people and families. Analysts are trying to determine how services can best be coordinated to fundamentally improve the overall environment for at-risk children and youth. One of the most thoughtful documents has been prepared by Richard Weissbourd, who summarized the results of three years of discussion among a group of concerned practitioners, scholars, and policy makers.

T oo often services are driven by legislative, funding, professional and bureaucratic requirements, rather than by the needs of children and families themselves. Because of legislative and bureaucratic requirements, for example, most public institutions and programs today isolate and react rigidly to a narrowly defined need, ducking problems that do not fall neatly within their jurisdictions. Schools deal with school problems. Health agencies deal with health problems. Drug programs treat drug problems. Yet children's needs are commonly untidy, and many children have multiple and interconnected problems. A child's diarrhea, for example, may be connected to an emotional crisis caused by a divorce at home or by a transition to a new school. Further, the problems of children are frequently enmeshed with the problems of their families. A young teenage girl's failure in school may be directly connected to her mother's alcoholism, or her father's sudden disappearance, or to constant conflict between her mother and her mother's boyfriend at home. Alternatively, this girl may be failing school because she has to stay home to take care of a younger sibling, or because she is unable to get needed reading help at home because both of her parents are illiterate. Yet our current service system tends to treat

Partly for this reason, increasing numbers of Title 1 schools are reporting impressive achievement gains. Other changes in federal legislation provide for participation of more low-achieving students in Title 1 through the secondary level as well as for improvements in program design and implementation. Data collected during the next few years may show whether these changes are having a positive impact.[33]

Behavioristic vs. cognitive approaches

2. *What type of early instruction should be provided?* Much of the uncertainty in early compensatory education involves the issue of whether programs should use a behavioristic direct-instruction approach, which focuses on basic skills such as decoding of words or simple computation in math, or instead should emphasize conceptual development and abstract thinking skills. Some direct-instruction programs have had excellent results through the third grade, but performance levels usually fall when participating children enter the middle grades. Results in cognitive-oriented programs stressing independent learning and thinking skills generally have not been as successful in terms of mastery of "mechanical" skills in

[33]Mary Jean LeTendre, "Improving Chapter 1 Programs," *Phi Delta Kappan* (April 1991), pp. 577–581. For examples of schools reporting gains in student performance, see material at **www.starcenter.org**.

each family member in isolation — a program for every person, a program for every problem.

This report outlines the shape of a system that would take as its starting point and as its map the interwoven needs of children and families. The model we propose is undergirded by five principles: *prevention, comprehensiveness, continuity, effective accountability,* and *enhancing the dignity and authority of families.* Further, this report describes concrete and far-reaching reforms that flow from these principles. Primarily, we argue that the service system needs to be a good deal more dynamic and flexible at many different levels. Most important, we need to untie the hands of human service workers — teachers, counselors, social workers, health care professionals. To provide preventive and comprehensive services, these workers need the authority, the skills and the support to respond flexibly and improvisationally to children and family needs. Program and city administrators need far more freedom — more freedom, for example, to shift resources into preventive efforts and to change direction when new problems suddenly spring up. This report argues that one promising way of giving city and agency administrators more latitude is "decategorization," providing them with single, flexible grants that pool, for

example, child welfare, foster services, Chapter I, Maternal and Child Health, and/or Head Start funds.

Questions

1. Why do various social and educational agencies usually function so separately from one another? How does this history of isolation impede the delivery of services?

2. What particularly might be done to enhance the "dignity and authority of families"?

3. When you become a teacher, what can you do to help coordinate social and educational services for students who are experiencing serious problems at home or in their neighborhoods?

4. To what extent is it the teacher's or the school's responsibility to address social and economic conditions and problems that interfere with learning? How much help can a teacher provide for "needy" students?

Source: Richard Weissbourd, "Making the System Work for Poor Children," a report of the Executive Session on *Making the System Work for Poor Children,* Wiener Center for Social Policy, Kennedy School of Government, Harvard University. Reprinted by permission. Cover and p. i reprinted by permission.

the primary grades, but some of the best cognitive approaches have resulted in gains that show up later.[34]

Uncertainty about secondary schools

3. *What should be done at the secondary school level?* Although most sizable programs of compensatory education have been carried out at the elementary level, a few secondary programs have reported promising results. Some success has been achieved in individual classrooms and in "schools within a school" in which a selected group of teachers work intensively with a relatively small number of low-achieving students. However, researchers still know relatively little about the best compensatory approaches for secondary school students.[35]

4. *Is it financially feasible to include most economically disadvantaged students in effective compensatory education programs?* Effective programs for the most economi-

---

[34]Sharon L. Kagan, "Early Care and Education," *Phi Delta Kappan* (November 1993), pp. 184–187; Rebecca A. Marcon, "Doing the Right Thing for Children," *Young Children* (November 1994), pp. 8–20; and David P. Weikart, "High/Scope Study Raises Direct-Instruction Questions," *Education Week,* July 8, 1998.

[35]Daniel U. Levine, "Educating Alienated Inner City Youth: Lessons from the Street Academies," *Journal of Negro Education* (Spring 1975), pp. 139–149; Daniel U. Levine, "Implementation of an Urban School-Within-a-School-Approach," in Hersholt C. Waxman et al., eds., *Students at Risk in At-Risk Schools* (Newbury Park, Calif.: Sage Corwin, 1992); and Kevin Haney, "Hornbeck Credits His Reform Plan," *Philadelphia Daily News,* August 24, 1998.

High costs

cally disadvantaged students tend to be expensive because they require prolonged intervention in the home and family environment. Some estimates indicate that only about one-third of students eligible for Head Start and 50 percent of those eligible for Title 1 are being served. To include most eligible children, these estimates say, would require billions of additional dollars a year.

The basic question: can it really work?

5. *Can compensatory education result in permanent, meaningful gains for most disadvantaged students?* This, of course, is the most fundamental question about compensatory education. Data indicate that the performance of many disadvantaged students entering secondary schools is still unacceptably low regardless of whether they have been in Title 1 or other compensatory programs. In most inner-city schools, for example, the average reading score of ninth graders remains at about the seventh-grade level. This means in turn that a substantial proportion of these students are unable to read well enough to succeed in school or obtain rewarding jobs later in life.

In view of such findings, some educators question whether compensatory education, even if designed for maximum effectiveness, can significantly improve a student's chances of succeeding in school and in later life — especially a minority student living in a neighborhood of concentrated poverty. As described in Chapter 10, revisionist critics argue that U.S. public schools have failed to provide equal opportunity and will continue to fail in the absence of fundamental reforms in society as a whole. Thus many observers believe that it may be necessary to improve parents' economic opportunities before children's school achievement will rise significantly.[36] It remains to be seen whether efforts to improve education for disadvantaged students can be sufficiently effective to disprove these skeptics' pessimism.

Multicultural Education

Our multiethnic population

Diversity within minority groups

More than most other countries, the United States consists of a large number of ethnic and racial groups with diverse histories and origins. Many of these are considered to be "minority" groups because in one way or another they have been placed at a disadvantage compared with "mainstream" groups whose ancestry and heritage are primarily European.

Minority groups in turn include a variety of racial and ethnic subgroups. For example, African Americans include people whose ancestors were brought here as slaves and people with family origins in the Caribbean, Latin America, Africa, and elsewhere. Hispanics (or "Latinos") include Cuban Americans, Mexican Americans, Puerto Ricans, and numerous other subgroups originating in Spanish-speaking cultures in Central and South America and in Spain. Asian Americans include people from scores of distinct cultures and societies of the Far East (such as China and Japan), the Indian subcontinent (for example, India and Pakistan), Southeast Asia (including Cambodia, Laos, Vietnam), and Hawaii and other Pacific Islands. Native Americans include American Indians from more than two hundred tribal-language groups, as well as Alaskan Aleuts and Eskimos. (On the basis of blood types and other genetic evidence, some scientists believe that Amerindians are closer to the Japanese than to any other racial or ethnic group.) Students from all these minority

---

[36]John Ogbu, "Racial Stratification and Inequality in the United States," *Teachers College Press* (Winter 1994), pp. 264–298; and John Ogbu and Herbert D. Simons, "Voluntary and Involuntary Minorities," *Anthropology and Education Quarterly* (June 1998), pp. 155–188.

groups are expected to constitute more than 40 percent of public-school enrollment early in the next century.[37]

Growth in minority population

As we point out in Chapter 10 and elsewhere in this book, many U.S. minority groups and subgroups are disproportionately low in socioeconomic status, and many children and youth from these groups are very low in educational achievement and attainment. Moreover, because of immigration and other factors, the minority population of the United States has been growing rapidly in recent years, so that the largest minority groups now constitute about 31 percent of the U.S. population. It is increasingly important, therefore, that the educational system accommodate the needs of diverse groups of students.

Multicultural education is a term that refers to the variety of ways in which the schools can take productive account of cultural differences among students and improve opportunities for students with cultural backgrounds distinct from the U.S. mainstream. Some aspects of multicultural education focus on improving instruction for students who have not learned Standard English or who have other cultural differences that place them at a disadvantage in traditional classrooms. Educators also are concerned with the larger implications of multicultural education that make it valuable for *all* students. By fostering positive intergroup and interracial attitudes and contacts, multicultural education may help all students function in a culturally pluralistic society. (From this point of view, the movement toward desegregation can be considered a part of multicultural education.) Before discussing multicultural instruction, we will review some historical trends in the development of a pluralistic society in the United States.

Multicultural goals for all students

From Melting Pot to Cultural Pluralism

Although the population of the United States always has been pluralistic in its composition, the emphasis throughout much of our history (as noted in Chapter 5) has been on assimilating diverse ethnic groups into the national mainstream rather than on maintaining group subcultures. As early as 1782 St. John de Crèvecoeur commented that the colonists were being "melted" into a "new race" of men. Israel Zangwill's 1908 play *The Melting Pot* popularized this term and called attention to the challenge of "Americanizing" the large streams of immigrants who were entering the United States at the turn of the century. In educating diverse groups of immigrants, the public school system has stressed the development of an American identity. Students learned how "Americans" were supposed to talk, look, and behave, sometimes in classes of fifty or sixty pupils representing the first or second generation of immigrants from ten or fifteen countries.[38]

Historical emphasis on assimilation

Pros and cons of past assimilation efforts

From our vantage point today, the schools' emphasis on a particular set of behaviors and standards may have been partially counterproductive. For example, Mexican American students in the Southwest frequently were alienated from education when they were prohibited from speaking Spanish even on the playground.

---

[37]William P. O'Hare and Judy C. Felt, *Asian Americans: America's Fastest Growing Minority Group* (Washington, D.C.: Population Reference Bureau, 1991); William O'Hare, "Managing Multiple Race Data," *American Demographics* (April 1998), available at **www.demographics.com**; and Gabriel Escobar, "Immigrants' Ranks Tripled in 29 Years," *Washington Post,* January 9, 1999.

[38]Joan Strouse, "Continuing Themes in Assimilation Through Education," *Equity and Excellence* (Spring 1987), pp. 105–112; and T. Alexander Aleinikoff, "A Multicultural Nationalism?" *American Prospect* (January–February 1998), pp. 80–86.

In general, however, the public schools and other institutions were successful in acculturating and socializing the children of generations of immigrants. Except for the most segregated minorities ethnic groups were able to achieve substantial socioeconomic mobility. An expanding economy, cheap land on the frontier, free public schools, and other opportunities made it possible for them to enter the mainstream of society. In the process they acquired many of the attitudes and behaviors of the typical American while enriching American culture with their contributions in language, the arts, food, sports, entertainment, and scholarship.[39]

Limitations of the "melting pot"

Nevertheless, beginning in the 1950s and 1960s many scholars and laypeople pointed out that the melting pot had not totally assimilated all its ingredients. In fact ethnic identity seemed to be undergoing a resurgence by that time, partly as a result of increased immigration and a decline in traditional forms of patriotism. Other observers have pointed out that African Americans, Asian Americans, Hispanics, Native Americans, and some European ethnic groups were systematically discriminated against in a manner that revealed the shortcomings of the melting pot concept.[40]

In the 1960s, as leaders of the civil rights movement fought to reduce the exclusion of minority groups, emphasis shifted (in some interpretations) from the stress on assimilation to a stress on diversity and cultural pluralism. In place of the metaphor of the melting pot, the concept of **cultural pluralism** introduced new metaphors, such as a "tossed salad" or a "mosaic," that allow for distinctive group

Valuing diversity

characteristics within a larger whole. According to the American Association of Colleges for Teacher Education (AACTE), "to endorse cultural pluralism is to endorse the principle that there is no one model American." From this viewpoint, the differences among the nation's citizens are "a positive force."[41]

It should be emphasized that stress on cultural pluralism does not mean that one supports a philosophy aimed at cultural, social, or economic separation. De-

Between assimilation and separation

pending on how cultural pluralism is defined, it may or may not stress integration in cultural, social, or economic matters, but generally it lies somewhere between total assimilation and strict separation of ethnic or racial groups. Cultural pluralism is more important than ever before as the United States becomes transformed into what some observers call the first "universal nation."

In response to these trends, educators have been developing ways to build the goals of a constructive pluralism into the school system. The AACTE sees this task as

Building a constructive pluralism

a major educational responsibility, and its president has stated that diversity in the educational community must be a central element in carrying out restructuring,

---

[39]Historical mobility data for some ethnic and racial groups in the United States are reviewed in Alice Kessler-Harris and Virginia Yans-McLaughlin, "European Immigrant Groups," in Thomas Sowell, ed., *American Ethnic Groups* (Washington, D.C.: Urban Institute, 1978), pp. 107–137. See also Nathan Glazer, ed., *Clamor at the Gates* (San Francisco: Institute for Contemporary Studies, 1985); and Margarita Calderon, "Adolescent Sons and Daughters of Immigrants," in Kathryn Borman and Barbara Schneider, eds., *The Adolescent Years* (Chicago: University of Chicago Press, 1998), pp. 65–87.

[40]Howard Bahr, Bruce A. Chadwick, and Joseph H. Strauss, *American Ethnicity* (Lexington, Mass.: D.C. Heath, 1979); Ilan Stavans, *The Hispanic Condition* (New York: HarperCollins, 1995); K. Anthony Appiah, "The Multiculturalist Misunderstanding," *New York Review of Books,* October 9, 1997; and Min Zhou and Carl L. Bankston, III, *Growing Up American* (New York: Russell Sage, 1998).

[41]"No One Model American: A Statement of Multicultural Education" (Washington, D.C.: American Association of Colleges for Teacher Education, 1972), p. 9. See also Nathan Glazer, *We Are All Multiculturalists Now* (Cambridge, Mass.: Harvard University Press, 1997); and John J. Miller, *The Unmaking of Americans* (New York: Free Press, 1998).

PROFESSIONAL
PLANNING

for your first year

What Can You Do
to Help Provide
Equal Educational
Opportunity?

The Situation

Assume you have just obtained your first teaching job in a city or suburban school with a relatively diverse mixture of students. You have been given a school profile indicating that about half the students are nonminority whites and the remaining half are minority students, including African Americans, Asian Americans, and Hispanic Americans. Many of the minority students are from low-income families, as are some of the white students, particularly those from families that recently immigrated from Bosnia and Greece. The profile also states that the average class size is thirty students, that emphasis is placed on including disabled students in regular classes as much as possible, and that the staff includes several Title 1 teachers as well as specialists who work with students who speak little English. It seems certain that your class or classes will include students who differ greatly from each other in current achievement level, racial and ethnic background, and readiness to benefit from curriculum materials commonly used in your grade and subject.

Thought Questions

1. Who on the staff might you want to ask how you can best work with a class that includes a very wide range of achievement levels?
2. Where might you find curriculum materials that can be used effectively with limited-English students or with learning-disabled students?
3. To what extent will the preparation program at your college or university help you prepare for this teaching assignment? What more can you do while you are in the program to build your skills in handling so much diversity among students in a classroom?
4. What attitudes should you cultivate that might help you succeed? To what extent can you overcome the feelings of failure you may well experience occasionally or even frequently as you cope with a very challenging beginning to your career in teaching? Which, if any, of your attitudes do you think are likely to be modified as you confront difficult problems in your own classroom?

school renewal, and other reforms. Many other observers also see multicultural education as an important task for teachers in every subject area.[42]

Multicultural Instruction

One key area in multicultural education concerns instructional approaches for teaching students with differing ethnic and racial backgrounds. Some of the most frequently discussed approaches have to do with student learning styles, recognition of dialect differences, bilingual education, and multiethnic curriculum.

[42]"No One Model American." If cultural pluralism were defined more narrowly as involving or advocating separation, segregation, or isolation of racial or ethnic groups, most Americans would see it as pernicious and undesirable. See also James A. Banks and Cherry A. M. Banks, eds., *Multicultural Education,* 3rd ed. (Boston: Allyn and Bacon, 1997).

Student Learning Styles.   In the preceding chapter we briefly described behavioral patterns and learning styles that appear to be correlated with students' socioeconomic status and, perhaps, with their race or ethnicity. We also mentioned attempts to modify instruction to accommodate different learning styles. One good example of research on this subject was provided by Vera John-Steiner and Larry Smith, who worked with Pueblo Indian children in the Southwest. They concluded that schooling for these children would be more successful if it took better account of their "primary learning" patterns (learning outside the school) and thereby emphasized personal communication in tutorial (face-to-face) situations. Other observers of Native American classrooms, including Frederick Erickson, reported that achievement rose substantially when teachers interacted with students in ways that were culturally appropriate: that is, social control was mostly indirect, and teachers avoided putting students in competitive situations. Similarly, several researchers have reported that cooperative learning arrangements are particularly effective with some Mexican American students whose cultural background deemphasizes competition.[43]

Accommodating cultural learning patterns

Another approach that modifies instruction to fit students' cultural learning styles is the Kamehameha Early Education Program (KEEP) in Hawaii. The KEEP approach combines whole-group direct instruction with individualized work in learning centers. The program addresses the students' cultural backgrounds by emphasizing student-produced stories in language arts, instant feedback, no penalty for "wrong" answers, and discussion of students' responsibilities as group members. According to the research, this attempt to capitalize on the informal interaction characteristic of native Hawaiian culture has improved student achievement. Educators working with Navajo students and other culturally distinctive groups are adapting the KEEP approach at other locations.[44]

The KEEP program

Analysts also have examined research on the performance of Asian American students. Several observers believe that some subgroups of Asian students (for example, Koreans and Vietnamese) tend to be nonassertive in the classroom, and that this reluctance to participate may hinder their academic growth, particularly with respect to verbal skills. However, some research suggests that such behavioral patterns diminish or disappear as Asian American students become more assimilated within U.S. society.[45]

Recognition of Dialect Differences.   Teachers generally have tried to teach "proper" or Standard English to students who speak nonstandard dialects. Frequently, however, a simplistic insistence on proper English has caused students to reject their own cultural background or else to view the teachers' efforts as demeaning and hostile. In recent years, educators have been particularly concerned with learning problems encountered by students who speak Black English. Research shows that Black English is not simply a form of slang; rather, it differs systemati-

Black English

---

[43]Vera John-Steiner and Larry Smith, "The Educational Promise of Cultural Pluralism" (Paper prepared for the National Conference on Urban Education, St. Louis, 1978); Frederick Erickson, *Qualitative Methods in Research on Teaching* (East Lansing, Mich.: Institute for Research on Teaching, 1985), p. 55; Kay M. Losey, "Mexican American Students and Classroom Interaction," *Review of Educational Research* (Fall 1995), pp. 283–318; and Barbara J. Snade, ed., *Culture, Style, and the Educative Process* (Springfield, Ill.: Thomas, 1997).

[44]Kathryn H. Au and Alice J. Kawakami, "Research Currents," *Language Arts* (April 1985), pp. 406–411; and Kathryn H. Au and Jacqueline H. Carroll, "Improving Literary Achievement through a Constructivist Approach," *Elementary School Journal* (January 1997), pp. 203–221.

[45]Ester Lee Yao, "Asian-Immigrant Students' Unique Problems That Hamper Learning," *NASSP Bulletin* (December 1987), pp. 82–88; Don T. Nakanishi and Tinya Y. Nishida, eds., *The Asian American Educational Experience* (New York: Routledge, 1995); and Li-Rong Lilly Cheng, "Enhancing the Education Skills of Newly-Arrived Asian American Students," *ERIC Clearinghouse on Urban Education Digest* (No. 136, 1998), available at **eric-web.tc.columbia.edu**.

cally from standard English in grammar and syntax. Because Black English seems to be the basic form of English spoken by many low-income African American students who are not succeeding academically, some educators have proposed that schools use Black English as the language of instruction for these students until they learn to read. Although this approach seems logical, research has not provided much support for it.[46]

Building bridges for students with nonstandard dialects

Even without conclusive research on the use of dialects in instruction, educators should seek constructive ways to overcome the learning problems that many students with nonstandard dialects encounter. This task became particularly important when a federal judge ruled in 1979 that the Ann Arbor, Michigan, school district must recognize that students who speak Black English may need special help in learning standard English. The district was ordered to identify children who speak Black English and then take their dialect into consideration in teaching them to read. Although the decision is not binding outside the Ann Arbor schools, it has influenced a number of other school districts. Guidelines often stress building "associative bridges" between a child's dialect and Standard English, as well as helping children develop skills in switching to Standard English.[47]

Ebonics in Oakland

Analysis of the dialect of many African American students (i.e., Black English) frequently is referred to as "Ebonics." An important controversy regarding **Ebonics** and its possible use in improving instruction for African American students — particularly low-achieving black students in socially isolated poverty neighborhoods — arose in 1997 after the Oakland, California, school board declared that Black English is a distinctive language. The board requested state and federal bilingual education funds (see the following section in this chapter) to help teachers use Black English in implementing approaches for improving black students' performance with respect to Standard English and reading. After television sound bites and brief newspaper reports allowed for the interpretation that Oakland schools were abandoning the goal of teaching "good" English, numerous national figures (including Reverend Jesse Jackson) criticized and even ridiculed the board for its policies regarding the use of Ebonics in teaching. Although the Linguistic Society of America declared that Oakland's policy was "linguistically and pedagogically sound," the Board of Education responded by removing terminology involving Ebonics from its policies and setting aside $400,000 for a "Standard English Proficiency" program designed to help teachers understand and build on dialect characteristics in instructing students whose language patterns strongly emphasize Black English.[48]

[46]J. R. Harber and D. N. Bryan, "Black English and the Teaching of Reading," *Review of Educational Research* (Summer 1976), pp. 397–398; Jane W. Torrey, "Black Children's Knowledge of Standard English," *American Educational Research Journal* (Winter 1983), pp. 627–643; Vivian L. Gadsden and Daniel A. Wagner, eds., *Literacy Among African-American Youth* (Creskill, N.J.: Hampton, 1995); and Charles J. Fillmore, "A Linguist Looks at the Ebonics Debate" (1997 posting at the Internet site of the Center for Applied Linguistics), available at **www.cal.org/ebonics.**
[47]Toya A. Wyatt and Harry N. Seymour, "The Implications of Code-Switching in Black English Speakers," *Equity and Excellence* (Summer 1990), pp. 11–18; Donna Christian, "Vernacular Dialects in U.S. Schools," *ERIC Digests* (May 1997), ED 406846; and Theresa Perry and Lisa Delpit, eds., *The Real Ebonics Debate* (Boston: Beacon, 1998).
[48]"Linguistic Society of America's Resolution on Ebonics," *Rethinking Schools* (Fall 1997); Charles Fillmore, "A Linguist Looks at the Ebonics Debate" (1997 Internet posting by the Center for Applied Linguistics), available at **www.cal.org/ebonics**; Wayne O'Neill, "If Ebonics Isn't a Language, Then Tell Me, What Is?" *Rethinking Schools* (Fall 1997), available at **www.rethinkingschools.org**; and Rene Sanchez, "After Ebonics Controversy, Oakland Seeks Viable Lesson Plan," *Washington Post,* April 19, 1998. For a dissenting analysis concerning the value of attending to Black English in teaching, see John H. McWhorter, "Throwing Money at an Illusion," *The Black Scholar* (January 1997), available at **www-learning.berkeley.edu.**

Lau v. Nichols requirements

Bilingual Education.   **Bilingual education,** which provides instruction in their native language for students not proficient in English, has been expanding in U.S. public schools. In 1968, Congress passed the Bilingual Education Act, and in 1974 the Supreme Court ruled unanimously in *Lau* v. *Nichols* that the schools must take steps to help students who "are certain to find their classroom experiences wholly incomprehensible" because they do not understand English. Congressional appropriations for bilingual education increased from $7.5 million in 1969 to more than $200 million in 1995. Although the federal and state governments fund bilingual projects for more than sixty language groups speaking various Asian, Indo-European, and Native American languages, the large majority of children served by these projects are Hispanic.

Rise of bilingual programs

The Supreme Court's unanimous decision in the *Lau* case, which involved Chinese children in San Francisco, did not focus on bilingual education as the only remedy. Instead, the Court said, "Teaching English to the students of Chinese ancestry is one choice. Giving instruction to this group in Chinese is another. There may be others." In practice, federal regulations for implementing the *Lau* decision have tended to focus on bilingual education as the most common solution for limited-English-proficient (LEP) and non-English-proficient (NEP) students. The regulations generally suggest that school districts initiate bilingual programs if they enroll more than twenty students of a given language group at a particular grade. Bilingual programs have proliferated accordingly. Since 1983 the federal government has indicated willingness to accept English-as-a-second-language (ESL) instruction or other nonbilingual approaches for providing help to LEP and NEP students. Nevertheless, data collected by the Council of Chief State School Officers and other organizations indicate that large numbers of LEP students are not receiving significant specialized assistance to help them learn English and other subjects.[49]

One advantage frequently attributed to bilingual education is its potential for emphasizing comprehension and thinking skills in the students' native language while they are learning to function fluently in English. *(© Elizabeth Crews)*

---

[49]Cynthia G. Brown, *The Challenge and State Response* (Washington, D.C.: Council of Chief State School Officers, 1990); Eugene E. Garcia and René Gonzalez, "Issues in Systemic Reform for Culturally and Linguistically Diverse Students," *Teachers College Record* (Spring 1995), pp. 418–430; and Ethan Bronner, "Bilingual Education Has Fallen Into Disfavor," *New York Times,* May 30, 1998.

Controversies: how much English, how soon?

Controversies over bilingual education have become increasingly embittered. As in the case of teaching through dialect, there are arguments between those who would "immerse" children in an English-language environment and those who believe initial instruction will be more effective in the native language. Educators and laypeople concerned with LEP and NEP students also argue over whether emphasis should be placed on teaching in the native language over a long period of time, called **first-language maintenance**, or providing intensive English instruction and then proceeding to teach all subjects in English as soon as possible, called **transitional bilingual education (TBE)**. The latter approach has been supported by federal guidelines and by legislation in some states. Those who favor maintenance believe that this will help sustain a constructive sense of identity among ethnic or racial minority students and/or will provide a better basis for learning higher-order skills such as reading comprehension while they acquire basic English skills. Their opponents believe that maintenance programs are harmful because they separate groups from one another or discourage students from mastering English well enough to function successfully in the larger society.[50]

Staffing disputes

Adherents and opponents of bilingual education also differ on staffing issues. Those who favor bilingual and bicultural maintenance tend to believe that the schools need many adults who can teach LEP or NEP students in their own language. Some advocates of transitional or ESL programs, on the other hand, feel that only a few native language or bilingual speakers are required to staff a legitimate program. Some critics of bilingual education go so far as to claim that bilingual programs are primarily a means of providing teaching jobs for native language speakers who may not be fully competent in English.

How much improvement?

Educators are particularly concerned with the effectiveness of bilingual education in improving the performance of low-achieving students. Some scholars believe that bilingual education has brought about little if any improvement. Several researchers in this group have reviewed the research and concluded that "structured immersion" (placement in regular classes with special assistance provided inside and outside of class) and "sheltered immersion" (using principles of second-language learning in regular classrooms) are more successful than TBE.[51] Other scholars disagree, arguing that well-implemented bilingual programs do improve achievement, and several reviews of research have reported that bilingual education worked significantly better than immersion or other mostly monolingual programs.[52] Part of the reason for these differences in conclusions involves disagreements about which studies should be reviewed and the criteria for selecting them.

Marks of good programs

A number of researchers have identified specific characteristics that help make programs for LEP and NEP students successful. They include continuity in enroll-

---

[50]Noel Epstein, *Language, Ethnicity, and the Schools* (Washington, D.C.: George Washington University Institute for Educational Leadership, 1977); Rosalie P. Porter, *Forked Tongue* (New York: Basic Books, 1990); Linda Chavez, *Out of the Barrio* (New York: Basic Books, 1991); and Glenn Garvin, "Loco, Completamente Loco," *Reason* (January 1998), pp. 18–29; available at **www.reasonmag.com.**

[51]Christine H. Rossell, "The Research on Bilingual Education," *Equity and Excellence* (Winter 1990), pp. 29–36; Rosalie P. Porter, "Language Choice for Latin Students," *The Public Interest* (Fall 1991), pp. 48–60; and Rosalie P. Porter, "The Case Against Bilingual Education," *Atlantic* (May 1998), pp. 28–38.

[52]Heidi Dulay and Marina Burt, "Bilingual Education: A Close Look at Its Effects," *Focus of the National Clearinghouse for Bilingual Education* (January 1982), pp. 1–4; Ann C. Willig, "A Meta-Analysis of Selected Studies on the Effectiveness of Bilingual Education," *Review of Educational Research* (Fall 1985), pp. 269–317; J. P. Greene, "Bilingual Education," *Policy Brief* (March 1998), pp. 1–6; and "Bilingual Education Beneficial in Early Grades," *School Reform News* (April 1998), available at **www.heartland.org.**

ment for a given student, frequent monitoring of progress, and open-ended assistance (rather than the elimination of assistance at an arbitrary point). For bilingual programs in particular, success is more likely if the program features "active" teaching, provision of services over a significant period of time, communication of high expectations to the students, emphasis on higher-order skills, and coordination of English-language development with academic studies.[53]

Special assistance needed

Stressing thinking skills

Despite disagreements on the effects of existing programs, most researchers agree that LEP and NEP students should be given special assistance in learning to function in the schools. According to the research, "submersion" approaches, which simply place LEP and NEP students in regular classrooms without any special assistance or modifications in instruction, frequently result in failure to learn. In addition, numerous researchers report that it is critically important to stress cognitive development and higher-order skills in bilingual education. Indeed, one advantage frequently attributed to bilingual education is its potential for emphasizing comprehension and thinking skills in the students' native language while they are learning to function in English.[54]

California restricts bilingual education

Following a frequently heated debate that received unprecedented national attention, in 1998 California voters supported legislation designed to eliminate bilingual education and restrict special programs for non-English-speaking students to one year of intensive instruction (i.e., "sheltered immersion"). This instruction would develop their English skills while continuing to focus part of the time on their native language.

Uncertain future

Arguments on each side basically paralleled and extended those outlined in the preceding pages. In particular, supporters of the legislation argued that although bilingual education was attractive in theory, it generally was not working in practice. Opponents emphasized the difficulties that NEP and LEP students experience when taught in a language they do not understand. (Hispanic parents were deeply divided on the issue. Many felt that bilingual education had helped their children, but many others felt that local programs took too many years to prepare their children for regular instruction.) Following passage of the new law, educators in many school districts sought to obtain waivers, and some decided to challenge the law in the courts. It probably will take some time to detremine exactly how the law will be implemented; meanwhile these developments generally do not appear to be having much influence on bilingual programming outside of California.[55]

Bilingual education for everyone

Many scholars believe that bilingual education ideally should be provided for all students, regardless of their ethnic group. In part this argument stems from the

---

[53]William J. Tikinoff, *Applying Significant Bilingual Instruction Features in the Classroom* (Roslyn, Va.: Inter-America Research Association, 1985); Thomas P. Carter and Michael L. Chatfield, "Effective Bilingual Schools," *American Journal of Education* (November 1986), pp. 200–232; Catherine Minicucci et al., "School Reform and Student Diversity," *Phi Delta Kappan* (September 1995), pp. 77–80; and Rita Karam, Douglas E. Mitchell, and Tom Destino, "Factors Impacting the Effectiveness of Language Development Programs" (Paper presented at the annual meeting of the American Educational Research Association, San Diego, April 1998).

[54]Kenji Hakuta, *Mirror of Language* (New York: Basic Books, 1986); Kenji Hakuta and Lois J. Gould, "Synthesis of Research on Bilingual Education," *Educational Leadership* (March 1987), pp. 38–45; and Guadalupe Valdés, "The World Outside and Inside the Schools," *Educational Researcher* (August–September 1998), pp. 4–9.

[55]Ethan Bronner, "Bilingual Education's Supporters Sue to Block Ban," *New York Times,* June 4, 1998; Louis Sahugan, "Responses to Prop. 227 All over the Map," *Los Angeles Times,* September 2, 1998; Lynn Schnaiberg, "In Battle over Prop. 227, Both Sides Command Armies of Statistics," *Education Week,* April 29, 1998; Don Terry, "Latino Community Remains Divided over Future of Bilingual Education," *New York Times,* June 5, 1998; Keith Baker, "Structured English Immersion," *Phi Delta Kappan* (November 1998), pp. 199–204; and Louis Sahugan, "L.A. Students Take to English Immersion," *Los Angeles Times,* January 13, 1999.

international economic advantages of a nation's citizens knowing more than one language. Programs to provide education in both English and another language for all students at a multiethnic school are sometimes referred to as "two-way" bilingual immersion. To make this type of education a positive force in the future, several groups of civic leaders have recommended stressing multilingual competence, rather than just English remediation, as well as insisting on full mastery of English.[56]

Multiethnic Curriculum and Instruction. Since the mid-1960s, educators have been striving to take better account of cultural diversity by developing multiethnic curriculum materials and instructional methods. Many textbooks and supplemental reading lists have been revised to include materials and topics relating to diverse racial and ethnic groups. In-service training has helped teachers discover multiethnic source materials and learn to use instructional methods that promote multicultural perspectives and positive intergroup relations.[57]

New multiethnic materials and methods

Efforts to implement multiethnic curricula have been particularly vigorous with respect to Native American students. For example, educators at the Northwest Regional Education Laboratory have prepared an entire Indian Reading Series based on Native American culture. Mathematics instruction for Native American students sometimes uses familiar tribal symbols and artifacts in presenting word and story problems, and local or regional tribal history has become an important part of the social studies curriculum in some schools. Many observers believe that such approaches can help Native American students establish a positive sense of identity conducive to success in school and society.[58]

Approaches for Native Americans

However, multiethnic curricula are not intended merely to bolster the self-image and enhance the learning of minority students. A crucial purpose is to ensure that each group of students acquires knowledge and appreciation of other racial and ethnic groups. Guidelines for attaining this goal typically stress building skills and understandings such as the following:[59]

Components for building multicultural understanding

- *Human relations skills* involving development of students' self-esteem and interpersonal communications
- *Cultural self-awareness* developed through students' research on their ethnic or racial group, family history, and local community
- *Multicultural awareness* derived in part from historical studies and literary or pictorial materials incorporating diverse racial and ethnic points of view
- *Cross-cultural experiences* including discussions and dialogue with students and adults from different ethnic and racial groups

[56]*What Works in Education: A Symposium* (Washington, D.C.: U.S. Government Printing Office, 1990); and Wayne P. Thomas and Virginia P. Collier, "Two Languages Are Better Than One," *Educational Leadership* (January 1998), pp. 23–26.
[57]Sara Bullard, "Sorting Through the Multicultural Rhetoric," *Educational Leadership* (January 1992), pp. 8–11; Gloria Ladson-Billings, "Toward a Theory of Culturally Relevant Pedagogy," *American Educational Research Journal* (Fall 1995), pp. 465–491; and Stephen May, *Towards Critical Multiculturalism* (Bristol, Pa.: Falmer, 1998).
[58]Lee Little Soldier, "The Education of Native American Students," *Equity and Excellence* (Summer 1990), pp. 66–69; *Indian Reading Series* (Portland, Oreg.: Northwest Regional Educational Laboratory, 1990); and Lee Little Soldier, "Is There an Indian in Your Classroom?" *Phi Delta Kappan* (April 1997), pp. 650–653.
[59]James A. Banks, *Multiethnic Education* (Needham Heights, Mass.: Allyn and Bacon, 1988); Ellen Wolpert, "Using Pictures to Combat Bias," *Rethinking Schools* (Summer 1995), p. 25; Deirdre A. Almeida, "Countering Prejudice Against American Indians and Alaska Natives Through Antibias Curriculum and Instruction," *ERIC Digest* (October 1996), EDO-RC-96-4, available at **www.ed.gov**; and Wilbert J. McKeachie, *Teaching Tips* (Boston: Houghton Mifflin, 1999).

Reducing Eurocentrism

Recent Controversies. In recent years particular attention has been given to ensuring that curriculum and instruction are not overwhelmingly *Eurocentric* (reflecting the culture and history of ethnic groups of European origin) but instead also incorporate the concerns, culture, and history of ethnic and racial groups of different origins. For example, *Afrocentric* programs focus on the history and culture of African Americans. Such approaches not only introduce materials dealing with the history and status of minority groups, but also involve activities such as community service assignments and cooperative learning tasks that are thought to acquaint students with minority cultures.[60]

Efforts to introduce Afrocentric and other minority-oriented themes have provoked controversy in California, New York, and other states, as well as in individual school districts. Critics of minority-oriented projects have voiced a number of strong objections:[61]

Critiques of Afrocentric and other minority-oriented approaches

■ Many of the materials being introduced or recommended embody an overly broad rejection of both the traditional curriculum and of existing efforts to make the school constructively multicultural. In constantly criticizing Europeans and European traditions and concentrating almost entirely on minority themes, Afrocentric and related approaches encourage racial and ethnic separation and animosity. For example, Diane Ravitch concluded that some of the new materials espouse a "version of history in which everyone is either the descendant or victim of oppressors," thereby recreating and fanning "ancient hatreds" and conflicts.

■ Many of the new materials are historically inaccurate. For example, some of these materials are based on the recent theories about Egypt discussed in Chapter 3: namely, that the culture and population of ancient Egypt were predominantly African and that ancient Greece derived much of its culture from Egypt. According to John Leo, classical scholars believe these generalizations are exaggerated.

■ Beliefs and attitudes presented as typical of minority racial and ethnic groups do not represent the diversity of opinions within each group.

■ Emphasis on minority culture and history sometimes becomes a substitute for the difficult actions required to improve minority students' academic performance.

Responding to these kinds of attacks, supporters of Afrocentric and related approaches make the following points:[62]

---

[60]Marge Scherer, "School Snapshot: Focus on African-American Culture," *Educational Leadership* (January 1992), pp. 17, 19; Frank J. Yurco, "How to Teach Ancient History, A Multicultural Model," *American Educator* (Spring 1994), pp. 32–37; and S. Kifano, "Afrocentric Education in Supplementary Schools," *Journal of Negro Education* (Spring 1996), pp. 209–218. For a selection of relevant source materials, see Molefi Kete Asante and Abu S. Abarry, eds., *African Intellectual Heritage: A Book of Sources* (Philadelphia: Temple University Press, 1996); and James A. Banks, *Multicultural Education*, 3rd ed. (Boston: Allyn and Bacon, 1997).
[61]Lynne V. Cheney, "Beware the PC Police," *The Executive Educator* (January 1992), pp. 31–34; Erich Martel, "How Valid Are the Portland Baseline Essays?" *Educational Leadership* (January 1992), pp. 20–23; John Travis, "Schools Stumble on an Afrocentric Science Essay," *Science*, November 12, 1993, pp. 1121–1122; Ellen Coughlin, "Not Out of Africa," *Chronicle of Higher Education*, February 16, 1996, pp. A6–A7; and Richard Bernstein, "Dictatorship of Virtue," *American Experiment Quarterly* (Summer 1998), available at **www.amexp.org**.
[62]Molefi Asante, *The Afrocentric Idea* (Philadelphia: Temple University Press, 1987); Molefi Asante, "Afrocentric Curriculum," *Educational Leadership* (January 1992), pp. 28–31; Anna D. Wilde, "Mainstreaming Kwanzaa," *The Public Interest* (Spring 1995), pp. 68–79; and Maulana Karenga, "An Idea Worth Considering," *Black Issues in Higher Education* (June 11, 1998), p. 25.

Responses to the critiques

- Few Afrocentric supporters advocate eliminating Western culture and history from the curriculum. Molefi Asante argues that the Afrocentric movement strives to de-bias the curriculum by adding appropriate Afrocentric materials, not by eliminating Western classics.

- Few if any supporters of Afrocentric or related approaches minimize the importance of academic achievement or advocate its deemphasis in the curriculum. Instead, stress on the history and contributions of one's racial or ethnic group is viewed as a way to enhance motivation while challenging students to perform to their fullest potential.

Initial reports promising

Although the research is not conclusive, some initial reports suggest that Afrocentric and related approaches may help improve the performance of low-achieving students. For example, educators in some big cities have concluded that including materials on minority history and culture can help raise students' motivation to learn. Both attendance and reading scores appear to have improved at some Atlanta and Detroit schools that introduced Afrocentric themes, and an assessment of college students who participated in an Afrocentric studies program for one year found that their grades improved substantially.[63]

Multiculturalism for the Future

Continuing controversies

The controversies about multicultural education as a whole follow some of the same lines as the specific arguments about Afrocentric and other minority-oriented curricula. Critics worry that multicultural education may increase ethnic separatism, fragment the curriculum, and reinforce the tendency to settle for a second-rate education for economically disadvantaged or minority students. To avoid such potential dangers, the director of an institute for civic education has provided some useful guidelines for multicultural programs:

Guidelines for multicultural programs

Maintain openness. . . . courses should have detailed syllabi available for any citizen to see at any time. A reasonable syllabus would outline the content, indicate the major topics and subtopics . . . and specify the required reading or other activities. . . .

Find out what positive aspects of Western civilization are being taught. If students are not learning that constitutional government, the rule of law, and the primacy of individual rights are among the hallmarks of Western civilization, then they are not learning the essential features of their heritage. . . .

Find out if students are being taught that racism, sexism, homophobia, and imperialism are characteristics of all cultures and civilizations at some time — not culture-specific evils. . . . America's failings should not be taught in isolation from the failings of other countries — no double standard.

Insist that all students study both Western and non-Western cultures. Students need solid academic courses in Latin American, African, and Asian history, in addition to European history.[64]

---

[63]Charles Devarics, "Afro-centric Program Yields Academic Gains," *Black Issues in Higher Education,* December 6, 1990, pp. 1, 34; Molefi Asante, "The Movement Toward Centered Education," *Crisis* (April–May 1993), pp. 18–20; and Marjorie Coeyman, "Black Pride Drives This Public School," *Christian Science Monitor,* October 6, 1998.

[64]Sandra Stotsky, "Cultural Politics," *American School Board Journal* (October 1991), p. 28. See also Diane Ravitch, "A Culture in Common," *Educational Leadership* (January 1992), pp. 8–11; and James A. Banks, "The Lives and Values of Researchers," *Educational Researcher* (October 1998), pp. 4–16.

TABLE 11.3	Number of Students Receiving Public Special-Education Services, by Type of Disability, 1977 and 1995*		
Type of Disability	**1977**	**1995**
Speech or language impaired	1,302,666	1,023,665
Mentally retarded	969,547	570,855
Learning disabled	797,213	2,513,977
Emotionally disturbed	283,072	428,168
Other health impaired	141,417	106,509
Hearing impaired	89,743	65,568
Orthopedically impaired	87,008	60,604
Visually handicapped	38,247	24,877
Total	3,708,913	4,794,223

*Tabulations for several categories mostly involving severe physical handicaps and multihandi-capped status are not included in this table. Adding them would bring the 1995 total to 4,915,168.

Source: U.S. Department of Education, *"To Assure the Free Appropriate Education of All Handicapped Children"* (Washington, D.C.: U.S. Department of Education, 1996); other U.S. Department of Education sources.

School as an extension of community

Despite the controversies, most influential educators believe there is an urgent need for comprehensive multicultural approaches that give attention to minority experiences. "If children are to do well academically," says former New York State Commissioner of Education Thomas Sobol, "the child must experience the school as an extension, not a rejection, of home and community." A central goal, Sobol contends, should be to "develop a shared set of values and a common tradition" while also helping "each child find his or her place within the whole."[65]

For many educators, commitment to multicultural education reflects a healthy recognition of the need to promote positive intergroup relationships and more effective educational opportunities for all groups of students. As with desegregation and compensatory education, educators will disagree among themselves on just what steps are needed. For years to come, however, the goal of attaining equal opportunity through multiculturalism will continue as a prominent theme in U.S. education.

Education for Students with Disabilities

Some of the major developments in education in the past twenty years have involved schooling for children with disabilities. Large gains have been made in providing and improving special-education services for these students. (Placement in "special education" usually means that a disabled student receives separate, specialized instruction for all or part of the day in a self-contained class or a resource room.) Table 11.3 shows the numbers of students with selected disabilities served in

[65]Thomas Sobol, "Understanding Diversity," *Educational Leadership* (February 1990), pp. 27–30. See also Michael Lind, *The Next American Nation* (New York: Free Press, 1995), and T. Alexander Aleinikoff, "A Multicultural Nationalism?" *American Prospect* (January–February 1998), pp. 80–86.

Growth of special education

or through public education in 1977 and 1995. As indicated, the total number served during this time increased by more than one million children and youth. Analysis conducted by the U.S. Department of Education indicates that about 72 percent of students with disabilities receive most or all of their education in regular classes (with or without assignment to part-time resource rooms); approximately 25 percent are in self-contained classes; and the rest are in special schools or facilities.[66]

Legal background

The growth of special education has been associated with the civil rights movement and its concern with equal educational opportunity. The U.S. Supreme Court's 1954 decision in *Brown* v. *Board of Education,* which addressed the segregation of African American children in separate schools, also served as a precedent in establishing the rights of students with disabilities. This right was explicitly affirmed in 1974 when a U.S. district court ruled in *Pennsylvania Association for Retarded Children, Nancy Beth Bowman et al.* v. *Commonwealth of Pennsylvania, David H. Kurtzman* that the state had an "obligation to place each mentally retarded child in a free, public program of education and training appropriate to the child's capacity."

PL 94-142 and IDEA

The Pennsylvania case and similar judicial decisions reflect federal laws based on the Fifth and Fourteenth Amendments to the Constitution, which state that no person can be deprived of liberty and of equal protection of the laws without due process. Federal requirements for the education of students with disabilities were enumerated systematically in the **Education for All Handicapped Children Act** of 1975 (often known by its public law number, PL 94-142), the **Individuals with Disabilities Education Act** (IDEA) of 1990, and the 1997 Reauthorization of the IDEA. The basic requirements spelled out in these acts, as well as by other laws and judicial interpretations, are as follows:

Basic requirements for special services

1. Testing and assessment services must be fair and comprehensive; placement cannot be based on a single criterion such as an IQ score.

2. Parents or guardians must have access to information on diagnosis and may protest decisions of school officials.

3. The team of persons that prepares an individualized education program (IEP) for each participating student must include a general educator.

4. Individualized education programs (IEPs) that include both long-range and short-range goals must be provided.

5. Educational services must be provided in the **least restrictive environment,** which means that children with disabilities may be placed in special or separate classes only for the amount of time judged necessary to provide appropriate services. If a school district demonstrates that placement in a regular educational setting cannot be achieved satisfactorily, the student must be given adequate instruction elsewhere, paid for by the district.

Progress still needed

Although there now are nearly 5 million students receiving special-education services, much progress still needs to be made in expanding participation in many school districts that tend to have high percentages of students with mental retardation, learning disabilities, and emotional problems. For example, recent reports have indicated that tens of thousands of children with disabilities are on waiting

---

[66]U.S. Department of Education, *To Assure the Free Appropriate Education of All Handicapped Children* (Washington, D.C.: U.S. Department of Education, 1996); and Lynne A. Weikart, "Segregated Placement Patterns of Students with Disabilities," *Educational Policy* (July 1998), pp. 432–448.

lists for placement in special education programs, and that federal and local monitoring and enforcement activities are weak and inadequate. Various analyses also indicate that the disability laws have been implemented much more successfully in some locations than in others, and that implementation in big cities has been particularly inadequate.[67]

Classification and Labeling of Students

Classification difficulties

Many of the problems associated with improving education for children with disabilities are related to difficulties in identifying students who require special-education services. It is very hard to be certain, for example, whether a child is mentally retarded and could benefit from special services or is simply a slow learner who requires more time and guidance to learn. Similarly, it is difficult to determine whether a child who is working below capacity has brain impairment or some other learning disability or is performing poorly because he or she is poorly motivated or poorly taught. (Of course, all these reasons may apply to the same child.) Although "learning disability" is currently the most-used label — covering students with specific deficits in reading, math, writing, listening, or other abilities — experts disagree among themselves not only on what constitutes such a disability but also on what services should be provided to ameliorate it. Similar problems are encountered in distinguishing between severe and mild emotional disturbances or between partial and complete deafness. Children who fall close to some borderline in disability status (a borderline that may be very fuzzy) are especially difficult to classify.[68]

Growth of the vague "LD" category

As many analysts have pointed out, the vagueness of the learning disabilities (LD) category has encouraged school districts to use this classification to obtain federal funds to improve educational services. Since most LD students spend much of their time in regular classes but receive extra assistance in resource rooms, LD services are often a form of compensatory education for disadvantaged or low-achieving students who do not qualify for Title 1 services. This helps to explain why the number of students in the LD category has grown so large. Research indicates that half or more of the LD students in the schools may not meet criteria commonly accepted by experts in special education.

Dangers in labeling

Critics also are concerned that classification may become a self-fulfilling prophecy. Students labeled as "disturbed," for example, may be more inclined to misbehave because the label makes unruly behavior acceptable and expected.[69] Researchers have tried to determine whether placement in a special class or program has either a positive or a detrimental effect on students. Among the variables they

---

[67]Judith D. Singer and John A. Butler, "The Education for All Handicapped Children Act: Schools as Agents of Social Reform," *Harvard Educational Review* (May 1987), pp. 125–152; Douglas Fuchs and Lynn S. Fuchs, "What's 'Special' About Special Education?" *Phi Delta Kappan* (March 1995), pp. 522–530; and "Examining the Relationship Between Housing, Education, and Persistent Segregation" (Undated paper posted at the Internet site of the Institute for Research on Poverty), available at **www1.umn.edu/irp.**

[68]Maynard C. Reynolds, "Classification of Students with Handicaps," in Edmund W. Gordon, ed., *Review of Research in Education* (Washington, D.C.: American Educational Research Association, 1984), p. 89. See also James J. Gallagher, "New Patterns in Special Education," *Educational Researcher* (June–July 1990), pp. 34–36; and Paul W. Newacheck and Neal Halfon, "Prevalence and Impact of Disabling Chronic Conditions in Childhood," *American Journal of Public Health* (April 1998), pp. 610–617.

[69]Perry A. Zirkel, "Offensive Parents," *Phi Delta Kappan* (March 1992), pp. 572–574; John O'Neil, "Can Inclusion Work?" *Educational Leadership* (December 1994–January 1995), pp. 7–11; and Kimberly Fornek, "Rockford Coins a Term," *Catalyst* (June 1998), available at **www.catalyst-chicago.org.**

Inconclusive research

have considered are peer acceptance and effects on self-concept. On the whole, the research is inconclusive.[70] (This type of research is difficult to conduct because of problems in defining terms, measuring program effects, and allowing for students' differing reactions to a given program.) Some researchers report that special education classes limit the progress of many students, but others have found that special-class placement can be beneficial when instruction is well planned and appropriate.

An Optimal Learning Environment?

Requirements of PL 94–142, IDEA, and related legislation specify that school officials must prepare an individualized educational plan for students with disabilities, including special services to help achieve educational goals specified in the plan. These requirements have frequently been interpreted as indicating that an "appropriate" free education for children with disabilities requires whatever services are necessary to help them derive as much benefit from education as do other students — perhaps establishing an optimal learning environment for every student who requires special assistance.

Rights vs. expenses

However, providing an optimal learning environment for students with severe disabilities (or, perhaps, for any student) can be very expensive. Arguments have arisen between school officials, who claim they cannot afford to provide maximally effective education for some students with disabilities, and parents or other advocates who believe that such students have a constitutional right to whatever services are needed to ensure maximum educational gains.

The Rowley *decision*

The issue went to the U.S. Supreme Court in 1982, when the parents of a deaf first grader named Amy Rowley demanded that she be provided with a sign-language interpreter in academic classes. Local educators argued that they had provided a hearing aid, a tutor of the deaf, and a speech therapist but could not provide an interpreter. In *Board of Education of Hudson Central School District* v. *Rowley,* the Court ruled that although the law requires the provision of such "supportive services" as "may be required to assist a handicapped child to benefit from public education," it does not require a particular level of benefit above the "basic floor of opportunity." In effect, according to constitutional scholars, the Court said that school officials may decide whether the additional costs are worthwhile in terms of the educational payoff for the child. Although *Rowley* requires a program "reasonably calculated" to enable the child to receive educational benefits, it does not require the best program that might be possible.[71]

---

[70]Gaea Leinhardt and Allan Pallay, "Restrictive Educational Settings: Exile or Haven?" *Review of Educational Research* (Winter 1982), pp. 557–578; (Menlo Park, Calif.: SRI International, Douglas Fuchs and Lynn S. Fuchs, "Sometimes Separate Is Better," *Educational Leadership* (December 1994–January 1995), pp. 22–26; and Naomi Zigmond, "Special Education in Restructured Schools" (Paper prepared for New Horizons for Learning, Seattle, 1997), available at **www.newhorizons.org.**

[71]However, the Supreme Court later reaffirmed that certain supportive services might be required to make basic educational opportunities truly available for a child with disabilities. In deciding the case of Amber Tatro, an eight-year-old with spina bifida, the Court ruled that school officials must provide intermittent catheterization. On the other hand, a 1991 U.S. appeals court decision interpreted the *Rowley* ruling as meaning that a school district did not have to pay tuition costs for a severely retarded student's attendance at an expensive private school. See Martha M. McCarthy, "Severely Disabled Children: Who Pays?" *Phi Delta Kappan* (September 1991), pp. 66–71; David A. Splitt, "Waist Deep," *The Executive Educator* (October 1995), pp. 17, 47; and Stephen B. Thomas and Mary J. K. Rapport, "Least Restrictive Environment," *Journal of Special Education* (Summer 1998), pp. 66–78.

Mainstreaming and Inclusion

Mandate for regular class settings

Despite the lack of conclusive data about the effects of separate settings for students with disabilities, some courts have weighed the evidence and concluded that separate placement probably does have detrimental effects for many students. This may be particularly true for those classified as having only mild disabilities. Federal legislation, as we have mentioned, also now requires that students with disabilities be placed in the least restrictive environment. As a result of these legal mandates, school districts throughout the country have made efforts to accommodate students with disabilities in regular class settings for all or most of the school day.

Mainstreaming and inclusion

The term **mainstreaming** was originally used to describe such efforts. More recently, the term **inclusion** has been applied. Inclusion usually denotes an even more strenuous effort to include disabled students in regular classrooms as much as is possible and feasible. However, neither mainstreaming nor inclusion approaches are necessarily intended to eliminate special services or classes for children with exceptional needs. Extra support may include a wide range of services, from consultation by specialists skilled in working with a particular disability to provision of special equipment. Even if a disability is severe and a child needs to spend a substantial amount of time away from the regular classroom, he or she can still be encouraged to take part in activities, such as art or music, that are open to other children.[72]

Studies ambiguous

Research on mainstreaming and inclusion has produced ambiguous results. Early studies generally failed to find evidence that placement of disabled students in regular classes for most or all of the day consistently improved their academic performance, social acceptance, or self-concept. But critics of these studies argued that most classrooms examined in the research did not provide a fair test because too little had been done to train teachers, introduce appropriate teaching methods, provide a range of suitable materials, or otherwise ensure that teachers could work effectively with heterogeneous groups of disabled and nondisabled students. Reflecting such criticism, several recent studies were limited to districts and states thought to be outstanding in providing mainstreamed or inclusive opportunities for disabled students. Again, results generally were disappointing: there were few indications that mainstreaming or inclusion has been consistently beneficial for disabled students.[73]

Model efforts based on systematic reforms

On the other hand, several recent assessments of individual schools are more promising. In general, these schools have been described as models of restructuring: systematic reforms were made in preparing teachers to work with heterogeneous groups, in providing special resources to assist both students and teachers who need help, in individualizing instruction and introducing cooperative learning, and in keeping class size relatively small. The researchers tend to agree that successful implementation of arrangements for mainstreaming or inclusion on a

---

[72]Christine L. Salisbury and Barbara J. Smith, "The Least Restrictive Environment: Understanding the Options," *Principal* (September 1991), pp. 24–27; Reinhard Nickisch, "Strategies for Integrating Handicapped Students," *Principal* (January 1992), pp. 20–21; and Joetta L. Sack, "Role of Spec. Ed. Teacher Changing," *Education Week*, March 25, 1998.
[73]Andrew R. Brulle, "Appropriate, with Dignity," *Phi Delta Kappan* (February 1991), p. 487; Justine Maloney, "A Call for Placement Options," *Educational Leadership* (December 1994–January 1995), p. 31; Naomi Zigmond et al., "Special Education in Restructured Schools," *Phi Delta Kappan* (March 1995), pp. 531–540; and Leslie Farlow, "A Quartet of Success Stories," *Educational Leadership* (February 1996), pp. 51–55.

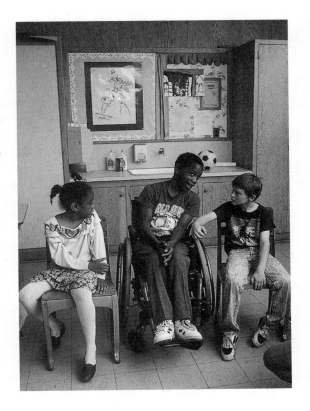

Effective mainstreaming of students with disabilities into regular classroom settings requires a variety of special resources, relatively small classes, and educators skilled in and dedicated to creating an effective learning environment and acceptance for all students. *(© Elizabeth Crews)*

national basis will require such effective restructuring of schools throughout the United States.[74]

Issues and Dilemmas

We have touched on a number of issues involved in special education, mainstreaming, and inclusion. In this section we focus on three issues or dilemmas that may have particular prominence in the next several years. Teachers and administrators throughout the educational system will be affected by the way these issues are resolved.

Financial dilemmas

1. *How will costs be handled?* As discussed above, services for severely disabled students can be very expensive, either in a separate setting or in a regular classroom. Further, if successful inclusion requires systematic restructuring of schools, placing even mildly disabled students in regular classes will consume large amounts of resources. Administrators face a series of dilemmas here. Federal laws require that disabled students receive meaningful services to support their education,

---

[74]Allan Gartner and Dorothy Kerzner Lipsky, "Beyond Special Education: Toward a Quality System for All Students," *Harvard Educational Review* (November 1987), pp. 367–395; Ray Van Dyke, Martha A. Stallings, and Kenna Colley, "How to Build an Inclusive School Community," *Phi Delta Kappan* (February 1995), pp. 475–485; and Linda L. Hansen and Robert M. Boody, "Special Education Students' Perceptions of Their Mainstreamed Classes," *Education* (Summer 1998), pp. 610–615.

but Congress has provided only a fraction of the funds needed to support these services. Upon studying this issue, one congressman confessed that federal failure to fund implementation of disability regulations "has to be the mother of all unfunded mandates in this country."[75]

One possible response is to divert local funds. Another is to classify more students as learning disabled in order to receive additional federal funding. Still another possibility involves including disabled students in regular classes *without* providing costly additional services there or undertaking systematic restructuring. There is reason to believe that responses along all these lines have been common in many school districts.[76]

Potential effects on nondisabled students

2. *To what extent are arrangements and services for educating disabled students detracting from the education of nondisabled students?* If school officials divert substantial amounts of money from regular budgets to pay for separate placements or special services for disabled students, or if school officials assign students with severe disabilities to regular classes where teachers are not able to address their problems efficiently, will classroom conditions for nondisabled students suffer? Observers disagree. Some believe that mainstreaming and inclusion have not substantially detracted from opportunities and outcomes for nondisabled students. Other observers believe that because regular classroom teachers often receive little or no help in dealing with students who have severe mental or emotional problems, they have more difficulty delivering effective instruction for all students.[77]

Many questions about implementation

3. *What services should be provided for which students, where, when, and how?* Posing this omnibus question indicates that many issues of the kind discussed in the preceding pages have not been satisfactorily resolved. For example, to what extent should differing arrangements be made for severely and mildly disabled students, or for differing students within either category? To what extent should schools implement "full inclusion" arrangements for all or most of the day, as contrasted with "partial inclusion" that assigns students to resource rooms or separate schools for significant amounts of time? To what extent should such decisions be made by parents, who may not have much understanding of their schoolwide effects, or by professionals, who may not be very sensitive to the particular problems of an individual student? To what extent is it desirable to provide regular classroom support services, such as a sign language interpreter for deaf students or a nurse to assist incontinent students, and to what extent is it feasible to do so? To what extent does the use of resource rooms complicate and disrupt the operation of the school as a whole — or is it more disruptive to bring a range of support services into the regular classroom? Will schoolwide restructuring carried out partly to accommodate full inclusion result in substantially improved schooling for all students, or is it unreasonable and unrealistic to expect widespread restructuring

---

[75]Joetta L. Sack, "GOP Puts Priority on Raising IDEA Funding," *Education Week,* May 20, 1998; and "What the Numbers Say," *Curriculum Review* (April 1998), p. 2.

[76]David A. Splitt, "The Special Ed Bill Comes Due," *The Executive Educator* (January 1994), pp. 11–35; Albert Shanker, "Full Inclusion Is Neither Free Nor Appropriate," *Educational Leadership* (December 1994–January 1995), pp. 18–21; and Robert C. Johnston, "Mich. Districts Chart Course After Spec. Ed. Rulings," *Education Week,* June 24, 1998.

[77]Lawrence Baines, Coleen Baines, and Carol Masterson, "Mainstreaming One School's Reality," *Phi Delta Kappan* (September 1994), pp. 38–40, 57–64; Debbie Staub and Charles A. Peek, "What Are the Outcomes for Nondisabled Students?" *Educational Leadership* (December 1994–January 1995), pp. 36–40; Albert Shanker, "A Double Standard," *New York Times,* February 11, 1996, p. E7; and Ann D. Lipsitt, "A Teacher's View," *Brown University Child and Adolescent Behavior Letter* (February 1998), pp. 1–3.

in the foreseeable future? These are a few of the questions for which educators do not have good answers.

Given the uncertainties that school officials confront in struggling to provide equal opportunity for students with disabilities, it would be useful to have policies and guidelines for deciding what to do. Some informed observers believe that such policies and guidelines should include the following:[78]

Suggested policies and guidelines

- Congress should provide more funds to help schools implement its mandates.

- Legislation should require that teachers receive adequate training.

- Mechanisms should be devised to expedite quick identification of classrooms or schools where full inclusion or other arrangements are not working well.

- Legislation should be passed to expedite quick removal from regular classes of disabled students who are violent or extremely disruptive (see Chapter 8).

- Schools opting to pursue full inclusion should receive whatever technical help is necessary.

- In inclusive classrooms, appropriate instructional strategies (such as peer-mediated instruction, mastery learning, and cooperative teaching) should be introduced to enable heterogeneous groups of students to master basic and advanced learning skills.

- Students with disabilities should be included in district, state, and national testing programs (which frequently is not the case now) in order to help determine whether their performance is improving or declining.

Disproportionate Placement of Minority Students

Use of "retarded" label for minorities and poor

Data on special-education placement show that students from some racial minority groups are much more likely to be designated for mental retardation programs than are non-Hispanic white students. African American students, for example, are nearly three times as likely as white students to be in "educable mentally retarded" classes. Placement in mental retardation categories is also highly correlated with students' socioeconomic background and poverty status.

Causes and effects

Many analysts believe that placement in classes for the retarded has been too dependent on intelligence tests, which have been constructed for use with middle-class whites. Some also believe that disproportionate numbers of minority students are shunted into classes for the emotionally disturbed or the retarded mainly to alleviate teachers' problems in dealing with culturally different children and youth. Many educators and parents worry that such placements may constitute a new version of segregation and discrimination, by which minority students are sentenced to special classes with low or nonexistent educational expectations.[79]

---

[78]Shanker, "Full Inclusion Is Neither Free Nor Appropriate"; Gail Lieberman, "States Must Provide Leadership," *Education,* February 22, 1995, p. 32; Pete Idstein, "Swimming Against the Mainstream," *American Educator* (Winter 1995–1996), pp. 28–31, 46; *The Inclusion of Students with Disabilities and Limited English Proficient Students in Large-Scale Assessments* (Washington, D.C.: National Center for Education Statistics, 1997), available at **nces.ed.gov**; and Joyce S. Choate and Thomas A. Rakes, *Inclusive Instruction for Struggling Readers* (Bloomington, Ind.: Phi Delta Kappa, 1998).

[79]James Lytle, "Is Special Education Serving Minority Students?" *Harvard Educational Review* (February 1988), pp. 116–120; Beth Harry and Mary G. Anderson, "The Disproportionate Placement of African American Males in Special Education Programs," *Journal of Negro Education* (Fall 1994), pp. 602–619; and Herbert Grossman, *Ending Discrimination in Special Education* (Springfield, Ill.: Thomas, 1998).

Court intervention

Several courts, sympathetic to this criticism, have issued rulings to make it less likely that students will be misassigned to special education classes. In the 1970 case *Diana* v. *Board of Education,* for example, a California court ruled that (1) all children whose primary language is not English must be tested in both their primary language and English; (2) the tests cannot depend solely on vocabulary, general information, or other experience-based items; and (3) districts that have a disparity between the percentage of Mexican American students in regular classes and in classes for the retarded must be able to show that this disparity is due to valid classification methods. In another case, *Larry P.* v. *Riles,* a California court heard evidence indicating that the dialect and family environment of many African American students produced invalid scores on IQ tests. The court then ruled that these students could not be placed in classes for the educable mentally retarded on the basis of IQ tests "as currently administered." Like the other controversies concerning special education, this one will continue in the future.[80]

Summing Up

1. Concern for equal educational opportunity has been expanding to emphasize issues involving racial and ethnic desegregation, achievement levels of students from low-income families, introduction of bilingual education and other aspects of multicultural education, and inclusion of students with disabilities in regular classrooms. Each of these and related sets of issues involve sizable expenditures to enlarge opportunities and ensure that the benefits of education are realistically available to all students. Teachers who enter the educational system in the next decade will play an important role in determining the extent to which such efforts will be successful or unsuccessful.

2. Although much desegregation has been accomplished in smaller school districts, the concentration of minority students and economically disadvantaged students in big-city districts has made it difficult to bring about stable desegregation.

3. Compensatory education seemed to be unsuccessful until evidence accumulating in the 1980s began to justify a more positive conclusion. However, many serious questions remain concerning the degree to which compensatory education can have substantial and lasting results on a large scale.

4. Efforts to contribute to constructive cultural pluralism through education include multicultural education approaches that take account of student learning styles, recognize differences in dialect, provide for bilingual education, and introduce methods and materials involving multiethnic curriculum and instruction. These approaches can help improve the performance of economically disadvantaged minority students and otherwise contribute to the attainment of a productive pluralistic society.

5. Legislative and court mandates have led to a large expansion in education for students with disabilities. As part of this process, educators are trying to mainstream these students as much as possible to avoid the damaging effects of labeling and separation. But research is not clear concerning the overall gains and losses associated with mainstreaming or inclusion, and many questions remain.

[80]John T. Affeldt, "It Is No Time to Reinstate Discriminatory I.Q. Tests," *Education Week,* November 2, 1994, p. 51; and Julia Washington, "African American English Research," *Perspectives* (Spring 1998), pp. 1–6.

Key Terms

desegregation *(347)*

integration *(347)*

de jure segregation *(349)*

de facto segregation *(349)*

magnet schools *(352)*

controlled choice *(357)*

compensatory education *(357)*

Title 1 *(358)*

Head Start *(358)*

Follow Through *(358)*

ecological intervention *(360)*

coordinated human services *(361)*

pullout approach *(361)*

multicultural education *(365)*

cultural pluralism *(366)*

Ebonics *(369)*

bilingual education *(370)*

first-language maintenance *(371)*

transitional bilingual education (TBE) *(371)*

Education for All Handicapped Children Act (PL 94-142) *(377)*

Individuals with Disabilities Education Act (IDEA) *(377)*

least restrictive environment *(377)*

mainstreaming *(380)*

inclusion *(380)*

Discussion Questions

1. What actions and policies are most important in bringing about successful desegregation? In what situations is it most difficult to implement desegregation effectively?

2. Why is compensatory education an important national issue? What approaches are most promising for improving the achievement of low-income students?

3. What are some of the major goals and components of multicultural education? What can teachers in predominantly nonminority schools do to advance its goals?

4. What can teachers in regular classrooms do to help disabled students who are included in their classes? What difficulties are they likely to encounter? How can these difficulties be overcome?

Suggested Projects for Professional Development

1. Interview teachers in nearby elementary schools to determine whether they are using, or considering, inclusion arrangements. What are their attitudes toward inclusion? What can you learn from them that may be useful in your own career?

2. Use Internet resources to find out what various school districts are doing to implement Title 1. Do improvements seem to be occurring? What changes have taken place during the past few years? Are similar changes taking place in districts in which you may apply for a position?

3. If a nearby school district operates magnet schools, visit one of them. Ask students and faculty what the magnet school is accomplishing and how it differs from a regular, nonmagnet school. Ask administrators how the school's goals were defined by the school district. Does the school seem to be successful in meeting these goals? Do you think you would enjoy working there? Why or why not?

4. Organize and participate in a debate about the desirability of bilingual education. As part of your preparation for the debate, identify articles and books that help you reach valid conclusions.

5. For your portfolio, begin preparing a section that will show your experience and studies with respect to topics considered in this chapter.

Suggested Readings and Resources

Internet Resources

In addition to federal-government and ERIC sites and other more specialized Internet locations identified elsewhere in this text, the important policy issues introduced in this chapter can be researched at Web sites emphasizing public-policy analysis. These sites include **www.brook.edu**, **www.heritage.org**, **www.ncpa.org**, **www.rand.org**, and **epn.org**. Electronic journals such as *Educational Policy Analysis Archives* also address issues reviewed in this chapter. Relevant research centers located on the Internet include the Center for Multilingual, Multicultural Research at **www-ref.usc.edu/~cmmr**, and the National Clearinghouse for Bilingual Education at **www.ncbe.gwu.edu**.

Video

Prejudice: The Eye of the Storm. VHS, 25 minutes (1981). Insight Media, 2162 Broadway, New York, NY 10024. Phone: 212–721–6316. *This Peabody Award winner describes how an elementary school teacher helped students understand the stereotypes that can limit the opportunities available to groups of people.*

Publications

Banks, James A., and Cheryl A.M. Banks, eds. *Handbook of Research on Multicultural Education.* New York: Macmillan, 1995. *A wide variety of research-based chapters deal with cultural diversity and learning, effective instruction for low-income students, desegregation, the history and performance of minority groups, multicultural instruction, and related topics.*

Gibson, Margaret A., and John U. Ogbu, eds. *Minority Status and Schools.* New York: Garland, 1991. *In addition to providing a general analysis of the experience of minority students in several countries, this book deals specifically with African American, Hispanic, Korean, Sikh, Ute Indian, and West Indian students in the United States.*

Levine, Daniel U., and Rayna F. Levine. *Society and Education.* 9th ed. Needham Heights, Mass.: Allyn and Bacon, 1996. *This text on the sociology of education provides detailed analysis of topics discussed in this chapter.*

Lind, Michael. *The Next American Nation.* New York: Free Press, 1995. *Provides detailed descriptions and discussions of topics involving immigration, multiculturalism, desegregation, affirmative action, sex equity, social class, and related issues.*

McLeod, Beverly. *School Reform and Cultural Diversity.* Santa Cruz, Calif.: National Center for Research on Cultural Diversity and Second Language Learning, no date. *Subtitled "Exemplary Schooling for Language Minority Students," this report identifies successful practices for students who speak little English. Available at zzyx.ucsc.edu/Cntr.*

PART FIVE

Philosophical and Curricular Foundations

CHAPTER TWELVE

Philosophical Roots of Education

Teachers face the important everyday challenges of preparing lessons, assessing student performance, and creating and maintaining a fair and equitable classroom learning environment.[1] How well you succeed in meeting these challenges determines the degree of success you will have as a teacher. From informal conversations in the teachers' lounge to professional workshops and institutes, many opinions are offered on how to meet these challenges. Often because of the urgent problems teachers face each day, these opinions, lying at the surface of education, are not examined and reflected upon. But upon reflection, the seemingly everyday issues take on a deeper and more philosophical dimension. This chapter examines educational philosophy's role in helping teachers move from unexamined opinions to such philosophical questions as the following:

- What is truth, and how do we know and teach it?
- What is right and wrong, and how can we teach ethical moral values?
- How can schools and their curriculum exemplify what is true and valuable?
- How do teaching and learning reflect one's beliefs about truth and value?

[1]Useful books on the philosophy of education are Robert D. Heslep, *Philosophical Thinking in Educational Practice* (Westport, Conn.: Praeger Publishers, 1997); and Nel Noddings, *Philosophy of Education* (Boulder, Colo.: Westview Press, 1995).

Throughout the chapter, we shall refer to these as "the basic questions." As a future teacher, you will be asked to answer them, not in so many words perhaps, but through all of your daily actions. The policies and procedures of the school in which you teach will then reflect an underlying philosophy.[2]

These are not easy questions to answer. They cannot be answered in true-false, multiple-choice format. Most likely, your answers to these questions will change over time, become more complex, and upon reflection result in the creation of your own philosophy of education. In today's educational practice, portfolios are used for ongoing student assessment. Teachers also keep journals with daily entries about classroom events, successes, and problems. Both portfolios and journals provide a personal framework of educational events upon which you can reflect. In much the same way, you can build a personal philosophy of education. It will not be easy or quick, but it will be rewarding both personally and professionally. It will help move your professional development from opinion to more reflective beliefs.

Basic questions and philosophical issues

Although philosophical issues can be found throughout this book, they are especially relevant to Chapter 13 on the goals of education and to Chapter 14 on curriculum. This chapter will provide you with a philosophical and theoretical map, a kind of grid, upon which you can examine your opinions about education and transform them into your own philosophy of education. The following questions can guide you in reading the chapter and also serve to aid you on the journey to building your own philosophy of education:

1. What are the areas of philosophy, how are they defined, and what are my beliefs about them?

2. What philosophies of education are found in human culture? Do I find certain philosophies in my educational experiences? Do I find these philosophies useful in examining and explaining beliefs about education?

3. What theories guide educational practice — curriculum, teaching, and learning? Do I find these theories present in my educational experiences? Are these theories useful in examining and explaining my beliefs about education?

4. How do philosophies and theories of education influence teaching and learning in the classroom? For example, how does a teacher's educational relationship to students reflect his or her ethics and values?

5. How does a teacher's method of instruction reflect a particular theory of knowledge and human understanding? How does a teacher's attitude to cultural diversity reflect his or her conception of a just society?

Philosophies and theories

This chapter examines four educational philosophies and five educational theories. Systematic **philosophies**, such as idealism and realism, refer to complete bodies of thought that present a worldview of which education is a part. In contrast, educational **theories** focus on education itself and on schools. (See Figure 12.1.) There are close links between the general philosophies examined in this chapter and the more specific theories of education. The theories are the school-based components of the philosophical approaches. For example, the theory of essentialism is closely related to the philosophy of realism. Similarly, the theories of progressivism and reconstructionism both derive from the general philosophy of pragmatism.

---

[2]For the relevance of educational philosophy to classroom practices, see Tony W. Johnson, *Discipleship or Pilgrimage? The Study of Educational Philosophy* (Albany, N.Y.: State University of New York Press, 1995).

FIGURE 12.1	Differences Between "Philosophies" and "Theories" of Education

GENERAL	SPECIFIC
Philosophies	**Theories**
Wide-ranging, systematic, complete, global	Focused on education; no complete philosophical system offered
Components related to metaphysics, epistemology, axiology, and logic	Components related to specifics of education, such as curriculum, teaching, and learning
Insights derived from the general system	Insights derived from more general philosophies or from school contexts

To understand current disputes about educational goals and curricula, we need to explore these often conflicting philosophical roots. Before doing so, we must define certain terms and areas of philosophy.

Special Terminology

Reality and existence

Every field of inquiry has a special terminology. Philosophy of education uses the basic terms *metaphysics, epistemology, axiology,* and *logic.*

Metaphysics examines the nature of ultimate reality. What is real and what is not real? Is there a spiritual realm of existence separate from the material world? Idealists, for example, see reality primarily in nonmaterial, abstract, or spiritual terms. Realists see it as an objective order that exists independently of humankind. Much instruction in schools represents the efforts of curriculum makers, teachers, and textbook writers to describe "reality" to students. As a teacher you will find that different textbooks have competing interpretations of reality, or at least different emphases.

Knowledge and knowing

Epistemology, which deals with knowledge and knowing, influences methods of teaching and learning. It raises such questions as: On what do we base our knowledge of the world and our understanding of truth? Does our knowledge derive from divine revelation, from ideas latent in our own minds, from empirical evidence, or from something else? Again, different philosophies hold different epistemological conceptions.

Teachers who believe that human ideas should conform to the ordered structure of reality will stress orderly and sequential teaching of subjects. In contrast, teachers who believe that the process (*how* we know) is more important than the content (*what* we know) will stress inquiry or problem solving.

What is of value?

Axiology, which prescribes values, is divided into *ethics* and *aesthetics.* **Ethics** examines moral values and the rules of right conduct; **aesthetics** addresses values in beauty and art. Whether a school explicitly teaches such values or not, teachers — like parents and society in general — convey values implicitly by re-

PROFESSIONAL PLANNING
for your first year

How Can You Implement Your Personal Philosophy of Education?

The Situation

Throughout a teacher's professional career, decisions need to be made regarding curriculum and instruction. These decisions reflect a personal philosophy of education. Consider, for example, Amanda Scott, a seventh-grade English and social studies teacher in her first year of teaching. The building principal has appointed Amanda to a three-person committee to review and make recommendations for revising the literature course. Amanda brings with her many progressive and critical theory ideas from her teacher-education program. For example, she believes that her own study of literature in middle and secondary school overemphasized historical rather than contemporary books and that too many selections were written by white Euro-American males. Inclined to a progressive philosophy and some critical theory ideas, she would like to revise the course to include more selections from contemporary Asian and African American writers, especially women.

At the committee's first meeting, the three members — Clara Emerson, a teacher with fifteen years of service in the school, David Senko, a teacher in his fifth year of teaching and committee chairperson, and Amanda — share their opinions. Mrs. Emerson says that the present literature curriculum represents selections from the finest writers in the American past — James Fenimore Cooper, Ralph Waldo Emerson, Louisa May Alcott, and Henry David Thoreau. Speaking as an experienced teacher, she says that these important works carry with them enduring perennial themes that should be the core of any literature program. Amanda then gives her opinion but is somewhat overwhelmed by Mrs. Emerson, who speaks with a sense of authority. Mr. Senko, who spends much of his time on administrative responsibilities, takes a neutral position and concludes the first meeting by saying, "Both points of view are interesting and useful. The committee will meet next week to draft the general principles that will guide our work. Before our next meeting, it would be a good idea for Mrs. Emerson and Ms. Scott to meet informally over coffee to discuss their apparently opposing viewpoints."

Thought Questions

1. In what philosophies or theories of education is each divergent view located? For example, is Mrs. Emerson speaking as a perennialist? What philosophy or theory is represented by Amanda's point of view?
2. Do you believe that Amanda, who is a first-year teacher, should continue to argue for curriculum change against Mrs. Emerson, an experienced teacher? If not, why not? If yes, how should she proceed?
3. Mr. Senko appears to be neutral. Is his kind of neutrality philosophically and professionally defensible, or should he take more of a stand?
4. Do you see any ways in which the committee can work out a philosophical compromise? What might be the effects of such a compromise on the students and teachers, especially Amanda and Mrs. Emerson?

warding or punishing behavior depending on whether it conforms to their conceptions of what is right, good, and beautiful. Moreover, the school climate as a whole represents the values of the educational community.

Deductive and inductive thinking

Logic, which is concerned with correct and valid thinking, examines the rules of inference that enable us to correctly frame our propositions and arguments. **Deductive logic** moves from general statements to particular instances and applications. **Inductive logic** moves from the particular instance to tentative generalizations subject to further verification. Curriculum and instruction are both based on conceptions of logic. Does something in the subject itself logically dictate how material should be organized and presented to students (the deductive approach)? Or should teachers take their cue from students' interest, readiness, and experience in deciding how to present instruction (an inductive approach)?

With this background in terminology, we can examine different philosophies and theories. After discussing the key concepts of each one, we will see how it answers the basic questions raised at the beginning of the chapter and helps a teacher create his or her own philosophy of education. (See Overview 12.1 for the philosophies discussed in this chapter.)

Idealism

Notable idealist thinkers

Idealism, one of the oldest of the traditional philosophies, goes back to Plato, who developed idealist principles in ancient Athens. In Germany, Georg W. F. Hegel created a comprehensive philosophical worldview based on idealism, and in the United States, Ralph Waldo Emerson and Henry David Thoreau developed a transcendentalist variety of idealism. Friedrich Froebel based his kindergarten theory on idealist metaphysics.[3] Asian religions such as Hinduism and Buddhism also rest on the spiritual outlook associated with idealism.

Key Concepts

Universal, eternal truth

Metaphysics. Idealists, holding that only the mental or spiritual is ultimately real, see the universe as an expression of a highly generalized intelligence and will — a universal mind. The person's spiritual essence, or soul, is the permanent aspect of human nature that provides vitality and dynamism. This mental world of ideas is eternal, permanent, regular, and orderly. Truth and values are absolute and universal.

Macrocosm and microcosm

Idealists, such as the transcendentalists, have used the concepts of the macrocosm and the microcosm to explain their version of reality. **Macrocosm** refers to the universal mind, the first cause, creator, or God. Regardless of the particular name used, the macrocosmic mind is the whole of existence. It is the one, all-inclusive, and complete self of which all lesser selves are parts. The universal, macrocosmic mind is continually thinking and valuing. The **microcosm** is a limited part of the whole — an individual and lesser self. But the microcosm is of the same spiritual substance as the macrocosm.

Latent knowledge

Epistemology. Idealism emphasizes the recognition or reminiscence of ideas that are latent — already present but not evident — in the mind. Such ideas are **a priori;** that is, they concern knowledge that exists prior to and independent of human ex-

---

[3]For a discussion of the leading contributors to idealism, see Howard A. Ozman and Samuel M. Craver, *Philosophical Foundations of Education,* 5th ed. (Columbus, Ohio, and Englewood Cliffs, N.J.: Merrill/Prentice-Hall, 1995), pp. 1–15.

OVERVIEW 12.1   Philosophies of Education

Philosophy	Metaphysics	Epistemology	Axiology	Educational Implications	Proponents
Idealism	Reality is spiritual or mental and unchanging	Knowing is the rethinking of latent ideas	Values are absolute and eternal	A subject-matter curriculum emphasizing the great and enduring ideas of the culture	Butler Emerson Froebel Hegel Plato
Realism	Reality is objective and is composed of matter and form; it is fixed, based on natural law	Knowing consists of sensation and abstraction	Values are absolute and eternal, based on nature's laws	A subject-matter curriculum stressing humanistic and scientific disciplines	Aquinas Aristotle Broudy Martin Pestalozzi
Pragmatism (experimentalism)	Reality is the interaction of an individual with environment or experience; it is always changing	Knowing results from experiencing; use of scientific method	Values are situational or relative	Instruction organized around problem solving according to the scientific method	Childs Dewey James Peirce
Existentialism	Reality is subjective, with existence preceding essence	Knowing is to make personal choices	Values should be freely chosen	Classroom dialogues stimulate awareness that each person creates a self-concept through significant choices	Sartre Marcel Morris Soderquist

perience about them. Through introspection the individual examines his or her own mind and finds a copy of the macrocosmic mind. Since what is to be known is already present in the mind, the teacher's challenge is to bring this latent knowledge to consciousness. The goal of education is to help students arrive at a broad, general, and unifying perspective of the universe.[4]

Hierarchy of subjects

Idealist teachers prefer a hierarchical curriculum based on traditional disciplines or subject matter. At the top of the hierarchy are the most general disciplines, philosophy and theology. These general and abstract subjects transcend the limitations of time, place, and circumstance, and they transfer to a wide range of situations. Mathematics is valuable, too, because it cultivates the power to deal with abstractions. History and literature also rank high as sources of moral and cultural

---

[4]Gerald L. Gutek, *Philosophical and Ideological Perspectives on Education,* 2nd ed. (Boston: Allyn and Bacon, 1997), pp. 13–25.

models. Somewhat lower in the curriculum, the natural and physical sciences address particular cause-and-effect relationships. Language is important because it is an essential tool at all levels of learning. For the idealist, the highest level of knowledge recognizes the relationships among all these subject matters and integrates them.

Enduring values

Axiology. Because idealists see the universe in universal and eternal terms, they prescribe values that are unchanging and applicable to all people. Thus ethical behavior reflects the enduring knowledge and values of human culture. Philosophy, theology, history, literature, and art are rich sources for transmitting this heritage of values. This kind of education requires that students be exposed to worthy models, especially the classics — the great works that have endured over time.

The Basic Questions

Knowledge of universal ideas

If you were to ask an idealist teacher, "What is knowledge?" he or she would reply that knowledge concerns the spiritual principles that are the base of reality. This knowledge of reality takes the form of ideas. If knowledge is about universal ideas, then education is the intellectual process of bringing ideas to the learner's consciousness.

Schooling: an intellectual pursuit of truth

In answering the question "What is schooling?" the idealist educator would say that the school is a social agency where students seek to discover and pursue truth. It is an intellectual institution where teachers and students explore the questions Socrates and Plato first asked: What is truth? What is beauty? What is the good life? These answers, although hidden, are present in our minds, and we need to reflect deeply to bring them to our consciousness. Nothing should be allowed to distract us from the intellectual pursuit of truth.

Who should attend school? The idealist would say everyone. Not all students have the same intellectual aptitude, but all need to cultivate their minds to the limits of their capacities. Gifted students need the greatest intellectual challenges that the teacher can provide.

Socratic method

How should teaching be carried on? The idealist would say that thinking and learning are names for the process of bringing ideas to consciousness. A very effective means of doing this is the **Socratic method**, a process by which the teacher stimulates the learner's awareness of ideas by asking leading questions. Another important aspect of idealist methodology is modeling. Teachers should be models worthy of imitation by students; they should have wide knowledge of the cultural heritage and lead an exemplary life.

High standards

Idealists want to safeguard the quality of education by maintaining high intellectual standards and resisting any tendency toward mediocrity. In Plato's *Republic*, for example, intellectual standards were so high that only a gifted minority entered the ruling elite of philosopher-kings. Today's idealists would not go that far, but they define educational goals as the developing of intellectual capacity, and they generally accept the fact that not all students will go on to the highest stages of education.

Implications for Today's Classroom Teacher

Intellectual development, not vocational training

Idealism offers significant possibilities for today's classroom teacher. It seeks to create an intellectual environment for teaching and learning. It rejects the consumerism and vocationalism that often shape attitudes in contemporary society. It sees teachers as vital agents in helping students realize their fullest potential, and it encourages teachers to acquaint themselves and their students with the finest elements of the cultural heritage. By immersing themselves in the great ideas of the heritage, learners prepare to contribute to the heritage in their own right.

Important subjects

Idealist teachers see certain subjects as especially powerful in stimulating thinking and developing identification with the cultural heritage. For example, they use mathematics to develop students' powers of abstraction. History is seen as the study of the contributions made by the great women and men of the past. Teachers expose students to the classics — great and enduring works of art, literature, and music — so that they can experience and share in the time-tested values conveyed by these cultural works.

An idealist lesson

How might a teacher use idealism in developing a lesson? For example, a fifth-grade teacher might illustrate the power of ideas and the higher ethical law by a unit on the life and work of Dr. Martin Luther King, Jr. Students would study the biography of Dr. King and seek to discover the principles of nonviolence and justice that guided his actions during the civil rights movement. They would study and recite his "I have a dream" speech to discover the power of ideas in shaping behavior. Finally, Dr. King would serve as a model worthy of imitation.

Realism

A real world of objects

Realism, which stresses objective knowledge and values, was developed by the ancient Greek philosopher Aristotle. In the Middle Ages, Thomas Aquinas articulated a variety of religious realism, known as Thomism, which was a synthesis of Aristotelianism and Christian doctrine. Thomism emphasizes a dualistic conception of reality with a lower material and a higher spiritual dimension. Thomism became the philosophical basis for Roman Catholic education. Alfred North Whitehead continued the realist tradition. Realism holds that (1) there is a world of real existence that human beings have not made; (2) the human mind can know about the real world; and (3) such knowledge is the most reliable guide to individual and social behavior. These doctrines provide a starting point for considering realism's educational implications.

Key Concepts

Metaphysics and Epistemology.   For the realist, a material world exists that is independent of and external to the mind of the knower.[5] All objects are composed of matter. Matter, in turn, must assume the structure of particular objects.

Knowing: sensation, then abstraction

Human beings can know these objects through their senses and their reason. Knowing is a process that involves two stages: sensation and abstraction. First, the knower perceives an object and records sensory data about it, such as color, size, weight, smell, or sound. The mind sorts these data into those qualities that are always present in the object and those that are sometimes present. By abstracting out the necessary qualities (those that are always present), the learner forms a concept

---

[5]For an analysis of realism, see two books by Roy Bhaskar, *Scientific Realism and Human Emancipation* (London: Verso, 1986), and *Reclaiming Reality: A Critical Introduction to Contemporary Philosophy* (London: Verso, 1989). Bhaskar's conception of realism is analyzed in David Corson, "Education Research and Bhaskar's Conception of Discovery," *Educational Theory* (Spring 1991), pp. 189–198.

of the object and recognizes it as belonging to a certain class. With this classification of the object, the learner understands that it shares certain qualities with other members of the same class but not with objects of a different class.

Curriculum of organized subjects

Like idealists, realists believe that following a curriculum of organized, separate subjects is the most effective way of learning about reality. Organizing subject matter, as scientists and scholars do, is a sophisticated method of classifying objects. For example, the past experiences of humankind can be organized into history. Plants can be studied systematically according to their classifications in botany. Units of political organization such as nations, governments, legislatures, and judicial systems can be grouped into political science. For the realist, the way to acquire knowledge about reality is through systematic inquiry into these subjects.

Rational behavior, based on reality

Axiology.   In the realist's conception of knowledge, certain rules govern intelligent behavior. For example, human beings ought to behave in a rational way, and behavior is rational when it conforms to the way in which objects behave in reality. From their study of reality, people can develop theories based on natural, physical, and social laws. Since natural laws are universal and eternal, so are the values based on them.

The Basic Questions

Knowledge concerns objects

To begin our philosophical cross-examination, we again ask, What is knowledge? Realists would reply that knowledge concerns the physical world in which we live. When we know something, our knowledge is always about an object. Our concepts are valid when they correspond to those objects as they really exist in the world.[6]

Education via subject-matter disciplines

Formal education, the realists would say, is the study of the subject-matter disciplines into which knowledge has been organized and classified. History, languages, science, and mathematics are organized bodies of knowledge. If we know them, we will know something about the world in which we live. This knowledge is our best guide in conducting our daily affairs.

For realists, societies have established schools, as primarily academic institutions, to provide students with knowledge about the objective world. Since all persons have a rational potentiality, schooling should be available to all, with students pursuing the same academic curriculum that will prepare them to make rational decisions. Realist teachers should be subject-matter experts who combine their disciplinary expertise with effective teaching methods.[7]

Implications for Today's Classroom Teacher

Classrooms for learning, not therapy

In realist classrooms, the teacher's primary responsibility is to teach some skill, such as reading, writing, or computation, or some body of disciplined knowledge, such as history, mathematics, or science. Although they appreciate that their students are emotional as well as rational persons, realist teachers do not turn classrooms into therapeutic centers for emotional or behavioral adjustment. Realist teachers would oppose those nonacademic activities that interfere with the school's primary purpose as a center of academic learning.

Teachers as subject-matter experts

In order to perform their primary educational responsibility, realist teachers need to be knowledgeable in the content of their subject. For example, the teacher

---

[6]David Kelley, *The Evidence of the Senses: A Realist Theory of Perception* (Baton Rouge: Louisiana State University Press, 1986).
[7]William O. Martin, *Realism in Education* (New York: Harper and Row, 1969).

of history should be a historian who possesses a thorough background in that discipline. In addition, the realist teacher should have a general education in the liberal arts and sciences — a background that will enable the teacher to demonstrate relationships between her or his area of expertise and other subject-matter areas. Realist teachers may employ a wide repertoire of methods, such as the lecture, discussion, demonstration, or experiment. Mastery of content is most important, and methodology is a necessary but subordinate means to reach that goal.

Example of a realist approach

How might a high-school physics teacher with a realist philosophical orientation plan a unit on Isaac Newton's laws of motion? First, the teacher would historically locate Newton and comment on his scientific contributions. Second, the teacher might illustrate the laws of motion in a laboratory demonstration. Third, the students might discuss the demonstration and frame the scientific generalization that it illustrated. Finally, students would take a test to demonstrate their understanding of Newton's laws of motion.[8]

Because of their stress on the teacher's expertise and the academic learning of students, realists tend to favor competency testing for both teachers and students. They also believe that administrators and school boards should maintain strong academic standards and encourage a high level of achievement.

Pragmatism

Pragmatism, a philosophy developed in the United States, emphasizes the need to test ideas by acting on them. Among its founders were Charles S. Peirce (1839–1914), William James (1842–1910), George Herbert Mead (1863–1931), and John Dewey (1859–1952). Peirce stressed using the scientific method to validate ideas, and James applied pragmatic interpretations to psychology, religion, and education. Mead emphasized the development of the child as a learning and experiencing human organism. Dewey, in particular, wrote extensively on education.[9]

Founders of pragmatism

Chapter 4 examined Dewey's work as an educational pioneer. Here we will focus on his pragmatic or experimentalist philosophy, which featured change, process, relativity, and the reconstruction of experience.

Organism and environment

Influenced by Charles Darwin's evolutionary theory, Dewey applied the terms *organism* and *environment* to education. Dewey saw human beings as biological and sociological organisms who possess drives or impulses that sustain life and promote growth and development. Every organism lives in a habitat or environment. Education, so conceived, was to promote optimum human growth.

Rejecting the a priori foundation of the older idealist and realist perspectives, Dewey's test of experience meant that human purposes and plans could be validated only by acting on and judging them by their consequences. The need to judge by consequences also applied to educational programs. Did a particular educational program, curricular design, or methodological strategy achieve its anticipated goals and objectives? For Dewey, the only valid test was to try out the proposal and judge the results.[10]

Problem solving

Whereas idealism and realism emphasized bodies of substantive knowledge or subject-matter disciplines, Dewey stressed the process of problem solving. For

---

[8]Philip H. Phenix, *Philosophies of Education* (New York: Wiley, 1961), pp. 22–24.
[9]John Dewey, *The Child and the Curriculum* (Chicago: University of Chicago Press, 1902); John Dewey, *Democracy and Education* (New York: Macmillan, 1906); John Dewey, *The School and Society* (Chicago: University of Chicago Press, 1923); and John Dewey, *Experience and Education* (New York: Macmillan, 1938).
[10]Stephen M. Fishman and Lucille McCarthy, *John Dewey and the Challenge of Classroom Practice* (New York: Teachers College Press, 1998).

Dewey, learning occurs as the person engages in problem solving. In Dewey's experimental epistemology, the learner, as an individual or as a member of a group, uses the scientific method to solve both personal and social problems. For Dewey, the problem-solving method can be developed into a habit that is transferable to a wide variety of situations.[11]

Key Concepts

Metaphysics and Epistemology.   Whereas idealism and realism emphasize an unchanging reality, pragmatism or experimentalism sees epistemology as a process of examining a constantly changing universe. In Dewey's philosophy of experimentalism, the epistemological, or knowing, situation involves a person, or organism, and an environment. **Experience,** defined as the interaction of the person with the environment, is a key concept. The person interacts with the environment to live, grow, and develop. This interaction may alter or change both the person and the environment. Knowing is thus a *transaction,* a process, between the learner and the environment. Although each interaction has some generalizable aspects that carry over to the next problem, each episode will differ somewhat. Effective people, by using the scientific method, can solve problems and add the features of a particular problem-solving episode to their ongoing experiences.[12]

Experience

If reality is continually changing, then a curriculum claiming to be based on permanent realities is foolish. Concepts of unchanging or universal truth become untenable. The only guides that human beings have in their interaction with the environment are tentative assertions that are subject to further research and verification. Therefore, according to pragmatists, what is needed is a method for dealing with change in an intelligent manner. The Deweyites stress problem solving as the most effective method for directing change toward desired outcomes. Even though reality involves constant transformation or *reconstruction* of both the person and the environment, humankind can benefit from the process. Each time a human experience is reconstructed to solve a problem, a new contribution is added to humanity's fund of experience.

No permanent realities

"Reconstruction" of person and environment

Axiology and Logic.   Pragmatic axiology is highly situational. Since we inhabit a constantly changing universe, values, too, must change. Values are relative to time, place, and circumstance. What contributes to personal and social growth is valuable; what restricts or limits experience is unworthy. Further, we can clarify our values by testing and reconstructing them in the same way scientific claims are verified.[13]

Relativity of values

Following the scientific method, experimentalist logic is inductive. Tentative assertions are based on empirical experience and must be tested. Experimentalist logic is suspicious of a priori truths and deductions based on them.

Inductive logic

---

[11]Lawrence J. Dennis and George W. Stickel, "Mead and Dewey: Thematic Connections on Educational Topics," *Educational Theory* (Summer–Fall 1981), pp. 320–321.

[12]Tom Colwell, "The Ecological Perspective in John Dewey's Philosophy of Education," *Educational Theory* (Summer 1985), p. 257.

[13]William R. Caspary, "Judgements of Value in John Dewey's Theory of Ethics," *Educational Theory* (Spring 1990), pp. 155–169. See also Robert B. Westbrook, *John Dewey and American Democracy* (Ithaca, N.Y.: Cornell University Press, 1991), pp. 151–156.

The Basic Questions

Knowledge is tentative

The pragmatist's answers to questions about knowledge, education, schooling, and instruction are very different from those of more traditional philosophies. Since knowledge is tentative and subject to revision, pragmatists are more concerned with the process of using knowledge than with truth as a body of knowledge. In contrast, traditional philosophers emphasize truth as a permanent body of knowledge.

An experimental process

For the pragmatist, education is an experimental process — a method of dealing with problems that arise as people interact with their world. Dewey argued that human beings experience the greatest personal and social growth when they interact with the environment in an intelligent and reflective manner. The most intelligent way of solving problems is to use the scientific method.

Interdisciplinary approach

When you face a problem, the pragmatists say, the information needed to solve it usually comes from many sources, not from a single discipline or academic subject. For example, to define the problem of pollution of the physical environment and to suggest ways of solving it, we must consider sources that are historical, political, sociological, scientific, technological, and international. An educated person, in the pragmatic sense, knows how to use information from all these sources. Pragmatists therefore favor interdisciplinary education. Idealists and realists, in contrast, are suspicious of interdisciplinary education because they believe students must first study organized subjects.

School as microcosm of society

Pragmatists such as Dewey see the school as a miniature community, a microcosm of the larger society. For them, no true separation exists between school and society. The school exercises three major functions: to simplify, purify, and balance the cultural heritage. To simplify, the school selects elements of the heritage and reduces their complexity to units appropriate to learners' readiness and interest. To purify, it selects worthy cultural elements and eliminates those that limit human interaction and growth. To balance, the school integrates the selected and purified experiences into a harmony.

Transmitting cultural heritage

Cultural diversity, but shared learning processes

Since many diverse cultural groups participate in society, the pragmatic school helps children of one culture understand and appreciate members of other cultures. Although cultural diversity is regarded as enriching the entire society, pragmatists want all cultural groups to use the scientific method. They also see schools as building social consensus by stressing common processes of learning. As genuinely integrated and democratic learning communities, schools should be open to all.

Combining quality and equity

As a proponent of an open and sharing society, Dewey did not regard quality and equity as mutually exclusive. To offer equal opportunity for all, schools would not need to compromise educational quality. In Dewey's view, a society and its schools reach their zenith when they provide for the widest possible sharing of resources among people of all cultures in the community. Sharing does not diminish quality but enriches it.

Implications for Today's Classroom Teacher

Subject matter as instrumental

Unlike idealist and realist teachers, who see teaching subject matter as their primary responsibility, pragmatist teachers are more concerned with the process of solving problems intelligently. While not ignoring subject matter, they use it instrumentally in problem-solving activities. They do not dominate the classroom but guide learning as facilitators of the students' research and activities.

Applying the scientific method

For students in a pragmatist classroom, the main objective is to share the experience of applying the scientific method to a full range of personal, social, and intellectual problems. By using the problem-solving method, it is expected that students will learn to apply the process to situations both in and out of school and thus to reduce the separation of the school from society.

Classroom as community

Pragmatist teachers work to transform classrooms into learning communities by encouraging students to share their interests and problems. Pragmatist educators also encourage both cultural diversity and commonalities. Although they recognize that each culture has something of value to share with other cultures, they stress shared communication between members of different cultures so that all students together can help create the larger democratic community of shared interests and values. Instead of simply preserving the status quo, pragmatist teachers need to take risks. They must see knowledge as indeterminate and open-ended, and their educational goals must constitute an ongoing inquiry that leads to action.

Teachers as risk takers

A pragmatist lesson

How might pragmatism be applied to classroom teaching? Although pragmatism is applicable to all levels of schooling, we can use the example of a college teacher-education class that defines the study of local school governance as its problem and project. The class does preliminary reading about school district organization and then attends a meeting of the board of education. After this experience, the class divides itself into research committees to investigate specific areas of local district goverance, such as (1) the roles, functions, and responsibilities of the board of education, the central office, and the building principals; (2) the development and review of curriculum and instruction; (3) teacher staffing, in-service training, and organization; (4) the composition, organization, and academic assessment of students; and (5) the role of community organizations. After completing the necessary research, each committee shares its findings with the class. Then an editorial committee prepares a collaborative paper on school governance. This project, illustrative of the pragmatist approach, is especially useful to future teachers' professional development.

Existentialism

Personal reflection

The philosophy of **existentialism**, representing both a feeling of desperation and a spirit of hope, examines life in a very personal way. An existentialist education encourages deep personal reflection on one's identity, commitments, and choices.

Key Concepts

The existentialist author Jean-Paul Sartre (1905–1980) stated that "Existence precedes Essence." This means that human beings are born and enter the world without being consulted. They simply are here in a world that they did not make or shape. However, they possess volition, or will, which gives them the freedom to make choices and to create their own purposes for existence. As people live, they are thrust into choice-making situations. Whereas some choices are trivial, those that deal with the purpose and meaning of life lead to personal self-definition. A person *creates* his or her own definition and makes his or her own essence. You are what you choose to be. Human freedom is total, say the existentialists, and one's responsibility for choice is also total.[14]

Creating one's essence through choices

This conception of a human being as the creator of his or her own essence differs substantially from that of the idealists and realists, who see the person as a uni-

---

[14]Ozman and Craver, *Philosophical Foundations of Education*, pp. 243–253.

For existentialists, education should help students develop consciousness about the freedom to choose and allow them to experiment with artistic media to dramatize their feelings and insights. (© Winter/The Image Works)

Existential Angst

versal category. Moreover, whereas the idealist or realist sees the individual as an inhabitant of a meaningful and explainable world, the existentialist believes that the universe is indifferent to human wishes, desires, and plans. Existentialism focuses on the concept of *Angst,* or dread. Each person knows that his or her destiny is death and that his or her presence in the world is only temporary. It is with this sense of philosophical dread that each person must make choices about freedom and slavery, love and hate, peace and war. As one makes these choices, a question is always present: What difference does it make that I am here and that I have chosen to be what I am?

Choosing self-determination

According to the existentialists, we must also cope with the fact that others — persons, institutions, and agencies — are constantly threatening our choice-making freedom. But existentialism does see hope behind the desperation. Each person's response to life is based on an answer to the question, Do I choose to be a self-determined person or do I choose to be defined by others? Each person has the potential for loving, creating, and being. Each can choose to be an inner-directed, authentic person. An authentic person, free and aware of this freedom, knows that every choice is really an act of personal value creation.[15]

Creating personal values

Since existentialists have deliberately avoided systemization of their philosophy, it is difficult to categorize its metaphysical, epistemological, axiological, and logical positions. However, some comments on these areas can illustrate the existentialist point of view. As already stated, each person creates his or her own self-definition, or essence, by the personal choices he or she makes. Epistemologically, the individual chooses the knowledge that he or she wishes to possess. It is axiology that is most important for existentialists, because human beings create their own values through their choices.

---

[15]Maxine Greene, *Landscapes of Learning* (New York: Teachers College Press, 1978); and Van Cleve Morris, *Existentialism in Education* (New York: Harper and Row, 1966).

The Basic Questions

Awakening consciousness of the human condition

Existentialists realize that we live in a world of physical realities and that we have developed a useful and scientific knowledge about these realities. However, the most significant aspects of our lives are personal and nonscientific. Thus, to our questions about knowledge and education, existentialists would say that the most important kind of knowledge is about the human condition and the personal choices we make. Education's most significant goal is to awaken human consciousness to the freedom to choose. Education should create a sense of self-awareness and contribute to our authenticity.

Questioning and dialogue

An existentialist teacher would encourage students to philosophize, question, and participate in dialogues about the meaning of life, love, and death. The answers to these questions would be personal and subjective, not measurable by standardized tests. An existentialist curriculum would consist of whatever might lead to philosophical dialogue. Particularly valuable are those subjects that vividly portray individual men and women in the act of making choices, including subjects that are emotional, aesthetic, and poetic.[16] Literature and biography are important for revealing choice-making conditions. Drama and films that vividly portray the human condition and human decision making ought to be seen and discussed by students. In addition to literary, dramatic, and biographical subjects, students need to create their own modes of self-expression.[17] They should be free to experiment with artistic media and to dramatize their emotions, feelings, and insights.

An existential curriculum

Same opportunities for all

The school, for the existentialists, is where individuals meet to pursue discussion about their own lives and choices. Since every person is in the same predicament and has the same possibilities, every individual should have opportunities for schooling. In the school, both teachers and students should have the chance to ask questions, suggest answers, and engage in dialogue.

Implications for Today's Classroom Teacher

Teacher encourages awareness

Teaching from an existentialist perspective is not easy because teachers cannot specify goals and objectives in advance — these are determined by each student as an individual person. Rather than imposing goals on students, the existentialist teacher seeks to create an awareness in each student that she or he is ultimately responsible for her or his own education and self-definition. In creating this awareness, the teacher encourages students to examine the institutions, forces, and situations that limit freedom of choice. Further, existentialist teachers seek to create open classrooms to maximize freedom of choice. Within these open learning environments, instruction is self-directed.

An existentialist lesson

Literature, drama, and film are especially powerful in existentialist teaching. An example of existentialist teaching might be a senior high school history class that is studying the Holocaust, the genocide of six million Jews in Europe during World War II. The class views Steven Speilberg's movie, *Schindler's List,* in which an industrialist, Oscar Schindler, who initially profits from the forced labor of Jewish concentration camp inmates, makes a conscious decision to save his workers from

[16]Maxine Greene, *The Dialectic of Freedom* (New York: Teachers College Press, 1988).
[17]For an approach that uses narrative and dialogue to examine philosophical issues in education, see Carol Witherell and Nel Noddings, eds., *Stories Lives Tell: Narrative and Dialogue in Education* (New York: Teachers College Press, 1991).

OVERVIEW 12.2	**Theories of Education**			
Theory	**Aim**	**Curriculum**	**Educational Implications**	**Proponents**
Progressivism (rooted in pragmatism)	To educate the individual according to his or her interests and needs	Activities and projects	Instruction that features problem solving and group activities; teacher acts as a facilitator	Dewey Kilpatrick Parker Washburne
Social reconstructionism (rooted in pragmatism)	To reconstruct society	Social sciences used as reconstructive tools	Instruction that focuses on significant socioeconomic problems	Brameld Counts Stanley
Perennialism (rooted in realism)	To educate the rational person	Subject matter that is hierarchically arranged to cultivate the intellect (great books, etc.)	Focus on enduring human concerns as revealed in great works of the Western cultural heritage	Adler Bloom Hutchins Maritain
Essentialism (rooted in idealism and realism)	To educate the useful and competent person	Basic education: reading, writing, arithmetic, history, English, science, foreign languages	Emphasis on skills and subjects that transmit the cultural heritage and contribute to socioeconomic efficiency	Bagley Bestor Conant Morrison
Critical Theory (rooted in neo-Marxism and postmodernism)	To raise consciousness about critical issues	Autobiographies about oppressed peoples	Focus on social conflicts	McLaren Giroux

death in the Nazi gas chambers. The class then probes the moral situation of one man, Schindler, and the choice that he made in a senseless and cruel world.

Educational Theories

In the following sections, we examine five educational theories: progressivism, perennialism, essentialism, social reconstructionism, and critical theory (see Overview 12.2). Rather than being comprehensive statements about metaphysics, epistemology, axiology, and logic, theories are ideas that are specific to particular institutions and processes. Educational theories are specific to schooling, curriculum, teaching, and learning. Sometimes theories are derived from philosophies. At other times, they arise from practice.

Progressivism

A widespread reform movement

Progressives in education

Progressive education was part of the general reform movement in American life in the late nineteenth and early twentieth centuries. Political progressives such as Robert La Follette and Woodrow Wilson wanted to curb powerful financial and industrial trusts and monopolies to make the democratic political system truly operative. Meanwhile, social welfare progressives, such as Jane Addams in the settlement house movement, worked to improve living conditions in Chicago and other urban areas.

Although the educational theory of **progressivism** is often associated with John Dewey's experimentalism, the progressive education movement wove together a number of diverse strands. Whereas some progressives sought to change the curriculum and instruction in the interests of social reform, other progressives, especially administrators, concentrated on making schools more efficient and cost effective. Administrative progressives sought to build larger schools that could house more class sections and create more curriculum diversity.[18]

Progressive education arose from a rebellion against traditional schooling. Educators such as G. Stanley Hall, Francis Parker, and William H. Kilpatrick argued against mindless routine, rote memorization, and authoritarian classroom management. Progressive teachers developed teaching styles and methods that emphasized students' own interests and needs. Their classrooms were flexible, permissive, and

Here, elementary pupils are engaged in hands-on process learning in a progressive science class. (© *Bob Daemmrick/Stock Boston*)

[18]Arthur Zilversmit, *Changing Schools: Progressive Education Theory and Practice, 1930–1960* (Chicago: University of Chicago Press, 1993).

open-ended. Marietta Johnson, founder of the School of Organic Education, described progressive educational principles as follows:

Emphasis on child's needs

> We believe the educational program should aim to meet the needs of the growing child. We believe that childhood is for itself and not a preparation for adult life. Therefore, the school program must answer the following questions: What does the child of any particular age need to minister to the health of his body, to preserve the integrity of the intellect, and to keep him sincere and unself-conscious of spirit?
>
> The answers to these questions will constitute the curriculum of the school, and as we grow in understanding of the nature and needs of childhood, the curriculum will change.[19]

Key Concepts

The Progressive Education Association, an organization that incorporated a number of varieties of progressivism, did not fashion a comprehensive educational philosophy because progressive educators often disagreed about both theory and practice.

Practices opposed by progressives

Nevertheless, they generally condemned the following traditional school practices: (1) authoritarian teachers, (2) book-based instruction, (3) passive memorization of factual information, (4) the isolation of schools from society, and (5) using physical or psychological coercion to manage classrooms. Although they had more difficulty in agreeing about what they favored, members of the Progressive Education Association

Practices favored by progressives

generally believed that (1) the child should be free to develop naturally; (2) interest, stimulated by direct experience, is the best stimulus for learning; (3) the teacher should be a facilitator of learning; (4) there should be close cooperation between the school and the home; and (5) the progressive school should be a laboratory for pedagogical reform and experimentation.[20]

Progressive reforms in schools

Opposing the conventional subject-matter curriculum, progressives experimented with alternative curricula, using activities, experiences, problem solving, and projects. Child-centered progressive teachers also emphasized collaborative learning rather than competition. More socially oriented progressives sought to make schools centers of larger social reforms.[21] Moreover, progressive schools, especially those that were private, often sought to free children from conventional restraints and repression. Critics saw these schools as eroding adult authority and undermining traditional values.

The Basic Questions

Eschewing dogma and often disagreeing among themselves, progressives would not have answered questions about knowledge, education, the school, teaching, and

Antitraditional

learning with a single voice. While united in opposition to traditionalism and authoritarianism, some emphasized children's freedom and others emphasized social

---

[19]Marietta Johnson, "The Educational Principles of the School of Organic Education, Fairhope, Alabama," in Harold Rugg, ed., *The Foundations and Technique for the Study of Education,* National Society for the Study of Education, Part I (Bloomington, Ind.: Public School Publishing, 1926), p. 349.

[20]Stephen J. Brown and Mary E. Finn, eds., *Readings from Progressive Education: A Movement and Its Professional Journal* (Lanham, Md.: University Press of America, 1988).

[21]The definitive history of progressive education remains Lawrence A. Cremin, *The Transformation of the School* (New York: Random House, 1961).

Child-centered and social reformist

reform. Progressives viewed knowledge as relative, arising from human experience, rather than in universal terms. Education was a means of liberating human creativity in its various cognitive and affective dimensions. Progressives believed that all children had the human right to attend schools. Child-centered progressives wanted schools in which children were free to experiment, play, and express themselves. Social reformist progressives wanted schools to be agencies of social reform. (A discussion of social reformist tendencies in social reconstructionism, which is derived from progressivism, follows later in the chapter.)

Readiness, interests, and needs

For progressives, children's readiness and interests, rather than predetermined subjects, shaped curriculum and instruction.[22] Instructionally flexible, progressive teachers used a repertoire of learning activities such as problem solving, field trips, creative artistic expression, and projects. They saw teaching and learning as an active, exciting, and ever-changing process. As educational community builders, progressive teachers wanted students to work collaboratively on projects based on their shared experience.

Constructing reality

Constructivism, a currently popular epistemology similar to progressivism and to John Dewey's pragmatism, rests on four major premises: (1) learners do not passively receive and store information in their minds but actively create meaning from their own construction of concepts about reality; (2) though knowledge is shaped by a person's prior experience, learners continually reconstruct their concepts; and (3) the construction of new knowledge — new concepts — is located in the social situations and interactions in which it is acquired.[23] Constructivism, like progressivism, emphasizes socially interactive and process-oriented "hands-on" learning in which students work collaboratively to expand and revise their knowledge base.[24]

Implications for Today's Classroom Teacher

Example of a progressive approach

How does a progressively oriented approach work in today's schools?[25] As an example, a junior-high or middle-school social studies program might examine the African American contribution to American life. Students might be organized in research teams, with each team focusing on particular problems and contributing collaboratively to the total project. The team activities might include the following:

Group A would trace the origins of African Americans to Africa and the slave trade. Such an investigation would involve research and reading in geography, economics, anthropology, and history. Each student in Group A would investigate a particular phase of the problem, and the results would then be integrated into the whole project.

Group B might identify the leading African American contributors to U.S. culture and prepare biographical sketches for class presentations. The group could also arrange an exhibit including photographs and evidence of each leader's contribution.

---

[22]For a Deweyan-progressive framework for assessing current educational reforms, see Richard A. Gibboney, *The Stone Trumpet: A Story of Practical School Reform, 1960–1990* (Albany, N.Y.: State University of New York Press, 1994).
[23]Constructivism is treated in Catherine Twomey, *Constructivism: Theory, Perspectives, and Practice* (New York: Teachers College Press, 1996).
[24]For a discussion of the challenges of translating constructivist epistemology into classroom practice, see Peter W. Airasian and Mary E. Walsh, "Constructivist Cautions," *Phi Delta Kappan* 78 (February 1997), pp. 444–449.
[25]See Kathe Jeris and Carol Montag, eds., *Progressive Education for the 1990s: Transforming Practice* (New York: Teachers College Press, 1991).

Group C might research current issues facing African Americans. The students could consult current newspapers and magazines and prepare a scrapbook of clippings.

As the various groups worked on their projects, the teacher would serve as a resource facilitator. Working with each group individually, he or she would suggest sources and help students discover ways of pursuing the project and solving the problems it presented.

Social Reconstructionism

As mentioned earlier, some progressive educators emphasized children's freedom; others, however, wanted education and schools to be agencies for social reform aimed at creating a new society. This **social reconstructionism** soon developed into a separate educational theory.

Cultural crisis

Social reconstructionism argues that humankind has reached a serious cultural crisis of global dimensions. If schools continue to reflect traditional concepts and values, they will transmit the social ills — exploitation, war, violence — that are symptoms of our cultural crisis. Reconstructionists argue that education should reconstruct society by integrating new technological and scientific developments with those parts of the culture that remain viable. For them, education's overriding goal is to create a world order in which people control their own destiny by applying their practical intelligence. In an age of nuclear weaponry, ecological deterioration, and pandemic disease, reconstructionists see education as a means of preventing global catastrophe. They see an urgent need for society to reconstruct itself before it self-destructs.[26]

Reconstructing society through education

Outdated values

According to the reconstructionists, human civilization made a great technological leap when it moved from an agricultural and rural to an urban and industrial society. However, preindustrial ideas and values have persisted into the modern era. Some of these values, such as individualism and competition, are ill suited to solve modern problems. In the reconstructionist view, schools must help reduce the cultural gap so that our values can catch up with our technology.

Reconstructionist Thinking

Identifying social problems

Reconstructionists urge teachers to lead their students on a searching examination of culture and society, both domestically and globally. As students identify and analyze major issues, they are locating social areas that need reconstruction. For example, certain nations enjoy plenty while others face the constant threat of starvation. A few people enjoy luxury, but many live with disease and poverty. Education should expose these socioeconomic inconsistencies and work to resolve them.

Need for a global curriculum

Reconstructionists see the technological era as one of tremendous interdependence. Events in one area of the globe will have an impact on other areas. The depletion of the ozone layer, for example, is not restricted to a single place but endangers the entire planet. With ever-increasing global interdependence, the inherited patterns of education that stress individualism, isolationism, or nationalism

[26]For an analysis of reconstructionism in global perspective, see Carole Ann Ryan, "George S. Counts: Dare Educators Inspire World Vision?" in David B. Annis, ed., *Proceedings of the Annual Conference of the Midwest Philosophy of Education Society (1990–1991)*, Ames, Iowa: Midwest Philosophy of Education Society, 1991, pp. 11–17.

DARE
THE SCHOOL
BUILD A NEW
SOCIAL ORDER?

By
GEORGE S. COUNTS
Author of The American Road to Culture,
The Soviet Challenge to America, etc.

New York
THE JOHN DAY COMPANY

GETTING TO THE SOURCE

Dare the School Build a New Social Order?

GEORGE S. COUNTS

George S. Counts (1889–1974) played multiple roles in American education. He was a professor of education at Columbia University's Teacher College, an expert on Soviet education, a president of the American Federation of Teachers, and an originator of the theory of social reconstructionism. Among his many books, *Dare the School Build a New Social Order?*, published in 1932, is frequently cited as an argument that teachers and schools should originate rather than reflect sociopolitical and economic ideas and values. In the following selection, Counts argues that teachers should seek to shape the society and not fear imposing their views in the educational process.

That the teachers should deliberately reach for power and then make the most of their conquest is my firm conviction. To the extent that they are permitted to fashion the curriculum and the procedures of the school they will definitely and positively influence the social attitudes, ideals, and behavior of the coming generation. In doing this they should resort to no subterfuge or false modesty. They should say neither that they are merely teaching the truth nor that they are unwilling to wield power in their own right. The first position is false and the second is a confession of incompetence. It is my observation that the men and women who have affected the course of human events are those who have not hesitated to use the power that has come to them. Representing as they do, not the interests of the moment or of any special class, but rather the common and abiding interests of the people, teachers are under heavy social obligation to protect and further those interests. In this they occupy a relatively unique position in society. Also since the profession should embrace scientists and scholars of the highest rank, as well as teachers working at all levels of the educational system, it has at its disposal, as no other group, the knowledge and wisdom of the ages. It is scarcely thinkable that these men and women would ever act

Survival depends on education

are dangerously obsolete. The reconstructionist would globalize the curriculum so that men and women will learn that they live in a global village.

For our own survival, the social reconstructionists believe, we must become social engineers, plotting our future and then using our scientific and technological expertise to reach the defined goal. In sum, a reconstructionist program of education will (1) critically examine the culture, even the most controversial issues; (2) cultivate a planning attitude; and (3) enlist students and teachers in social, educational, political, and economic change as a means of total cultural renewal.[27]

---

[27]Among important sources of reconstructionist education are Theodore Brameld, *Toward a Reconstructed Philosophy of Education* (New York: Holt, Rinehart and Winston, 1956); George S. Counts, *Dare the School Build a New Social Order?* (New York: John Day, 1932); and William O. Stanley, *Education and Social Integration* (New York: Teachers College Press, 1952).

as selfishly or bungle as badly as have the so-called "practical" men of our generation — the politicians, the financiers, the industrialists. If all of these facts are taken into account, instead of shunning power, the profession should rather seek power and then strive to use that power fully and wisely and in the interests of the great masses of the people.

The point should be emphasized that teachers possess no magic secret to power. While their work should give them a certain advantage, they must expect to encounter the usual obstacles blocking the road to leadership. They should not be deceived by the pious humbug with which public men commonly flatter the members of the profession. . . . Moreover, while organization is necessary, teachers should not think of their problem primarily in terms of organizing and presenting a united front to the world, the flesh, and the devil. In order to be effective they must throw off completely the slave psychology that has dominated the mind of the pedagogue more or less since the days of ancient Greece. They must be prepared to stand on their own feet and win for their ideas the support of the masses of the people. Education as a force for social regeneration must march hand in hand with the living and creative forces of the social order.

Questions

1. According to Counts, why should teachers reach for power?
2. How can education be a force for social reconstruction?
3. Is Counts's argument relevant to teachers' ongoing professional organization and development?
4. If you agree with Counts, how would you, as a beginning teacher, empower teachers?

Source: George S. Counts, *Dare the School Build a New Social Order?* (Carbondale, Ill.: Southern Illinois University Press, 1978), pp. 26–28. Reprinted by permission of Martha L. Counts. Cover from the 1932 edition, published by The John Day Company, New York.

The Basic Questions

Instrumental view of knowledge

Social reconstructionists are convinced that a new social order will be created only when educators challenge obsolete conceptions of knowledge, education, schooling, and instruction. Like the pragmatists and progressives, social reconstructionists see knowledge as an instrument to be used for a purpose. The knowledge areas that are particularly useful are the social sciences, including anthropology, economics, sociology, political science, and psychology. These disciplines provide insights and methods for planning social change.

Challenging the status quo

Education, for social reconstructionists, is to arouse students' social consciousness and to engage actively in solving social problems. Teachers encourage students to investigate controversial issues in economics, politics, society, and education in order to develop alternatives to the status quo. As a social agency open to all, the school is not only an academic institution but also a "think tank" in which students and teachers formulate hypotheses for social reform. Located on the cutting edge of change, reconstructionist schools will often be centers of controversy.

When this happens, conflict resolution should be carried out according to agreed-upon, democratic processes.

Implications for Today's Classroom Teacher

Role of the reconstructionist taecher

Since reconstructionist teachers see schools as agencies that will create a new social order, they do not define education in exclusively academic terms. Instead, reconstructionist teachers encourage students to diagnose the major problems confronting human beings on planet Earth: pollution of the environment, warfare, famine, terrorism and violence, and the spread of epidemic diseases such as AIDS. Limitations posed by socioeconomic class and discrimination by race or gender should be identified and examined so that we can begin eradicating them. Rather than be neutral observers of world problems, reconstructionists want to be committed to solving these problems for human betterment.

As another example, reconstructionist teachers might focus on the current debate between proponents of an American cultural core and advocates of cultural diversity.[28] Seeing this debate as a cultural war over national identity, they would lead students on a searching inquiry into such questions as: Who were Americans in the past? Who are Americans in the present? Who will we be in the future? To answer these questions, they would encourage students to analyze the claims of both camps. The goal would be to reconstruct inherited cultural beliefs and values to provide a larger sense of national identity and purpose. Teachers would encourage students to share their cultural heritages and to build a knowledge base incorporating the contributions of many diverse ethnic, racial, social, and language groups. Throughout this process, reconstructionist teachers would stress the use of democratic procedures.

Perennialism

Truth in the classics

Perennialism, a culturally conservative educational theory, centers on the authority of tradition and the classics. It believes that (1) truth is universal and does not depend on circumstances of place, time, or person; (2) a good education involves a search for and an understanding of the truth; (3) truth can be found in the great works of civilization; and (4) education is a liberal exercise that develops the intellect.

Perennialism draws heavily on realist principles. Since there are educational similarities between idealism and realism, some educational theorists also relate perennialism to idealism. However, leading perennialists such as Robert Hutchins and Mortimer Adler based their theory of education on Aristotle's realism.

Schools cultivate rationality

Agreeing with Aristotle that human beings are rational, perennialists see the school's primary role as the cultivation of rationality. Perennialists therefore oppose political, social, and economic theories that seek to use schools as multipurpose agencies. They do not want schools to stress students' emotional adjustment or to be vocational training centers for the marketplace. Although perennialists understand that emotional wellness and vocational competency are necessary for people to function in society, they believe that agencies other than schools should attend to these activities. To put extra nonacademic demands on teachers and schools takes away energy, time, and resources from the primary academic purpose.

---

[28]For an analysis of this cultural conflict, see James Davison Hunter, *Culture Wars: The Struggle to Define America* (New York: Basic Books/HarperCollins, 1991).

Perennial curriculum

For perennialists, the most important educational goals are searching for and disseminating truth. Since they believe that truth is universal and unchanging, a genuine education is also universal and constant. Thus the school's curriculum should consist of permanent, or perennial, studies that emphasize the recurrent themes of human life. It should contain cognitive subjects that cultivate rationality and the study of moral, aesthetic, and religious principles to cultivate ethical behavior. Like idealists and realists, perennialists prefer a subject-matter curriculum. This curriculum includes history, language, mathematics, logic, literature, the humanities, and science. The content of these subjects should come from the classical works of literature and art. Mastering these subjects is regarded as essential for training the intellect.

Hutchins: education develops the mind

Robert Hutchins, a president of the University of Chicago, was a highly articulate perennialist theorist. Hutchins described the ideal education as "one that develops intellectual power. . . . The ideal education is not an *ad hoc* education, not an education directed to immediate needs; it is not a specialized education, or a preprofessional education; it is not a utilitarian education. It is an education calculated to develop the mind."[29]

Great books of Western civilization

Believing that the rationality of human nature is universal, Hutchins stressed education's universality. Since reason is our highest power, the cultivation of the intellect should be education's highest priority. Hutchins particularly recommended intensive study and discussion of the great books of Western civilization. The great books, he reasoned, place the members of each generation in dialogue with the great minds of the past. These classic works, containing persistent or perennial themes, help to make a person a genuine cultural participant. They cultivate the intellect and prepare students to think critically. In addition to the classics, he urged the study of grammar, rhetoric, logic, mathematics, and philosophy.

Critique of great books curriculum

Postmodernist critics argue that Hutchins's great books curriculum is really an attempt to give Western European culture predominance over other cultures, such as those of Asia and Africa. In this view, Hutchins's prized great books merely asserted dominant class interests at a given time in history. For example, critical theorists, as we will see later in the chapter, seek to deconstruct the texts of the great books to find their historically based meaning.

The Paideia Proposal

Mortimer J. Adler's **The Paideia Proposal:** *An Educational Manifesto* is a revival of perennialism.[30] *Paideia,* a Greek word, means the total educational formation of a person. Affirming the right of all people to a general education, Adler wants all students in America's democratic society to have the same high quality of schooling.

Paideia curriculum

The *Paideia* curriculum includes language, literature, fine arts, mathematics, natural sciences, history, geography, and social studies. These studies are a means to develop a repertoire of such intellectual skills as reading, writing, speaking, listening, calculating, observing, measuring, estimating, and problem solving, which lead to higher-order thinking and reflection.[31]

---

[29]Robert M. Hutchins, *A Conversation on Education* (Santa Barbara, Calif.: The Fund for the Republic, 1963), p. 1. See also Robert M. Hutchins, *The Learning Society* (New York: Praeger, 1968); and Hutchins, *The Higher Learning in America* (New Haven, Conn.: Yale University Press, 1962).

[30]Mortimer J. Adler, *The Paideia Proposal: An Educational Manifesto* (New York: Macmillan, 1982); see also Mortimer J. Adler, *Paideia Problems and Possibilities* (New York: Macmillan, 1983).

[31]Adler, *Paideia Proposal,* pp. 22–23.

The Basic Questions

A general education

Progressives criticize perennialism for fostering educational elitism. Denying this allegation, perennialists defend their program as genuinely democratic, arguing that all persons have the right to the same high-quality education. Students, they contend, should not be grouped or streamed into "tracks" that prevent some from acquiring the general education to which they are entitled by their common humanity. To track some students into an academic curriculum and others into vocational curricula denies genuine equality of educational opportunity.

Against cultural relativism

Perennialists strongly oppose **cultural relativism**, which is associated with pragmatism, progressivism, social reconstructionism, and critical theory (some of which are examined later in this chapter). According to cultural relativism, our "truths" are temporary statements based on our coping with changing circumstances. Since environments change over time and differ from place to place, truth, rather than being permanently and universally valid, is temporarily and situationally valid. Perennialists, like Allan Bloom in *The Closing of the American Mind,* condemn cultural relativism for weakening ethical character. They claim it denies universal standards by which some actions are consistently either morally right or wrong.[32]

Implications for Today's Classroom Teacher

Perennialists, like idealists and realists, see the classroom as an environment for students' intellectual growth. To stimulate students' intellects, teachers must be liberally educated people who have a love of truth and a desire to lead a life based on it. Indeed, a liberal education is more important for perennialist teachers than courses in educational methods.

Enduring human concerns

In primary grades, the perennialist teacher would emphasize learning fundamental skills, such as reading, writing, and computation, which contribute to a person's literacy and readiness to begin the lifelong quest for truth. Perennialist secondary teachers would structure lessons around the enduring human concerns explored in the great works of history, literature, and philosophy. Like idealists, perennialists emphasize the classics that have engaged the interest of people across generations. In perennialist schools, administrators, teachers, and students maintain high standards for academic work.

A perennialist lesson

An illustration of the perennialst emphasis on recurring human concerns and values can be seen in a middle school literature class that is reading and discussing Louisa May Alcott's *Little Women*. The students have discussed the main characters — Marmie, Jo, Beth, Meg, and Amy — and the issues the March family faced. The class discussion reveals that the sad times and the happy times experienced by the March family are found in family life today. Sometime later, when Alice, a student in the class, is asked at a family dinner, "What are you studying in school?" She replies, "We just finished reading *Little Women*." Alice's mother and grandmother both say that they, too, read and enjoyed the book when they were girls. A conversation then ensues in which Alice, her mother, and grandmother share their impressions of the book. In this way, perennial themes can become memories that transcend time and generations.

---

[32]Allan Bloom, *The Closing of the American Mind* (New York: Simon and Schuster, 1987).

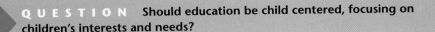

TAKING ISSUE

Education: Child-centered or Subject Matter?

A persistent issue in American education is whether the focus of curriculum and instruction should be on the child's interests and needs or on the transmission of the culture. Pragmatists and progressives contend that education should arise from children's interests. These interests, they say, will lead to projects that will bring children into contact with the larger world. Idealists, realists, perennialists, and essentialists disagree, arguing that schools should prescribe subjects that transmit the cultural heritage from adults, society's mature members, to children, its immature members.

Arguments PRO

1 Experience in their immediate environment leads children to realize needs and interests in learning skills and knowledge. Children learn most effectively when guided by interests arising from their own direct experience.

2 Learning arising from interests is a process that engages children with their environment; projects are a hands-on, process way of learning by which children create their own concepts about reality.

3 As a result of following their interests, children will expand the effort that they need to solve problems and work on projects.

4 Child-oriented, process learning results in collaborative learning that brings about a genuine community of learners.

Arguments CON

1 Over time, civilized people have developed culture, often through trial and error. Thus, relying primarily on children's interests and needs to repeat this trial and error is a needlessly inefficient waste of time. It is crucial to transmit this cultural heritage from adults to children deliberately and efficiently.

2 Certain skills, especially literacy and numeracy, and certain subjects, such as mathematics, science, language, and history, have been developed by the culture's great thinkers. This organized knowledge needs to be taught deliberately and sequentially to children. Children should not be allowed to generate their own, possibly erroneous, ideas.

3 Even if children are not initially interested in learning the culture's skills and subjects, these need to be transmitted to them so they can participate in society.

4 To rely on children's interests as the foundation of the curriculum is to jeopardize the transmission of the culture from one generation to the next.

Essentialism

Essentialst goals

Rooted in both idealism and realism, **essentialism,** a conservative educational theory, emphasizes an academic subject-matter curriculum and encourages teachers to stress order, discipline, and effort. For essentialists, the important goals of education are (1) to transmit the basic skills and knowledge in the cultural heritage; (2) to emphasize skills and subjects that can lead learners to higher-order skills and knowledge; and (3) to use education as a civilizing agency that emphasizes continuity between the knowledge and values of the past and the requirements of the present.

Mastering basic skills and subjects

For essentialists, education involves learning the basic skills, arts, and sciences that sustain civilization.[33] Mastering these skills and subjects prepares students to function effectively as members of civilized society. Since learning the essential curriculum requires discipline and hard work, teachers should be skilled professionals both in subject matter and in teaching.

Core subjects

Arthur Bestor, an advocate of basic education in the 1950s, argued that the liberal arts and sciences, as intellectual disciplines, were the necessary core subjects of general education. Bestor and the Council on Basic Education contended that the lowering of academic standards places American education in jeopardy.[34] For them, the schools' essential responsibility is to introduce students to organized, coherent, and structured subjects. Bestor and other essentialists want elementary schools to teach the indispensable areas of reading, writing, computation, and research skills. In high school, science, mathematics, history, English, and foreign languages are the emphasized intellectual disciplines.

Basic Education

Critique of academic weakness

The **"back-to-basics" movement** derives from essentialist principles.[35] Back-to-basics proponents contend that social experimentation and untested innovations have lowered academic standards. They charge that many children in elementary schools have not mastered basic literary and computational skills and that academic weaknesses in high schools result from the absence of a prescribed curriculum. The back-to-basics position is that schools should concentrate on the essential skills and subjects that contribute to literacy and to social and intellectual efficiency.

Homework and testing

Back-to-basics proponents want teachers restored as educational authorities. Teachers must be well prepared and accountable for children's learning. Regular assignments, homework, recitations, and frequent testing and evaluation should be standard practices.

Neoessentialism

Revival of essentialism

In the 1980s and 1990s, a series of national reports on the condition of American education generated a period of neoessentialist educational reforms. The term *neoessentialist* indicates that this movement reiterated themes from earlier essentialists. These essentialist themes were prescribed as remedies for certain economic and social problems facing the United States, such as lowered productivity and increasing violence.

---

[33]Gerald L. Gutek, *Basic Education: A Historical Perspective* (Bloomington, Ind.: Phi Delta Kappa Educational Foundation, 1981).
[34]Arthur E. Bestor, Jr., *The Restoration of Learning* (New York: Knopf, 1955).
[35]Ben Brodinsky, "Back to the Basics: The Movement and Its Meaning," *Phi Delta Kappan* (March 1977), pp. 523–527.

Here elementary pupils are working at a geography lesson on map skills illustrating emphasis on essential skills. *(© Bob Daemmrick/ Stock Boston)*

Neoessentialism was clearly evident in the 1983 report *A Nation at Risk,* examined in Chapter 13, which recommended a high school curriculum of "five new basics": English, mathematics, science, social studies, and computer science. Of these subjects, only computer science was really new; the others had all been emphasized by earlier essentialists.[36]

Essential knowledge

E. D. Hirsch, who criticizes the decline of **cultural literacy** in the United States, also echoes neoessentialist themes. Hirsch argues that Americans need to possess a core of essential background knowledge. This core contributes to cultural literacy, which, in turn, is necessary for functional literacy and national discourse and communication. Without the transmission of such a cultural core by education, American society will become culturally fragmented.[37]

Common themes run through the variations of essentialism: (1) the elementary school curriculum should cultivate basic skills that contribute to literacy and to mastery of arithmetical computation; (2) the secondary curriculum should cultivate knowledge of history, mathematics, science, English, and foreign languages; (3) schooling requires discipline and a respect for legitimate authority; and (4) learning requires hard work and disciplined attention.

The Basic Questions

Common essentialist and perennialist themes

Since the perennialists and essentialists share many ideas about knowledge, education, schooling, and instruction, their views can be examined as a shared educational defense of cultural conservatism. For them, knowledge lies in the cultural heritage, the tested wisdom of the human race accumulated over time. They differ,

---

[36]National Commission on Excellence in Education, *A Nation at Risk: The Imperative for Educational Reform* (Washington, D.C.: U.S. Government Printing Office, 1983), pp. 23–31.
[37]E. D. Hirsch, Jr., *Cultural Literacy: What Every American Needs to Know* (Boston: Houghton Mifflin, 1987).

however, in that perennialists see wisdom originating with human rationality and essentialists see it coming from tested human experience. Both see the school as society's agency for transmitting the cultural heritage from adults to the young.

Perennialists and essentialists are suspicious of those who want to use schools as agencies of socialization or vocationalism. They are critical of those who promote multiculturalism without first establishing an integrating cultural core based on the Western and American heritage. For them, the school as a civilizing agency brings children and adolescents into contact with the fundamental processes of language and numeracy and with great works of art, music, and literature. Warning against the rising tide of violence in modern society, they urge schools to require behavior based on a civility that is rooted in Western culture.

Five new basics

Essentialists believe the curriculum should consist of basic skills, especially literacy and computation, and academic subjects such as the "five new basics" recommended in *A Nation at Risk*. Teaching and learning should focus on mastery of skills and subjects. Although all children and adolescents should attend school, they should meet rigorous academic standards. Promotion and graduations should require mastery of needed skills and subjects. Social promotion, based on age rather than academic achievement, should be ended since it places unprepared people in society and the workplace. The competency testing many states require for both students and teachers reflects contemporary essentialism.

Implications for Today's Classroom Teacher

Essentialist curriculum

Essentialist teachers, preferring a structured curriculum, seek to transmit the cultural heritage to students by means of carefully sequenced basic skills and subjects. The teacher is to be a specialist in subject-matter content and skilled in organizing it into instructional units. In the essentialist classroom, students devote their energy to learning academic skills and subjects rather than to currently popular fads. Reading, writing, and arithmetic and subject-matter disciplines such as English, foreign languages, mathematics, history, science, and geography are emphasized.

"Effective" schools and teachers

Much of the contemporary "effective schools" movement is based on the way essentialists define effectiveness. Schools are judged effective when principals and teachers hold high expectations of academic achievement and see the school's function as preparing students to be academically competent. Effective teachers know their subjects well, are committed to teaching them as academic disciplines, and succeed in having students do well on measures of academic achievement.

An essentialist lesson

The essentialist emphasis on first mastering facts and then basing generalizations on those facts can be illustrated in a high-school American history class that is studying the differences between the two African American leaders Booker T. Washington and W. E. B. Du Bois. First, the teacher assigns reading on both men. Then he or she leads a discussion in which the students carefully identify Washington's and Du Bois's differences in background, education, and policy. After such teacher-led research, the students are to reach a judgment about why Washington and Du Bois acted as they did and to assess their influence in African American and United States history.

Critical Theory

Neo-Marxism

Critical theory, a highly influential contemporary educational theory, relates to Marxism, especially to current neo-Marxism. Karl Marx, an important nineteenth-century German philosopher, argued that all social institutions rested on an eco-

Conflict theory

nomic base and that human history was a struggle of socioeconomic classes for economic and social control. For example, Marx's concept of class struggle is important for **conflict theory,** a focusing theme in critical theory.[38] Using conflict theory, critical theorists believe that dominant social and economic classes use social institutions, such as schools, to maintain their control of society. Dominated classes, if conscious of their repressed condition, can change the conditions that exploit and disempower them.[39] Critical theorists see the school as a place where different groups are in conflict over control of curriculum and teaching.[40] For example, civil rights, environmentalist, feminist, counterculture, gay and lesbian, and antiwar groups are in conflict with neoconservatives, who emphasize fundamentalist religious values, nationalist patriotism, economic competition, and basic education. In the cultural conflict, critical theorists support disempowered groups such as the poor, minorities, and women by challenging the status quo that traditional schools reproduce.

Key Concepts

Who controls the schools?

Critical theory involves both critique and reform. As critique, it examines the issue of control of educational institutions and agendas. Critical theorists ask the following crucial questions: Who controls the schools? Who makes policies that govern schools? Who determines the ethical, social, and economic goals of education? Who sets the curriculum? Once the question of control is answered, critical theorists turn to the motivations behind this control.[41]

Powerful groups dominate

Critical theorists contend that many structures in contemporary society, including educational institutions, are used by powerful groups to control those who lack power. The power holders seek to impose their knowledge, beliefs, and values on those who lack economic and political power. The power holders in the corporate capitalist sector dominate political processes and the media. In the United States, those who have power have traditionally been white males of European ancestry. The dispossessed have been women; unskilled and service workers; small farmers; and Asian, African, and Native Americans. Extending the critique globally, critical theorists divide nations into the powerful industrial ones and those, often in the southern hemisphere, that are less technologically developed. On the basis of their critique, critical theorists advocate a reform agenda to empower those who lack control over their own lives and destinies.

The Basic Questions

Postmodernism

Seeking to create a "new public philosophy" for the "postmodern" twenty-first century, critical theorists challenge traditional beliefs about knowledge, especially the

---

[38]For an assessment of Marxist educational theory, see Frank Margonis, "Marxism, Liberalism, and Educational Theory, *Educational Theory* (Fall 1993), pp. 449–465.

[39]Martin Carnoy, "Education, State, and Culture in American Society," in Henry A. Giroux and Peter L. McLaren, eds., *Critical Pedagogy, the State, and Cultural Struggle* (Albany: State University of New York Press, 1988), pp. 6–7.

[40]James Davison Hunter, *Culture Wars: The Struggle to Define America* (New York: Basic Books/HarperCollins, 1991), pp. 52–64. See also Valerie L. Scatamburlo, *Soldiers of Misfortune: The New Right's Culture War and the Politics of Political Correctness* (New York: Peter Lang, 1998).

[41]For an analysis of power relations, domination, and empowerment, see Seth Kreisberg, *Transforming Power: Domination, Empowerment, and Education* (Albany: State University of New York Press, 1992).

GETTING TO THE SOURCE

Critical Pedagogy and the Cultural Struggle

HENRY A. GIROUX AND PETER MCLAREN

Critical
Pedagogy,
the State,
and Cultural
Struggle

Henry A. Giroux
and Peter McLaren
EDITORS

Henry A. Giroux is the director of the Center for Education and Culture Studies at Miami University of Ohio, and Peter McLaren is the associate director. Both are recognized authorities in critical theory. In the following excerpt, they criticize the current wave of neoconservatism in American education.

[We] want to argue that the current debate about education represents more than a commentary on the state of public education in this country; it is fundamentally a debate about the relevance of democracy, social criticism, and the status of utopian thought in constructing both our dreams and the symbols and stories we devise in order to give meaning to our lives. The debate has taken a serious turn in the last decade. Under the guise of attempting to revitalize the language of conservative ethics, the [neoconservative] agenda has, in reality, launched a dangerous attack on some of the most fundamental aspects of democratic public life. What has been valorized in this language is not the issue of reclaiming public schools as agencies of social justice or critical democracy, but a view of schooling that disdains the democratic implications of pluralism, rejects a notion of learning which regards excellence and equity as mutually constitutive, and argues for a return to the old transmission model of learning.

It is worth noting that since the early 1980s the conservatives have dominated the debate over public education and have consistently put liberals and other groups of progressive stripe in the uncomfortable position of defending failed, abandoned, or unpopular policies and programs initiated in the 1960s, even

Deconstruction

major literary and philosophical texts of the old order. Rather than valuing these works as cultural classics, as do idealists, realists, essentialists, and perennialists, they see them as the constructions of dominant and often oppressive groups at a particular time in history.[42] They argue that the conventional curriculum has been dominated by a Eurocentric, white male perspective that is contaminated by racism, sexism, and imperialism. Rejecting the perennialist argument that the curriculum must feature the classics of Western civilization, critical theorists see these classics as period pieces that legitimate the cultural dominance of one group over another. The curriculum needs to be deconstructed, or taken apart, and then reconceptualized to include different cultural experiences and perspectives, especially those neglected in the past by the dominant power structures.[43] Supportive of multicultural education, critical theorists emphasize learning rooted in the students' own autobiographies and family and community experiences.

[42]Henry A. Giroux and Peter L. McLaren, "Schooling, Cultural Politics, and the Struggle for Democracy," in Henry A. Giroux and Peter McLaren, eds., *Critical Pedagogy, the State, and Cultural Struggle,* (New York: State University of New York Press, 1989), pp. xi–xii.
[43]For reconceptualizing the curriculum, see Audrey Thompson and Andrew Gitlin, "Creating Spaces for Reconstructing Knowledge in Feminist Pedagogy," *Educational Theory* (Spring 1995), pp. 135–150.

though it is recognized that many of these programs and policies were either never properly implemented or were not given an adequate chance at achieving their expected results. The power of the conservative initiative resides, in part, in its ability to link schooling to the ideology of the marketplace and to successfully champion the so-called virtues of Western civilization. In addition, it has doggedly defended a programmatic policy of school reform based on jargon-filled and undifferentiated conceptions of authority, citizenship, and discipline. . . .

In our view, the debate over public education has been predictably one-sided in that the conservatives have set the agenda for such a debate and initiated a plethora of policy studies designed to implement their own educational initiatives. The success of the conservative educational agenda also points to a fundamental failure among progressive and radical educators to generate a public discourse on schooling. This is not to suggest that there has been an absence of writing on educational issues among leftist critics. In fact, the body of literature that has emerged in the last decade is duly impressive. One major problem facing the recent outpouring of critical discourse on schooling is that over the years it has become largely academicized. It has lost sight of its fundamental mission of mobilizing public sentiment toward a renewed vision of community; it has failed to recognize the general relevance of education as a public service and the importance of deliberately translating educational theory into a community-related discourse capable of reaching into and animating public culture and life. In effect, critical and radical writings on schooling have become ghettoized within the ivory tower, reflecting a failure to take seriously the fact that education as a terrain of struggle is central to the reconstruction of public life and, as such, must be understood in vernacular as well as scholarly terms.

Questions

1. How do Giroux and McLaren characterize the current debate over education?
2. What are the major elements in their critique of neoconservatism?
3. What emphases would critical theorists such as Giroux and McLaren recommend in a teacher's professional development?

Source: Reprinted by permission of the State University of New York Press from *Critical Pedagogy, the State, and Cultural Struggle* by Henry A. Giroux and Peter L. McLaren, eds. © 1989 State University of New York. All rights reserved.

Public spheres

Critical theorists want all children and adolescents to attend school, but they also want schools to become liberating rather than indoctrinating agencies. They contend that schools have been and continue to be controlled by dominant groups that impose their version of knowledge as a means of social control. Children of subordinate groups, usually economically disadvantaged and politically weak, are indoctrinated to believe that they live in the best of all possible worlds. The approved textbooks and other educational materials confirm, or legitimate, this "sanitized" version of social reality. The "hidden curriculum" (see Chapter 9), with its emphasis on individual competition and private property, reinforces corporate values. Critical theorists want schools to be transformed into "democratic public spheres" where young people become conscious of the need to create a more equitable society for all people.[44]

Teachers, like students, need to be empowered so that they can use methods that open students to social alternatives rather than mirroring the status quo. Critical theorists attack such mechanisms as standardized testing, teacher competency assessment, and top-down administrator-controlled schools as disempowering teachers.

---

[44]Giroux and McLaren, p. xxi.

Implications for Today's Classroom Teacher

Agenda for teacher empowerment

Critical theorists want teachers to examine the ideologies that connect education to wider social and political issues. Their agenda for teacher empowerment includes (1) fighting for genuine school reform that will give teachers power over the conditions of teaching and learning; (2) engaging in collaborative research with other teachers to reconceptualize curriculum and instruction; (3) studying the culturally diverse people in the communities whose children the schools educate; (4) organizing community centers for collaborative action with community members; (5) engaging in critical dialogues with students about the realities of American politics, economics, and culture; (6) redistributing power in schools between teachers and administrators; and (7) involving schools in attempts to solve society's major problems, such as drug abuse, teenage pregnancy, illiteracy, malnutrition, and inadequate health care.[45]

Emphasizing diversity

Emphasizing cultural diversity, the critical theorist would lead students on knowledge explorations that begin with their own unique multicultural experiences. The curriculum would stress study of the students' histories, languages, and cultures, as well as analysis of the persistent issues of American life, particularly those that empower some and disempower others.[46]

Building Your Own Philosophy of Education

We now return to the questions posed at the beginning of this chapter and the realization that educational philosophers and theorists often provide conflicting answers. What is truth and how do we know and teach it? Do you believe that there are universal truths, as do idealists, realists, perennialists, and essentialists? Or do you think of truth as depending on changing circumstances, as do pragmatists and progressives? Your answers, reflecting your perception of reality, will influence your approach to teaching. They will also determine your view of equity and justice issues in schools and shape your attitudes about fairness and appropriate behavior in your own teaching and classroom. Your answers to these questions are part of your on-going quest to create your own philosophy of education.

Summing Up

1. To provide an orientation for developing your own philosophy of education, the text defined such terms as *metaphysics, epistemology, axiology* (*ethics* and *aesthetics*) and *logic*. It then related these terms to education, schooling, knowledge, and teaching and learning.

2. To provide a frame of reference for developing your own philosophy of education, we examined such philosophies of education as idealism, realism, pragmatism, and existentialism and educational theories such as perennialism, essentialism, progressivism, social reconstructionism, and critical theory.

3. By studying these philosophies and theories of education, you can work toward formulating your own philosophy of education and come to understand the the underlying philosophical bases of curriculum and teaching and learning.

[45]Ibid., p. xxiii.
[46]Christine E. Sleeter and Peter L. McLaren, eds., *Multicultural Education, Critical Pedagogy, and the Politics of Difference* (Albany: State University of New York Press, 1995).

Key Terms

philosophies *(389)*

theories *(389)*

metaphysics *(390)*

epistemology *(390)*

axiology *(390)*

ethics *(390)*

aesthetics *(390)*

deductive logic *(392)*

inductive logic *(392)*

idealism *(392)*

macrocosm *(392)*

microcosm *(392)*

a priori ideas *(392)*

Socratic method *(394)*

realism *(395)*

pragmatism *(397)*

experience *(398)*

existentialism *(400)*

progressivism *(404)*

constructivism *(406)*

social reconstructionism *(407)*

perennialism *(410)*

The Paideia Proposal *(411)*

cultural relativism *(412)*

essentialism *(414)*

"back-to-basics" movement *(414)*

cultural literacy *(415)*

critical theory *(416)*

conflict theory *(417)*

Discussion Questions

1. Reflect on your own ideas about knowledge, education and schooling, and teaching and learning. What would you say is your philosophy of education? If you have the opportunity, share your thoughts with your classmates. Then listen to their philosophies and discuss the agreements and disagreements that emerge.

2. Reflect on how your philosophy of education has been influenced by significant teachers in your life or by books and motion pictures about teachers and teaching. Share and discuss such influences with your classmates.

3. Can you identify underlying philosophical orientations in the courses you are taking or in your teacher-education program as a whole? What are they?

4. Of the philosophies and theories examined in Chapter 12, which is most relevant and which is most irrelevant to contemporary American education? Why?

Suggested Projects for Professional Development

1. In your field-based or clinical experience, keep a journal that identifies the philosophy or theory underlying the school, curriculum, and teaching-learning methods you have observed. Share and reflect on these observations with the members of the class.

2. Create and maintain a clippings file of articles about education that appear in the popular press — newspapers and magazines — either critiquing schools or proposing educational reforms. Then analyze the philosophical and theoretical positions underlying these critiques and proposed reforms. Share and reflect on your observations with the members of the class.

3. Create and maintain a clippings file of articles about education that appear in local newspapers of the community in which the school where you are doing clinical experience, student teaching, or teaching is located. Then analyze the

philosophical and theoretical positions underlying these articles. Share and reflect on your observations with the members of the class.

4. Research and prepare a statement on the philosophy of education approved by the board of education in the school district in which you are doing clinical experience, student teaching, or teaching. Compare and contrast the board's philosophy of education with the philosophies and theories discussed in this chapter. Share and reflect on your observations with the members of the class.

5. Prepare a set of questions that can be used as a guide for interviewing key educators — deans, department chairs, professors — at your college or university about their educational philosophies. Share and reflect on your observations with the members of the class.

6. Prepare a set of questions that can be used as a guide for interviewing administrators and teachers in the school district in which you are engaged in clinical experience, student teaching, or teaching. The questions should relate to their educational philosophies. Share and reflect on your observations with the members of the class.

7. Prepare a set of questions that can be used as a guide for interviewing key community leaders — editors, politicians, media persons, officers of service organizations and unions — about their educational philosophies. Then assign members of the class to report the findings of their interviews.

8. Prepare a set of questions that can be used as a guide for interviewing key campus leaders who represent a wide cultural diversity — officers of the African American, Hispanic, and Asian American organizations; gay or lesbian alliance; Young Republicans; Young Democrats; Socialist youth groups; leftist organizations; right-wing organizations; religious fundamentalists; Right to Life groups; Freedom of Choice groups — about their educational philosophies. Then assign members of the class to report the findings of their interviews.

Suggested Readings and Resources

Internet Resources

For information about neoprogressive and constructivist theories of education, consult the Association for Experiential Education at Princeton University: **www.princeton.edu/rcurtis/aee.html.**

For the Great Books approach associated with perennialism, consult Mercer University: **httkkpk//roger.vet.uga. edu/%7 Elnoles?grtbks.html.**

For information on basic education related to essentialism and neoessentialism, consult the Council for Basic Education: **www.c-b-e.org.**

For information related to critical theory, consult the electronic journal *Postmodern Culture:* **www.jefferson. village. edu/pmc.**

For information on the discussion of philosophical topics, consult the University of Chicago Philosophy Project: **csmaclab:www.uchicago.edu/philosophyProject/ philos.html.**

For teaching and learning related to critical thinking, consult the Critical Thinking Community: **www.sonoma.edu/cthink.**

Links to resources on all aspects of philosophy can be found at: **www/bris.ac.uk/Depts/Philosophy/VL.**

Videos

Transformation. VHS, 25 minutes (1995). Insight Media, 2162 Broadway, P.O. Box 621, New York, NY 10024-0621. Phone: 212-721-6316. *Designed to assist teachers in developing a philosophy of education, the program examines key ideas and philosophers.*

The Progressives. VHS, 24 minutes (1988). Insight Media, 2162 Broadway, P.O. Box 621, New York, NY 10024-0621. Phone: 212-721-6316. *Explores the lives and philosophies of leading progressive educators.*

Professional Ethics. VHS, 22 minutes (1990). Insight Media, 2162 Broadway, P.O. Box 621, New York, NY 10024-0621. Phone: 212-721-6316. *Explores ethical situations and decisions in teaching.*

Publications

Bloom, Allan. *The Closing of the American Mind.* New York: Simon and Schuster, 1987. *In his widely read book, Bloom attacks the effects of relativism on American education.*

Fishman, Stephen M., and Lucille McCarthy. *John Dewey and the Challenge of Classroom Practice.* New York: Teachers College Press, 1998. *The authors examine key Deweyan concepts such as student-curriculum integration, interest and effort, and continuity and interaction in terms of schools and classrooms.*

Gutek, Gerald L. *Philosophical and Ideological Perspectives on Education.* Boston: Allyn and Bacon, 1997. *Gutek examines the major philosophies, ideologies, and theories of education.*

Heslep, Robert D. *Philosophical Thinking in Educational Practice.* Westport, Conn.: Praeger Publishers, 1997. *Heslep, a well-respected educational theorist, relates the philosophy of education to classroom practices.*

Hinchey, Patricia H. *Finding Freedom in the Classroom: A Practical Introduction to Critical Theory.* New York: Peter Lang, 1998. *Hinchey's book examines critical theory in ways that are applicable to schools and classrooms.*

Hirsch, Jr., E. D. *Cultural Literacy: What Every American Needs to Know.* Boston: Houghton Mifflin, 1987. *An essentialist notion of what a good education is about and what every young American needs to know about Western culture.*

Hunter, James Davison. *Culture Wars: The Struggle to Define America.* New York: Basic Books/A Division of HarperCollins Publishers, 1991. *Hunter's book carefully examines the philosophical roots of the current conflict over culture and cultural values in the United States.*

Jervis, Kathe, and Carol Montag, eds. *Progressive Education for the 1990s.* New York: Teachers College Press, Columbia University, 1991. *This contemporary treatment of progressive education approaches the subject from both historical and practical perspectives that can guide schooling, teaching, and learning.*

Johnson, Tony W. *Discipleship or Pilgrimage? The Study of Educational Philosophy.* Albany: State University of New York Press, 1995. *In his critique of educational philosophy and the assumptions of educational philosophers, Johnson argues that it is necessary to rethink the field in terms of school practices.*

Kanpol, Barry. *Critical Pedagogy: An Introduction.* Westport, Conn.: Bergin and Garvey, 1994. *Kanpol's book provides a useful and readable treatment of critical theory, a highly significant contemporary educational theory.*

Noddings, Nel. *Philosophy of Education.* Boulder, Colo.: Westview Press, 1995. *In her well-reviewed book, Noddings relates general issues in the philosophy of education to important questions of educational policy making and classroom practices.*

Ozmon, Howard A., and Samuel M. Craver. *Philosophical Foundations of Education,* 5th ed. Columbus, Ohio, and Englewood Cliffs, N.J.: Merrill, an imprint of Prentice Hall, 1995. *In their widely used text, Ozmon and Craver present a first-rate analysis of the important educational philosophies.*

The Purposes of Education

Contemporary society changes fundamentally and rapidly. As it changes, we must fit ourselves into the present and project ourselves into the future. We look to the schools to help us cope with the climate of change. As a society, we react to change and social pressures by revising our educational purposes, and the schools respond by changing their programs.

Where *are* we going? As teachers and educators, what are our real purposes, and how should they be guiding our work?

Chapter 13 will begin to focus your thinking on important issues. As you read, think about the following questions:

- How do social forces combine with philosophies of education to shape our educational purposes?
- How are our goals and objectives formulated?
- What groups of students have been targeted for special treatment in recent decades?
- What are the major themes of recent policy reports on education?
- What goals will be most important in the future?

This chapter was revised by Dr. James Lawlor, Towson University

In this continual revision of educational priorities, the basic philosophies and theories examined in Chapter 12 play a strong role. People respond differently to the same events; they appraise, reflect on, and react to the tendencies of the times according to their own philosophies and values. Moreover, certain eras in American education have been dominated by particular philosophical approaches. As times change, the dominant philosophy or theory often changes, and the impact is felt in classrooms across the country — classrooms like yours. As a new teacher you will need to look for a "fit" between your philosophy of education and the educational values of the school district in which you teach. Examine your school district goals as well as those of your school. How do these goals translate into curriculum and teaching methods, and, most importantly, how comfortable are you philosophically with the answers to these questions?

This chapter shows how philosophies and theories of education interact with social forces to influence the purposes of American education. After describing the purposes that have prevailed at different times in the history of American education, we examine the important changes of recent years. First, however, the chapter shows how educational purposes are defined in terms of goals and objectives.

Establishing Goals and Objectives

Levels of educational purpose

Effect of social forces and philosophies

Three influential forces

When we talk about the purposes of education, we may be referring to purposes at one or more of the following levels: nation, state, school district, school, subject/grade, unit plan, or lesson plan. Although there is no perfect agreement, most educators use the terms **goals** and **objectives** to distinguish among levels of purpose, with goals being broader and objectives being more specific. Both terms are used to describe a direction — what we are seeking to accomplish. Many educators refer to goals and objectives as "ends" or "end points" of education.

All end points, however, are influenced by social forces and by prevailing philosophies or theories of education. Social forces and philosophies combine to shape the goals adopted at the national or state level; these goals in turn affect the more specific goals and objectives adopted in particular schools and classrooms. Over time, changes in social forces can also lead to modifications in prevailing philosophies and theories. There are three main types of influential forces: society in general, developments in knowledge, and beliefs about the nature of the learner.[1]

Changes in *society* include shifts in emphasis among the various influences examined in Chapters 9 and 10, such as the family, peer groups, social class, and the economy. Changes in *knowledge* include new developments in science and technology, new methods of processing and storing information, and new methods of defining or organizing fields of study. Finally, changes in beliefs about the nature of the *learner,* such as new theories of the learning process, may also produce changes in educational theories and purposes.

Goals

Goals as broad statements of purpose

Although goals are important guides in education, they cannot be directly observed or evaluated; rather, they are broad statements that denote a desired and valued

---

[1]The concept of three sources of change is rooted in the ideas of Boyd Bode and John Dewey, who wrote some eighty years ago. These ideas, popularized by Ralph Tyler in 1949, have been developed by contemporary curriculum theorists such as Allan Ornstein, J. Galen Saylor, and Robert Zais.

Aims, goals, and objectives — which help teachers define educational purposes — are influenced by social forces and prevailing theories of education. *(© Robert Finken/ The Picture Cube)*

competency, a theme or concern that applies to education in general. Sometimes the most general goals are called *aims*.

Goals or aims are formulated at the national and state levels, often by prestigious commissions or task forces. Here is one example of a goal at the national level, from the *National Education Goals Report:* "By the year 2000, all children in America will start school ready to learn."[2] Another national or state goal might be "to prepare students for democratic citizenship." Although both of these are admirable goals, it is unclear how local school districts might achieve them. They merely suggest a general direction to follow.

National or state goals

Goals at the school district level begin to narrow in focus. For example, a school district goal related to the national goal of school readiness might be that "all children will have access to high-quality and developmentally appropriate preschool programs that help prepare children for school." A more sharply focused example of the national citizenship goal might be that "students will participate actively in the political and social life of the community." Each of these goals helps to point teachers, principals, and superintendents toward certain general ends.

District goals

Goals at the school level usually narrow in focus even more, translating national, state, and district goals into statements that coincide more closely with the philosophy and priorities of the local school community.[3] Often, school-level goal statements are found in documents known as *school improvement plans*. These goal

School goals

---

[2]National Education Goals Panel, *The National Education Goals Report, 1997* (Washington, D.C.: U.S. Government Printing Office, 1997), pp. 1–4.
[3]Elliot W. Eisner, *The Educational Imagination,* 3rd ed. (New York: Macmillan, 1993); and Allan C. Ornstein and Francis P. Hunkins, *Curriculum: Foundations, Principles and Issues,* 3rd ed. (Boston: Allyn and Bacon, 1998).

statements flow from an overall school *mission statement,* which articulates the school's role in educating the community's youth.[4] An example of a school-level goal related to the national goal of school readiness might be that "kindergarten will be expanded from a half-day program to a full-day program."

In the late 1940s Ralph Tyler developed an outline for school goals that is still influential today. Tyler identified four fundamental questions that need to be considered:

Tyler's four questions

1. What educational purposes should the school seek to attain?
2. What educational experiences can be provided to help attain these purposes?
3. How can these educational experiences be effectively organized?
4. How can we determine whether [and to what extent] the purposes have been attained?[5]

Goodlad's twelve major goals

A generation later, another influential educator, John Goodlad, studied lists of school goals published by local boards of education across the country and identified a cluster of twelve that represented the spirit of the total list. Each of the twelve can be further defined by a rationale statement, as shown in Table 13.1. These goals have not changed much since then; rather, the emphasis has varied depending on a school district's or school's philosophy and the way it interprets the forces of social change.

Citizen input

The process of developing goals for a school district or individual school should permit citizens, parents, and, at times, students to have meaningful input. Working in partnership with professional educators who understand child development and the learning process, citizens can provide a valuable perspective in helping to decide what public schools are to teach.[6]

Goals are not behavioral

Whether formulated at the national, state, school district, or school level, goals are usually written in nonbehavioral terms, not tied to particular content or subject matter. By describing what schooling is intended to accomplish, goals provide a direction, but they are too vague for teachers and students to apply directly in the classroom. Thus for classroom use, goals must be translated into more specific objectives.

Objectives

Objectives are generally written at three levels of instruction: subject/grade level, unit plan level, and lesson plan level.[7] Although objectives are more specific than goals, educators disagree about how detailed they ought to be. Some prefer fairly general objectives; others advocate objectives precise enough to be measured in behavioral terms — that is, by the observable behavior of the student.

Classroom objectives

In practice, most educators at the classroom level organize instruction with a combination of general and specific objectives in mind. General objectives are char-

---

[4]Maryland State Department of Education, *The Comprehensive Plan for the Maryland School Performance Program* (Baltimore: Maryland State Department of Education, 1996), pp. 1–24.
[5]Ralph W. Tyler, *Basic Principles of Curriculum and Instruction* (Chicago: University of Chicago Press, 1949), p. 1.
[6]Ronald S. Brant and Ralph W. Tyler, "Goals and Objectives," cited in Allan C. Ornstein and Linda S. Behar-Horenstein, *Contemporary Issues in Curriculum* (Boston: Allyn and Bacon, 1999, pp. 20–29.
[7]George J. Posner and Alan N. Rudnitsky, *Course Design: A Guide to Curriculum Development for Teachers,* 4th ed. (New York: Longman, 1992); and Hilda Taba, *Curriculum Development: Theory and Practice* (New York: Harcourt, Brace, 1962).

TABLE 13.1	Major Goals of American Schools

1. *Mastery of basic skills or fundamental process.* In our technological civilization, an individual's ability to participate in the activities of society depends on mastery of these fundamental processes.

2. *Career or vocational education.* An individual's satisfaction in life will be significantly related to satisfaction with her or his job. Intelligent career decisions will require knowledge of personal aptitudes and interests in relation to career possibilities.

3. *Intellectual development.* As civilization has become more complex, people have had to rely more heavily on their rational abilities. Full intellectual development of each member of society is necessary.

4. *Enculturation.* Studies that illuminate our relationship with the past yield insights into our society and its values; further, these strengthen an individual's sense of belonging, identity, and direction for his or her own life.

5. *Interpersonal relations.* Schools should help every child understand, appreciate, and value persons belonging to social, cultural, and ethnic groups different from his or her own.

6. *Autonomy.* Unless schools produce self-directed citizens, they have failed both society and the individual. As society becomes more complex, demands on individuals multiply. Schools help prepare children for a world of rapid change by developing in them the capacity to assume responsibility for their own needs.

7. *Citizenship.* To counteract the present human ability to destroy humanity and the environment requires citizen involvement in the political and social life of this country. A democracy can survive only through the participation of its members.

8. *Creativity and aesthetic perception.* Abilities for creating new and meaningful things and appreciating the creations of other human beings are essential both for personal self-realization and for the benefit of society.

9. *Self-concept.* The self-concept of an individual serves as a reference point and feedback mechanism for personal goals and aspirations. Facilitating factors for a healthy self-concept can be provided in the school environment.

10. *Emotional and physical well-being.* Emotional stability and physical fitness are perceived as necessary conditions for attaining the other goals, but they are also worthy ends in themselves.

11. *Moral and ethical character.* Individuals need to develop the judgment that allows us to evaluate behavior as right or wrong. Schools can foster the growth of such judgment as well as a commitment to truth, moral integrity, and moral conduct.

12. *Self-realization.* Efforts to develop a better self contribute to the development of a better society.

Source: Adapted from John I. Goodlad, *What Are Schools For?* (Bloomington, Ind.: Phi Delta Kappa, 1979), pp. 44–52. Reprinted with permission.

acterized by "end" terms such as to *know, learn, understand, comprehend,* and *appreciate.* Such objectives help a teacher develop a sequenced curricula for a grade level or a unit.

Lesson plan objectives

At the level of the individual lesson plan, objectives usually become very specific, as recommended by Robert Mager. They use precise wording (often action words) such as *discuss, describe in writing, state orally, list, role-play,* and *solve.* Sometimes called *behavioral* or *performance objectives,* these statements are content or skill specific, require particular student behavior or performance, and are observable and measurable. Both the teacher and the learner can evaluate the amount or degree of learning.[8]

---

[8]Robert F. Mager, *Preparing Instructional Objectives,* rev. 3rd ed. (Atlanta: Center for Effective Performance, 1997); Robert Kibler, Larry L. Baker, and David T. Miles, *Behavioral Objectives and Instruction,* 2nd ed. (Boston: Allyn and Bacon, 1981); and W. James Popham, *Modern Educational Measurement,* 2nd ed. (Englewood Cliffs, N.J.: Prentice-Hall, 1990).

OVERVIEW 13.1	Goals and Objectives of Education		
Ends	**Level of Direction**	**Developed by**	**Example(s)**
National and state goals	Nation, state	Commissions, task force groups, broad professional associations	Improving basic literacy skills
Local goals	School district, school	Groups of administrators, teachers, and/or community members; broad professional associations	Acquiring information and meaning through reading, writing, speaking, and mathematical symbols
General objectives	Subject/grade	Subject-centered professional associations; curriculum departments or committees of state departments of education; large school districts	Improving reading comprehension Appreciating the reading of whole books
	Unit plan	Textbook authors; teachers	Developing word recognition skills Listening to stories read
Specific objectives	Lesson plan	Textbook authors; teachers	Identifying the main ideas of the author Writing ten new vocabulary words

Examples of objectives

An example of a general unit objective might be that "students will understand why American colonists wanted to separate from Great Britain in the 1770s." Transposing this general objective into a specific lesson objective, we might obtain "Students will describe in writing three reasons American colonists gave in favor of separation from Great Britain." This objective refers to a specific kind of knowledge, states what is expected of students, and gives a precise criterion of three reasons.

Overview 13.1 summarizes the differences among the various levels of goals and objectives. As we move from national goals to lesson objectives, the examples become more specific — that is, easier to observe and/or measure.

Historical Perspective

We live in an era when educators and the public at large are questioning the purposes of American education. What is it that our schools should be trying to do? The answers are varied, and the debate has often been heated. To understand this debate, we need to know how educational purposes have developed and changed over the years. As the following sections illustrate, the goals of American education have undergone many transformations.

The Mental Discipline Approach

Mental discipline: exercising the mind

Before the twentieth century, the perennialist theory generally dominated American education. Subject matter was organized and presented as a mere accounting of information. Proponents of the **mental discipline approach** believed that the mind is strengthened through mental activities, just as the body is strengthened by exercising. Traditional subjects, such as languages (Latin, Greek, French, and German), mathematics, history, English, physics, chemistry, government, and biology, were valued for their cultivation of the intellect; the more difficult the subject and the more the student had to exercise the mind, the greater the value of the subject.[9]

Committee of Ten's recommendations

The mental discipline approach is best exemplified by the National Education Association's Report of the Committee of Ten on Secondary School Studies (1894). This approach established a curriculum hierarchy, from elementary school through college, that promoted academics and college preparation, ignoring the majority of students who were not bound for college.

Progressive demands for reform

Gradually demands were made for various changes in schooling to meet the needs of a changing social order. The pace of immigration and industrial development led a growing number of educators to question the classical curriculum and the emphasis on mental discipline and repetitive drill. Adherents of the new pedagogy represented the progressive voice in education. They emphasized schoolwork and school subjects designed to meet the needs of everyday life for all children. By the early twentieth century, the effort to reform the schools along more progressive lines was well under way.

The Progressive Approach: The Whole Child

The most widely accepted list of educational purposes in the twentieth century was compiled by the NEA's Commission on the Reorganization of Secondary Education in 1918. Its influential bulletin, which reflected the rise of progressivism, was entitled ***Cardinal Principles of Secondary Education.*** The Cardinal Principles emphasized educating all youth for "complete living," not just college-bound youth for mental rigor. Cited in 1918, these purposes are still found in one form or another in most statements of educational goals today (see Table 13.2.)

The Cardinal Principles

The Ten Imperative Needs

Influenced by World War II, the Educational Policies Commission of the NEA issued its most influential report, ***Education for all American Youth.*** It stressed goals related to democracy and world citizenship as well as those related to the general needs of children and youth. The Commission's most influential report, *Education for All American Youth* (1944), contained the "Ten Imperative Needs of Youth" (see Table 13.2). Like the Cardinal Principles, the Ten Imperative Needs included such matters as health, family life, ethics, and the wise use of leisure, and added the importance of rational thinking and the arts.

Concern for the whole child

In contrast to the perennialist philosophy and mental discipline approach that prevailed before World War I, the period from World War I until after World War II was dominated by the philosophy of progressivism and the science of child psychology. During this period, emphasis was placed on the **whole-child concept** and on life adjustment. The prevailing view held that schools must be concerned with the growth and development of the entire child, not just with certain selected mental

---

[9]Ellwood P. Cubberley, *Public Education in the United States,* rev. ed. (Boston: Houghton Mifflin, 1947), p. 543.

Underlying the whole-child movement is the view that schools should be concerned with the development of the entire child, not just with selected aspects of the child's growth. Here, seventh graders are being taught folk dancing.
(© Elizabeth Crews)

aspects. Goals related to cognitive or mental growth had to share the stage with other important purposes of education, including goals involving social, psychological, vocational, moral, and civic development. The whole-child concept and the corresponding growth of child psychology had a tremendous impact on the schools that is still felt today.

Focus on the Academically Talented

During the era of the Cold War and the Soviet *Sputnik* flight (1957), international events gave major impetus to the U.S. movement to reexamine academic disciplines as the focus of schooling. The country was appalled at the notion of losing technological superiority to the Soviets; national pride was challenged, and national goals were threatened.

Return to academic essentials

Influenced by the perennialist and essentialist theories of education, critics called for a return to academic essentials and mental discipline. "Concern with the personal problems of adolescents [had] grown so excessive as to push into the background what should be the school's central concern, the intellectual development of its students," stated noted historian Arthur Bestor.[10] Admiral Hyman Rickover wondered why Johnny could not read while Ivan could and did. Rickover de-

[10]Arthur Bestor, *The Restoration of Learning* (New York: Knopf, 1956), p. 120.

TABLE 13.2 Goals of Education: Two Major Statements of the Progressive Approach

Cardinal Principles of Secondary Education (1918)	Ten Imperative Needs of Youth (1944)
1. *Health:* provide health instruction and a program of physical activities; cooperate with home and community in promoting health	Develop skills and/or attitudes that enhance the following:
2. *Command of fundamental processes:* develop fundamental thought processes to meet needs of modern life	1. Productive work experiences and occupational success
3. *Worthy home membership:* develop qualities that make the individual a worthy member of a family	2. Good health and physical fitness
4. *Vocation:* equip students to earn a living, to serve society well through a vocation, and to achieve personal development through that vocation	3. Rights and duties of a democratic citizenry
	4. Conditions for successful family life
	5. Wise consumer behavior
5. *Civic education:* foster qualities that help a person play a part in the community and understand international problems	6. Understanding of science and the nature of man
	7. Appreciation of arts, music, and literature
6. *Worthy use of leisure:* equip people to find "recreation of body, mind, and spirit" that will enrich their personalities	8. Wise use of leisure time
	9. Respect for ethical values
7. *Ethical character:* develop ethical character both through instructional methods and through social contacts among students and teachers	10. The ability to think rationally and communicate thoughts clearly

Source: Commission on the Reorganization of Secondary Education, *Cardinal Principles of Secondary Education,* Bulletin no. 35 (Washington, D.C.: U.S. Government Printing Office, 1918), pp. 11–15; and Educational Policies Commission, *Education for All American Youth* (Washington, D.C.: National Education Association, 1944).

manded a return to the basics, a beefing up of science and mathematics courses, and a "de-emphasis of life-adjustment schools and progressive educationalists."[11]

National legislation

Hard on the heels of *Sputnik* came national legislation to support training, equipment, and programs in fields considered vital to defense. The National Defense Education Act singled out science, mathematics, modern languages, and guidance (often considered a way to steer youth into the three former fields and into college). The scientific community, university scholars, and curriculum specialists were called upon to reconstruct subject-matter content, especially on the high-school level, while government and foundation sources provided the funds.[12]

Challenging the academically talented

The new educational climate included an increasing emphasis on providing topnotch education for the academically talented child. In 1959, James Conant, president of Harvard University, after visiting fifty-five high schools with "good reputations" across the country, stated that "the academically talented student, as a

---

[11]Hyman G. Rickover, *Education and Freedom* (New York: Dutton, 1959), p. 190.
[12]William Van Til, "In a Climate of Change," in E. F. Carlson, ed., *Role of Supervisor and Curriculum Director in a Climate of Change,* 1965 ASCD Yearbook (Washington, D.C.: Association for Supervision and Curriculum Development, 1965), p. 21.

rule, is not being sufficiently challenged, does not work hard enough, and his program of academic subjects is not of sufficient range."[13] Conant's influential book, *The American High School Today,* was a blueprint for moderate reform — for upgrading the curriculum in general, especially mathematics, science, and foreign language; and grouping students according to their abilities.

Focus on Disadvantaged Students

Concern for non-college-bound students

During the 1960s the social conscience of America burst forth, bringing increased concern about poverty, racial discrimination, and equal educational opportunity. In this new climate, new educational priorities surfaced, often related to the progressive and social reconstructionist theories of education. Educators noted that most students did not go on to college and that many dropped out of school or graduated as functional illiterates. Under those circumstances, serious problems could be anticipated if educational goals continued to be narrowly directed toward the most able students.[14]

"Social dynamite"

James Conant shifted his position somewhat and in the 1961 book *Slums and Suburbs* urged educators and policy makers to pay closer attention to the inner city and disadvantaged child and to the "social dynamite" accumulating in our large cities.[15]

Given the student unrest and urban riots of the 1960s, it was easy to accept the arguments of an impending crisis and a shift in educational goals to focus on the disadvantaged. To some educators, however, it appeared that the new emphasis tended to overlook the average and above-average student.

Expanded Priorities

Multicultural and bilingual programs

The focus on disadvantaged students extended into the 1980s and was expanded to include multicultural and bilingual students and students with disabilities. The nation's multicultural and bilingual efforts were characterized by increased federal funding for Hispanic, Asian American, and Native American students, and by legal support for students with limited English skills (*Lau* v. *Nichols,* U.S. Supreme Court, 1974).

Students with disabilities

During the 1970s and 1980s, much concern also surfaced for special education, especially for students with learning disabilities or other special needs. The cornerstone of these new policies and programs was the Education for All Handicapped Children Act, passed in 1975 (described in Chapter 11). This legislation mandated a free and appropriate public education for all children and youth with disabilities. The act was amended in 1986 to extend the full rights and protection of this law to children aged three through five. It also permitted the schools to identify these young children as "developmentally delayed" rather than by the category of disability.[16]

By the 1990s the term *at risk* began to replace the older term *disadvantaged,* and the definition of students covered by the term has continued to expand. A category

[13]James B. Conant, *The American High School Today* (New York: McGraw-Hill, 1959), p. 40.
[14]See, for example, John W. Gardner, *Excellence: Can We Be Equal and Excellent Too?* (New York: Harper and Row, 1961), pp. 28–29, 77.
[15]James B. Conant, *Slums and Suburbs* (New York: McGraw-Hill, 1961), p. 2.
[16]Cheryl M. Jorgenson et al., "Curriculum and Its Impact on Inclusion and the Achievement of Students with Disabilities," *CISP Issue Brief* (July 1997), pp. 1–21.

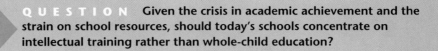

TAKING ISSUE

The Intellect Versus the Whole Child

Since World War I, there has been an underlying conflict concerning the aims of American education. One argument states that the schools should emphasize social experiences and personal development as well as academics. This position has been called the whole-child concept of education. The opposing argument insists that schools focus strongly on intellectual competence instead of trying to incorporate nonacademic concerns.

Arguments PRO

1 Schools are having a hard time maintaining basic academic standards. Many students cannot even read and write acceptably. Devoting school time to personal and social development undercuts attempts to improve achievement.

2 Whole-child education often intrudes into the proper domains of parents, church, and community. A child's moral instruction, for example, should be determined by his or her parents, not by teachers, curriculum planners, or any other agency of government.

3 The whole-child concept is often used to justify unnecessary school activities (such as driver's education) or to guarantee jobs for special interest groups (such as counselors, psychologists, and health educators). The strain on school finances would be reduced if such marginal programs were eliminated.

4 If schools would concentrate on a general humanities curriculum, the needs of the whole child would in fact be served. Almost every moral, social, or personal dilemma a student might encounter is addressed in the classic and modern works of Western civilization.

Arguments CON

1 Concentration on achievement and basic skills develops only a partial person. Students who do not fit socially, morally, or personally into society will not lead a rewarding life or act as responsible citizens.

2 The modern home and the institutional structures of contemporary society can no longer perform the same roles as in the past. Consequently, children are growing up in a developmental vacuum. The schools seem to be the only institutions able to fill students' needs.

3 Students today grow up faster than ever before. Society hurries them into coping with psychological and social pressures that are difficult even for adults. Specialists like counselors and psychologists therefore play an increasingly vital role in education.

4 To trust academic courses to promote nonacademic development is to divorce thought from action, speculation from experience. Reading great works of moral thought does not necessarily make one a moral person. Students need help in applying ideas to their own lives.

Students "at risk"

of the "new needy" has emerged, including homeless children, crack-exposed babies, and children of migrant workers.[17] Latchkey children, who constitute perhaps 60 to 65 percent of all American students, are also held to be potentially at risk because they lack adult supervision after school.[18] Some educators would further expand the at-risk category to include students who fall into any of these groups: (1) abused or neglected, (2) substance addicted, (3) pregnant, (4) gang or cult members, (5) HIV virus infected or (6) living in a single-parent family.[19]

Commitment to all children

These needs are recognized in the first goal of the *National Education Goals* (see Table 13.3 on p. 447), which states that "by the year 2000, all children in America will start school ready to learn." This goal represents a national commitment to *all* young children. The accompanying statements call for education and support for parents, attention to health and prenatal care, and universal access to appropriate preschool environments and the importance of reading in the life of the child. This goal underscores the critical role of parents in the educational process.[20]

Ongoing controversies

In the 1990s, however, conservative reactions against these trends have also increased. As noted in Chapter 11, multicultural and bilingual programs have been heavily criticized as contributing to fragmentation and separatism rather than cultural unity. Educators concerned about children at risk and limited-English-speaking students have fought back, some of them warning that race discrimination issues (and not solely those pertaining to African Americans) are still with us more than forty years after *Brown v. Board of Education*.[21] Educators have also split into factions over the most effective way to conduct special education: some want full inclusion (elimination of self-contained classrooms for special education students and assignment of special education teachers to coteach regular classrooms); others support partial inclusion (whereby students with learning disabilities are placed in general education classrooms as much as possible); and still others favor maintaining mostly separate classes for special education students.[22]

---

[17]Adele M. Brodkin and Melba Coleman, "Kids in Crisis: How Can I Help a Homeless Child?" *Instructor* (November–December 1994), pp. 17–18; Joe R. Feagin and Melvin P. Sikes, *Living with Racism: The Black Middle Class Experience* (Boston: Beacon Press, 1994); Comer School Development Program, *Achieving Nationwide School Improvement Through Widespread Use of Effective Programs and Practices* (Baltimore: CRESPAR Publications Department, The Johns Hopkins University, 1997).

[18]Bobbie Rowley, "Home Away from Home," *Executive Educator* (October 1993), pp. 39–40; SECA Public Policy Institute, "The Latchkey Solution: School Age Care Comes of Age," *Dimensions of Early Childhood* (Summer 1993), pp. 5–8; and Debra A. Brass, *Programs, Problems and Policies: A Study of Latchkey Children in Ohio Public Libraries*. ERIC Document Number ED 413912.

[19]Allan C. Ornstein, "Enrollment Trends in Big-City Schools," *Peabody Journal of Education* (Summer 1989), pp. 64–71; and David C. Smith and Edward E. Greene, "Preparing Tomorrow's Principals Today," *Principal* (September 1990), pp. 20–24.

[20]Sharon L. Kagan, "Early Care and Education: Beyond the Fishbowl," *Phi Delta Kappan* (November 1994), pp. 184–187; and Shanna Shulman, *Kids Count in Colorado, 1997* (Denver: Colorado Children's Campaign, 1997).

[21]Michael Apple, "The Politics of Official Knowledge: Does a National Curriculum Make Sense?" *Teachers College Record* (Winter 1993), pp. 222–241; John I. Goodlad, ed., *Access to Knowledge: The Continuing Agenda for Our Nation's Schools* (New York: College Entrance Board, 1994); Jay P. Heubert, "Brown at 40: The Tasks Remain for Educators and Lawyers" (Paper presented at the annual meeting of the National Organization on Legal Problems of Education, San Diego, November 17, 1994); and Jose A. Cardenas, *Multicultural Education: A Generation of Advocacy* (Needham Heights, Mass.: Simon and Schuster, 1995).

[22]Douglas Fuchs and Lynn S. Fuchs, "What's 'Special' About Special Education?" *Phi Delta Kappan* (March 1995), pp. 522–529; James William Noll, ed., "Is Full Inclusion of Disabled Students Desirable?" in *Taking Sides: Clashing Views on Educational Issues* (Guilford, Conn.: Dushkin/McGraw-Hill, 1999), pp. 224–238.

Focus on outcomes

Finally, as the late 1980s and 1990s brought increased demands for educational accountability (demands expressed by elected officials and business leaders as well as by laypeople), many argued that education should focus more clearly on *outcomes* or outputs — that is, on meaningful, measurable academic results — rather than on inputs such as money, programs, efforts, and intentions. According to some of these critics, mere completion of a curriculum means little if students cannot use their education in real-life contexts. As a result of this new focus, twenty-five states have developed or implemented an **outcomes-based education (OBE)** approach, and eleven others have made outcomes a part of the state assessment process. Of course, although many educators believe the focus on student outcomes is a sensible way to look at educational goals, OBE is not without its critics. Some fear that it emphasizes affective outcomes and critical thinking to the detriment of religious faith and family values. Others claim that OBE promotes minimal academic standards, "dumbing down" the curriculum. Still other critics claim that OBE involves higher costs without corresponding results.[23]

The Call for Excellence

Keeping in mind how American educational goals have changed over time, we can look more closely at the contemporary demand for reform in the schools. How do various recent proposals reflect important changes in American educational purposes? How well do particular reforms fit your own ideas about the purpose of education?

Overview of Policy Reports

National reports call for reform

By the early 1980s national attention began to focus on the need for educational excellence and higher academic standards for all students — particularly the neglected "average" student — and not just the disadvantaged or the talented. In the years since then, a number of national policy reports, most of them reflecting what has been called a neoessentialist perspective, have called urgently for reforms to improve the quality of education in the United States. To support their proposals, the reports have presented devastating details and statistics indicating a serious decline in American education. For example:

Declining achievement and competency

1. Average achievement scores on the Scholastic Aptitude Test (SAT) declined steadily from 1963 to 1995. Average verbal scores fell 34 points (466 to 432), and mathematics scores dropped 10 points (492 to 482).[24]

2. By 1996 only 24 percent of eighth-grade students achieved math competency for their grade level. Among twelfth-grade students, only 14 percent could perform at grade level, and only 7.4 percent were capable of advanced work such as probability and statistics.[25]

---

[23]Bruno V. Manno, "The New School Wars: Battles over Outcome-Based Education," *Phi Delta Kappan* (May 1995), pp. 720–726; and Paul M. Terry, "Outcome-Based Education: Is It Mastery Learning All Over Again,Or Is It a Revolution to the Reform Movement?" (Paper presented at the Annual Meeting of the Midwest Regional Comparative International Education Society, Fort Wayne, Indiana, October 11–13, 1996.)
[24]*Digest of Education Statistics, 1997* (Washington, D.C.: U.S. Government Printing Office, 1997), Table 129, p. 133; and Steve Stecklow, "SAT Scores Rise Strongly After Test Is Overhauled," *The Wall Street Journal,* August 24, 1995, pp. B1, 11.
[25]*Digest of Education Statistics, 1997* Tables 120 and 123, pp. 125,128.

PROFESSIONAL PLANNING

for your first year

Really – What Is Your Educational Philosophy?

The Situation

Amanda Scott, a brand new eighth-grade teacher at Oxford Middle School, just finished her first postobservation conference with Ms. Renee, her principal. Although a positive and upbeat conference, Ms. Renee's comments keep ringing in Amanda's head. "Amanda," Ms. Renee said, "it's clear that you enjoy your students and that they respond well to the structure and expectations you've created. I was pleased with the flow of the lesson and the attention the students paid to you and to each other. But when you interviewed for this position, you described yourself as a 'facilitator of active learning,' and your portfolio showed you understood that approach. Now, though, what I see in your class is mostly teacher directed: lecture, vocabulary drills, worksheets, and so on. How are you building the students' capacities for creativity, autonomy, and critical thinking? Where's the Amanda Scott we interviewed? Next time I visit, I would like to see *that* Amanda in action."

"How could I get away from what I believe in?" Amanda scolds herself. The problem, she realizes, was that in her first few weeks as a teacher, feeling unsure of herself, she tried to be safe, to make sure her students were getting a basic foundation. Now it is time to challenge them and herself.

Later that day, while Amanda and several other teachers were eating lunch in the teacher's lounge, someone picked up the local morning paper, which had a lead article about the results of a statewide assessment program administered to eighth graders. Composite scores for every middle school in the metropolitan region were listed, and Oxford Middle was ranked in the bottom third. Amanda's school made marginal improvements over last year's tests in reading and math scores, but lost ground on the writing portion of the test.

Everyone in the lounge lamented the newspaper's remark that the school's progress was "not significant." They expressed pride in the advances their students made. They argued that most schools with comparable populations of low-income and culturally diverse students have not shown gains as great as Oxford Middle.

Bill O'Connell pointed to another article in the paper. This one featured members of a Citizen's Educational Advisory Council complaining about the schools' performance on the assessment program. Their demand was for a back-to-basics approach with more emphasis on factual knowledge and less on critical thinking and innovative and time-consuming teaching strategies.

Amanda asked herself, "What should I do?"

Thought Questions

1. What philosophical orientation is being expressed by each party in this dilemma (Amanda, Ms. Renee, the Citizen's Educational Advisory Council)?
2. Which of the orientations above best reflects your own personal philosophy of education?
3. If none does, can you think of someone who would represent your philosophy in this dilemma, such as a concerned parent or business leader in the community?
4. What would you do if you were a teacher at Oxford Middle School faced with this conflict in educational goals? Do you see any way to achieve both goals? What would you do if you were Amanda's principal? What do you think Amanda should do?

International comparisons

3. International comparisons of student achievement in the last two decades have revealed that on nineteen academic tests U.S. students were never first or second and, in comparison with other industrialized nations, were last seven times.[26] (See Chapter 15 for further discussion of international comparisons.)

Functional illiteracy

4. Some 21 to 23 percent of the 191 million U.S. adults are functionally illiterate by the simplest tests of everyday reading and writing. Moreover, about 13 percent of all seventeen-year-olds in the United States are considered functionally illiterate, and this illiteracy rate jumps to 40 percent among minority youth.[27] More alarming is that the average literacy skills of young adults (age sixteen to twenty-four) in 1993 were lower than they were in 1986, as reported in National Assessment of Educational Progress studies.[28]

Student-teacher ratios

5. These problems have occurred despite a relatively good student-teacher ratio: approximately 16 to 1 students per teacher in the United States, compared to ratios of over 25 to 1 in Japan and Korea. Moreover, our per-pupil expenditures for education K–12 have been the second highest in the world (second only to Finland).[29]

Reports' common themes

Six of the national reports from which these statistics are taken are summarized in Overview 13.2. All of these reports emphasize the need to strengthen the curriculum in the core subjects of English, math, science, foreign language, and social studies. Technology and computer courses are mentioned often, and at the dawn of the twenty-first century the need to improve students' technology skills and to upgrade schools technologically is almost a "mantra" — the fourth "R" as some call it. High-level cognitive and thinking skills are also stressed. Although some of the reports are also concerned with programs and personnel for disadvantaged students and students with learning disabilities, this message is not always loud and clear.

Importance of technology

Higher standards, more rigorous requirements

The reports further emphasize tougher standards and tougher courses, and a majority propose that colleges raise their admission requirements. Most of the reports also talk about increasing homework, time for learning, and time in school, as well as instituting more rigorous grading, testing, homework, and discipline. They mention upgrading teacher certification, increasing teacher salaries, increasing the number of science and math teachers and paying higher salaries, and providing merit pay for outstanding teachers. Overall, the reports stress academic achievement, not the whole child, and increased productivity, not relevancy or humanism.

Schools play too many roles

Most of the reports express concern that the schools are pressed to play too many social roles; that the schools cannot meet all these expectations; and that the schools are in danger of losing sight of their key purpose — teaching basic skills and core academic subjects, new skills for computer use, and higher-level cognitive skills for the world of work and technology. Many of the reports, concerned not only with academic productivity but also with national productivity, link human capital with economic capital. Investment in schools would be an investment in the economy and in the nation's future stability. If education fails, so do our work

---

[26]*The Condition of Education, 1997* (Washington, D.C.: U.S. Government Printing Office, 1997), pp.78–79; *Digest of Education Statistics, 1997*, Figures 31 and 32, p. 437.
[27]National Center for Educational Statistics, *Adult Literacy in America* (Washington D.C.: Office of Educational Research and Information, 1993).
[28]National Education Goals Panel, *Data Volume for the National Goals Report, Volume I, National Data, 1994* (Washington D.C.: U.S. Government Printing Office, 1994), pp. 92–94.
[29]*Digest of Education Statistics, 1997*, Table 393, p. 443; Table 399, p. 429. See also John Hood, "Education: Money Isn't Everything," *The Wall Street Journal*, February 9, 1990, p. 14.

OVERVIEW 13.2 Selected Recommendations of Six Reports on Education, 1983–1997

Report and Sponsor	Basic Recommendations	Content Emphasis	School Organization	Government-Business Role
Action for Excellence Education Commission of the States (1983)	Establish minimum competencies in reading, writing, speaking, listening, reasoning, and economics Strengthen program for gifted students Raise college entrance standards	English, math, science, foreign language, history, computer literacy	Consider longer school day Emphasize order and discipline More homework More rigorous grading with periodic testing Independent learning	Foster partnerships between private sector and education Increase federal funds for education
Educating Americans for the 21st Century National Science Foundation (1983)	Devote more time to math and science in elementary and secondary schools Provide more advanced courses in science and math Raise college entrance standards	Math, science, technology, computers	Consider longer school day, week, and/or year Twelve-year plan for math and science	With federal input, establish national goals for education Increase NSF role in curriculum development and teacher training
High School Carnegie Foundation for Achievement in Teaching (1983)	Stress mastery of language, including reading, writing, speaking, and listening Expand basic academic curriculum Aid student transition to work and further education Strengthen graduation requirements	Core of common learning, including English, history, civics, math, science, technology Computer literacy	Improved working conditions for teachers Use of technology to enrich curriculum Flexible schedules and time allotments One track for all students School-community learning activities Greater leadership role for principal	Make "connections" between school and community, business, and universities Increase parent and community coalitions with and service to schools Use retired personnel from business and colleges Give federal scholarships to science and math teachers

Report and Sponsor	Basic Recommendations	Content Emphasis	School Organization	Government-Business Role
A Nation at Risk National Commission on Excellence in Education (1983)	Improve textbooks and other instructional materials Provide more rigorous courses in vocational education, arts, and science Strengthen graduation requirements Raise college entrance requirements	Five new basics: English, math, science, social studies, and computer science	Consider seven-hour school day Tighten attendance and discipline More homework More rigorous grading and periodic testing Group students by performance rather than age	Increase federal cooperation with states and localities Meet needs of disadvantaged student populations as well as gifted and talented Establish national standardized tests
First Lessons: A Report on Elementary Education in America The Secretary of Education (1986)	Improve basic skills for young children Improve complex learning tasks and abilities for older children Increase knowledge base essential for democratic society and national identity Improve textbook and workbook writing and selection Raise academic standards	Basic skills, especially reading through phonics Problem-solving skills in mathematics and hands-on learning and discovery in science Unified sequence stressing history, geography, and civics Computer literacy and cultural literacy	Longer school day More homework More rigorous testing Parental choice in children's schools Rewards for teacher performance	Increase communitywide and parental responsibility in education Require teacher and school accountability Improve training programs for elementary teachers; emphasize arts and science rather than methods courses
The National Educational Goals U.S. Department of Education (1990, 1994, 1997)	Focus on all students, with emphasis on at-risk students Equip students with knowledge and skills necessary for responsible citizenship and world of work Ensure readiness for school; upgrade school standards and student achievement	Basic knowledge and skills Reasoning and problem-solving skills Math, science, English, history, and geography Drug and alcohol prevention programs	Preschool programs for all disadvantaged learners Parental training for child's early learning; parental choice in children's schools Up-to-date instructional technology Multilayer system of vocational, technical, and community colleges	Inspire reform at the federal, state, and local levels Enlist assistance of parents, community, business, and civic groups; involve all parts of society

OVERVIEW 13.2   **Selected Recommendations of Six Reports on Education, 1983–1997** (*continued*)

Report and Sponsor	Basic Recommendations	Content Emphasis	School Organization	Government-Business Role
The National Educational Goals U.S. Department of Education (1990, 1994, 1997) (*continued*)	Improve adult literacy and lifelong education Provide a safe and drug-free school environment Strengthen teacher education and development and increase parental involvement	Citizenship, community service, cultural literacy, and knowledge of the international community	More student loans, scholarships, and work study programs in higher education Upgrade teacher preparation; reward teachers but hold them accountable	Create effective apprenticeships, job training, teacher-employee exchanges, and adopt-a-school programs Increase flexibility, innovation, accountability, and results Targets established for the year 2000

force and nation. Hence business, labor, and government must work with educators to help educate and train the U.S. population.

In the following sections, we will look more closely at the two most popularized and influential reports: *A Nation at Risk,* published in 1983, and ***The National Education Goals,*** a 1994 revision of a report first published in 1990.

Rising tide of mediocrity

A Nation at Risk.   The report by the National Commission on Excellence in Education, compiled by a panel appointed by the Department of Education, indicates that the well-being of the nation is being eroded by a "rising tide of mediocrity."[30] This mediocrity is linked to the foundations of our educational institutions and is spilling over into the workplace and other sectors of society. The report lists several aspects of educational decline that were evident to educators and citizens alike in the late 1970s and early 1980s: lower achievement scores, lower testing requirements, lower graduation requirements, lower teacher expectations, fewer academic courses, more remedial courses, and higher illiteracy rates. It states that the United States has compromised its commitment to educational quality as a result of conflicting demands placed on the nation's schools and concludes that the schools have attempted to tackle too many social problems that the home and other agencies of society either will not or cannot resolve.

Recommendations of A Nation at Risk

The report calls for, among other things, tougher standards for graduation, including more courses in science, mathematics, foreign language, and the "new ba-

---

[30]National Commission on Excellence in Education, *A Nation at Risk: The Imperative for Educational Reform* (Washington, D.C.: U.S. Department of Education, 1983).

sics" such as computer skills; a longer school day and school year; far more homework; improved and updated textbooks; more rigorous, measurable, and higher expectations for student achievement; higher teacher salaries based on performance, and career ladders that distinguish among the beginning, experienced, and master teacher; demonstrated entry competencies and more rigorous certification standards for teachers; accountability from educators and policy makers; and greater fiscal support from citizens.

Reports such as *A Nation at Risk* and Educational Policies Commission reports often spring from a broad-based concern about the quality of public education in changing times. The goal of these reports is to make practical recommendations for educational improvement and, as such, provide guidance to state and local boards of education, school districts, and ultimately teachers as they plan for instruction. The impact of *A Nation at Risk* has been substantial, driving increases in high school graduation requirements, increases in mathematics and science courses, a return to academic basics, changes in technology, and increased college entrance requirements. Most of these changes occurred at the local school district level.

The National Education Goals.   In 1990, President George Bush announced the establishment of national goals for education that would serve as guidelines for state and local education agencies. The overriding theme of the published document was the push for an educated citizenry, well trained and responsible, capable of adapting to a changing world, knowledgeable of its cultural heritage and the world community, and willing to accept and maintain America's leadership position in the twenty-first century. The contention was that "sweeping changes" in schools must be made if we are "to maintain our strength and international competitiveness."[31] Educators must be given greater flexibility to devise teaching and learning strategies that serve all students, regardless of abilities or interests; at the same time, they should be held responsible for their teaching. Parents must become involved in their children's education, especially during the preschool years. Community, civic, and business groups all have a vital role to play in reforming education. Finally, students must accept responsibility for their education, and this means they must work hard in school.

The original report outlined six national goals to be reached by the year 2000. In 1994 Congress passed **Goals 2000:** Educate America Act, which added two new goals to address the critical areas of teacher education and professional development and parental participation. The complete set of goals, published as *The National Education Goals* and often referred to simply as Goals 2000, is listed in Table 13.3.

In 1997, the National Education Goals Panel issued a progress report on the 8 goals and 26 "indicators" in Goals 2000. They found 6 indicators that had improved significantly: infants with health risks, 2-year-old immunization, families reading to children, mathematics achievement, degrees granted in math and science, and incidents of threats and injuries to students in school. Correspondingly, the Panel found 7 areas in which performance has declined: grade 12 reading achievement, percent of secondary teachers with degree in main teaching assignment, participation in adult education programs, student drug use, sale of drugs at school, threats and injuries to public school teachers, and classroom disruptions

"Sweeping changes" demanded

Developing national standards

---

[31]*National Goals for Education* (Washington, D.C.: U.S. Department of Education, 1990), pp. 1–2.

GETTING TO THE SOURCE

A Nation at Risk

Issued in 1983, the landmark report *A Nation at Risk* alerted Americans to the dangers of an inadequate educational system. Stressing the challenge of international economic competition, the report emphasized the need to prepare a skilled work force for the "information age." Many subsequent reports and commentaries have sounded familiar calls for educational reform.

Our Nation is at risk. Our once unchallenged pre-eminence in commerce, industry, science, and technological innovation is being overtaken by competitors throughout the world. This report is concerned with only one of the many causes and dimensions of the problem, but it is the one that undergirds American prosperity, security, and civility. We report to the American people that while we can take justifiable pride in what our schools and colleges have historically accomplished and contributed to the United States and the well-being of its people, the educational foundations of our society are presently being eroded by a rising tide of mediocrity that threatens our very future as a Nation and a people. What was unimaginable a generation ago has begun to occur — others are matching and surpassing our educational attainments.

If an unfriendly foreign power had attempted to impose on America the mediocre educational performance that exists today, we might well have viewed it as an act of war. As it stands, we have allowed this to happen to ourselves. We have even squandered the gains in student achievement made in the wake of the *Sputnik* challenge. Moreover, we have dismantled essential support systems which helped make those gains possible. We have, in effect, been committing an act of unthinking, unilateral educational disarmament. . . .

Progress report on National Goals

that interfere with teaching. Another 7 indicators showed no change. While the *National Education Goals* report shows positive gains in math and science proficiency, American students barely perform at the international average in comparisons. Obviously, areas of decline continue to be a source of concern. In an effort to address these concerns, the Goals Panel is proposing tougher standards, comparable to the best in the world; aligning all components of the education system with these standards; and strengthening teachers' subject-matter knowledge and teaching skills.[32]

The Educate America Act also formalized the development of national standards, such as content, performance, and opportunity-to-learn standards, and authorized the development of standards for students not bound for college. Although the program was voluntary, states were to receive money if their standards were certified by national panels; $5 billion was authorized over the first five years.[33]

---

[32]National Education Goals Panel, *The National Education Goals Report: Building a Nation of Learners* (Washington, D.C.: U.S. Government Printing Office, 1997).
[33]*The National Education Goals* (Washington, D.C.: U.S. Department of Education, 1994), pp. 1–4; and Stephen Arons, *Short Route to Chaos: Conscience, Community and the Re-Constitution of American Schooling* (Amherst: University of Massachusetts Press, 1997).

History is not kind to idlers. The time is long past when America's destiny was assured simply by an abundance of natural resources and inexhaustible human enthusiasm, and by our relative isolation from the malignant problems of older civilizations. The world is indeed one global village. We live among determined, well-educated, and strongly motivated competitors. We compete with them for international standing and markets, not only with products but also with the ideas of our laboratories and neighborhood workshops. America's position in the world may once have been reasonably secure with only a few exceptionally well-trained men and women. It is no longer.

The risk is not only that the Japanese make automobiles more efficiently than Americans and have government subsidies for development and export. It is not just that the South Koreans recently built the world's most efficient steel mill, or that American machine tools, once the pride of the world, are being displaced by German products. It is also that these developments signify a redistribution of trained capability throughout the globe. Knowledge, learning, information, and skilled intelligence are the new raw materials of international commerce and are today spreading throughout the world as vigorously as miracle drugs, synthetic fertilizers, and blue jeans did

earlier. If only to keep and improve on the slim competitive edge we still retain in world markets, we must dedicate ourselves to the reform of our educational system for the benefit of all — old and young alike, affluent and poor, majority and minority. Learning is the indispensable investment required for success in the "information age" we are entering.

Questions

1. What new skills are needed for the information age? Are they indeed *new*?
2. In your view, what educational reforms are most important for improving our "competitive edge"?
3. Should American students and schools be judged competitively today with students of other nations? Explain why or why not.
4. Which philosophy of education mentioned in Chapter 12 most closely reflects the views expressed in *A Nation at Risk*? How comfortable are you with this phylosophy?

Source: National Commission on Excellence in Education, *A Nation at Risk: The Imperative for Educational Reform* (Washington, D.C.: U.S. Department of Education, 1983), cover, pp. 1–2, 5.

Assessment and Action

As mentioned above, national reports often address the educational concerns of the times and make recommendations for educational improvement. These recommendations, however, do not always filter down to the school district and classroom level.

Criticisms of the reports

Criticisms of the various national reports by the educational community tend to center on three major points: (1) the reports are too idealistic and therefore unrealistic; (2) they put too much emphasis on excellence at the expense of equity; and (3) they are enormously expensive to implement. Although it is true that school districts can easily "accomplish" such changes as more rigorous homework or graduation requirements by mandating them, the history of school improvement shows that substantial funding is required to support effective change on a school-by-school basis. The Goals 2000 act did provide $5 billion in focused aid to states, but critics contended that was not nearly enough.

Ignoring complex realities?

Some educators point out that the reports ignore a basic fact about school change and improvement: that the process is complex and involves the cooperation of teachers, administrators, parents, and community members, all of whom

The demand for highly skilled workers is accelerating rapidly amid growing concern that the United States is being overtaken by other nations in commerce, industry, science, and technology. (© Peter Menzel/Stock Boston)

often have different agendas and ideas about reform.[34] Others say the reports ignore the realities of students' situations — the "whole-child" view. Why talk about raising standards when most at-risk students cannot even meet existing standards because of their difficult social and home environments?[35] Seasoned educators have learned, sometimes the hard way, that there are no "magic bullets" for reforming schools. David Cohen notes that "America is awash with competing schemes to save the schools," and Goals 2000 "seems like just another voice in the babel of reform proposals."[36] Moreover, the education highways are cluttered with reforms that have run out of gas — the "wrecks" of famous bandwagons.[37] Why should today's reform movement be any different?

A new consensus   One reason, according to former NEA president Mary Futrell, is that there seems to be a new consensus on the necessity of providing high-quality education for *all* students. Reflecting this new consensus, coalitions are now being formed among government, corporate, and educational groups.[38] It has taken many years to reach this point of cooperation.

[34]See, for example, Thomas R. Guskey, "Guidelines for School Innovation," *Education Digest* (October 1990), pp. 23–27.
[35]Iris R. Weiss, *The Status of Science and Mathematics Teaching in the United States: Comparing Teacher Views and Classroom Practice to National Standards* (Madison, Wisc.: National Institute for Science Education, 1997).
[36]David Cohen, "What Standards for National Standards?" *Phi Delta Kappan* (June 1995), pp. 751–757; Herbert London, "National Standards for History Judged Again" (January–February 1997), pp. 26–28.
[37]Ron Brandt, Keynote Address to Washington State Association for Curriculum Development and Supervision, Seattle, February 11, 1983; and Howard D. Mehlinger, *School Reform in the Information Age* (Bloomington: Center for Excellence in Education, 1995).
[38]Mary Hatwood Futrell, "Mission Not Accomplished: Education Reform in Retrospect," *Phi Delta Kappan* (September 1989), pp. 1–4; and Laura Miller, "Focus on Student Learning Is Key to School Restructuring," *Education Week,* November 8, 1995, p. 6.

TABLE 13.3   The National Education Goals

Goal 1   School Readiness
By the year 2000, all children in America will start school ready to learn.

Goal 2   School Completion
By the year 2000, the high school graduation rate will increase to at least 90 percent.

Goal 3   Student Achievement and Citizenship
By the year 2000, all students will leave grades 4, 8, and 12 having demonstrated competency over challenging subject matter including English, mathematics, science, foreign languages, civics and government, economics, arts, history, and geography, and every school in America will ensure that all students learn to use their minds well, so they may be prepared for responsible citizenship, further learning, and productive employment in our Nation's modern economy.

Goal 4   Teacher Education and Professional Development
By the year 2000, the Nation's teaching force will have access to programs for the continued improvement of their professional skills and the opportunity to acquire the knowledge and skills needed to instruct and prepare all American students for the next century.

Goal 5   Mathematics and Science
By the year 2000, United States students will be first in the world in mathematics and science achievement.

Goal 6   Adult Literacy and Lifelong Learning
By the year 2000, every adult American will be literate and will possess the knowledge and skills necessary to compete in a global economy and exercise the rights and responsibilities of citizenship.

Goal 7   Safe, Disciplined, and Alcohol- and Drug-free Schools
By the year 2000, every school in the United States will be free of drugs, violence, and the unauthorized presence of firearms and alcohol and will offer a disciplined environment conducive to learning.

Goal 8   Parental Participation
By the year 2000, every school will promote partnerships that will increase parental involvement and participation in promoting the social, emotional, and academic growth of children.

Source: Goals 2000: Educate America Act (March 31, 1994); *The National Education Goals* (Washington, D.C.: U.S. Department of Education, 1994).

Reasons for optimism

Furthermore, as educators assert, the political force driving educational reform is another basis for optimism. Reforms in the past were based on educational ideas that did not necessarily have widespread support from legislators or policy makers, much less the public.[39] Today, the fear about American decline touches far more people than ever before, and they seem willing to do something about it. People are now making the connection between education and economics, realizing that school failures are tied to economic failures and that it is time to invest in children and youth. There seems to be a guarded willingness on the part of the public to spend money on education, as long as educators show substantive results.[40] Some recent findings offer at least a taste of the results the public wants to see. SAT scores rose significantly in 1995 for the first time in years. The 1998 elections reflected this

[39]David S. Seeley, "Carrying School Reform into the 1990s," *Education Digest* (May 1990), pp. 3–6; and Albertina Bailey et al., *School Reform: The Legal Challenges of Change* (Alexandria: National School Boards Association, 1996).
[40]Lonnie Harp, "State Results Called a Vote for Moderation," *Education Week*, November 15, 1995, p. 16; Drew Lindsay, "Mills Calls for Higher Standards for N.Y. Students, Schools," *Education Week*, November 15, 1995, p. 17; and Jessica Sondham, "Moderation the Theme in Gubernatorial Races," *Education Week*, November 11, 1998, pp. 13–14.

Signs of improvement

willingness to commit additional financial resources to public education at both the national and state levels.[41] In addition, a study of high-school students ten years after *A Nation at Risk* showed several positive indicators of change. First, high-school students were taking more courses, particularly in academic areas. Second, NAEP scores showed increased student learning in math and science, even among lower-ability students. Third, fewer students were dropping out of high school, and finally, student educational aspirations were increasing. These were changes of a positive nature, even though much concern remained for the high level of eighth- and ninth-grade dropouts, especially in urban schools.[42]

State reform efforts

Overall, the national reports on education have captured public attention, spotlighted concern for the quality of education, and helped to upgrade school standards. In the last decade and a half, nearly all the states have revised their curricula, raised high-school graduation requirements (especially in math and science), established competency testing for teachers and students, or adopted other well-publicized reform measures. In the view of many educators these reforms merely scratch the surface. Nevertheless, we may now have the best opportunity we have had in generations for a comprehensive and effective reform of American schools.

Swings of the Pendulum

Old themes reemerge

In examining educational goals from the turn of the twentieth century until today, we see considerable change but also old ideas reemerging in updated versions. For example, a stress on rigorous intellectual training, evident in the early twentieth century, reappeared in the 1950s during the Cold War and again in the 1980s and 1990s as a result of concern over economic competition with foreign countries. Similarly, as the social ferment of the 1960s and 1970s brought increasing concern for the rights and aspirations of low-income and minority groups, the ideas of the early progressive educators resurfaced, and a renewed stress was placed on educating the disadvantaged. Although this concern for disadvantaged or at-risk students remains, the pendulum has now swung closer to the center: our current priorities are more diffuse, and there is growing concern for various kinds of students, including average and academically talented groups.

Too much expected of schools?

In looking at the broad sweep of American educational purposes, you may ask yourself whether schools are expected to do more than is feasible. The schools are often seen as ideal agencies to solve the nation's problems, but can they do so? Many people throughout society refuse to admit their own responsibility for helping children develop and learn. Similarly, parents and policy makers often expect teachers and school administrators to be solely responsible for school reform. In fact, without significant cooperation from parents and community members, schools cannot do a good job, and reform efforts will fail.

Coping with change

Unquestionably, the goals of education must be relevant to the times. If the schools cannot adapt to changing conditions and social forces, how can they expect to produce people who do? Today we live in a highly technical, automated, and bureaucratic society, and we are faced with pressing social and economic problems — aging cities, the effects of centuries of racial and sexual discrimination, an aging population, economic dislocations, and the pollution of the physical envi-

---

[41]Stecklow, "SAT Scores Rise Sharply."
[42]*The Condition of Education, 1997*, pp. 1–15; and Chester Finn, Michael Petrilli, Susan Pimentel, and Leslye Arsht, "The State of State Standards," *Education Week*, November 11, 1998, pp. 56; 39,40.

ronment. Whether we allow the times to engulf us, or whether we can cope with our new environment, will depend to a large extent on what kinds of skills are taught to our present-day students — and on the development of appropriate priorities for education.

Summing Up

1. The purposes of education are influenced by changing social forces as well as by educational philosophies and theories.

2. Broad statements of educational purpose, generated at the national or state level, are usually translated into more specific goals by the school district or individual school. These goals, in turn, are developed into even more specific objectives at the subject/grade, unit plan, and lesson plan levels.

3. Since the turn of the century, the goals of American education have gone through at least five periods, each with a different focus of attention: academic rigor and mental discipline; the whole child; academically talented students; disadvantaged and minority students and children with disabilities; and, in the 1980s and 1990s, tougher academic standards for all students.

4. Most of the major reports released since 1983 have emphasized the need for educational excellence and higher standards. Although educators disagree about many of the reports' recommendations, most states have already implemented changes based on these reports.

5. We must learn to live with some disagreement about the purposes of schooling. Various groups of people need to work together in formulating future educational priorities.

6. We often expect schools to be a key instrument for solving our technological or social problems and preparing our work force for the future. The years ahead will severely test this expectation.

Key Terms

goals *(426)*

objectives *(426)*

mental discipline approach *(431)*

Cardinal Principles of Secondary Education (431)

Education for All American Youth (431)

whole-child concept *(431)*

outcomes-based education (OBE) *(437)*

A Nation at Risk (442)

The National Education Goals (442)

Goals 2000 *(443)*

Discussion Questions

1. In terms of the various types and levels of educational goals, why is the question "What are schools for?" so complex?

2. Are the goals of the Educational Policies Commission, as summarized in the right-hand column of Table 13.2, desirable for education today? Based on your personal philosophy of education, how might you modify them?

3. Who should have educational priority: below-average students, average students, or above-average students? What philosophical leanings and social forces influence your answer to the question?

4. What is your opinion of the National Education Goals? Discuss your thinking with another student in class, if possible with several students. What other national goals might you suggest? How do these goals align with your emerging philosophy of education?

5. What argument could you make for or against computer technology and skills as a "new basic" or "fourth R"?

Suggested Projects for Professional Development

1. As you visit schools, ask to examine any goal statements that are available, such as position papers, mission statements, and school improvement plans. How do teachers and administrators think the goals will be implemented? How would you implement them?

2. Select a school with yearly goals and ask to see its goal statements. Talk with teachers and administrators to find out the following: the process by which the goals were developed, who developed them, how parents and the community were involved in the process, and how assessment of goals takes place. How would you feel about this process if you were participating? What would you see as your role?

3. Write Goals 2010. Be as idealistic as you like, but also realistic. How do you believe you, as a teacher, would work toward your Goals 2010?

4. In groups of two or three, work with classmates to analyze how the National Education Goals address the needs of diverse student populations, particularly students with disabilities and the educationally disadvantaged. Select one National Goal and describe how a local school district might meet it.

Suggested Readings and Resources

Internet Resources

Access the federal Department of Education's Web sites (**www.ed.gov** or **gopher.ed.gov**) for the full texts of the Goals 2000: Educate America Act, the Improving America's Schools Act of 1994, and the National Educational Goals Panel Report of 1997. Up-to-date status reports on the Goals 2000 project are offered at the subsidiary Web page **www.ed.gov/legislation/GOALS 2000/index.html.** One starting point for general information about educational reform is the index at **www.io.org/~ klima/ed.html.** Topics such as "accountability" and "gifted students" can be pursued by searching the Department of Education's sites or by starting with a search for "ASK ERIC." General Internet searches for key terms such as *educational technology, school reform* and *national/state standards* can also be useful.

Videos

Visions of Literacy. VHS (1993). Hineman Educational Books, 361 Hanover St., Portsmouth, NH 03801. Phone: 800–541–2086. *A series with a number of individual programs relevant to issues raised in this chapter: for example,* Children at Risk *(30 minutes) and* Multicultural Education *(28 minutes).*

Reinventing Our Schools. VHS, 28 to 29 minutes per program (1994). Agency for Instructional Technology and Phi Delta Kappa, P.O. Box 789, Bloomington, IN

47402. Phone: 800–766–1156. *An excellent series of six videotapes in which renowned educators present their views on the reform process in American education.*

Publications

Conant, James B. *The American High School Today.* New York: McGraw-Hill, 1959. *A classic written during the* Sputnik *era, this book offers many recommendations for upgrading the high-school curriculum.*

Duke, Daniel, and Robert L. Canady. *School Policy.* New York: McGraw-Hill, 1991. *A compact book on federal, state, and local school policy — and on how to formulate, evaluate, and revise goals of education.*

Gardner, John W. *Excellence: Can We Be Equal and Excellent Too?* New York: Harper and Row, 1961. *Another classic text, this book remains relevant today. The questions and issues it raises are still of deep concern in American schools and society.*

Goals 2000: Educate America Act. Washington, D.C.: U.S. Government Printing Office, 1994. *Describes Goals 2000, detailing the eight major goals for improving American schools.*

National Commission on Excellence in Education. *A Nation at Risk: The Imperative for Educational Reform.* Washington, D.C.: U.S. Department of Education, 1983. *Among the recent reports on American education, this one has had the most political impact.*

National Education Goals Panel. *The National Education Goals Report: Building a Nation of Learners.* Washington, D.C.: U.S. Government Printing Office, 1997. *An Evaluation of Goals 2000 and Its Twenty-Six Indicators.*

Ravitch, Diane, and Maris A. Vinovskis, eds. *Learning from the Past: What History Teaches Us About School Reform.* Baltimore: Johns Hopkins University Press, 1995. *An excellent work on standards in American education; issues of federal, state, and local control; equity and the changing conception of multiculturalism; and school reform strategies.*

Spring, Joel. *American Education.* 7th ed. Hightstown, N.J.: McGraw-Hill, 1996. *A concise look at the purposes of public schooling and multicultural education issues.*

Spring, Joel. *Wheels in the Head: Educational Philosophies of Authority, Freedom, and Culture from Socrates to Human Rights.* 2nd ed. New York: McGraw-Hill, 1999. *A wonderful little book dealing with philosophies of schooling and critical questions educators need to think about as they shape teaching and learning in classrooms, school districts, and society.*

CHAPTER FOURTEEN

Curriculum and Instruction

Perhaps more than the citizens of any other country, Americans have demanded the utmost from their schools. We ask the schools to teach children to think, to socialize them, to alleviate poverty and inequality, to reduce crime, to perpetuate our cultural heritage, and to produce intelligent, patriotic citizens. Inevitably, American schools have been unable to meet all of these obligations. Nonetheless, the demands persist, and the **curriculum** — the planned experiences provided through instruction — is their focal point. Consequently, the curriculum is continuously modified as the goals of education are revised, as student populations change, as social issues are debated, and as new interest groups are activated.

The goals of education have shifted as national priorities and social pressures have changed. In this chapter we will look at several major curricular approaches of recent decades. You will see that they are closely related to the philosophies and theories discussed in Chapter 12 and to the various goals of education described in Chapter 13.[1] You might begin to think about these curricular approaches in light of your own emerging philosophy of education.

As we examine curriculum, we will also examine instructional activities that relate to curriculum. This chapter will help you answer the following questions:

- How does curriculum content reflect changes in society?

- What are some of the ways in which curriculum is organized?

- How might the use of cooperative learning or mastery learning influence your work as a teacher?

- How can computers and other electronic resources be used in the classroom to improve instruction?

- What are some trends that seem likely to affect curriculum and instruction in the future?

This chapter was revised by Dr. James Lawlor, Towson University

[1]See R. Freeman Butts, *The Revival of Civic Learning* (Bloomington, Ind.: Phi Delta Kappa, 1980); Lawrence A. Cremin, *American Education: The National Experience* (New York: Harper and Row, 1980); and Lawrence A. Cremin, *The Transformation of the School* (New York: Random House, 1964).

Curriculum Organization

Subject matter vs. student needs

Curriculum blends

Organization by subjects

Arguments pro and con

Drawing on the classical tradition

The various types of curriculum organization in American schools can be viewed from two perspectives. One emphasizes the subject to be taught; the other emphasizes the student. In the first case, the curriculum is seen as a body of content, or subject matter, that leads to certain achievement outcomes or products. The second approach defines curriculum in terms of the needs and attitudes of the student; the concern is with process — in other words, how the student learns and the climate of the classroom or school.

Actually, the two views represent the extremes of a continuum, and most practitioners (and researchers) rely on some curriculum blend within this continuum. Few schools employ pure subject-centered (cognitive) or pure student-centered (psychological) approaches in the teaching-learning process. Even though most teachers tend to emphasize one approach over the other, they incorporate both choices in the classroom.

Subject-Centered Curricula

Subject matter is both the oldest and most contemporary framework of curriculum organization. It is also the most common — primarily because it is convenient, as evidenced by the departmental structure of secondary schools and colleges. Curricular changes usually occur at the departmental level. Courses are added, omitted, or modified, but faculty members rarely engage in comprehensive, systematic curriculum development and evaluation. Even in elementary schools, where self-contained classrooms force the teachers to be generalists, curricula are usually organized by subjects.

Proponents of **subject-centered curricula** argue that subjects are a logical way to organize and interpret learning, that teachers are trained as subject-matter specialists, and that textbooks and other teaching materials are usually organized by subject. Critics claim that subject-centered curricula are often a mass of facts and concepts learned in isolation. They see this kind of curriculum as deemphasizing life experiences and failing to consider the needs and interests of students. In subject-centered curricula, the critics argue, the teacher dominates the lesson, allowing little student input.

The following sections discuss several variations of subject-centered approaches to curricula, such as the subject-area approach, back-to-basics, and the core curriculum. These are not the only possible variations, nor do they represent hard-and-fast categories. Many schools and teachers mix these approaches, drawing from more than one of them.

Subject-Area Approach to Curriculum. The subject-area approach is the oldest and most widely used form of curriculum organization. It has its roots in the seven liberal arts of classical Greece and Rome: grammar, rhetoric, dialectic, arithmetic, geometry, astronomy, and music. Modern subject-area curricula trace their origins to the work of William Harris, superintendent of the St. Louis school system in the 1870s. Steeped in the classical tradition, Harris established a subject orientation that has virtually dominated U.S. curricula from his day to the present. For example, consider Table 14.1, which shows the recommendations of the Committee of Fifteen in 1895. Although the committee's proposal is more than a century old, the subject categories are quite recognizable. Students today are still introduced to "algebra" and "English grammar," "reading" and "writing," as well as "geography" and "history."

TABLE 14.1 The Elementary School Curriculum Proposed by the Committee of Fifteen in 1895

Branches	1st year	2nd year	3rd year	4th year	5th year	6th year	7th year	8th year
Reading	10 lessons a week		5 lessons a week					
Writing	10 lessons a week		5 lessons a week		3 lessons a week			
Spelling lists				4 lessons a week				
English Grammar	Oral with composition lessons				5 lessons a week with textbook			
Latin								5 lessons a week
Arithmetic	Oral, 60 minutes a week		5 lessons a week with textbook					
Algebra							5 lessons a week	
Geography	Oral, 60 minutes a week		*5 lessons a week with textbook				3 lessons a week	
Natural science and hygiene	60 minutes a week							
U.S. history							5 lessons a week	
U.S. Constitution								*5 lessons a week
General history	Oral, 60 minutes a week							
Physical culture	60 minutes a week							
Vocal music	60 minutes a week divided into 4 lessons							
Drawing	60 minutes a week							
Manual training or sewing and cooking							One-half day each	
Total hours of recitation	12	12	11	13	16¼	16¼	17½	17½

Questions

1 If your major is early childhood or elementary education, study the Committee of Fifteen's proposals for grades 1–5. How do the suggested subjects and their treatment compare with curriculum treatment you believe students should receive today? List specific additions and deletions.

2 If your major is secondary education, do the same as in question 1 for grades 6, 7, and 8. How do the committee's suggested subjects and treatment compare with the curriculum treatment you feel students should receive today? List specific additions and deletions.

3 Which theories of education described in Chapter 12 best fit the Committee of Fifteen's proposals? What evidence in Table 14.1 supports your choice of theories?

*Begins in second half of year.

Source: Committee of Fifteen, "Report of the Sub-Committee on the Correlation of Studies in Elementary Education," *Educational Review* (March 1895), p. 284.

Categories of subjects

The modern **subject-area curriculum** treats each subject as a specialized and largely autonomous body of knowledge. Some subjects, often referred to as the "basics," are considered essential for all students; these usually include the three Rs at the elementary level and English, history, science, and mathematics at the secondary level. Other specialized subjects develop knowledge and skills for particular vocations or professions — for example, business mathematics and physics. Finally, elective content affords the student optional offerings, often tailored to student interests and needs.

Exploratory subjects

A newer term, *exploratory subjects,* refers to subjects that students are allowed to choose from a list of courses designed to suit a wide range of learning styles, needs, and interests. These courses, which can include such subjects as study skills, computer science, creative writing, and drama, are a way for the school to diversify its offerings and are most often found in middle school and late elementary school curricula.[2] Schools that include exploratory subjects in the curriculum tend to be more progressive in outlook than schools that still favor the traditional core academic subjects.

Perennialism: the best of the past

Perennialist and Essentialist Approaches to Curriculum. Two of the educational theories described in Chapter 12 are fundamentally subject centered: perennialism and essentialism.[3] Believing that the main purpose of education is the cultivation of the intellect and of certain timeless values concerning work, morality, and family living, the perennialists concentrate their curriculum on the three Rs, Latin, and logic at the elementary level, adding study of the classics at the secondary level. The assumption of the **perennialist approach to curriculum**, according to Robert Hutchins, is that the best of the past — the so-called permanent studies, or classics — is equally valid for the present.[4]

Essentialism: major disciplines, cultural literacy

Essentialists believe that the elementary curriculum should consist of the three Rs, and the high-school curriculum of five or six major disciplines: English (grammar, literature, and writing), mathematics, the sciences, history, foreign languages, and, geography.[5] Adherents of the **essentialist approach to curriculum** believe these subject areas constitute the best way of systematizing and keeping up with the explosion of knowledge. They argue that mere "basic" skills are insufficient preparation for life. Students need an academic knowledge base — what they call "cultural literacy" or "essential knowledge" — to deal with new ideas and challenges.[6]

Rigorous intellectual training and grading

Essentialism shares with perennialism the notion that the curriculum should focus on rigorous intellectual training, a training possible only through the study of certain subjects. Both perennialists and essentialists advocate educational meritocracy. They favor high academic standards and a rigorous system of grading and

---

[2]Allan C. Ornstein, *Middle and Secondary School Methods* (New York: Harper and Row, 1992); Paula DeHart and Perry Cook, "Transforming Middle Schools Through Integrated Curriculum," *Voices from the Middle* (April 1997) pp. 2–6.
[3]These two terms were coined by Theodore Brameld in *Patterns of Educational Philosophy* (New York: Holt, 1950).
[4]Robert M. Hutchins, *The Higher Learning in America* (New Haven, Conn.: Yale University Press, 1936). See also Allan Bloom, *The Closing of the American Mind* (New York: Simon and Schuster, 1987); and E. D. Hirsch, *Cultural Literacy: Rediscovering Knowledge in American Education* (Boston: Houghton Mifflin, 1987).
[5]For classic statements of this approach, see Arthur Bestor, *The Restoration of Learning* (New York: Knopf, 1956); and James B. Conant, *The American High School Today* (New York: McGraw-Hill, 1959).
[6]See, for example, E. D. Hirsch, "The Core Knowledge Curriculum — What's Behind Its Success?" *Educational Leadership* (May 1993), pp. 23–25, 27–30; Norman Bauer, *Essential Schools and the Basics; Resisting Technocratic Rationality, 1993* ERIC Document Number 356560).

testing to help schools sort students by ability. Today, many parochial schools and academically oriented public schools stress various aspects of the perennialist and essentialist curricula.

Public opinion favoring "basics"

Back-to-Basics Approach to Curriculum. In recent years many educators and laypeople have called for a **back-to-basics curriculum.** Between 1976 and 1998, in annual Gallup Polls that asked the public to suggest ways to improve education, "devoting more attention to teaching the basics" and "improving curriculum standards" ranked no lower than fifth in the list of responses.[7]

Stress on solid subjects

Like the essentialist curriculum approach, back-to-basics connotes a heavy emphasis on reading, writing, and mathematics. So-called solid subjects — English, history, science, and mathematics — are required in all grades, and the back-to-basics proponents are even more suspicious than the essentialists of attempts to expand the curriculum beyond this solid foundation. Critics of this approach worry that a focus on basics will suppress students' creativity and shortchange other domains of learning, encouraging conformity and dependence on authority.[8]

Standards and testing

Back-to-basics proponents insist on the need to maintain minimum standards, and much of the state school reform legislation passed in the 1980s and 1990s reflects this popular position. The push for national tests in major subject areas by the Clinton administration further emphasized the importance of mastery of basic subjects. In most states, standardized tests serve a "gatekeeping" function at selected

A back-to-basics curriculum places heavy emphasis on reading, writing, and mathematics. *(© Charles Gupton/ Stock Boston)*

---

[7]See the annual Gallup Polls published in the September or October issues of *Phi Delta Kappan*, 1976 to 1998.
[8]For various perspectives on the debate, see Wendy Schiller, "The Arts: The Real Business of Education," *Early Child Development and Care* 90 (1993), pp. 5–13; Elliot W. Eisner, "What Really Counts in School," *Educational Leadership* (February 1991), pp. 10–17; and Bruce R. Joyce, "The Doors to School Improvement," *Educational Digest* (May 1991), pp. 59–62.

points on the educational ladder. Forty-five states also require students to pass a statewide exit test before receiving a high-school diploma.[9]

Core Approach to Curriculum.   The importance of basic subjects in the curriculum is also expressed by the term *core curriculum*. Unfortunately, in the post–World War II era, this term has been used to describe two different approaches to organizing curricula.

The first core curriculum

The first approach, which we will call *core curriculum*, originally developed in the 1940s and 1950s and is popular again today, especially in middle schools. In this approach, students study two closely related subjects taught by the same instructor (for example, math and science, or English and social studies). The teacher organizes instructional units in an interdisciplinary manner, showing how diverse subjects relate to one another.[10] This approach, sometimes called block scheduling (a block of time for math and a block for science), is tied to a progressive theory of education.

The new core curriculum

The second approach, in contrast, was born out of the educational reform movement of the 1980s and reflects the more conservative theory of essentialism. In this version, which we will call the **new core curriculum** or **core subjects approach**, the desire is for students to experience a common body of required subjects — subjects that advocates believe are central to the education of all students.[11] Mortimer Adler is best known for popularizing this new core curriculum idea at the elementary school level. Ernest Boyer, John Goodlad, and Theodore Sizer are best known for their similar influence on high schools; they believe that the typical secondary school curriculum fails to offer an overall conceptual framework or a balanced preparation for further academics or for the world of work. Boyer and Sizer contend that high schools should focus on the education of the intellect rather than offer learning in all domains of life.[12]

Expanding the core units

Both Boyer and Sizer emphasize the humanities, communication and language skills, science, math, and technology. Boyer believes that the core units required for graduation should be expanded from one-half of the total curriculum (now the norm) to about two-thirds. Goodlad would like to see about 80 percent of the curriculum devoted to core courses, with only 20 percent reserved for the development of individual talents and interests.[13]

Stiffer requirements

The proponents of a new core curriculum have helped to bring about changes in subject-matter requirements in many districts throughout the nation. Between 1982 and 1997 the average number of years of coursework required for high-school graduation increased from 1.6 to 2.6 in mathematics, from 1.5 to 2.3 in science, and from 3.6 to 3.9 in English. (Social studies has remained relatively stationary at

---

[9]Allan C. Ornstein, "National Reform and Instructional Accountability," *High School Journal* (October–November 1990), pp. 51–56; "State Testing," *Education Week*, October 5, 1994, p. 4; and Jo Anne Natale, "Write This Down," *American School Board Journal* (December 1995), pp. 16–20.
[10]Allan C. Ornstein and Francis Hunkins, *Curriculum: Foundations, Principles and Theory*, 2nd ed. (Boston: Allyn and Bacon, 1993), pp. 160–161.
[11]Richard W. Riley, "World Class Standards: The Key to Educational Reform" (Washington, D.C.: Department of Education, 1993); and John I. Goodlad, "A New Look at an Old Idea: Core Curriculum," *Educational Leadership* (December 1986–January 1987), pp. 8–16.
[12]Ernest L. Boyer, *High School* (New York: Harper and Row, 1983); Theodore R. Sizer, *Horace's Compromise: The Dilemma of the American High School*, rev. ed. (Boston: Houghton Mifflin, 1985); and Joseph Creech, *High School Graduation Standards: What We Expect and What We Get* (Atlanta: Southern Regional Educational Board, 1996).
[13]Boyer, *High School;* Sizer, *Horace's Compromise;* John I. Goodlad, *A Place Called School* (New York: McGraw-Hill, 1984); and Ernest L. Boyer, *The Basic School: A Community of Learning* (Princeton: Carnegie Foundation, 1995).

TAKING ISSUE

State Competency Tests for Students

One feature of the back-to-basics movement has been a rise in statewide testing of students. The failure of many students to master even the most basic skills, especially in reading, writing, mathematics, and history, has prompted state legislators to demand proof that schools are meeting minimum standards. All states now employ statewide testing at one or more stages in the educational process. Many states, in fact, have established minimum-competency tests that students must pass before graduating from high school.

Arguments PRO

1 Statewide testing for high-school graduation forces schools to improve their minimum standards. Students are no longer passed automatically through the system, and every student is taught the skills required for basic literacy.

2 The rise in minimum standards brought about by statewide testing is especially important for students from disadvantaged backgrounds. To break the cycle of poverty and joblessness, these students must be given the skills needed for productive employment.

3 Besides improving minimum standards, statewide testing helps to shift curriculum emphasis back to the basics. All of our students need a firmer grounding in such essential subjects as reading, writing, and mathematics.

4 Testing for graduation shows the public that schools are being held accountable for their performance. The test results help to identify schools that are not doing their jobs properly.

5 Using the data provided by statewide testing, educators can discover where the overall problems lie. Policies can be modified accordingly, and curricula can be designed to address the problem areas.

Arguments CON

1 Statewide testing is cumbersome, costly, and may not lead to much improvement in minimum standards. The effort must come from the local level, where educators know the strengths and weaknesses of their own schools.

2 Statewide tests discriminate against minorities and the urban and rural poor, who fail the tests in disproportionate numbers. This failure stigmatizes them unjustly and further damages their prospects for employment.

3 When schools try to focus on "basics," they often neglect other important elements of education, such as problem solving and creative thinking. These higher-order abilities are increasingly important in a technological society.

4 Test scores by themselves cannot identify ineffective schools, and it is dangerous to use them for that purpose. There are too many complicating factors, such as the students' home environment and socioeconomic background.

5 Most teachers already know where the problems lie. Moreover, soon after a statewide test is established, many teachers begin to "teach the test." Thus, the data obtained from such examinations become meaningless or misleading.

2.8.)[14] In the decade after 1982 the percentage of high-school graduates who completed a basic curriculum in core subjects increased from 15 percent to over 40 percent.[15]

Critiques of new core curriculum

The new core curriculum approach has drawn some of the same criticisms as the back-to-basics curriculum. It may be argued that the new core curriculum turns the clock back to the turn of the century, when subject-matter emphasis and academic rigor were the order of the day. Compared to 1900, there are more students today who are college bound, and for them the academic core courses may be appropriate; yet there increasing numbers of students who graduate from our schools as functional illiterates. To have value for all students, a core curriculum should take into account diverse populations of students, their individual differences and career preferences.

Student-Centered Curricula

As we have seen, the subject-centered curricula focus on cognitive aspects of learning as represented in traditional subject disciplines. A direct contrast can be found in the various types of **student-centered curricula.** The student-centered approach emphasizes students' interests and needs, including the affective aspects of learning. At its extreme the student-centered approach is rooted in the philosophy of Jean Jacques Rousseau, who encouraged childhood self-expression. Implicit in Rousseau's philosophy is the necessity of leaving the child to his or her own devices, allowing the creativity and freedom essential for children's growth.

Stressing students' needs

Progressive education gave impetus to student-centered curricula. Progressive educators believed that when the interests and needs of learners were incorporated into the curriculum, students would be intrinsically motivated and learning would be more successful. This does not mean that students' whims or passing fads should dictate the curriculum. However, one criticism of student-centered curricula is that they sometimes overlook important cognitive content.

Influence of progressivism

John Dewey, one of the chief advocates of student-centered curricula, attempted to establish a curriculum that balanced subject matter with students' interests and needs. As early as 1902, he pointed out the fallacies of either extreme. The learner was neither "a docile recipient of facts" nor "the starting point, the center, and the end" of school activity.[16] Dewey tried to emphasize that a balance was necessary.

Dewey's call for balance

There are at least five major approaches to organizing student-centered curricula: activity-centered approaches, relevant curriculum, the humanistic approach, alternative or free schools, and values-centered curricula.

Activity-Centered Approaches. The movement for an **activity-centered curriculum** has strongly affected the public elementary schools. William Kilpatrick, one of Dewey's colleagues, was an early leader. In contrast to Dewey, Kilpatrick believed that the interests and needs of children could not be anticipated and that therefore any preplanned curriculum was impossible. Thus he attacked the typical school

---

[14]*The Condition of Education 1987* (Washington, D.C.: U.S. Government Printing Office, 1987), Table 1.37 B, p. 84; and *Digest of Education Statistics* (Washington, D.C.: U.S. Government Printing Office, 1997), Table 155, pp. 149–154.

[15]"By the Numbers — Key Subjects," *Education Week,* June 14, 1995, p. 4.

[16]John Dewey, *The Child and the Curriculum* (Chicago: University of Chicago Press, 1902), pp. 8–9.

The activity-centered curriculum generated a host of teaching strategies — including lessons based on life experiences, group games, dramatizations, story projects, field trips, social enterprises, and interest centers. (© A. Carey/The Image Works)

Lifelike, purposeful activities

curriculum as unrelated to the problems of real life. Instead, he advocated purposeful activities that were relevant and as lifelike as possible and that were tied to a student's needs and interests,[17] such as group games, dramatizations, story projects, field trips, social enterprises, and interest centers. All of these facets of the activity-centered curriculum involved problem solving and active student participation. They also emphasized socialization and the formation of stronger school-community ties.

Constructivism

The recent development of *constructivist learning theory*, described in Chapter 12, draws on these and similar concepts. Constructivists favor an activity-centered curriculum in which students actively (mentally and physically) interact with knowledge and each other to construct meaning and new knowledge for themselves.[18]

Relevant Curriculum.   By the 1930s, some reformers complained that the traditional school curriculum had become irrelevant: it had failed to adjust to social change, and therefore it emphasized skills and knowledge that were not pertinent to modern society. The 1960s and 1970s saw a renewed concern for a **relevant curriculum**, but with a somewhat different emphasis. There was less concern that the curriculum reflect changing social conditions and more concern that the curriculum be relevant to the students' personal needs and interests.

Requirements for a relevant curriculum

Proponents of this approach today see the following needs: (1) the individualization of instruction through such teaching methods as independent inquiry and

---

[17]William H. Kilpatrick, "The Project Method," *Teachers College Record* (September 1918), pp. 319–335.
[18]Lois T. Stover, Gloria A. Neubert, and James C. Lawlor, *Creating Interactive Environments in the Secondary School* (Washington, D.C.: National Education Association, 1993), pp. 20–23; and Catherine Fosnot, *Constructivism: Theory, Perspectives and Practices* (New York: Teachers College Press, 1996).

special projects; (2) the revision of existing courses and the development of new courses on such topics of student concern as environmental protection, drug addiction, urban problems, and cultural pluralism; (3) the provision of educational alternatives (such as electives, minicourses, and open classrooms) that allow more freedom of choice; and (4) the extension of the curriculum beyond the school's walls.[19]

Humanistic Approach to Curriculum.   Like many other modern curriculum developments, humanistic education began as a reaction to what was viewed as an overemphasis on cognitive learning in the late 1950s and early 1960s.

Psychological foundation

A **humanistic approach to curriculum** emphasizes affective rather than cognitive outcomes. Such a curriculum draws heavily on the work of psychologists Abraham Maslow and Carl Rogers.[20] Its goal is to produce "self-actualizing people," in Maslow's words, or "total human beings" as Rogers puts it. The works of both psychologists are laden with such terms as *choosing, striving, enhancing,* and *experiencing* — as well as *independence, self-determination, integration,* and *personal relationships.*

Higher domains of consciousness

Advocates of humanistic education contend that the present school curriculum has failed miserably, that teachers and schools are determined to stress cognitive behaviors and to control students *not* for students' good but for the good of adults. Humanists emphasize more than affective processes; they seek higher domains of spirit, consciousness, aesthetics, and morality.[21] They stress more meaningful relationships between students and teachers; student independence and self-direction; and greater acceptance of self and others. The teacher's role would be to help learners cope with their psychological needs and problems and to facilitate self-understanding among students.

Alternative or Free Schools Programs.   Some student-centered curriculum programs today are found in **alternative** or **free schools.** These are often private or experimental institutions, and some have been organized by parents and teachers who are dissatisfied with the public schools. These schools are typified by much freedom for students, noisy classrooms, and a learning environment where students are free to explore their interests. The teaching and learning process is unstructured. Most of these schools are considered radical and antiestablishment, even though many of their ideas are rooted in the well-known student-centered doctrines of progressivism.

Freedom for students

---

[19]Maxine Green, "Education, Art and Mastery: Toward the Spheres of Freedom," in H. Svi Shapiro and David E. Purpel, eds., *Critical Social Issues in American Education* (New York: Longman, 1993), pp. 330–344; Michael W. Apple and Linda Christian-Smith, *The Politics of the Textbook* (New York: Routledge, 1991); and Arthur Powell, Eleanor Farrar, and David Cohen, *The Shopping Mall High School* (Boston: Houghton Mifflin, 1985).

[20]Abraham H. Maslow, *Toward a Psychology of Being* (New York: Van Nostrand Reinhold, 1962); Abraham H. Maslow, *Motivation and Personality,* 2nd ed. (New York: Harper and Row, 1970); and Carl Rogers, *Freedom to Learn,* 2nd ed. (Columbus, Ohio: Merrill, 1983).

[21]Elliot Eisner, *The Educational Imagination,* 3rd ed. (New York: Macmillan, 1993); John Miller, *The Holistic Curriculum: Revised and Expanded Edition* (Ontario: OISE Press, 1996); and Carol Witherell and Nel Noddings, *The Challenge to Care in Schools* (New York: Teachers College Press, 1992). See Paul Freire, *Pedagogy of the Oppressed* (New York: Herder and Herder, 1970); Henry A. Giroux, *Teachers as Intellectuals* (Granby, Mass.: Bergin and Garvey, 1988); Ivan Illich, *Deschooling Society* (New York: Harper and Row, 1971); Herbert R. Kohl, *The Open Classroom* (New York: Random House, 1969) and *On Teaching* (New York: Schocken Books, 1976); Jonathan Kozol, *Free Schools* (Boston: Houghton Mifflin, 1972); and Jonathan Kozol, *Savage Inequalities: Children in America's Schools* (New York: Crown Publishers, 1991).

Controversy about free schools

Paul Freire, Henry Giroux, Ivan Illich, Herbert Kohl, and Jonathan Kozol have stressed the need for, and in many cases have established, student-centered alternative or free schools.[22] Critics, however, condemn these schools as places where little cognitive learning takes place and where there is little discipline and order. Proponents counter that children do learn in student-centered alternative schools, which — instead of stressing conformity — are made to fit the student.

Public alternative schools

A second type of alternative school is that run by public-school systems for students who have or present persistent discipline problems (and who often also have learning problems). These schools start from the premise that schools must be changed to provide a more flexible approach to learning. They generally stress greater collaboration among staff members and between staff and students in terms of both curriculum and instructional methods. Many of the schools that have developed highly creative approaches are among the best examples of *restructured schools* in the country — that is, schools reorganized around improved student achievement, effective teaching, and improved school organization.[23] (See Chapter 16 for further discussion of restructuring.)

Restructuring

Value confusion

Values-Centered Curriculum.   As a result of the fast pace of modern society, the breakdown of the nuclear family, and the decline in church influence, people today often suffer from value confusion, which can cause apathy, uncertainty, and inconsistency. A **values-centered curriculum** — or, as it is more popularly known, **character education** — attempts to lessen the confusion by placing special emphasis on moral and ethical issues. For example, advocates of multicultural education stress not only knowledge of the diverse cultures and ethnic experiences of American society, but also appreciation and respect for cultures other than one's own. In this re-

Multiculturalism and values

Many curricular programs actively engage students in meaningful community service projects, which extend beyond the classroom and address social, moral and ethical concerns. *(© Bob Daemmrick/Stock Boston)*

---

[22]See, for instance, Diane Ravitch, *The Troubled Crusade* (New York: Basic Books, 1983); and Frank Smith, *To Think* (New York: Teachers College Press, 1990).

[23]Jon Harford and Mary Anne Raywid, "Are Alternative Schools Dumping Grounds for Problem Students?" *American Teacher* (September 1993), p. 6.

Sense of right and wrong

spect, multicultural education fits into a values-centered curriculum. Even more fundamentally, some educators, parents, and community members have come to the conclusion that too many students lack a strong sense of right and wrong. It is up to the schools, these people argue, to teach such basic values as honesty, responsibility, courtesy, self-discipline, compassion, tolerance, and respect for the rights of others.[24]

No quick fix

Kevin Ryan, director of the Center for the Advancement of Ethics and Character, says that the school curriculum, now increasingly devoid of moral authority and ethical language, has become sterile and meaningless. But Ryan warns that character education cannot be achieved through a quick-fix approach. Educators and their communities must define character education clearly and make it a focal point of the school's mission, finding a common ground of civic values that do not transgress upon religious and family values.[25]

What values should be taught?

One potential drawback to values-centered curricula, like humanistic curricula, is a lack of attention to cognitive learning. Even more important, educators and community members often do not concur about the values to be taught or how to teach them. Parents may be offended if a school attempts to teach values that differ from those of the home and family. In such controversial areas as sex, religion, and social justice, values education may become a minefield.

Finding a consensus

Despite these problems, many educators contend that it is possible — even with our multicultural, multireligious population — to establish a set of values that represent an American consensus.[26] Table 14.2, for example, lists a "common core of values" developed by the school system in Baltimore County, Maryland. These values are emphasized throughout the curriculum, especially in social studies and English. Although the exact definitions of concepts like "freedoms," "patriotism," and "tolerance" may be hard to determine, many educators believe that finding such a common core is an urgent responsibility of American schools.

Curriculum Contrasts: An Overview

In summary, subject-centered and student-centered curricula represent extremes on a continuum. Most schooling in the United States falls somewhere between the two — keeping a tenuous balance between subject matter and student needs, between the cognitive and affective dimensions of students' development.

Influence of school philosophy

Decisions about what is taught and how curriculum is organized are usually influenced by the philosophical orientation of the school. More traditional schools that subscribe to a perennialist or essentialist philosophy generally lean toward a subject-centered curriculum. Schools that are oriented more toward progressive or reconstructionist education tend to use a student-centered approach. Overview 14.1 summarizes the various subject-centered and student-centered approaches to curricula and their corresponding philosophies, content emphases, and instructional emphases. As you begin to think seriously about which district and in which school you want to teach, consider asking interviewers questions about curricular

[24]See, for example, Task Force on Values Education and Ethical Behavior, *How to Establish a Values Education Program in Your School* (Towson, Md.: Baltimore County Public Schools, 1991); "Fostering Civic Virtue: Character Education in the Social Studies," *Social Studies Review* (Fall–Winter, 1997), pp. 23–25.
[25]Kevin Ryan, "Character and Coffee Mugs," *Education Week*, May 17, 1995, pp. 37, 48.
[26]Ibid., pp. 37, 48; Keith Geiger, "Who Says Character Doesn't Count?" *Education Week*, January 11, 1995, p. 26; and Thomas Lasley, "The Missing Ingredient in Character Education," *Phi Delta Kappan* (April, 1997), pp. 654–655.

TAKING ISSUE

Character Education

Over the past quarter-century, many educators have asserted that schools should be neutral when it comes to teaching what is "right" and "good." Emphasis has been placed on fostering skills that students need to make their own decisions about values. Now, however, a growing number of educators, with some public support, are abandoning that position and calling for a return of character education in the public schools.

Arguments PRO

1 In the face of rising crime, youth violence, drugs, teen pregnancy, and other social problems, schools are being blamed for the decline of traditional values. Recent Gallup polls show that as many as 84 percent of parents with school-age children want public schools to provide "instruction that will deal with morals and moral behavior."

2 There is a body of core values that bind Americans together as a people, transcending barriers of class, creed, and ethnicity. Without schooling in these principles, young people cannot prepare themselves for the responsibilities of democratic citizenship.

3 Although terminology may differ, virtually everyone can agree on certain basic and traditional virtues: for example, honesty, respect, tolerance, and peaceful resolution of conflicts. In conveying such values, schools can unite people without interfering with any group's unique culture or beliefs.

4 Programs in values clarification, humanistic education, and multicultural education, among other recent efforts, have demonstrated that values can be taught successfully in the classroom. Character education can be integrated, in fact, throughout the entire curriculum.

Arguments CON

1 If people blame the schools for declining morality, it is only because schools are an easy target for almost any complaint. In fact, problems of values are not the schools' fault, nor are the schools equipped to address them. Character education should be handled by the institutions where values begin — namely, the family and the religious community.

2 The notion that schools could teach basic "American" values led to some of the worst abuses in the history of U. S. education. Schools helped to suppress the cultures of minority groups such as Native Americans, Hispanics, and Asians. We cannot risk letting that happen again.

3 People who believe in a substantial common core of beliefs are deluding themselves. Our society is simply too diverse for all to agree on any particular virtue. Moreover, character education is all too likely to be hijacked by the extreme right or extreme left, producing more divisiveness instead of unity.

4 Even some supporters of character education realize that more research is needed on a very basic question: whether such education has any genuine effect. Until the research is conclusive, educators should not water down the curriculum by sprinkling it with "values."

TABLE 14.2	A "Common Core of Values," as Defined by the Baltimore County (Md.) Public Schools		
Compassion	Reasoned argument		Justice
Due process procedures	Responsibility		Loyalty
Freedoms	Tolerance		Rational consent
Human worth and dignity	Courtesy		Respect for rights of others
Knowledge	Critical inquiry		Responsible citizenship
Patriotism	Honesty		Peaceful resolution of conflict

Questions

1. Which of the core values in Table 14.2 do you feel are most important and why?
2. What core values do you feel should be added to Table 14.2?

Source: Task Force on Values Education and Ethical Behavior, *1984 and Beyond: A Reaffirmation of Values* (Towson, Md.: Baltimore County Public Schools, 1994).

organization, so that there is a "fit" between your philosophy and that of the district or school. In the next section we move on to the process of curriculum development and the main issues it raises.

Issues in Curriculum Development

Curriculum at national and state levels

Whether the curriculum is subject centered or student centered, the process of developing it involves (1) assessing the needs and capabilities of the learners (including those of culturally diverse populations, learners with disabilities, gifted and talented students, college-bound students, and those who wish to enter the work force) and (2) selecting or creating the instructional materials and activities. At the national level, curriculum making is minimal and indirect, despite the recent work on national goals and standards. At the state level, curriculum development is often limited to the publication of curriculum guides and booklets. These are prepared by a professional staff in the state department of education, assisted by curriculum consultants and college professors. The state publications tend to focus on large-scale concerns, such as the need for stronger curricula in math and science. In many states, however, the guidelines are more specific, including lists of instructional materials that are either mandated or recommended or in some cases forbidden. The greatest responsibility for curriculum development generally falls on the local school district — or, as school-based management becomes more widespread, on the schools themselves. Large school districts often employ personnel who specialize in curriculum development, including subject-matter specialists and test consultants. In the smaller school districts, curriculum development is generally handled by a group of teachers organized by subject or grade level; sometimes parents, administrators, and even students are also involved.

Curriculum at the local level

College admission standards exert a strong influence on curriculum choices. Increasingly, too, local curriculum developers must pay close attention to standards and academic requirements established by the state (including voluntary national standards).

Influence of textbooks

Another major influence on curriculum — one whose importance is often underrated — is the textbook. Traditionally, textbooks have been the most frequently

OVERVIEW 14.1 — Curriculum Organization Approaches

Curriculum Approach	Corresponding Philosophy or Theory	Content Emphasis	Instructional Emphasis
Subject-Centered			
Subject-area	Perennialism, essentialism	Three Rs; academic, vocational, and elective subjects	Knowledge, concepts, and principles; specialized knowledge
Perennialist	Perennialism	Three Rs; liberal arts; classics; timeless values; academic rigor	Rote memorization; specialized knowledge; mental discipline
Essentialist	Essentialism	Three Rs; liberal arts and science; academic disciplines; academic excellence	Concepts and principles; problem solving; essential skills
Back-to-basics	Essentialism	Three Rs; academic subjects	Specific knowledge and skills; drill; attainment of measurable ends or competencies
New core curriculum (core subjects)	Perennialism, essentialism	Common curriculum for all students; focus on academics	Common knowledge; intellectual skills and concepts; values and moral issues
Student-Centered			
Activity-centered	Progressivism	Student needs and interests; student activities; school-community activities	Active, experimental environment; project methods; effective living
Relevant	Progressivism, social reconstructionism	Student experiences and activities; felt needs	Social and personal problems; reflective thinking
Humanistic	Progressivism, social reconstructionism, existentialism	Introspection; choice; affective processes	Individual and group learning; flexible, artistic, psychological methods; self-realization
Alternative or free schools	Progressivism	Student needs and interests; student experiences	Play oriented; creative expression; free learning environment
Values-centered (character education)	Social reconstructionism, existentialism	Democratic values; ethical and moral values; cross-cultural and universal values; choice and freedom	Feelings, attitudes, and emotions; existentialist thinking; decision making

used instructional medium at all levels beyond the primary grades. As such, they can dominate the nature and sequence of a course and profoundly affect the learning experiences of students. Since courses are often based on the knowledge and biases of the textbook's author, curriculum developers often shape the entire course

PROFESSIONAL PLANNING

for your first year

Keeping Up with the Curriculum

The Situation

Ella Johnstone was fresh out of college. On her first day at Lincoln Middle School, she met with the principal and eighth-grade team leader, received her teaching assignment, picked up textbooks, and visited her own classroom for the first time. It was an exciting day, but it held some surprises and challenges.

Ella had majored in history, and her teaching assignment was the history and regional geography of the United States. She had good grades in her history and social science courses and felt prepared to teach them. However, the team leader talked less about the subject matter than about ways to involve students in the learning process. The emphasis clearly was on student-centered instruction.

Ella wondered how to develop a student-centered approach to these subjects when her university's emphasis had been on mastering information in her major. Would the textbooks help? She hoped they would be treasure troves of activities and teaching suggestions, though she suspected they were not. However, the team leader had promised to introduce her to videodisk collections and show her how to find lesson plans and curriculum projects on the Internet. For instance, students could access electronic images of the Grand Canyon and interact with a U.S. Park Service geologist about its origins. That sounded fascinating! She also promised to introduce Ella to the Internet as a research tool for students.

Overall, as Ella prepared for her first class, she no longer felt like an "expert" ready to convey her knowledge to students; rather, she saw the curriculum and learning process as an ongoing challenge for teacher and students alike. In this era of shifting curriculum, innovative instructional approaches, and rapidly changing technology, Ella discovered that she needed to know less about specific, factual content and more about current trends and about using technology as a resource for teaching her subject.

Thought Questions

1. Do you believe you would be comfortable in a school like Ella's — one that emphasizes student-centered instruction? Why or why not?
2. What elements of the student-centered approach described in this chapter might Ella adopt as she plans her history and geography classes?
3. How do you intend to stay apprised of the current trends in curriculum, instruction, and resources (particularly technological resources) after you finish your college coursework?

just by choosing the textbook. For this reason, it is important to understand some of the factors that govern textbook writing and publication.

Limitations of textbooks

In order to have wide application and a large potential market, textbooks tend to be general, noncontroversial, and bland. Since they are usually written for a national audience, they do not consider local issues or community problems. And because they are geared for the greatest number of "average" students, they may not

GETTING TO THE SOURCE

Fundamental Questions on Curriculum

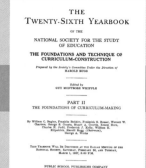

THE
TWENTY-SIXTH YEARBOOK
OF THE
NATIONAL SOCIETY FOR THE STUDY
OF EDUCATION

THE FOUNDATIONS AND TECHNIQUE OF
CURRICULUM-CONSTRUCTION

Prepared by the Society's Committee Under the Direction of
HAROLD RUGG

Edited by
GUY MONTROSE WHIPPLE

PART II
THE FOUNDATIONS OF CURRICULUM-MAKING

By William C. Bagley, Franklin Bobbitt, Frederick G. Bonser, Werrett W.
Charters, George S. Counts, Stuart A. Courtis, Ernest Horn,
Charles H. Judd, Frederick J. Kelly, William H.
Kilpatrick, Harold Rugg (Chairman),
George A. Works

THIS YEARBOOK WILL BE DISCUSSED AT THE DALLAS MEETING OF THE
NATIONAL SOCIETY, SATURDAY, FEBRUARY 26, AND TUESDAY,
MARCH 1, 1927, 8:00 P.M.

PUBLIC SCHOOL PUBLISHING COMPANY
BLOOMINGTON, ILLINOIS
1930

The twenty-sixth yearbook of the National Society for the Study of Education, published in 1930, is considered a landmark book on curriculum; it was the first attempt by a group of curriculum scholars to synthesize the meaning and practice of curriculum making. Volume II presented a list of "fundamental questions" on curriculum making, intended to stimulate discussion among teachers and curriculum leaders. The questions have stood the test of time; they are relevant even today.

1. What period of life does schooling primarily contemplate as its end?
2. How can the curriculum prepare for effective participation in adult life?
3. Are the curriculum-makers of the schools obliged to formulate a point of view concerning the merits or deficiencies of American civilization?
4. Should the school be regarded as a conscious agency for social improvement?
   a. Should the school be planned on the assumption that it is to fit children to "live in" the current social order or to rise above and lift it after them? Are children merely to be "adjusted" to the institutions of current society or are they to be so educated that they will be impelled to modify it? Are they to accept it or to question it?
5. How shall the content of the curriculum be conceived and stated?
6. What is the place and function of subject matter in the educative process?
7. What portion of education should be classified as "general" and what portion as "specialized" or "vocational" or purely "optional?" To what extent is general education to run parallel with vocational education and to what extent is the latter to follow on the completion of the former? . . .

---

meet the needs and interests of any particular group or individual.[27] In summarizing large quantities of data, they may become superficial and discourage conceptual thinking, critical analysis, and evaluation. Furthermore, with the possible exception of those on mathematics, most textbooks quickly become outdated. Because they are expensive, however, they are often used long after they should have been replaced.

Advantages of textbooks

Considering these criticisms, why do teachers rely so heavily on textbooks? The answer is that textbooks do have many advantages. A textbook provides an outline that the teacher can use in planning lessons; summarizes a great deal of pertinent information; enables the student to take home most of the course material in a convenient package; provides a common resource for all students to follow; includes pictures, graphs, maps, and other illustrative material that facilitate understanding; and frequently includes other teaching aids, such as summaries and review ques-

---

[27]Allan C. Ornstein, "Textbook Instruction: Processes and Strategies," *NASSP Bulletin* (December 1989), pp. 105–111; and Elliot W. Eisner, "Who Decides What Schools Will Teach?" *Phi Delta Kappan* (March 1990), pp. 523–525.

11. To what extent should traits be learned in their "natural" setting (i.e., in a "life-situation")?

12. To what degree should the curriculum provide for individual differences? . . .

14. What should be the form of organization of the curriculum? Shall it be one of the following or will you adopt others?

   a. A flexibly graded series of suggestive activities with reference to subject matter which may be used in connection with the activities? Or,

   b. A rigidly graded series of activities with subject matter included with each respective activity? Or,

   c. A graded sequence of subject matter with suggestion for activities to which the subject matter is related? Or,

   d. A statement of achievements expected for each grade, a list of suggestive activities, and an outline of related subject matter, through the use of which the grade object may be achieved? Or,

   e. A statement of grade objectives in terms of subject matter and textual and reference materials which will provide this subject matter without any specific reference to activities?

15. What, if any, use shall be made of the spontaneous interests of children?

Questions

1. What principles of psychology and school of philosophy do the questions reflect?

2. To what extent would you modify the questions set forth in the statement? Which questions do you find relevant? Irrelevant?

3. What groups are most appropriate to ask and answer these questions?

4. As you grow professionally, which of these questions will most influence what you teach and how you teach?

Source: "A Composite Statement by the Members of the Society's Committee on Curriculum Making," in G. M. Whipple, ed., *The Foundations of Curriculum Making,* Twenty-sixth Yearbook of the National Society for the Study of Education. Part II (Bloomington, Ill.: Public School Publishing Co., 1930), cover, pp. 9–10. Reprinted by permission.

tions.[28] In short, the textbook is an acceptable tool if it is selected and used properly. However, it should not be the only source of knowledge for students, and it should not define the entire curriculum.

Censorship trends

Another issue in curriculum development is the question of censorship. In the states that prepare lists of instructional materials for their schools, the trend is growing to "limit what students shall read."[29] As Chapter 8 indicated, the list of objectionable works has sometimes included such classics as *Little Red Riding Hood* and *Huckleberry Finn.* Today, almost any book that contains political or economic messages, obscenity, sex, nudity, profanity, slang or questionable English, ethnic or racially sensitive material, or any material that could be interpreted as antifamily, antireligious, or anti-American is subject to possible censorship.

---

[28]Allan C. Ornstein, "The Textbook-Driven Curriculum," *Peabody Journal of Education* (Spring 1994), pp. 70–85.

[29]*Attack on the Freedom to Learn, 1989–90* (Washington, D.C.: People for the American Way, 1990); and John S. Simmons, *Censorship: A Threat to Reading, Learning, Thinking* (Newark: International Reading Association, 1994).

Subtle censorship   Although censorship is often overt, it can operate in subtle ways as well. Curriculum developers may quietly steer away from issues and materials that would cause controversy in the community. Moreover, textbooks often omit topics that might upset potential audiences or interest groups. Even pictures are important, for some organizations count the number of pictures of one ethnic group versus another group, of boys versus girls, of business versus labor. Professional associations can also exert a type of censorship when they recommend certain changes in subject content and implicitly discourage other approaches. Educators must be sensitive to censorship because it is always there in one form or another. In dealing with such issues, we often find that Herbert Spencer's fundamental question "What knowledge is of most worth?" becomes "Whose knowledge is of most worth?"[30]

As teaching becomes more professionalized, teachers are increasingly expected to deal with curriculum choices and the complex issues they present. To avoid letting curriculum become "a political football," as Michael Apple terms it,[31] today's teachers need a full understanding of community concerns, statewide standards and goals, and student needs.

Instructional Approaches

Interrelationship of curriculum and instruction

Although educators differ in the definition of curriculum, most recognize that curriculum and instruction are interrelated. To carry out the curriculum one must rely on instruction — programs, materials, and methods. The search for new programs and methods of instruction is continual. The last four decades, in particular, have witnessed a major effort to improve learning outcomes, integrate technology into the lesson, and have students participate firsthand with the new tools of instruction.

Although we cannot survey all the major instructional innovations, the following sections describe several that have drawn considerable attention from educators. Chapter 16 will return to the subject of instructional approaches in the context of school reform and school effectiveness.

Individualized Instruction

In recent decades, several models have been advanced for **individualized instruction.** Although these approaches vary, they all try to provide a one-to-one student-teacher or student-computer relationship. Students are allowed to proceed at their own rate, and the instructional materials are carefully sequenced and structured, usually with an emphasis on practice and drill.

IPI   One of the early examples, the Project on Individually Prescribed Instruction (IPI), was developed at the University of Pittsburgh in the late 1950s and early 1960s.[32] For every student, an individual plan was prepared for each skill or subject based on a diagnosis of the student's needs. Objectives were stated in behavioral terms, and specific proficiency levels were identified. Learning tasks were individualized, and the student's progress was continually evaluated.

---

[30]Joan DelFattore, *What Johnny Shouldn't Read: Textbook Censorship in America* (New Haven: Yale University Press, 1992); Edward Jenkinson, "Myths and Misunderstandings Surround the School Protest Movement," *Contemporary Education* (Winter 1995), pp. 70–73.
[31]Michael Apple, "Is There a Curriculum Voice to Reclaim?" *Phi Delta Kappan* (March 1990), pp. 526–530.
[32]Robert Glaser and Lauren B. Resnick, "Instructional Psychology," *Annual Review of Psychology* (no. 23, 1972), pp. 207–276.

Significant gains reported

Field testing of individualized instruction programs has generally been positive. Some reports on IPI and other approaches have shown significant gains in student achievement. Adaptive instruction seems to benefit all kinds of students, especially low-achieving ones or students with mild disabilities.[33] Nevertheless, individualized plans are expensive to implement because of materials cost and one-to-one teacher-student relationships. Most schools today continue to employ group methods of instruction and group expectations.

Cooperative Learning

Cooperative, rather than competitive, learning is also becoming more and more accepted as an important way to instruct students. In the traditional classroom structure, students compete for teacher recognition and grades. The same students tend to be "winners" and "losers" over the years because of differences in ability and *Competition vs. cooperation* achievement. High-achieving students continually receive rewards and are motivated to learn, whereas low-achieving students continually experience failure (or near failure) and frustration. The idea of **cooperative learning** is to change the traditional structure by reducing competition and increasing cooperation among students, thus diminishing possible hostility and tension among students and raising academic achievement.

Benefits of competition

This does not mean that competition has no place in the classroom or school. The chief advocates of cooperation tell us that competition can be used successfully to improve performance on simple drill activities and speed-related tasks (such as spelling, vocabulary, and simple math computations), in low-anxiety games and on the athletic field.[34] Under the right conditions, competition can be a source of fun, excitement, and motivation.

Benefits of cooperation

In cooperative learning, however, competition takes second place. According to a review of the research, cooperation among participants helps build (1) positive and coherent personal identity, (2) self-actualization and mental health, (3) knowledge and trust of one another, (4) communication with one another, (5) acceptance and support of one another, and (6) wholesome relationships with a reduced amount of conflict. The data also suggest that cooperation and group learning are considerably more effective in fostering these social and interpersonal skills than are competitive or individualistic efforts.[35]

STAD

Of all the cooperative instructional arrangements, the two developed by Robert Slavin are most popular: Student-Teams Achievement Divisions (STAD) and Team-Assisted Individualization (TAI). Both methods have increased student achievement

---

[33]William Malloy, *Inclusion: An Educational Reform Strategy for All Children* (ERIC Document 379856, 1994); Peggy Dettmer, "IEP's for Gifted Secondary Students: Instruments for Enhancing Potential," *Journal of Secondary Gifted Education* (Summer 1994), pp. 52–59; Herbert J. Klausmeier, *Learning and Teaching Concepts* (New York: Academic Press, 1980); and Melanie Driesbach, "A Description of an Inclusion Model That Is Working in a Rural Area," in *Reaching to the Future: Boldly Facing Challenges in Rural Communities* (Las Vegas, Nev.: Conference Proceedings of the American Council on Rural Special Education, March 15–18, 1995).
[34]David W. Johnson and Roger T. Johnson, *Learning Together and Alone: Cooperative, Competitive, and Individualistic Learning,* 4th ed. (Needham Heights, Mass.: Allyn and Bacon, 1994); and Robert E. Slavin, *School and Classroom Organization* (Hillsdale, N.J.: Erlbaum, 1988).
[35]Robert E. Slavin, *Cooperative Learning: Theory, Research, and Practice* (Boston: Allyn and Bacon, 1995); Robert J. Stevens and Robert E. Slavin, "Effects of a Cooperative Learning Approach in Reading and Writing on Academically Handicapped and Nonhandicapped Students," *Elementary School Journal* (January 1995), pp. 241–262; and Robert Slavin, "Cooperative Learning and Intergroup Relations" (ERIC Document Number 382730, 1995).

when the proper procedures have been followed.[36] In STAD, teams are composed of four or five members, preferably four (an arrangement that contradicts other research indicating that groups of four tend to pair off). Teams are balanced by ability, gender, and ethnicity. Team members provide assistance and feedback to each other and receive a group performance score on quizzes. They also receive recognition via bulletin boards, certificates, special activities and privileges, and letters to parents. The teams are changed every five or six weeks to give students an opportunity to work with others and to give members of low-scoring teams a new chance.[37]

TAI

The TAI approach puts more emphasis on mastery of particular skill sheets and on individual diagnosis through pre- and post-testing. Students first work on their own skill sheets and then have their partners or team members check their answers and provide assistance. Not until the student scores 80 percent or higher on a practice quiz is the student certified by the team to take the final test. Teams are scored and recognized in the same way as with STAD, but criteria are established for "superteams" (high performance), "great teams" (moderate performance), and "good teams" (minimum passing grade). Every day the teacher spends 5 to 15 minutes of the 45-minute lesson period with two or three groups that are at about the same point in the curriculum. The other teams work on their own during this time.[38]

Mastery Instruction

Mastery instruction is an instructional plan for all grade levels and subjects. The approach being used most widely in the public schools is the Learning for Mastery (LFM) model, often referred to as mastery learning and associated originally with John Carroll and later with James Block and Benjamin Bloom. Their ideas have gained supporters particularly in some urban school districts that have an obvious and urgent need to improve academic performance.

Varying time needed to learn

Carroll pointed out that nearly all students (assuming no major learning disability) can succeed if given sufficient time. He also maintained that if a student does not spend sufficient time to learn a task, he or she will not master it. However, students vary in the amount of time needed to successfully achieve or complete a task.[39] Thus Carroll distinguished between *time needed* to learn (based on student characteristics) and *time available* for learning (under the teacher's control). High-achieving students need less time for learning the same material than low-achieving students do. The teacher can vary instructional time for different individuals (or groups of students), depending on the learners' needs and the teacher's own judgment.

---

[36]Robert E. Slavin, "When Does Cooperative Learning Increase Student Achievement?" *Psychological Bulletin* (November 1983), pp. 429–445; Robert E. Slavin, "Synthesis of Research on Cooperative Learning," *Educational Leadership* (February 1991), pp. 71–82; and Thomas Brush, "The Effectiveness of Cooperative Learning for Low- and High-Achieving Students Using an Integrated Learning System," In Proceedings of the National Convention of the Association for Educational Communications and Technology, Indianapolis, Indiana, 1996. (ERIC Document Number 397780).

[37]Robert E. Slavin, *Using Student Team Learning,* 3rd ed. (Baltimore: Johns Hopkins University Press, 1986).

[38]Thomas L. Good and Jere E. Brophy, *Looking in Classrooms,* 5th ed. (New York: HarperCollins, 1991); and Robert E. Slavin, "Team-Assisted Individualization: Combining Cooperative Learning and Individualized Instruction in Mathematics," in R. E. Slavin, ed., *Learning to Cooperate, Cooperating to Learn* (New York: Plenum, 1985), pp. 177–209.

[39]John B. Carroll, "A Model of School Learning," *Teachers College Record* (May 1963), pp. 723–733; and John B. Carroll, "The Carroll Model: A 25 Year Retrospective and Prospective View," *Educational Researcher* (January–February 1989), pp. 26–31.

Block and Bloom's approach is also based on the central argument that 90 percent of public-school students can learn much of the curriculum at practically the same level of mastery. Although slower students require a longer period of time to learn the same materials, they can succeed if their initial level of knowledge is correctly diagnosed and if they are taught with appropriate methods and materials in a sequential manner, beginning with their initial competency level.[40]

To accomplish this goal, attention must be focused on small units of instruction, and criterion-referenced tests must be used to determine whether a student has the skills required for success at each step in the learning sequence. An entire course such as third-grade mathematics is too complex to be studied in large units. Instead, it should be broken into smaller modules, and the students should be maximally successful (scoring 80 to 90 percent correct) before moving to the next module.

There have been hundreds of studies on mastery learning. After reviewing this broad span of literature, several observers have concluded that mastery strategies do have moderate to strong effects on student learning when compared to conventional methods.[41] When entire school districts are studied, the results show that mastery approaches are also successful in teaching basic skills, such as reading and mathematics, that form the basis for later learning; moreover, inner-city students profit more from this approach than from traditional groupings of instruction,[42] and even students at risk and those with learning disabilities achieve at mastery levels.[43]

Data favorable to mastery learning do not mean that all the important questions have been answered or that mastery strategies do not have critics. Many educators, for example, are not convinced that mastery approaches can accomplish "higher-order" learning, even though Bloom has reported positive gains in higher-order thinking skills correlated with the mastery learning approach.[44] Educators are also uncertain how well the various mastery approaches work for affective learning or for different types of students. Moreover, it is unknown to what extent teachers are teaching a test to their students to avoid blame for students' failure to master the material.[45] Other critics claim that even though reading, writing, and mathematics are being broken down into discrete skills that are mastered, the students still cannot read, write, or compute any better. Although students show gains on

---

[40]James H. Block, *Mastery Learning: Theory and Practice* (New York: Holt, Rinehart and Winston, 1971); Benjamin S. Bloom, *Human Characteristics and School Learning* (New York: McGraw-Hill, 1976); and Thomas R. Guskey, "Mastery Learning in the Regular Classroom: Help for At-Risk Children," *Teaching Exceptional Children* (Winter 1995), pp. 15–18.

[41]See, for instance, Lorin W. Anderson, "Values, Evidence, and Mastery Learning," *Review of Educational Research* (Summer 1987), pp. 215–223; Benjamin S. Bloom, "The Search for Methods of Instruction," in Allan C. Ornstein and Linda S. Behar, eds., *Contemporary Issues in Curriculum* (Boston: Allyn and Bacon, 1995), pp. 208–225; and Stephen Anderson, "Synthesis of Research on Mastery Learning" (ERIC Document Number ED 382567, 1994).

[42]Daniel U. Levine, "Achievement Gains in Self-Contained Chapter I Classes in Kansas City," *Educational Leadership* (March 1987), pp. 22–23; Daniel U. Levine and Allan C. Ornstein, "Research on Classroom and School Effectiveness," *Urban Review* (June 1989), pp. 81–94.

[43]Perry D. Passaro et al., "Instructional Strategies for Reclaiming Schools," *Journal of Emotional and Behavioral Problems* (Spring 1994), pp. 31–34; and Perry D. Passaro et al., "Using Mastery Learning to Facilitate Full Inclusion of Students," *Rural Special Education Quarterly* (Summer 1994), pp. 31–39.

[44]Bloom, "The Search for Methods," pp. 220–222; and Robert Slavin, "Mastery Learning Re-Reconsidered," *Review of Educational Research* (Summer 1990), pp. 300–302.

[45]Herbert J. Walberg, "Productive Teaching," in Allan C. Ornstein, ed., *Teaching: Theory into Practice* (Boston: Allyn and Bacon, 1995), pp. 43–44, 49; Allan C. Ornstein, "Emphasis on Student Outcomes Focuses Attention on Quality of Instruction," *NASSP Bulletin* (January 1987), pp. 88–95; and Robert E. Slavin, "Mastery Learning Re-Reconsidered."

small skill-acquisition items, this does not necessarily prove learning.[46] Finally, mastery learning and other individualized instructional systems are not easy to implement. Responsibility is placed on the teacher, who must adapt the instruction to each student. The teacher must continually monitor each student's work, determine what skills and tasks each student has mastered, and provide immediate feedback — not an easy instructional task in a class of twenty-five or more students.

Critical Thinking

Intelligence that can be taught

Critical thinking and *thinking skills* are terms used today to denote problem-solving ability. Interest in this concept is evidenced by an outpouring of articles in the professional literature, by a host of conferences and reports on the subject, and by steps taken in a majority of states to bolster critical thinking for all students.

Most of the commentators argue that **critical thinking** is a form of intelligence that can be taught. The leading proponents of this school are Matthew Lipman and Robert Sternberg.[47] Lipman seeks to foster thirty critical skills, generally designed for elementary school grades. These skills include understanding concepts, generalizations, cause-effect relationships, analogies, part-whole and whole-part connections, and applications of principles to real-life situations.[48]

Metacognition

Lipman's strategy for teaching critical thinking has children spend a considerable portion of their time thinking about thinking (a process known as *metacognition*)[49] and about ways in which effective thinking is distinguished from ineffective thinking. After reading stories in Lipman's text, children engage in classroom discussions and exercises that encourage them to adapt the thinking process depicted in the stories.[50] The assumption is that children are by nature interested in such philosophical issues as truth, fairness, and personal identity. Therefore, they can and should learn to think for themselves, to explore alternatives to their own viewpoints, consider evidence, make distinctions, and draw conclusions. Additionally, most research studies have found that cooperative learning is more effective than other modes of instruction for higher-level thinking tasks.[51]

Criticisms of critical thinking

Some critics of critical thinking approaches contend that teaching a person to think is like teaching someone to swing a golf club or tennis racket; it involves a holistic approach, not the piecemeal effort implied by proponents like Lipman. Critical thinking, the critics say, is too complex a mental operation to divide into small processes; the result depends on "a student's total intellectual functioning, not on a set of narrowly defined skills."[52] Moreover, as Sternberg has cautioned, crit-

[46]Linda Darling-Hammond, "Mad-Hatter Tests of Good Teaching," *New York Times,* January 8, 1984, sect. 12, p. 57; and Marilyn Cochran-Smith, "Word Processing and Writing in Elementary Classrooms," *Review of Educational Research* (Spring 1991), pp. 107–155.

[47]See, for example, Matthew Lipman et al., *Philosophy for Children,* 2nd ed. (Philadelphia: Temple University Press, 1980); and Robert J. Sternberg, "How Can We Teach Intelligence?" *Educational Leadership* (September 1984), pp. 38–48.

[48]Matthew Lipman, "The Cultivation of Reasoning Through Philosophy," *Educational Leadership* (September 1984), pp. 51–56; Matthew Lipman, "Critical Thinking — What Can It Be?" *Educational Leadership* (September 1988), pp. 38–43; and Missy Garrett, "A Community of Learners: Empowering the Teaching/Learning Process," *Research and Training in Developmental Education* (Spring 1993), pp. 45–54.

[49]Matthew Lipman, "Critical Thinking," in Ornstein and Behar, *Contemporary Issues,* p. 149.

[50]Lipman et al., *Philosophy for Children.*

[51]Catherine Lee et al., "Cooperative Learning in the Thinking Classroom: Research and Theoretical Perspectives," Paper Presented at the 7th International Conference on Thinking, Singapore, June 1–6, 1997 (ERIC Document Number ED 408570).

[52]William A. Sadler and Arthur Whimbey, "A Holistic Approach to Improving Thinking Skills," *Phi Delta Kappan* (November 1985), p. 200.

ical thinking programs that stress "right" answers and objectively scorable test items may be far removed from the problems students face in everyday life.[53] Thus many educators believe that attempts to teach critical thinking as a separate program or as a particular group of defined skills are self-defeating. Ideally, one might argue, critical thinking should be integrated into all courses throughout the curriculum so that students are continually challenged to develop an inquiring attitude and a critical frame of mind.

Computerized Instruction

The role of computers in our schools continues to increase. In 1980 some 50,000 microcomputers were used by the nation's schools, and by 1995 it had soared to 5 million.[54] In 1994 schools spent $2.4 billion on computers, laser disks, CD-ROMs, and similar technology.[55]

CAI

Patrick Suppes, an early innovator of computer use in schools, coined the term *computer-assisted instruction (CAI)*. Suppes defined three levels of CAI: practice and drill, tutoring, and dialogue.[56] At the simplest level, students work through computer drills in spelling, reading, foreign languages, simple computations, and so forth. At the second level, the computer acts as a tutor, taking over the function of presenting new concepts; as soon as the student shows a clear understanding, he or she moves to the next exercise. The third and highest level, dialogue, involves an interaction between the student and the computer. The student can communicate with the machine — not only give responses but ask new questions — and the computer will understand and react appropriately.

Hypermedia browsing

More recent applications often involve the use of a **hypermedia** approach, which represents a significant shift in how information is presented and accessed by students. With hypermedia, information is structured nonsequentially around "nodes" (information chunks) connected through associative links and presented in the program through text, illustrations, or sound. Thus the hypermedia approach allows learners to browse through an information base to construct their own relationships. Through this process, learning becomes more meaningful because it is related to the knowledge structure of the student rather than to the structure presented by the teacher or a textbook.[57] Many educational CD-ROMs use a hypermedia approach. So, of course, does the World Wide Web, with its rapid links to diverse and far-ranging sites.

Problem of equal access

Many teachers, once skeptical of computers, are abandoning the chalkboard in favor of the computer terminal because they see computers as adding a challenging and stimulating dimension to classroom learning. Now it is the problem of computer access that concerns many educators: as former NEA president Keith Geiger put it, the challenge is "how to ensure every student — rural or urban, rich or poor — access to the most important learning tool of our time."[58] Limited funding, lack of equipment or outdated equipment, too few terminals or access points, and a

---

[53]Robert J. Sternberg, "Thinking Styles: Key to Understanding Student Performance," *Phi Delta Kappan* (January 1990), pp. 366–371.
[54]Peter West, "Wired for the Future," *Education Week,* January 11, 1995, p. 8.
[55]John Merrow, "Four Million Computers Can't Be Wrong," *Education Week,* March 29, 1995, pp. 39, 52.
[56]Patrick Suppes, "Computer Technology and the Future of Education," *Phi Delta Kappan* (April 1968), pp. 420–423.
[57]Simon Hooper and Lloyd P. Rieber, "Teaching Instruction and Technology," in Ornstein and Behar, *Contemporary Issues,* pp. 258–259.
[58]Keith Geiger, "Computer Learning Achieves Lift Off," *Education Week,* May 24, 1995, p. 11.

High potential costs

shortage of teacher in-service training all present barriers to students' use of "the information superhighway." Indeed, few classrooms come equipped with cable television, telephones, or modems, and even fewer are wired for new technologies.[59] The cost of wiring schools (many of them old buildings) for cable and fiber optics is a major concern. Low-end estimates provided by Secretary of Education Richard Riley start at $10 billion, and high-end estimates range into the hundreds of billions of dollars.[60] This problem, however, could be lessened by AT&T's recent announcement that it will provide more than 100,000 public and private schools nationwide with easy access to the Internet, including software and free dial-up Internet services.[61]

Access improving

Changes are coming, however, and quickly. The National Center for Educational Statistics reported that, in 1998, 78 percent of the nation's schools were connected to the Internet (up from 35 percent in 1994), and projections are this figure will be 95 percent by 2000. Although only about 14 percent of the nation's classrooms had Internet access in 1996, it is increasing rapidly, as is the percentage of students with computer access at home (36 percent in 1993 and projected to be 50 percent by 2000).[62]

Impersonal machine or increased human contact?

Early in the computer revolution, some educators worried that computerized instruction involved students with machines and materials that, in themselves, had minimal emotional and affective components. Such critics justifiably contended that substituting a machine for a human teacher left the student with no true guidance and with too little personal interaction. The expansion of the Internet and the increasing access to it in schools across the country should help combat this impersonal aspect of computers. With e-mail and other electronic means of contact, students can reach other people, not merely other collections of information.[63] Moreover, the computer can be used to build a sense of inquiry, to "mess about," to explore, and to improve thinking skills. When students learn how to think and explore with the computer, their potential for innovation and creativity is unlimited.[64]

Video and Satellite Systems

Along with the computer, advances in video technology have brought many other valuable tools for instruction. In foreign language, English, science, history, geography, government, and even the arts (music, drama, dance, creative writing, visual arts), teachers have discovered considerable value in the use of videotapes, videodisks, CD-ROMs, satellite links, telecommunication networks (Channel 1 for news and current events), and even cable TV, and have felt that this technology makes instruction more accessible and productive.[65]

Widespread use of videos

Videotapes, cassettes, and disks can be used for instruction in classrooms, libraries, resource centers, and students' homes. A 1997 study by the Corporation for

---

[59]Peter West, "Logged On for Learning," *Education Week,* January 11, 1995, p. 10.; and U.S. General Accounting Office, *School Facilities: America's Schools Not Designed or Equipped for 21st Century* (Washington: U. S. General Accounting Office, 1995).
[60]West, "Wired for the Future," p. 8.
[61]Peter West, "AT&T to Offer All Schools Free Access to Internet Services," *Education Week,* November 8, 1995, p. 11.
[62]Deb Reichmann, "Nerd Discipline Needed in Schools," *The Sun,* September 7, 1998, p. C4; *Digest of Education Statistics, 1997,* pp. 457–458; Table 421, p. 467.
[63]Odvard E. Dyrli, "Surfing the World Wide Web to Education Hot Spots," *Technology and Learning* (October 1995), pp. 44–51.
[64]Robert C. Johnston, "Connecting with Technology," *Education Week,* May 10, 1995, pp. 27–28.
[65]Dennis Knapczyk, "Staff Development in Rural Schools Through Distance Education," *Educational Media International* (June 1993), pp. 72–82.

Public Broadcasting showed that TV, video, and the Internet are more widely used and more fully integrated into the curriculum than previously.[66] And some studies show increased student achievement in courses with integrated video segments.[67] Since videos can be played at any convenient time, students never have to miss a lesson. Hundreds of catalogs offer videos on a wide range of subjects; in addition, many school systems and teachers have begun to produce their own videos for specific instructional purposes. With the help of a videoprinter, individual images from the screen — photographs, tables, graphs, or any other useful picture — can be printed on paper for further study. Educators are also investigating ways to use the popularity of videogames for teaching purposes. Math, reading, and writing lessons can be written in a videogame format, and the student will find practice and drill more lively in a game atmosphere.

Interactive videos

More and more, videos are designed to be interactive — that is, to respond to the student's input. The term *interactive video instruction (IVI)* has been applied to realistic simulations and action-reaction situations that are presented as part of an instructional program. The program can tell the viewer if a response is right or wrong; or the viewer can be offered a choice of options and the program will then display the outcome of the option chosen. Interactive videos can be used either for individual lessons or for instruction in small groups.

Virtual reality

As one educator says, video technology "is the next best thing to being there." In fact, in some applications students enter a *virtual reality* far from their classroom. They might interact with zookeepers at the San Diego Zoo, plan their upcoming field trip with local museum staff, or interact directly with White House staffers on a "hot" issue before the Congress. Video use in schools has increased at such a staggering rate that teachers must plan ways to integrate it into the curriculum.[68] In an era when the number of videos rented from video stores surpasses the total number of books checked out of libraries, teachers should help students become critical video consumers, aware of how visual images affect us as individuals and as a society.[69]

Distance Education.   Many of the electronic systems discussed in the last two sections have the potential for transporting educational materials and instruction across long distances. The term **distance education** refers to the many ways in which schools make use of this technology.

Educational TV via satellite or cable

For example, schools may select television programs specifically developed for educational purposes and have them beamed into the classroom by satellite. This is particularly useful for small, rural schools with limited local resources, as well as for colleges and universities as they reach beyond their traditional service areas.[70]

---

[66]Corporation for Public Broadcsting, *Study of School Uses of Television and Video: 1996–1997 School Year Summary Report* (Washington, D.C.: Corporation for Public Broadcasting, 1997).
[67]William Harwood and Maureen McMahon, "Effects of Integrated Video Media on Student Achievement and Attitude in High School Chemistry," *Journal of Research in Science Teaching* (August 1997), pp. 617–631.
[68]George Peterson, "Geography and Technology in the Classroom," *NASSP Bulletin* (October 1994), pp. 25–29; Kerry O'Dell et al., "Instructional Technology: The Information Superhighway, the Internet, Interactive Video Networks," *Agricultural Education Magazine* (August 1994), pp. 5–11, 15–17; and "Windows on the World," *Education Week*, February 8, 1995, pp. 36–37.
[69]Allan C. Ornstein, "Video Technology and the Urban Curriculum," *Education and Urban Society* (May 1991), pp. 335–341.
[70]Jerry D. Pepple, Dale A. Law, and Sheri Kallembach, "A Vision of Rural Education for 2001," *Educational Horizons* (Fall 1990), pp. 50–58; and *Master Plan for Distance Learning: An Evolving Technological Process* (Austin, Tex: Texas Higher Education Coordinating Board, 1996).

Teleconferences

Schools can also make use of home cable systems that carry educational programming, such as the Discovery, Learning, and History channels, each of which offers special programs on a wide range of subjects.

Widely used in business and industry, teleconferences have also begun to appear in school systems. In a typical conference, a resource person, teacher, or group of students is viewed through the television screen talking to or instructing other students or participants. Viewers can watch as if they were across the table, even though they may be thousands of miles away. The viewing audience can ask questions and make decisions about what further information should be presented.[71]

Rapid spread of distance education

With the expansion of video phone links and the Internet, distance education is becoming a resource not just for isolated or small schools but for any school that wants to extend its students' horizons. U.S. schools currently spend $500 million annually on distance education, and projections are that the figure will reach $2 billion by the turn of the century.[72] Today teachers are using electronic technology to put their students in touch with experts, teachers, and other students around the globe. The point of contact can be as close as an adjacent school or as far away as the frigid Antarctic.[73]

Teachers need technological competence

To some educators, our rapid technological advances spell the eventual demise of "pencil technology." In the twenty-first century, the textbook may not be the norm that it once was; it may be incidental, or it may take on different forms — talking to the student, monitoring his or her progress, and presenting information in a highly visual and stimulating way. What experts agree, however, is that technological knowledge and skills will be an essential component in the preparation and repertoire of all teachers.

Emerging Curriculum Trends: An Agenda for the Future

Computer knowledge as fundamental skill

In discussing computer links and communications technology, we have already begun to step from the present into the future. What other trends, we may ask, will the future bring to American classrooms? Some of the most important likely trends are described in the following list.

1. *Electronic education and technical literacy.* Because of the revolution in technology, computer literacy stands beside the three Rs as a fundamental skill.[74] According to government projections, of the ten fastest-growing occupations, four require knowledge of computers (technician, systems analyst, programmer, and operator).[75] Other trends suggest a heavy high-tech influence in such growth areas as biogenetics, biotechnology, health care, computer and video software, robotics,

---

[71]Allan C. Ornstein, "Curriculum Trends Revisited," *Peabody Journal of Education* (Summer 1994), pp. 4–20; and Allan C. Ornstein, "Bringing Telecommunications and Videos into the Classroom," *High School Journal* (April–May 1990), pp. 252–257.
[72]Peter West, "Satellite Space Crunch Seen Impeding Distance Learning," *Education Week*, March 22, 1995, p. 3.
[73]"Distance Learning," *The Electronic School*, a supplement to *American School Board Journal* (January 1998), pp. A1–40.
[74]Tweed W. Ross and Gerald D. Bailey, "Wanted: A New Literacy for the Information Age," *NASSP Bulletin* (September 1994), pp. 31–35; Ora Silverstein, "Imagery in Scientific and Technical Literacy for All," in *Imagery and Visual Literacy* (Conference of the International Visual Literacy Association, Tempe, Arizona, October 12–16, 1994); and National Center for Education Statistics, *Student Use of Computers* (Washington, D.C.: National Center for Education Statistics, 1995).
[75]Suneel Ratan, "A New Divide Between Have's and Have Nots?" *Time,* Special Issue: Welcome to Cyberspace (Spring 1995), p. 25; and *Occupational Projections and Training Data* (Washington, D.C.: U.S. Department of Labor, 1990).

Government projections and other trends suggest high-tech influence in growth areas such as biogenetics, robotics, and computer and video software. *(© Peter Menzel/Stock Boston)*

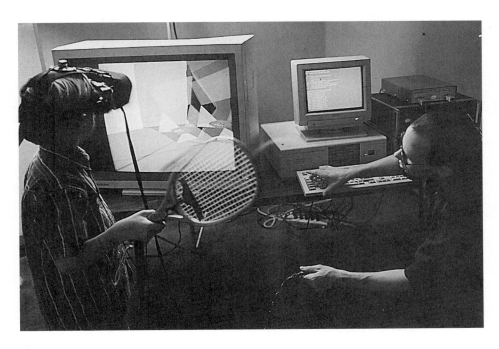

telecommunications, microelectronics, environmental science and engineering, toxic waste and pollution, space, and the oceans.[76] Soon there will be technical occupations for which we do not even have names.

Preparing students to use technology

In cooperation with industry and government, schools must identify the emerging technologies and services and provide a curriculum that prepares students for viable careers. In part, this means educating future scientists who can design, develop, and apply the new technology. But not everyone needs to become a scientific expert. For many occupations, people simply need to understand the technological basics — what buttons to push under what conditions and how to make machines provide the service or information they were designed to offer.[77]

2. *Lifelong learning.* The trend toward lifelong learning is occurring in all modern societies as a result of the knowledge explosion and the rapid social, technological, and economic changes that force people to prepare for second or third careers and to keep themselves updated on new developments that affect their personal and social goals. Therefore, it is not surprising to find lifelong learning an important element in the federal government's Goals 2000, and an especially important element in the professional life of a teacher.[78] Taking note of this trend, the Carnegie Commission has developed the concept of a "step-in, step-out" educational system for lifelong learning. This means that people could move in and

Education at many stages of life

---

[76]Patrick L. Sheetz, *Recruiting Trends, 1993–94: A Study of Business, Industries and Government Agencies Employing New College Graduates* (East Lansing: Michigan State University, Career Development and Placement Services, 1993); and Daniel Tomal, "Biotechnology Career Education: Educational Technology Imperative for the 21st Century," *Technology Teacher* (September–October 1992), pp. 7–9.

[77]Margaret Riel, "Educational Change in a Technology Rich Environment," *Journal of Research on Computing in Education* (Summer 1994), pp. 452–474; and Ornstein, "Curriculum Trends Revisited," pp. 4–20.

[78]*National Goals for Education: Goals 2000* (Washington, D.C.: Department of Education, 1994); and *The National Educational Goals Report; Building a Nation of Learners* (Washington, D.C.: The National Educational Goals Panel, 1996).

out of educational programs throughout their lives. Accelerating developments in technology, specifically personal computers in homes and access to the Internet, help to make such learning individualized, relevant, and very convenient.[79]

Some observers believe that much of the learning that has been provided by elementary, secondary, and postsecondary schools may be provided by business and industry in the future, especially to meet the needs of a skilled work force in high-tech and information-based industries.[80] Still other scenarios envision educating adolescents and adults through a network of community resources and small learning centers and libraries.

Geographic illiteracy

3. *The restoration of geography.* Geography gradually disappeared from the school curriculum in the 1960s and 1970s. Absorbed into social studies, it was often delegated to teachers who preferred to emphasize history, and it also soon disappeared as a requirement for college admission. As a result of this neglect, American students became geographically illiterate. The National Assessment of Educational Progress revealed abysmal performance by students in the area of geography.

Nationwide efforts

The publication of *A Nation at Risk* in 1983 sounded the alarm. In 1984 the National Geographic Association, in concert with the Association of American Geographers and the Association for Geographic Education, began a national program to improve understanding of the basic principles of geography and special methods for teaching the discipline. As a result of these efforts, geography is undergoing a renaissance in the school curriculum and is being linked to various curriculum foci, such as back-to-basics, multicultural education, environmental education, and global education.[81] Additionally, geography is one of the core subjects in the America 2000 and Goals 2000 reform plans. Therefore, many educators expect this trend to continue and expand in the future.[82]

4. *National curriculum standards.* As a by-product of the 1990 National Governor's Conference and its report, *Goals 2000,* the U.S. Department of Education funded the development of national curriculum standards in seven subject fields: history, geography, economics, English, foreign languages, mathematics, and science. Many of these efforts have been spearheaded by professional organizations in the respective disciplines, such as the American Historical Association, the National Academy of Science, and the National Council of Teachers of Mathematics.

Ongoing discussion of national standards

When draft standards were circulated for feedback in the mid-1990s, they aroused much controversy, particularly the history, English, and math standards. Nevertheless, back-to-basics proponents are promoting national curriculum standards as a way to restore the primacy of basic content to the curriculum. In 1994 the Clinton administration, as part of the National Goals Project, offered financial incentives for states to adopt the national curriculum standards. The concept of national curriculum standards has not, however, been sufficiently accepted for

---

[79]*Understanding Information Technology in Kindergarten Through Grade 12, 1994–1995* (Wellesley, Mass: CCA Research, 1996).

[80]Michael W. Apple, "Curriculum in the Year 2000," *Phi Delta Kappan* (January 1983), pp. 321–326; Barbara L. McCombs, "Motivation and Lifelong Learning," *Educational Psychologist* (Spring 1991), pp. 117–128; and Roger J. Vaughan, "The New Limits to Growth," *Phi Delta Kappan* (February 1991), pp. 446–449.

[81]Donald N. Rallis and Helen Rallis, "Changing the Image of Geography," *The Social Studies* (July–August 1995), pp. 167–168; and Karen Diegmueller, "Developers Set Final Standards for Geography," *Education Week,* October 26, 1994, pp. 1, 14–15.

[82]Norman Bettis, "The Renaissance of Geography Education in the United States," *International Journal of Social Education* (Fall–Winter 1996), pp. 61–72.

states to buy into national standards; thus it remains a subject of considerable discussion among curriculum developers at the national, state, and local levels.[83]

Status of foreign language study

5. *International education.* As many educators and laypeople have pointed out, the increasing interdependence among nations demands that Americans become more knowledgeable about distant lands. One area of international education that U.S. schools may particularly need to address is foreign language instruction. Although forty states require schools to offer two years of foreign language study, only twenty-seven states offer it as part of the core curriculum, on an equal footing with other major disciplines. In 1994, 35 percent of U.S. secondary students were enrolled in foreign language classes, and at the elementary level the percentage was a miniscule 4.5 percent.[84]

Most common languages

When students do study foreign languages, they do not necessarily concentrate on those that are most important in the current world economy. The most common spoken language in the world is Mandarin, followed by English, Hindi, and Spanish; Japanese ranks tenth, and German and French rank even lower. Nearly all foreign language programs in American schools offer Spanish and French; but few offer Japanese, even fewer teach Mandarin, and practically none offer Hindi. Failure to train students in some of the world's most common languages may severely limit the future growth of U.S. trade. However, surveys show that students do link selection of a foreign language to occupational considerations, and helping students see this connection can increase the study of foreign languages, especially those that are traditionally less common in American schools.[85]

U.S. education will probably become more international in other ways as well. Educators may expand travel exchange programs and perhaps make study in another culture a requirement for graduation. Emphasis on international geography, history, political science, and economics may increase. As the world becomes more interconnected and interdependent, such needs will become more evident and more funds may be devoted to the area of global curriculum.

AIDS epidemic

6. *Health education and physical fitness.* Trends in the health of the U.S. population are producing new pressures to expand or change the curriculum. For example, the epidemic of AIDS (acquired immunodeficiency syndrome), with its dire risk to sexually active adolescents, has forced educators to confront the issue of student health in a new way. Predictions are that by the year 2000 almost 50 million people around the world will be affected by the disease, and almost two million will be Americans. The Center for Disease Control and Prevention (CDC) states that the annual number of AIDS cases attributed to heterosexual transmission is very likely to continue increasing, with 86 percent of all sexually transmitted cases of the disease occurring among people in the fifteen to twenty-nine age group. Although the Goals 2000: Educate America Act urges that a drug and alcohol curriculum be taught as an integral part of comprehensive health education, it

---

[83]Meg Sommerfield, "Sciences Group Quietly Unveils Final Standards," *Education Week,* December 13, 1995, p. 1, 9; Karen Diegmueller, "Report Offers Ways to Improve History Standards," *Education Week,* January 17, 1996, p. 8; and Nell Noddings, "Thinking About Standards," *Phi Delta Kappan* (November 1997), pp. 184–189.

[84]"Foreign Languages: State of the States," *Education Week,* February 8, 1995, p. 4.

[85]William R. Connors, "Linking Foreign Language to Occupational Education in a Rural High School" (ERIC Document 369644, 1994); John Watzke, "Less Commonly Taught Languages Taught in High School," *Education Digest* 58 (1992), pp. 69–72; Ronald A Walton, *Expanding the Vision of Foreign Language Education* (Washington, D.C.: Johns Hopkins University, National Foreign Language Center, 1992).

Reasons for inadequate AIDS education

is silent regarding AIDS.[86] Some educators see the AIDS epidemic as literally a life-or-death matter for their students, but schools have been slow to include AIDS education in the curriculum.[87] One reason for the lack of AIDS education is the continued controversy over the disease and the recommended preventive measures. Many parents and educators have been particularly incensed by programs that distribute condoms in schools. A more basic reason for the lack of AIDS education, however, is that only twenty-seven states require any form of health or sex education, and when health education is offered, it is more likely to be taught by science, physical education, or other subject-area teachers than by certified health teachers. Elementary teachers are generally poorly trained in this field.[88] Many educators believe that this problem must and will be addressed in the future.

Drug use

Drugs are another critical matter. As detailed in Chapter 9, after a decade of decline in illicit drug use among teenagers, there is a disturbing trend toward increased use of marijuana, tobacco, and other drugs. For example, marijuana use among teenagers nearly doubled from 1992 to 1994.[89]

Diet and exercise

Dietary habits and exercise are yet another health concern. Citing medical evidence of high blood pressure and elevated blood fats among American youngsters, physicians have criticized the high-fat, burgers-and-fries diet common among school-age children. A recent federal study showed that American high-school students are exercising less than in the past and watching television or playing video games three or more hours every school day.[90] In addition, schoolchildren have been increasingly unable to pass basic physical fitness tests, and they do poorly on measures of body development, strength, and flexibility.[91] As one report summed up the situation, "We presently have a generation of adolescents that is heavier, less physically active and that is smoking more than its parents were at the same age." For that reason, the American Cancer Society and American Public Health Association have developed a draft set of national standards for health education and have called for its inclusion in the high-school curriculum as a core subject.[92]

High immigration rate

7. *Immigrant education.* The education of immigrant children in America has growing implications for curriculum. The United States is currently in the midst of the second largest immigration wave since the beginning of the twentieth century. Legal immigration now accounts for up to one-half of the annual growth in the

---

[86]Clark Robenstine, "The School and HIV Education After the First Decade of AIDS" (ERIC Document 379250, 1994), pp. 1–25; W. James Popham, "Wanted: AIDS Education That Works," *Phi Delta Kappan* (March 1993), pp. 557–562; and Danielle Skripak and Liane Summerfield, *HIV/AIDS Education in Teacher Preparation Programs* (Washington, D.C.: ERIC Clearinghouse on Teaching and Teacher Education, 1996).

[87]David Sumpter and Tammy Benson, "Aids Education in the Middle School Language Arts Program? Yes!" *Rural Educator* (Fall 1995), pp. 1–2,4.

[88]Robenstine, "The School and HIV," p. 8.

[89]"A Disturbing Trend: Drug Use Among Teenagers Rises for Third Straight Year," *Education Week*, January 11, 1995, p. 10; and Lauran Neergaard, "Survey: Teens' Marijuana Use Nearly Doubled over Two Years," *Philadelphia Inquirer*, September 13, 1995, p. A9.

[90]"High School Students Are Exercising Less, Federal Study Shows," *Education Week*, November 16, 1994, p. 7; and James Story et al., "School-Based Weight Management Services: Perceptions and Practices of School Nurses and Administrators," *American Journal of Health Promotion* (January–February 1997), pp. 183–185.

[91]Nancy Benac, "Diet Guide for Kids Targets Cholesterol, Heart Disease," *Chicago Sun Times*, April 9, 1991, p. 22; Dick Thompson, "A How To Guide on Cholesterol," *Time*, October 19, 1987, p. 215; and "Time Out for Fitness," *Health Magazine* (April 1991), pp. 10, 11.

[92]"Core Subjects Status for Health Education Sought," *Education Week*, May 10, 1995, p. 5.

U.S. population. In fact, nearly one in eleven U.S. residents in 1994 was foreign born — nearly double the 1970 figure.[93]

Sources of immigration

The new immigrant population differs in ethnic origins from that of the past. Previously 80 percent of immigrants to the United States came from Western Europe and Canada. By 1994, however, the leading source countries (in rank order) were Mexico, the Philippines, South Korea, Taiwan/China, India, Cuba, the Dominican Republic, Jamaica, Canada, Vietnam, the United Kingdom, and Iran. Today as many as 78 percent of immigrants come from non-Western or underdeveloped countries. Moreover, about 300,000 people per year arrive as illegal immigrants, mainly from Mexico, Central America, and the Caribbean.[94] At present,

Growth of school "minorities"

U.S. public schools are 34 percent "minority"; this percentage will reach almost 40 percent by 2000,[95] and in many areas minorities will be in the numerical majority.

For some recent immigrants, life in America has been a remarkable success story. Many, however, face language barriers, ethnic prejudice, health problems,

Difficulties faced by immigrant families

and a lack of good jobs. A significant number of immigrant families who arrived in the late 1980s and 1990s are worse off economically than comparable U.S. natives. In addition, because of cultural differences in learning styles or thinking patterns, immigrant children may be labeled "learning disabled" or "slow." Even when this is not the case, value hierarchies vary widely across cultures, so that immigrant children have diverse attitudes about school, teacher authority, gender differences, social class, and behavior, all of which have implications for success in school.[96]

Studies show that after about fifteen years of living in the United States immigrants are about as well off as comparable natives. After twenty-five years the immigrants often pull ahead.[97] Nevertheless, few educators would argue that the first generation of immigrant children should be allowed to flounder on the assumption that the next generation will catch up. Many educators believe that immigrant children need special programs, such as expanded bilingual and multicultural education, to help them acclimate themselves. Other educators, however, believe English language immersion should take place as soon as possible. California's Proposition 227, enacted in 1998, requires the state's one thousand school districts to place limited-English-proficient students in English

Debate about special programs

immersion classes rather than in bilingual classes (as described in Chapter 11).[98] Multicultural programs also help longer-established groups understand how much the new immigrants can contribute to American society. However, as we saw in Chapter 11, multicultural education remains a controversial subject, and schools are still working out their responses to the new rise of immigration.

---

[93]Center for Immigration Studies, "Immigration Related Statistics," *Backgrounder* (July 1995), pp. 6, 11; Augie Cannon, "One in Eleven U.S. Residents Born Abroad — Double 1970 Level," *Philadelphia Inquirer*, August 29, 1995, p. A16.
[94]Harold Hodgkinson, "A True Nation of the World," *Education Week*, January 18, 1995, p. 32; John Fallows, "The New Immigrants," *Atlantic* (November 1983), pp. 45–68, 85–89; and Jason Juffus, *The Impact of the Immigration Reform and Control Act on Immigration* (Washington, D.C.: Urban Institute, 1991).
[95]*State Indicators in Education* (Washington, D.C.: National Center for Education Statistics, 1997), p. 137; and Hodgkinson, "A True Nation," p. 32.
[96]Xue Lan Rong and Judith Prelssle, *Educating Impaired Students* (Thousand Oaks, Calif: Corwin Press, 1998).
[97]Cannon, "One in Eleven U.S. Residents," p. A16; and Gary Imhoff, *Learning in Two Languages* (New Brunswick, N.J.: Transaction Press, 1990).
[98]Lynn Schnalberg, "Schools Gear Up as Bilingual Education Law Takes Effect," *Education Week*, August 5, 1998, p. 29.

Words of Caution

Although curriculum should evolve to serve a changing society, we caution the reader on several fronts. Change for the sake of change is not good. Schools throughout the ages have viewed their programs as being on the cutting edge of progress, and they have often been wrong.

Balancing old and new

New knowledge, indeed, is not necessarily better than old knowledge. Are we to throw away most of Aristotle, Galileo, Kepler, Darwin, and Newton merely because they are not part of this century? If we stress only scientific and technological knowledge, we could languish physically, aesthetically, morally, and spiritually. We must learn to prune away old and irrelevant parts of the curriculum and integrate and balance new knowledge. As we modify and update content, we need to protect schools and students against fads and frills, and especially against extremist points of view. We must keep in perspective the type of society we have, the values we cherish, and the educational goals we wish to achieve.

Summing Up

1. In organizing the curriculum, most educators hold to the traditional concept of curriculum as the body of subjects, or subject matter. Nevertheless, a number of contemporary educators who are more concerned with the experiences of the learner regard the student as the focus of curriculum.

2. Examples of a subject-centered approach include the following types of curriculum: (1) subject-area, (2) perennialist and essentialist, (3) back-to-basics, and (4) new core.

3. Examples of a student-centered approach include the following types of curriculum: (1) activity-centered approaches, (2) relevant curriculum, (3) the humanistic approach, (4) alternative or free schools programs, and (5) values-centered curriculum.

4. Recent decades have produced a number of significant instructional innovations, including (1) individualized instruction, (2) cooperative learning, (3) mastery instruction, (4) critical thinking, (5) computerized instruction, and (6) the use of video and satellite systems. The last two areas of innovation have made distance learning an increasingly important resource.

5. Future curricular trends will probably include the following: (1) electronic education and technical literacy, (2) lifelong learning, (3) return of geography, (4) national curriculum standards, (5) international education, (6) health education and physical fitness, and (7) immigrant education.

Key Terms

curriculum (452)

subject-centered curricula (453)

subject-area curriculum (455)

perennialist approach to curriculum (455)

essentialist approach to curriculum (455)

back-to-basics curriculum (456)

new core curriculum (core subjects) (457)

student-centered curricula (459)

activity-centered curriculum (459)

relevant curriculum (460)

humanistic approach to curriculum (461)

alternative or free schools (461)

values-centered curriculum *(462)*

character education *(462)*

individualized instruction *(470)*

cooperative learning *(471)*

mastery instruction *(472)*

critical thinking *(474)*

hypermedia *(475)*

distance education *(477)*

Discussion Questions

1. What are the benefits and limitations of using a single textbook as the basis of course curriculum?

2. Does your teacher-education program seem to favor one curriculum approach over another? Why might this be so? What kind of curriculum approach would you recommend for a teacher-education program? Relate your approach to your philosophy of education.

3. Which of the instructional approaches discussed in this chapter best fits your teaching style? Why? Share your thinking with a classmate.

4. List the curriculum changes you expect to see in the future. How will these affect your work as a teacher?

Suggested Projects for Professional Development

1. How is curriculum organized in the schools you visit? Ask to see a curriculum guide for your subject field. Is it a general outline of content and activities, or is it a detailed list of objectives, activities, and materials and resources? Which approach do you feel is better for students? More helpful to teachers?

2. In your visits to schools this semester, talk with teachers about the curriculum they teach. Do they use a subject-centered approach, and, if so, which of the four subject-centered approaches described in this chapter best describes their procedure? If they use a student-centered approach, which of the five student-centered approaches best describes what they do? Of the several schools you have visited, explain which school's approach best fits your own ideas for a curriculum.

3. Talk with members of the educational faculty at your college. What do they see as the pros and cons of subject-centered versus student-centered curricula?

4. Draw up your own version of Table 14.1, reflecting what you see as the proper division of time for today's elementary schools. (Or do a similar chart for high schools or middle schools.) Show your chart to one or more classmates and defend your decisions.

5. Explore the Internet and other electronic resources for learning. Identify a series of topics about which you would like to know more to further your professional knowledge and development.

6. Using the following Internet Resources section, select a topic or unit of instruction and develop a portfolio of resources and sample lesson plans to use as a teacher.

Suggested Readings and Resources

Internet Resources

The development of national curriculum standards can be followed by checking the latest documents on the subject at the U.S. Department of Education's Internet site **www.ed.gov** or **gopher.ed.gov.** For particular types of curricular or instructional resources, the Ask ERIC Virtual Library (accessible via **ericir.syr.edu**) is a treasure trove, and there are hundreds of other interesting offerings on the World Wide Web, with new ones appearing every month. For a sample, you might look at these sites: Academy One (**www.nptn.org:80/cyber. serv/AOneP**); the JASON Project (**seawifs.gsfc.nasa.gov/scripts/JASON.html**); Kids on Campus (**www.tc.cornell.edu/Kids.on.Campus/WWWDemo**); EdWeb (**edweb.cnidr.org:90**); and Explorer (**unite.ukans.edu**). Information on curriculum and instruction can also be found by exploring state-level sites and other agencies accessible at **info.asu.edu:70//asu-cwis/education/other/sea** or by using Infoseek, Yahoo, or other search engines for "education journals."

Videos

Active Learning. VHS, 22 minutes (1993). The Learning Channel and the National Education Association, NEA Professional Library, P.O. Box 509, West Haven, CT 05616. Phone: 800-229-4200. *A look at learning through the eyes of students, with emphasis on active learning strategies and their pros and cons.*

Censorship or Selection: Choosing Books for Public Schools. VHS, 60 minutes (1992). PBS Video, 1320 Braddock Place, Alexandria, VA 22314. Phone: 800-739-5269. *Fred W. Friendly hosts a debate about the selection and censorship of books for public schools.*

Explicit Thinking Skills (Teachers Teach Thinking). VHS, 20 minutes (1991). Skylight Publishing, 200 East Wood St., Suite 274, Palatine, IL 60067. Phone: 800-343-4474. *A program illustrating how a fifth-grade math teacher teaches for, of, about, and with "thinking"; offers a look at some current methods in critical thinking and metacognition.*

Publications

Altbach, Philip G., ed. *Textbooks in American Society.* Albany: State University of New York Press, 1991. *Focusing on how textbooks are produced and selected, this book explains the pressures placed on textbook authors and publishers.*

Beyer, Barry K. *Critical Thinking.* Fastback #385. Bloomington, Ind.: Phi Delta Kappa Educational Foundation, 1995. *A cogent monograph on the essential features of critical thinking and ways to use it in classrooms.*

Boyer, Ernest L. *High School: A Report on Secondary Education in America.* New York: Harper and Row, 1983. *An analysis of high-school curricula in the United States and proposals for a new core curriculum.*

Boyer, Ernest L. *The Basic School: A Community of Learning.* Princeton, N.J.: The Carnegie Foundation, 1995. *A description of Boyer's proposed eight core commonalities in curriculum.*

Connelly, Michael F., and D. Jean Claudinin. *Teachers as Curriculum Planners.* New York: Teachers College Press, 1988. *Offers a number of case studies on the role of teachers in planning and developing the curriculum.*

Doll, Ronald C. *Curriculum Improvement: Decision Making and Process.* 8th ed. Boston: Allyn and Bacon, 1992. *Provides an excellent overview of curriculum improvement, with emphasis on practical principles, problems, and solutions.*

The Electronic School, 1998. Supplement to the *American School Board Journal.* This *periodical offers excellent suggestions for electronic educational resources for schools.*

Johnson, David W. *Reaching Out: Interpersonal Effectiveness and Self-Actualization,* 5th ed. Needham Heights, Mass.: Allyn and Bacon, 1993. *Describes the theory and practice of cooperative learning and how to enhance student self-actualization.*

Marzano, Robert J. *A Different Kind of Classroom: Teaching with Dimensions of Learning.* Alexandria, Va.: Association for Supervision and Curriculum Development, 1992. *Describes teaching, the psychology of learning, curriculum planning, and assessment.*

Sizer, Theodore R. *Horace's Compromise: The Dilemma of the American School.* Rev. ed. Boston: Houghton Mifflin, 1985. *A book on school reform that is still quite relevant.*

Sizer, Theodore R. *Horace's School: Redesigning the American High School.* Boston: Houghton Mifflin, 1992. *Looks at the goals of U.S. secondary education and at high schools in particular, with a special focus on mastery learning.*

Slavin, Robert J. *Cooperative Learning: Theory Research and Practice.* Boston: Allyn and Bacon, 1995. *An excellent book on cooperative learning theory and practice.*

PART SIX

Effective Education

INTERNATIONAL AND AMERICAN PERSPECTIVES

CHAPTER FIFTEEN

International Education

Many educational reformers have suggested that the United States could improve its educational system by emulating other countries. Japanese education has received particular attention because it appears to have contributed in large measure to Japan's economic success during the past fifty years. But it is not a simple matter to imitate educational practices from other countries. Would they work in an American context? Do they mesh with American beliefs and values?

Before beginning to answer such questions, educators need to understand the varieties of educational systems that exist in other countries: how they resemble one another, how they differ, and which particular features are most effective in which contexts. In this chapter we offer an introduction to that kind of analysis. We then consider education in developing countries and international studies of school improvement. Finally, we offer a brief comment on the accomplishments of U.S. schools in an international context. As you read the chapter, try to work toward answers to the following basic questions:

- What do educational systems in various countries have in common? In what respects do they differ?

- How do educational systems differ with respect to the resources they devote to education and the percentage of students they enroll?

- How does the achievement of U.S. students compare with that of students in other countries?

- Which countries provide examples of outstanding educational activities that may be worth emulating elsewhere?

- What should be done to improve education in developing countries?

- How do the purposes and attainments of U.S. schools compare with those of other countries?

Commonalities in Educational Systems

Despite the great variety in educational systems worldwide, certain commonalities exist. The following sections describe some characteristics and problems that are virtually universal: the strong relationships between students' social-class origins and their success in school; the educational challenges posed by multicultural populations; the typical teaching approaches and the professional conditions that teachers face; and dilemmas arising from the relationship between education and economic development.

Social-Class Origins and School Outcomes

Privileged vs. less privileged students

As we noted in Chapter 10, strong relationships between students' socioeconomic background and their success in school and in the economic system have been reported in various national and international studies. For example, World Bank studies have reported that family socioeconomic background is a salient predictor of students' achievement in both industrialized and developing countries. Similarly, Donald Treiman found that individuals' social-class origins and background are related to their educational and occupational attainment regardless of whether their society is rich or poor, politically liberal or conservative.[1] A multitude of studies such as these also demonstrate that the family and home environments of low-income students in other countries generate the same kinds of educational disadvantages as in the United States.[2]

Multicultural Populations and Problems

Rising diversity

Except in a few homogeneous countries, nationwide systems of education enroll diverse groups of students who differ significantly with respect to race, ethnicity, religion, native language, and cultural practices. (Because of its geographic isolation and cultural insularity, Japan is one of the exceptions to this generalization.) Most large nations historically have included numerous racial/ethnic and cultural subgroups, but the twentieth century seems to have greatly accelerated the mixture of diverse groups across and within national boundaries. World and regional wars, global depressions and recessions, migration and immigration to large urban centers that offer expanded economic opportunity — these and other destabilizing forces have led some historians to see recent decades as the era of the migrant and the refugee.[3]

Multicultural challenges

Not surprisingly, then, other countries encounter challenges in multicultural education similar to those of the United States (see Chapters 11 and 13). This is partly because minority racial, ethnic, and religious groups in most nations

[1]Donald J. Treiman, *Occupational Prestige in Comparative Perspective* (New York: Academic Press, 1977); and Marlaine E. Lockheed, Bruce Fuller, and Ronald Nyirongo, *Family Background and School Achievement* (New York: The World Bank, 1988). See also Daniele Checchi, "Education and Intergenerational Mobility in Occupations," *American Journal of Economics and Sociology* (July 1997), pp. 331–350.

[2]Alan C. Purves and Daniel U. Levine, eds., *Educational Policy and International Assessment* (Berkeley, Calif.: McCutchan, 1975); Marilyn Osborn, Patricia Broadfoot, Charles Planel, and Andrew Pollard, "Social Class, Educational Opportunity and Equal Entitlement," *Comparative Education* (November 1997), pp. 375–393; and Carole Bellamy, *The State of the World's Children 1999* (New York: UNICEF, 1999).

[3]Marcelo M. Suarez-Orozco, "Migration, Minority Status, and Education," *Anthropology and Education Quarterly* (June 1991), pp. 99–118; and "Workers of the World," *Economist,* May 30–June 6, 1998.

GETTING TO THE SOURCE

Social Class and English Schools

GENE MAEROFF

Gene Maeroff, a senior fellow at the Carnegie Foundation for the Advancement of Teaching, participated in a study group that visited English schools in 1990. Members of the study group were struck by the extent to which many working-class students in England were alienated from education. Comparing what he saw and heard with our situation in the United States, Maeroff found both similarities and differences.

An American visitor to one high school asked a small group of students who had stayed on after age 16 why they thought their fellow students had left school. This particular school served some 900 students in a working-class neighborhood, in which an estimated 20% of the fathers were unemployed because the economy had shifted and former employers had closed down production. The students said of the school leavers:

"Many of them lacked confidence that they could do the schoolwork."

"They wanted to make money."

"They were tired of school."

"Their parents may have needed them at home."

"They may have wanted more independence than there is in school."

There appeared to be a tendency among students in such schools to hide their interest in education and in achievement. Said one teacher, speaking of those who remained enrolled after age 16: "A potential achiever must be strong-willed. He could be subject to ridicule. We chaperone them and provide them with a haven from the others [those not yet eligible to leave school]. There are instances of the others destroying the folders of the achievers on the way to and from school."

In Japanese elementary schools, not all lessons are designed to develop students' thinking and problem-solving skills. Many lessons are geared to educating the "whole person." (*© Charles Gupton/Stock Boston*)

What are we hearing here? Clearly, England and the U.S. share problems when it comes to the schools in which students are having the least success. Peer pressure against academic achievement, especially among disadvantaged students, is an obstacle to learning in both countries. Whether in England or in the U.S., the outlook for such young people once they leave school is grim. Legions of youths in both countries depart school utterly unequipped to make their way in a world that demands certain skills and attitudes on the job and that expects a kind of mainstream socialization to fit comfortably into society.

In England, there is the overlay of a historically intractable system of social class that has a devastating effect on the aspirations of young people in the lower class, who in England are overwhelmingly white. These students assume that social mobility is nearly impossible and appear not to aspire to higher education to the degree that poor Americans do. In turn, higher education in England does not play the role that it does in the U.S., where the educational hopes of the disadvantaged are reinforced by nonselective admissions policies and lots of available spaces.

Questions

1. In what ways do working-class students in England appear to exemplify the operation of "resistance theory" as described in Chapter 10? What might you do as a teacher to counteract this tendency and help alienated students stay in school?
2. Why do working-class students in England seem particularly likely to "assume that social mobility is nearly impossible" and to have little hope for advancement through higher education? Do you think that working-class students in the United States hold similar views? In your opinion, to what extent are such views accurate for the United States?
3. Why are educators and public officials in England and many other countries particularly concerned with improving opportunities for working-class students?

Source: Gene I. Maeroff, "Focusing on Urban Education in Britain," *Phi Delta Kappan* (January 1992), p. 357. Reprinted by permission of the author.

frequently are low in socioeconomic status. Familiar issues arise: the ineffectiveness of traditional instruction, the provision of bilingual education, and the desegregation of minority students. England, France, the Netherlands, and other European countries have to cope with a large influx of students from Africa, Asia, the Caribbean, and other distant locations. Germany is struggling to provide effective education for the children of Romany (Gypsy), Slavic, and Turkish migrants, and most West African nations include students from numerous disadvantaged tribal and minority-language groups.[4]

Teaching Approaches and Conditions

Similar teaching practices

Although instructional approaches vary considerably from one teacher to another and the conditions for teaching and learning change accordingly in different classrooms and schools, there is much similarity in the practices typically emphasized around the world. From some points of view, in fact, there is relatively little international variation in the teaching practices most commonly used and the types of challenges and problems that teachers find rewarding or frustrating. Thus two

---

[4]Malcolm Cross, ed., *The Threatening Minority* (Utrecht: ERCOMEB, 1996); and Nigel Grant, "Some Problems of Identity and Education," *Comparative Education* (March 1997), pp. 9–28.

researchers who analyzed data on fifth- through ninth-grade classes in mathematics, social studies, and science in ten countries found "remarkable similarity with respect to the teaching and learning process." In general, in all ten participating countries, the primary classroom activities included teacher-presented lectures or demonstrations plus seatwork activity.[5]

Similar pros and cons for teachers

Scholars in many countries report that teachers typically cite the following sources of "professional discouragement": lack of time to accomplish priority goals, a multiplicity of sometimes conflicting role demands, and lack of full support from administrators. Sources of "professional enthusiasm" generally center on relationships with students and satisfaction with students' accomplishments. Just as in the United States, these sources of teacher enthusiasm and discouragement reflect "the reality of schools."[6]

Education and Economic Development

All countries, whether wealthy or poor, confront difficult decisions in determining how to provide educational services that can improve the economic and social well-being of their populations. Expending resources to provide one type of program usually requires deemphasizing or eliminating others that also may be beneficial. In addition, a particular program may prove ineffective because its prerequisites have been neglected. The most central dilemmas include the following:[7]

Allocating limited resources

Emphasize early years or later years?

1. Should special emphasis be placed on preschool and primary education to ensure a high degree of basic literacy so that secondary and postsecondary schools will draw from a well-developed pool of talent? Or should resources be allocated more to secondary or postsecondary schools to make sure that graduates can compete with the most skilled people in other nations?

Vocational or general education?

2. Should priority be placed on vocational and technical education in order to encourage economic growth and prosperity, which in turn may eventually provide resources to improve general education? Or is it better to emphasize general education now to ensure that the labor force will have strong reading and math skills that will help workers adapt to changes in the future?

Centralized or decentralized?

3. Should decisions about curriculum, instructional methods, and teacher selection be made centrally to ensure that students receive equal opportunities wherever they attend school? Or should decisions be decentralized so that educators can determine what works best in their own buildings or communities?

---

[5]Angela Hilgard and Sid Bourke, "Teaching for Learning: Similarities and Differences Across Countries" (Paper presented at the annual meeting of the American Educational Research Association, Chicago, April 1985), p. 17. See also Max Angus, "Metarules and School Reform" (Paper presented at the annual meeting of the American Educational Research Association, San Diego, April 1998).

[6]Herbert Eibler et al., "A Cross-Cultural Comparison of the Sources of Professional Enthusiasm and Discouragement" (Paper presented at the annual meeting of the American Educational Research Association, San Francisco, April 1986), p. 21. See also Max Angus, *The Rules of School Reform* (London: Falmer, 1998).

[7]Adrian M. Verspoor, *Accelerated Educational Development* (Washington, D.C.: The World Bank, 1990); *Adult Illiteracy and Economic Performance* (Washington, D.C.: Center for Educational Research and Innovation, 1992); Bryan T. Peck, "Compulsory Schooling in Europe," *Phi Delta Kappan* (January 1995), pp. 418–419; and Joseph P. Farrell, "A Retrospective on Educational Planning in Comparative Education," *Comparative Education Review* (August 1997), pp. 277–313.

Differences in Educational Systems and Outcomes

Expenditures for education

Better student-teacher ratios in wealthy regions

Higher enrollment in wealthy regions

Increasing female enrollment

Although the commonalities described above are present in educational systems throughout the world, each system also differs in important ways from other systems. Some of the most significant differences are discussed in the following sections.

Resources Devoted to Education

One fundamental way in which nations differ is in the percentage of their resources devoted to education rather than to other priorities such as highways, health care, and military forces. As a percentage of gross domestic product (wealth produced annually), public expenditures on K–12 and higher education range from 3 to 4.5 percent in nations that are low in average income and/or place relatively little priority on education, to more than 7 percent in some nations that have high average income and/or emphasize education. In the world's poorest countries, average per capita expenditures on military forces are nearly one-third greater than per capita spending for education.[8]

Student-Teacher Ratios at the Primary Level.   Relatively wealthy nations, as well as nations that allocate many of their resources to education, are able to provide a higher level of services than poor nations that mobilize relatively few resources for their schools. For example, average student-teacher ratios at the primary level tend to be much higher in poorer regions than in wealthier regions. More than half of African nations report an average student-teacher ratio of more than 30 to 1, whereas most European and North American nations have average ratios of 20 to 1 or less. There also are large differences, however, when wealthy countries are compared with each other, and when poor countries are compared with other poor countries:[9]

Enrollment Ratios.   The amount of resources devoted to education also helps determine whether most children and youth attend school and whether they obtain diplomas or degrees. As Table 15.1 shows, in some regions nearly all children between the ages of 6 and 11 attend school (Northern America, Oceania), but less than two-thirds of their counterparts in Africa do. Similarly, nearly all young people from age 12 through 17 and more than 60 percent between 18 and 23 in the relatively wealthy nations of Northern America are enrolled in school, compared with much lower percentages for less wealthy regions. The table also shows, however, that the percentage of children and youth enrolled in school has increased substantially since 1960 in all regions. This trend has continued in the 1990s.[10]

Male-Female Enrollment.   Table 15.1 shows that the expansion in the availability of education since 1960 generally has involved both male and female students. For example, enrollment of boys between 12 and 17 in Africa increased from 23 percent in 1960 to 49 percent in 1992, and enrollment of girls of comparable ages increased from 11 percent to 37 percent. However, enrollment ratios for girls still are substantially lower than those for boys in many countries, even though female enrollment is increasing more rapidly in some regions. Many analysts believe that the low

---

[8]George Psacharopoulos, *Planning of Education: Where Do We Stand?* (Washington, D.C.: The World Bank, 1985); and Nancy Matheson et al., *Education Indicators* (Washington, D.C.: U.S. Department of Education, 1996).
[9]Matheson, *Education Indicators;* and *Education Indicators at a Glance: OECD Indicators 1998* (Washington, D.C.: OECD Washington Center, 1998).
[10]*UNESCO Statistical Yearbook 1998* (Paris: UNESCO, 1998).

TABLE 15.1	Estimated Enrollment Ratios by Region, Age Group, and Sex, 1960 and 1992					
	Ages 6–11		Ages 12–17		Ages 18–23	
Region and Year	Male	Female	Male	Female	Male	Female
Africa						
1960	40	24	23	11	03	01
1992	61	52	49	37	13	07
Asia						
1960	62	42	49	32	11	06
1992	87	76	52	41	17	11
Europe						
1960	87	87	63	58	16	10
1992	89	89	80	84	35	36
Latin America						
1960	58	57	39	34	08	04
1992	88	87	69	67	25	25
Northern America						
1960	100	100	99	90	33	27
1992	100	100	97	94	63	70
Oceania						
1960	89	89	63	58	12	05
1992	100	97	73	75	27	29

Note: Enrollment ratios show the percentage of the appropriate population that is enrolled in school. Data for Europe include the former USSR. "Latin America" includes Central and South America, Mexico, and the Caribbean. "Northern America" includes Bermuda, Canada, Greenland, St. Pierre, and the United States. "Oceania" includes Australia, Guam, Polynesia, Samoa, Tonga, and other Pacific Islands.

Source: UNESCO Statistical Yearbook 1994 (Paris: UNESCO, 1994), Table 2.9, pp. 2–26 and 2–27. Copyright © UNESCO, 1994. Reproduced with the permission of UNESCO. See also the 1998 Yearbook for data on overall enrollment growth between 1980 and 1986, by nation and region.

enrollment ratio for girls compared to boys in many low-income countries in Africa and Asia is both a cause and an effect of economic development problems.[11]

The United States Among Industrial Nations.   For some purposes it is instructive to compare wealthy or highly industrialized nations with each other rather than with poor or economically underdeveloped nations. Other things remaining equal, nations that have less wealth and fewer resources have a much harder time supporting education or other government services than do those with a strong eco-

---

[11]Partha S. Dasgupta, "Population, Poverty, and the Local Environment," *Scientific American* (February 1995), pp. 40–45; and Carol Bellamy et al., *The State of the World's Children 1998,* at **www.unicef.org**.

nomic base. Thus, to analyze how well the United States mobilizes resources for education, we should compare it with other highly industrialized countries.[12]

Several recent controversies have erupted about this subject. Although some critics of public schools have claimed that American expenditures on education are "unsurpassed," many researchers disagree. When funding for higher education is subtracted, the United States does not rank high on education expenditures. Figure 15.1 shows such a comparison in graphic form. In terms of expenditures on public education from first grade through grade twelve as a percentage of gross domestic product, the United States ranks only sixth among twelve industrial countries.[13]

U.S. rank in expenditures

Analysts also debate whether teacher salaries in the United States are high or low in comparison with those of other industrial countries. Data on the average salaries of teachers indicate that for both beginning and experienced teachers, average salaries in some countries (such as Ireland and Norway) are a good deal lower than in the United States, but in other countries they are generally higher.[14]

Comparing teacher salaries

Sometimes the comparisons are expanded to other types of resources that support children's well-being and development. For example, Timothy Smeeding, comparing the United States with Australia, Canada, Germany, Sweden, and the United Kingdom, found that U.S. government expenditures on children's education and health services as a percentage of gross domestic product are about the same as the average for these five countries. However, he also found that U.S. government expenditures to help provide income security for children's families are less than half the average for these countries. Smeeding concluded that because high rates of divorce, out-of-wedlock births, and other social forces are creating a larger "urban and rural underclass," it is "becoming increasingly hard to argue that all U.S. children have equal life chances."[15]

Comparing social-welfare expenditures

Extent of Centralization

All governments must decide whether to emphasize decentralized decision making, which allows for planning and delivering instruction in accordance with local circumstances, or centralized decision making, which builds accountability up and down a national or regional chain of command. Examples go far in either direction. In the United States, most important decisions are decentralized across thousands of diverse public school districts. At the other extreme, as in France, Greece, and Japan, educational systems and decisions have been highly centralized, following nationwide policies concerning acceptable class size and what will be taught in a given subject at a particular grade and time. In some countries, one result of centralization is that long lines of citizens from all parts of the nation can be seen waiting outside the ministry of education for appointments with central school

Decentralized vs. centralized systems

---

[12]"Developed" nations as classified by the United Nations Educational, Scientific, and Cultural Organization (UNESCO) include Australia, Canada, Europe except for Yugoslavia, Israel, Japan, South Africa, the former USSR, the United States, and New Zealand. All others are classified as "developing" nations.

[13]Joel Sherman and Marianne Perie, *International Resources and Expenditures for Elementary and Secondary Education* (Washington, D.C.: Pelavin Research Center, 1998).

[14] Daniel U. Levine, "Educational Spending: International Comparisons," *Theory into Practice* (Spring 1994), pp. 126–131; and F. Howard Nelson, *How and How Much the U.S. Spends on K–12 Education* (Washington, D.C.: American Federation of Teachers, 1996).

[15]Timothy Smeeding, "Social Thought and Poor Children," *Focus* (Spring 1990), p. 14. See also Keith Bradsher, "America's Opportunity Gap," *New York Times,* June 4, 1995, p. E4, and William Finnegan, "Prosperous Times, Except for the Young," *New York Times,* June 12, 1998.

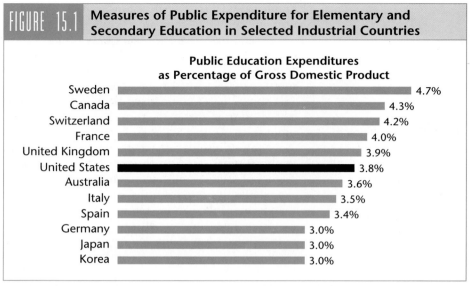

FIGURE 15.1   Measures of Public Expenditure for Elementary and Secondary Education in Selected Industrial Countries

Public Education Expenditures as Percentage of Gross Domestic Product

Country	Percentage
Sweden	4.7%
Canada	4.3%
Switzerland	4.2%
France	4.0%
United Kingdom	3.9%
United States	3.8%
Australia	3.6%
Italy	3.5%
Spain	3.4%
Germany	3.0%
Japan	3.0%
Korea	3.0%

Note: Expenditure data are for first grade through high school but exclude capital outlay and debt service. Student-teacher ratios are adjusted for part-time vocational enrollment. Various other adjustments have been made to enhance comparability of the original data.

Source: Joel Sherman and Marianne Perie, *International Resources and Expenditures for Elementary and Secondary Education* (Washington, D.C.: Pelavin Research Center, 1998), Figure 3.1, p. 4.

officials who determine what schools children will attend and how students will be treated.[16]

Curriculum Content and Instructional Emphasis

Although, as we have seen, much instruction worldwide consists of teacher lectures and student seatwork, nations do differ with regard to curriculum content and instructional emphasis. The following are some well-known practices that make some countries distinctive:[17]

Distinctive types of curriculum and instruction

■ New Zealand primary schools are known for their systematic emphasis on learning to read through "natural language learning." Using this approach, children learn to figure out words in context as they read, rather than through phonics and decoding instruction.

■ British "infant schools" historically have emphasized personal and social development and creative learning in preschools and in the primary grades.

■ Schools in some Islamic countries build much of the curriculum around religious content and emphasize didactic memorization of religious precepts.

[16]Ami Voollansky and Daniel Bar-Elli, "Moving Toward Equitable School-Based Management," *Educational Leadership* (December 1995–January 1996), pp. 60–62; and Geoff Whitty, "Education Policy and the Sociology of Education," *International Studies in Sociology of Education* (September 1997).
[17]Elaine Jarchow, "Ten Ideas Worth Stealing from New Zealand," *Phi Delta Kappan* (January 1992), pp. 394–395; Charles Patterson, "A Visit to London," *Educational Leadership* (February 1996), pp. 80–83; and Aziz Talbani, "Pedagogy, Power, and Discourse," *Comparative Education Review* (February 1996), pp. 66–82.

Vocational Versus Academic Education

Divergence after primary years

School systems around the world also differ greatly in the way they are organized to provide education through the postsecondary level. Although most nations now provide at least four years of first-level education during which all students attend "primary" or "elementary" schools, above that level systems diverge widely. Most students continue in "common" first-level schools for several more years, but in many countries students are divided between academic-track schools and vocational-type schools after four to eight years of first-level education. This arrangement, which corresponds to the traditional European dual-track pattern described in Chapter 3, is often known as a **bipartite system.**

Wide variations in tracking

The proportion of secondary students enrolled in primarily vocational programs varies from less than one-tenth in some industrial countries (such as Austria and Denmark) to more than one-fifth in others (such as Germany and Spain). Similar variation can be found in academic tracks. In some countries, beginning at the secondary level and extending into postsecondary education, large proportions of students are enrolled in academic schools designed to produce an "elite" corps of high-school or college graduates. In other countries, such as Canada and the United States, most secondary students continue to attend "common" or "comprehensive" schools, and many enroll in colleges that are relatively nonselective.[18]

Enrollment in Higher Education

Factors affecting enrollment in higher education

Countries that channel students into vocational programs tend to have low percentages of youth attending institutions of higher education. By contrast, in countries that provide general academic studies for most high-school students, more youth go on to higher education. Other factors that help determine enrollment in higher education include a nation's investment of resources in higher education, stress on postsecondary learning rather than entry into the job market, traditions regarding the use of higher education to equalize educational opportunities, and the extent to which colleges and universities admit only high-achieving students.

Developing vs. industrial nations

Developing countries that have relatively little funding available for higher education, and in any case are struggling to increase enrollments at the elementary and secondary levels, predictably have low proportions of youth participating in higher education. Thus Afghanistan, China, Ethiopia, Ghana, and many other developing nations enroll less than 10 percent of their eighteen- to twenty-one-year-olds in higher education. Most industrial countries provide postsecondary education for much higher proportions of youth and young adults (see Table 15.1). In most industrial nations, one-fourth to one-third of eighteen- to twenty-one-year-olds are attending postsecondary schools, but in two countries — Canada and the United States — this proportion is nearly two-thirds.[19]

Once high-school graduates are enrolled in postsecondary institutions, numerous considerations determine whether they will stay enrolled and eventually gain

---

[18]Elliott A. Medrich and Susan A. Kagehiro, *Vocational Education in G-7 Countries: Profiles and Data* (Washington, D.C.: U.S. Department of Education, 1994); and *Education at a Glance* (Paris: OECD, 1997).

[19]Richard P. Phelps, Thomas M. Smith, and Nabeel Alsalam, *Education in States and Nations* (Washington, D.C.: National Center for Education Statistics, 1996); and Ethan Bronner, "Other Countries Catching Up to U.S. in Education, Study Finds," *New York Times*, November 24, 1998.

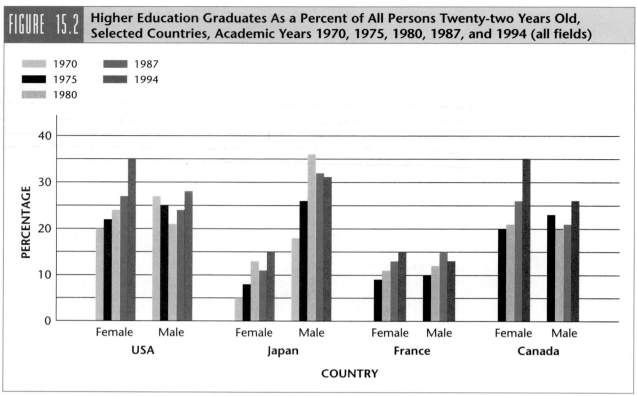

FIGURE 15.2 Higher Education Graduates As a Percent of All Persons Twenty-two Years Old, Selected Countries, Academic Years 1970, 1975, 1980, 1987, and 1994 (all fields)

Source: Postsecondary Education (Washington, D.C.: U.S. Government Printing Office, 1991), Chart 2:8, p. 37; Laura Hersh Salganik et al., *Education in the States and Nations* (Washington, D.C.: U.S. Government Printing Office, 1993), Table 10a, p. 60; and *Education at a Glance* (Paris: OECD, 1996), Table R12, p. 181.

Differences among industrial nations

their degrees: the rigor of the curriculum, the availability of financial support, the extent to which they are motivated, and the accessibility of preferred institutions and courses. Industrial nations differ greatly in the proportion of young people who obtain postsecondary degrees, as well as in the educational opportunities available for women. As shown in Figure 15.2, for example, Canada, Japan, and the United States graduate a much higher percentage of twenty-two-year-olds from postsecondary institutions than does France. However, Japan's high percentage can be accounted for by the relatively high percentage of young men who obtain degrees; young women in Japan are significantly less likely to complete higher education than are their counterparts in Canada and the United States.

Nonpublic Schools

Proportion of students in private schools

Depending on their histories, political structures, religious composition, legal frameworks, and other factors, nations differ greatly in the size and functioning of nonpublic sectors of education. In a few countries, such as the Netherlands, more than half of elementary and secondary students attend private schools. At the other extreme, governments in Cuba, North Korea, and some other nations have prohibited nonpublic schools in order to suppress ideologies different from those supported by the state. In most countries, private-school students constitute less than 10 percent of total enrollment.[20]

Nations also vary widely in the extent to which they provide public support for nonpublic schools or students. They differ as to government regulation of nonpublic systems, people's perceptions of public and nonpublic schools, and the role that private schools are expected to play in national development. In some countries, nonpublic schools enroll a relatively small, elite group of students who later enter the most prestigious colleges; in others they serve a more representative sample of the nation's children and youth. Given this variety, it is not possible to say exactly what a "private school" is internationally, or to generalize about cross-national policies that encourage or discourage nonpublic schools. Clearly, productive national policies on nonpublic schools must reflect each country's unique mix of circumstances and challenges.

Problems in defining a "private school"

Achievement Levels

Differences in school achievement among nations have received considerable attention since the **International Association for the Evaluation of Educational Achievement (IEA)** began conducting cross-national studies in the 1960s. One of the first major IEA projects collected and analyzed data on the achievement of 258,000 students from nineteen countries in civic education, foreign languages, literature, reading comprehension, and science. This study showed a wide range in average achievement levels across nations. In general, the United States ranked close to the middle among the nations included in the study. Later studies also have found that our students generally rank near the average for industrial countries in reading, but we frequently rank far below the highest-scoring countries in mathematics and science.[21]

IEA studies

Assessment of mathematics achievement has been particularly emphasized in IEA activities, partly because math is widely viewed as a "gatekeeper" subject that helps determine later success in scientific and technical studies. Mathematics also lends itself to international comparisons because its content is relatively standard across cultures. The first International Study of Achievement in Mathematics reported that high-ability students performed well in nearly all participating countries. A second such study assessed the performance of twelve- and thirteen-year-olds in educational systems in eighteen countries. Japanese students had the highest average scores in arithmetic, algebra, geometry, and measurement. Students in Hungary and the Netherlands also did unusually well in several of these categories. Eighth graders in the United States scored close to the overall average in arithmetic and algebra, and close to the bottom in geometry and measurement.[22]

Math comparisons

---

[20]T. Neville Postlethwaite, ed., *International Encyclopedia of National Systems of Education*, 2nd ed. (New York: Pergamon, 1995); and Sheryl L. Lutjens, "Education and the Cuban Revolution," *Comparative Education Review* (May 1998), pp. 197–224.

[21]Purves and Levine, *Educational Policy and International Assessment;* Lawrence C. Stedman, "The Achievement Crisis is Real," *Educational Policy Analysis Archives,* January 23, 1996, pp. 1–11, available at Internet site **www.asu.edu;** Patricia Murphy, "The IEA Assessment of Science," *Assessment in Education* (July 1996), pp. 213–232; and Business Coalition for Education Reform, *The Formula for Success* (Washington, D.C.: U.S. Department of Education, 1998).

[22]Curtis C. McKnight et al., *The Underachieving Curriculum* (Champaign, Ill.: Stipes, 1987); Thomas M. Smith et al., *The Condition of Education 1994* (Washington, D.C.: U.S. Government Printing Office, 1994); Margaret Brown, "FIMS and SIMS," *Assessment in Education 1998* (July 1996), pp. 193–212; and Thomas D. Snyder et al., *The Condition of Education 1998* (Washington, D.C.: U.S. Government Printing Office, 1998), available at **nces.gov/pubs98.**

IAEP studies

Several years after the second study, the IEA and the U.S. National Assessment of Educational Progress (NAEP) worked together to help produce the first and second **International Assessments of Educational Progress (IAEP)**, which compared math and science achievement among elementary and middle-level students. Results from the Third International Mathematics and Science Study (TIMSS) of achievement among fourth and eighth graders and high-school students were released in 1996 and subsequent years. As shown in Table 15.2 (which reports data for countries that met TIMSS guidelines for data collection), U.S. students scored well below students in the highest-scoring nations. Some analysts have concluded that U.S. curricula and instruction in math and science generally are a "mile wide and an inch deep" and that the low performance resulting from this superficial teaching poses a serious threat to our international competitiveness.[23]

Researchers' conclusions

Analyzing data from these international studies, other scholars also have tried to determine whether or how aspects of curriculum and instruction are associated with national performance levels. Some of their analyses support the following conclusions:[24]

1. Instructional characteristics (including class size, amount of time allocated to instruction, teachers' experience, and amount of homework) generally were not correlated with average math and science scores.

2. As in most other countries studied, mathematics instruction in the United States generally employed "tell and show" approaches that emphasize passive, rote learning. Since scores in some of these countries were considerably higher, such approaches could not account for low U.S. performance levels except in interaction with other variables.

3. In contrast to many other nations, the U.S. mathematics curriculum is "dramatically differentiated." That is, our middle-level students tend to be sorted into mathematics tracks that stress algebra and other advanced topics for high-achieving students and simple arithmetic for low achievers. Thus many students with low or medium achievement levels have little opportunity to proceed beyond basic skills. This is in marked contrast to Japan and some other locations where most students are challenged to perform at a higher level. Most analysts who have reviewed these patterns believe that action must be taken to reduce this kind of curriculum differentiation.

4. Improvement in the performance of U.S. students will require systemic change involving setting of standards, assessment of students, preparation of teachers, instructional methods, and other aspects of our educational system.

Publication of the IEAP and TIMSS studies has helped ignite some emotional controversies. On one side, some observers claim that our educational system is not as unsatisfactory as it is often portrayed. While admitting that major improvements are needed, these observers point to factors like the following:[25]

---

[23]Archie E. Lapointe, Nancy A. Mead, and Gray W. Phillips, *A World of Differences* (Princeton, N.J.: Educational Testing Service, 1989); and Pascal D. Forgione, Jr., "Responses to Frequently Asked Questions About 12th-Grade TIMSS," *Phi Delta Kappan* (June 1998), pp. 769–772.

[24]Ina V. S. Mullins, Eugene H. Owen, and Gary W. Phillips, *Accelerating Academic Achievement* (Princeton, N.J.: Educational Testing Service, 1991); and Edward A. Silver, *Improving Mathematics in Middle School* (Washington, D.C.: U.S. Department of Education, 1998), available at **www.ed.gov.**

[25]Purves and Levine, *Educational Policy and International Assessment;* and Debra Viadero, "New Questions Raised About the Validity of TIMSS Comparisons," *Education Week,* May 27, 1998, p. 7.

TABLE 15.2	Average Mathematics and Science Proficiency Scores for Eighth Graders Scoring at the Fiftieth Percentile in Sixteen Nations	
Country	**Mathematics**	**Science**
Korea	607	565
Japan	605	571
Czech Republic	564	574
Slovak Republic	547	544
France	538	498
Hungary	537	554
Russian Federation	535	538
Sweden	518	535
New Zealand	508	525
Norway	503	527
United States	500	534
Spain	487	517
Iceland	487	494
Lithuania	477	476
Portugal	454	480
Iran	428	470
International Average	513	516

Source: Adapted from *Mathematics and Science Achievement for the 21st Century* (Washington, D.C.: National Education Goals Panel, 1997), Figure 8, p. 20.

Defense of U.S. schools

- Our students generally perform at a relatively high level in reading.
- International studies may underestimate the performance of our high schools in relation to other countries because these studies may be comparing our students with more elite groups of students elsewhere.
- Much of the relatively low performance of our students may be due to cultural factors, not deficiencies in the schools. For example, the very high levels of mathematics achievement reported for Hungary, Japan, and Korea may be attributable primarily to the great value their cultures attach to mathematics performance and to strong family support for achievement.
- Contrary to the statements of some critics, achievement in U.S. schools has improved during the past few decades, particularly considering the increased enrollment of minority students from low-income families. These improvements may be attributable in part to the positive effects of compensatory education and school desegregation (see Chapter 11) and to efforts at educational reform.
- Analyses of relatively low performance among U.S. students typically fail to take account of the fact that, by some measures, expenditures for elementary and secondary education are low compared with those for some other industrial nations (see earlier sections in this chapter).
- Assessments of the U.S. educational system should highlight the fact that our system produces higher percentages of high-school graduates and college entrants than most other countries.

PROFESSIONAL PLANNING

for your first year

Why Is Achievement in Japan So High, and What May Be Some Implications?

The Situation

Imagine you are sitting at lunch one day with two of your friends. One of them has just read a newspaper article pointing out that Japanese students score much higher on science and math tests than U.S. students. The article also explains that Japan has a national curriculum dictating what will be taught in every classroom, that Japanese students attend schools many more days per year than American students, and that Japanese schools have very few discipline problems. Maybe these facts are the clue to school reform in the United States, your friend suggests.

You are inclined to agree, but it happens that your other friend at the lunch table spent part of her childhood in Japan. From her own experiences she describes some further differences. Teachers in Japan have very high status, she says, and they pay attention to their students' social relationships and moral development as well as academic needs.

You begin to wonder, then, whether such differences in teaching—rather than factors like curriculum and discipline—might be the keys to Japanese achievement. Is it possible to isolate the characteristics that count? Also, can they be copied in the United States, or are there too many differences between the societies for the same methods to work in both countries?

Thought Questions

1. Do you believe that our schools should try to use methods and approaches that appear to be successful in Japan and other countries? What might be some reasons for being cautious about such methods and approaches? What special problems might be encountered in trying to implement them?
2. What methods and approaches that are widely used in our schools do you think are most valuable for consideration elsewhere? What difficulties might educators in other countries experience in trying to introduce them?
3. Can you identify a method or approach that is relatively unique to a specific country or group of countries? What historical and social circumstances might account for its unique emergence?
4. Isn't teaching and learning the same everywhere? To the extent that this generalization is valid, why are there so many differences internationally? Is the generalization invalid?
5. When we examine educational systems in other parts of the world, should we be most concerned about assessing practices that have helped boost economic productivity or, instead, give priority to practices that are advancing social and economic equity? Which countries may be making an effort in both directions?

Critique of U.S. schools

However, critics of U.S. performance have been unappeased by such arguments. Frequently pointing to the particularly low scores that our students register on tests assessing higher-order skills such as math problem solving, they reiterate the importance of improving students' skills in comprehension, geography, math, science, and other subjects. They also stress bottom-line findings, such as the fact that less than 10 percent of U.S. high-school juniors can designate the amount of a loan to be repaid after calculating the interest. They conclude that the low rankings of U.S. students in international achievement studies represent a deplorable performance level that cannot be corrected without radical efforts to reform or even replace our current system of education.[26]

Testing Policies and Practices

Countries vary widely in the methods used to measure student achievement, from the types of tests used and the grade levels tested to whether the tests are administered nationally or locally. They also differ in the degree to which tests are used to make final decisions about students' placement and careers, and the extent to which improved testing is seen as a means of reforming schools.[27]

Debate over national tests and curriculum

As we discuss elsewhere in this book, U.S. educators and political and civic leaders have been debating whether to establish national tests of certain skills and knowledge. Once these tests were in place, teachers everywhere would be expected to emphasize those elements of skill and knowledge. In effect, national tests would both reflect and facilitate the development of a **national curriculum**, which some policy makers strongly support and others just as strongly oppose. Many countries with centralized educational systems already use national tests to determine whether students are mastering a standard curriculum. Examining the results in such countries, Thomas Kellaghan, George Madaus, and Richard Wolf have identified the following potential problems associated with national tests or other "external examinations" administered across a diverse group of schools:[28]

Potential problems of national tests

1. The costs of testing practical and oral skills are so high that those skills tend to be left untested.

2. It is extremely difficult, if not impossible, to prepare external exams that conclusively assess such aspects of student performance as perseverance in executing projects.

3. External exams reinforce tendencies to emphasize low-order skills that are most easily taught and tested.

4. Since external exams in effect determine much of the curriculum, they diminish the professional role of teachers.

5. Whether a nation has a national test or national curriculum is not related to its achievement levels on international comparisons.

Kellaghan, Madaus, Wolf, and other scholars have been particularly interested in developments in England and Wales, which have implemented a type of testing that resembles plans being considered in the United States. During the 1980s and early 1990s, the British government established a required national curriculum that

The British experience

[26]Chester E. Finn, Jr., *We Must Take Charge* (New York: Free Press, 1991); and Albert Shanker, "Where We Stand," available at **www.aft.org.**

[27]Marilyn R. Binkley, James W. Guthrie, and Timothy J. Wyatt, *A Survey of National Assessment and Examination Practices in OECD Countries* (Lugano, Switzerland: OECD, 1991); Debra Viadero, "Study Finds Variations in Math, Science Tests in 7 Nations," *Education Week,* January 10, 1996, p. 13; and Max A. Eckstein, "A Comparative Assessment of Assessment," *Assessment in Education* (July 1996), pp. 233–240.

[28]Thomas Kellaghan and George F. Madaus, "National Testing: Lessons for America from Europe," *Educational Leadership* (November 1991), pp. 87–90. See also Richard M. Wolf, "National Standards: Do We Need Them?" *Educational Researcher* (May 1998), pp. 22–25.

is monitored and assessed partly through a new national testing system. In line with much current thinking about the disadvantages of standardized multiple-choice exams, the new tests are designed to assess a wide range of abilities and skills, such as students' ability to apply conceptual knowledge, to perform in both written and oral modes, and to understand complex subject matter. Methods of assessment require students to write essays, participate in group interviews, perform experiments, and compile portfolios or exhibits to demonstrate their ability to carry out meaningful projects over a significant period of time.

Pros and cons of British system

According to some analysts who have examined the early results from England, the system may be helping to establish and communicate nationwide standards for teaching and learning. However, researchers also report that large amounts of time, work, and money are required to select appropriate objectives and curricula, assess students' performance without dreadfully overloading teachers, and plan and deliver large-scale staff development. In addition, many observers believe, the national examinations often stimulate teachers to deemphasize meaningful learning and damage teachers' efforts to deliver a coherent curriculum.[29]

Exemplary Reforms: A Selection

Many nations have introduced substantial reforms in their educational systems. Some countries have been respected for many decades for the quality and effectiveness with which they provide early childhood opportunities, mathematics instruction, vocational schooling, or other important educational experiences. In this section we will briefly review several such exemplary features of education in other countries. The term *potentially exemplary* might be better, however, because some reforms have been introduced only recently or may have little relevance to other, very different countries.

Early Childhood Education in France

Recognizing the critical importance of the preschool years in a child's social, physical, and educational development, many countries have taken steps to provide stimulating learning opportunities and positive day-care arrangements for most or all young children. For example, more than 90 percent of three- to five-year-olds in Belgium, Hong Kong, and Italy are enrolled in early childhood programs, compared with little more than half in the United States. Outstanding child-care arrangements for infants are easily accessible to families throughout Scandinavia. The mix of preschool and day-care programs varies considerably from one country to another, as does the extent to which early childhood educators work with parents and families. Overall, however, early childhood education has become a topic of urgent interest throughout much of the world.

Varying child-care arrangements

French preschool programs

France has what many observers consider a "vintage" approach to preschool services. Nearly all three- to five-year-olds are enrolled in preschool programs, and average salaries of preschool teachers are considerably higher than in the United States or most other countries. Stimulating activities are conducted for participating children before and after school, during vacation, and at other times when school is

---

[29]Gene I. Maeroff, "Assessing Alternative Assessment," *Phi Delta Kappan* (December 1991), pp. 273–280; Sarah W. Freedman, "Exam-Based Reform Stifles Student Writing in the U.K.," *Educational Leadership* (March 1995), pp. 26–29; and Angela M. Ferree, *Literature Instruction and Assessment: A Cross-National Study* (Washington, D.C.: ERIC ED413346, 1998).

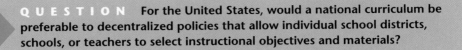

TAKING ISSUE

Establishment of a National Curriculum

In some countries in which public education is highly centralized, teachers generally are expected to follow a national curriculum that specifies the topics to be taught and the objectives and materials to be emphasized in each subject and grade level. In other countries that follow a decentralized pattern, decisions about subject matter and materials are made primarily at the level of a regional group of schools (such as a school district) or by individual faculties or teachers. Government officials in some highly centralized nations such as the United States are considering whether a national curriculum should be established to provide for a more standardized approach in planning and delivering instruction.

Arguments PRO

1 Availability of a national curriculum is partly responsible for the high achievement levels attained in Japan, Korea, and some other countries.

2 A national curriculum based on the careful deliberation of subject-area specialists and experienced teachers makes it easier to achieve in-depth teaching of well-sequenced objectives and materials.

3 Uniformity in objectives and materials reduces the inefficiencies and learning problems that occur when students move from one classroom, school, or district to another.

4 A national curriculum will facilitate improvements in teacher education because preparation programs can concentrate on objectives and materials that trainees will be required to teach when they obtain jobs.

5 Because it draws on a large base of resources, national curriculum planning can incorporate the best current thinking in each subject area and can be carried out in conjunction with the preparation of technically excellent tests.

Arguments CON

1 Establishment of a national curriculum runs counter to promising trends toward school-based management and professional autonomy for teachers.

2 A national curriculum is undesirable because it results in the use of objectives and materials that are too difficult for many students in some classrooms and too easy for many students in other classrooms.

3 Particularly in large and diverse countries such as the United States, the standardized materials that form the basis for a national curriculum will be uninteresting and demotivating for many students.

4 Even if the national curriculum allows some flexibility in objectives and materials, teachers will be pressured to follow the same path as everyone else, and funds probably will not be available for alternative materials. Therefore students and classes that might benefit from alternatives will suffer.

5 Since it is very difficult to prepare challenging materials that are appropriate for use across a wide range of classrooms, a national curriculum will reinforce tendencies to emphasize low-level skills and uncreative materials.

not in session. Equally important, parents are given financial incentives to enroll their children in high-quality programs that provide pediatric and other preventive health services. Child-care specialists and civic leaders who examined the French system have reported that the following aspects of French programs are worth considering in the United States:[30]

Positive features of French programs

- A coordinated system linking early education, day care, and health services is accessible to virtually all children.

- Paid parental leave from jobs after childbirth or adoption helps to nurture positive parent-child relationships.

- Good salaries and training for early childhood teachers help to keep turnover low and program quality high.

- Nearly all young children are enrolled in preschool facilities.

Vocational and Technical Education in Germany

Advantages and disadvantages

Most European countries and many developing countries channel a high percentage of high-school and postsecondary students into vocational or technical schools. There students receive high-quality training for specific occupations, which they enter immediately upon receiving their diplomas or certificates. The "up" side of this bipartite system — early separation into vocational and technical versus academic tracks — is that many students who will not complete college can be successfully prepared for employment. Thus the transition from adolescence or young adulthood to work is smooth and easy. The "down" side is that these young people do not have many opportunities to pursue academic studies and obtain a college degree, as they do in Canada, the United States, and a few other countries.

Responding to this dilemma, government officials in many countries with severe tracking arrangements are introducing general studies programs into vocational education, expanding opportunities to attend academic high schools and postsecondary institutions, and establishing "informal" mechanisms such as correspondence courses for obtaining college degrees. Conversely, officials in the United States are beginning to establish apprenticeship programs and other vocational or technical courses that may help prepare high-school students for employment without placing them in separate tracks that exclude them from higher education.[31]

German apprenticeship program

Many authorities on vocational education see the traditional apprenticeship program in Germany as one of the most effective in the world. Only about a third of German students of high-school age attend college-preparatory institutions; the remainder are enrolled in vocational and technical schools that combine academics with job training as an apprentice. Their work is supervised by experienced personnel and monitored by appropriate organizations, such as state agencies for health workers or industrial associations for students with jobs in commerce. The responsible organizations also administer exams that lead to completion certificates and

---

[30] Hillary Rodham Clinton, "In France, Day Care Is Every Child's Right," *New York Times*, April 7, 1990, p. 15; Karen Whiten, *Promoting the Development of Young Children in Denmark, France, and Italy* (Washington, D.C.: U.S. Government Accounting Office, 1995); and Thomas M. Smith and Nabeel Alsalam, *Education Indicators: An International Perspective* (Washington, D.C.: National Center for Education Statistics, 1996).

[31] John R. McKernan, Jr., *Making the Grade* (Boston: Little, Brown, 1994); Wayne Rowley, Terry Crist, and Leo Presley, "Partnerships for Productivity, *Training and Development* (January 1995), pp. 53–55; and *Pathways and Participation in Vocational and Technical Education and Training* (Washington, D.C.: OECD, 1998).

Many believe that certain elements of the German apprenticeship system—such as close supervision of apprentices by veterans and certification of employability—can be adapted and emulated successfully elsewhere. *(© Owen Franken/Stock Boston)*

often directly to employment. Although analysts recognize that the German apprenticeship system evolved gradually over centuries and cannot be simply recreated in other countries, many believe that certain elements, such as close supervision of apprentices by skilled veterans and certification of a young person's employability, can be adapted successfully elsewhere.[32]

Comprehensive Schools in Sweden

As we pointed out earlier, there is a strong relationship worldwide between students' socioeconomic background and their educational performance and attainment. In many nations this pattern, combined with the practice of dividing secondary (or upper-level) students into academic and vocational/technical tracks, has meant that students with high socioeconomic status have been much more likely than their peers to enter and graduate from academic high schools — and later from colleges and universities.

Detracking in Sweden

Sweden has been a leader in offering more effective and equalized opportunities for students of all social backgrounds. In the 1960s Swedish elementary and middle-level schools were detracked. Since that time, high and low achievers for the most part have attended the same schools and studied the same curriculum in heterogeneous classes until the age of fourteen. Reports indicate that standards of performance for many low-achieving students have increased substantially; critics believe that further progress is needed.[33]

---

[32]Harvey Kantor, "Managing the Transition from School to Work," *Teachers College Record* (Summer 1994), pp. 442–461; Tim Hatcher, "From Apprentice to Instructor," *Journal of Industrial Teacher Education* (Fall 1995), p. 44; and Wanda Menke-Ghickert, "Wanted: A New Humboldt," *Europe* (September 1997), p. 28.

[33]Wilfried Hartmann, Robert Erikson, and Jan O. Jonsson, "Can Education Be Equalized?" *Comparative Education Review* (May 1997, pp. 235–236).

Mathematics and Science Education in Japan

High performance

The international achievement studies indicate that Japanese students consistently attain very high scores in mathematics, science, and some other subject areas. For example, the second International Study of Achievement in Mathematics reported that eighth graders in Japan on average answered 62 percent of the test items correctly, compared with 45 percent in the United States and 47 percent across the eighteen countries included in the study. With respect to science achievement among eighth graders, Japanese students attained an average score of 571, compared with an average of 541 for other industrial nations included in the third assessment.[34]

Possible reasons for Japanese success

Some aspects of Japanese education and society may help account for high achievement levels among Japanese youth. Most of the characteristics highlighted in the following list apply to Japanese education in general, not merely to math and science programs. The list of pertinent factors is long, and researchers are not yet sure which of these characteristics are important. Perhaps they all are.[35]

Parental involvement

[handwritten: Population 135 million about as big as California]

■ Intense parental involvement is expected. In particular, mothers feel great responsibility for children's success in school. Families provide much continuing support and motivation, ranging from elaborate celebration of entry into first grade to widespread enrollment of children in supplementary private cram schools (*juku*), which students attend after school and on weekends. Compared with U.S. parents, Japanese parents stress "effort" more and "ability" less when asked to identify causes of success or failure in school.

Long school year

■ Students attend school 240 days a year (compared with less than 200 in the United States).

National curriculum

■ Careful planning and delivery of a national curriculum help students acquire important concepts within a sequential and comprehensive framework.

■ Large amounts of homework correlated with classroom lessons contribute to high student performance.

■ Partly because much time and support are available to help slower students, there is less variability in achievement than in the United States and most other countries. There are relatively few very low achievers in Japanese schools.

Stress on character

■ The schools emphasize the development of students' character and sense of responsibility through such practices as assigning students chores and having them help each other in learning.

■ Educators tend to take responsibility for students' learning. For example, many teachers contact parents to recommend homework schedules and curfews.

Status of teachers

[handwritten: Teachers come from top 1/3 of graduates]

■ Japanese educators have relatively high social status, which enhances their authority in working with students and parents. Partly for this reason, there are numerous applicants for teaching positions, thus allowing administrators to select highly qualified candidates.

■ School schedules provide considerable time for counseling students, planning instruction, and engaging in other activities that make teachers more effective.

---

[34]*Digest of Education Statistics 1991* (Washington, D.C.: U.S. Government Printing Office, 1991); Barbara J. Reyes and Robert E. Reyes, "Japanese Mathematics Education," *Teaching Children Mathematics* (April 1995), pp. 474–475; and *The Condition of Education 1997* (Washington, D.C.: U.S. Government Printing Office, 1997).

[35]Robert D. Hess and Hiroshi Azuma, "Cultural Support for Schooling," *Educational Researcher* (December 1991), pp. 2–12; Thomas P. Rohlen, "Differences That Make a Difference: Explaining Japan's Success," *Educational Policy* (June 1995), pp. 129–151; and Sonni Efron, "Japan's Example," *Los Angeles Times*, May 19, 1998.

- Socialization practices in the family and in early childhood education help students learn to adapt to classroom situations and demands. By way of contrast, U.S. schools tend to attain good discipline by making instruction attractive and by "bargaining" with students to obtain compliance (see Chapter 9), at great cost to academic standards and rigor.

- Compared with elementary-school practices in the United States and in many other countries, lessons deemphasize rote learning.

- Prospective teachers must pass rigorous examinations and then are intensely supervised when they enter the profession.

- Language patterns in Japan and other Asian countries facilitate academic learning. For example, math may be easier to learn in Japanese than in English because numbers are designated in a "ten plus one, two, etc." system.

- Outstanding day care helps prepare children for success in the schools.

Criticisms of Japanese system

However, people familiar with the Japanese educational system also point out some apparently negative characteristics:[36]

Too little divergent thinking

- There appears to be relatively little emphasis on divergent thinking. Some observers believe that insufficient emphasis on creativity may severely hamper future social and economic development in Japan.

Class and gender limitations

- Opportunities for working-class students and women to attend postsecondary institutions and gain high occupational status appear to be severely limited. For example, one study found that only 11 percent of students in academic high schools that stress college preparation were from families in which the father had not completed high school, compared with 32 percent of students in less academic high schools.

- Partly because of the restricted opportunities for higher education, secondary education is exam driven in the sense that instruction is geared to covering very large quantities of factual information likely to be tested on entrance examinations. In turn, examination pressures further stifle divergent thinking and frequently lead to mental distress and even suicide.

- Relatively few demands are made of students once they are admitted to colleges and universities.

Behavioral conformity

- Behavioral standards and expectations in many Japanese schools are so narrow and rigid that some educators believe they generate too much conformity. In accordance with the old Japanese proverb "The nail that sticks out gets hammered down," students are told what school uniform to wear at each grade. In some cases, they have been required to dye their hair to conform to school regulations. However, rules governing student appearance and the details of their behavior have been significantly loosened in recent years.

- More than ever before, young people in Japan seem to be rejecting the traditional customs and values on which the educational system is founded.

- Many students with disabilities receive little help.

---

[36]Ken Schoolland, *Shogun's Ghost: The Dark Side of Japanese Education* (New York: Bergin and Garvey, 1990); Maso Miyamoto, *Straitjacket Society* (Tokyo: Kodansha, 1994); and Michael Zielenziger, "Youth Violence Tears at Fabric of Japan," *Miami Herald,* May 4, 1998; and Mary Jordan and Kevin Sullivan, "In Japan Schools, Discipline in Recess," *Washington Post,* January 24, 1999.

GETTING TO THE SOURCE

THE Public Interest

NUMBER 76, SUMMER 1984

CONTENTS

THE PUBLIC INTEREST (ISSN-0033-3557) is published quarterly by National Affairs, Inc. and appears in Spring, Summer, Fall, and Winter issues. Its office of publication is located at 10 East 53rd Street, New York, NY 10022. Subscription price: $16.00 for one year; $32.00 for two years. Add $2.00 annually for Canadian and foreign subscriptions.

Snapshot of an Elementary Classroom in Japan

MERRY WHITE

After visiting Japan in the early 1980s, Merry White of the Harvard Graduate School of Education challenged the widely held myth that students in Japan spend most of their time in highly disciplined drill and practice. Although there is some truth to this stereotype at academic secondary schools in Japan, White and other scholars have shown that Japanese educators place great emphasis on developing learning-to-learn skills and helping students acquire mastery of complex concepts and understandings. The following excerpt describes White's visit to a fifth-grade math class.

The day I visited, the class was presented with a general statement about cubing. Before any concrete facts, formulae, or even drawings were displayed, the teacher asked the class to take out their math diaries and spend a few minutes writing down their feelings and anticipations over this new concept. It is hard for me to imagine an American math teacher beginning a lesson with an exhortation to examine one's emotional predispositions about cubing (but that may be only because my own math training was antediluvian).

After that, the teacher asked for conjectures from the children about the surface and volume of a cube and asked for some ideas about formulae for calculation. The teacher asked the class to cluster into its component *han* (working groups) of four or five children each, and gave out materials for measurement and construction. One group left the room with large pieces of cardboard, to construct a model of a cubic meter. The groups worked internally on solutions to problems set by the teacher and competed with each other to finish first. After a while. the cubic meter group returned, groaning under the bulk of its model, and everyone gasped over its size. (There were many comments and guesses as to how many children could fit inside.) The teacher then set the whole class a very challenging problem, well over their heads,

- Japanese schools have done relatively little to introduce computers and other aspects of modern technology.

In reviewing its various strengths and weaknesses, several thoughtful observers have concluded that we have much to learn from the Japanese educational system, but they add that we should make sure that promising practices from elsewhere are workable and appropriately adapted to our own situation. Likewise, government commissions in Japan have been considering reform proposals that incorporate the more positive aspects of education in the United States (for example, to reduce the emphasis on conformity). A professor of Japanese studies at Harvard University has summarized the situation in this way: "As a mirror showing us our weakness and as a yardstick against which to measure our efforts," Japanese education has great value for us. But we should not "allow ourselves either to ignore or to imitate" its approach. Instead, we should "look periodically into the 'Japanese mirror' while we quite independently set out to straighten our schools and our system within our own cultural and social context."[37]

Neither ignore nor imitate

[37]Thomas P. Rohlen, "Japanese Education: If They Can Do It, Should We?" *The American Scholar* (Winter 1985–86), p. 43. See also Catherine C. Lewis, *Educating Hearts and Minds* (Cambridge: Cambridge University Press, 1995); and Michael D. Usdan, "Is the Grass That Much Greener?" *Education Week,* October 21, 1998.

and gave them the rest of the class time to work on it. The class ended without a solution, but the teacher made no particular effort to get or give an answer, although she exhorted them to be energetic. (It was several days before the class got the answer—there was no deadline but the excitement did not flag.)

Several characteristics of this class deserve highlighting. First, there was attention to feelings and predispositions, provision of facts. and opportunities for discovery. The teacher preferred to focus on process, engagement, commitment, and performance rather than on discipline (in our sense) and production. Second, the *han*: Assignments are made to groups, not to individuals (this is also true at the workplace) although individual progress and achievement are closely monitored. Children are supported, praised, and allowed to make mistakes through trial and error within the group. The group is also pitted against other groups, and the group's success is each person's triumph, and vice versa. Groups are made up by the teacher and are designed to include a mixture of skill levels—there is a *hancho* (leader) whose job it is to choreograph the group's work, to encourage the slower members, and to act as a reporter to the class at large.

Questions

1. Why has it been so difficult to dispel the myth that Japanese schools concentrate primarily on producing miniature soldiers who mostly repeat back material introduced by their teachers?
2. Teachers in Japan frequently refer to John Dewey in describing their methods and objectives. What Deweyesque ideas and practices are apparent in White's snapshot? What other practices might they be using that are in line with Dewey's philosophy as described in Chapter 5 of this book?

Source: Merry I. White, "Japanese Education: How Do They Do It." Reprinted with permission from *The Public Interest*, No. 76 (Summer 1984) pp. 87–101. Copyright © 1984 by National Affairs Inc.

Multicultural Education in Europe and North America

Probably no country has responded adequately to the challenges posed by multicultural populations. However, many nations have made important efforts to deliver educational services suitable for diverse groups of students, particularly minority students who experience racial, ethnic, or religious discrimination or who do not learn the national language at home. Approaches like the following may become future models:[38]

Model multicultural programs

- As we discussed at length in Chapter 11, the United States is trying to provide bilingual education for millions of limited-English-proficient and non-English-proficient students, even in California, where state legislation has eliminated many bilingual programs.
- Canada has implemented sizable bilingual education programs, as well as numerous approaches for promoting multiethnic curriculum and instruction.
- France has provided in-service training nationwide to help teachers learn to teach French as a second language.

[38]Bruce Carrington and Alastair Bonnett, "The Other Canadian 'Mosaic,'" *Comparative Education* (November 1997), pp. 411–432.

■ Belgium provides **reception classes** in which immigrant children receive six months to two years of instruction from both a Belgian teacher and a native-language assistant teacher.

Problems and Prospects in Developing Countries

Education and economic development

Problems in upgrading education

Recommendations for developing countries

Earlier in this chapter we saw that educational inadequacies in developing countries are both a cause and a result of poverty. For this reason, national governments and international organizations have placed great stress on bolstering the economies of developing countries by expanding and improving their educational systems. Education usually is considered critical for economic development because it can give people the skills and knowledge to compete in international markets and because it can help bring about a more equitable distribution of wealth and power, which in turn contributes to political stability and long-term economic growth.

However, it has proved exceedingly difficult to achieve widespread, lasting, and balanced improvement of educational systems in many developing countries. For example, extreme poverty in countries such as Rwanda has been partly responsible for restricting the availability of funds to less than $100 per primary student per year. Numerous developing countries also confront a so-called **brain drain:** the number of high-school and university graduates increases, but since well-paid jobs suitable to their level of education are not available, these well-trained people emigrate to wealthier countries with better employment opportunities. Some developing countries (such as India and Nigeria) also are struggling to overcome educational problems associated with the use of dozens or even hundreds of different languages among their multiethnic populations.

To improve education in developing countries, researchers have suggested the following steps:[39]

1. Invest more in primary schools to broaden the base of students who can participate in higher levels of education

2. Avoid emphasizing enrollment in higher education, since students will tend to study abroad and may not return

3. Make private schools an integral part of educational expansion plans

4. Expand efforts to improve students' cognitive functioning

5. Work on overcoming obstacles that limit the education of girls and women

6. Substantially improve the preparation of teachers

7. Use modern technologies to expand educational opportunities at all levels.

School Improvement Projects and Research

As in the United States, educators in other parts of the world are introducing reforms to make schools more effective. One interesting topic is how unusually successful schools function. As we point out in the next chapter, research on these so-called **effective schools** has identified certain characteristics that help account

---

[39]Gary Stix and Paul Wallich, "A Digital Fix for the Third World?" *Scientific American* (October 1993), p. 89; Muain Jamian, "Proposal for an Open University in the Arab World," *T.H.E. Journal* (January 1995), pp. 53–57; and Lynn Davies and Zafar Iqbal, "Tensions in Teacher Training for School Effectiveness," *School Effectiveness and School Improvement* (June 1997), pp. 254–266.

Worldwide research on effective schools

for their unusual success. Although most of the studies have been conducted in the United States, important research also has taken place in Australia, Canada, the Netherlands, the United Kingdom, and elsewhere. Most studies indicate that effective school reform requires systematic change and long-term commitment rather than quick fixes.[40] Chapter 16 will explore this topic in detail.

Conclusion: U.S. Schools in an International Context

Growing similarities among nations

Some observers believe that international study of education is becoming increasingly useful because developed societies are growing more alike. Throughout the world, more citizens are becoming middle class, and school systems and other institutions are emphasizing preparation for dealing with advanced technology and rapid social change. Mass media and other technologies exert a common influence across national borders. This does not mean that societies ever will be exactly alike or that cultural and social differences will disappear entirely, but it does seem likely that characteristics of social institutions (including the family and the school) will converge. For example, Kenichi Ohmae has remarked that the "Nintendo Kids" in Japan — the youngsters who have grown up with computers, video games, and global media — "have more in common with similar youngsters outside Japan than with other generations within Japan."[41]

Much to learn, much to offer

If that is true, we have much to learn from studying effective education in other nations. In some ways, too, other nations can learn from the United States. Despite the many shortcomings of U.S. education described in this book, the United States has been an international leader in striving to educate all students regardless of their social background or previous achievement. As Glen Latham has put it, "The American system of education, with all its faults, is still the most remarkable system on the face of the earth. It serves more children, with a broader range of ability, over a longer period of their lives, in the most enriched educational setting, for less money per pupil, than any educational system that has ever existed in the history of humankind."[42]

Summing Up

1. Although educational systems differ considerably internationally, they tend to confront the similar problem of providing effective instruction for large numbers of students whose opportunities and performance are related to their social and cultural background.
2. Teaching conditions throughout the world appear to be fundamentally similar. In most countries, teachers and curricula emphasize presentation of information, and teachers struggle to find time to accomplish difficult and sometimes conflicting goals.

---

[40]Peter Mortimore et al., *School Matters* (Berkeley: University of California Press, 1988); Daniel U. Levine, "Creating Effective Schools Through Site-Level Staff Development, Planning and Improvement of Organizational Culture," in David H. Hargreaves and David Hopkins, eds., *Development Planning for School Improvement* (London: Cassell, 1994), pp. 37–48; and Tony Townsend, "What Makes Schools Effective?" *School Effectiveness and School Improvement* (September 1997), pp. 311–326.

[41]Kenichi Ohnae, "China's 600,000 Avon Ladies," *New Perspectives Quarterly* (Winter 1995), p. 15. See also Pico Iyer, "The Diversity Debate: Point," *The Utne Reader* (January–February 1996), pp. 35–36; and Jeffrey Klein, "Fire Fighting," *Mother Jones* (July–August 1998), pp. 3, 5.

[42]Glenn Latham, "Amerika Ni Dekimassen," *Principal* (February 1992), pp. 52–53. See also Stephen R. Graubard, "Preface," *Daedalus* (Fall 1995), pp. v–xxx; and William F. Bennett et al., "A Nation Still at Risk," *Policy Review* (July–August 1998), available at **www.heritage.org**.

3. Decision makers everywhere face difficult choices in the relative allocation of resources to early childhood education; to elementary, secondary, and postsecondary schools; and to vocational education.

4. School systems around the world differ greatly with respect to the resources they devote to education, enrollments, student-teacher ratios, proportions of male and female students, the extent of centralization or decentralization, curriculum content and instructional emphasis, higher education and vocational education opportunities, the availability and role of nonpublic schools, student achievement, and national testing policies and practices.

5. A number of countries have educational services or practices that appear to be exemplary: early childhood education in France, vocational and technical education in Germany, comprehensive schools in Sweden, mathematics and science education in Japan, and multicultural education in Europe and North America. Researchers can learn much from studying educational systems in other countries, but it is not always easy to identify the reasons for a system's success or failure or its implications for different societies.

6. Scholars studying education in developing countries believe that emphasis should be placed on improving teacher preparation and primary education, developing the cognitive functioning of students, and expanding education for girls and women.

7. The United States is an international leader in the effort to provide equal and effective educational opportunities for all groups of students.

Key Terms

bipartite system *(499)*

International Association for the Evaluation of Educational Achievement (IEA) *(501)*

International Assessments of Educational Progress (IAEPs) *(502)*

national curriculum *(505)*

reception classes *(514)*

brain drain *(514)*

effective schools *(514)*

Discussion Questions

1. Why is the distribution of curriculum subjects so similar from one country to another? Who decides what subjects should be taught? Who should decide?

2. What are the most important educational problems in developing countries? What policies might be most appropriate in addressing these problems?

3. To what extent should education policies and practices in the United States emulate those in Japan? Which practices might be most "transportable," and which may be undesirable?

4. What are the advantages and disadvantages of offering higher education opportunities for a large proportion of young people? What might or should be done to counteract the disadvantages?

Suggested Projects for Professional Development

1. Use Internet resources to find recent arguments for and against national tests and/or a national curriculum. Does the current seem to be moving toward or away from national standards and curricula? (Hint: Searching ERIC for these terms at **www.ed.gov** can provide a useful start.)
2. Examine one or more international studies of educational achievement (such as the ones cited in this chapter) to determine how far the United States ranks from the top or bottom. Has the U.S. position been improving or declining?
3. Research two or three educational policies or approaches used in other countries but not in the United States. Do they seem applicable to the United States? If so, what problems might there be in implementing them? How would you prepare a plan to convince school officials to let you try such a policy or approach in your subject or teaching field?
4. Are citizens in other countries more or less satisfied with their schools than in the United States? Find some data relevant to this question, and assess their implications. (Hint: Use FirstSearch, Infotrac, Ebsco, or other electronic approaches for searching periodical data bases.) What philosophical differences in ideas about the importance and purpose of education do you suppose contribute to relative levels of satisfaction?

Suggested Readings and Resources

Internet Resources

Good sources of information regarding developments in educational systems elsewhere include publications such as the *Daily Telegraph* (**www.telegraph.co.uk**) and *The Economist* (**www.economist.com**), organizations such as the Organization for Economic Co-operation and Development (**www.oecd.org**) and the federal government site at **www.ed.gov**. The home page of the International Association for the Evaluation of Educational Achievement (IEA) at **uttou2.to.utwente.nl/** is worth frequent visits.

Publications

Caldwell, Brian J., and David Hayward. *The Future of Schools.* London: Routledge, 1998. *Particular attention is given to recent school reform efforts in Australia and the United Kingdom.*

Comparative Education Review. *This journal emphasizes such topics as the development of national school systems, education and economic development, comparisons across nations, and international aspects of multicultural education.*

Hargreaves, David H., and David Hopkins. *The Empowered School.* London: Cassell, 1991. *Drawing on research from many countries, this volume provides recommendations for improving instruction through development of individual school plans.*

Husen, Torsten, Albert Tuijnman, and William Halls. *Schooling in Modern European Society.* Oxford: Pergamon, 1992. *Discusses trends in curriculum and testing, economics and education, schooling for minorities, and other contemporary issues.*

International Journal of Educational Research. *Recent theme issues have dealt with equal opportunity, giftedness, private education, science education, and other topics of worldwide concern.*

Lane, John J., ed. *Ferment in Education: A Look Abroad.* Chicago: University of Chicago Press, 1995. *In addition to several general essays, this book includes chapters dealing with Africa, China, Israel, Japan, and Russia and Eastern Europe.*

McAdams, Richard P. *Lessons from Abroad.* Lancaster, Pa: Technomic, 1993. *Subtitled "How Other Countries Educate Their Children," this volume includes chapters on Canada, Denmark, England, Germany, Japan, and the United States.*

Wilson, Maggie. *Girls and Young Women in Education.* Oxford: Pergamon, 1990. *Educational systems in nine European countries are analyzed with reference to the performance and attainment of girls and young women, provision of equal opportunity for female students, and impacts of national policy on career opportunities.*

CHAPTER SIXTEEN

School Effectiveness and Reform in the United States

Much of this book has been concerned with problems and trends in the reform of elementary and secondary schools. Chapter 1 described recent efforts to improve the teacher work force in response to widespread dissatisfaction with the schools, and Chapter 2 considered merit pay and other methods of motivating teachers. Chapters 9, 10, and 11 examined reasons for the low performance of many disadvantaged students and explored the goal of educational equity. Chapter 13 summarized major national reports on school reform, and Chapter 14 discussed trends in curriculum and instruction.

The material in this chapter deals even more explicitly with selected issues in school effectiveness and reform. After highlighting several major challenges that confront the U.S. educational system, we will examine research into the characteristics of effective instruction and effective schools. We will also look at the process of school improvement and reform and a number of other important areas often discussed under the heading of school effectiveness.

Debates about school reform cannot be resolved without analyzing actual research evidence. This chapter cannot discuss every change that has been suggested, but it will examine the proposals that seem to have particular promise or that have received widespread attention. As you read, try to determine which ideas have solid evidence to support them. For each suggested reform, think also about the prerequisites for success, the underlying conditions that may help make it appropriate or inappropriate, and how it may affect your career as a teacher. Keep the following basic questions in mind:

- Why is educational reform so important?
- What are the characteristics of effective instruction and effective schools?
- How can rural schools be made more effective?
- What is the role of magnet and alternative schools?
- Are nonpublic schools more effective than public schools?
- Will expansion of school choice plans improve education?
- What should be done for gifted and talented students?

Imperatives to Improve the Schools

Underprepared workers

Compelling need for equity

CCSSO recommendations

Much of the concern about American schools focuses on the need to bolster the nation's international economic competitiveness by teaching students skills they will need as members of the work force, and on the related imperative to improve the performance of disadvantaged students.

Several major national reports and studies have suggested that American students are leaving school unprepared to participate effectively in jobs that will, in an increasingly sophisticated and technology-based world economy, require them to "reason and perform complex, non-routine intellectual tasks." For example, one 1998 survey of employers reported that more than half of current workers are deficient in basic skills.[1]

In addition to their worries about deficits in basic-skills education, many educational policy makers are also concerned that schools are not doing enough to prepare youth for using the technologies of the future. In the words of U.S. Secretary of Education Richard Riley, "Possibilities for introducing technological improvements are receiving increasing attention in school reform efforts throughout the United States."[2]

Nearly all the recent reports and studies dealing with educational reform call for improving the performance of economically disadvantaged students in order to make educational outcomes more equitable. In addition to the desire for fairness, educational equity has also been related to the need for economic competitiveness. For example, the Forum of Educational Organizational Leaders concluded that "if we wish to maintain or improve our standard of living, we must work smarter . . . [but] it is not possible to succeed if only middle class people from stable families work smarter. . . . [This capacity] must — for the first time in human history — be characteristic of the mass of our population."

Specific areas of concern for educators working to reform educational opportunities for disadvantaged students include the following:

- *At-risk students.* The social and economic opportunities of low-achieving students and those without good postsecondary credentials have declined rapidly. Perhaps the most far-reaching set of proposals for helping at-risk and disadvantaged students are in the policy statements of the Council of Chief State School Officers (CCSSO). CCSSO's statements argue that state laws should "guarantee" educational programs and other services "reasonably calculated to enable all persons to graduate from high school." Such a guarantee policy, the CCSSO has indicated, may require such strong measures as "state takeovers" of distressed school districts, support for students to transfer from low-achieving schools or districts to "successful" locations elsewhere, and reduction in the concentration of students at low-income schools.[3]

---

[1]Carnegie Task Force on Teaching as a Profession, *A Nation Prepared: Teachers for the 21st Century* (New York: Carnegie Corporation, 1986), pp. 12, 14; and Richard W. Riley, "Regarding the 1994 NAEP Reading Assessment" (Statement posted on the World Wide Web, May 1995). See also *Human Resources Competitive Profile* (Washington, D.C.: Council on Competitiveness, 1995); and Franca Gargiulo, "High-Tech Edge Depends on Education and Immigration," *San Francisco Business Times*, June 1, 1998.
[2]"Schools Falling Behind As House Threatens Technology Funds" (U.S. Department of Education Press Release, March 7, 1998); "Bridging the Technology Gap in Schools," *Community Update* (July–August 1998), available at **www.ed.gov**; and Richard A. Melcher, "Education Prognosis 1999," *Business Week*, January 11, 1999, pp. 132–133.
[3]*Assuring Educational Success for Students at Risk* (Washington D.C.: Council of Chief State School Officers, 1987); and *State Responsibility for Student Opportunity,* (Washington D.C.: Council of Chief State School Officers, 1995, available at **www.ccso.org**.

Inner-city poverty. As we pointed out in Chapter 10 and elsewhere, educational problems are particularly severe in inner-city minority neighborhoods of concentrated poverty. A workable response to the problems of inner-city neighborhoods will require coordinated efforts involving employment, transportation, housing, social welfare, desegregation and deconcentration of poverty populations, crime and delinquency, affirmative action, and other components — and there is no doubt that elementary and secondary education must play a pivotal part.[4]

Concentrated rural poverty. Some rural areas have communities of concentrated poverty similar in many respects to those in big cities. Among these are the Appalachian region in the eastern United States and the Ozarks region in the South. Although many poor rural communities have mostly nonminority populations, indicators of social disorganization — high teenage pregnancy rates, widespread juvenile delinquency, very low school achievement, and pervasive feelings of hopelessness — are as high or nearly as high as those in poor minority neighborhoods in big cities. For the U.S. economy as a whole to "work smarter," these rural students, like their inner-city counterparts, need effective education.[5]

Many observers believe that our response to these challenges will be of historic importance in determining whether the United States prospers or declines in the twenty-first century.

Coordinated reform needed to combat declining opportunities

Pockets of rural poverty

Characteristics of Effective Classrooms and Schools

The push for greater educational effectiveness became a national growth industry in 1983, and since then has generated hundreds of research studies as well as thousands of discussion papers and improvement plans. The following sections describe some of the most important findings from this vast flood of materials.

Effective Teaching and Instruction

Much has been learned

Recent research suggests that much has been learned about effective delivery of instruction in the classroom. This section summarizes what this research into effective teaching and instruction has to say about classroom management, pedagogical methods, grouping of students, and related issues.

Classroom Management. Research on classroom management indicates that effective teachers use a variety of techniques to develop productive climates and to motivate students. Effective teachers emphasize practices like the following:[6]

---

[4]Carolyn Cody, "Teachers Need Help, Not Accusations," *Black Issues in Higher Education,* January 2, 1992, p. 22; and *The State of the Cities—1998* (Washington, D.C.: U.S. Department of Housing and Urban Development, 1998), available at **www.huduser.org.**

[5]Maureen Sullivan and Danny Miller, "Cincinnati's Urban Appalachian Council and Appalachian Identity," *Harvard Educational Review* (February 1990), pp. 106–124; Alan J. DeYoung and Barbara K. Laurence, "On Hoosiers, Yankees, and Mountaineers," *Phi Delta Kappan* (October 1995), pp. 104–112; and Sarah G. Thomason, "Language Variation and Change" (Undated Internet posting by the author), available at **www.lsadc.org/web2/fldfr.htm.**

[6]Jere Brophy, "Classroom Management Techniques," *Education and Urban Society* (February 1986), pp. 182–195; Anne Reynolds, "What Is Competent Beginning Teaching? A Review of the Literature," *Review of Educational Research* (Spring 1992), pp. 1–36; and Jere Brophy and Janet Alleman, "Classroom Management," *Social Education* (January 1998), pp. 56–58.

1. Making sure that students know what the teacher expects
2. Letting students know how to obtain help
3. Following through with reminders and rewards to enforce the rules
4. Providing a smooth transition between activities
5. Giving students assignments of sufficient variety to maintain interest
6. Monitoring the class for signs of confusion or inattention
7. Being careful to avoid embarrassing students in front of their classmates
8. Responding flexibly to unexpected developments
9. Designing tasks that draw on students' prior knowledge and experience
10. Helping students develop self-management skills
11. Ensuring that all students are part of a classroom learning community

Time of active engagement

Time-on-Task. Effective teaching as portrayed in a number of studies brings about relatively high student **time-on-task** — that is, time engaged in learning activities. As one would expect, students who are actively engaged in relevant activities tend to learn more than students who are not so engaged. Studies of time-on-task have pointed out that classrooms can be managed to increase the time students spend on actual learning activities. However, student learning is not simply a function of the time spent on academic work. Other variables, such as the suitability of the activities, the students' success or failure in the tasks attempted, and the motivating characteristics of methods and materials, are also important.[7]

Skillful questioning and wait time

Questioning. One way to stimulate student engagement in learning is to ask appropriate questions in a manner that ensures participation and facilitates mastery of academic content. Several studies have identified questioning skills as an important aspect of effective teaching. In particular, research indicates that longer "wait time" (the interval between the posing of a question and selecting or encouraging a student to answer it) significantly improves student participation and learning. Some research also indicates that "higher-order" questioning that requires students to mentally manipulate ideas and information is more effective than "lower cognitive" questioning that focuses on verbatim recall of facts.[8]

Direct Instruction and Explicit Teaching. The terms **direct instruction** and **explicit teaching** (frequently used as synonyms) usually refer to teacher-directed instruction that proceeds in small steps. (Direct instruction also is sometimes referred to as "active teaching.") Research has shown a link between this method, properly implemented, and high levels of student achievement. Barak Rosenshine identified the following six teaching "steps" or "functions" as central to direct instruction:[9]

---

[7]Mary Rohrkemper and Lyn Corno, "Success and Failure in Classroom Tasks: Adaptive Learning and Classroom Teaching," *Elementary School Journal* (January 1988), pp. 297–311; Robert E. Slavin, "A Model of Effective Instruction," *Educational Forum* (Winter 1995), pp. 166–176; and Michael Sadowski, "Time and Learning," *Harvard Education Letter* (March–April 1998).
[8]Kenneth R. Chuska, *Improving Classroom Questions* (Bloomington, Ind.: Phi Delta Kappa, 1995); Barry Beyer, "Improving Student Thinking," *Clearing House* (May–June 1998), pp. 262–267; and Susan M. Glazer, "Using KWL Folders," *Teaching K–8* (January 1999), pp. 106–107.
[9]Barak Rosenshine, "Explicit Teaching and Teacher Training," *Journal of Teacher Education* (May–June 1987), pp. 34–36. See also Barak Rosenshine, "Advances in Research on Instruction," in J. W. Lloyd, E. J. Kameanui, and D. Chard, eds., *Issues in Educating Students with Disabilities* (Mahwah, N.J.: Erlbaum, 1997), pp. 197–221; and "Direct Instruction" (1998 posting at the Internet site of the Education Commission of the States), available at **www.ecs.org**.

Six teaching steps

1. Begin lessons with a review of relevant previous learning and a preview and goal statement
2. Present new material in small steps, with clear and detailed explanations and active student practice after each step
3. Guide students in initial practice; ask questions and check for understanding
4. Provide systematic feedback and corrections
5. Supervise independent practice; monitor and assist seatwork
6. Provide weekly and monthly review and testing

Several other prominent advocates of explicit teaching, such as Jere Brophy, Thomas Good, Madeline Hunter, and Jane Stallings, have outlined similar components of direct instruction.[10]

Explicit Comprehension Instruction and Strategic Teaching. Explicit teaching has often been criticized for its tendency to neglect important higher-order learning (reasoning, critical thinking, comprehension of concepts) in favor of small-step learning of factual material. In many schools where teachers have been told to follow a prescribed sequence of this kind, the practice emphasizes low-level learning and mindless regurgitation of facts and leaves little room for "individualism, individual freedom, creativity, [and] analytical thinking."[11]

Critique of explicit teaching

Questioning skills—such as ensuring long "wait times" and asking "higher-order" questions—are an important aspect of effective teaching. *(© Elizabeth Crews)*

----

[10]Jere Brophy and Thomas I. Good, "Teacher Behavior and Student Achievement," in Merlin C. Wittrock, ed., *Handbook of Research on Teaching,* 3rd ed. (New York: Macmillan, 1986); Steven A. Stahl and David A. Hayes, eds., *Instructional Models in Reading* (Mahweh, N.J.: Erlbaum, 1996); and James M. Cooper, ed., *Classroom Teaching Skills* (Boston: Houghton Mifflin, 1999).

[11]Arthur E. Wise, "Legislated Learning Revisited," *Phi Delta Kappan* (January 1988), pp. 328–329; Robert Rothman, *Measuring Up* (San Francisco: Jossey-Bass, 1995); and Ervin F. Sparapani, "Encouraging Thinking in High School and Middle School," *Clearing House* (May–June 1998), pp. 278–280.

Higher-order focus

However, direct instruction does not have to be concentrated on low-level learning. Indeed, much has been accomplished during the last decade in refining classroom techniques for explicitly teaching comprehension in all subject areas. David Pearson and his colleagues refer to many such approaches as **explicit comprehension instruction**. Barak Rosenshine has characterized the development of this approach since 1970 as an "enormous accomplishment" in which educators should take great pride.[12]

Like explicit teaching, explicit comprehension instruction emphasizes review and preview, feedback and correctives, and guided as well as independent practice, but it also systematically stresses teacher modeling of conceptual learning, linking of new knowledge to prior learning, monitoring of students' comprehension, and systematic training for students in summarizing, inferencing, and other learning strategies. Techniques and strategies associated with explicit comprehension instruction include the following:[13]

Techniques for explicit comprehension instruction

- "Prediction" activities in which students predict what will be found in the text based on their prior knowledge
- "Reciprocal teaching," student team learning, and other approaches to cooperative learning, through which students learn to take more responsibility for helping each other comprehend material
- "Semantic maps" and "semantic networks" that organize information
- Computer simulations designed to develop concepts and thinking skills
- "Metacognitive" learning strategies through which students monitor and assess their own learning processes
- "Learning to learn" strategies
- Problem-solving models that help students analyze learning situations
- Collaborative study of increasingly complex questions and problems

Teachers as strategists

Beau Jones and her colleagues have described the effective use of such techniques as **strategic teaching**, a "concept which calls attention to the role of the teacher as strategist." Emphasis in strategic teaching is on the student's construction of meaning and growth in independent learning, with the teacher serving as a model and mediator of learning. As noted in Chapter 1, many analysts use the term *reflective teaching* in describing this kind of instructional approach.[14]

Cognitive Instruction for Low-Achieving Students.   Emphasis on passive learning of low-level skills seems to be particularly pervasive in schools with concentrations of working-class students and low achievers. A change in this pattern will require

---

[12]P. David Pearson and Janice A. Dole, "Explicit Comprehension Instruction," *Elementary School Journal* (November 1987), pp. 151–165; Ann L. Brown, "The Advancement of Learning," *Educational Researcher* (November 1994), pp. 4–12; and Barak Rosenshine, "The Case for Explicit, Teacher-Led Cognitive Strategy Instruction" (paper presented the annual meeting of the American Educational Research Association, Chicago, 1997).
[13]Barbara Z. Presseisen, *Thinking Skills: Research and Practice* (Washington, D.C.: National Education Association, 1986); Barak Rosenshine and Carla Meister, "Reciprocal Teaching: A Review of the Research," *Review of Educational Research* (Winter 1994), pp. 479–530; and Miriam Alfassi, "Reading for Meaning," *American Educational Research Journal* (Summer 1998), pp. 309–332.
[14]Michael Pressley, Rachel Brown, Peggy Van Meter, and Ted Schuder, "Transactional Strategies," *Educational Leadership* (May 1995), p. 81; and Michael Pressley, *Reading Instruction That Works* (Washington, D.C.: International Reading Association, 1998).

new approaches for delivering cognitive instruction, as well as fundamental improvements in programming throughout the educational system.[15]

Approaches to improve thinking skills

In addition to the comprehension-enhancement strategies described in the preceding sections, several other learning approaches offer promise for improving the thinking skills of low achievers. *Cognitive apprenticeships* immerse students in a motivating, real-world setting. *Cognitively guided instruction* builds on existing knowledge and intuitive reasoning to develop skill and understanding in problem solving. *Scaffolded instruction* provides step-by-step modeling and other forms of intellectual support that are gradually withdrawn as students acquire independent learning skills. *Situated learning* involves multimedia simulations that are highly motivating and help students master learning-to-learn strategies.[16]

Specific programs aimed at improving the thinking skills of low achievers include the Higher Order Thinking Skills Program (discussed later in this chapter), the Productive Thinking Program, and the Chicago Mastery Learning Reading (Insights) Program. Research suggests that such approaches have indeed improved performance. However, some specific obstacles need to be addressed, including the preference many students have developed for low-level learning, the low expectations many teachers have for low achievers, and the high financial cost of effective instruction that stresses cognitive development.[17]

Grouping and Tracking. **Homogeneous grouping** of students by ability or previous achievement frequently is used on the grounds that it facilitates teaching and learning. Most research, however, has found that it has little or no consistent positive effect. In fact, some studies have concluded that it improves the performance of high achievers but depresses outcomes for low achievers. Teachers may have low expectations for low-achieving groups and pace instruction very slowly, and students in those groups may be deprived of positive peer reinforcement and assistance.[18]

Low expectations, low outcomes

Nevertheless, as we pointed out in Chapter 10, the implications of research on grouping are neither simple nor obvious. One can argue that individualized and small-group instruction in heterogeneous classes should have better results than homogeneous grouping, but such instruction is expensive and difficult to deliver

---

[15]Jean Anyon, "Social Class and the Hidden Curriculum of Work," in Henry Giroux and David Purpel, eds., *The Hidden Curriculum and Moral Education* (Berkeley, Calif.: McCutchan, 1983), pp. 143–167; Daniel U. Levine, "Teaching Thinking to At-Risk Students: Generalizations and Speculation," in Barbara Z. Presseisen, ed., *At-Risk Students and Thinking: Perspectives from Research* (Washington, D.C.: National Education Association and Research for Better Schools, 1988); Linda Darling-Hammond, *The Right to Learn* (San Francisco: Jossey-Bass, 1997); and Eric J. Cooper and Daniel U. Levine, "Teaching for Intelligence," in Barbara Presseisen, ed., *Teaching for Intelligence: A Collection of Articles* (Arlington Heights, Ill.: Skylight, 1999).

[16]Barak V. Rosenshine and Carla Meister, "The Use of Scaffolds for Teaching Higher-Level Cognitive Strategies," *Educational Leadership* (April 1992), pp. 26–33; Kathleen Hogan and Michael Pressley, eds., *Scaffolding Student Learning* (Cambridge, Mass.: Brookline, 1987); and Michael E. Cena and Judith P. Mitchell, "Anchored Instruction," *Journal of Adolescent and Adult Literacy* (April 1998), pp. 559–561.

[17]Stanley Pogrow, "Challenging At-Risk Students," *Phi Delta Kappan* (January 1990), pp. 389–397; Stanley Pogrow, "Making Reform Work for the Educationally Disadvantaged," *Educational Leadership* (February 1995), pp. 20–24; and Stanley Pogrow, "What Is an Exemplary Program?" *Educational Researcher* (October 1998), pp. 22–29.

[18]Robert E. Slavin, "Achievement Effects of Ability Grouping in Secondary Schools: A Best-Evidence Synthesis," *Review of Educational Research* (Fall 1990), pp. 471–499; Elizabeth G. Cohen, "Restructuring the Classroom: Conditions for Productive Small Groups," *Review of Educational Research* (Spring 1994), pp. 1–35; Alfie Kohn, "Only For My Kid," *Phi Delta Kappan* (April 1998), pp. 110–120; and Anne Wheelock, "Keeping Schools on Track," *Rethinking Schools* (Winter 1998–1999), p. 22.

Improved grouping methods

effectively, and many schools have been unsuccessful at it. In addition, some research suggests that homogeneous grouping can be much more successful than it has been in the past. The effects of grouping practices depend on a complex set of interacting considerations, such as the pacing and quality of instruction, adequacy of materials, class size, number of low achievers, instructional methods, and so on. Much more needs to be learned.[19]

Opportunity limited by tracking

The term **tracking**, as we have noted in earlier chapters, usually refers to the practice of separating high-school students into different curriculum paths, such as an academic track for college-bound students, a general track for "business" students, and a vocational track for students who will enter a trade. Most of the research on tracking supports the conclusion that students in the general or business track have less opportunity to learn academic subject matter and make smaller academic gains than college-track students with similar family and socioeconomic backgrounds. For this reason, many recent proposals for educational reform strongly recommend that enrollment in general/business or vocational tracks be reduced or eliminated.[20]

Effective Schools

Focusing on larger contexts

The preceding sections addressed effective teaching and instruction at the classroom level. However, reformers must also pay attention to the school as an institution and, in the final analysis, to the larger context of the school district and the environment in which schools operate. The effectiveness of the school and of the district as a whole helps to determine what happens in each classroom.

Edmonds's research

Elementary Schools. Most of the recent research on effective schools focuses on elementary education. Effectiveness is usually defined at least partly in terms of outstanding student achievement. For example, Ronald Edmonds and other researchers described an effective school as having characteristics such as the following:[21]

Characteristics of effective schools

1. A *safe and orderly environment* that is not oppressive and is conducive to teaching and learning

2. A *clear school mission* through which the staff shares a commitment to instructional priorities, assessment procedures, and accountability

3. *Instructional leadership* by a principal who understands the characteristics of instructional effectiveness

[19]Gaea Leinhardt and Allan Pallay, "Restrictive Educational Settings: Exile or Haven?" *Review of Educational Research* (December 1982), pp. 199–210; Elizabeth G. Cohen and Rachel A. Lotan, *Working for Equity in Heterogeneous* (New York: Teachers College Press, 1997); and Elizabeth G. Cohen, "Making Cooperative Learning Equitable," *Educational Leadership* (September 1998), pp. 18–21.
[20]James E. Rosenbaum, *Making Inequality* (New York: Wiley, 1976); Jeannie Oakes, "Can Tracking Research Inform Practice?" *Educational Researcher* (May 1992), pp. 12–21; Richard McAdams, "Improving America's Schools," *Principal* (November 1994), pp. 34–35; and C. Anne Brossard and Alfred L. Joseph, "Tracking," *Social Work in Education* (April 1998), pp. 110–121.
[21]Joan Shoemaker, "Effective Schools: Putting the Research to the Ultimate Test," *Pre-Post Press* (1982), p. 241. See also William J. Gauthier, Jr., Raymond I. Pecheone, and Joan Shoemaker, "Schools Can Become More Effective?" *Journal of Negro Education* (Summer 1985), pp. 388–408; and Philip Hallinger, Leonard Bickman, and Ken Davis, "School Context, Principal Leadership, and Student Reading Achievement," *Elementary School Journal* (May 1996), pp. 528–549.

PROFESSIONAL PLANNING

for your first year

How Will You Participate in School Reform?

The Situation

In the middle of your first year in teaching, while you are still struggling to learn how to teach well in your own classroom, the school reform movement hits you head on. Your principal has just conducted a special faculty meeting at which she informs you and your colleagues that several of the trends and developments discussed in this chapter will affect your school directly.

For one thing, state government officials have announced that your school will be designated as producing inadequate achievement and will have to meet standards set by external teams of educators who will frequently observe your classes.

Second, district officials have decided that your faculty must develop a "whole-school" reform approach (discussed later in this chapter) that involves substantial staff development designed to bring about "systemic" improvement. All faculty will have to participate.

Third, your principal has suggested that the reform effort should include a major emphasis on technology, so that all faculty can work to improve achievement. She also has decided that planning for this effort should involve research on unusually effective schools.

Thought Questions

1. Has your teacher-preparation program prepared you well to work with new technologies? Would you be willing to provide leadership in this part of your school's improvement effort?
2. Are there some topics you studied in your preparation program, such as unusually effective schools, that you wish you would have given more time to pursuing on your own?
3. To what extent can you help provide leadership in developing a comprehensive plan that will involve all faculty? To do so, do you need to learn more about what other teachers are doing?
4. Will you feel comfortable being observed frequently by "outsiders" who you think are likely to be critical in their evaluations?
5. Are you ready to try new methods and approaches while you are still coping with the basics of learning to teach? What methods and approaches might be most feasible for you?

4. A climate of *high expectations* in which the staff demonstrates that all students can master basic skills

5. High *time-on-task* brought about when a large percentage of students' time is spent "engaged" in planned activities to master basic skills

6. Frequent *monitoring of student progress,* using the results to improve both individual performance and the instructional program

7. Positive *home-school relations* in which parents support the school's basic mission and play an important part in helping to achieve it

Coordinating methods and materials

Another characteristic that contributes to school effectiveness is **curriculum alignment** — the coordination of instructional planning, methods, materials, and testing. When staff development focuses on such coordination, teachers are less likely to rely solely on textbooks and more likely to select or create materials that are most appropriate for teaching a specific skill to a particular group of students.[22]

Other key factors

According to several recent research reviews, other key features of unusually effective schools are (1) attention to goals involving cultural pluralism and multicultural education; (2) emphasis on responding to students' personal problems and developing their social skills; (3) faculty who strive to improve students' sense of efficacy; and (4) continuous concern for making teaching tasks realistic and manageable. Researchers at the Northwest Regional Educational Laboratory have identified more than one hundred specific practices, grouped in eighteen categories, that contribute to school effectiveness.[23]

Secondary Schools.   Relatively few studies have concentrated solely on the characteristics of unusually effective secondary schools. (Our use of the term *secondary schools* refers to middle schools, which usually include a combination of grades six through eight; junior highs, which usually include grades seven through nine; and senior highs, which include grades nine or ten through twelve.) Because the goals and programs of most secondary schools are so diverse and complex, it is difficult to conclude that one school is more effective than another, particularly when the social class of the student body is taken into account. In addition, hardly any secondary schools enrolling mostly working-class students stand out as being relatively high in achievement.[24]

Major modifications

One of the few senior high schools for which concrete data indicate unusual effectiveness is South Boston High School, which was able to generate substantial improvement during a time of continuing turmoil in the Boston school system. The changes that appear to account most for these improvements include the following:[25]

Significant reforms at South Boston

1. A new principal made major changes in organizational patterns and insisted that staff reexamine their methods.

2. More than two-thirds of the faculty were replaced by teachers willing to discard ineffective traditional methods.

---

[22]Daniel U. Levine and Joyce Stark, "Instructional and Organizational Arrangements That Improve Achievement in Inner-City Schools," *Educational Leadership* (December 1982), pp. 41–48. See also Daniel U. Levine and Lawrence W. Lezotte, *Unusually Effective Schools* (Madison, Wisc.: National Center for Effective Schools Research and Development, 1990); Craig Spilman, "Transforming an Urban School," *Educational Leadership* (December 1995–January 1996), pp. 34–39; and Lawrence W. Lezotte, "Effective Schools Process" (Undated posting at the Internet site of Effective Schools Inc.), available at **www.effectiveschools.com.**

[23]Daniel U. Levine, "Update on Effective Schools: Findings and Implications from Research and Practice," *Journal of Negro Education* (Fall 1990), pp. 577–584; Kathleen Cotton, *Effective Schooling Practices: A Research Synthesis 1995 Update* (Portland, Oreg.: Northwest Regional Educational Laboratory, 1995); Gerald R. Richardson, "Sustaining State Reform Through Research and Recognition," *CEIC Review* (August 1997); and Daniel U. Levine and Rayna F. Levine, "Two Routes to Unusual Effectiveness" (1999 posting at **www.pdkintl.org).**

[24]Daniel U. Levine and Eugene E. Eubanks, "Organizational Arrangements in Effective Secondary Schools," in John J. Lane and Herbert J. Walberg, eds., *Organizing for Learning* (Reston, Va.: National Association of Secondary School Principals, 1988); Edys Quellmalz and Patrick M. Shields, *School-Based Reform* (Washington, D.C.: U.S. Government Printing Office, 1995), available at **www.ed.gov/pubs/Reform;** and Charles Teddlie and David Reynolds, eds., *Research on School Effectiveness* (Levittown, Pa.: Falmer, 1998).

[25]This portrayal of South Boston is drawn from the authors' personal observations and from Geraldine Kozberg and Jerome Winegar, "The South Boston Story: Implications for Secondary Schools," *Phi Delta Kappan* (April 1981), pp. 565–569; and Daniel U. Levine and Allan C. Ornstein, "What Research Says About Success," *High School Magazine* (December 1993), pp. 32–34.

3. Nearly all ninth and tenth graders were placed in reading and writing courses rather than in traditional English classes.

4. Students were placed in mathematics courses rather than in "business mathematics," which for the most part repeated beginning arithmetic.

5. A number of in-school and out-of-school alternatives were established. These included a school-within-a-school that emphasized academic learning and a minischool that emphasized experiential learning and instruction.

Support from research

Comparable changes have taken place at several other inner-city high schools, including George Washington Preparatory High School in Los Angeles and Ribault High School in Jacksonville, Florida. Since no two schools share exactly the same problems and possibilities, we cannot say that other secondary schools should introduce exactly the same set of changes. However, research on effective approaches supports a number of the changes listed above, including emphasis on firm but fair discipline, personalized guidance for students, increased stress on reading and math for students far below grade level, and activities to build school spirit. Overall insistence on more rigorous standards is also considered important.[26]

According to several reviews of the literature, two of the most promising structural changes are a **school-within-a-school** and **achievement centers**.[27]

School-within-a-school

1. *School-within-a-school for low achievers.* Students who can read but are more than two or three years below grade level are assigned to a school-within-a-school serving 80 to 120 students and staffed by four or five teachers (English, reading, math, science, and social studies) and a coordinator. If teachers are selected for their ability and willingness to work with low achievers, the students can make large gains in reading and other basic skills.

Special assistance in achievement centers

2. *Achievement centers.* After specific learning objectives are identified for a given grade and subject area (for example, tenth-grade English), an achievement center is established for both remedial and developmental purposes. Students who do not have the prerequisite skills for a particular unit or who need special assistance in developing their full potential will attend the achievement center instead of or in addition to the regular class.

High-School Reform Proposals.   In addition to recommendations contained in the national reports, several prominent educators have offered proposals for comprehensive reform of high schools. Two of the most highly publicized proposals are those of Ernest Boyer and Theodore Sizer.

Boyer's proposals

Boyer's book *High School* was based on a three-year study that collected data at fifteen diverse senior high schools. Boyer stressed these major themes:[28]

---

[26]U.S. Department of Education, *Schools That Work* (Washington, D.C.: U.S. Government Printing Office, 1987); Gary Wehlage, Gregory Smith, and Pauline Lipman, "Restructuring Urban Schools: The New Futures Experience," *American Educational Research Journal* (Spring 1992), pp. 51–96; and "City-As-School" (Undated Internet posting at **www.sharingsuccess.org**).
[27]Gary G. Wehlage et al., *Reducing the Risk* (New York: Falmer, 1989); Daniel U. Levine, "Implications of an Urban School-Within-a-School Approach," in Hershholt C. Waxman et al., eds., *Students at Risk in At-Risk Schools* (Newbury Park, Calif.: Sage Corwin, 1992); Amy P. Dietrich and Elsie L. Bailey, "School Climate," *NASSP Bulletin* (January 1996), pp. 16–25; and Mary A. Raywid, "Taking Stock" (Undated Internet posting at **eric-web.tc.columbia.edu**).
[28]Ernest L. Boyer, *High School* (New York: Harper and Row, 1983). See also Ernest L. Boyer, *The Basic School* (New York: Carnegie Foundation for the Advancement of Learning, 1995); and Courtney Leatherman, "The Legacy of Ernest Boyer," *Chronicle of Higher Education*, January 5, 1996, p. A18. See also Shirley M. Hord, "Professional Learning Communities" (Undated Internet posting available at **www.sedl.org/siss**.

1. Goals must be more clearly focused on mastery of reading and writing, preparation for work and further education, and community service.

2. The core curriculum should expand from about half the units required for graduation to about two-thirds.

3. Working conditions of teachers must be improved.

4. Improvements must be made in instructional methods and materials.

5. Technology should be used to enrich curriculum.

6. More flexibility is needed in school size, schedules, and other arrangements.

Sizer's recommendations

Sizer recommends that the curriculum be divided into four major areas: inquiry and expression, mathematics and science, literature and the arts, and philosophy and history. He also advocates more active learning and less emphasis on minimal competency testing. Sizer particularly wants to eliminate the tacit understanding between students who say, "I will be orderly . . . if you don't push me very hard" and teachers who respond, "You play along with my minimal requirements and I will keep them minimal."[29]

Teams of teachers and students

Perhaps the greatest virtue of Sizer's proposals is that they explicitly recognize the difficulties of high-school teaching. After pointing out that teachers cannot provide appropriate coaching to 150 to 180 students a day, he suggests that teams of seven or eight teachers should work with groupings of 100 students or less. This might be made possible by eliminating the specialized positions of teachers now assigned to counseling, the arts, physical education, and other non-academic areas.

CES

To implement his ideas, Sizer organized the Coalition of Essential Schools (CES). His book, *Horace's School: Redesigning the American High School,* and articles by him and his colleagues describe developments at hundreds of schools that have joined the coalition. These studies document the difficulty of reform and discuss reasons why many CES schools have not changed very much.[30]

Evaluation of Effective Schools Research. In evaluating research on effective schools, a number of points should be kept in mind. First, we should recognize the widespread confusion about definitions. There are nearly as many definitions of effective schools as there are people discussing them. Some people have in mind a school with high academic achievement (taking account of social class), but others are thinking about a "self-renewing" school that can identify and solve internal problems, a school that promotes students' personal growth, a school that has shown improvement in achievement, or a school that concentrates on developing independent study skills and love for learning.

Definitions differ

Research focused on poverty schools

Second, most of the rigorous studies have focused on high-poverty elementary schools in which academic achievement is higher than at most other schools with similarly disadvantaged students. It is more difficult to identify unusually effective high schools and schools outside the inner city, where high achievement is more

---

[29]Theodore R. Sizer, *Horace's Compromise: The Dilemma of the American High School* (Boston: Houghton Mifflin, 1984). See also Reba N. Page, "Cultures and Curricula," *Educational Foundations* (Winter 1990), pp. 49–76; Theodore Sizer, *Horace's Hope* (Boston: Houghton Mifflin, 1996); and William G. Wraga, "The Comprehensive High School and Educational Reform in the United States," *High School Journal* (February–March 1998), pp. 121–132.

[30]Theodore R. Sizer, "No Pain, No Gain," *Educational Leadership* (May 1991), pp. 32–34; Theodore R. Sizer, *Horace's School: Redesigning the American High School* (Boston: Houghton Mifflin, 1992); and Donna E. Muncey and Patrick J. McQuillan, *Reform and Resistance in Schools and Classrooms* (New Haven: Yale University Press, 1996).

common. In addition, the key components of effectiveness outside the inner city may differ somewhat from those at poverty schools.[31]

Problems in research methods

Third, other methodological problems have left much of the research vulnerable to criticism. For example, schools identified as effective in a given subject (say, reading) during a given year may not be effective on other measures or in the next year. In addition, controls for students' social class and family environment are frequently inadequate. For instance, magnet schools enrolling inner-city students may be judged as unusually effective; but if later research shows that those schools draw their students from highly motivated poverty families dissatisfied with neighborhood schools, the high achievement might be attributable more to the students' background than to the characteristics of the school.[32]

Begging the question

Fourth, the literature often tends to beg the question of what teachers and principals should do in the schools. For example, the claim that a school requires good leadership and a productive climate does not specify exactly what these are or how to accomplish them.[33]

Despite these qualifications, the research on effective schools has identified a number of characteristics that deserve to be considered, and some projects have met with notable successes. The next section will examine more of these success stories and the changes that lie behind them.

Recent Efforts to Increase School Effectiveness

Many attempts to increase school effectiveness are under way. Educators in Chicago, Detroit, Milwaukee, Memphis, New York, and elsewhere are trying to create more successful schools by introducing practices identified in effective schools research. Departments of education in California, Connecticut, Florida, New Jersey, Ohio, and other states are providing services to help low-performing schools become more effective.

Successful Effectiveness-Improvement Projects and Approaches

Milwaukee project

Encouraging data for achievement gains among disadvantaged students have been reported in a number of locations. For example, among eighteen Milwaukee elementary schools participating in a project to raise achievement, the percentage of fifth-grade students reading in the lowest performance category decreased from 55 percent in 1979 to 30 percent in 1985, and the comparable decline in math was from 42 percent to 18 percent. Probably the most impressive large-scale project has been the **Achievement Goals Program** (AGP), which includes twenty-three schools in San Diego. The San Diego approach was twofold: (1) use of effective

AGP

---

[31]Daniel U. Levine and Robert S. Stephenson, "Are Effective or Meritorious Schools Meretricious?" *The Urban Review* (no. 1, 1987), pp. 25–34; Thomas Corcoran and Margaret Goetz, "Instructional Capacity and High Performance Schools," *Educational Researcher* (December 1995), pp. 27–31; and Larry Cuban, "How Schools Change Reforms," *Teachers College Record* (Spring 1998), pp. 453–477.

[32]John H. Ralph and James Fennessey, "Science of Reform: Some Questions About the Effective School Model," *Phi Delta Kappan* (June 1983), pp. 689–694; Robert G. Owens, *Organizational Behavior in Education,* 3rd ed. (Needham Heights, Mass.: Allyn and Bacon, 1995); and William L. Yancey, "Identifying Exceptional Schools in Urban Areas" (Paper presented at the annual meeting of the American Educational Research Association, San Diego, April 1998).

[33]Judith Chapman, "Leadership, Management, and the Effectiveness of Schooling," *Journal of Educational Administration* (vol. 31, no. 4, 1993), pp. 4–18; and Karen Louis, "Improving Urban and Disadvantaged Schools," *Knowledge and Policy* (no. 94, 1995), pp. 34–55.

schools research on mastery learning, classroom management, time-on-task, direct instruction, provision of staff development, and other topics; and (2) a radical curriculum alignment that made it difficult for teachers to overemphasize low-level skills. Large gains in reading comprehension (along with language and math) were registered at every grade. Throughout the ten years of the program, for example, the percentage of students in grades five, nine, and eleven who scored above the national median on standardized reading comprehension tests jumped by over 10 percent.[34]

Unfortunately, however, school improvement projects do not seem to have been implemented successfully in many locations. Thus the low achievement patterns and other educational problems that we cite elsewhere in this book do not appear to have changed significantly on a national basis. In order to attain national goals for cognitive growth of students, international competitiveness, and socioeconomic equity, more schools must make better use of the research on effective schooling.

Exemplary Instructional Interventions

Numerous recent intervention approaches appear to improve the cognitive functioning and performance of low achievers when educators implement them well. This section briefly describes several such types of intervention.

HOTS components

Higher Order Thinking Skills (HOTS) Program.   Developed by Stanley Pogrow and his colleagues, the HOTS program is specifically designed to replace remedial-reading activities in grades four through six. The HOTS approach has four major components: (1) use of computers for problem solving; (2) emphasis on dramatization techniques that require students to verbalize, thereby stimulating language development; (3) Socratic questioning; and (4) a thinking-skills curriculum that stresses metacognitive learning, learning-to-learn, and other comprehension-enhancement techniques of the kind described earlier. Now used in nearly 2,000 schools, HOTS frequently has brought about very large improvements in student performance in both reading and math.[35]

A faster pace

The developers of HOTS also have devised a thinking-based math curriculum and identified materials and methods for improving low-achievers' comprehension in science, social studies, and other subjects. According to Pogrow, results of the HOTS program show that at-risk students have "tremendous levels of intellectual and academic potential" but that many do not "understand 'understanding.'" This "fundamental learning problem can be eliminated if enough time and enough resources are made available."[36]

Success for All.   Probably the most comprehensive intervention for improving the achievement of disadvantaged students, Success for All provides intensive instruc-

---

[34]Daniel U. Levine and Eugene E. Eubanks, "Achievement Improvement and Non-Improvement at Concentrated Poverty Schools in Big Cities," *Metropolitan Education* (Winter 1986– 87), pp. 92–107; Barbara S. Taylor, ed., *Case Studies in Effective Schools Research* (Madison, Wisc.: National Center for Effective Schools Research and Development, 1990); and "Successful Texas Schoolwide Programs" (1997 Internet posting at **www.starcenter.org/promise/research.htm**.
[35]"Important Basic Information About the HOTS Program" (Undated Internet posting at **www.hots.org).**
[36]Stanley Pogrow, "What to Do About Chapter 1," *Phi Delta Kappan* (April 1992), pp. 624–630; Stanley Pogrow, "Helping Students Who 'Just Don't Understand,'" *Educational Leadership* (November 1994), pp. 62–68; and "For Low Achievers, Some Like It Hots," *Education Digest* (January 1997).

Comprehensive changes

tional support along with family assistance for children in preschool classes and the primary grades. Curriculum and instruction stress language development and learning-to-learn skills, and students receive individualized help in small classes. Success for All also emphasizes cooperative learning and mastery instruction, with technical support and staff development provided by full-time coordinators and resource persons assigned to participating schools. Measurable improvements in student achievement have been documented at numerous low-income schools in both urban and rural districts. According to its developers, Success for All demonstrates that success for disadvantaged students can be routinely ensured in schools that are not exceptional or extraordinary. However, the program does require a serious commitment to restructure elementary schools and to reconfigure the use of available funds.[37]

Individual tutoring in reading

Reading Recovery. Using linguistic theories originally elaborated in New Zealand, Reading Recovery provides systematic help for first graders who experience serious problems learning to read. Participating students receive individual tutoring every day for twelve to twenty weeks from a trained reading teacher. (A few students participate in additional tutoring after the first grade.) The emphasis is on learning to read through oral and written expression, diagnosis and correction of individual learning problems, and use of short paperback books or other materials with only a few lines per page. In contrast to many compensatory education programs, in which students have registered substantial gains but later declined in performance, Reading Recovery students have maintained relatively high reading scores in later grades.[38]

Stressing real-life comprehension

Degrees of Reading Power Comprehension Development Approach. Based in part on the Degrees of Reading Power (DRP) test originally developed by the College Board, the DRP approach is being implemented successfully at many urban schools. The test is unlike other standardized reading measures in that it assesses how well a student actually can comprehend written prose he or she encounters in or out of school, not just whether the student is above or below some abstract grade level. After using the DRP to determine their students' comprehension levels, teachers in all subject areas align their instruction accordingly. For homework and other independent assignments, they select materials that are not so difficult as to frustrate students; for classwork, they use materials slightly beyond students' comprehension in order to help them improve.[39]

Anchored Instruction and Other Technology-Based Approaches. As we pointed out in earlier chapters, numerous approaches attempt to improve student achievement

---

[37] Robert E. Slavin, "Neverstreaming," *Educational Leadership* (February 1996), pp. 4–7; Robert E. Slavin, "Can Education Reduce Social Inequity?" *Educational Leadership* (December 1997–January 1998); and Sharon Cromwell, "What Makes 'Success For All' So Successful?" *Education World,* October 26, 1998, available at **www.education-world.com.**

[38]Gay Su Pinnell, "Success for Low Achievers Through Reading Recovery," *Educational Leadership* (September 1990), pp. 17–21; Soundaram Ramaswami, *The Differential Impact of Reading Recovery on the Achievement of First Graders in the Newark School District* (Newark, N.J.: Newark Public Schools, 1995); and Stanley E. Swartz and Adria E. Klein, eds., *Research in Reading Recovery* (Westport, Conn.: Heinemann, 1997).

[39]Daniel U. Levine and John K. Sherk, "Implementation of Reforms to Improve Comprehension Skills at an Unusually Effective Inner City Intermediate School," *Peabody Journal of Education* (Summer 1989), pp. 87–106; Daniel U. Levine, "Instructional Approaches and Interventions That Can Improve the Academic Performance of African American Students," *Journal of Negro Education* (Winter 1994), pp. 46–63; and Eric J. Cooper, "Advanced Thinking for All Students" (Paper presented at the Fourth International Teaching for Intelligence Conference, New York, April 1998).

Using technology to teach problem solving

by using computers, interactive video, multimedia, and other technological innovations. Many of these approaches have particular relevance to low achievers. For example, the Anchored Instruction approach devised by the Cognition and Technology Group aims to improve the problem-formulating and problem-solving skills of low achievers by using videodisk and computerized materials that help students explore "authentic" tasks. Researchers report that students have been participating actively and becoming more proficient at complex problem solving.[40]

Comer School Development Program.   Developed by James Comer and his colleagues at Yale University, the School Development Program aims to improve achievement at inner-city elementary schools through enhanced social and psychological services for students, emphasis on parent involvement, and encouragement and support for active learning. Participating faculties involve parents in all aspects of school operation (including governance), and teachers, parents, psychologists, social workers, and other specialists form "Mental Health Teams" that design and supervise individualized learning arrangements for students with unusual problems. Curriculum and instruction are coordinated across subject areas to emphasize language learning and social skills. A number of schools in various school districts have produced large improvements in student achievement and behavior after implementing the School Development Program along with other innovations.[41]

Comer's approach

Algebridge and Equity 2000.   Jointly developed by the Educational Testing Service and the College Board, Algebridge was created to help students succeed in the transition from arithmetic to algebra. It since has evolved into the Equity 2000 project, which addresses additional aspects of mathematics education in secondary schools. Students receive assistance in prealgebra, algebra, geometry, and other courses. Recent data suggest that students frequently register large gains in mathematics performance, and that many are succeeding in algebra and other advanced math courses they otherwise would not be taking.[42]

Transition to algebra

Cooperative Learning.   For two decades, educators at Johns Hopkins University have been developing and refining techniques and materials for cooperative learning. As we pointed out earlier in the book, cooperative learning approaches can help teachers motivate students and respond to differences in learning styles. Student Team Learning (STL) provides techniques for implementing cooperative learning in any grade or subject. Drawing on STL, Cooperative Integrated Reading and Composition (CIRC) uses specially prepared materials and comprehension-enhancement strategies at the elementary-school level, and Team Accelerated Instruction (TAI) combines STL with individualized mastery instruction in middle-

Cooperative learning approaches

[40]The Cognition and Technology Group at Vanderbilt, "Anchored Instruction and Its Relationship to Situated Cognition," *Educational Researcher* (August–September 1990), pp. 2–10; Marcia Linn, "The Art of Multimedia and the State of Education," *Educational Researcher* (February 1992), pp. 30–32; and "Looking at Technology in Context," in David C. Berliner and Robert C. Calfee, eds., *Handbook of Educational Psychology* (New York: Macmillan, 1996), pp. 807–840.
[41]James P. Comer, "Educating Poor Minority Children," *Scientific American* (November 1988), pp. 42–48; and Catherine Sullivan-DeCarlo, Karol DeFalco, and Verdell Roberts, "Helping Students Avoid Risky Behavior," *Educational Leadership* (September 1998) pp. 80–82.
[42]"Algebridge Users Report Success," *Mathematics Education News* (Spring 1992), pp. 1–2; "Curriculum Gates Unlocked as Algebra Numbers Soar," *Equity and Choice* (Spring 1994), pp. 3–4; and "Equity 2000" (1998 posting at the Internet site of the Education Commission of the States), available at **www.ecs.org**; click to "information clearinghouse," then "best practices," then "secondary education."

At-risk students, such as those with English-as-a-second language, can benefit from programs such as Head Start. *(© Elizabeth Crews/Stock Boston)*

grade mathematics. All three approaches, when implemented well, have produced sizable gains among low achievers.[43]

Combinations of Approaches.   Exemplary interventions such as those described above are not mutually exclusive. Educators frequently combine promising approaches to school-based management, comprehensive staff development, changes in testing, and mastery instruction with other innovations and interventions described elsewhere in this book. For example, HOTS incorporates computer technology, and faculties using the School Development Program can use student team learning, mastery learning, and other innovations in curriculum and instruction. School faculties throughout the United States are combining these kinds of exemplary interventions as part of districtwide or multischool projects.[44]

Frequent combinations of approaches

At-Risk Students and Dropouts

In addition to the reform projects already discussed, many efforts have focused on *at-risk students*. The term is often not defined very specifically, but it usually refers to students who are low achievers and/or are alienated from school. They are considered to be at risk either of dropping out or of not acquiring enough education to

---

[43]Robert E. Slavin, ed., *School and Classroom Organization* (Hillsdale, N.J.: Erlbaum, 1989); Robert J. Stevens and Robert E. Slavin, "The Cooperative Elementary School," *American Educational Research Journal* (Summer 1995), pp. 321–351; and Olatokunbo S. Fashola and Robert E. Slavin, "Promising Programs for Elementary and Middle Schools," *Journal of Education for Students Placed at Risk* (no. 3, 1997), pp. 251–307. Information on CIRC is available at **www.successforall.org.**

[44]Thomas R. Guskey, Perry D. Passaro, and Wayne Wheeler, "The Thorpe Gordon School," *Principal* (September 1991), pp. 36–38; James H. Block, Susan I. Everson, and Thomas R. Guskey, eds., *School Improvement Programs* (New York: Scholastic, 1995); and Robert E. Slavin and Olatokunbo S. Fashola, *Show Me the Evidence* (Thousand Oaks, Calif.: Corwin, 1998).

Defining "at risk" succeed in the economy. A high proportion of at-risk, low achievers consists of economically disadvantaged minority students.

Some of the approaches most often advocated for at-risk students are listed below. These are not mutually exclusive.

- *Alternative opportunities* such as career academies, in-school suspension programs, magnet schools, and schools-within-a-school[45]

- *Employment linkages* to provide part-time employment training and/or improvement in vocational education[46]

Approaches for at-risk students

- *Special social services and counseling programs* such as those for delinquents or pregnant girls[47]

- *Modifications in curriculum and/or instruction* to make education more motivating and relevant for uninterested students[48]

- *Smaller classes and schools* that allow more personal contact between teachers and students and so create supportive communities[49]

- *Selection of dedicated teachers* who are willing and able to work with potential dropouts[50]

- *Experiential learning* that provides for active engagement in interesting activities[51]

- *Mentoring and advocacy assistance* from sympathetic adults[52]

The Process of School Improvement and Reform

Promulgating, legislating, and even packaging change are not the same as actually changing. Analysis of past efforts to improve schools has resulted in a much better understanding of the steps that must be taken to ensure that reform efforts have a significant and lasting impact. Some of the lessons that can be learned from past efforts are described below.

---

[45]Charles Dayton et al., "The California Partnership Academies," *Phi Delta Kappan* (March 1992), pp. 539–545; and Mary A. Raywid, "Small Schools," *Educational Leadership* (January 1998).

[46]W. Norton Grubb, "Giving High Schools an Occupational Focus," *Educational Leadership* (March 1992), pp. 36–37, 40–43; "Second-Chance Schools," *The Executive Educator* (March 1995), pp. 27–29; and Olatokunbo S. Fashola and Robert E. Slavin, "Effective Dropout Prevention and College Attendance Programs for Latino Students" (1997 paper prepared for the Hispanic Dropout Project), available at **www.ncbe.gwu.edu.**

[47]Dale Mann, "Can We Help Dropouts?" *Teachers College Record* (Spring 1986), pp. 307–323; and Samantha Morrisey, "Mat-Su," *Northwest Education* (Summer 1998), available at **www.nwrel.org.**

[48]Russell W. Rumberger, "High School Dropouts: A Review of Issues and Evidence," *Review of Educational Research* (Summer 1987), pp. 101–121; and Lee Sherman, "Meridian Academy," *Northwest Education* (Summer 1998), available at **www.nwrel.org.**

[49]Mary Koepke, "All in the Family," *Teacher Magazine* (March 1992), pp. 21–22; Craig Howley, "The Academic Effectiveness of Small-Scale Schooling," *ERIC Clearinghouse on Rural Education and Small Schools* (1997); and Mary A. Raywid, "Synthesis of Research," *Educational Leadership* (December 1997–January 1998), pp. 34–39.

[50]Patricia S. Miller, "Increasing Teacher Efficacy with At-Risk Students," *Equity and Excellence* (Fall 1991), pp. 30–35; and Suzie Boss, "Portland Night School," *Northwest Education* (Summer 1998), available at **www.nwrel.org.**

[51]Stan Bernard, "A Day at the Box Factory," *Educational Leadership* (March 1992), pp. 50–51; and Catherine Paglin and Jennifer Fager, *Alternative Schools* (Portland, Oreg.: Northwest Regional Educational Laboratory, 1997).

[52]Stephen F. Hamilton and Mary Agnes Hamilton, "Mentoring Programs: Promise and Paradox," *Phi Delta Kappan* (March 1992), pp. 546–550; Janet Testerman, "Holding At-Risk Students," *Phi Delta Kappan* (January 1996), pp. 364–366; and Shannon Priem, "Mansion on the Bluffs Catches Lives on the Edge," *Northwest Education* (Summer 1998), available at **www.nwrel.org.**

Solving day-to-day problems

1. *Adaptive problem solving.* An innovation frequently has little or no effect on students' performance because a host of problems arise to stifle practical application. For example, experts may devise a wonderful new science curriculum for fourth graders and school districts may purchase large quantities of the new curriculum materials, but teachers may choose not to use the materials or may not know how to use them. Innovations are not likely to work unless the organization introducing them is adaptive in the sense that it can identify and solve day-to-day problems.[53]

Focus on individual schools

2. *School-level focus.* Because the innovating organization must solve day-to-day problems, the focus must be at the level of the individual school, where many of the problems occur.[54]

Compatibility and accessibility

3. *Potential for implementation.* Successful school reform also depends on whether changes can be implemented feasibly in typical schools. Three characteristics that make successful implementation more likely are an innovation's *compatibility* with the social context of potential users, its *accessibility* to those who do not already understand or share the underlying ideas, and its *doability* in terms of demands on teachers' time and energy. Levine and Levine have pointed out that many approaches have high "potential for mischief" because they are so difficult to implement.[55]

Sharing a vision

4. *Leadership and shared agreements.* Meaningful innovation requires change in many institutional arrangements, including scheduling of staff and student time, selection and use of instructional methods and materials, and mechanisms for making decisions. In this regard the building principal usually is the key person, but the faculty also must have a shared vision of the changes that are possible and necessary. Otherwise, staff members are likely to discount proposals that ask them to make significant changes.[56]

Giving teachers a voice

5. *Teacher involvement.* Because people who are expected to alter their working patterns will not cooperate fully unless they have a voice in designing and implementing change, teachers must have an opportunity to help select and evaluate innovations.[57]

---

[53]Michael G. Fullan, *The New Meaning of Educational Change* (New York: Teachers College Press, 1991); Joseph F. Johnson, Jr., "The Promise of School Reform in Texas" (1997 posting at the University of Texas Star Center), available at **www.starcenter.org**; and Linda Lambert, *Building Leadership Capacity in Schools* (Alexandria, Va.: Association for Supervision and Curriculum Development, 1998).

[54] Daniel U. Levine, "Creating Effective Schools Through Site-Level Staff Development, Planning and Improvement of Organizational Cultures," in David H. Hargreaves and David Hopkins, eds., *Development Planning for School Improvement* (London: Cassell, 1994), pp. 37–48; and Glibel Gomez and Heidi H. Mickelson, "Successful Strategies for Schools Serving At-Risk Children," *City Schools* (Spring 1998), pp. 33–37.

[55]David P. Crandall, Jeffrey W. Eiseman, and Karen E. Louis, "Strategic Planning Issues That Bear on the Success of School Improvement Efforts," *Educational Administration Quarterly* (Summer 1986), pp. 21–53; Jane Foley, "A Recipe for Restructuring," *The School Administrator* (January 1996), p. 30; Daniel U. Levine and Rayna F. Levine, "Romantic and Pragmatic Approaches to Improving Instruction" (Paper presented at the Fourth International Teaching for Intelligence Conference, New York, April 1998), available at **www.pdkintl.org**; and Jonathan Kozol, "Kozol on Kids," *Teacher Magazine* (January 1999).

[56]Kenneth A. Leithwood, "The Move Toward Transformational Leadership," *Educational Leadership* (February 1992), pp. 8–12; Marilyn Korostoff, Lynn Beck, and Sharon Gibb, "Supporting School-Based Reform" (Paper presented at the annual meeting of the American Educational Research Association, San Diego, 1998); and Vince Molinaro and Susan Drake, "Successful Educational Reform," *International Electronic Journal for Leadership in Learning* (October 1998), available at **www.acs.ucalgary.ca.**

[57]Susan Moore Johnson, *Teachers at Work* (New York: Basic Books, 1990); and Richard A. Schmuck and Philip J. Runkel, *The Handbook of Organizational Development in Schools,* 4th ed. (Prospect Heights, Ill.: Waveland, 1998).

Staff development essential

6. *Training of staff.* Staff development is a core activity in the school improvement process. In an elementary school, the entire staff should participate; in secondary schools, departments may be the appropriate unit for some activities. Staff development should be an interactive process in which teachers and administrators work together at every stage.[58]

Related Efforts to Improve School Effectiveness

Besides the innovations we have described so far, there are many related proposals. We do not have space to describe all of them, but several of the more important efforts are discussed briefly in the following pages.

Cooperation with Other Institutions

Many schools and school districts are attempting to improve the quality of education by cooperating with other institutions, particularly those in business and industry. Some of the most promising efforts include the following:[59]

Types of cooperation

■ "Partnership" or "adopt-a-school" programs in which a business, church, university, or some other community institution works closely with an individual

Many school districts are cooperating with business and industry to improve the quality of education in their schools. *(© Bob Daemmrich/ The Image Works)*

[58]Bruce B. Joyce and Marcia Weil, *Models of Teaching*, 2nd ed. (Englewood Cliffs, N.J.: Prentice-Hall, 1991); and Rebecca Jones, "What Works," *American School Board Journal* (April 1998), available at **www.asbj.org.**
[59]Celia B. Richardson, "Gift-In-Kind Clearing House," *Phi Delta Kappan* (June 1995), pp. 792–793; Karen Smith, "Tech Corps," *T.H.E. Journal* (October 1998), available at **www.thejournal.com.** "1,400 Employers Agree: School Is on the Record," *Work America* (March 1998), available at **www.nab.com/publications;** and "New Breed of Business Partners," *American School Board Journal* (January 1999).

school, providing assistance such as tutors or lecturers, funds or equipment for vocational studies, computer education, or help in curriculum development

- Cooperative activities such as health or drug education
- Operation of professional development schools at which teachers and teacher educators work together to improve training and instruction
- Joint conduct of school improvement projects in which the emphasis is on helping faculty use research to improve curriculum and instruction
- Funding of student awards for reading books or other positive behaviors
- Provision of surplus equipment and supplies
- Development of approaches that enable employers to check students' school performance records before making hiring decisions

Boston Compact

An even more far-reaching example of cooperation with public schools is the Boston Compact. In forming the Compact in 1982, business leaders agreed to recruit at least two hundred companies that would hire graduates of the Boston public schools and also provide employment for students. In return, school officials agreed to establish competency requirements for graduation, increase placement rates of graduates into higher education as well as into full-time employment, and reduce dropout and absenteeism rates. The message sent to city students is "If you stay in school, work hard, and master the basics, you will be helped to find a job."

Expansion of the compact

By 1995 approximately four hundred companies were participating in the compact. Activities had expanded to include more than twenty local colleges and universities, and tens of thousands of Boston students had been placed in summer jobs programs or had received help in obtaining full-time jobs after graduation. Data collected by Compact officials indicate that very high proportions of high-school graduates in Boston either enter college or are employed full time, and most college entrants are persisting to graduation.[60]

Corporate projects

The apparent success of the Boston Compact has helped stimulate similar projects elsewhere. Among the other projects started by corporations in the late 1980s and 1990s are these:[61]

- RJR Nabisco allocated $30 million to help implement educational improvements.
- General Electric committed nearly $20 million to assist disadvantaged college-bound youth.
- Many corporations are cooperating with schools in developing the Work Keys assessment system to prepare young people for skilled and well-paid employment.

Support from foundations

Philanthropic foundations also have become much more active (and generous) in providing funds to help improve education at all levels. For example, the MacArthur Foundation is providing $40 million to support reform efforts in the Chicago Public Schools, the Coca-Cola Foundation donated $50 million to support

---

[60]Robert Schwartz and Jeannette Hargroves, "The Boston Compact," *Metropolitan Education* (Winter 1986–87), pp. 14–25; Randy L. Dewar and Barbara Sprong, "No Diploma, No Job," *American School Board Journal* (October 1991), pp. 38–39; and Sandra A. Waddock, "Schools and the System," *Education Week*, August 2, 1995, p. 53.

[61]Mary A. Zehr, "'Work Keys' Job Skills Assessment Finally Catching On," *Education Week*, March 4, 1998.

education-improvement activities, and the Annenberg Foundation is providing hundreds of millions of dollars to improve schools in Chicago, Los Angeles, New York, and a number of other school districts.[62]

Contracts with a private agency

Privatization.   Recent efforts to involve business and other external agencies in public education have extended beyond the provision of financial support and staff assistance to the **privatization** of educational services. In privatization arrangements, the funds and the responsibilities for operating a school or some of its programs are contracted out to private agencies. Several prominent analysts have argued that privatization can produce higher student performance at a lower cost than most public schools.

Dade County's experience

One of the best-known privatization experiments to date took place in the Dade County (Florida) Public Schools, where a corporation called Educational Alternatives, Inc., contracted to operate an elementary school. Educational Alternatives promised to generate high achievement levels regardless of students' socioeconomic background. However, the Board of Education did not renew the five-year contract, largely because of dissatisfaction with the achievement results.[63]

The Edison Project also has been prominent in the movement to sign contracts with corporations that operate public schools for profit. By 1999, Edison had contracted to operate more than fifty schools in various parts of the United States. As in the case of Educational Alternative, there has been considerable controversy regarding student performance at participating schools.[64]

Guaranteed Postsecondary Access for High-School Graduates.   As noted above, a key component in the Boston Compact (and other similar projects elsewhere) is guaranteed support from business to help students attend postsecondary schools. In a growing number of communities, similar support is being provided by wealthy individuals, foundations, community agencies, colleges and universities, and state or local governments.

Rapid spread of programs

Programs that guarantee postsecondary access proliferated rapidly in the 1990s. By 1998, sponsors were helping to support programs similar to I Have a Dream in more than sixty cities. As the U.S. Government General Accounting Office reported, these programs generally combine "a financial aid guarantee, personal, often intense, mentoring, and a wide range of program elements aimed at increasing both motivation and academic skills."[65]

Technology in School Reform

Earlier in this chapter we noted that some approaches to school reform make use of computers, multimedia, and other evolving digital technologies. Educators confront many questions and challenges with respect to the introduction of new

---

[62] Rosalind Rossi, "School Reform Gets Big Boost," *Chicago Sun-Times*, January 22, 1995, p. 3; and Lynn Olson, "The Importance of 'Critical Friends,'" *Education Week*, May 27, 1998.
[63] Myron Lieberman, *Prioritization and Educational Choice* (New York: Saint Martin's Press, 1989); Willis D. Hawley, "The False Premises and False Promises of Movement to Privatize Public Education," *Teachers College Record* (Summer 1995), pp. 735–742; and Richard C. Seder, "Organizing Principals," *Reason* (January 1998), available at **www.reasonmag.com.**
[64] Rene Sanchez, "Edison Project to Double Number of Schools," *Washington Post*, May 27, 1998; and John Chubb, "Edison Scores and Scores Again in Boston," *Phi Delta Kappan* (November 1998), pp. 205–212.
[65] Eleanore Chelimsky, *Private Programs Guaranteeing Student Aid for Higher Education* (Washington, D.C.: General Accounting Office, 1990), p. 2. See also "The 'I Have a Dream' Foundation" (1998 Internet posting at **www.ihad.org**).

and emerging technologies as part of reform efforts in the schools. We will consider several major topics, including the effective introduction of new technologies in schools and classrooms, equity and technology use in education, and cautions regarding developments that have occurred during the past decade.

Policies for technology

Effective Introduction of Computers and Other Technologies.   Analysts have identified many of the considerations that determine whether the introduction of computer-based technologies will produce or help produce substantial improvements in the performance of elementary and secondary students. It is useful to view such considerations as having implications for policy and practice at each level of the educational system: federal, state, district, school, and classroom. Federal officials and legislators have been grappling with broad issues, such as how to make Internet connections affordable for schools, how to obtain and disseminate research dealing with the effective use of computers, and how to help colleges and universities improve teacher education with respect to instructional technologies. State and district decision makers have been considering and often acting on recommendations such as the following:[66]

- State leaders must have a clear plan for supporting district efforts in introducing new technologies.
- Teachers must receive ongoing training and technical support in how to use technologies effectively. Technical support staff should be available at both the district and school levels.
- There should be a good balance between investing in hardware and software, and training.
- Teacher licensing standards should include assessment of knowledge and skills involving incorporation of technology in classsroom lessons.
- Schools should have community partners who provide expertise and support.

At the district and school levels, much is being learned about what to do and what not to do in bringing computer-based technologies into schools and classrooms. In a paper subtitled, "Creating a Community of Technology Users Leads to Some Hard-Won Realizations," Cooley summarized some of these lessons as follows:[67]

Success not assured

1. "Technology will not [by itself] transform a mediocre school into a good one." Success depends on a "number of factors including curriculum instructional leadership, personnel evaluations, staff development, and school environment." (These factors involve general characteristics of unusual effectiveness that were enumerated earlier in this chapter.)

2. "Understand why you are investing in technology." When school boards invest millions of dollars in technology without a clear and workable plan for how this money will be used, much of it will be poorly used or even unused, and teachers will become cynical about the supposed benefits of computers.

---

[66]John Cradler, "Implementing Technology in Education" (1996 posting at the Internet site of the Far West Laboratory), available at **www.fwl.org/techpolicy/recapproach.html;** "Highlights of National Forum Sessions and Events" (Meeting summary of the Education Commission of the States National Forum held in Portland, Oregon, July 1998); and *National Educational Technology Standards for Students* (Eugene, Oreg.: International Society for Technology in Education, 1998), available at **www.iste.org.**
[67]Van E. Cooley, "Technology Lessons," *Electronic School* (June 1998), available at **www.electronic-school.com.** See also Sylvia Charp, "Classrooms of Tomorrow," *T.H.E. Journal* (January 1999), available at **www.thejournal.com.**

3. "Be aware of school culture — it is either a friend or an enemy." If administrators behave like dictators and do not involve teachers in decisions about selecting and using technology, many teachers will be uncooperative and may sabotage proposed changes.

Hire support staff

4. "Hire technology staff now, or pay a high price later." Unless adquate technical support is provided, which itself will entail significant additional costs, "teachers and administrators — and ultimately students, too — will stop using the technology."

5. "Don't start until a staff development program is in place." The federal Office of Technology recommends spending 30 percent of total project funds on staff development, but most districts allocate no more than 15 percent, and many set aside less than 10 percent for staff development related to the introduction of new technologies.

At the classroom level, researchers have found that variables associated with the successful implementation of computer-based technologies include the following:[68]

Some concentration needed

- Computers must be sufficiently concentrated to make a difference. For example, one study found that placing one computer in a classroom did not change student achievement but that providing classrooms with three or more computers did produce better outcomes.

- Training must be sufficiently intensive to make a difference. For example, several studies found that providing teachers with more than ten hours of training results in much more change in instruction than shorter training periods.

- How teachers use computers helps determine student outcomes. For example, one major study using data from hundreds of schools supported the obvious conclusion that eighth graders whose teachers emphasized problem solving and learning of concepts using computers learned significantly more than did those whose teachers emphasized low-level "drill and kill" exercises. (This does not mean that repetitious exercises emphasizing memorization have no place in the instructional program, but rather that they should not be overdone and should not substitute for higher-order assignments.)

Coordination needed

- Plans for computer use must be coordinated with arrangements for scheduling, testing, class size, and other aspects of instruction. If class periods are too short or classes are too large to allow the teacher to deliver a lesson effectively, or if teachers are preoccupied with preparing students for tests or with other urgent tasks, the availability of computers may make little or no difference.

If there is a predominant theme present throughout the preceding review of what has been learned regarding computer-based technologies and successful school reform, it is that substantial, appropriate teacher training is definitely a prerequisite. Topics and considerations that should receive attention in planning and delivering such training include the following:[69]

Training needed

---

[68]Dale Mann and Edward A. Shafer, "Technology and Achievement," *American School Board Journal* (July 1997), available at **www.asbj.com**; Harold Weglinsky, *Does It Compute?* (Princeton, N.J.: Education Testing Service, 1998), available at **www.ets.org**; and Gary Lilly, "Tech Coaches," *Electronic School* (January 1999), available at **www.electronic-school.com**.
[69]Fred Reiss, "Project T.E.A.C.H.—Technology Enrichment and Curriculum Help," *T.H.E. Journal* (October 1998), pp. 70–71, available at **www.thejournal.com**; and James P. Tenbusch, "Teaching the Teachers," *Electronic School* (March 1998), available at **www.electronic-school.com**.

- Knowledge and skills involving the use of computers in the classroom
- Examination of best practices with respect to the use of computers
- Opportunities to personally experience the application of new skills
- Availability of feedback regarding efforts to apply the skills
- Guidance in learning how to incorporate the skills within one's current instructional repertoire

Equity and the Use of Technology.   Another key issue, particularly at the national and state levels, is ensuring equal opportunity for all students to access the benefits of technology improvements. Whether in their schools or homes, low-income students generally have less access to some kinds of computer-based learning opportunities than do middle-income students. Until recently, computers clearly have been unaffordable for many or most low-income families. At schools enrolling high percentages of low-income students, computers usually have been available, but in recent years the movement toward Internet and multimedia usage in U.S. schools has mostly bypassed high-poverty schools in big cities. Thus U.S. Secretary of Education Richard Riley has pointed out that the percentage of classrooms that are located in low-income communities and have Internet access is about half the percentage for classrooms nationwide. According to Riley, "[This is] a divide centered largely on racial, economic, and other demographic lines. But it is a divide that doesn't have to be. . . . We, as a nation, are missing the opportunity of a lifetime . . . [to make sure that all students] whether they are from a small town, a city, a rural area, or suburb — learn at the highest levels with the greatest resources and have the promise of real opportunity. . . . It is time to break the cycle of technological inequity — not perpetuate it."[70]

Poverty schools bypassed

As Secretary Riley recognized, inequities regarding the availability and use of computer-based technologies involve not just socioeconomic background but also race, ethnicity, and geographic location. In addition, as we noted in Chapter 9, girls also lag behind boys in some indicators involving access to and the use of computers. Educators at the National Educational Technology Consortium have been studying disparities among groups of students in opportunities to learn with and from computer-related technologies. They have offered many recommendations, such as the following, for addressing the situation in a school or district:[71]

Addressing inequities

- Gather usage and course enrollment data . . . and examine the data on the basis of race, gender, language status, disability status, and income.
- Collect and disseminate information on promising intervention strategies, and discuss these possibilities with the staff.
- Assist faculty in developing plans for advancing equity.
- Evaluate staff on how well they incorporate activities ensuring the equitable use of computers.

Much of what is being done to enhance equity in technology access involves opportunities available not in schools but in community locations. Neighborhood

---

[70]Richard W. Riley, "Technology and Education: An Investment in Equity and Excellence" (Remarks at the National Press Club, Washington, D.C.: July 29, 1998), available at **www.ed.gov/Speeches/980729.html;** and Michael Dertouzos, "The Rich People's Computer?" *Technology Review* (January–February 1999), available at **www.techreview.com.**
[71]"Closing the Equity Gap in Technology Access and Use" (Undated posting at the Internet site of the National Educational Technology Consortium), available at **www.netc.org/equity.**

Community technology centers

computer centers in low-income urban and rural communities are providing opportunities for residents — both adults and children — to learn about and benefit from advanced technologies. One researcher commented that "community technology centers ensure that we don't leave part of our population behind with nineteenth-century skills as we move into a twenty-first-century economy." This approach may become widespread in the future, and may be tied in with school-based efforts to reduce inequities related to computer-based technologies.[72]

Cautions Regarding Computer-Based Technologies in Education. Not everyone is optimistic about the likelihood that technology will produce productive reforms in the educational system. Skeptics abound, and their ranks include some of the most knowledgeable analysts of recent developments in the schools and of the evolution of computers in general. For example, Clifford Stoll, widely known for his contributions to the development of the Internet, has written a book titled *Silicon Snake Oil* in which he points out that, although computers may be fun to use in the classroom, entertainment is not synonymous with learning. Stoll sees computers as potentially equivalent to the grainy films and the disjointed film strips that some teachers used years ago mainly to keep their students occupied.[73]

Silicon snake oil?

Idle clicking?

Similarly, Jane Healy had become well known as an enthusiast about the potential of computers for opening new worlds to students and then shocked many of her readers with a 1998 book in which she questioned the effects that new technologies are having on children both inside and outside the schools. After two years spent visiting classrooms, she concluded that computers in many classrooms are supervised by "ill-prepared teachers" whose students engage mostly in mindless drills, games unrelated to coherent learning objectives, "silly surfing," and/or "idle clicking." Some other analysts, also on the basis of visits to numerous schools and classrooms, have reached the conclusion that expensive multimedia setups frequently are serving more as a medium for classroom control than as a tool for learning. In reaching such conclusions, Healy and other skeptics typically offer such cautions and criticisms as the following regarding computer-based technologies in the schools:[74]

- Research that supports the conclusion that computers are producing widespread gains in student performance generally is badly flawed and mostly invalid.

Creativity reduced?

- Computers too often detract from students' creativity by constraining them within prescribed boundaries of thought and action.

- Responding to perceived or real public demands and expectations that classrooms should be loaded with advanced technologies, schools are buying expensive equipment that will soon be obsolete.

---

[72]Mitchell Resnick and Natalie Rusk, "Computer Clubhouses in the Inner City," *American Prospect* (July–August 1998), available at **www.epn.org/prospect/educ.html**; and "Low-Income Americans Pursue Career and Personal Goals at Community-Based Technology Centers, According to New EDC Study," *Spotlight News* (August 1998).

[73]Clifford Stoll, *Silicon Snake Oil: Second Thoughts on the Information Superhighway* (New York: Doubleday, 1995). See also Todd Oppenheimer, "The Computer Delusion," *Atlantic* (July 1997), available at **www.theatlantic.com/issues97/computer.htm**.

[74]Stoll, *Silicon Snake Oil;* David Tyack and Larry Cuban, *Tinkering Toward Utopia* (Cambridge, Mass.: Harvard University Press, 1995); Oppenheimer, "The Computer Delusion"; Chris Dede, "Six Challenges for Educational Technology" (1998 Internet posting at **virtual.gmu.edu/ascdpdf.htm**); Jane M. Healy, *Failure to Connect* (New York: Simon and Schuster, 1998); Pamela Mendels, "Once a Champion of Classroom Computers, Psychologist Now Sees Failure," *New York Times,* September 16, 1998; and Paul Saffo, "Neo-Toys," *Civilization* (November 1998), available at **www.civmag.com/articles**.

- The high costs of these soon-to-be-outdated technologies are forcing schools to severely cut back on industrial arts, art and music, and other "frills."
- Particularly for young children, time on the computer too often replaces time needed to develop motor skills and logical thinking.

Reduced attention span of screenagers?

- Much of students' time online involves commercial sources that are mainly trying to develop loyal customers.
- Even more than television, digital technology is reducing the attention span of children and "screenagers" (adolescents growing up in the Internet era).
- Fantasy worlds and other imaginary digitized environments are distorting childrens' sense of reality.
- According to Paul Saffo, digitized technologies are an "even more potent time-sink" than television, "serving up parent-fretting violence and vapid, content-less drivel" that constitutes a vast, "cyberspace wasteland."

Scaling up a problem

- Isolated examples of a few classrooms, schools, and even districts in which computer-based technologies are being used effectively do not tell us anything about what is happening or likely to happen in most situations. Indeed, the educational system has a long and inglorious history of failure in half-hearted attempts to "scale up" from a few promising implementations to widespread use throughout the system.

In reviewing these cautions, we should keep in mind preceding parts of this section as well as earlier parts of this chapter that identified actions associated with the successful implementation of computer-based technologies and other substantial efforts to bring about reform in the schools. Will schools and districts provide large-scale and ongoing training and the meaningful technical support required if teachers are to use technology effectively? Will the introduction of such technologies be carefully aligned and coordinated with curriculum objectives, testing, and school climate improvements? Fortunately, many educators are working to make this happen.[75]

Rural Education

Rural diversity

More than one-third of public-school students attend rural schools, and about one-half of school districts are rural. In trying to improve rural education, educators must confront the extreme diversity of rural locations, which makes it difficult to generalize across communities. One group of observers defined rural school districts as those that have fewer than 150 residents per square mile and are located in counties in which at least 60 percent of the population resides in communities with populations under 5,000. Even within this fairly restricted definition, rural communities exemplify hundreds of "subcultures" that differ in racial and ethnic composition, extent of remoteness, economic structure, and other characteristics.[76]

Partly because of this diversity, the particular problems of rural schools have received relatively little attention during the past fifty years. Recently, however, a small

[75]Philip Yam, "Bracing for (Educational) Impact," *Scientific American* (January 1999).
[76]Michael Newman, "Too Many Districts?" *Teacher* (March 1990), pp. 12–13; Jennifer Loven, "On the Back Roads, Not the Infobahn," *The Executive Educator* (August 1995), pp. 12–13; "Characteristics of Small and Rural School Districts," *Statistical Analysis Report* (May 1997), available at **nces.ed.gov**; and Robert C. Johnston, "Rural Education," *Education Week*, December 16, 1998.

group of scholars has been trying to determine what should be done to provide high-quality education in a rural setting. They have reached several major conclusions:[77]

Conclusions about rural schools

1. The critical elements for rural school improvement are community dependent. For this reason, some innovations that are effective in urban areas tend not to work well in rural areas.

2. Because of the tremendous diversity in rural America, school improvement efforts also should be diverse, and they should address the goals of multicultural education.

3. The small scale of rural schools offers advantages. Teachers can know students and parents personally, and schools can work closely with community agencies.

4. Cyclical economic recessions have made public education an even more important force than before in providing skilled personnel and jobs in rural communities.

5. Educators should make sure that children and youth in rural communities feel appreciated. They should understand that they have a part to play in the future of their communities.

Other authors have concluded that teacher-training programs for rural areas should prepare teachers in a larger number of content areas for a broader age range of students than do conventional programs. As Chapter 6 points out, educators also are reassessing the desirability of school consolidation in light of the possible advantages of very small schools.

Teacher shortages and distance education

Many rural schools face serious problems in attracting qualified teachers. Because many states have increased certification requirements and reduced the flexibility that allowed teachers to be employed without proper certification, some rural districts have been unable either to find or to afford sufficient teaching personnel, particularly in science, math, and foreign languages. This problem can be overcome, in part, by the use of television, interactive computers, and other forms of **distance education** that deliver instruction in a cost-effective manner. In addition to expanding access to high-quality teachers, distance education can facilitate contact between schools, prepare students for high-skilled employment, deliver staff development programs, and provide specialized courses.[78]

Cooperation among districts

Cooperation among school districts also appears to be expanding. Rural districts frequently share specialists in staff development, evaluation, and other areas, and many work together to provide services like vocational education and special education. Cooperation with business also may be helpful in developing more financial and community support.[79]

---

[77]Paul W. Nachtigal, ed., *Rural Education* (Boulder, Colo.: Westview, 1982); Craig Howley, *Charting New Maps: Multicultural Education in Rural Schools* (Washington, D.C.: U.S. Department of Education, 1993, ERIC Digest 348196); Craig R. Howley, "Studying the Rural in Education," *Education Policy Analysis Archives* (April 30, 1997), available at **elem.ed.asu.edu;** and Toni Haas and Paul Nachtigal, *Place Value* (Charleston, W.Va.: Appalachian Educational Laboratory, 1998).

[78]Bruce O. Barker, *The Distance Education Handbook* (Washington, D.C.: ERIC, 1992); Kenna R. Seal and Hobart L. Harmon, "Realities of Rural School Reform," *Phi Delta Kappan* (October 1995), pp. 119–125; "How Rural Schools Use Technology," *The Executive Educator* (August 1995), p. 13; and Troy K. Corley, "Tapping into Technology in Rural Communities," *Educational Leadership* (May 1998), pp. 71–73.

[79]Andy Sommer, *Rural School District Cooperatives* (Portland, Oreg.: Northwest Regional Educational Laboratory, 1990); Judi Repman, "Will Distance Learning Go the Distance?" *T.H.E. Journal* (February 1996), pp. 11–12; and Craig Howley and Bruce Barker, "The National Information Infrastructure," *ERIC Clearinghouse on Rural Education and Small Schools Digest* (No. EDRC9-3, 1997).

Adapting curriculum and instruction

For low-income students in Appalachia and other areas of rural poverty, educators are trying to find ways to adapt curriculum and instruction to their students' social and cultural backgrounds. Examples of such adaptation can be found in the Foxfire approach, which uses oral history and local cultural materials to help improve students' understanding and motivation inside and outside the school.[80]

Effectiveness of Nonpublic Schools

Vouchers and tax credits

As we mentioned in Chapter 7, proposals have been made to provide families with vouchers and tuition tax credits to support attendance at nonpublic schools, and some movement is occurring in these directions. To some extent, the desirability of such proposals hinges on the argument that nonpublic schools tend to be more effective than public schools.

Coleman's studies

Debate about the effectiveness of nonpublic schools has been spurred by studies in which James Coleman and his colleagues compared nonpublic and public schools. Among the major conclusions of these studies were the following: (1) when family background variables are accounted for, students in nonpublic schools have higher achievement than students in public schools; (2) nonpublic schools provide a safer and more orderly environment; (3) except for Catholic schools, nonpublic schools are smaller, have smaller classes, and encourage more student participation than do public schools; (4) nonpublic schools require more homework and have better attendance; and (5) superiority in school climate and discipline accounts for the higher achievement of students in nonpublic schools.[81]

Conclusions by Chubb and Moe

John Chubb and Terry Moe of the Brookings Institution also have studied achievement differentials between public and nonpublic schools. They, too, concluded that nonpublic schools produce higher achievement. A major reason for this difference, they said, is that nonpublic schools tend to function more autonomously and with less bureaucracy. For example, principals of public schools are much more constrained than their counterparts in nonpublic schools with respect to hiring and firing teachers. In addition, public schools tend to be more complex and more susceptible to pressures from a variety of external constituencies (such as central offices, state government officials, or groups representing taxpayers). As a result, teachers and students in public schools are more likely to receive mixed messages about the priority goals in their schools, and they are less inclined to work together to achieve these goals.[82]

Debate about research findings

However, many educators disagree with the conclusion that nonpublic schools produce higher achievement than public schools. Critics give the following reasons for their disagreement: (1) obtaining better measures or otherwise taking better

---

[80]Jane H. Arends, *Building on Excellence: Regional Priorities for the Improvement of Rural, Small Schools* (Washington, D.C.: Council for Educational Development and Research, 1987); Eliot Wigginton, "Foxfire Grows Up," *Reform Report* (January 1993), pp. 1, 4–7; and Betty A. Starnes, "It's Deja Vu All Over Again" (Paper posted at the Foxfire, Inc. Internet site, no date), available at **www.foxfire.org.**

[81]James Coleman, Thomas Hoffer, and Sally Kilgore, *Public and Private Schools* (Washington, D.C.: National Center for Education Statistics, 1981); James S. Coleman, *Equality and Achievement in Education* (Boulder, Colo.: Westwood, 1990); and Barbara Schneider, Kathryn S. Schiller, and James S. Coleman, "Public School Choice," *Educational Evaluation and Policy Analysis* (Spring 1996), pp. 19–29.

[82]John E. Chubb and Terry M. Moe, *Politics, Markets, and America's Schools* (Washington, D.C.: The Brookings Institution, 1990). See also Edith Pasell and Richard Rothstein, eds., *School Choice* (Washington, D.C.: Economic Policy Institute, 1994); "Interview with David W. Kirkpatrick" (1998 posting in the *School Choice Newsletter*), available at **www.schoolreport.com;** and Paul E. Peterson, "Vouchers and Test Scores," *Policy Review* (January–February 1999), available at **www.policyreview.com.**

account of family background variables virtually eliminates the achievement superiority of nonpublic students; (2) taking account of achievement level upon entry to high school also eliminates or greatly reduces the achievement difference between public and nonpublic students; (3) the statistical methods the researchers employed were inappropriate and led to misleading and unjustified conclusions; and (4) whatever differences may exist between Catholic or other nonpublic schools on the one hand and public schools on the other are trivial and have few long-term effects.[83]

Coleman and his colleagues as well as Chubb and Moe have responded with more data and further arguments supporting their original conclusions. In particular, they have argued that nonpublic schools enhance achievement by placing a relatively high percentage of students in college-bound programs. But since it is difficult to isolate differences in student motivation even after one has taken account of family background and social class, researchers probably will continue to argue over the relative effectiveness of public and nonpublic schools.[84]

Magnet and Alternative Schools

Many efforts to reform the public schools have involved the establishment of magnet and alternative schools.

Today's magnet schools

Magnet schools, as described in Chapter 11, are designed to attract voluntary enrollment by offering special programs or curricula that appeal to students from more than one neighborhood. They are often established as part of a reform effort aimed at increasing desegregation and with providing students with opportunities to participate in instructional programs not available in their local schools. **Alternative schools** provide learning opportunities that are not available in the average public school. From this point of view, magnet schools are a type of alternative school. So, too, are many parochial and other nonpublic schools; institutions such as street academies, storefront schools, and high-school "outposts" designed to make education more relevant for inner-city students; and "schools without walls," which draw heavily on community resources for learning. Studies of alternative schools have indicated that they usually enroll students who have not succeeded in traditional schools or who want a different kind of education. Compared to traditional schools, alternative schools allow for greater individualization, more independent study, and more openness to the outside community. They tend to offer small size, high staff morale, high attendance, satisfied students, freedom from external control, and strong concern for noncognitive goals of education.[85]

Types of alternative schools

Advantages of alternative schools

---

[83]Ellis B. Page and Timothy Z. Keith, "Effects of U.S. Private Schools," *Educational Researcher* (August–September 1981), pp. 7–22; Timothy Z. Keith and Ellis B. Page, "Do Catholic High Schools Improve Minority Student Achievement?" *American Educational Research Journal* (Fall 1985), pp. 337–349; and David Baker and Cornelius Riordan, "The 'Eliting' of the Common American Catholic School and the National Education Crisis," *Phi Delta Kappan* (September 1998), pp. 16–23.

[84]James S. Coleman and Thomas Hoffer, "Response to Taeuber-James-Cain-Goldberger and Morgan," *Sociology of Education* (October 1983), pp. 218–234; and Lee Shumow, Deborah L. Vandell, and Kyungseok Kang, "School Choice, Family Characteristics and Home-School Relations" *Journal of Educational Psychology* (no. 18, 1996), pp. 451–460.

[85]Daniel U. Levine, "Educating Alienated Inner City Youth: Lessons from the Street Academies," *Journal of Negro Education* (Spring 1975), pp. 139–148; Timothy W. Young, *Public Alternative Education* (New York: Teachers College Press, 1990); Mary Anne Raywid, "Alternative Schools: The State of the Art," *Educational Leadership* (September 1994), pp. 28–31; Louann A. Bierlin, "Catching on but the Jury's Still Out," *Educational Leadership* (December 1995–January 1996), pp. 90–91; Suzie Boss, "Learning from the Margins," *Northwest Education* (Summer 1998), available at **www.nwrel.org**; and Kimberly Fornek, "Crawford a Nurturing but Strict Place," *Catalyst* (February 1999), available at **www.catalyst-chicago.org**.

Advocates of alternative schools point out that only one model of education typically is available to parents in any given public-school neighborhood. Some advocates argue for creating alternative schools within the system; others contend that the only true alternatives are outside the system. Either way, both types of advocates generally stress the value of providing students with opportunities to choose the type of school they wish to attend. This consideration brings us to the hotly debated topic of school choice.

School Choice

In recent years, **school choice** plans have been advocated as a way to introduce greater flexibility and accountability into education. The basic idea is to enhance students' opportunities to choose where they will enroll and what they will study. Recent developments include the following:

- Legislators in Colorado, Minnesota, Washington, and other states have either introduced or approved laws expanding students' attendance options. Colorado's legislation requires that all districts allow students to transfer freely within their boundaries. Minnesota's comprehensive choice plan not only supports both intradistrict and interdistrict transfers but also expands alternative schools and programs. Washington's legislation provides students who experience a "special hardship or detrimental condition" with an absolute right to enroll in another school district that has available space; it also requires districts to accept students who transfer to locations close to their parents' place of work or child-care site.[86]

- After stating that business involvement in education had produced little basic reform in the schools, the chairman of the Golden Rule Insurance Company announced that his company would provide $1.2 million to help low-income children transfer to nonpublic schools. Similarly, Robert and Peggy Wegman (of Wegmans Food Markets) provided $25 million to enable low-income children to attend Catholic schools in Rochester, N.Y., and philanthropists in numerous other locations offered to provide vouchers to enable students to attend nonpublic schools. By 1998, there were more than forty such privately funded voucher plans nationwide.[87]

- After a group of business executives provided funding for scholarships that enabled 2,200 New York City students (out of more than 40,000 applicants) to attend nonpublic schools in 1998 and 1999, a larger group committed themselves to raise $200 million for a national program in which 50,000 inner-city students will receive scholarships to nonpublic schools.[88]

---

[86]Ross Corson, "Choice Ironies: Open Enrollment in Minnesota," *The American Prospect* (Fall 1990), pp. 94–99; Cheryl Lange and James E. Ysseldyke, "How School Choice Affects Students with Special Needs," *Educational Leadership* (November 1994), pp. 84–85; and Steven Glazerman, "School Quality and Social Stratification" (Paper presented at the annual meeting of the American Educational Research Association, San Diego, April 1998).
[87]Hilary Stout, "Business Funds Program in Indianapolis Letting Poor Children Flee Public Schools," *The Wall Street Journal,* February 27, 1992, pp. B1, B5; Laura Miller, "Couple Gives $25 Million for Catholic School Vouchers," *Education Week,* September 13, 1995, p. 5; Christine Foster, "The Power of Choice," *Forbes,* June 15, 1998, p. 16; and Adam Meyerson, "A Model of Cultural Leadership," *Policy Review* (January–February, 1999), available at **www.policyreview.com.**
[88]Diane Ravitch and Joseph Viteritti, "A New Vision for City Schools," *The Public Interest* (Winter 1996), pp. 3–16; Mark Walsh, "Court Allows Vouchers in Milwaukee," *Education Week,* June 17, 1998; and Benjamin Dowling-Sendor, "A Victory for Vouchers," *American School Board Journal* (January 1999).

■ The Wisconsin legislature approved a plan providing funds to help transfer a limited number of low-income students from the Milwaukee Public Schools to nonsectarian private schools. More than 1,500 students participated in 1995. The legislature subsequntly expanded the plan to provide for participation of up to 15,000 students and to allow for enrollment in religious schools. Similarly, the Ohio legislature initiated a plan that enables 2,000 elementary students to attend nonpublic schools in Cleveland.[89]

As actions such as these expand school choice, vast numbers of recommendations for and against additional action are being put forward. Those who support complete choice recommend enrollment within and across school district boundaries, vouchers to attend nonpublic schools, magnetization of entire school districts and regions, and creation of alternative-school networks. Supporters of choice emphasize the following arguments:[90]

Arguments favoring choice

■ Providing choice for disadvantaged students will enable them to escape from poorly functioning schools.

■ Because public schools generally are not very successful in working with low achievers, there is little to lose in facilitating their transfer to other schools.

■ Achievement, aspirations, and other outcomes will improve for many students because they will be more motivated to succeed at schools they select voluntarily.

■ Both existing public schools and alternative learning institutions (whether public or nonpublic) will provide improved education because their staffs will be competing to attract students.

■ Increased opportunities will be available to match school programs and services with students' needs.

■ Parents will be empowered and encouraged to play a larger role in their children's education.

Critics of school choice plans question these arguments, particularly in cases that involve public financing of nonpublic schools. The critics maintain the following:[91]

Arguments against choice

■ Choice plans will reinforce stratification and segregation because highly motivated or high-achieving white and minority students will be disproportionately likely to transfer out of schools that have a substantial percentage of students with low achievement or low social status.

[89]John E. Coons and Stephen D. Sugarman, "The Private School Option in Systems of Educational Choice," *Educational Leadership* (January 1991), pp. 54–56; Herbert Gintis, "The Political Economy of School Choice," *Teachers College Record* (Spring 1995), pp. 491–510; Peter W. Cookson, Jr., and Sonali M. Shroff, "Recent Experience With Urban School Choice Plans," *ERIC Clearinghouse on Urban Education Digest* (No. 127, 1997), available at **eric-web.tc.columbia.edu**; "School Choice," *Workforce Economics* (June 1998), pp. 9–15; and David Hill, "Clippings," *Teacher Magazine* (January 1999).
[90]Jacques Steinberg, "Voucher Program for Inner-City Children," *New York Times,* June 10, 1998; and Sol Stern, "The Schools That Vouchers Built," *City Journal* (January 1999), available at **www.city-journal.org.**
[91]Herbert J. Grover, "Private School Choice Is Wrong," *Educational Leadership* (January 1991), p. 51; Associated Press, "Witches Plan School If New System Passes," *The Billings Gazette*, July 17, 1993, p. 5A; Jeffrey R. Henig, *Rethinking School Choice* (Princeton, N.J.: Princeton University Press, 1994); Clint Bolick, "Blocking the Exits," *Policy Review* (May–June 1998), available at **www.heritage.org**; and Barbara Miner, "Vouchers in Legal Limbo," *Rethinking Schools* (Winter 1998–1999), p. 3.

- Much of the student movement will consist of middle-class students transferring to nonpublic schools. That will reduce the middle class's willingness to support the public schools.

- Public financial support for nonpublic schools is unconstitutional.

- Competition among schools to attract transfer students will not by itself result in improved achievement; other emerging reforms described in this chapter are more important.

- The opening and closing of numerous schools based on their competitive attractiveness will disrupt the operation of the entire educational system.

- There is little or no reason to believe that most schools that presently enroll relatively few disadvantaged students will be more successful with such students than are their present schools.

- Even if one assumes that schools capable of substantially improving the performance of low achievers are widely available in a choice plan, many students and parents lack the knowledge necessary to select them, and these outstanding schools may not accept many low achievers.

- Although accountability may increase in the sense that unattractive schools will lose students and may even be closed, overall accountability will be reduced because nonpublic schools receiving public funds will not be subject to government standards.

- Public financing of nonpublic institutions will result in the establishment of "cult" schools based on divisive racist or religious ideologies.

- Nonpublic schools' participation will result in greater regulation by state and local governments.

Fear of increased separatism

These worries about school choice are shared even by some people who have supported proposals to expand student options. For example, John Leo thinks that school choice is "reform's best choice" but also is education's "new 600-pound gorilla." He believes it may harm education by funding schools that encourage social, racial, and economic separatism. In this context, many analysts have been trying to identify policies that could make choice plans as constructive as possible. They have suggested policies like the following:[92]

Policies for constructive school choice

- Ensure that students and parents receive adequate counseling and information

- Provide free transportation, scholarships, and other support to make sure that choices are fully available and do not depend on social status

- Include guidelines to avoid segregation and resegregation

- Ensure that enrollment and admissions procedures are equitable and do not exclude large proportions of students from the most desirable schools

- Include provisions to release government-operated schools from regulations not imposed on nonpublic schools

- Do not ignore other reform necessities and possibilities; instead, treat choice as part of a comprehensive reform agenda

---

[92]John Leo, "School Reform's Best Choice," *U.S. News and World Report,* January 14, 1991, p. 17; Tim W. Ferguson, "Getting an Education," *Reason* (November 1993), pp. 27–32; Stacy Smith, "The Democratizing Potential of Charter Schools," *Educational Leadership* (October 1998), pp. 55–58; Barbara Miner, "$22 Million Siphoned from MPS to Pay for Private Schools," *Rethinking Schools* (Winter 1998–1999), p. 3; and Frank B. Murray, "What's So Good About Choice?" *Education Week,* January 27, 1999.

Extended School Schedules and Year-Round Schools

Extending time controversial

Several national reports, including *A Nation at Risk* and *Prisoners of Time,* have recommended extending the school year and/or the school day to provide more time for teaching and learning.[93] Some of these reports also have recommended going to **year-round schools** that run on rotated schedules so that three-quarters of students attend for nine weeks while the remaining quarter are on vacation for three weeks. Year-round schools have usually been established where schools are very overcrowded. More than two million students now attend year-round schools. Numerous school districts also have lengthened the school day or the school year. However, movement in these directions usually is controversial because these changes require a significant increase in staff costs and also may disrupt parents' child-care arrangements. Action to extend time for learning also will require substantial changes in curriculum and instruction if it is to improve student achievement.[94]

Gifted and Talented Students

Trends in gifted education

Research on the education of gifted and talented students has increased. There are several widespread program trends: "radical acceleration" of learning opportunities for gifted and talented students; provision of special "mentoring" assistance; increased emphasis on independent study and investigative learning; use of individualized education programs (IEPs), as with students with disabilities; provision of opportunities to engage in advanced-level projects; delivery of instruction in accordance with students' learning styles; establishment of special schools, Saturday programs, and summer schools; increased use of community resources; and "compacting" of curriculum to streamline content that students already know and replace it with more challenging material.[95]

Differing approaches

One of the major issues involving gifted and talented students is the selection of effective approaches to curriculum and instruction. In general, educators have tended to emphasize either acceleration through the regular curriculum or enrichment that provides for greater depth of learning, but some have argued for a "confluent" approach that combines both. Developing this idea, some analysts have advocated combining elements like these: (1) a "content" model, which emphasizes accelerated study; (2) a "process-product" model, which emphasizes enrichment through independent study and investigation; and (3) an "epistemological" model, which emphasizes understanding and appreciation of systems of knowledge.[96]

---

[93]Larry Hayes, "Support for a Longer School Year," *Phi Delta Kappan* (January 1992), p. 413; National Education Commission on Time and Learning, *Prisoners of Time* (Washington, D.C.: U.S. Department of Education, 1994); and "History of Year-Round Education" (Internet posting of the National Association for Year-Round Education, 1998), available at **www.nayre.org.**
[94]"Year-Round Schooling Rejected," *Teacher Magazine* (February 1996), pp. 10–11; and "Quotes" (Internet posting of the National Association for Year-Round Education, 1998), available at **www.nayre.org.**
[95]E. Paul Torrance, "Teaching Creative and Gifted Learners," in Merlin C. Wittrock, ed., *Handbook of Research on Teaching,* 3rd ed. (New York: Macmillan, 1986); John F. Feldhusen, "How to Identify and Develop Special Talents," *Educational Leadership* (February 1996), pp. 66–69; Karen L. Westberg and Francis X. Archambault, Jr., "A Multi-Site Case Study of Successful Classroom Practices for High Ability Students," *Gifted Child Quarterly* (Winter 1997, pp. 42–51; and Sally M. Reis et al., "Equal Does Not Mean Identical," *Educational Leadership* (November 1998), pp. 74–77.
[96]Joyce Van Tassel-Baska, "Effective Curriculum and Instructional Models for Talented Students," *Gifted Child Quarterly* (Fall 1980), pp. 162–168; Bruce N. Berube, "Talent Development for Everyone," *National Research Center on the Gifted and Talented Newsletter* (Spring 1997); and Ann Robinson and Pamela R. Clinkenbeard, "Giftedness," *Annual Review of Psychology* (No. 49, 1998), pp. 117–139.

More Time in School

One suggestion for improving student achievement has been to increase the amount of time students spend in school by lengthening the school day or school year or both. This idea is based in part on observations of countries such as Japan, where students spend considerably more time in school than do American students. It also reflects research indicating that time-on-task is an important determinant of students' performance.

Arguments PRO

1 Extending the school year or school day will give teachers more contact time and an opportunity to teach students in depth. This is particularly vital for at-risk students, who need special services and remedial work.

2 Experience in countries such as Japan indicates that increased time spent in school can assist in raising achievement scores. Many national task-force reports have also recommended that time in school be extended.

3 The extension of school time can help to solve the problems of latchkey children, who must look after themselves while their parents work. In this way, schools can benefit the family as well as improve education.

4 Lengthening students' time in school will indicate to taxpayers that schools are serious about raising educational standards. Taxpayers will therefore be more willing to support the schools.

5 The present system of school attendance originated in an agrarian period when children were needed to assist in farm tasks. In an industrial society, the best use of students' time is to give them additional schooling that prepares them for the world of the twenty-first century.

Arguments CON

1 Extending time in school will not compensate for the poor teaching that takes place in too many schools. The problem is not quantity but quality of schooling, and longer hours could well mean *reduced* quality.

2 So many social and cultural differences exist between Japan and the United States that simple comparisons are not valid. There is little hard evidence that increasing students' time in school will raise achievement levels in the United States.

3 The growing institutional interference with basic family life will be increased by extending the time children spend in school. Such interference, however well intentioned, contributes to the fragmentation of the modern family.

4 Extending school time will require major new expenditures to increase salaries and refurbish buildings. Taxpayers will not willingly pay for these expenses.

5 We know too little about the effects of lengthening the school day or year. Do children in our culture *need* ample breaks from school? Do their originality and creativity suffer when they are kept too long in classes? Until we have answers, we should not make students spend more time in school.

Including more minority students

Much concern has been expressed about the low participation of minority students and economically disadvantaged students in gifted education. Evidence indicates that selection criteria frequently fail to identify disadvantaged students who might benefit from participation. For this reason, many efforts are under way to broaden definitions of giftedness to include indicators such as very strong problem-solving skills, high creativity, high verbal or nonverbal fluency, and unusual artistic accomplishments and abilities.[97]

Systemic Restructuring and Reform

Throughout this chapter and the book as a whole, we have discussed many innovative proposals to reform the educational system. Efforts are being made to improve the preparation and professionalism of teachers, modify the organization and financing of school districts, empower faculties and parents as part of school-based management, and devise more successful policies on compensatory education, special education, and multicultural education. Reformers are also urging educators and state officials to alter testing and assessment of students to place greater emphasis on higher-order skills, establish magnet and alternative schools to enhance opportunities for at-risk students, and upgrade the capabilities of teachers and entire faculties in accordance with research on effective instruction and effective schools.

Improving the entire system

In recent years many of these reform efforts have been discussed in terms of **restructuring** all or part of the educational system. Although this term has been interpreted in as many different ways as the term *reform,* it increasingly is used to indicate the need for systemic improvement — that is, reform that simultaneously addresses all or most major components in the overall system. For example, officials of the Education Commission of the States have stated that all parts of the educational system from "schoolhouse to statehouse" must be restructured to bring about systematic improvement in teaching and learning. Systemic restructuring deals with instructional methods; professional development; assessment of student, teacher, and/or school performance; curriculum and materials; school finance; governance; course requirements; and other aspects of education.[98]

Making reforms coherent

When many changes are introduced simultaneously, restructuring and reform activities must be coherent; they must be compatible with and reinforce each other, rather than becoming isolated fragments that divert time and energy from priority goals. Recognizing this imperative, analysts and decision makers have been trying to identify packages of changes that are sufficiently comprehensive and coherent to be successful.

Origins of Kentucky reform

State-Level Systemic Reform. A good example of a coherent systemic plan at the district level can be found in the Rochester Public Schools, which we reviewed in Chapter 1. Probably the best example of such a plan at the state level is in Kentucky, where in 1989 the state supreme court declared the state's "system of common schools" unconstitutional on the grounds that it was ineffective and inequitable.

[97]James J. Gallagher, "Education of Gifted Students: A Civil Rights Issue?" *Phi Delta Kappan* (January 1995), pp. 408–410; Stephanie McIntosh, "Serving the Underserved: Giftedness Among Ethnic Minority and Disadvantaged Students," *The School Administrator* (April 1995), pp. 25–29; and Wendy Schwartz, "Strategies for Identifying the Talents of Diverse Students," *ERIC Clearinghouse on Urban Education* (May 1997), available at **www.ed.gov**.
[98]"Reforming Science, Mathematics, and Technology Education," *CPRE Policy Briefs* (May 1995), pp. 1–10; Dianne Massell, Michael Kirst, and Margaret Hoppe, "Persistence and Change," *CPRE Policy Briefs* (March 1997), available at **www.negp.org**; and Ronald A. Wolk, "Empower Schools," *Teacher Magazine* (January 1999).

The court then instructed the legislative and executive branches to improve the "entire sweep of the system — all its parts and parcels." As a result, the following changes, among others, have been phased in as part of the Kentucky Education Reform Act (KERA):[99]

Provisions of Kentucky plan

- Curriculum, instruction, and student assessment are performance-based, stressing mastery-oriented learning and criterion-referenced testing.

- Schools have established governance councils with authority to make decisions on curriculum and instruction and on how budgets are allocated.

- Parents can transfer their children out of schools they consider unsatisfactory.

- Faculty at unsuccessful schools receive help from state-appointed teachers and administrators.

- Youth and family service centers have been established in communities where 20 percent or more of students are from low-income families.

- All districts offer at least half-day preschool programs for all disadvantaged four-year-olds.

- The state's new school finance formula provides additional funds for low-wealth districts.

- Taxes have been increased by billions of dollars to pay for the changes.

Although some KERA reforms have been in place for several years, and it is not yet clear whether they will produce gains in student and school performance, political support for implementing them seems to have remained fairly strong.[100]

Educators and legislators in Texas also have been striving to introduce many of the components of systemic reform on a statewide basis. Testing is one key to the Texas reform effort. The Texas Assessment of Essential Skills (TAAS) is used to identify and provide support for modifying instruction at low-performing schools and districts. Between 1994 and 1998, large gains were reported for the state as a whole, but gains were greatest for minority students and students from low-income families.[101] Among students in El Paso, for example, intensive staff development, tutoring for low achievers, and other reform efforts helped increase the percentage of *Reduced achievement gap* African American and Hispanic students who attained passing scores, from 34 percent in 1993 to 86 percent in 1998. Although some observers complained that too much time is being spent preparing students for the TAAS and that too many low achievers are being excluded from testing by being designated as learning disabled or limited in English, most analysts have applauded teachers' efforts to help low achievers improve their performance.[102]

School-Level Systemic Reform.   At the same time that systemic reform efforts are being emphasized at the state level, educators have been initiating comparable *Whole-school reform* efforts at individual schools. These efforts are variously referred to as "whole-school

---

[99]Chris Pipho, "Re-Forming Education in Kentucky," *Phi Delta Kappan* (May 1990), pp. 662–663; Thomas R. Guskey and Kent Peterson, "The Road to Classroom Change," *Educational Leadership* (December 1995–January 1996), pp. 10–15; Marc S. Tucker and Charles S. Clark, "The New Accountability," *American School Board Journal* (January 1999); and Kerry A. White, "What to Do When All Else Fails," *Education Week Quality Counts 99,* January 7, 1999.
[100]Sam Staley, "Kentucky Reforms No Panacea for School Reform," *Business First,* December 8, 1997; and Debra Viadero, "In the Field," *Education Week,* January 14, 1998.
[101]"TAAS Scores Show Rise for Fourth Year in Row," *San Antonio Expressnews,* May 21, 1998.
[102]"El Paso Closing the Gap," *Thinking K–16* (Summer 1998), p. 14; and Tyce Palmaffy, "The Gold Star State," *Policy Review,* March–April 1998), available at **www.heritage.org.**

EVERY CHILD READING:
AN ACTION PLAN OF THE LEARNING FIRST ALLIANCE

Learning First Alliance
1001 Connecticut Avenue, N.W.
Suite 335
Washington, DC 20036

June 1998

Every Child Reading: An Action Plan

The Learning First Alliance is an organization of twelve collaborating national educational associations. At its January 1998 Summit on Reading and Mathematics, the alliance developed "action papers" on reading and mathematics. The following excerpts are from its plan for improving students' reading performance.

If we started today, we could ensure that virtually every healthy child born in the 21st century would be reading well by age nine, and that every child now in elementary school would graduate from high school a reader. . . . [In view of this situation, the Alliance calls on educators and policy makers to carry out the following strategies, among others:]

1. Base educational decisions on evidence, not ideology. It is time to call off the endless reading wars [among advocates of differing approaches to teaching reading]. . . . The famous pendulum of educational innovation swings more wildly in reading than in any other subject. . . . Educational practice must come to be based on evidence—not ideology. . . .

2. Promote adoption of texts based on the evidence of what works. Historically, reading textbooks have been adopted primarily based on criteria that have little to do with evidence: attractiveness, cost, supplements, and so on. This must change. . . .

3. Provide adequate professional development. . . . Teachers and paraprofessionals must receive quality staff development on instructional strategies. . . .

4. Promote whole-school adoption of effective methods. Some of the most effective approaches to early literacy instruction are comprehensive methods that . . . are adopted by the entire school, providing a common focus and extensive assistance in implementing a well-integrated design for change.

5. Involve parents in support of their children's reading. Research shows that parent involvement, especially in activities that directly support their children's school success, is correlated with reading achievement. . . .

reform," "comprehensive building reform," and "school-level restructuring." Such initiatives generally reflect research-based recognition (described earlier in this chapter) that faculty at the building level ultimately determine whether change efforts are successful. They also allow for the intensive, ongoing staff development and technical assistance required to help teachers master new or different instructional approaches. Two of the most prominent of these initiatives involve the New American Schools project in Memphis and elsewhere, and the Comprehensive School Reform Development Program.

6. Improve preservice education and instruction . . . on the research base about learning to read . . . [and] applications of that research in the classroom. . . .

7. Provide additional staff for tutoring and class-size reduction. . . .

8. Improve early identification and intervention. Diagnostic assessments should be administered regularly to kindergartners and first-graders. . . . Such tools can tell us which children are having reading difficulties and enable teachers to provide immediate and high-quality interventions if necessary.

9. Introduce accountability measures for the early grades. . . . Usually, the earliest assessments are of third- and fourth-graders [but appropriate tests also should be developed and used in kindergarten and grades one and two].

10. Intensify reading research. If early reading were as high a priority in our society as, say, space exploration was in the 1960s, there is little question that early reading failure could be virtually eliminated. . . .

[Among the most important additional actions are the following involving Early Childhood and Community Outreach:]

■ Promote family literacy programs to help parents develop in their young children a love of reading. . . .

■ Provide full-day kindergarten, with a curriculum designed to have all children ready to read by first grade.

■ Assist at-risk families in providing their children with the health care and rich cognitive experiences they will need to enter school ready to learn.

■ Provide high-quality prekindergarten programs to all four-year-olds and to younger children.

■ Improve the quality and availability of early child care, afterschool programs, summer programs, and other out-of-school opportunities to promote literacy and healthy development.

Questions

1. In what ways is this action plan connected with material in this chapter and earlier chapters, particularly Chapters 1 and 11?

2. Do you think the plan as presented in this excerpt represents "systemic" reform? What might be added to make it more systemic?

3. Do you agree that all future teachers, whatever their subject area or grade level, should be required to learn about the "research base" concerning "learning to read"? Why or why not?

4. How would you rank the ten strategies presented by the alliance in order of importance? Which would you postpone if resources were not sufficient to deal with all of them?

5. Do you think this paper is likely to have an influence on what you do when you become a teacher?

Source: Every Child Reading: An Action Plan (Washington, D.C.: Learning First Alliance, 1998), available at **www.learningfirst.org.** Reprinted with permission. Members of the alliance include the American Association of Colleges of Teacher Education; American Association of School Administrators; American Federation of Teachers; Association for Supervision and Curriculum Development; Council of Chief State School Officers; Education Commission of the States; National Association of State Boards of Education; National Association of Elementary School Principals; National Association of Secondary School Principals; National School Boards Association; National Parent Teachers Associations; and National Education Association.

New American schools

The New American Schools (NAS) is a nonprofit organization that was established in 1991 to support educational reform through widespread implementation of specific approaches (called "designs" by the NAS) that address all aspects of participating schools. With funds from the federal government and several foundations, the NAS sponsored nine "whole school" designs, which it helps schools implement during an initial three-or-more-year period. Research conducted during the first phase indicated that approximately 50 percent of participating schools were making substantial progress, and that schools scoring high in implementation had benefited from having a stable team of external design consultants who communicated effectively with faculty and provided substantial staff development and planning time for the entire faculty.[103]

Core features of successful reform

Having learned something about considerations that are central for successful implementation, NAS began taking designs that have been successful in a few schools and introducing them at many schools. During this second phase, analysts identified the following core set of features that must be present for schools to succeed in introducing a given design: an effective process for matching schools and designs; an ability to obtain sufficient focused resources; adequate school-based authority; an accountability system based on assessment of student and school performance; and coordination of professional development activities and external assistance. The NAS now is trying to incorporate these features as it implements its designs in a large number of schools.[104]

Reform in Memphis

The NAS designs are an important part of the Memphis Public Schools Restructuring Initiative established in 1995. As part of this effort, thirty-four schools introduced one or another of eight of the nine NAS designs. Data collected after the first year indicated that many teachers felt revitalized and were trying new or different instructional strategies, but there also was a need for more focused training, more time for collaboration, and better alignment of curriculum, instruction, and testing. Analysts also concluded that "restructuring a school requires tremendous energy, time, and commitment from the teachers, administrators, and school communities." By 1998, researchers reported that twenty-five schools were beginning to register measurable gains in student achievement. Meanwhile, the school board and central administration moved to require that all 160 schools in Memphis adopt a whole-school improvement approach by the end of 1999.[105]

Federal support for whole-school reform

The Comprehensive School Reform Development Program (CSRDP), initiated by the federal government in 1998, provides up to $50,000 per year to help participating schools introduce "whole-school-reform" models that affect all aspects of the school's operation and that have had documented success in improving student performance at other locations. For the first year, Congress provided $120 million for Title 1 schools and $25 million for non-Title schools. Applicants were encouraged to select among twenty-seven models for which data were available to support their potential effectiveness.[106]

Conclusion: The Challenge for Education

To help meet national challenges to compete internationally and to address the problems of disadvantaged citizens, education in the United States will have to become more effective than it is today. This is particularly true with respect to the development of higher-order skills among all segments of the student population and specifically among disadvantaged students.

---

[103]Thomas J. Glennan, Jr., *New American Schools After Six Years* (Santa Monica, Calif.: Rand Organization, 1998), available at **www.rand.org**.
[104]Susan J. Bodily, *Lessons from New American Schools' Scale-Up Phase* (Santa Monica, Calif.: Rand Organization, 1998) available at **www.rand.org**.
[105]Lana J. Smith et al., "Activities in Schools and Programs Experiencing the Most, and Least, Early Implementation Successes," *School Effectiveness and School Improvement* (March 1997), p. 148; and Lynn Olson, "Memphis Study Tracks Gains in Whole-School Reform," *Education Week,* May 27, 1998.
[106]"States and Districts and Comprehensive School Reform," *CPRE Policy Briefs* (May 1998), pp. 1–6; and Brent R. Kettner, *Funding Comprehensive School Reform* (Santa Monica, Calif.: Rand Organization, 1998), available at **www.rand.org**.

Key role for new teachers

Recent national proposals for educational reform have reflected these emerging concerns. During the same time, much has been learned about improving educational effectiveness at the school and classroom levels. However, using this knowledge to fundamentally improve the schools is a difficult and complex task. New teachers will play an important part in determining whether the reform effort is successful.

Summing Up

1. The educational system is being challenged to improve achievement in order to keep the United States internationally competitive and to provide equity for disadvantaged and other at-risk students.

2. Research on effective teaching and instruction provides support for appropriate emphasis on efficient classroom management, direct instruction, high time-on-task, frequent questioning of students, explicit comprehension instruction, and other methods that promote achievement.

3. Research indicates that schools that are unusually effective in improving student achievement have a clear mission, outstanding leadership, high expectations for students, positive home-school relations, high time-on-task, monitoring of students, and an orderly, humane climate. Research also has identified somewhat more specific characteristics such as curriculum alignment and schoolwide emphasis on higher-order skills.

4. It now seems possible to create more effective schools, provided educators use what has been learned about the school improvement process.

5. Emerging technologies offer great potential for improving elementary and secondary education, but effective use of technologies will require considerable effort and resources.

6. Greater cooperation with other institutions and establishment of magnet and other alternative schools may help to improve the effectiveness of our educational system.

7. Some research indicates that nonpublic schools are more effective than public schools, but many researchers question this conclusion.

8. Many possibilities exist for improving education through expanding school choice, but there also are many potential dangers.

9. Much needs to be done to improve rural education and education for gifted and talented students.

10. Efforts now under way to bring about systemic, coherent restructuring and reform offer great promise.

Key Terms

time-on-task *(522)*

direct instruction *(522)*

explicit teaching *(522)*

explicit comprehension instruction *(524)*

strategic teaching *(524)*

homogeneous grouping *(525)*

tracking *(526)*

curriculum alignment *(527)*

school-within-a-school *(529)*

achievement centers *(529)*

Achievement Goals Program *(531)*

privatization *(540)*   school choice *(549)*

distance education *(546)*   year-round school *(552)*

magnet schools *(548)*   restructuring *(554)*

alternative schools *(548)*

Discussion Questions

1. What are some of the major obstacles in working to improve students' higher-order skills? What can be done to attain this goal at the school and classroom levels?

2. Why is school effectiveness so dependent on what happens in the school as a whole, not just in individual classrooms? What are the most important things a teacher can do to help improve the effectiveness of the school?

3. What does research say about the effectiveness of nonpublic schools? Do they produce higher achievement than public schools? If yes, what considerations account for the difference?

4. Why should educators be somewhat cautious in interpreting research on effective schools? What mistakes in interpretation are most likely?

5. Would you be willing to work in a high-poverty school even though teaching there might be more difficult and frustrating than in a middle-class school? What philosophical commitments might be important in undertaking such an assignment?

Suggested Projects for Professional Development

1. Collect and analyze information about cooperation between schools and other institutions (such as businesses and colleges) in your community. To what extent has such cooperation been helpful to the schools?

2. Visit a nearby school with a high proportion of low-income students. Talk with both teachers and students. Write a description of the school comparing its programs and practices with the characteristics of unusually effective schools discussed in this chapter. Organize your material for inclusion in your personal portfolio.

3. List the first actions you would take to improve the effectiveness of a typical high school. Defend your list. How do your proposals reflect research on school effectiveness? How do they reflect your personal philosophy of education?

4. In a recent book or journal, or in an article available on the Internet, find a proposal for a basic reform or restructuring in the public schools. What does the author propose to reform? How? Is the proposal realistic? What philosophic perspectives does it represent? What conditions or resources would be required to implement it successfully? What is the likelihood of success?

5. Using Internet and library resources, obtain information about the implementation and results of the Comer approach (**info.med.edu/comer**), HOTS (**www.hots.org**), Success for All (**www.successforall.org**), or other interventions discussed in this chapter. What are their major advantages and disadvantages? Would you want to teach in a participating school?

Suggested Readings and Resources

Internet Resources

Full texts of important studies and reports dealing with school effectiveness and reform can be obtained by calling up publications menus at Internet site **www.ed.gov**. Other sites for relevant documents include federally supported clearinghouses and research and development agencies such as the North Central Regional Educational Laboratory (NCREL). You can access these sources by starting at the **www.ed.gov** site or by doing a general search using terms such as "ASK ERIC" or "NCREL."

There are so many excellent Internet resources dealing with topics in this chapter that you usually can find relevant materials by starting with widely used search engines. In particular, we have had much success by starting at **www.nlsearch.com**.

Video

Effective Schools for Children at Risk. VHS, 25 minutes (1991). Association for Supervision and Curriculum Development, Alexandria, VA. Phone: 703-549-9110. *Based on James Comer's ideas about the key characteristics of effective schools, this video explores ways of organizing public schools to meet the needs of at-risk students.*

Publications

Block, James H., Susan I. Everson, and Thomas R. Guskey, eds. *School Improvement Programs.* New York: Scholastic, 1995. *Describes and analyzes many of the topics discussed in this chapter, as well as numerous others.*

Fullan, Michael. *The New Meaning of Educational Change.* New York: Teachers College Press, 1991. *Excellent analysis of both the theoretical basis and the practical implications of research on the school change process.*

Healy, Jane M. *Failure to Connect.* New York: Simon and Schuster, 1998. *Many of Healy's classroom observations raise important questions about the appropriate use of computers and other digital media.*

Jones, Beau Fly, and Lorna Idol, eds. *Dimensions of Thinking and Cognitive Instruction.* Hillsdale, N.J.: Erlbaum, 1990. *Here is much of what you always wanted to know about instruction to develop higher-order skills.*

Loveless, Tom, "The Tracking and Ability Grouping Debate" (Paper prepared for the Thomas B. Fordham Foundation, July 1998). *A useful, detailed review and analysis of research on this important topic, available at **www.edexcellence.net/library**.*

Oakes, Jeannie, and Karen Hunter Quartz, eds. *Creating New Educational Communities.* Chicago: University of Chicago Press, 1995. *Includes descriptions of approaches that use heterogeneous grouping successfully and/or provide special help for low achievers in heterogeneous settings.*

GLOSSARY

Academic freedom A protection permitting teachers to teach subject matter and choose instructional materials relevant to the course without restriction from administrators or other persons outside the classroom.

Academy A type of private or semipublic secondary school that was dominant in the United States from 1830 through 1870.

Accountability Holding teachers, administrators, and/or school board members responsible for student performance or for wise use of educational funds.

Acculturation The process beginning at infancy by which a human being acquires the culture of his or her society.

Activity-centered curriculum A type of student-centered curriculum that emphasizes purposeful and real-life experiences and, more recently, student participation in school and community activities.

Aesthetics The branch of axiology that examines questions of beauty and art.

Affirmative action A method of redressing the wrongs of past discrimination against minorities and women in employment and education by giving preferential treatment to selected groups on the basis of sex, race, and ethnic background. Usually such plans require goals and timetables.

Alternative certification Teacher certification obtained without completing a traditional teacher-education program at a school or college of education.

Alternative school A school, public or private, that provides learning opportunities different from those in local public schools. Some such schools follow a student-centered curriculum characterized by a great deal of freedom for students and a relative lack of structure.

At-risk students Students who are low achievers and/or are alienated from school; students considered to be at risk of either dropping out of school or of not acquiring sufficient education to succeed in the economy.

Axiology The area of philosophy that examines value issues, especially in ethics and aesthetics.

Back-to-basics curriculum A type of subject-centered curriculum that emphasizes the three Rs at the elementary level and academic subjects at the secondary level; also includes a defined minimum level of academic standards.

Bilingual education Instruction in their native language provided for students whose first language is not English.

Block grants Grants for a general purpose from the federal government to the states, allowing each state considerable freedom to choose the specific programs for which the funds will be spent.

Board of education (local) See School board, local.

Brahmins Members of the highest caste and the primary recipients of education in ancient India.

Career ladder The arrangement of teaching positions in a series of steps, with inexperienced teachers at the bottom and the most highly qualified at the top. Promotion from one step to the next usually brings additional responsibilities as well as a higher salary.

Caste A system of social stratification traditionally used in India.

Categorical grants Grants designated for specific groups and purposes; the standard method of federal education funding before the 1980s.

Certification State government review and approval providing a teaching candidate with permission to teach.

Chapter 1 See Title 1.

Character education. See Values-centered curriculum.

Charter school A public school governed by a community group that has been granted a special contract (charter) by the state or the local school board. Charter schools are often formed to offer alternative types of education not available in the regular public schools.

Chief state school officer A person serving as chief executive of the state board of education; sometimes called the state superintendent or commissioner of education.

Choice of schools See School choice.

Collective bargaining A procedure for resolving disagreements between employers and employees through negotiation. For teachers, such negotiation pertains to many aspects of their work and salary as well as their relationship with students, supervisors, and the community.

Common school A publicly supported and locally controlled elementary school.

Compensatory education An attempt to remedy the effects of environmental disadvantages through educational enrichment programs.

Competency-based teacher education An approach that requires prospective teachers to demonstrate minimum levels of performance on specified teaching tasks in actual or simulated situations.

Comprehensive high school A public high school that offers a variety of curricula, including a common core, to a diverse student population.

Confucius (551–478 B.C.)   Chinese philosopher and government official who devised an ethical system still in use in China today and in other parts of the world.

Consolidation   The combining of small or rural school districts into larger ones.

Constructivism   A learning theory that emphasizes the ways in which learners actively create meaning by constructing and reconstructing ideas about reality.

Continuing teacher contract   An employment contract that is automatically renewed from year to year without need for the teacher's signature.

Cooperative learning   A form of instruction in which students are assigned to teams whose members work cooperatively on specific tasks or projects.

Core subjects   A curriculum of common courses that all students are required to take. Emphasis is usually on academic achievement and traditional subject matter.

Critical theory (critical pedagogy)   An interpretation of schooling that views public school systems as functioning to limit opportunities for low-income students. Proponents argue that teachers should be "transformative intellectuals" who work to change the system. Also known as "critical discourse."

Critical thinking   Solving problems by means of general concepts or higher-order relationships. Instruction in critical thinking generally emphasizes basic analytical skills that can be applied to a wide variety of intellectual experiences.

Cultural pluralism   Acceptance and encouragement of cultural, ethnic, and religious diversity within a larger society.

Curriculum   Planned experiences provided through instruction that enable the school to meet its goals and objectives.

Curriculum alignment   Coordination of instructional planning, methods, materials, and testing in order to accomplish important learning objectives.

Decentralization   The division of large school districts into smaller units. Although these smaller units have certain powers, the primary focus of authority generally remains in the central administration.

De facto segregation   Segregation associated with and resulting from housing patterns.

De jure segregation   Segregation resulting from laws or government action.

Department of Education   See State department of education; U.S. Department of Education.

Desegregation   Attendance by students of different racial backgrounds in the same school and classroom.

Direct instruction   A systematic method of teaching that emphasizes teacher-directed instruction proceeding in small steps, usually in accordance with a six- to eight-part lesson sequence.

Distance education   Instruction by people or materials that are distant from the learner in space or time; many distance education projects use interactive television, the Internet, and other modern communication technologies.

Dual-track system   The traditional European pattern of separate primary schools for the masses of population and preparatory and secondary schools for the upper socioeconomic classes.

Due process   A formalized legal procedure with specific and detailed rules and principles designed to protect the rights of individuals.

Ebonics   Frequently used as a synonym for Black English, Ebonics also refers to analysis of a dialect used by many African Americans and of how it might play a part in teaching standard English.

Education   The lifelong process of acquiring knowledge, skills, and values, whether by formal means such as schooling or by informal means such as discussion and personal experience.

Educational voucher   A flat grant or payment representing a child's estimated school cost or portion of the cost. Under a typical voucher plan, the parent or child may choose any school, public or private, and payment is made to the school for accepting the child.

Effective schools   Schools that are unusually successful in producing high student performance, compared with other schools that enroll students of similar background; sometimes defined as schools in which working-class students achieve as well as middle-class students.

Elementary school   An educational institution for children in the earliest grades, generally grades one through six or one through eight; often includes kindergarten as well.

Epistemology   The area of philosophy that examines knowing and theories of knowledge.

Essentialism   An educational theory that emphasizes basic skills and subject-matter disciplines. Proponents generally favor a curriculum consisting of the three Rs at the elementary level and five major disciplines (English, math, science, history, and foreign language) at the secondary level. Emphasis is on academic competition and excellence.

Ethics   The branch of axiology that examines questions of right and wrong and good and bad.

Ethnic group   A group of people with a distinctive history, culture, and language.

Exclusive product rights   Special privileges conferred upon commercial enterprises whereby the right to market their product exclusively (e.g., Pepsi Cola) in the school district is given in exchange for a fee.

Existentialism   A philosophy that examines the way in which humans define their own selves by making personal choices.

Experience   The interaction of a person with his or her environment.

Explicit teaching   See Direct instruction.

Expulsion   Dismissal of a student from school for a lengthy period, ranging from one semester to permanently.

Goals   Broad statements of educational purpose.

Head Start   A federal government program that provides preschool education for economically disadvantaged students.

Hidden curriculum   What students learn, other than academic content, from what they do or are expected to do in school.

High school   A school for the upper grades of secondary students, commonly serving grades nine or ten through twelve.

Higher Education Reauthorization Act of 1998   Federal legislation that substantially expands attention and resources devoted to improving the preparation and skills of teachers.

Homogeneous grouping   The practice of placing together students with similar achievement levels or ability.

Hornbook   A single sheet of parchment, containing the Lord's Prayer, letters of the alphabet, and vowels, covered by the flattened horn of a cow and fastened to a flat wooden board. It was used during the colonial era in primary schools.

Humanistic curriculum approach   A student-centered curriculum approach that stresses the personal and social aspects of the student's growth and development. Emphasis is on self-actualizing processes and on moral, aesthetic, and higher domains of thinking.

Idealism   A philosophy that construes reality to be spiritual or nonmaterial in essence.

Inclusion   Educating students with disabilities in regular classrooms in their neighborhood schools, with collaborative support services as needed.

Independent school   A private school not sponsored by a church or religious group.

Individualized instruction   Curriculum content, instructional materials, and activities designed for individual learning. The pace, interests, and abilities of the learner are taken into consideration.

In loco parentis   A Latin term meaning "in the place of a parent"; a concept whereby a teacher or school administrator assumes the rights, duties, and responsibilities of a parent during the hours the child attends school.

Instruction   The methods and materials of the teacher designed to implement the curriculum.

Integration   The step beyond simple desegregation whereby effective action is taken to develop positive interracial contacts and to improve the performance of low-achieving minority students.

Intermediate unit   An educational unit or agency in the middle position between the state department of education and the local school district; usually created by the state to provide supplementary services and support staff to local school districts.

Islam   Religion founded by Mohammed (569–632); currently practiced in many Middle Eastern countries and in many other countries.

Junior high school   A two- or three-year school between elementary and high school, commonly for grades seven through nine.

Kindergarten   A school or division of a school for children below the first grade, usually for children between the ages of four and six; an educational environment first designed by Froebel in the mid-nineteenth century.

Land grant   An arrangement used to found many of today's state universities. The Morrill Act of 1862 granted 30,000 acres of public land for each senator and representative in Congress, the income from which was to be used to support at least one state college for agricultural and mechanical instruction.

Land-grant college   A state college or university, offering agricultural and mechanical curricula, funded originally by the Morrill Act of 1862.

Latin grammar school   A college preparatory school of the colonial era that emphasized Latin and Greek studies.

Lead teacher   *See* Master (or lead) teacher.

Least restrictive environment   A term used in the education of students with disabilities to designate a setting that is as normal or regular as possible. Federal law requires that children with disabilities be placed in special or separate classes only for the amount of time necessary to provide appropriate services.

Magnet school   A type of alternative school that attracts voluntary enrollment from more than one neighborhood by offering special instructional programs or curricula; often established in part for purposes of desegregation.

Mainstreaming   Placing students with disabilities in regular classes for much or all of the school day, while also providing additional services, programs, and classes as needed.

Master (or lead) teacher   A teacher at the top rung of a career ladder who receives additional remuneration in return for increased responsibilities such as training beginning teachers or consulting on effective teaching methods.

Mastery instruction   An approach in which students are tested after initial instruction, and those who did not master the objectives receive corrective instruction and retesting. Emphasis is on short units of instruction and learning of defined skills.

Merit pay   A plan that rewards teachers partially or primarily on the basis of performance or objective standards.

Metaphysics   The area of philosophy that examines issues of a speculative nature dealing with ultimate reality.

Middle school   A two- to four-year school between elementary and high school, commonly for grades six through eight.

Multicultural education   Education that focuses on providing equal opportunity for students whose cultural and/or language patterns make it difficult for them to succeed in traditional school programs. Many multicultural programs also emphasize positive intergroup and interracial attitudes and contacts.

National Assessment of Educational Progress (NAEP)   A periodic assessment of educational achievement under the jurisdiction of the Educational Testing Service, using nationally representative samples of elementary and secondary students.

National Board for Professional Teaching Standards (NBPTS)   A national nonprofit organization that issues certificates to teachers who meet its standards for professional ability and knowledge.

National curriculum   A standard curriculum established by a national government and implemented in schools throughout the country; usually linked with a nationwide testing program to determine whether students are mastering the curriculum.

New core curriculum   *See* Core subjects.

Normal school   A two-year teacher-education institution that was popular in the nineteenth century.

Objectives   Specific statements of educational purpose, usually written for a particular subject, grade, unit, or lesson; commonly defined in behavioral terms so that student experiences and performance can be observed and measured.

Outcomes-based education   Education guided by the principle that success should be judged by student "outcomes" (generally seen in terms of abilities to function in real-life contexts) rather than by "inputs" such as programs, courses, or funding. Many proponents would revise traditional curricula that fail to produce desired outcomes.

Parochial school   A school governed and operated by a religious denomination.

Perennialism   An educational theory that emphasizes rationality as the major purpose of education, asserting that the essential truths are recurring and universally true. Proponents generally favor a curriculum consisting of the three Rs at the elementary level and the classics at the secondary level.

Philosophies   Fully developed bodies of thought each representing a generalized worldview.

Pragmatism   A philosophy that judges the validity of ideas by their consequences in action.

Profession   An occupation that is rated high in prestige and requires extensive formal education and mastery of a defined body of knowledge beyond the grasp of laypersons. Members of many professions control licensing standards and have autonomy in their work environment.

Professional development school   An elementary or secondary school operated jointly by a school district and a teacher-training institution, stressing thoughtful analysis of teaching and learning. The participants usually include future teachers as well as practicing teachers, administrators, and teacher educators.

Professional practice board   A state or national commission that permits educators to set professional standards and minimal requirements of competency.

Progressivism   An antitraditional theory in American education associated with child-centered learning through activities, problem solving, and projects. As an educational movement, progressivism was promoted by the Progressive Education Association.

Realism   A philosophy that construes reality to be dualistic in nature. That is, it considers reality to have both a material and a formal or structural component.

Reflective teaching   A style of teaching that emphasizes reflective inquiry and self-awareness. Reflective teachers analyze their own teaching behavior and consider the factors that make their teaching effective or ineffective.

Relevant curriculum   A type of student-centered curriculum that pays close attention to the interests and experiences of the student; often consists of numerous course electives, extension courses, minicourses, and alternative courses.

Resistance theory   The view that working-class students resist the school, in part because a hegemonic traditional curriculum marginalizes their everyday knowledge.

Scholasticism   The intellectual and educational approach used by educators in medieval universities, involving the study of theological and philosophical authorities.

School-based management   A system of school governance in which many important decisions are made at the level of the individual school rather than by the superintendent or board of education. This system usually gives teachers substantial decision-making responsibility.

School board, local   A group of people, elected or appointed, given authority by the state to operate the schools within a defined school district or location.

School choice   A system that allows students or their parents to choose the schools they attend.

School code   *See* State school code.

School superintendent   *See* Superintendent of schools.

Scientific method   A systematic approach to inquiry in which hypotheses are tested by replicable empirical verification. Although usually identified with the laboratory method in the natural sciences, the scientific method is also used in philosophy, where it is associated with pragmatism.

Secondary school A post-elementary school, such as a middle school or a junior or senior high school.

Sex roles Socially expected behavior patterns for girls and boys, men and women.

Site-based management *See* School-based management.

Social class A ranking of people according to their status in society. Common divisions include upper class, middle class, and working class. *See also* Socioeconomic status (SES).

Socialization The process of preparing persons for a social environment.

Social reconstructionism A theory of education advocating that schools and teachers act as agents of deliberate social change.

Socioeconomic status (SES) Relative ranking of individuals according to economic, social, and occupational prestige and power; usually measured in terms of occupation, education, and income and generally viewed in terms of social-class categories ranging from working class to upper class.

Socratic method An educational method attributed to the Greek philosopher Socrates by which the teacher encourages the student's discovery of truth by asking leading and stimulating questions.

Staff development Continued education or training of a school district's teaching staff. Such programs often stress teacher input as well as collaboration between the school district and a college or university.

State board of education An influential state education agency that serves in an advisory function for the state legislature and establishes policies for implementing legislative acts related to education.

State department of education An agency that operates under the direction of the state board of education. Its functions include accrediting schools, certifying teachers, apportioning state school funds, conducting research, issuing reports, and coordinating state education policies with local school districts.

State school code A collection of laws that establish ways and means of operating schools and conducting education in a state.

Student-centered curricula Curricula that focus on the needs and attitudes of the individual student. Emphasis is on self-expression and the student's intrinsic motivation.

Subject-area curriculum A type of subject-centered curriculum in which each subject is treated as a largely autonomous body of knowledge. Emphasis is on the traditional subjects that have dominated U.S. education since the late nineteenth century, including English, history, science, and mathematics.

Subject-centered curricula Curricula that are defined in terms of bodies of content or subject matter. Achievement is judged according to defined outcomes such as test scores, correct answers, or responses deemed appropriate.

Superintendent of schools The executive officer of the local school district, whose function is to implement policies adopted by the school board.

Suspension Dismissal of a student from school on a temporary basis.

Tax base Basis upon which taxes for public schools are assessed at state and local levels — e.g., property tax, sales tax, transportation taxes, and special fees.

Teacher empowerment The process of increasing the power of teachers and their role in determining school policies and practices.

Tenure Permanence of position granted to educators after a probationary period, which prevents their dismissal except for legally specified causes and through formalized due process procedures.

Theories Sets of ideas or beliefs, often based on research findings or generalizations from practice, that guide educational policies or procedures.

Title 1 A portion of the federal Elementary and Secondary Education Act that provides funds to improve the education of economically disadvantaged students.

Town school The eighteenth- and early-nineteenth-century elementary school of New England that educated children living in a designated area.

Tracking Separation of students into different curriculum paths. The term usually refers to the high-school level, where students are often separated into an academic track, a general or business track, and a vocational track.

Transitional bilingual education (TBE) A form of bilingual education in which students are taught in their own language only until they can learn in English.

Tuition tax credits Tax reductions offered to parents or guardians of children to offset part of their school tuition payments.

Underclass Section of the lower working class that is subject to intergenerational transmission of poverty.

U.S. Department of Education A cabinet-level department in the executive branch of the federal government, in charge of federal educational policy and the promotion of educational programs.

Values "Should" or "ought" imperatives that relate to moral and ethical behavior or aesthetic appreciation.

Values-centered curriculum A type of student-centered curriculum that emphasizes affective learning and personal growth, focusing on morality, personal biases, personal choice, value clarification, and the social world in general.

Vedas One of the key religious texts used in Hinduism; the focus of ancient Indian education.

Voucher *See* Educational voucher.

Whole-child concept The view that schools must concern themselves with all aspects of students' growth and development, not merely with cognitive skills or academic learning.

INDEX

PROFESSIONAL PLANNING

for your first year

Teaching Students Who Are Socially Disadvantaged

The Situation

Suppose you are assigned as a student teacher to a school in a low-income neighborhood. Most of the students are from minority groups, and their backgrounds often include one or more of the social disadvantages identified in Chapter 9. In your first class, you give your best lesson: challenging, upbeat, informative, imaginative. The students pay attention and several participate, responding to questions and asking their own. You feel you've done a good job. But as the students leave the room, one of them — a quiet, rather thoughtful young person — stops to say this to you: "I can see you're tryin'. But pretty soon you'll quit on us like others do. We're the wrong type or the wrong color, and some of us don't talk your language. Everybody knows we ain't going anywhere but out on the streets."

The comment upsets you. You want to respond that it's not true: these students *can* go somewhere. You feel challenged by the student's bleak outlook.

Thought Questions

The following questions should be useful to keep in mind as you read not just this chapter but subsequent chapters in this book.

1. To what extent is it true that middle-class student teachers do not "speak the same language" as students from low-income families? Should teachers try to do this? How might doing so affect the teacher's relationships with his or her students?
2. If you were to face a situation like this, what would you say or do to reassure the student?
3. What would your reaction be if most of the students in the class indicated they were not interested in the lesson you had worked so hard to prepare? Who might you turn to for help?
4. How might the teacher in this latter situation (question 3) try to modify his or her lesson to stimulate more interest among students?
5. What are some of the things you might do to ensure that all the students in your classroom have an equal opportunity to achieve?

A divided population

For educators, the challenge is to imdents, from whatever ethnic group. Th
more divided, with a growing high-inc
ment, and a shrinking middle segmen
Secretary of Labor Robert Reich: "If we
tiered society, we not only risk the nati
herence and stability. As the economy
clean the offices and provide the basic
the gains, but that hasn't been happeni

[24]Quoted in Keith Bradsher, "Productivity Is
June 25, 1995, p. 4E. See also Keith Bradsher,
June 4, 1995, p. E4; and Peter Passell, "Benefi
Wages," *New York Times*, June 14, 1998.

New to this edition
Professional Planning for Your First Year
features teaching situations and encourages reflection about key issues.

Suggested Projects for Professional Development

1. Find out the teacher tenure regulations in your state and in one or two nearby states. Do the states differ with respect to probationary period, cause for dismissal, or other matters? Are teachers in your community aware of these policies?
2. From a nearby school district, collect and analyze information about teachers' responsibilities for identifying and reporting child abuse. What are the district's explicit policies? Have any teachers been released or otherwise disciplined for failure to meet these responsibilities?
3. Survey several nearby school districts regarding their policies on student and teacher dress codes. Find out whether and how these policies have changed in the past ten or fifteen years. Do you expect to see further changes in the near future?
4. For your portfolio, prepare a lesson plan dealing with religious holidays in a manner that does not unconstitutionally promote or inhibit religion.

Suggested Readings and Resources

Internet Resources

Useful sources dealing with material in this chapter — particularly with major Supreme Court and federal court decisions — can be found by going to the Web page of the Emory University School of Law at **www.law.emory.edu**. Any relevant ERIC digest is quickly and easily downloadable using the search procedure at **www.ed.gov**. The American Civil Liberties Union at **www.aclu.org**, also gives considerable attention to education-related cases. A wealth of law-related material involving school safety and student discipline is available at **www.keepschoolsafe.org**. You can take a virtual tour of the U.S. Supreme Court and listen to the statements and arguments of plaintiffs and defendants in some of the Court's major cases at **court.it-services. nwv.edu/oyez**.

Publications

Alexander, Kern, and David M. Alexander. *American Public School Law*. 4th ed. Belmont, Calif.: Wadsworth, 1998. *This venerable text has been providing solid and reliable information and analysis regarding school law for decades.*

LaMorte, Michael W. *School Law: Cases and Concepts*. 4th ed. Needham Heights, Mass.: Allyn and Bacon, 1995. *A comprehensive text that uses excerpts from judicial opinions to convey important legal principles.*

Provenzo, Eugene F., Jr. *Religious Fundamentalism and American Education*. Albany: State University of New York Press, 1990. *Describes and analyzes major Supreme Court decisions dealing with church and state censorship, family rights and education, and related issues.*

Rossow, Lawrence F., and Janice A. Hiniger. *Students and the Law*. Bloomington, Ind.: Phi Delta Kappa, 1991. *This slim "Fastback" includes chapters on freedom of speech, student publications, search and seizure, drug testing, religious activity, discipline in special education, and expulsions and suspensions.*

Wills, Garry. "H. R. Clinton's Case." *New York Review of Books*, March 5, 1992, pp. 3–5. *This article describes legal theories developed by attorney Hillary Rodham Clinton with respect to protecting the rights of children and adolescents in schools and other institutions.*

New end-of-chapter section
Suggested Projects for Professional Development *provides opportunities to extend knowledge through activities such as debating, conducting surveys, and role-playing.*